The Business of Food

THE BUSINESS OF FOOD

Encyclopedia of the Food and Drink Industries

Edited by Gary Allen and Ken Albala

Foreword by Marion Nestle

GREENWOOD PRESS
Westport, Connecticut • London

Library of Congress Cataloging-in-Publication Data

The business of food : encyclopedia of the food and drink industries / edited by Gary Allen and Ken Albala.

    p. cm.

"More than 150 signed essay entries make up this encyclopedia"—P.   .

Includes bibliographical references and index.

ISBN 978-0-313-33725-3 (alk. paper)

1. Food industry and trade. 2. Food industry and trade—Social aspects. 3. Food industry and trade—Environmental aspects. 4. Beverage industry and trade. 5. Beverage industry and trade—Social aspects. 6. Beverage industry and trade—Environmental aspects. I. Allen, Gary (Gary J.) II. Albala, Ken, 1964- III. Title: Encyclopedia of the food and drink industries.

HD9000.5.B875 2007

338.4′766400973—dc22   2007026091

British Library Cataloguing in Publication Data is available.

Library of Congress Catalog Card Number: 2007026091

ISBN-13: 978-0-313-33725-3

First published in 2007

Greenwood Press, 88 Post Road West, Westport, CT 06881

An imprint of Greenwood Publishing Group, Inc.

www.greenwood.com

Printed in the United States of America

The paper used in this book complies with the Permanent Paper Standard issued by the National Information Standards Organization (Z39.48-1984).

10   9   8   7   6   5   4   3   2   1

CONTENTS

LIST OF ENTRIES

LIST OF ENTRIES BY TOPIC

FOREWORD

The food industry—encompassing businesses that produce, package, prepare, and serve foods and beverages—brings us a food supply so abundant, readily available, and low in cost that only the poorest segments of the world's populations cannot obtain enough to meet daily needs. In the United States, this industry sells more than 300,000 food and beverage products, and an average supermarket might offer as many as 50,000. By any standard, this industry has been outstandingly successful in providing more than enough quantity and variety to meet nutritional needs.

Thus, it is highly ironic that this success causes so many problems. Today, consumers are overwhelmingly confused by the plethora of food choices. Many people eat more than is necessary, gain weight, and become obese. Groups of people throughout the world participate in social movements aimed at creating new systems of food production and marketing that are healthier for people, food animals, and the planet.

The problems can be traced to policy changes of the early 1980s—the dawn of the obesity epidemic. These marked a turning point in the way food businesses operated. Farm policies changed to encourage farmers to produce more food. From 1980 to 2000, the number of calories available in the food supply (the amount produced in the United States, less exports, plus imports) rose from 3,200 per capita per day to 3,900—an amount roughly twice average need. The early 1980s also marked the advent of the "shareholder value movement" demanding higher immediate returns on investment. The result was that food companies not only had to sell products in an absurdly competitive marketplace, but also had to report growth to Wall Street every ninety days.

To grow sales, food companies increased portion sizes, encouraged snacking, introduced food into formerly forbidden places (such as bookstores and libraries), placed vending machines in schools and workplaces, and fostered social changes that encouraged people to eat more often, in more places, and in larger amounts. Rates of obesity rose in parallel with these changes. Food executives were not scheming to make Americans fat; they were merely trying to expand sales. In this situation, obesity was just collateral damage.

Indeed, obesity poses an impossible dilemma for food companies. They are businesses and corporate regulations require them to place stockholder interests—

growth—above all other considerations. But to prevent or reverse obesity, people must eat less, and eating less is very bad for business.

If this encyclopedia has one overarching theme, it is surely to explain how the food industry arrived at this dilemma and how companies cope with the problems it causes. The essays in this volume reveal much about how business interests interact—sometimes positively, sometimes negatively—with public concerns about health, animal welfare, and the environment. The information provided here is essential for consumers as well as food business leaders if we as citizens are to develop and maintain an adequate, health-promoting, sustainable food system capable of meeting the needs of the twenty-first century.

—Marion Nestle

PREFACE

What we eat and drink, how our food is grown and processed, and where it comes from are vital concerns for our health, the economy, and the well-being of the planet. In the course of the past century, our food and drink supply has increasingly been controlled by larger and larger corporate interests whose primary concern has been making a profit rather than supplying people with good food. This has had dramatic consequences, for while our grocery shelves are loaded with a staggering quantity and variety of products, often drawn from the far corners of the globe, it is becoming increasingly apparent that this abundance comes at a great cost.

Food and beverages seem to be fairly cheap, yet there are many hidden costs, such as unfair and dangerous labor practices, fertilizer runoff and pesticide poisoning, transportation pollution, excess packaging, animal suffering, and marketing and advertising onslaughts, as well as the price of increasing health care due to diet-related illness such as obesity and diabetes. On top of this, our tax dollars support farm subsidies and our politicians make decisions that ultimately reflect the interests of their campaign contributors, by and large the food and drink industries.

The business of food and drink is for better and worse the business of our nation and our planet, and to most consumers how it works remains largely a mystery. For example, we are intentionally kept in the dark about the ways genetically engineered crops enter our food system. Few people care to know how the animals that end up on our plates are treated, let alone the people whose labor transforms the raw ingredients into our sustenance. We hope this encyclopedia will address many of the most important questions we will be facing in the coming decades concerning our food supply and the business of food and drink.

There are, of course, many outspoken critics of our food system who point out that the way we eat is unsustainable, that our current practices cannot continue without dire consequences. At best, we are passing on the burden of our short-sighted choices to our progeny and future generations. They recognize that, while we seem to have a lot of cheap food, this is not the case around the world. Americans have relatively high wages and decent working conditions, yet again, people elsewhere, many of whom grow our food, are often not so fortunate.

Many alternatives have been proposed. The increasing market share of organic foods, local and sustainable agriculture, the growth of farmers' markets, and even what appears to be a growing awareness of the dangers of highly processed junk and fast food, all show signs of promise. Yet when buzzwords like "organic" become merely another way for large corporations to sell food in the same factory-farmed industrial model, whether this profit-driven system is in anyone's best interest is open to debate.

This encyclopedia is meant to be a source of information, laying out the facts in a clear and accessible manner so readers as consumers can make more informed choices. Ultimately we hope readers will have a better sense of what truly constitutes *good food*, meaning food that both tastes good and is good for our bodies, our neighbors, and the creatures with whom we share this planet.

The scope of this encyclopedia is intentionally broad, covering topics from food companies and brands to the environment, health, science and technology, culture, finance, and more. We chose not to create a comprehensive list of every food and beverage company and trend, which would have proven not only tedious and redundant but also probably out of date before it went to press. In fact, the rapid mergers and acquisitions of food companies are a running theme of this encyclopedia. We decided that thoughtful, short introductory essays on the most pressing issues in the food industry would better serve the average reader and student. This work presents those issues that have been of perennial importance to our food supply and those that are likely to continue to continue to be of great concern in the decades to come. Thus we have included topics such as famine and obesity, which might not at first seem directly connected to the food industry.

This encyclopedia also contains a good deal of history, because in a certain sense the current state of the food and drink industries is the product of conscious choices made in the past, just as the future will be the product of those we make today. Although the scope covers primarily the United States, contributors have taken a more global approach when appropriate.

The contributors themselves come from a wide variety of disciplines. There are historians and sociologists, nutritionists and journalists, food service professionals and hard scientists. They have all sought to offer the basic facts in clear prose free of academic jargon, in objective and succinct entries.

More than 150 signed entries make up this encyclopedia. Most include books, articles, or websites for further reading on the subject. The front matter includes an alphabetical list of entries and a topical list of entries to allow the reader to quickly find items of interest. Numerous cross-references in the entries and blind entries provide other search strategies. Words that appear in **bold** refer to main entries. The index is another in-depth search tool.

Additives Additives are a substance or combination of substances that are mixed with food products as a result of production, processing, **packaging**, or storage. The total market for food additives was estimated at $4 billion in 2006 in the United States and grows at an approximate rate of 4.8 percent annually. Additives are included among ingredients for any number of reasons, ranging from improving nutritional value to enhancing quality or consumer acceptability. There are many categories of food additives, including preservatives, processing aids, coloring agents, flavorings, and nutritional supplements. There are also growing concerns over the increasing use of additives and their relation to allergic-like reactions, cancer, and other illnesses. Some additives have been banned outright due to insufficient testing or dangerous problems related to their use.

History of Additives and Legal Background

As with many other elements used in food processing, additives originate very early in human history. For example, people learned in prehistoric times that adding salt to meat would preserve it. Likewise, smoke, which also acts as a preservative, might be considered an early food additive. Over time, additives have come to thoroughly influence our eating habits, our taste preferences, and our sociocultural development.

The earliest legislation controlling the use of food additives took place in Britain in the 19th century, following the work of Frederick Accum, though its original impetus was the prevention of food adulteration. In the United States, the Food and Drug Administration (FDA) oversees the regulation of ingredients that can be added to food. It was not until 1958 that legislation was adopted requiring food and chemical manufacturers to test their additives before they were submitted to the FDA. Before that law, the FDA itself was responsible for testing the submitted additives. Thereafter, Congress established a Generally Recognized as Safe (GRAS) list. This list recognized that many substances that had been added to food for a long time were commonly seen as safe by qualified scientists, which exempted them from premarket clearance. This list was revised in 1969 and as of 1980 contained 415 substances that were originally included in the 1958 project. Today, manufacturers are responsible for demonstrating their GRAS status and providing evidence (such as scientific literature) to support it. Approximately 100 new substances are presented to the FDA for GRAS certification every year.

Also included in 1958 law was an amendment called the Delaney Act; it stipulated that "no additives may be permitted in any amount if the tests show that it produces cancer when fed to man or animals or by other appropriate test." Many manufacturers, as well as some FDA commissioners, have criticized this amendment as being unenforceable. Instead, in 2003, the FDA adopted a "no residue" clause; this clause provided that the FDA could approve an animal feed additive or drug that induces cancer if there is "no residue" of the additive found after slaughter. The FDA maintains that the risk is slight or nonexistent if humans consume meat or drink milk from an animal with a minuscule amount of a carcinogen present.

Uses and Categories of Food Additives

Additives are used in foods for a wide array of purposes. Some of these include improving nutritional value, enhancing taste or consumer acceptability, improving storage potential, making the food more readily available, and facilitating its preparation. Food additives can be categorized by function; the main categories explored here are preservatives, appearance additives, and **nutritional** supplements.

Preservatives are added to food substances to slow spoilage and deterioration. Some sources estimate that there are about 100 common preservatives being used by the food industry. Preservatives are specific to the food being preserved; antioxidants are used in fatty products, for example, while breads often have "mold inhibitors." Other common multipurpose preservatives are familiar ingredients such as salt, **sugar**, and vinegar. All of these extend the shelf life of food products and reduce the risk of food-related disease. Some preservation techniques, such as **irradiated** food, aseptic processing, and microwave pasteurization, reduce the need for conventional food additives used to reduce spoilage, but their safety is sometimes debated.

Appearance additives include texturizers, coloring agents, and flavorings. These additives enhance the look, mouthfeel, or taste of foods without changing other characteristics. Texturizers are put into food products to maintain a desired texture, and sodium nitrate is used to develop and stabilize the pink color in meats. Coloring agents are used to increase attractiveness of food to consumers; foods that are frequently colored include **candy**, **soft drinks**, and **dairy** products such as butter, cheese, and cream. Flavoring additives are the most common type of additive approved for human consumption. Of the roughly 3,000 additives currently approved, about 2,000 are flavorings used to replace the **flavors** lost during processing. Hence this category of additives is used mainly to appeal to user tastes and to enhance purchasing of the target food product.

Nutritional supplements are another major type of additive. **Breakfast cereals**, which often make extensive nutritional claims, rely heavily on such additives. Many of the additives used are **vitamins** (such as vitamin C) and are intended to make the product a better source of nutrition. Other uses include moisture control, thickening, and processing aids.

To regulate all these additives, and to help consumers sort through the complex and confusing terminology, each additive is assigned a unique number. This codification (also called E numbers in Europe) is recognized internationally and is managed by the **Codex Alimentarius Commission**. The Food and Agriculture Organization and the World Health Organization created this commission in 1963. Its mission is to develop food standards and guidelines for identification worldwide. For example, aspartame, a popular artificial sweetener, is coded E951, while monosodium glutamate (MSG) is coded E621.

This classification identifies all existing additives, regardless of whether they are approved for use or not. Hence, an additive might be approved for use in one country but banned in another. This is why universal classification is required. In some cases, a product that is approved in some countries but not in Europe will have a unique number but no corresponding E number. For example, acetic acid, which is approved in Australia, is additive 103, but does not have an E103 number.

Additives can be either synthetic (i.e., chemically produced, artificial) or natural in origin. A 2006 study found that participants significantly preferred foods with natural additives over those with synthetic ones.

Critics and Dangers Related to Additives

Criticisms directed toward food additives are abundant. The most common criticisms focus on allergic-like reactions, carcinogenic properties, and a causal relationship to attention deficit hyperactivity disorder (ADHD). Growing concerns have also been related to additive overuse.

Over the years, many people have reported adverse reactions to certain food additives, including aspartame and MSG. To date, no consistent pattern of symptoms can be attributed to the use of aspartame, and carefully controlled clinical studies have shown that it is not an allergen. MSG, sulfites (used as colorants), and FD&C yellow #5 also cause "allergic-like" reactions but have not been given allergen status. For now, agencies require producers using these ingredients to carefully label their products while they continue monitoring the situation.

There are also concerns about food additives and cancer. A few additives have been linked to certain forms of cancer, but some scientists believe that the amount needed to cause harm is so excessive that there is no real danger; most additives that involve risk are allowed in foods only at levels less than a hundredth those at which the risk is still known to be zero. Hence, in these situations, the benefits outweigh the risks. Once the risk is too high, these additives are usually banned from use in food products.

Finally, some people think that certain food additives, especially artificial colors, can cause hyperactivity in children or may exacerbate ADHD. At the moment, there is not enough scientific evidence to support a connection between these additives and hyperactivity or ADHD in children. Research is ongoing.

Although the use of single food additives at their regulated concentrations is believed to be relatively safe, their effects when combined remain unclear. Hence, there are concerns that cytotoxicity (toxicity to the cells) might be amplified when the number of different additives consumed increase. As the number of approved additives grows, the risks of combined cytotoxicity also increases.

Moreover, some believe that if adverse reactions to additives seem statistically rare, it is only because they are underdiagnosed in part due to a low index of suspicion. But once a specific additive is identified as causing an adverse reaction, basically all its forms are avoided and consequently banned.

See also Food Laws and Regulations; Food Safety.

FURTHER READINGS: Center for Science in the Public Interest. "Food Additives." http://www.cspinet.org/reports/chemcuisine.htm; Devcich, Daniel A., Irene K. Pedersen, and Keith J. Petrie. "You Eat What You Are: Modern Health Worries and the Acceptance of Natural and Synthetic Additives in Functional Foods." *Appetite* 48, no. 3 (May 2007): 333–37; Lau, K., W. G. McLean, D. P. Williams, and C. V. Howard. "Synergistic Interactions between Commonly Used Food Additives in a Developmental Neurotoxicity Test." *Toxicological Sciences* 90, no. 1 (March 2006): 178–87; Wilson, B. G., and S. L. Bahna. "Adverse Reactions to Food Additives." *Annals of Allergy, Asthma & Immunology* 95, no. 6 (December 2005), 499–507; Winter, Ruth. *A Consumer's Dictionary of Food Additives.* 6th ed. New York: Three Rivers Press, 2004.

Jean-François Denault

Advertising More than in any other nation, American foodways have been formed and nurtured by advertising and media. The birth of the hype machine can be traced to the mid-19th century, when revolutions in transportation, settlement patterns, and cheap newsprint led to enormous changes in eating patterns. In the post–Civil War era, railroads had begun to send oranges from Florida and grain from the Midwest to the urban centers of the northern United States even as those very cities were becoming engorged from an influx of ex-farmers and immigrants. Mass-market magazines were at the ready to instruct the new urban middle classes in ways of preparing the brand-new, industrially produced foods that flooded the market.

The invention of modern advertising can largely be credited to patent medicine sellers of the Reconstruction era. They came up with all sorts of spurious and even dangerous cures for such ill-defined diseases as neuralgia and dyspepsia, which seemed epidemic in that unsettled time. To promote their nostrums, the hucksters scared their customers with "facts" almost guaranteed to induce psychosomatic symptoms, printed advertisements offering miraculous cures (showman P. T. Barnum was a one-time copywriter), enlisted celebrities as spokesmen, and sponsored traveling medicine shows where quack doctors and their accomplices testified to the efficacy of their potions. Early **soft drinks** were sold and marketed as patent medicines. An 1892 advertisement for Coca-Cola was typical of the genre: the carbonated potion was recommended as "the Ideal Brain Tonic for Headache & Exhaustion." **Coffee** substitutes were originally promoted in much the same way. As late as 1951, the Federal Trade Commission was investigating the **Post** Company for running ads for its Postum beverage claiming that drinking coffee discourages marriage or that it results in "divorces, business failures, factory accidents, juvenile delinquency, traffic accidents, fire or home foreclosures."

Postum, created in 1895 by Charles W. Post, was just one of many new foods concocted around the turn of the 20th century. The most notable of these were **breakfast cereals** like Post's own Grape-Nuts, Kellogg's Corn Flakes, and the products of the Shredded Wheat Company. Advertising was the heart and soul of the cereal business from the beginning. The pioneer in this regard was Henry Crowell of the Quaker Oats Company. He was the first to register a trademark for a cereal, in 1877, and he promoted his brand by plastering signs on barns, trains, and even the white cliffs of Dover. Crowell came up with the idea of giving away bowls and saucers as a premium. In imitation of the patent medicine sellers, his ads made various unsubstantiated medical claims. Before Crowell's campaign, oatmeal had been relatively rare in the United States, but now who could turn down a food that promised to "supply what brains and bodies need ... with more proteids [*sic*], more phosphorus, more lecithin than any other food"? A generation later, when Kellogg's Corn Flakes hit the market, the advertising onslaught only intensified. In 1912, Kellogg's erected a 50- by 106-foot sign in New York's Times Square—at that time the largest billboard in the world. In Chicago, a moving electric sign was installed atop a building at State and Adams streets. By 1942, Kellogg Company figures showed that they had spent approximately $100 million on advertising. For most of the 19th century, there was no such thing as a breakfast cereal; by the mid-20th century, 50 percent of Americans would be eating an ounce or so of it every day.

Other hitherto unknown foods were introduced to a public unschooled in advertising. "An Absolutely New Product," proclaimed the full-page 1912 ad for Crisco in *Ladies Home Journal*, describing hydrogenated vegetable shortening as a "A Scientific Discovery Which [would] Affect Every Kitchen in America." This and subsequent campaigns succeeded in substituting Crisco for lard as the country's favorite shortening. Mass-market chocolate bars were a novelty when introduced by Milton Hershey in 1905. He convinced customers to try his three-cent chocolate bars by riding around in a horseless carriage, commissioning promotional dioramas to decorate grocers' windows, and encouraging tours of his factory. Advertising's influence extended even to infant nutrition. One of the new products of the industrial era was infant formula, which was touted by its manufacturers as healthier and "more scientific" than old-fashioned breast milk. Subsequently, several generations of mothers were convinced of the superiority of formula to breast milk.

Others who did not have a new product to sell found that **packaging** goods that had hitherto been sold in bulk could create a brand image (and loyalty) with catchy names, clever slogans, or targeted scare tactics. The crackers sold by the National Biscuit Company were common enough but were typically sold in open cracker barrels. These would soon go the way of stagecoaches when the company introduced "sanitary" packages of Uneeda Crackers in 1898. **Nabisco** drove home the advantage of their packaging with the slogan "Whatever the weather, always fresh." Others took advantage of the new emphasis on hygiene and the limited understanding of microorganisms to mount a frontal assault on their competitors. The **sugar** trust (under the brand name Domino) mounted a campaign to denigrate brown sugar, whose refining it did not completely control, by reproducing blown-up photographs of horrible-looking but harmless little microbes. So successful was this effort that in 1900 the hugely popular *Mrs. Lincoln's Boston Cook Book* accepted this as scientific wisdom, warning readers that brown sugar was inferior in quality to white sugar and was prone to infestation by "a minute insect."

The primary targets for food advertising then, as now, were women. In their transformation from farmwife to urban homemaker, middle-class women's place in the economy changed from producer (on the farm) to consumer of industrial goods. In order to fulfill their new job requirements, women had to be taught to need all 57 varieties of **Heinz** products and instructed in the myriad uses of Royal Baking Powder. One gimmick that proved a perennial favorite throughout the first half of the 20th century was the premium cookbook, sold or offered free as an incentive to use a company's products. Nearly every manufacturer printed these by the tens of thousands, but none was as influential as the cookery guides put out by **Campbell's Soup** Company. By the 1950s, the canned soup manufacturer was selling more than a million books per year. As a result, an estimated 1 million cans of soup were used each day solely as recipe ingredients. In a similar vein, recipes were actually printed on the packaging, assuring ready access to instructions for making the likes of Nestlé's chocolate chip cookies and Rice Krispies Squares.

The food industry found an ideal medium for getting its message across in the women's magazines that flourished after the turn of the 20th century. Not only did the manufacturers finance the publications with advertising and contribute many recipes, but the editors themselves were paid to promote products. The 1913 *The Story of Crisco*, with its 250 recipes using the mock lard, was penned by Marion Harris Neil, the food editor of *Ladies Home Journal*, the top women's magazine of its day. Others journalists gave demonstrations. In the post–World War II era, the magazine's recipes included so many of the advertisers' products that it would become almost impossible to distinguish editorial from advertising in many publications.

As those early admen saw it (and it was almost exclusively men who molded the campaigns), women desired "luxury and daintiness" and were best reached by appealing to their feminine, motherly side with delicate drawings, pastel colors, and serif typefaces. Small children were popular, too, enlisted to sell everything from Morton's salt to Campbell's soup. And sex was also used to sell products as varied as Nabisco Sugar Wafers and Jell-O; the come-ons becoming increasingly explicit as the 20th century advanced. A 1912 ad for the wafers was relatively subtle with its picture of a shirtless and well-muscled Hiawatha. By 1959, the text of a Jell-O ad made it explicit just how sexy the wobbly gelatin dessert could be: "A would-be bride can use it to bait a date and a bride of a few years can use it to remind her mate how lucky he is."

Seeking to put a face on their industrially produced foods, many advertisers sought out spokespeople to promote their wares. Nancy Green became the face of Aunt Jemima after cooking up mountains of flapjacks to promote the company's new pancake mix at the 1893 Chicago Columbian Exposition. The entirely fictional Betty Crocker was created in 1921 to promote Gold Medal flour. She went on to author several cookbooks and became so popular that she apparently even received proposals of marriage. In later years, movie stars and other celebrities were enlisted to sell everything from hot chocolate to low-fat foods. Madison Avenue even signed up cartoon animals to make their pitch. Tony the Tiger—the cartoon feline used to advertise Kellogg's Frosted Flakes—became as recognizable as Mickey Mouse after his introduction in 1952.

The advent of radio in the late 1920s mostly reinforced the promotional innovations of the previous quarter-century. In the United States, the transition from print to broadcasting was relatively seamless, in part because the model developed for funding radio programming was essentially the same as that used for magazines. Whereas in Europe most radio was state funded, here advertising paid the bills and determined what would and would not be heard over the airwaves. Some early advertisers even created the programs themselves. Most of the early radio shows were sponsored by a single company, but soon spot ads became common. Typically, these were woven directly into the script so that the fictional character in a radio play, for example, would segue into praise for the sponsor's product. Early forms of cross-media advertising also hammered home the connection between a product and radio show. Campbell's, which sponsored the Burns and Allen radio show in the 1930s, ran print ads featuring the Campbell's kids listening to the radio. By this time, daytime soap operas had also been invented to target homemakers with ads for not only soap but a whole range of kitchen and household products.

The changes of the post–World War II era echoed the transformations of the late 1800s. A spate of new products and cooking technologies came onto the market.

Women changed their living patterns by moving away from urban communities to larger, but more isolated, homes in the suburbs. The newly invented field of consumer surveys gives us a snapshot of the insecure suburban housewife. In 1951, when the Gallup organization asked married women about their cooking abilities, only 23 percent claimed they were better than their mothers while 58 percent feared they were worse. Little wonder that they were happy to load their brand-new freezers with **frozen foods** and seek advice from the women's magazines on how to combine canned tuna with cream of mushroom soup. The suburbs led to larger, broad-aisled supermarkets, which in turn necessitated bigger, bolder packaging. The car-based culture and new mobility created a demand for standardized **fast food** across the United States. Fast food chains like Kentucky Fried Chicken (first **franchised** in 1952) and **McDonald's** (founded in 1955) had the advertising budgets to promote their **restaurants** nationally.

The 1950s also ushered in the new medium of **television**. At first, both programs and ads on TV simply imitated what had worked on radio, but, with rising costs, it was no longer economically viable for one company to sponsor a whole program. By the 1960s, the now familiar sequence of commercials interspersed with programming became the norm. The 1970s brought cable television and hundreds of channels to a medium that had hitherto been dominated by only three networks. Traditionally, food and kitchen appliance advertising funded daytime television, while products aimed at a male market dominated evening television. But as the market increasingly splintered, the food industry could reach their sought-after demographic with ever increasing precision. With the advent of the Food Network in 1993, sellers of barbecue equipment or Lean Cuisine had finely defined audiences for their wares.

Whereas print ads for food were primarily directed at wives and mothers, the visual form of television made it possible to reach consumers at earlier and earlier ages. One 1991 study counted 222 junk food ads in one Saturday morning's set of cartoon shows. Many fast food chains used toy giveaways—generally cross-marketed with television or movie characters—to encourage children to eat at their outlets. Schools were paid by soft drink manufacturers to stock their brands exclusively in order to build brand loyalty. This approach has proven effective, as children increasingly influence their own and even their family's dining choices. According to one survey of children in the 1990s, some two-thirds claimed to influence their family' s choice of restaurant.

Advertisers have undergone scrutiny for the ways they market their wares to both children and adults, but with little real effect. Intermittently, the government has stepped in to limit just what benefits advertisers could claim for their products. Congress passed major legislation on several occasions between 1906 and 1967 to restrict the most brazen practices and unsubstantiated claims, but the deregulatory climate of the 1980s and '90s once again expanded the manufacturers' options. In an echo of the patent medicine sellers, foods were once again touted for their supposed health attributes. Around the turn of the millennium, Lipton tea made claims that its beverage was an anticarcinogen and Cheerios breakfast cereal blithely claimed that it lowered the incidence of heart disease.

But the business did not entirely stand still. Food companies emblazoned their names on everything from high school cafeterias to sports arenas. Coke, Pepsi, Bacardi rum, and others got into the business of sponsoring pop music tours. Products were routinely placed in feature films and television shows. Particularly successful was the use of Reese's Pieces candy in the 1982 movie *E.T.*, which led to an 85 percent sales increase.

In the 1990s, the coming of the **Internet** promised to deliver consumers with ever-greater accuracy, although there is some question about the effectiveness of this marketing technique when it comes to mass-market foods. There is no doubt, however, that it has allowed marketers of niche products such as heirloom turkeys and artisanal cheeses to promote their products at modest cost.

Early on in the 20th century, food advertising was largely instrumental in creating a common culinary culture out of a nation of immigrants. Subsequently, it projected that culture abroad. To most of the world, Coke and McDonald's are the American Way.

See also Cultural Imperialism; Marketing to Children.

FURTHER READINGS: Cayton, Mary Kupiec, and Peter W. Williams, eds. "Television" in *Encyclopedia of American Social History.* New York: Thomson-Gale (Charles Scribner's Sons), 2001; Manring, M. M. *Slave in a Box: The Strange Career of Aunt Jemima.* Charlottesville: University Press of Virginia, 1998; Parkin, Katherine. *Food Is Love: Advertising and Gender Roles in Modern America.* Philadelphia: University of Pennsylvania Press, 2006.

Michael Krondl

African American Food Business African American business activities with food have existed since black settlement on American shores. Early African Americans, slave and free, established businesses, enterprises, assumed risks associated with granting and receiving credit, and generating markets for their goods and services. African American business activities in general and those involving food in particular are notable primarily because they were small in scale and usually informal. As a result, black entrepreneurship in food service has gone unnoticed, despite its historical importance.

Precolonial Africans in the Food Business

Those Africans who came directly from the continent to the English colonies could count among their talents agricultural skills and competence in trade and marketing. In precolonial Africa, men were mostly merchants and traders while women participated in the market where they bartered and sold agricultural goods. In western Africa, these goods and provisions might include yams, plantains, okra, onions, and malaguetta peppers. Livestock dealers made lucrative profits from trading cattle, and the waterways and lakes yielded major fishing opportunities enabling salting, smoking, and sun drying of the fish. Where food was plentiful, African traders would provision slave ships that were preparing for the transatlantic voyage.

Provisioning Colonial America

It was previously assumed that small garden plots primarily provided a means of self-provisioning. While true, this was not the sole purpose of these gardens. With land in abundance, many enslaved people used the excess they produced to enter the market economy as hawkers and traders. Though the practice varied over time and space, depending upon one's location and the agricultural schedule of the plantation, sometimes barter and trade were possible. According to early traveler's accounts it was not an unfamiliar sight to see African American women, slave and free, vending and hawking food items while walking the streets of major towns. Plantation as well as nonplantation households had to be provisioned on a daily and sometimes on a weekly basis, consequently, average-sized plantations along with wealthier homesteads like Carter Burwell's Carter's Grove and Thomas Jefferson's Monticello sometimes increased their foodstuffs from the provision grounds of their slaves.

Economic opportunities for blacks were severely limited. Nonetheless, the pre-Revolutionary War years witnessed some of the earliest known black food enterprises. Not only did enslaved and free blacks participate in the marketing and trading of agricultural surplus but also they would take part in vending prepared foods—smoked fish, chicken, and even soup. Free blacks, in particular, used their knowledge and skills in cooking and preparing foods to open restaurants, inns, boardinghouses, and catering houses. Proprietors who gained a reputation for providing good food and drink could make substantial profits. One such restaurant owner was Samual Fraunces, who in the 1750s opened Fraunces Tavern in New York City. Fraunces considered himself both a caterer and an innkeeper and was said to operate one of the finest hostelries in colonial America.

Even before Fraunces, however, there were other leaders in the catering field, specifically in the oyster trade and in the pastry making sector. In 1736, for example, using a small amount of start-up capital from Mary's bootlegging business, Emanuel Bernoon and his wife went on to open an oyster and ale house. Duchess Quamino, a slave in the home of William Channing, was celebrated as the best pastry chef in Rhode Island. With the proceeds of her sales she was able to eventually buy her freedom. Cyrus Bustill is considered another successful baker. The son of the white lawyer Samuel Bustill and one of his slaves, Cyrus learned the trade of a baker from a Quaker. Bustill served as a baker for a period during the Revolutionary War after which he moved to Philadelphia, retired, and opened a Quaker school. Most of these caterers provided food services almost exclusively to elite whites. However, there were some African Americans in food service who had a more general clientele.

Provisioning during the Antebellum Years

Prior to the Civil War, African Americans maintained a virtual stranglehold on the catering business. This is hardly surprising given that food service was an area where most African Americans were expected to dominate. It was, however, an industry that provided enterprising opportunities for black women either to hire out their time from the plantation owner and set up small-scale cookshops or to enter the trade as free women. Though overwhelmingly small-scale, these enterprises provided proceeds that were used to purchase personal freedom and the freedom of family members. In instances of free women, profits were used to better the lives and opportunities of one's family.

Local newspapers, travel memoirs, and slave's narratives are replete with stories of African American women who would anticipate the opening of the daily marketplace by selling their wares ahead of time. Many free black women would prepare the food at home or in their stall and sell to busy travelers throughout urban centers and rural travelways. At times, the African Americans were so astute that they would command whatever price they wanted. In return, these women would secure money, food, and in some cases presents. In Fort Washington, Maryland, for example, the mother of late nineteenth-century journalist and self-trained historian John E. Bruce used her skills as a cook at the Marine Corps garrison. Her business was so profitable that she had to purchase a horse and wagon to convey and sell her goods.

Some of the most successful black women in the food service field combined food with the operating of inns and taverns. Some were owned legally and many others illegally. The most successful inns did not cater to slaves or free blacks, perhaps because it was illegal to sell liquor to them. In order to be profitable, a liquor permit was necessary. Consequently, owners limited their clientele. The Washington, D.C., Wormley Hotel, established by James Wormley, a wealthy black caterer, largely attracted politicians and foreign dignitaries. The elegant, upscale hotel survived throughout the closing decades of the nineteenth-century, setting some of the standards for turn of the twentieth-century luxury hotels. In all, however, the services of elite black caterers were no longer needed or wanted by wealthy whites as the United States rapidly moved toward the Jim Crow Era.

Black Food Business from 1865–1900

Whereas previously some whites sought the services of elite African American catering houses to provide for their needs, the closing decades of the nineteenth-century found requests waning in the face of competition from newer and larger luxury hotels established by whites. But African American caterers continued to move forward. By 1869, the Corporation of Caterers was founded by 12 African American caterers in New York City. Their desire was not only to consolidate their interests but also to control the quality of services being dispensed. In Philadelphia, the epicenter of the catering industry prior to the Civil War, two additional black catering organizations were founded—the Philadelphia Caterers Association (1866) and the Caterers Manufacturing and Supply Company (1894). Again the goal was cooperative enterprise and quality control.

Some African American caterers continued to flourish despite the lack of demand. Among them were Thomas Dorsey, Levi Cromwell, and Henry Minton. These African American men offered catering services that afforded them a comfortable net worth and a place in history. Others, including Chicagoan Charles Smiley, changed the face of African American catering by offering a full range of services including food, cakes, and floral arrangements. As such, he maintained not only a white clientele but also a number of elite African Americans. African American caterers found themselves in the situation where they were primarily limited to servicing small dinner parties and other social occasions for middle-class whites. As a result, some African Americans with an interest in food service went into the hotel business while others simply chose to rely on all black patrons.

Similar to the culinary turmoil taking place in urban centers, those in rural areas experienced overt hostility at times even though they were involved in more informal trades. African American women could be found offering foods and food services in more unceremonious ways at whistle-stops and train junctions. As they sold their pies, hot coffee, fried chicken, and other foodstuffs they were in direct competition with tavern owners. Often times they were denied permits to vend and hawk their wares, forcing them to develop alternative and creative ways of entering the capitalist economy. One of the most documented trade sites is Gordonsville, Virginia, where a group of women were called "waiter carriers." A multigenerational enterprise, the participants used the proceeds from their trade to open restaurants and to secure material goods to better their way of life.

From the antebellum period through Reconstruction, black business activity continued in earnest. Following the Civil War a new black planter class emerged that was comprised of former slaves, tenant farmers, or independently hired farm laborers. Benjamin Montgomery, for example, owned plantations and dry-goods stores. While such successes were few and far between compared to the number of whites who succeeded as merchants, some blacks did prevail. Perhaps the most triumphant stories are of black commercial farmers engaged in **agribusiness,** which ranged from **sugar** production to livestock. Known as "The Negro Potato King," for example, Junius Groves owned a general merchandise store and several apple orchards. In one year he is documented as having produced over 700,000 bushels of potatoes.

Black Food Business, 1900–1950

Considered the "golden age of black business" by one historian, the first half of the twentieth century found many African Americans emerging as leading capitalists. Though locked out the economic exchanges fueled by industrialization—the production of iron, oil, steel, and coal—some African Americans managed to establish million-dollar enterprises. Most, however, were relegated to the food service sector where they were able to excel.

The Great Migration and World War I contributed in no small part to the concentration of African Americans in various residential areas. This, in turn, prompted the emergence of several creative capitalist food ventures. Banks Fried Chicken and Restaurant Company open in 1913. Starting from a pushcart, Thomas Banks, went on to establish four restaurants by 1919. A precursor to successful contemporary chicken chains, Banks' enterprise was short-lived with the advent of Prohibition. Unable to sell liquor, his ability to also sell chicken was affected.

By the Great Depression a number of African American cooperatives had emerged. Each member paid a few dollars to join, which was then used as venture capital to establish a business wherein each member shared in the profits. Largely organized by black churches, these co-ops established grocery and meat markets. The black Florida Farmers' Cooperative Association, for example, was founded in 1918 and by five years later they had branches in almost a dozen counties. Other co-ops included the Victory Poultry Production Enterprises and the People's Cooperative **supermarket,** established by Tuskegee Institute.

There were several additional food ventures that were attempted during this period. Black food-processing companies like Henry Armstrong Beer Distributing Company in Kansas City, Colony House Premium Beer, a black-owned brewery, and others were started but were slow to catch on. On the other hand, companies like Minnie Lee Pie Company, established by Minnie Lee Fellings around 1939, Parker House Sausage, and Baldwin Ice Cream all met with relative success.

Contemporary Black Food Business

Participation by African Americans in corporate America and in the food business industry rose to varying levels of success in the second half of the twentieth century; still few blacks are in ownership positions. Of notable exception was Reginald Lewis, who in October 1987 purchased the international division of Beatrice Foods. With holdings in 31 countries, the company became known as TLC Beatrice International. At the time, the deal was considered the largest leveraged buyout by an American company. By 1992, the company had sales of over $1.6 billion annually, making TLC black America's first billion-dollar corporation.

Franchising has provided a major entryway into corporate America for many African Americans, particularly those interested in food service supply. Franchises that are owned by African Americans include **McDonald's,** 7-Eleven stores, Burger King, and Godfather's Pizza. Wallace Amos, Jr. established Famous Amos Chocolate Chip Cookie Company in 1975. Initially, his cookies could be found in upscale department stores—Bloomingdales, Neiman Marcus, and Macy's. But after failing to expand his franchising operations Amos declared bankruptcy.

In 1988, a joint venture partnership was formed between Earvin "Magic" Johnson and Starbucks, the leading retailer of specialty coffee in the United States. The enterprise, known as Urban Coffee Opportunities, locates Starbucks stores in diverse urban and suburban neighborhoods throughout the United States. With over 100 stores nationwide, the goal of the venture is to bring quality products and services to minority communities, increasing exposure as well as economic advancement and opportunity.

With a history and established tradition of business activity and entrepreneurship, African Americans have been active in gaining a foothold in corporate America. Numerous federal initiatives, access to capital, and joint ventures among other avenues have enabled African Americans to enjoy business success. These success, however, have not been without numerous challenges—many of which persist.

According to Oxfam and U.S. Agriculture census data, in 1910 a total of 218,000 black farmers owned 15 million acres of land. By 1978, black farmers owned less than 4.3 million acres of land. Today the numbers are in further decline with approximately 18,000 black farmers owning less than 2.4 million acres of land. In 1997, black farmers comprised less than 1% of the number of white farmers. Black farmers are being forced to leave a multigenerational livelihood. In 1982, the U.S. Commission on Civil Rights found that tactics implemented by the **U.S. Department of Agriculture (USDA)** were a major cause of land loss among black farmers. After years of having their USDA loan applications systematically denied or delayed, black farmers joined together and filed a Class Action Lawsuit (*Pigford v. Glickman*) against the USDA. Daniel Glickman was the Secretary of Agriculture under the Clinton administration. In April 1999 the USDA and black farmers reached a settlement. The Black Farmers Association, founded by John Boyd Jr., has since filed motions in federal court noting the flaws and defects in the settlement decree.

Aside from agribusiness, African Americans are sorely missing from the fine dining realm. Contemporary African American chefs find themselves either pigeonholed into positions that limit them to cooking southern foods or not being taken seriously for their craft. In some instances, African American chefs are constantly associated with stereotyped images like Aunt Jemima and Uncle Rastus. In other instances, African Americans wanting to enter culinary schools meet with resistance from family members who remember the age when blacks could find employment only in low-paying cooking establishments. Few, if any blacks have been publicly recognized as notable chefs. Edna Lewis, who died in 2006 at the age of 89, and Tavern on the Green's Patrick Clark, who died in 1998 at the age of 42, were two of the few considered bona fide celebrity chefs.

Almost unilaterally, African Americans who have worked in the food service industry have done so through small businesses. Strides have been made and contributions noted, but there is even more to the heritage that African Americans bring to American food business no matter how small.

FURTHER READINGS: Bower, Anne, ed. *African American Foodways: History and Culture.* Urbana: University of Illinois Press, 2007; Harris, Jessica. *Iron Pots and Wooden Spoons.* New York: Simon and Schuster. Fireside edition, 1999; Spivey, Diane M. *The Peppers, Crackling, and Knots of Wool Cookbook: The Global Migration of African Cuisine.* New York: State University of New York Press, 1999; Walker, Juliet K. "Racism, Slavery, and Free Enterprise: Black Entrepreneurship in the United States Before the Civil War." *Business History Review* 60 (Autumn 1986): 343–82; Walker, Juliet K. *The History of Black Business in America.* New York: Twayne Publishers, 1998; Williams-Forson, Psyche. *Building Houses Out of Chicken Legs: Black Women, Food, and Power.* Chapel Hill: University of North Carolina Press, 2006.

Psyche Williams-Forson

Agribusiness The term *agribusiness* refers to those farms and firms directly involved with agricultural production. This emphasis on production is what distinguishes agribusiness from other aspects of the food business, which focus on consumption. Of course, business integration across the food supply system blurs this distinction, making it difficult to identify agribusiness apart from the food business as a whole. Firms that supply farms with seed, **fertilizers**, pesticides, and transportation services, such as Cargill, Archer Daniels Midland, and Syngenta, often market food products. Alternatively, companies such as Nestlé, **Kraft**, **Heinz**, and **Campbell's**, which sell foods under familiar brand names, are also directly involved in agriculture—engaged in contract farming or with divisions that provide agricultural technology. This integration is a key component of agribusiness today, as it illustrates a common set of values running through both modern farming and many food corporations. Both enterprises stress volume, efficiency, and profitability above all, and celebrate technology as the best way to achieve these goals. Agribusiness, then, refers not just to those firms concerned in some direct way with farming but also to a set of values—efficiency, productivity, and technological innovation—that are central to the contemporary food industry.

History

The history of agribusiness assumes a vastly different form in Europe and other parts of the world than it does in the United States. Globally, one can see parts of the agrarian sector isolated from the full impact of the market even through the 20th century. In the United States, on the other hand, farmers in the United States have always been deeply capitalistic, and agrarianism has seldom existed apart from commercial considerations. So the history of agribusiness centrally involves the United States.

Agribusiness began in the United States when mid-19th-century mechanization and the advent of rail transportation inalterably transformed the scope of agriculture. As railroads extended the market-oriented farmers' reach, increasing competition and lowering farm prices, success required that farmers produce more crops and livestock, and produce it more cheaply. In order to maintain their place in the market, farmers found it necessary to acquire the new equipment being produced by companies such as McCormick (founded 1848) and John Deere (1868) and to intensify production using guano and sodium nitrate fertilizers being mined and mixed by firms such as W. R. Grace (1854).

After the Civil War, agriculture led the way to a modern, fully industrialized economy. Late 19th- and early 20th-century discoveries in the chemical industry involving pesticides and fertilizers, and the further mechanization of farming via the internal combustion engine, increased the economic complexity of agriculture. New advances in plant and livestock breeding brought nursery, seed, and stock businesses into the farm supply market. By the early 20th century, petroleum and chemical businesses not generally thought of as "agricultural" had joined equipment firms as participants in the farm economy. These include such firms as DuPont (famously starting as a gunpowder manufactory in 1802, but by the 1890s producing pesticides, and by the 1950s seeds and herbicides), Standard Oil of California–Chevron (from 1912, lubricants, then by the 1940s, fertilizer, pesticides, and animal feeds), and **Monsanto** (beginning with **artificial sweeteners** in 1899, but by the 1920s into pesticides, and by the 1960s herbicides and seeds).

As the business of supplying the farm increased in complexity, a corresponding trend occurred with marketing farm products. In the late 19th century, U.S. trading companies and product processors achieved an international scale and reached backward to integrate with farming enterprises. Cargill (founded in 1865), Archer Daniels Midland (1898), and General Mills (1928, but with roots in the Minneapolis Milling Company founded in 1856) can trace their prominence back to their successful integration of shipping, milling, and marketing grain. **Meatpackers** and processors such as **Armour** (1883) and **Swift** (1885) employed rails, **refrigeration**, and "dis-assembly" lines to transform beef ranching and pig raising. Also in the late 19th century, the industrialized **canning** of fruits and vegetables spawned such firms as Heinz (1869), Campbell's (1869), **Dole** (1851), and **Del Monte** (founded as California Fruit Canner's Association, 1899). These processors and marketers all engaged in contract farming and eventually became involved in agricultural research.

The final component of today's agribusiness sector also took shape in the late 19th century with the move of the **U.S. Department of Agriculture** (USDA; est. 1862) into research and technological development. By the 1890s, the USDA had sent researchers and "plant explorers" around the world to acquire new crop varieties and genetic material. It had also set up a system of agricultural experiment stations around the country. Many of these became associated with the large state universities, supported by government land grants, "for the benefit of Agriculture and the Mechanic Arts" as established by the 1863 Morrill Act. Universities in Illinois, Michigan, Texas, Iowa, and California, among others, still play a key role in developing new technologies for farming and new uses for farm products.

By the mid-20th century, then, there existed in America an enormously complex business sector associated with agriculture, driven by technology and based on the premise that market integration meant efficient production and assured profitability. Only those farms themselves most integrated into this system—up-to-date in equipment and chemical use, with enough land at their disposal to generate a large crop or handle a large herd—could successfully compete in the international marketplace, and so the scale of farming itself enlarged and intensified and often incorporated. Small farmers did not disappear, but they found it increasingly difficult to operate independently. Nowhere was this process of increasing scale more visible than in

poultry, pig, and beef cattle raising, which after World War II saw the rise of "confined animal feeding operations" or CAFOs, growing and slaughtering millions of animals a year. Independent poultry farmers were eventually driven out of business, while small hog farms and cattle ranches became a tiny cog in a fully industrialized system.

Changing Attitudes toward Agribusiness

Given that it had been developing for 100 years, it is striking testimony to the agrarian myth of the independent farmer that the term *agribusiness* was not employed until 1957, by Harvard business professor John H. Davis and Ray Goldberg. Davis was director of the Harvard program in agriculture and business, a postwar brainchild of business school dean Donald K. David, who had been an executive in the food processing industry. So, the book responsible for coining agribusiness, the term, was itself an example of the nexus of agriculture, business, and academic institutions it described. Davis and Goldberg used the word to refer in aggregate to the many enterprises involved in commodity production and processing, food and fiber manufacturing, and food distribution and retailing, and they pointed out that in the mid-1950s, the combined products and services generated involved 40 percent of total U.S. consumer expenditures. Interestingly, in light of subsequent critiques of global corporate control, Davis and Goldberg expressed some concern that what they saw as the disordered complexity of the agribusiness enterprise—its multiplicity of farms, companies, trade associations, government agencies, and academic training and research programs—would increase the uneven development of the farm sector and inhibit the efficient coordination of the nation's food supply. To meet the needs of both agribusiness and consumers, they argued for greater centralization, based on informed policies that reached across all elements of the economy.

Since the concept of agribusiness so clearly described the 20th-century realities of farming and food production, the term was quickly accepted and, in the years immediately after its conception, generally used favorably as indicative of a technologically up-to-date, modern food "system." Yet less than a decade after its coining, the word began acquiring perjorative connotations, and the interrelationships it described began coming under attack. These negative associations with agribusiness came partly from small farmers, worried about farm consolidation and still attracted to the agrarian image of virtuous, self-sufficient production; they emerged as well from the health fears spawned by extensive pesticide, herbicide, and chemical fertilizer use, fears that crystallized with the publication of Rachel Carson's *Silent Spring* (1964); they appeared, too, in the general public dismay over California farmowners' callous treatment of farmworkers revealed by the protests of Cesar Chavez and the United Farm Workers in the mid-1960s; and finally, if less specifically, they were influenced by a general distrust of big business and big government that characterized the social and political upheavals of the later 1960s.

Indicating a new attitude toward agribusiness in U.S. politics was the Agribusiness Accountability Group, a Washington public interest organization affiliated with consumer activist Ralph Nader and led by former congressional aide (and future Texas Commissioner of Agriculture) Jim Hightower. In its brief existence, from 1969 to 1974, it released a series of scathing, widely publicized reports on such topics as excessive pesticide use encouraged by firms such as Dow and Union Carbide; the domination of the grain market by big processors such as Cargill; and USDA neglect of independent farmers in favor of corporate farmers such as the Tenneco Oil Company. Hightower published his own report in 1973, which excoriated the agricultural research and training programs at the nation's land-grant universities, arguing that they ignored the public interest in the name of big business, leading to tasteless "hard tomatoes" for consumers and discriminatory "hard times" for small farmers.

In the next two decades into the 1990s, increasing numbers of critiques now exactly reversed Davis and Goldberg's concerns: far from being underorganized and inefficient, the problem with agribusiness was that it was dominated by a small set of centralized institutions driven only by productivity and greed. Late-20th-century anxieties concerning the rapid pace of economic globalization heightened these negative associations.

Agribusiness was by this time a **multinational** enterprise, and each firm had a lengthy and confusing pedigree, which only grew more tangled as mergers and acquisitions flew over national boundaries. For example, J. R. Geigy (founded 1758), a Swiss chemical firm and one of the developers of DDT's insecticidal uses, merged with chemical company Ciba (1884) in 1970, and as **Ciba-Geigy** marketed pesticides, fertilizers, and seeds. In 1996 the company merged with Swiss pharmaceutical firm Sandoz (1886) and became Novartis. In 2000 Novartis divested itself of its agribusiness and merged it with Zeneca Agrochemicals, which itself had been divested in 1994 from the English firm Imperial Chemical Industries (1926). Together, Novartis and Zeneca created Syngenta, a company now with thousands of employees, including those at nine locations in the United States, and billions of dollars in worldwide sales.

Equally huge and multinational were firms such as the Thai-based Charoen Pokphand Corporation, which had begun as a vegetable and seed shipper in the 1920s, but by the 1980s supplied seeds, fertilizer, and farm management to all of Asia. Another example is the Mexico-based Grupo Pulsar, a conglomerate formed in 1985 in part from Dutch, British, and American seed companies. It quickly became one of the world's largest seed marketers and vegetable **hybridizers**, via its subsidiaries Seminis and Savia. In 2005 Seminis was bought by Monsanto, which had by that time re-created itself after having been acquired and divested by Pharmacia. These bewildering shifts in corporate allegiances, and the size and scope of the organizations involved, added to the sense that agribusiness possessed a power beyond the reach of national governments.

By the 1990s, these firms' pursuit of the latest technology became part of the indictment against agribusiness, as well. Technology that had been celebrated for increasing production and combating world hunger in the 1960s "green revolution" now appeared a threat to indigenous farming practices, environmentally unsustainable because it required continuous chemical inputs. These fears only increased when breakthroughs in **genetic engineering** allowed firms like Monsanto to quickly alter plants' genome. Most notoriously, Monsanto created seeds that grew soybeans resistant to the herbicide the company produced, offering farmers the convenience of killing weeds chemically without fear of harming their crop—and, of course, increasing sales of Monsanto's herbicide. Such genetically modified products, however, alarmed consumers, adding distrust of "Frankenfoods" to the negative imagery associated with factory farms and global agglomeration. For many consumers, "agribusiness" had become an epithet, signifying a malevolent, shadowy corporatism.

Agribusiness Today: Issues and Concerns

The deep suspicion, even paranoia, about agribusiness's influence on the world's food supply that exists among some contemporary critics of the food system appears at times based on a reflexive anticapitalism that sees only exploitation in institutionalized market arrangements. Indeed, some of the pejorative associations with agribusiness come from a naive adherence to agrarian mythology, which ignores the deep historical interaction of business and agriculture, particularly in the United States. Reformers tend to exaggerate the degree of human concern and responsibility that existed when agriculture was more localized, and their proposals call for wholesale restructuring of the global economy.

In fact, reformers at times appear to overestimate the power of agribusiness firms to control the world's food supply. Monsanto, for example, was thrown on the defensive by world rejection of the soybeans it had successfully marketed in the United States and Canada. Domestically, it also failed to win a market for its genetically engineered **wheat** seed. In fact, the heavy consumer orientation of the current food system, and its relative responsiveness to health and food security fears, especially as revealed in the reaction to genetically engineered crops, suggest real limits to agribusiness power. At the same time, the increasing power of retail outlets in the food business (albeit themselves worldwide conglomerates) appears as a barrier to further consolidation of the food industry from agribusiness firms. That the rapid growth of **organic food** in response to consumer concerns about health and the environment occurred even within an agribusiness context that discouraged organic farming suggests a level of consumer power that is reassuring.

Yet it would be equally naive to dismiss critics' concerns about the nature of agribusiness. Indeed, as doubters of the recent "greening" of agribusiness have pointed out, the commitment to organic production and sustainability on the part of agricultural and food corporations is often shallow, eschewing pesticide use, for example, but still practicing intensive monoculture—that is, growing one kind of one crop exclusively. Multinational firms, even while marketing organic products, continue to exploit **labor** and undermine local farming across the world, and by operating at a scale beyond community or even national regulation, they can make claims without fearing close scrutiny from consumers. Even if consumers had the energy to investigate the agribusiness origins of their food, the size of the corporations involved—not to mention their renaming as they spin off, acquire, and merge—make such tracking and tracing of accountability difficult.

A balanced assessment must grant that today's abundance of food in the developed world stems from the efficiency and technological advancement promoted through the 20th century by corporate farms, agrochemical companies, and processing and marketing firms. Such an assessment must also recognize agribusiness's costs, which have included the ruin of small farmers, the destruction of workers' lives, and environmental damage around the world. For some time, both policy makers and the consuming public have judged that the benefits of productivity are worth its costs. There are indications, however, that the 21st century will see a new debate between company prerogatives, food policy makers, and consumer interests. Should this debate seriously challenge the overwhelming commitment to technology and high productivity, agribusiness and the food business as a whole will be transformed.

See also Boycotts and Consumer Protests; Corn.

FURTHER READINGS: *Agribusiness* [journal, 1985–]. Available online at http://www3.inter-science.wiley.com/cgi-bin/jhome/35917; Davis, John, and Ray Goldberg. *A Concept of Agribusiness.* Cambridge, MA: Harvard University, Division of Research, Graduate School of Business Administration, 1957; Fitzgerald, Deborah. *Every Farm a Factory: The Industrial Ideal in American Agriculture.* New Haven, CT: Yale University Press, 2003; Hightower, Jim. *Hard Tomatoes, Hard Times: A Report of the Agribusiness Accountability Project on the Failure of America's Land Grant College.* Cambridge, MA: Schenkman, 1973; Jansen, Kees, and Sietze Vellama. *Agribusiness and Society: Corporate Responses to Environmentalism, Market Opportunities and Public Regulation.* New York: Zed Books, 2004; Magdoff, Fred, John Bellamy Foster, and Frederick H. Buttel. *Hungry for Profit: The Agribusiness Threat to Farmers, Food, and the Environment.* New York: Monthly Review Press, 2000.

Jeffrey Charles

Agricultural Unions The types of agricultural unions within which workers organize are diverse and vary depending on local contexts. In developing countries, where agriculture is the dominant economic activity, the membership of national agricultural unions tends to consist of workers on commercial farms and plantations. These unions, which may organize workers across sectors or solely within specific sectors, are often the largest workers' organizations within their country. Examples include the Kenya Plantation and Agricultural Union in Kenya and the National Union of Plantation and Agricultural Workers in Uganda.

In countries where the agricultural workforce is proportionally small, notably the highly industrialized countries, members of different sectors are typically brought together in general national unions. Agricultural wageworkers compose sections or units within these broader general unions. Examples of such unions include Kommunal in Sweden and the United Food and Commercial Workers (UFCW) union in North America.

In developed countries that have undergone processes of deindustrialization, many agricultural workers have been organized within industrial unions that have diversified to maintain their membership. In Canada, agricultural workers have recently been organized within the Canadian Auto Workers (CAW), whose full name—the National Automobile, Aerospace, Transportation and General Workers Union of Canada—expresses its level of diversification. There has been some concern that the interests of agricultural workers are of lower priority than are those of the CAW's traditional industrial base, which still provides the union's core membership.

Nontraditional social movement unions have also played important parts in organizing to resist large **agribusiness** monopolies in specific sectors in wealthier countries. These unions have made innovative use of direct action tactics and consumer **boycotts** to win significant victories, including in the grape industry of California and the tomato fields in Florida. Recognizing their limited leverage to win strikes, these unions have operated like social movements, relying on alliances with other movements to bring broad-based pressure to bear on employers. Important examples include the United Farm Workers of America (UFW), founded by Cesar Chavez, and the Coalition of Immokalee Workers, whose members supply produce to the **fast food** giants.

In order to overcome the often contradictory relationship that separates agricultural wage earners and small farmers, some unions have become hybrid organizations representing both groups. These hybrid unions generally develop separate organizational and political structures to address the needs of their dual membership. These can be uneasy arrangements, especially where small farmer members employ wage laborers. Examples of such hybrid unions include the General Agricultural Workers Union (GAWU) of Ghana and CONTAG in Brazil, which is the largest such union, boasting a membership of three million wageworkers and six million small farmers.

Unions have also tried to build alliances with indigenous peoples. Until recently there has been little engagement between the labor movement and indigenous peoples' organizations in rural areas. In the current context of global capital and the enclosure of land by giant **multinational** agribusinesses, however, the labor movement and indigenous groups have come together around issues of land reform and sustainable indigenous development.

National agricultural unions may affiliate to the International Union of Food, Agricultural, Hotel, Restaurant, Catering, Tobacco and Allied Workers' Association (IUF), a global trade union federation founded in 1920. The IUF brings together a network of some 336 national unions. The member unions of the IUF represent workers in agriculture and plantations, the processing and manufacturing of food and beverages, and tobacco workers. The IUF focuses its efforts on building solidarity among agricultural workers at every stage of the food chain, whether planting, harvesting, processing, preparing, or serving food. In order to develop links most effectively between unions throughout the food chain, given available resources, the IUF has targeted six major crops—bananas, cocoa, **coffee**, cut flowers, **sugar**, and tea—for its organizing efforts and ongoing publicity campaigns. The stated goal of the IUF is to create an international union opposition to the power of the transnational corporations that currently dominate agricultural sectors. A major part of this is the struggle for union recognition at every level, including internationally, which is crucial given the low level of unionization within the industry. At the same time, the IUF organizes beyond immediate workplace issues to support broader struggles against oppression. This work involves building active alliances with environmental, human rights, and consumer groups and has taken on greater significance since the emergence of the alternative globalization movement in the 1990s.

The international union federations, such as the IUF, allow for the development of coordinated organizing of workers in multinational corporations and for the deployment of campaigns against the multinational companies that monopolize the agricultural industry. While national and regional trade unions and union federations can be successful in dealing with transnational corporations, they cannot achieve broader goals of internationally recognized rights and standards, for both labor and the environment, within global companies without the coordinated solidarity allowed through the resources of the international federations.

Agricultural work is highly dangerous, labor-intensive work. Agricultural workers are among the lowest paid workers, and they typically work longer hours—routinely more than 45 hours per week—than do workers in other industries. The right of workers to establish and join organizations of their own preference in order to improve working conditions and defend their interests as workers is a fundamental right enshrined in the principle of freedom of association as articulated in the International Labor Organization's (ILO) Right of Association (Agriculture) Convention, 1921 (Number 11) and the Freedom of Association and Protection of the Right to Organize Convention, 1948 (Number 87). Recognizing the limitations that are often imposed on these rights by national governments, the ILO instituted the Rural

Workers' Organizations Convention, 1975 (Number 141) in an effort to extend the principle of freedom of association to workers in the agricultural industry.

Despite this, violations of rights to freedom of association are frequently experienced by agricultural workers seeking to organize. The ILO Committee on Freedom of Association has accumulated enormous amounts of data documenting numerous violations of agricultural workers' rights to unionize. These violations range from state-initiated regulatory impediments to physical assaults and even assassinations of union organizers, again often under state sponsorship.

Most agricultural workers have only limited protection under national labor laws. Numerous countries simply exclude the agricultural sector from their regular labor legislation, often using the excuse that, as provision of a basic human need—food— the necessity of agricultural work takes precedence over the rights of workers within the industry. Specific limitations to general labor legislation are often applied on the basis of the size of the agricultural interest, such as family farms, or on the contractual status, such as seasonal labor, of the workers. Indeed, casual, temporary, and seasonal workers are often left with little or no labor protection.

This is not only true in poorer countries or countries ruled by less democratic forms of government. It is also true of wealthier countries with relatively well-developed and long-standing regimes of labor legislation. In Canada, for example, farm workers in the wealthiest province, Ontario, are specifically excluded from protection under the basic health and safety regulations that cover every other worker in the province. In addition, farm workers in Ontario are prohibited by law from organizing within a union. Approximately 13 percent of all occupational deaths in Canada are farm related.

Where legislation does exist, it is often difficult for inspection, regulation, or enforcement to be carried out given the dispersed nature of agricultural work across farms that may be separated by miles and are isolated from urban centers, or even from rural centers. These twin factors of dispersal and isolation have posed daunting challenges to union members attempting to organize farmworkers. Not only do these realities make it difficult to bring workers together, but the isolated environment also often allows farm owners and managers the opportunity to operate in ways that might otherwise result in penalty or sanction. Harassment, intimidation, and even physical violence are not uncommon means used by farm bosses to interfere with organizing efforts. Threats by management are worsened by the lack of citizenship status for migratory workers who face summary deportation simply on the basis of the boss's word.

Perhaps not surprisingly, trade union organizations are quite weak in rural areas, with a few exceptions in Latin America and central and eastern Europe. Only between 2 and 7 percent of the agricultural workforce is organized. The geographical dispersal of work sites, limited resources among what are often poorer unions, costs of transportation for organizers, issues of illiteracy, and the use of violence by bosses are all obstacles that make agricultural organizing difficult. The importance of unionization and collective bargaining in the food industries is reflected in the fact that wages, benefits, and working conditions are better within those sectors in which unionization is more prevalent than in the rest of the agricultural sector.

Levels of organizing are especially low among female agricultural workers, who make up approximately one-third of all wage employment in agriculture. This number has in fact been rising, reaching over 40 percent in Latin America and the Caribbean and probably more in Africa, where employment is often informal and confirmed data are lacking. The feminization of agricultural employment is an issue that unions have had to address recently, as agricultural enterprises turn to women as a lower-paid workforce. Unions have attempted to address a number of issues of concern to women through collective bargaining. Some of the issues pursued include maternity leave and benefits, equal opportunity employment, child care, reproductive health care, and pay equity. In addition, unions have become more sensitive to the gendered character of issues such as wages, overtime, bonuses, and discipline.

Where organizing has occurred, collective bargaining remains limited to larger workplaces and plantations. Unionization and the collective bargaining of contracts have been most commonly achieved in those sectors where full-time, regular employment is greatest. Even within those sectors, and even within the same enterprise, seasonal, temporary, and part-time workers tend not to be included within collective agreements that cover their full-time coworkers. In smaller farms and workplaces, the low levels of membership dues are sometimes reflected in the limited services provided by the unions.

In 2002, the IUF World Congress approved a proposal to address the difficulties facing migrant agricultural workers by developing a charter of rights for migrant workers in the industry. A draft charter of rights, which can be a useful tool for union organizing, was produced in 2003. In the United Kingdom, the Transport and General Workers Union (TGWU) has worked to develop the Seasonal Agricultural Workers Scheme, administered by the government, to ensure that migrant workers have the same rights and benefits as other workers in the industry.

In many countries, employment agencies and labor services contract with agricultural companies to supply seasonal labor, whether on farms, in horticultural businesses, or at packing houses. This is part of the broader casualization of labor in agriculture in which more workers are employed on a temporary contract basis with lower wages and often no benefits. These employment contractors often abuse workers through illegal deductions from pay; underpayment; withholding of wages; overcharging for transportation, housing, and food; and, where migrant workers are concerned, through threats of deportation. Many workers find themselves in positions of debt slavery in which they are forced to continue working, with their wages going solely to pay contractors' fees. In addition, workers contracted through employment agencies or labor contractors are often prohibited from registering as union members at their place of work because, technically speaking, they are employed by the agency or contractor rather than by the agricultural enterprise where their work is carried out.

Several unions, including the UFCW and the Industrial Workers of the World (IWW), have attempted to circumvent the employment agencies by developing hiring halls. These are worker-run labor centers which, by controlling the labor supply, allow agricultural workers some direct control over the conditions by which their labor is sold. In Britain, the TGWU has preferred the legislative route, campaigning for the registration of contractors or "gangmasters," albeit meeting with only limited success given the government's reluctance to enact such legislation.

Unions have also had to deal with the use of forced or even slave labor in agriculture. Cases of forced labor involving agricultural workers have been examined by the ILO in several countries. Indeed such cases appear to be growing within wealthier countries. Slave labor camps have been documented within agricultural industries in the United States as well. In June 2005, federal agents from the Department of Labor's Office of the Inspector General, along with members of the Drug Enforcement

Administration and the Environmental Protection Agency's Criminal Investigation Division, raided a Florida labor camp in which homeless men and women were being used as slave labor. This was only one part of an ongoing campaign to investigate the possibly extensive use of slave labor camps by crop producers in Florida. The presence of such situations suggests to some commentators that conditions of trade liberalization and global competition have encouraged a return to slavery as producers seek regular supplies of cheap labor. The Coalition of Immokalee Workers has recently begun a campaign against slavery in the U.S. produce industry.

Unions in agriculture face many challenges, but with the growing concentration of ownership in the agricultural sector, their development is likely to become more prominent. The monopolization of the industry by fewer but larger enterprises, replacing smaller producers and self-employed farmers, has increased the proportion of wageworkers in agriculture. There are currently more wageworkers in agriculture, approximately 450 million out of a total workforce of one billion, or 45 percent of the labor force, than at any previous time.

See also Labor and Labor Unions.

FURTHER READINGS: Edid, Marilyn. *Farm Labor Organizing: Trends and Prospects.* Ithaca, NY: ILR Press, 1994; Frank, Dana. *Bananeras: Women Transforming the Banana Unions of Latin America.* Boston: South End Press, 2005; Hurst, Peter. *Agricultural Workers and Their Contribution to Sustainable Agriculture and Rural Development.* New York: FAO/ILO/IUF, 2005; Royle, Tony. *Labour Relations in the Global Fast Food Industry.* London: Routledge, 2002.

Jeff Shantz

Airline Food These days, airline food is typically derided for its blandness and stinginess, conspicuous absence from flights, or cost above the ticket price, at least in economy ticket classes. But airline food has a fascinating history from the earliest commercial flights and, even today, in-flight catering represents an important multibillion-dollar segment of the aviation industry.

Early Days

The commercial airline industry in the United States developed after World War I when trained military pilots returning home applied their skills to moving mail and light cargo in airplanes. These planes typically had few passenger seats, and when passengers were aboard, little thought was given to servicing them. Passengers on long flights often brought a box lunch or snacks onboard.

It was not until the 1930s that the fledgling airline industry designed planes specifically with the idea of moving people as a core business, and with these planes, accompanying galleys were instituted. From the beginning, despite challenges like cramped spaces, weight restrictions, and lack of usable electricity onboard, airlines worked to compete with steamships and trains by providing full-service dining experiences to passengers, albeit with in-flight accommodations like pillows and lap trays rather than tables. Coffee was brewed onboard and in-flight meals were purchased from fine **restaurants** and hotels, kept warm where possible using piped water or glycol heated by the engines, and served on china and linen with real cutlery.

By the late 1930s, problems with the quality control, ground transportation, and timeliness of **food service** subcontracted from hotels and restaurants, as well as a more competitive marketplace, prompted United Airlines, closely followed by its major competitors, to create airport-based flight kitchens around the country. Airlines continued to buy from restaurants and hotels in smaller airports.

The late 1940s and 1950s prompted many of the in-flight dining innovations familiar today. Aircraft after World War II began to be constructed with attachable or attached tray tables, making the dining balancing act a bit easier for passengers. The ability for planes and later jets to generate usable electricity in flight made commercial kitchen equipment such as ovens and warming cabinets, as well as dry ice iceboxes, adaptable to the airplane galley.

While these innovations improved the quality and availability of airline food, problems remained. The short shelf life of **refrigerated** and reheated food, or food held warm, was acceptable for a short or even transcontinental flight but problematic for a transoceanic flight, on which two or even three meals might have been served en route. Furthermore, the increased popularity of air travel necessitated costly flight kitchens in nearly every airport, including those where access to reliable fresh food was a challenge. The increased frequency of transoceanic flights in the 1950s and '60s prompted a further innovation in in-flight dining: the **frozen** tray dinner (**TV dinner**), brought aboard frozen, shipped throughout the world, and heated in flight via convection oven. This last development, removing the restaurant chef from the process, developing standardized 1950s-style frozen entrees, and plating a complete meal service in a single dinner tray, complete with an individual cutlery and seasonings packet, represented a major innovation in in-flight dining efficiency but contributed to many of the negative associations with airline food today.

Logistics and Meal Structure

Serving quality airline food is a logistical challenge. If the number or variety of meals needed is inaccurately calculated, customer dissatisfaction ensues. Complicating this challenge is the large selection of specialty meals available, including diabetic, gluten-free, Hindu, kosher, lacto-ovo **vegetarian**, low-fat, low-sodium, Muslim, lactose-free, vegan, and vegetarian.

Despite the limitations of space, cooking technology, and cost, efforts are made to serve airline food consistent with a typical meal, especially on long flights encompassing one or more mealtimes. Such a meal may consist of a main dish protein item, vegetable, starch, salad, roll, and dessert. A recent meal served in coach or economy class on a transoceanic United Airlines flight consisted of chicken breast with white sauce, broccoli, carrots, wild rice, crackers with cheese, a salad, a roll, and strawberry ice cream. A first- or business-class meal typically conforms to the same structure but is more likely to use specialty ingredients and consist of multiple courses and is served on china rather than a tray. A recent meal served in business class on British Airways included:

Appetizer: King prawns with a mango and coriander salsa
Main course: Four-cheese ravioli and roast vegetables in a creamy Parmesan cheese and basil sauce
Dessert: Fresh fruit and cheese platter and assorted chocolates

Airline food is tightly regulated and monitored to avoid highly allergenic foods as well as Hazard Analysis and Critical Control Points (HACCP) **food safety** violations.

While not as critical, airlines also avoid particularly strong or potentially offensive foods such as raw onions and items like beans that are likely to cause flatulence.

As the airline industry strives for ever greater efficiencies, aircraft are at the gate for increasingly short time periods. During this intensive period of refueling, cleaning, and aircraft maintenance, in-flight caterers must be at the ready to load a well-calculated number of meals, as well as snacks, beverages, specialty meals, and crew meals, all at proper temperatures for food safety. Any misstep can cause a flight delay, and as timeliness ranks second only to passenger and crew safety in importance, a late caterer—or worse, one serving food that is physically, chemically, or biologically contaminated—can trigger millions of dollars in lawsuits, lost revenue, and lost contracts.

Safety and Security

Safety and security are critical for the airline industry in the terminal and onboard the aircraft. Food and beverages represent a risk to both safety and security and so are carefully monitored. Carelessness or malice on the part of the caterer or a criminal infiltration of the in-flight catering could result in hundreds of injuries or deaths from food contaminated by **bacteria** or viruses, foreign objects such as glass shards, or poisons. Often such injury can come from simple negligence, such as serving tainted food or miscalculating a cooking or holding temperature.

To ensure safety, food production facilities are carefully monitored, suppliers vetted and held to exacting specifications, employees checked for criminal background, and HACCP food safety plans written and followed for each menu item. A HACCP breach, such as food left at room temperature for longer than the time specified in the plan, may result in the entire batch of food being discarded.

For further safety, food safety specifications for crew members exceed those for passengers—restrictions on potentially hazardous eggs and **dairy**, for example. Airline regulations mandate that cockpit crew members eat at least two entirely different meals to minimize the likelihood of the entire crew contracting foodborne illness.

Blandness

A frequent criticism of airline food is its perceived blandness. There are three primary reasons for this. First, since airline meals need to appeal to a wide variety of people with a diverse range of cultural and taste sensitivities, airline meals are designed to be benignly acceptable. Strong spices and **flavorings** are avoided, as are strong smells that can permeate the cabin and may appeal to some but not all passengers.

Second, the body simply cannot physically taste as well at high altitudes, and the dry air in the cabin further impedes tasting as it causes dry mouth. **Wine** consultants to airlines recommend high-impact high-flavor wines for in-flight service and report a marked change in the flavor of the wine in flight.

Third, depending on the menu item, the long storage times and processing of the aircraft meal, potentially moving from raw, through flash frozen, reheated, and held, all within a relatively short time period, can result in additional flavor loss.

Short- and Long-Haul Flights

For a short-haul flight of a few hours or less, food and beverage service ranges from nothing, to a beverage with a small snack such as pretzels, to food available for purchase. In first- and business-class cabins, a light meal or full meal service is provided. Typically, alcohol is available for purchase in the coach cabin and provided free of charge in first and business classes. A few niche carriers highlight their food service for all passengers, such as chocolate chip cookies baked onboard (Milwaukee-based Midwest Airlines) or a wide selection of snacks with Dunkin' Donuts **coffee** (New York City–based JetBlue). Lately, in an effort to trim costs, airlines have increasingly been moving to food-for-purchase offerings in the main cabin, in some cases showcasing **gourmet** or **celebrity chef**–designed offerings.

For long-haul transcontinental or transoceanic flights, meals are often served in the main cabin, especially for international transoceanic flights, where as many as three meals may be served, depending on the length of flight. First- and business-class service consists of one or more full meals, usually with real china and glassware, with a selection of a few wines. Many international flights provide free alcoholic beverages in all classes of service.

International Flight Services Association and Major Players

Nowadays, most airlines contract out their food service to firms that specialize in in-flight services. These may be independent firms or airline subsidiaries. Their services may be limited to food and beverage catering or may encompass other onboard services such as cleaning and stocking reading material. The field is dominated by a number of leading firms—LSG Sky Chefs, Dobbs International Services, Ogden Aviation Services, and Gate Gourmet, to name a few—with numerous smaller and specialty firms servicing airlines worldwide or subcontracting to larger players.

Many airlines, caterers, and suppliers belong to the trade association for in-flight and rail caterers, the International Flight Services Association (IFSA), known at its inception in 1966 as the Inflight Food Service Association. The organization was founded by Gerald Lattin and a consortium of 43 industry professionals who gathered at Cornell University in Ithaca, New York, to discuss problems and opportunities unique to the in-flight catering industry. Today, IFSA is a major membership organization of airlines and railways, in-flight and rail caterers, and their suppliers that seeks to further **research** and quality in the field while advancing the interests of its membership.

The Future of Airline Food

Industry experts anticipate a further bifurcation of airline food. In an attempt to attract the top-dollar elite flier, such as frequent business travelers, airlines will continue to emphasize creative and specialty first- and business-class menus. In coach or economy class, food offerings will continue to be scarce on short-haul flights and adequate, if not delicious, on long-haul flights. Additional attention will likely be given to revenue-generating opportunities such as premium cocktails and purchase-on-board meals and snacks.

In light of a greater awareness of terrorism and airport safety, in-flight catering will gain even more attention from federal and airport authorities with regard to food safety and security in in-flight foodservice facilities.

FURTHER READINGS: Airlinemeals.net. http://www.airlinemeals.net; International Flight Services Association. http://www.ifsanet.com; McCool, Audrey C. *Inflight Catering Management.* New York: Wiley, 1995.

Jonathan M. Deutsch

Altria Group Until 2007, Altria Group was the parent company of **Kraft Foods**, the second largest food and beverage company in the world; Phillip Morris International, one of the foremost international tobacco companies; Phillip Morris USA, the largest tobacco company in the United States, with half of the U.S. cigarette market's retail share; and the Phillip Morris Capital Corporation, an investment company. It also holds a 28.7 percent economic and voting interest in SABMiller, the world's second largest brewer. Altria Group divested its majority stake in Kraft Foods in 2007.

In April 2002, shareholders granted the board of directors of the company formerly known as Phillip Morris Companies the authority to change the company's name to the Altria Group. Phillip Morris now refers only to the tobacco operating companies. Many observers regard the name change as a means of solving various company problems—in particular, the problem of the "taint of tobacco." The Wirthlin Group, the company's consultants, argued for a name change so that the parent company could secure more positive name recognition and improve its image. The name itself, according to Phillip Morris, is derived from the Latin *altus*, meaning "high," and is meant to represent the company's desire to "'reach higher' to achieve greater financial strength and corporate responsibility."

While the taint of tobacco may have been a point of concern in terms of renaming the parent company, many critics assumed that in previous years Kraft Foods served to shelter the company's tobacco interests. Critics pointed out that news media that advertised Kraft products would be less likely to fund and air exposés on the tobacco industry. As the world's second largest foodmaker, Kraft advertises its many brands widely. Seven of its brands secure annual revenues of more than a billion dollars: Kraft cheeses, salad dressings, dinners, and other products; Jacobs and Maxwell House **coffees**; Milka **chocolates**; Oscar Mayer meats; Philadelphia cream cheese; and **Post** cereals.

Many observers believe that the choice to rename the company came as a result of Altria's desire to obscure the fact that the company's main source of profit is from tobacco. As a result, public health advocates worked to ensure that the new name would continue to be linked to tobacco. To that end, the American Lung Association, American Cancer Society, American Heart Association, and Campaign for Tobacco-Free Kids ran an advertising campaign in national papers across the United States. Underneath the photograph of a snake, the first line of the advertisement reads, "No matter how often a snake sheds its skin . . . it's still a snake." This is followed by the announcement that "Altria is Phillip Morris," and the ad concludes: "More kids still smoke 'Altria's' Marlboros than all other brands combined. 2,000 kids still get hooked on tobacco every day. 1 in 3 will die prematurely."

Kraft Foods believes that its most important asset is its brands. Many of the brands, such as Kraft cheese and Philadelphia cream cheese, hold the top market share position. Brands such as Kool-Aid, Oscar Mayer, Oreo, Ritz, and, of course, Jell-O also are associated with American culture. Jell-O came on the market when the food industry was eager to demonstrate to America's homemakers that through the miracle of modern science, packaged foods not only would free them from the drudgery of kitchen work but also would provide them with a culinary product superior to made-from-scratch recipes. Marketed as "America's Most Famous Dessert," Jell-O has been on **supermarket** shelves for more than a hundred years. Jell-O brand building is so complete that in 1997 the Jell-O Museum opened its doors in Le Roy, New York, the birthplace of the gelatin salad and dessert.

Kraft is dedicated not only to ensuring the share position of its established brands but also to developing and marketing new products. For example, Kraft has teamed up with the developer of the South Beach Diet to capitalize on a new diet campaign that stresses foods with a low glycemic index, as these foods are digested more slowly and have less of an impact on the body's glucose concentration. As a result of the partnership with Arthur Agatston, Kraft has released a variety of "South Beach Diet–approved" products, along with new product lines of prepared South Beach Diet foods. Many of Kraft's South Beach–approved alternatives are outperforming their original counterparts; the reduced-calorie version of Cool Whip, for example, now makes up 40 percent of that brand's sales.

Amid concerns that packaged foods will become the "new tobacco," Kraft Foods has taken a number of steps in order to avoid potential lawsuits. Created from partially hydrogenated oils, trans fats had long been a staple in Kraft's packaged foods because these fats are cheaper, hold up better in food production, and have a longer shelf life. However, trans fats have been found to raise the level of "bad cholesterol" while lowering the level of "good cholesterol" in the bloodstream, thereby increasing the risk of diabetes and heart disease. As a result, Kraft cut out or reduced the trans-fat levels in about 650 of its **snack foods**.

Kraft Foods also has responded to concerns about childhood **obesity**. About 17 percent of youths ages 2–19 are overweight, and an additional 17 percent are at risk of becoming overweight. Kraft recently joined the Alliance for a Healthier Generation, created by the American Heart Association and the William J. Clinton Foundation, in order to combat the spread of childhood obesity. The company voluntarily signed an agreement to limit the amount of fat, **sugar**, and calories it will allow in its snack products sold in schools.

In another move to avoid the growing number of lawsuits against companies for selling unhealthy foods, Kraft also has agreed to change the way in which it **advertises** its products to children. The company promised to curtail print, **television**, and radio **marketing to children** under the age of 11. Kraft had already stopped marketing to children under the age of 6, but remained one of the heaviest advertisers to preteens. In addition, the company agreed to stop advertising Kraft foods or beverages in elementary schools, to promote only nutritious foods or healthy messages in interactive games, and to discontinue the use of licensed characters in ads for snack foods.

Altria Group decided to divest itself of Kraft Foods in 2007. According to analysts, the tobacco industry may be facing an improved litigation environment. For example, in November 2006, the U.S. Supreme Court refused to revive a $10.1 billion award against Philip Morris USA. Given such rulings, Altria's CEO, Louis Camilleri, announced that the parent company would move ahead in divesting itself of its 88.6 percent of outstanding Kraft common shares because Altria believed that Kraft Foods would be better able to work on brand building, as well as creating and marketing new products, as an independent company.

See also Kraft Foods; Multinationals.

FURTHER READING: Counihan, Carole M. *Food in the U.S.A.: A Reader*. New York: Routledge, 2002.

Cayo Gamber

Animal Rights "Animal rights" denotes a movement organized to increase the moral rights and prevent the suffering and abuse of animals at the hands of humans. In North America and Europe, around 17 billion animals are raised and killed for food each year. Additional hundreds of millions are killed in laboratory experiments or for their fur. Animal rights activists and groups in these locales seek to reform such practices and encourage people to consume in ways that do not use animals for food, entertainment, clothing, and laboratory research. Their broad goal is to influence people to change the way they live in a manner that considers the humane treatment of animals in the same light that we think of human rights. Thus, using animals as a means to our own ends—their death and use for human purposes—is considered wholly unjustifiable. Typically, such movements and groups make emotional appeals to their audiences to promote awareness of and regulations governing the legal rights of animals as being meaningful and necessary.

Through methods of educational and advertisement campaigns, investigations into practices that use animals, operating animal rescues, and grassroots activism, animal rights supporters' tactics vary along a spectrum of intensity. Their activities range from endorsing and eating a **vegetarian** or vegan diet, buying "cruelty-free" consumer products, displaying photographs depicting the atrocities of factory farms, and petitioning legislatures to reform social practices involving animals to breaking into laboratories or farms to free animals from confinement and destroying property. In relation to the food industry, books, pamphlets, videos, and websites created by activists describe in gruesome details the treatment and conditions of animals on factory farms.

The animal rights movement differs from the animal welfare movement, which acknowledges animal cruelty and suffering within systems such as the food industry but attempts to reduce cruelty and suffering through humane treatment rather than eliminate it outright. For example, a person who believes in animal welfare might be concerned that cows get enough space on farmland, are not given growth hormones, and are fed proper food, but would not deride the killing and eating of cows on principle, as long as the rearing and slaughter are done in a "humane" manner. The total elimination of the use and exploitation of animals, or assigning specific individual moral rights to them, are not the welfare movement's objectives.

Some members of the animal rights movement prefer using the term "liberation" instead of "rights" because it evokes images of previously successful liberation movements such as the liberation of slaves and women. The term *liberation* does not necessarily refer to the literal freeing of individual nonhuman animals, but rather to freedom from suffering more generally. The phrase "animal liberation" became popular with the 1975 publication of Peter Singer's popular book of that title, which is considered a mainstay of the animal rights movement and is often referred to in the activist press as the bible of the movement. Singer's main argument is that the rights that animals and humans possess should be determined by their interests and capacities. He recognizes that some rights, such as voting, would be irrelevant to animals because their interests are not the same as humans, but argues that animals merit equal consideration of their interests as living beings who have the capacity to feel pain and to suffer.

The Argument for Animal Rights

The concept of animal rights has a long and rich history. For centuries, thinkers have juxtaposed the role of mercy and compassion for animals with popular

Judeo-Christian conceptions of animals as lacking souls, existing solely for human benefit, and not being worthy of man's ethical consideration. Animal welfare and social reformist groups have made a range of attempts and provided various theoretical justifications for their advocacy to improve the lot of animals in society. Philosophers from Pythagoras in the 6th century B.C. to 18th-century thinkers Jean-Jacques Rousseau and Jeremy Bentham have argued that animals are sensitive beings with a capacity for suffering as real and morally relevant as human pain and, as such, that man is morally obliged to consider their rights.

The animal rights movement today extends the idea of minimally treating animals used as commodities well. This withholding of rights from animals is often denoted by advocates as "speciesism," a term coined by British psychologist Richard Ryder in a pamphlet about experiments on animals and later in his contribution to the influential 1972 book *Animals, Men and Morals*. Conceptually, speciesism follows suit with the principal arguments against racism or sexism, contending that human beings place greater moral significance on what happens to them than on what happens to nonhuman animals because of their belonging to a particular species. Speciesism uses the capacity for experiencing pain and pleasure as the measure of what defines having interests, positioning animals and humans as necessitating equal consideration when they have similar interests (such as avoiding pain).

Animal rights arguments for the prevalence of speciesism uphold the notion that being bred as a source of human food does not change an animal's biological or physical capacity to feel pain and experience fear. Besides basic criminal laws against cruelty to animals (particularly to companion animals such as dogs and cats) and laws that regulate the keeping of animals in cities and on farms, the interstate and international transport of animals, and sanitary-based quarantine and inspection provisions, animals raised for food receive little legal protection. Additionally, the effectiveness of any national food-related animal oversight law or federally instituted regulation in the United States (such as from the **U.S. Department of Agriculture**) typically depends on the willingness of the **agribusiness** industry in question to comply.

Animal Rights Groups and Controversies

The world's first animal welfare organization, the Society for the Prevention of Cruelty to Animals (SPCA), was founded in Great Britain in 1824. Similar groups arose elsewhere in Europe and North America, including the American Society for the Prevention of Cruelty to Animals (ASPCA) in 1866. One of the most recognized and successful animal rights groups in the United States today is People for the Ethical Treatment of Animals (PETA), founded in 1980. PETA operates under the basic principle that animals should not be eaten, worn, or used for experimentation or entertainment. It first uncovered animal abuse in laboratory experiments though undercover investigation in 1981, exposing the conditions and treatment of monkeys used in experiments funded by the National Institutes of Health. This activism resulted in the first arrest and criminal conviction in the United States on charges of cruelty to animals, the first reduction of federal funding for government-supported research and confiscation of laboratory animals because of abuse, and the first U.S. Supreme Court decision in favor of animals in laboratories. Since then, PETA has performed numerous undercover investigations of laboratories, circuses, and farms to denounce testing on animals and farm practices it considers to be cruel or brutal.

From the 1980s onward, the animal rights movement has employed controversial tactics and campaigns to maintain public visibility. It has been joined by a wide variety of academic and professional groups, including theologians, lawyers, psychologists, veterinarians, and, importantly, celebrities, who contribute their name and money to promote the cause of animal rights. Some writers, activists, and groups have drawn comprehensive analogies between the treatment of animals today and the treatment of Jews during the Holocaust. PETA often recruits film and music celebrities as spokespeople for its campaigns, relying on their popular appeal to correspond to mobilization of donation revenue and resource streams. For example, female celebrities and models are recruited to pose in the nude for PETA's provocative "I'd Rather Go Naked Than Wear Fur" ad campaigns.

Obstacles for the Animal Rights Movement

In comparison with other social movements for human rights or liberation, the animal rights movement has three key handicaps in gaining institutional and public support. First is the fact that nonhuman animals, as members of the exploited group, cannot organize themselves or protest against the treatment they receive. Second, animal rights movements that seek a new moral standing for animals confront humans who eat, and enjoy eating, meat, as well as cultural traditions and government policies that encourage the consumption of meat and other animal products.

The third handicap, and perhaps the one most relevant to the contemporary movement's internal cohesion as well as its public perceptions, is the disagreement among animal rights proponents about the methods used in movement activities, especially those that break the law. The animal rights movement is largely nonviolent, yet, like most large and diverse social movements, it has factions that believe in courses of action that engage the use of force, lawbreaking, or violence to fight what they believe to be injustice to animals. Individuals with extremist views who use force, violence, coercion, and intimidation to achieve their goals for animal rights, have, since 2002, been officially classified and investigated by the FBI as ecoterrorists.

Animal Rights' Relation to the Food Industry

The animal rights movement has achieved, and is achieving, numerous goals related to the food industry. One key challenge has been the creation of consumer awareness of animal cruelty in the food system and demand for non–animal-based products. The crux of the cruelty issue for the animal rights movement lies in a positive response to the question, "Do food production methods cause animals to feel pain and suffering, denying them their inherent rights as living beings?"

In recent years, increasing numbers of consumers in postindustrial societies have altered their purchasing habits because of concerns about health, the treatment of the animals used in research and production, and the production system's impact on the environment. Through resonance with these other social movement and consumer groups, such as the **organic** and sustainability movements, animal rights activists have been able to tap into preexisting mobilization networks around food issues, in addition to previous reliance on the cultural codes of other minority rights movements (such as women's liberation and antislavery campaigns) throughout history. Here, the animal rights movement publicly encourages people to consider every time they eat as an opportunity to make a political and moral statement about the suffering and rights of animals.

Companies producing consumer goods that were previously tested on animals have changed their practices to fit with such consumer demand. Large numbers of individuals in North America and Europe are converting to vegetarian and vegan diets, and many **restaurants** offer multiple vegetarian options. The **European Union** has enacted major changes in farm animal welfare policies. More individuals are asking government and industry organizations about the use and welfare of animals used in medical research and food production, and public support for animal experimentation has significantly declined.

Large food companies have instituted new guidelines for the treatment of animals that go into their food offerings. For example, both Burger King and **McDonald's** recently instituted new larger space guidelines for laying hens that provide eggs for use in their restaurants. Prominent chefs have additionally made promises to consider animal welfare in supplying their restaurants. Though this decision relates more to issues of animal welfare than animal rights, such new policies, given the size and scope of their presence in national and international food markets, have the potential to encourage even more change in favor of greater moral consideration of animals' lives.

FURTHER READINGS: Godlovitch, Stanley, Rosalind Godlovitch, and John Harris, eds. *Animals, Men, and Morals: An Enquiry into the Maltreatment of Non-humans.* New York: Tablinger, 1972; Singer, Peter. *Animal Liberation.* New York: New York Review, 1975. Reprint, New York: Ecco, 2002.

Michaela DeSoucey

Antibiotics An antibiotic is a biological substance (either synthetic or natural) that kills or inhibits the growth of microorganisms, usually **bacteria**. Most antibiotics are made from bacteria and fungi, but an increasing number are made synthetically from chemical compounds. They are relatively harmless to the hosts; hence they are prescribed widely for infections. However, there is growing concern that antibiotic over-prescription and their extensive use in food animals is leading to antibiotic resistance and the inability of the human immune system to fend off infection.

History of Antibiotics

Although there is debate in the scientific community about who discovered antibiotics, most historians credit Scottish scientist Alexander Fleming with the discovery of penicillin in 1928. This breakthrough provided the first effective countermeasure against bacteria that cause diseases such as gonorrhea, meningitis, diphtheria, and pneumonia. At the time, Fleming believed penicillin could be used as a disinfectant, as he did not believe it could last long enough in the human body to kill pathogens. Today, more than 100 different antibiotics exist that are able to cure anything from minor discomforts to life-threatening infections.

Description and Use of Antibiotics

There are two types of antibiotics. The first category consists of nonsynthetic antibiotics, which are usually prepared with natural by-products such as fungi and weakened bacteria. The other type is the synthetic antibiotics; these are prepared in a laboratory setting. A number of antibiotics being produced are semisynthetic, meaning that they are modified natural antibiotics. A few people refer to both compounds as *antibacterial* and define *antibiotics* as only nonsynthetic compounds, but most scientists use both words interchangeably.

Antibiotics can work two different ways. Several antibiotics are *bactericidal* and completely kill the bacteria in their host. Others are *bacteriostatic* and simply inhibit the growth and multiplication of bacteria, enabling the host's own immune system to overcome them. Prescription of antibiotics rarely exceeds five days.

Antibiotics are used to treat only bacterial infections; they are useless against other types of infection such as viruses like that of the common cold, fungal infections such as ringworm, and parasitic infections such as tapeworm. Common side effects of antibiotics include mild stomach upset and diarrhea. Sometimes allergic reactions occur, usually ranging from rashes to slight wheezing, but it is possible to have life-threatening allergic reactions such as anaphylaxis. Despite these side effects and allergic reactions, most doctors continue to prescribe antibiotics because of their numerous benefits.

The effectiveness of antibiotics varies according to the location of the infection, the ability of the antibiotic to reach the infection site, and the bacteria's ability to resist the antibiotic. There are three main drug delivery mechanisms: orally (administered as a pill, capsule, tablet, or liquid in the treatment), intravenously (through the blood stream by an injection), or topically (as eye drops or ointments).

Like other drugs, antibiotics usually have two names. The first is the trade or brand name, created by the manufacturing company to market and sell the antibiotic. The second name, its generic name, refers to the antibiotic's chemical structure or class. For example, cephalexin is the generic name of an antibiotic similar to penicillin in action and side effects. Different companies brand cephalexim under the names of Keflex, Keftabs, and Biocef, but all three brands refer to the same antibiotic.

Antibiotic Resistance

There are growing concerns relating to antibiotic resistance. In simple terms, if an antibiotic is used often and long enough, a variant of the bacteria will emerge that cannot be killed by that antibiotic. Tuberculosis, gonorrhea, malaria, and childhood ear infections are just a few of the diseases that have grown hard to treat with antibiotic drugs. Several explanations have emerged for the development of resistant bacteria. Foremost, there is a growing trend of overprescribing antibiotics, including prescribing them for cold or flu viruses; the use of antibiotics to treat these sicknesses is ineffective and serves only to increase antibiotic resistance.

In addition, food-producing animals are routinely given enormous doses of antibiotics, especially when they are reared in confined spaces where the likelihood of infection is great. It is not uncommon for a whole herd to be given antibiotics when only a single animal has displayed symptoms of illness. Antibiotics are also giving as a growth hormone. How it happens is not completely understood, but antibiotics increase the growth rate and feeding efficiency of farm animals. Hence, they are commonly given for non–disease-related purposes. This type of usage is directly linked to antibiotic resistance. High concentrations of antibiotics used for a short time, as when treating a sick animal, are much less likely to lead to antibiotic resistance than lower concentrations given over a long period of time, as when used as growth hormones. Although the link between this use of antibiotics and antibiotic resistance is unproven, European studies report than the banning of some antibiotics has led to decreased antibiotic resistance.

As for antibiotics found in genetically modified plants, most microbiologists agree that there is very little risk that these contribute to antibiotic resistance, although debate on this subject is ongoing.

FURTHER READINGS: Phillips, Ian, Mark Casewell, Tony Cox, Brad DeGroot, Christian Friis, Ron Jones, Charles Nightingale, Rodney Preston, and John Waddell. "Does the Use of Antibiotics in Food Animals Pose a Risk to Human Health? A Critical Review of Published Data." *Journal of Antimicrobial Chemotherapy* 53 (2004): 28–52; Salyers, Abigail A., and Dixie D. Whitt. *Revenge of the Microbes: How Bacterial Resistance Is Undermining the Antibiotic Miracle.* Washington, DC: ASM Press, 2005.

Jean-François Denault

Appellations. *See* Wine Business.

Applebee's. *See* Chain Restaurants.

Archer Daniels Midland. *See* Agribusiness; Corn.

Armour Philip Danforth Armour was born in Stockbridge, New York, in 1832 and as a teenager made a small fortune supplying miners with water during California's gold rush. With the money he earned from that venture, he built a soap company in Milwaukee that was later destroyed by fire. Armour went on to join a provisions firm and eventually came to the attention of Milwaukee's leading **meat packer**, John Plankinton, whose company he joined as a junior partner. Soon he was writing up and executing extremely lucrative pork contracts with the government, and with his share of the profits, Armour helped his younger brothers, Herman Ossian and Joseph Francis, start a grain provisioning firm in 1863 that eventually rented out a packinghouse at the newly established Union Stock Yards and began to handle hogs. They were extremely successful—handling 25,000 hogs in their first year—and the company grew quickly, so that by 1868 they were able to purchase their own, larger plant. The brothers renamed their firm that year and Armour & Company was born.

Armour & Company became one of the kings of the Chicago meatpacking scene, along with others such as **Swift**, Morris, and Hammond. Chicago itself became known as America's "Porkopolis" after the Civil War. The company continued its rapid expansion and by 1880 was one of Chicago's most important businesses, with branch packing plants in Kansas City, St. Louis, and Cincinnati, in addition to offices in New York, Liverpool, and London. The company-owned rail cars that carried Armour products at this time were proudly painted with the slogan "We Feed the World."

Looking for logical directions to grow and to make use of the huge amounts of animal waste that it generated, Armour & Company also processed animal by-products into such items as soap, glue, gelatin, and **fertilizer**. The company became so successful at this that Armour was known to boast that his company made use of "every part of the pig but the squeal." The persistent search for improved production and efficiency was a hallmark of Armour & Company. In fact, pig processing methods at Armour's packing plants set an example for others—industrialist Henry Ford was inspired by the pig disassembly line to manufacture his Model Ts on an assembly line of his own.

Like many successful businessmen of his time, though, Armour's savvy extended to more than just knowing how to use the whole hog—he also pioneered the use of **refrigerated** rail cars for shipping meat and had a **canning** operation as early as 1878. The advent of refrigerated rail cars made the establishment of distribution plants in the Eastern states possible, and these became the launch pad for exporting Armour products to Europe. At the same time, Armour & Company's cannery and canned meat products, as well as Philip's experience in writing and negotiating government contracts, positioned the firm to be a major supplier of meat products to the British military. Philip Armour was particularly proud of the fact that British troops deployed in Sudan at the time ate two million pounds of Armour canned meat.

Of course, the relentless drive for efficiency and maximum profits possessed a seamy underbelly. Operating in the era before stringent government regulations, Armour's meats were of inferior quality, often containing contaminants such as metal filings or toxic chemicals. Sanitation was nonexistent and the stench arising from the stockyards and packing plants (not just Armour's) was legendary. Working conditions were abominable, workers were paid poorly, accidents were common, and compensation rare. Upton Sinclair's influential book *The Jungle* was inspired by conditions in Chicago's meatpacking plants and shed a harsh light on the gory details of life in the yards. After its publication in 1906 and the subsequent public outcry, the government passed both the Meat Inspection Act and the Pure Food and Drug Act that same year.

Much as Armour is remembered as a meat baron, it is often forgotten that he never left the soapmaking business, either; in 1888, soon after Armour & Company was established, the firm came out with a laundry bar called Armour Family Soap. Company scientists developed the first antibacterial-deodorant soap in 1948. The product, which was given the name "Dial" in reference to the round-the-clock deodorant protection it offered, became so popular that the company changed its name from Armour & Company to the Armour-Dial Company. Armour-Dial was purchased by Greyhound Lines in 1970 to become Greyhound-Dial, but in 1987 the Greyhound unit was sold off and the company became the Dial Corporation.

Thus divested of its status as a conglomerate, today Armour is a brand of meat-based food products owned by Pinnacle Foods, which acquired it from Dial in 2006 when the latter company divested itself of its food-related brands. (The Dial Corporation is now a subsidiary of the Henkel Group/Germany and headquartered in Scottsdale, Arizona.) Armour's product line is much reduced from its former range and now includes Vienna sausage, potted meat, sliced beef, meat spreads, chili, luncheon meat, corned and roast beef hash, beef stew, and lunch buckets. In February 2007, Pinnacle announced its acquisition by a private equity and investment management firm, the Blackstone Group, for $2.16 billion.

FURTHER READINGS: Leech, Harper. *Armour and His Times.* New York: D. Appleton-Century Co., 1938; Wade, Louis Carroll. *Chicago's Pride: The Stockyards, Packingtown, and Environs in the Nineteenth Century.* Urbana: University of Illinois Press, 1987.

Karen Y. Lau

Baby Food Baby foods are very special products. The first nutrients to nourish new humans pass from mothers' blood through the umbilical cord to the fetus before birth. As the fetus floats in the amniotic sac, the surrounding amniotic fluid carries the tastes of the foods available in the world outside the womb. After birth, babies take in their first foods by mouth. As with all mammals, the product designed to be that first food is maternal breast milk.

Humans are omnivores, able to eat a wide range of foods culturally defined as edible, but the food needs of babies are more specialized and are limited to products such as human milk or a breastmilk substitute. Some adults survive very poor diets, but what a baby consumes during the first year of life shapes subsequent adult health. For that reason, commercial baby foods are doubly scrutinized by both producers and consumers and are expected to meet very high standards. When these standards are breached in any way, manufacturers may experience the wrath of mothers, citizen groups, and consumer advocates, in the form of protests or **boycotts** against their products.

Adults choose the foods deemed suitable for infants and toddlers, who may refuse to eat what they are given; thus adult perceptions about how children should be fed, and how baby foods differ from adult foods, determine what foods babies receive. For example, if adults don't eat fruits and vegetables, they are unlikely to feed them to infants. In some societies, meat may be considered too strong for infants. Generally, baby foods are finely textured, light, and simple in composition.

In the 20th century, parents turned to expert authorities to help them feed their infants. The choices of North American parents were shaped by advice books such as Dr. Spock's *The Common Sense Book of Baby and Child Care* (1946), instructions from the emerging specialty of pediatrics, and advertising for commercially produced baby foods.

Healthy Feeding Patterns

From the age of six months, babies need other foods in addition to breast milk to meet their nutritional needs, particularly foods rich in iron and zinc. These foods are referred to as complementary foods, as they are meant to complement rather than supplant breast milk. But if babies' stomachs are filled with poor quality foods, there will be less room for nutritionally superior breast milk. Thus, baby foods need to be high in nutrients, of a soft consistency, and fed carefully. In many parts of the world, baby foods are introduced either too early or too late.

The World Health Organization (WHO) and UNICEF define the ideal conditions for feeding infants in the *Global Strategy for Infant and Young Child Feeding*: After six months, babies should be introduced to appropriate and adequate complementary foods, with continued breastfeeding for up to two years and beyond. Sufficient quantities of human milk—about 500–600 cc a day, or at least three to six good, high-volume breastfeedings per day—should be supported for two years or longer while increasing to three to five nutrient-rich feedings with locally available household foods. The caregiver's attention and response to the child's needs and the child's developmental readiness to handle food consumption are also important. Caregivers are encouraged to introduce a variety of foods, but not to force-feed an older baby.

The quality of baby foods themselves is not the only factor determining infant health. Other factors include good hygiene and proper food handling, washing caregivers' and children's hands before food preparation and eating, serving foods immediately after preparation, using clean utensils to prepare and serve food, using clean cups and bowls when feeding children, and avoiding the use of feeding bottles, which are difficult to keep clean.

Caregivers are advised to gradually increase food consistency and variety as the infants get older, adapting to their requirements and abilities. By eight months, most infants can eat "finger foods" by themselves. By 12 months, most can eat the same types of foods as consumed by the rest of the family, keeping in mind the need for nutrient-dense food. Protein-rich foods such as meat, poultry, fish, or eggs should be eaten as often as possible. Generally, babies should get "the best bits" of whatever foods are available in the household; high rates of child malnutrition in many countries suggest that this seldom happens, however. Drinks with low nutrient value, such as tea, coffee, sugary drinks, and carbonated **soft drinks**, are unsuitable for infants and young children, but have been used inappropriately as breastmilk substitutes.

History

Throughout human history, there have always been alternatives available to maternal breast milk, including wet nursing and the use of animal milks. By 1500 B.C., terra-cotta feeding bottles were in use in Egypt. However, any alternatives to maternal breastfeeding were universally recognized as dangerous. Animal milks often played a role in feeding babies, and many European orphanages kept goats for rearing infants. However, most alternatives to breast milk used in the past were nutritionally inadequate and contributed to high rates of infant mortality. Feeding infants without maternal breast milk was referred to as "dry nursing" or "bringing the baby up by hand." It is only in the last century that improvements in baby foods permitted many infants to survive this feeding regimen.

Historically, the difference between breastmilk substitutes and complementary foods has not been clearly defined. Semisolid mixtures of grains, often mixed with animal milk or water, were given to infants to replace or supplement breast milk. These *paps*, *panadas*, and *beikost* were fed through feeding devices of horn or ceramic and are plentiful in the archaeological record. In some parts of the world, including Southeast Asia, and among many indigenous peoples of North America, mothers prechewed foods to make it of a consistency that infants could digest. While Western "experts" disparaged such practices as unhygienic, in fact the practice was a practical way to render adult food suitable for infants.

The first milk-based commercial infant formula was developed by Nestlé in 1867. Early formulas often included cereals and were marketed as foods, not liquid breast-milk substitutes. These proprietary milk products competed alongside condensed and evaporated milks and custom-made preparations around the end of the century. In 1928, Gerber developed and marketed specialty foods for babies such as strained vegetables, including peas, carrots, and spinach, and this successful innovation was emulated in the next decade by products developed by **Heinz**, **Beech-Nut**, and **Libby's** in North America. In 1931, Beech-Nut developed 13 varieties of strained baby foods and sold them in patented vacuum-sealed clear glass jars, replacing lead-soldered metal cans. Over the next 20 years, the use of commercial baby food increased in middle- and upper-income North American homes, where it was used not just to supplement but also to substitute for breast milk.

Specialty products such as preterm infant formula were developed in the 1960s. The 1980s saw the development of fortifiers to adapt human milk for low–birth-weight infants, now in use in intensive-care nurseries. Mothers' own milk is now the standard of care for these infants, with pasteurized or fresh donor human milk used when the mother's own milk is not available. More recently, soy-based products have come onto the market, along with follow-on formula for older infants. Similarly, in the mid-1980s, baby food companies promoted age-specific baby foods, including products for toddlers such as first dinners and junior foods.

In developing countries, nutrition projects sought to make local foods more nutrient dense, often by fortification or by the development of high-protein complementary foods. Current nutrition interventions stress micronutrient supplementation to prevent deficiencies where fortified complementary foods are not regularly consumed. While efforts to improve complementary foods through fortification have been of interest to international agencies, sufficient frequency and variety of age-appropriate foods, fed in a responsive manner by an interested caretaker, are the keys to improved infant growth and development.

Problems

The development of mass-produced baby foods has not been problem free. For example, they were often used as breastmilk substitutes, and given too early, replacing more nutritious breast milk. Since the development of commercial baby foods, there has been a steady decrease in the age of introduction of solids to infants. In North America, parents took pride in seeing infants eat strained baby foods at increasingly early ages. But commercial baby foods were often overcooked, with an attendant loss of nutrients; some contained too much salt, sugar, water, or starchy fillers. Gradually, in response to consumer demand, companies removed excessive salt, sugar, and starches from their products. Critics pointed out the potential dangers of artificial preservatives and **additives** for immature infant intestines. Consumer groups also exposed cases of fraud, such as replacing apple juice with sugar and using genetically modified rice in baby cereal.

Industrial accidents in the production of infant formulas and baby foods are not uncommon and require costly recalls; recent cases include baby rusks with pesticide traces, plastic and glass shards in jars of baby food and cans of infant formula, cadmium-laced carrots, soy formula containing cow's milk, and excessive amounts of vitamin D, aluminum, lead, and iodine (and insufficient amounts of other nutrients) in infant formula. In 2003, the **Codex Alimentarius Commission** (CAC) of the UN's Food and Agriculture Organization identified the harmful **bacteria** *Enterobacter saka-zakii* in powdered infant formula. The cultural perception that artificial feeding carries few risks persists to this day and is maintained by commercial marketing strategies. However, the risks of artificial feeding and the risks of not breastfeeding in both industrialized and resource poor settings are becoming more widely known.

Nevertheless, industrially processed complementary foods are an option for some mothers who have the economic means to buy them and the knowledge and facilities to prepare and feed them safely. These baby foods must be fortified to meet the food safety standards of the CAC. Resource-poor households and communities can make use of low-cost complementary food, prepared with locally available ingredients in the household, or in the community using suitable small-scale production technologies.

More recently, concerns about childhood **obesity** have drawn researchers to examine **television advertising** for high-fat, high-sugar **snack foods** targeting toddlers. Very young children cannot always distinguish sponsor messages or direct advertisements from cartoon characters. Thus, food advertising to young children, both directly and through the food provider, is of ongoing concern.

Protecting Baby Foods

To address the problem of the aggressive and unethical promotion of breastmilk substitutes, WHO and UNICEF jointly hosted an international meeting in 1979 on infant and young child feeding and called for the development of an international code to regulate the promotion and marketing of baby foods. Representatives of governments, technical experts, nongovernmental organizations, the infant food industry, and scientists working in infant nutrition attended the meeting, which led to the International Code of Marketing of Breast-milk Substitutes, passed at the World Health Assembly (WHA) in 1981. The rules for industry, health workers, and governments regulate the promotion of bottles, teats, and all breastmilk substitutes, not just infant formula. Subsequent WHA resolutions require that complementary food and drinks not be marketed in ways that undermine breastfeeding (WHA 49.15, 1996). Complementary foods should not be labeled, advertised, or commercially promoted as being suitable for infants under six months of age (WHA39.28, WHA54.2, 2001). The food industry is obligated to meet these regulations even when national legislation has not been implemented.

Future Trends

Euromonitor in 2001 estimated the annual world market for commercial baby milks and foods at just under $17 billion and forecast its increase to nearly $20 billion by 2005. Why have commercial baby foods been so successful? They clearly filled a need felt by parents in Europe and North America for safe, convenient, ready-to-eat foods for their infants. With women active in the formal and informal labor markets, and national policies on maternity entitlements lagging behind mothers' needs, the perceived time-saving and convenience of commercial baby foods had substantial appeal.

From Euro-American perspectives, two trends are visible: first is the growing consumer demand for **organic** baby foods and products with no genetically modified ingredients; second is the return to homemade baby foods, processed from household foods using small food grinders. Both options coexist, as women seek more ways to integrate child feeding with the many demands on their time.

See also Genetic Engineering; Marketing to Children.

FURTHER READINGS: Bentley, Amy. "Feeding Baby, Teaching Mother: Gerber and the Evolution of Infant Food and Feeding Practices in the United States." In Arlene Voski Avakian and Barbara Haber, eds., *From Betty Crocker to Feminist Food Studies: Critical Perspectives on Women and Food*, pp. 62–88. Amherst: University of Massachusetts Press, 2005; Fildes, Valerie. *Breasts, Bottles and Babies: History of Infant Feeding*. Edinburgh: Edinburgh University Press, 1986; *Global Strategy for Infant and Young Child Feeding*. Geneva: World Health Organization, 2002; Sokol, Ellen. *The Code Handbook: A Guide to Implementing the International Code of Marketing of Breastmilk Substitutes*. Penang, Malaysia: International Baby Food Action Network, 1997.

Penny Van Esterik

Bacteria Bacteria are microscopic, single-celled organisms. There are thousands of different types of bacteria. Some are found in the surrounding environment (such as in the soil or water), while others are found on living beings (in the mouth or digestive tract). Bacteria are usually distinguished by shape. Some have positive properties, especially when used in food and industrial settings; only a few kinds of bacteria are pathogenic, causing diseases in human beings. It is estimated that 500 to 1,000 different species of bacteria live in the human body (Sears, 2005).

History

Bacteria are thought to be the first organisms that lived on the planet; fossils of bacteria have been found dating to more than 3.5 billion years ago. Due to their simple physical structure, they were able to survive and evolve into more complex organisms.

Anton van Leeuwenhoek first observed bacteria through his single-lens microscope in 1674. Later, Louis Pasteur demonstrated that the fermentation process was caused by the growth of microorganisms or bacteria. This was followed by Robert Koch's experiments on bacteria as a source of disease, specifically the anthrax bacillus, for which he won the Nobel Prize in 1905. Gradually the beneficial role of bacteria was also recognized, and today beneficial bacteria or probiotics are sold as a component of nutraceutical products.

Physical Properties

Bacteria are usually very small organisms, sometimes measuring less than 5 μm each; there are typically billions of bacterial cells on a single grain of soil. Bacteria are usually classified by their different shapes. They can be of spherical shape (which are called *cocci*), rod-like (*bacilli*), or spiral/helical (*spirochetes*).

Being mostly unicellular organisms, they are usually simply organized, although unicellular bacteria are known to combine into bacterial colonies. These colonies have been known to become codependent. Bacteria have an external plasma membrane, which contains the internal content of the cell, such as the cytoplasm, ribosome, and DNA. Bacteria reproduce through asexual reproduction, creating two identical clone daughter cells; mutation in the reproduction cycle can lead to the creation of new bacteria.

Commercial Use of Bacteria

Bacteria (in combination with yeasts and molds) have been used for thousands of years to produce fermented foods such as cheese, **beer**, **wine**, and yogurt. As such, bacteria are a key element for the food industry. For example, cheese is created by fermentation, being the result of a specific bacterium being added to milk. Beer is also a product of fermentation, in this case of grains.

Fermenting bacteria thrive in environments with limited oxygen. They convert food molecules into useful energy and waste products; it is these various waste products that give fermented food its distinctive aromas and flavor that people have come to appreciate. Some of the bacteria used for this process include *Lactobacillus* (which converts sugars to lactic acids), *Pediococcus* (which produces lactic acids), and *Leuconostoc* (which converts malic acid to lactic acid). One of the advantages of bacterial presence in food is that these discrete microorganisms prevent other, less desirable bacteria from growing in the same product, thereby acting as a type of natural preservative.

Bacteria are also used in many industrial fields. For example, some bacteria are used in waste processing; they are able to digest the hydrocarbons in petroleum and hence are used during oil-spill cleanups. They are also used in the biopharmaceutical industry for production of antibodies and insulin; the enzymes created as a waste by-product are recuperated and converted into drugs.

Pathogenic Profile

A number of bacteria are pathogenic (i.e. capable of causing disease). These can infect people through many different pathways: direct contact, air, food, water, and bloodsucking insects. Cholera, leprosy, and tuberculosis are all bacterial diseases. The use of **antibiotics** is meant to limit the spread of harmful bacteria, but the overprescription of antibiotics has led to antibiotic resistance.

Most bacteria are beneficial. Out of the thousands of types of bacteria currently known to exist, only a small minority is harmful to humans. Furthermore, some bacteria that are pathogenic to one species may be harmless to another. Bacteria that harm human beings are sometimes harmless to other animals. The reverse is also true, animals can be a source of foodborne poisoning for human beings, as we consume food infected with a bacterium that lived in harmony with the consumed animal.

Probiotics

Probiotics are a special use of beneficial bacteria. In their common form, they are a dietary supplement containing potentially beneficial bacteria. Lactic acid bacteria are the most common. These supplements are taken for a variety of purposes, the most popular of which is to reinforce or strengthen the resident flora.

The digestive tract of each human being contains a bacteria colony, also called the *resident flora*. Between 300 and 1,000 different kinds of bacteria reside in this colony, but it is believed that 99 percent of the bacteria living in the resident flora are comprised of just 30 or 40 species. This flora protects the body against disease-causing organisms, as well as breaking down some nutrients (such as carbohydrates) that humans are not able to digest. They also train the immune system. Hence, this bacterial colony lives in symbiosis with the human body.

Some antibodies kill a large proportion of the beneficial resident flora, enabling other bacteria and fungi to take their place. Although there is no published evidence that probiotic supplements are able to replace the body's natural flora, there are data that demonstrate that probiotics can form temporary colonies, which assist the body while allowing the natural flora to recover from the antibiotics. Probiotics are believed by some to help manage lactose intolerance, prevent colon cancer, and lower cholesterol and blood pressure, but these are not yet clinically proven.

Foodborne Illnesses

Bacteria in food are a common source of **food poisoning**. As mentioned, most bacteria in food are benign, but a small number cause various forms of food poisoning. Sometimes the results are very mild, resulting in only a slight upset stomach, while more serious cases result in fever, diarrhea, vomiting, and dehydration. As most foodborne poisonings go unreported, it is difficult to estimate the exact number of poisoning each year; the Centers for Disease Control and Prevention estimates that 76 million people are infected each year in the United States and about 5,000 of these die.

Causes of food poisoning are multiple and vary from one food to the other. Some bacteria can be present on food when it is purchased; for example, raw meat can be contaminated during slaughter, or seafood can be contaminated during harvest. Other foods such as vegetables can be contaminated during growth, harvest, processing, storing, and shipping. Food can also be contaminated during kitchen preparation and cooking.

Food that is cooked and left at room temperature is especially vulnerable to bacteria that cause food poisoning. Freezing food slows down and even stops the growth of bacteria, but does not destroy them. Cooking at temperatures higher than 145°F for roasts, 160°F for pork, and 165°F for **poultry** is needed to completely destroy bacteria. Furthermore, all precooked food should be reheated above 165°F. Other tips to avoid foodborne bacteria include preventing cross-contamination (keeping raw food separated from cooked food), never defrosting food on the kitchen counter, and avoiding packing the **refrigerator** too full (as it prohibits the cool air from circulating).

See also Dairy Industry; Functional Foods and Nutraceuticals; Irradiation.

FURTHER READINGS: Dyer, Betsey Dexter. *A Field Guide to Bacteria.* Ithaca, NY: Cornell University Press, 2003; Ouwehand, A. C., S. Salminen, and E. Isolauri. "Probiotics: An Overview of Beneficial Effects." *Antonie Van Leeuwenhoek* 82 (2002): 279–89; Playfair, John. *Living with Germs: In Sickness and in Health.* New York: Oxford University Press, 2004; Sears, C. L. "A Dynamic Partnership: Celebrating Our Gut Flora." *Anaerobe* 11, no. 5 (October 2005): 247–51.

Jean-François Denault

Beech-Nut Although today the Beech-Nut Corporation sells only **baby foods**, the company's first products were smoked and cured hams and bacon. Twenty years after its founding as the Imperial Packing Company in 1891, the company had diversified its product line to include mustard, **peanut butter**, macaroni, marmalades, and **coffee**. It incorporated as the Beech-Nut Packing Company in 1899. The Canajoharie, New York, business took pride in maintaining a high standard of flavor by scrutinizing the quality of raw ingredients and developing unique processing. The company eventually expanded to a national market with many well-known brands, including Tetley Tea, Martinson's Coffee, and Table Talk Pie.

In 1931, Beech Nut was acquired by Life Savers and entered the baby food market with 13 varieties of strained baby food. Beech-Nut was the first company to sell baby food in clear glass jars, allowing the consumer to see the product.

Through the following decades, the company maintained its reputation for quality food products. In 1968, Squibb Beech-Nut Corporation was formed out of the larger parent company, Olin Matheson. In 1977, the Beech-Nut Corporation, selling exclusively baby food, was sold to an investment group led by Frank C. Nicholas, who became the company's chairman, president, and chief executive officer. In an effort to increase sales and distinguish the product in its market, Nicholas decided to remove salt, **sugar**, artificial flavors, monosodium glutamate (MSG), and hydrolyzed vegetable protein (HVP) from the product line. In 1979, when Nicholas sold the company to Nestlé, it had the second highest sales in baby food.

In a further effort to bolster lagging sales, in 1978 the company began purchasing a less expensive brand of wholesale apple juice. When executives realized that the product was not juice but colored sugar water, they continued to sell the mislabeled juice six months after a recall and outside the United States. This cover-up and violation of Food and Drug Administration regulations led the fines of $2.2 million.

In 1989, Beech-Nut was acquired by Ralston Purina, and the company continued to refine its line of baby foods, removing chemically modified starch, producing iron-fortified juices, and introducing foods in age-specific varieties, following the American Academy of Pediatrics feeding guidelines. Beech-Nut products today include cereals, vegetables, fruit, cookies, and meal combinations for children up to 18 months old. The company also marks its foods to suit cultural, religious, and dietary strictures, including kosher, gluten-free, and international flavors. Most recently Beech-Nut began adding DHA (docosahexaenoic acid) and ARA (arachidonic acid) fatty acids, which are found in breast milk and are the most prevalent structural fats in the brain.

FURTHER READINGS: Beech-Nut Corporation. http://www.beechnut.com; *The Story of a Pantry Shelf, an Outline History of Grocery Specialties.* New York: Butterick, 1925; Traub, James. "Into the Mouths of Babes." *New York Times,* July 24, 1988.

Claudia Kousoulas

Beef/Cattle Industry The North American cattle industry has changed dramatically since its inception. It has moved from geographically localized businesses, comprised of ranchers, butchers, and cowboys, to technologically specialized and internationally integrated commercial feeding, packing, and marketing operations.

The modern beef industry is best approached in terms of three interrelated parts: production, distribution, and consumption. Beef production includes cow calf operators (ranchers or farmers who raise cattle), feeders and feedlots, and **meatpacking** plants. Distribution includes modes of transportation and forms of packing, as well as retail outlets (**supermarkets**, **restaurants**, and other **food service industries**) that purchase beef products from meatpacking plants and make them available to consumers.

Consumption also plays a central role, as consumer tastes and concerns over **food safety**, nutrition, and animal welfare increasingly shape industry practices.

Early History

The North American cattle industry had two major cultural and economic paths of development: a western tradition from Spain and Mexico; and an eastern one from England. Cattle were first brought to the New World by Spanish explorers and missionaries. In the 15th and 16th centuries, longhorn cattle were introduced to Puerto Rico, Jamaica, Cuba, Argentina, Brazil, Paraguay, and Mexico. These herds belonged, primarily, to Spanish priests and social elites. In 1540, a ban was lifted on indigenous ownership of horses in Mexico. As a result, opportunities were created for indigenous people to become mounted horsemen, enabling the creation of the first cowboys of the Americas: the *vaqueros*.

By the 17th century, Spanish settlers had set up missions as far north as what is now Texas. After Mexico gained independence from Spain in 1821, the missions were secularized, leading to a mass exodus of priests who either left behind their herds or slaughtered them. The remaining herds were tended by vaqueros, who also provided a cheap labor pool for wealthy ranchers and (later) English cattlemen. When Texas gained independence, several Spanish ranchers also fled, leaving behind their herds. In 1836, the New Republic of Texas declared these cattle part of the public domain. Entrepreneurial businessmen began rounding up cattle and driving them inland for sale in Missouri, Ohio, and Louisiana. The Civil War, however, cut off this movement of longhorn cattle, and as a result, their populations multiplied. By the end of the war, Texan longhorns provided a lucrative market, contributing to the famous but short-lived "beef bonanza" of the late 19th century.

Spanish longhorns differed dramatically from eastern shorthorn breeds that were introduced to North America by the British in the 19th century. Britain and Scotland had a thriving history of cattle breeding. The growing demand for beef as well as decreased grazing lands in Europe and the United Kingdom forced the British government to seek new grazing lands: first in Scotland and Ireland in the 17th century, followed in the 19th century by colonization of North American plains, Argentine pampas, Australian outback, and New Zealand grasslands.

From the end of the Civil War until approximately 1890, cowboys drew large herds of cattle from feeding grounds in Texas and western plains to the meat packers in the north and east. In 1867, Joseph McCoy linked the western cattle drives with Eastern railroads, vastly improving the distribution networks for cattle. The north–south cattle trails met up with an east–west rail link in Abilene, Kansas. McCoy built stockyards in Abilene and encouraged western cattlemen to use this centralized system. Although it provided a sustained content for western movies and country songs, the open-range cattle drives had a very short history, lasting only until 1885. A series of events led to the demise of the open range: a harsh winter in 1885; improved railroad transportation lines; increased land used for farming; enclosure laws; and the invention of the barbed-wire fence.

Chicago's Union Stock Yards opened in 1865 and played a pivotal role in the formation of the modern beef industry. Prior to this, stockyards were owned by either railroads or private interests. In Chicago, shippers drove animals through crowded streets to reach one of several small stockyards scattered in various districts. The railroad reoriented these yards so that by 1850 all but the smallest had rail connections, allowing shippers to send meat and live animals east. However, the growth of the city made transportation of animals more difficult. Chicago's nine largest railroads, in conjunction with members of Chicago's Pork Packers Association, therefore created the Union Stock Yard and Transit Company, a central, integrated stockyard that would receive cattle from the west, store and process them, and ship them to markets throughout America.

The Union Stock Yards also facilitated the successful growth of the meatpacking industry. Meat packing was historically limited to small-scale butcher operations that used salt or smoke preservation techniques. Prior to 1825, most meat moved on the hoof, since major transportation routes were yet to be developed. The first meatpacking business was begun in 1692 by John Pynchon of Springfield, Massachussetts, who shipped meat to Boston in barrels filled with brine. This nascent industry was seasonal and weather dependent, with shipping confined to the winter months.

Early packinghouses were originally concentrated in New England. They shifted westward by the mid-19th century with the development of the livestock industry in Midwest. This shift was primarily due to **corn** production: farmers realized that more profit could be made by feeding corn to cattle or pigs, and then packing the meat into barrels to be shipped east. Commercial meat packing came into existence around 1818 in Cincinnati, which was called "Porkopolis" because by 1850, it controlled a third of the meatpacking industry in the West. With the development of the Union Stock Yards, Chicago surpassed Cincinnati as the meatpacking center of America.

Soon after the creation of the Stock Yards, various meatpacking companies established operations nearby. The earliest was the **Armour** plant, followed by **Swift**, Morris, and Hammond. The assembly line was first created by the packinghouses, which were forced to find ever faster ways to process the increasing amounts of cattle coming by rail. By the first decade of the 20th century, the skilled butcher was practically eliminated in the Chicago yards, replaced by teams of men whose labor was divided into specialized, mechanized tasks.

The Chicago packers had an advantage over other packing operations because they could search for the best prices in America and distribute their meat accordingly. They were also able to find specialized markets for the by-products of slaughter that would not have been consumed. Packers installed new chemical research laboratories during the 1880s and '90s, facilitating the development of the modern rendering industry. By-products were used to make soap, animal feed, pharmaceuticals, and cosmetics. The rendering industry provided an increased profit margin for the packers; it also offered a solution to the mounting pollution from the packinghouses as the waste products of slaughter were now sold as profitable commodities rather than dumped as waste.

The development of **refrigerated** cars as well as dressed beef dramatically altered the beef industry. In 1872, packers began using ice-cooled units to preserve meats. In 1882, Gustavus Swift developed the first refrigerated railroad car, making in possible to ship processed meat instead of live animals to eastern markets. As a result, Chicago's packing plants were no longer seasonally confined. Farmers could count on a year-round market for their corn-fattened animals.

Dressed beef refers to the portion remaining after removal of hides, hooves, and offal. It is fresh and uncured, not salted or dried. The packing industry faced major challenges with dressed beef, as they had to overcome consumer resistance to meat that was not freshly slaughtered. The railroads also resisted dressed beef because they had a great deal of investment in shipping live cattle. The Grand Trunk was the first railroad to ship dressed beef; less than a decade later, dressed rather than "on the hoof" was the common distribution method.

Once the geographical and shipping constraints were lifted, beef could be processed and shipped from any region, not just centrally located ones. By the late 1880s, packers moved from Chicago to Kansas City and Denver to take advantage of cheap grass, cost savings from shipping dressed beef by rail, less regulation, and a nonunion workforce. Urban growth, with its increase in land value, property taxes, and antipollution laws, contributed to the decline of the Union Stock Yards, which officially closed in 1971.

The Move to Rural Areas

After World War II, the rapid growth of the federal highway system and the development of the refrigerated truck enabled packinghouses to move out of the urban areas they had depended upon for railroad access. Sophisticated, mechanized plants were built in less-expensive rural areas. Additionally, meat packers began conducting business directly with farmers, thus bypassing the need for the stockyard. They also had better access to grain farmers, who provided the feed for the burgeoning feedlot industries. Cattle were raised in small cow calf operations, shipped to feedlots for fattening, and then sold to packing plants.

In the 1960s, the Iowa Beef Packers (IBP) led to a second revolution in the meatpacking industry. Until this time, cattle raised in the country were mainly brought by train to Omaha or Kansas City, where the animals were fed and slaughtered. In 1967, IBP refined its meatpacking process at Dakota City, Nebraska, by creating *boxed beef*. Carcasses were broken into smaller, vacuum-packed portions and shipped in boxes. Better **packaging** improved the shelf life and flavor of meats. Boxed beef allowed the packer to add more value to the product at the plant, to reduce transaction costs in shipping, and to reduce **labor** costs for urban retail grocery chains by allowing these stores to bypass the skilled labor unions and hire low-skilled workers.

The ruralization of the meat-processing industry has brought about a number of dramatic social, economic, and cultural changes in small communities of the Midwest. Changes have been introduced most notably by an influx of immigrant laborers and their families.

Beef consumption doubled from the 1950s to the mid-1970s, as the hamburger and beef on the grill captured the dominant North American cultural scene.

Corporate and Transnational Integration of the Beef Industry

The beef industry experienced unprecedented structural change during the 1980s. This was led by policies favoring trade liberalization, changes to domestic agriculture policy, the adoption of new technologies such as bioengineered seeds and information technologies, and increased competition from nonagricultural sectors for land and labor, as well as the emergence of a more powerful consumer market. The result was more corporate consolidation and integration in the beef sector. Regional trade agreements (such as the **North American Free Trade Agreement**), as well as the World Trade Organization's Agreement on Agriculture, increased the market integration in the United States, Canada, and Mexico. The general regulatory environment also changed as the move toward neoliberal economic policies resulted in a relaxation of antitrust statutes. Both the United States and Canada became net exporters of beef. Foreign export markets present the greatest opportunity for North American beef producers, as increasing incomes in developing countries allow consumers to increase their consumption of animal-source proteins.

Until recently, the beef industry has not been as integrated as the **poultry** or pork industries. These industries transformed their productive processes from a commodity-driven market to a supply-chain model, where each step of the production chain is aimed at producing a final consumer product. By coordinating the different sectors (cow calf operations, feeding, packing, retail), the beef industry is now moving toward more vertical integration, allowing for beef products that directly meet consumer demand while keeping overall production costs low.

Global consumer demand has shifted toward high-value processed foods that are healthy (low in fat) and convenient to prepare. In the United States and Canada, demand tends to favor branded or valued-added products (such as certified Angus beef or **organic** beef). Product development and promotion are central to the industry in order to address the increasing consumer demands for convenience, safety, and nutrition. New marketing initiatives have also been developed to coordinate production with consumer taste. For example, beef industry "check-off" programs collect money from the sale of cattle to fund **advertising** and promotional programs such as the popular "Beef: It's What's for Dinner" campaign. The production, marketing, and distribution of these products are capital and labor intensive; as such, they are dominated by large **multinational** corporations such as Tyson, Cargill, and ConAgra, which have the resources to absorb these costs.

The contemporary beef industry faces many challenges. Demand for red meat declined dramatically in the 1980s, due primarily to health concerns about fatty beef. The beef industry responded by producing leaner cuts, although it still faces competition from the poultry, pork, and seafood industries. In the 1990s, concerns over the safety of beef rose due to outbreaks of hamburger disease (*E. coli* 0157:H7 **bacteria**), listeria, and mad cow disease (**bovine spongiform encephalopathy**). Environmental concerns have been raised about the increased global production and consumption of beef, which is tied to deforestation, the overuse of water and grain resources, and the production of greenhouse gases.

Labor concerns have also been expressed, as meatpacking plants rely on immigrant workers who are often too economically and politically vulnerable to organize for change. The industry as a whole does not have equal distribution of wealth: although small-scale cow calf producers have suffered severe economic hardships in previous years due to drought and border closures, the major feedlots, meat packers, and retail outlets have turned record profits. Meatpacking industries are also beginning to move their operations out of North America, taking advantage of cheaper production costs in less-regulated countries.

Animal rights organizations, such as People for the Ethical Treatment of Animals, have raised public awareness about animal rights and welfare, leading some consumers either to become **vegetarians** or to demand more "humanely" raised and slaughtered animals.

Future technological innovations such as laboratory-derived tissue-cultured meat (or "meat in a vat") may present even deeper challenges to the livestock industries, taking "meat" even further away its natural source.

FURTHER READINGS: Carlson, Laurie Winn. *Cattle: An Informal Social History.* Chicago: Ivan R. Dee, 2001; Cockburn, A. "A Short, Meat-Oriented History of the World: From Eden to the Mattole." *New Left Review* 215 (1996): 16–42; Cronon, William. *Nature's Metropolis: Chicago and the Great West.* New York: W. W. Norton, 1991; Rifkin, Jeremy. *Beyond Beef: The Rise and Fall of Cattle Culture.* New York: Dutton Books, 1992; Schlosser, Eric. *Fast Food Nation: The Dark Side of the All-American Meal.* New York: Perennial, 2002; Sinclair, Upton. *The Jungle.* New York: Doubleday, Page, 1906; Skaggs, Jimmy M. *Prime Cut: Livestock Raising and Meatpacking in the United States, 1607–1983.* College Station: Texas A&M University Press, 1986; Stull, Donald D., Michael J. Broadway, and David Griffith. *Any Way You Cut It: Meat Processing and Small-Town America.* Lawrence: University Press of Kansas, 1995.

Gwendolyn Blue

Beer Beer is a beverage created by mixing water with fermentable sugars (traditionally from malted barley), hops, and yeast. Under proper conditions the yeast will convert the sugars to alcohol and carbon dioxide, yielding a mildly alcoholic drink.

The earliest records of beer brewing are found in ancient Mesopotamia. A Sumerian cylinder seal dating from the third millennium B.C. depicts individuals drinking beer through straws from a communal bowl (straws were an elegant way to avoid the sediment that settled at the bottom of the vessels—the rich coated their beer drinking reeds with gold). Sumerians cherished beer, dedicating nearly half of their barley harvest to its production and including it ceremonially in all matters of import. The oldest known recipe for beer, written in a Sumerian hymn around 2800 B.C., was dedicated to their goddess of brewing, Ninkasi, whose name translates to "the lady that fills the mouth." Brewing, in Sumerian culture, was the only craft that was overseen by a female goddess and was done by women only.

Around 1800 B.C. in the reign of King Hammurabi, women were responsible for selling and running alehouses, and the famous legal code of Hammurabi condemns any women who overcharged with being thrown into the water. Presumably public opinion against drunkenness was already being felt, as it also forbade priestesses, "sisters of gods," from operating—or even entering—an alehouse. The punishment for this violation was death by burning.

Beer brewing generally flourished in all the grain-growing agricultural societies of the Middle East and was probably taught by the Egyptians to the Greeks, who taught the Romans. Although the practical merits of beer making as a method to preserve the harvest and to render liquids sanitary would probably have ensured its continued development, no doubt its more esoteric side effects sealed the bargain.

By the Middle Ages, the Romans rejected beer in favor of wine. Beer, already a strong symbol of Germanic culture, was considered barbaric by the Byzantines and was used as a pawn in the ideological battle between the old religions and early Christianity. Pagan rituals went so far as to use beer as a deliberate alternative to wine, which was already sacred to Christianity, representing the blood of Jesus. Northern Europe remained devoted to beer brewing, though, grain being a more productive crop there than grapes.

The first recorded use of hops in beer dates to 822, although it did not become widespread until the 1700s. Prior to the fifteenth century in Europe, "beer" was a thick, unhopped ale. Subsequently, hopped ale was known as "beer." Lagers, which are the biggest sellers in the United States today, were developed in the 16th century.

Beer brewing had remained a home endeavor for thousands of years, but the introduction of hops to the brewing process rendered beer more stable, allowing it to be transported without degradation and kept for longer periods of time. The process was perfected in Germany, and small breweries consequently formed there. Eventually the process spread to throughout Europe, with artisan brewpubs and monasteries supplying beer for their communities.

Immigrants to North America brought with them their passion for beer, and brewing quickly took root in the colonies. By 1776, New York, Virginia, Massachusetts, Pennsylvania, Rhode Island, Georgia, New Hampshire, and North Carolina all had established breweries. Both the colonists and the British army built their own breweries in the New World to ensure a steady supply. The French also built a brewery in what was then Kaskaskia territory, now Illinois, to satisfy the fur traders and explorers there. Soldiers in the Revolutionary War were enticed and rewarded with the choice of a quart of beer or cider per day while in the army. Thomas Jefferson and George Washington both brewed their own beer, and in 1789 Washington issued a statement indicating that he would only drink beer that had been made in the United States.

The advent of the Industrial Revolution brought breweries efficient power in the form of the steam engine and consistent measurement with the introduction of the thermometer and hydrometer. In the early 1800s, the flavor of beer was improved with the invention of the drum roaster, used to roast malts while avoiding the unwanted smoky flavor previously picked up from the malt-roasting fires. And greater purity was achieved when Louis Pasteur discovered the role of yeast in fermentation, publishing *Studies on Beer* in 1876, showing how yeast organisms can be controlled.

By 1873, there were more than 4,300 breweries in the United States. But with the rise of the popularity of beer came a corresponding rise in the power of the Temperance Movement, which promoted banning the sale of alcoholic beverages. Their mission became known simply as Prohibition. By 1829, the American Temperance Society had 100,000 members, and by 1833, there were 5,000 temperance societies with a combined membership exceeding 1.25 million people.

Maine passed the first prohibition law in 1846. States across the country followed suit; Vermont, Massachusetts, Rhode Island, Minnesota, Michigan, and Connecticut all voted for prohibition by 1854. By the close of 1855, alcohol bans had been adopted in New York, New Hampshire, Delaware, Indiana, Iowa, and the Nebraska Territory.

It was the improvement in technology, rather than the Temperance Movement, that caused the number of breweries to drop from its all-time high in the 1870s to just 1,500 by 1910. Brewers were consolidating, buying up smaller breweries and using the strength of an ever-increasing distribution network. But the Temperance Movement was gaining strength.

Kansas, whose more than 90 brewing plants represented the fourth largest industry in the state in 1860, passed a prohibition amendment in 1881. Most breweries went out of business, but a few fought the ban. However, in 1887, the Supreme Court handed Kansas temperance supporters an important victory that enforced their crusade. In *Mugler v. Kansas* (123 U.S. 623), the Court found that in closing Mugler's brewery, enforcing that state's prohibition law, the state had not unfairly deprived Mugler of his property, but rather was "abating a nuisance" and protecting the public health. Another Kansas brewer, John Walruff, who was also battling in the courts to save his brewery, saw the writing on the wall and fled the state, abandoning his property and skipping bail, taking what was left of his fortune and starting another brewery, this time in Missouri.

With the passage of the 18th Amendment, brewers across the country were faced with the same economic disaster. The enterprising stayed afloat by converting to vinegar factories, soda bottlers, cold storage facilities, and whatever else they can manage. The rest went bankrupt.

Supporters of Prohibition referred to it as the "noble experiment," asserting that it would lead to the end of poverty and would afford the common man the dignity and ability to achieve his highest nature. But in reality, organized crime syndicates became wildly wealthy meeting the demand for alcohol. The Canadian border easily allowed smugglers through. Speakeasies (illegal taverns serving alcohol), illicit distilleries, and smuggling operations flourished. Eventually lawmakers realized that a mistake had been made and began work to repeal Prohibition. In 1933, the 21st Amendment, repealing the 18th Amendment, was passed, and breweries resumed production.

During World War II, the brewing industry was required to devote 15 percent of its production to the war effort. At the same time, women who had been thrust into the workforce developed a thirst for beer. Brewers begin brewing beer for women's tastes, and light lagers took over the field.

In general, the brewery consolidation continued until in 1983 there were only 80 breweries in the United States, with just 51 owners. The top six brewers (Miller, Pabst, Anheuser-Busch, Heileman, Stroh, and Coors) controlled 92 percent of the beer market in the United States.

However, a vacuum had been created, and specialty brewers were beginning to fill the void. In 1965, cheesemaker Fritz Maytag bought the Anchor Brewing Company in San Francisco. In 1976 Jack McAuliffe opened the New Albion Brewery in Sonoma, California. The New Albion closed after just a few years, but it became known as the first craft brewery or "microbrewery."

In 1984 microbreweries opened in seven different states, and the nation's first brewpub opened in Manhattan. In 1990 the Sierra Nevada Brewery, also in California, produced and sold so much beer (31,000 barrels), that it could no longer be considered a microbrewery (defined by producing 25,000 barrels per year or less). And by 1994 California alone hosted 84 microbreweries or brewpubs.

As of 2006, there were estimated to be 1,389 craft brewers, including microbreweries and brewpubs, in the United States. There were 20 large breweries, 24 regional breweries, and 4 other noncraft brewers, bringing the total number of U.S. breweries to 1,437. Together, they produced more than 210 million barrels of beer annually and generated $94 billion. Of this total, 6.7 million barrels were brewed in the craft brewery segment—3.2 percent of the share by volume, but almost 5 percent by dollar value.

Craft beer sales in 2006 represented a 31.5 percent increase over just the previous three years, causing the big breweries to take concerned notice. Large brewers began marketing small "specialty" brews of their own and also began purchasing the smaller breweries, folding them into their portfolios in a new round of consolidation.

FURTHER READINGS: EyeWitness to History. "Prohibition." http://www.eyewitnesstohistory.-com/snpmech2.htm; Flandrin, Jean-Louis. "The Humanization of Eating Behaviors." In Jean-Louis Flandrin and Massimo Montanari, eds., *Food: A Culinary History from Antiquity to the Present.* New York: Columbia University Press, 1999; Higgins, Cindy. *Kansas Breweries and Beer, 1854–1911.* Eudora, KS: Ad Astra Press, 1992; Montanari, Massimo. "Production Structures and Food Systems in the Early Middle Ages." In Jean-Louis Flandrin and Massimo Montanari, eds., *Food: A Culinary History from Antiquity to the Present,* 172. New York: Columbia University Press, 1999; Nasrallah, Nawal. *Delights from the Garden of Eden.* Bloomington, IN:

1stBooks, 2003; Papazian, Charlie. *The Complete Joy of Homebrewing*. 3rd ed. New York: Quill, 2003; Van Wieren, Dale P. *American Breweries II*. West Point, PA: Eastern Coast Breweriana Association, 1995.

Bonni J. Miller

Ben & Jerry's. *See* Ice Cream.

Betty Crocker Betty Crocker was one of the best-known **advertising** icons of the 20th century—an imaginary kitchen confidante and a role model to millions of American homemakers. Consumer surveys from the early 1940s showed that her name was familiar to 9 out of 10 homemakers; in 1945, *Fortune* magazine listed Betty Crocker as the second most popular woman in the United States (after First Lady Eleanor Roosevelt). Even in 1996, when her image was much less visible (having been largely replaced by the Red Spoon logo, first introduced in 1954), Betty Crocker was still ranked 16th on a list of "America's most powerful brands."

When she debuted in 1921, Betty Crocker was nothing more than a signature used by the Washburn-Crosby Company (millers of Gold Medal flour) to sign their replies to consumer letters. A promotional contest earlier that year had drawn thousands of entries, along with an influx of baking questions. The queries would be answered by the home economics staff, but company executives wanted to give each letter a personal touch—the signature of a helpful, reassuring friend. They chose the name "Betty" for its homey familiarity and "Crocker" to honor a director who had recently retired; then they asked the firm's female employees to sign the name and chose a distinctive signature from samples.

In 1936 Betty Crocker was given her first "official" face. Neysa McMein, an illustrator whose all-American beauties had graced many magazine covers, painted Betty as an earnest young matron whose gentle eyes and softly waved hair offset the sternness of her tight mouth and firm jaw. The portrait first appeared on packages of Softasilk cake flour in 1937, and in subsequent years Betty's name and image would identify many General Mills products, most notably a line of cake mixes; since 1946, the brand has been licensed to companies producing bakeware, small appliances, and other home products.

A slightly retouched portrait, with a bit more glamour about the eyes, gazed out from the jacket of *Betty Crocker's Picture Cook Book,* published in 1950 and destined to become a perennial best-seller. The cover copy refers to the fictitious author as a real person: "Year after year, in national surveys, she is chosen as the nation's most helpful cooking authority.... Into this—her Picture Cook Book—Betty Crocker has put the results of over a quarter of a century of scientific cooking experience." Nine editions later, the book is still a mainstay in millions of homes.

Betty Crocker's voice was first heard in 1924, when Washburn-Crosby launched "The Betty Crocker Cooking School of the Air" on its own local Minneapolis-St. Paul, Minnesota, radio station, WCCO. The program became part of the NBC network's national lineup in 1927 and was broadcast through 1951. Marjorie Husted was the voice of Betty Crocker on the radio. Encouraged by robust sales of the 1950 cookbook, General Mills put Betty Crocker on television in 1951, sharing cooking tips with the likes of George Burns and Gracie Allen. "The Betty Crocker Search for the All-American Homemaker of Tomorrow" began a 23-year run in 1954. Adelaide Hawley played Betty on TV from 1949 to 1964.

Over the years, the iconic Betty Crocker portrait has been modified and updated to present an image with which consumers can identify. In her most recent incarnation, Betty's features and complexion suggest a modicum of ethnic heritage—perhaps African American or Latina—created by computer "morphing" of photos of a cross-section of American women.

FURTHER READINGS: General Mills. http://www.generalmills.com; Inness, Sherrie A., ed. *Kitchen Culture in America.* Philadelphia: University of Pennsylvania Press, 2001; Marks, Susan. *Finding Betty Crocker: The Secret Life of America's First Lady of Food.* New York: Simon & Schuster, 2005; Smallzreid, Kathleen Ann. *The Everlasting Pleasure.* New York: Appleton-Century-Crofts, 1956.

Bonnie J. Slotnick

Beverages. *See* Bottling Industry; Coffee; Dairy Industry; Distilled Spirits; Soft Drinks; Wine Business.

Birds Eye The 75-year-old Birds Eye Foods Company is headquartered in Rochester, New York. The company's family of farms is composed of 1,500 growers located in nine major growing regions in the United States. Birds Eye maintains 195 sites for receiving, processing, and storage of vegetables. Its branded line includes Birds Eye, Birds Eye Fresh, Birds Eye Steamfresh, Birds Eye Voila!, C&W Freshlike, and McKenzie's. Processed foods include Comstock and Wilderness pie fillings, Nalley and Brooks chili products, Bernstein's and Nalley salad dressings, and Tim's and Snyder of Berlin **snacks**.

Adding to its early food freezing technology, Birds Eye Foods has recently taken on new cooking technology, using steam management similar to the process of microwaving popcorn. Called Steamfresh, it is a nine-variety vegetable collection of flash-frozen, ready-to-eat vegetables in a special microwave steam-in-its-bag unit. Additionally, the company has added a new Birds Eye Herb Frozen Garden Collection, six combinations of vegetables paired with fresh herbs and seasonings mixed with olive oil, citrus, and butter.

Birds Eye Foods grew from very small beginnings, the efforts of one man, Clarence "Bob" Birdseye (1886–1956) of New York City, a businessman and inventor. Originally a biology major at Amherst College, Birdseye dropped out of school and became a U.S. field naturalist in Labrador in 1920. There, he became impressed with the well-preserved cellular structure of cooked fish frozen naturally and rapidly in the Arctic outdoors. He noted that this freezing process caused less crystallization within the fish tissue.

Desiring to implement this theory into something everyone could enjoy, Birdseye returned to New York in 1915 and developed his crude "Multiplate Quick Freeze Machine." In it, he lowered food in tightly sealed cartons encased in metal into a low-temperature brine solution to freeze the foods. Later, he froze foods with calcium chloride brine chilled to −40°F.

By 1924, Birdseye was able to organize the General Seafood Corporation. He then turned his attention to developing **refrigerated** railroad boxcars to transport **frozen foods** nationwide. In 1929, Birdseye sold his company to Postum, which later became **General Foods** Corporation. Birdseye's line of frozen foods was renamed Birds Eye. Ultimately, in 1949, using the anhydrous freezing process, Birdseye managed to cut the initial freezing time of 18 hours to just 90 minutes.

Though not first in frozen foods, Birdseye's fame came from his rapid process for producing tasty, well-preserved fresh fish, fruits, and vegetables in retail-size containers. **Restaurants** profited greatly from his work. Birdseye held 300 patents in all, but the only other patent concerning food was a process for converting crushed sugarcane residue into paper pulp.

Dean Foods Vegetable Company purchased Birds Eye Foods in 1993. Plans now call for the company to concentrate on its branded businesses, with increased emphasis on new products and marketing, and selling off the nonbranded entities. Additionally, it will sell its 500-employee Watsonville, California, facility.

FURTHER READING: Elan, Elissa. "Clarence Birdseye." *Nation's Restaurant News* 30 (February 1996): 32.

Marty Martindale

Borden Gail Borden (1801–1874), best known for the invention and commercial production of condensed milk, was born in Norwich, New York. He moved west with his family as a young man and ultimately settled in Galveston, Texas. Borden was actively involved in civic life in Galveston, where he edited the town's first regular newspaper and helped draft the first state constitution. He had very little formal education, and no scientific training, but was a keen inventor and developed an early interest in food preservation.

In 1851 his "meat biscuit"—or "portable desiccated soup-bread"—won a gold medal at the Great Council Exhibition in London. It was, however, a commercial failure, and Borden changed his emphasis to the preservation of milk. His patent application for condensed milk was rejected three times until finally being accepted in 1856 at the recommendation of the editor of *Scientific American*. In 1858, Borden obtained financial backing from Jeremiah Milbank, a grocery wholesaler whom he had met by chance, and the New York Condensed Milk Company was formed. The company got off to a good start with two serendipitous events in 1858: Borden's milk was praised by the Committee of the Academy of Medicine, and one of the **advertisements** for the product appeared in the same issue of *Leslie's Illustrated Weekly* as a scathing indictment of the quality of the milk sold in most cities.

The Civil War was a huge boost to the company, and even after licensing other manufacturers to produce condensed milk, Borden could not keep up with the demand for supplies for troops on both sides of the conflict.

After the war, the business continued to innovate and expand: fluid milk was offered in 1875, glass **bottles** were pioneered in 1885, canned unsweetened condensed milk was produced in 1885, and evaporated milk in 1892.

The company was incorporated as the Borden Condensed Milk Company in 1899, and two years later the first international branch opened in Ontario. By 1929, the Borden Company, as it had been renamed in 1919, had absorbed more than 200 other businesses and had added **ice cream**, cheese, and powdered milk to its range, as well as an adhesives business that became the Borden Chemical Company.

There was another spate of acquisitions in 1986–1991, with 91 companies purchased at a cost of $1.9 billion. The company was not able to manage the rapid expansion, however, and suffered huge losses in 1992 and 1993. In 1995 Borden was taken over by the investment firm of Kohlberg, Kravis, Roberts (KKR), which reorganized the company and split it into 11 separate entities that were progressively sold off over the next few years. Borden's original **dairy** company is now Borden Milk Products, LP, and is now privately owned by the Dallas-based Milk Products, LP.

Janet Clarkson

Bottling Industry According to the **U.S. Department of Agriculture**'s Economic Research Service, the per capita consumption of carbonated beverages rose 5.9 percent between 1994 and 2004, from 49.4 gallons to 52.3 gallons. That means that, on average, every person in this country consumes roughly a gallon of soda every week. In the same period, the consumption of bottled water rose 115 percent, from 10.8 gallons per capita to 23.2 gallons; by 2006, this was up to about 28 gallons. Whatever this trend may forebode for human health, it has dramatically increased the demand for aluminum and plastic containers.

Globally, 41 billion gallons of bottled water were consumed in 2004, much of it in places where tap water is perfectly safe and good tasting. This means instead of drinking a gallon of water that should cost a few pennies at most from a faucet and through a system of distribution that is relatively inexpensive (pipes), people are paying two or three dollars for water in a container that is extremely expensive to manufacture and travels many miles on average, wasting fuel in its journey to the consumer. Moreover, the plastic itself is a form of polyester called polyethylene terephthalate (PET) that is made from crude oil, and despite efforts at recycling, most of this either ends up in landfills where it will never biodegrade, is incinerated, or becomes litter that often makes its way into our streams, rivers, and oceans, toxifying water and scenery for marine life, wildlife, and humans. The manufacturers and bottlers of **beer**, **soft drinks**, sports drinks, and water are hugely powerful interests that liberally fund lobbyists to squash current efforts to enact bottle bills in various states.

While few consumers consider soft drinks a health-promoting beverage option—even though there are brands that employ this marketing angle, especially **diet** and nutrient-fortified drinks—the general perception is that bottled water is good for you. Leading brands **advertise** micronutrients and essential minerals, which are often added to ordinary filtered tap water. Imported waters also carry the prestige of affluence, unspoiled tropical islands, pristine alpine springs, or sophisticated Old World spas. Ironically, the time spent in plastic bottles, being shipped from these sources or sitting on shelves, may leach toxins such as antimony and bisphenol A into the water. The plastics industry and the Food and Drug Administration assure consumers that plastic containers are safe, but there is increasing cause for concern. In other words, bottled water may be good neither economically, nor environmentally, nor for promoting health.

Another major trend in the bottling industry in the past decades has been the vertical integration by soft drink manufacturers. Strangely, while antitrust legislation prevented the largest manufacturers (Coca-Cola and Pepsi) from buying out all competitors and creating monopolies, it allowed these companies to purchase the bottling companies. Bottlers used to be **franchised** and allotted specific regional distribution rights. Today most are owned by the same companies that produce the syrups, and thus the soft drink industry follows trends in the wider food industry: increasingly, all stages in the growing, processing, distributing, and retailing of food are controlled by fewer and larger corporations.

Key Points in Bottling History

1820	Saratoga Springs is the first bottled mineral water.
1861	Ginger ale is first bottled.
1871	Lemon's Superior Sparkling Ginger Ale is the first trademarked soda.
1876	Charles E. Hires markets root beer extract.
1881	Cliquot Club markets ginger ale and sodas in other flavors.
1883	White Rock markets bottled mineral water.
1884	Hervey D. Thatcher invents the milk bottle in Potsdam, New York.
1885	Moxie is distributed.
1886	Automatic bottle filling and capping machines are patented. Coca-Cola is invented.
1888	Dr. Pepper, developed in 1885, is sold in bottles.
1889	Shasta Mountain Spring Water is bottled.
1892	William Painter invents crown bottle cap.
1893	Hires Root Beer is bottled.
1898	Pepsi is invented; its name is registered as a trademark in 1903.
1899	Machine for blowing glass bottles is patented.
1905	Royal Crown begins bottling ginger ale and root beer.
1906	Orange Crush is introduced in Chicago.
1907	Canada Dry, a new ginger ale, is introduced.
1911	Rotary bottle filling and capping machines are patented.
1919	The American Bottlers of Carbonated Beverages created.
1923	First six-pack cartons ("Hom-Paks") for soft drinks in use.
1924	Nehi is sold in $9\frac{1}{2}$-ounce bottles.
1928	7Up is invented.
1933	Mission Orange soda is sold in a black bottle.
1934	Baked-on color labels first applied to soft drink bottles; Royal Crown Cola is introduced.
1936	Cliquot Club Ginger Ale is the first canned soda tested; the tests fail.
1937	Dad's Old Fashion Root Beer is bottled.
1938	Squirt is marketed.
1940	Grapette is sold in a 6-ounce bottle.
1948	Pepsi-Cola attempts to market canned sodas, but fails.
1952	No-Cal Beverage is the first diet soda marketed.
1957	Aluminum cans in use for the first time.
1958	Fanta is introduced.
1962	Alcoa invents pull-ring tab for cans.
1963	First "pop top" can used by the Schlitz Brewing Company.
1965	Vending machines first used to dispense soft drinks in cans.
1970	First time that soft drinks are sold in plastic bottles.
1973	Improved bottles (made of PET—polyethylene terephthalate) are developed.
1974	Stay-on tabs for aluminum cans invented.

Sources: Museum of Beverage Containers and Advertising, "Soda Bottle History," http://gono.com/cc/bottle.htm
"Timeline." http://library.thinkquest.org/04oct/01795/timeline.htm

FURTHER READING: Container Recycling Institute. http://container-recycling.org.

Darius Willoughby

Bovine Spongiform Encephalopathy (BSE) Bovine spongiform encephalopathy emerged as a sudden epidemic in cattle in the United Kingdom in spring 1986. It was described in the press as "mad cow disease." The first known case was a cow that died in February 1985 after tremors of the head, loss of weight, and uncoordinated movements. In 1995, two British teenagers were diagnosed with Creutzfeldt-Jakob Disease (CJD), a related brain disease that ordinarily affects only older people. Although British government officials reassured the public that **beef** was safe, it was apparent to scientists that the variant form of CJD affecting younger people was almost certainly a result of eating beef from cattle carrying BSE.

By 2006, infected cattle had been identified in about 40 countries, including the United States and Japan, almost 200 people worldwide had died of variant CJD, and worldwide losses to the beef industry were estimated in the tens of billions of dollars. There have been three identified cases of BSE in the United States. The only known U.S. case of variant CJD was in a woman who had lived in England during the 1980s.

The disease in cattle was initially controlled by slaughtering infected herds, but more effective control has required banning feed made from slaughterhouse by-products. Nevertheless, new cases in cattle continue to appear, and it is impossible to predict the human death toll because so many questions about these new and slow-developing diseases are still unanswered. The peak years for BSE in Britain were 1992 and 1993, with almost 100,000 confirmed cases; overall, the United Kingdom total is about 200,000 cases. More than 4.5 million British cattle were slaughtered preemptively to control a disease with an apparently long incubation period.

The now-accepted scientific description of transmissible spongiform encephalopathies was published by Stanley Prusiner just before British cows began to stagger and die. Prusiner had been studying human CJD since 1972, and he discovered that the infectious agent was not a slow virus but a simpler protein fragment he named a "prion." He also noted that scrapie, a 250-year-old dementia endemic in sheep, was also a prion disease. Prions are thought to be chemically identical to protein fragments that are quite common in normal brain tissue, but the diseased prions are misfolded or reverse-folded such that they induce other proteins to misfold and cause brain tissue to die off. The dead areas form holes as in a sponge, hence the designation "spongiform encephalopathies." Because prions are tiny protein fragments, the immune system does not detect and resist them. They also do not break down under normal cooking or even the rendering of slaughterhouse scraps into animal feed.

Since scrapie did not apparently infect people who ate lamb or mutton, it was initially thought that mad cow disease, even if it were a prion disease, would not harm human consumers. The disease was controlled by slaughtering any affected cattle, and later—using the prion hypothesis—by banning the use of animal feed made from slaughterhouse by-products. It is now believed that BSE originally arose in cattle that ate feed made from parts of sheep with scrapie. However, it may be that BSE has been endemic in cattle at a low incidence for a long time and only became epidemic because of changes in the feeding practices.

British health officials publicly reassured the public that beef was safe, while scientists in 1990 quietly set up a watch for unusual human cases of dementia that might be caused by BSE. When unusually young people began dying of CJD in some numbers, the meat and grocery industry in Britain stopped selling brain and nervous tissues, which probably contain the most prions. Because the incubation periods of BSE, CJD, and the new variant CJD are long and not fully determined, no one knows whether the diseases are fully under control or how high the death toll might eventually rise. People and some cattle may be carrying the disease without symptoms for long periods of time. There are as yet no effective treatments for prion diseases, nor even real-time tests. It is unknown what produced CJD in humans prior to the BSE epidemic, because it is such a sporadic disease (one or two cases per million deaths). Other unknowns include how scrapie infects sheep, whether BSE/variant CJD prions can or have infected or reinfected sheep, how much BSE is transmitted from cow to calf, or why wild deer and elk in the United States are now showing a related chronic wasting disease.

The British cattle industry had lost $6 billion by 2000. By that time, BSE had appeared in European cattle, and the **European Union** instituted a purchase-for-destruction program and feed controls costing about $3 billion. Two cases in the United States led to a two-and-a-half-year Japanese ban on American beef (2004–2006) with an estimated loss of more than $4 billion in exports. In turn, a brief U.S. ban on Canadian beef in 2005 was estimated to cost the Canadian industry US$8 million per week.

In 1997, the new Labour government of Britain commissioned a $42 million investigation of the crisis, led by Lord Phillips. In its 16-volume report, the Phillips Commission criticized the previous Conservative government for neglecting public health and protecting the beef industry, but did not strongly criticize the food industry and praised retail **supermarket** chains. As a result of the report, the British government began paying compensation to the families of variant CJD victims. By way of comparison, about 200 cases of classical CJD occurred among fewer than 10,000 people treated in several countries with tainted human growth hormone prior to 1977, when a safer production process was mandated.

Although BSE appears to be coming under control and variant CJD remains a rare disease, the prospect of catching an untreatable and rapidly fatal dementia from something we eat arouses strong fears. The British experience shows a series of dangerous delays from when information became available to when government or industry took protective (and admittedly expensive) actions. For example, it was more than a year after the government knew that BSE was caused by recycling slaughterhouse scraps into cattle before the process was banned (in 1988), and another year before the ban was extended to feed for chickens or pigs, since these animals were not known to have similar diseases. Many cases of BSE after the feed ban are believed to have resulted from using up old feed stocks or the accidental or deliberate diversion of pig and chicken feed to cattle.

FURTHER READINGS: Brown, Paul, Robert G. Will, Raymond Bradley, David M. Asher, and Linda Detwiler. "Bovine Spongiform Encephalopathy and Variant Creutzfeldt-Jakob Disease: Background, Evolution, and Current Concerns." *Emerging Infectious Diseases* 7, no. 1 (January–February 2001). Available at http://www.cdc.gov/ncidod/eid/vol7no1/brown.htm.

Mark Zanger

Boycotts and Consumer Protests The term *boycott* derives from actions taken against the English land agent Charles Boycott, who in late 19th-century Ireland was ostracized as a protest against his failure to reduce rents. The term has subsequently been widely applied to describe economic or political protest through deliberate nonparticipation in a circumscribed activity. Food boycotts and other types of consumer food protests are forms of (usually) peaceful citizen action against food companies or governments whose policies and practices are judged to be unfair or unjust. Such protests can escalate into full-scale food riots, particularly in times of economic hardship. While food protests have occurred throughout the ages and in many parts of the world, consumer boycotts have become increasingly common in the last half-century. Consumer boycotts are usually aimed at specific commodities or private-sector businesses, whereas food protests more often target governments and government agencies; however, this is not a clear-cut distinction. Although they have many similarities, boycotts and other forms of food protest will be dealt with separately below.

Boycotts

A consumer boycott is an attempt by an organized group or groups to achieve certain moral or political objectives by urging individual consumers to refrain from making selected purchases in the marketplace. It is usually aimed at a specific business or market sector and provides a tangible way for consumers to collectively exert pressure on businesses by holding them to public account for their corporate practices. A boycott is accomplished by the simple withdrawal of economic support through refusal to purchase the company's products. Boycotts can also be directed against governments as a form of protest against perceived unjust political actions or causes.

Food is a common, though certainly not exclusive, vehicle for boycotts. There are both pragmatic and cultural factors that contribute to this, reflecting the fact that food is both a biological necessity and a powerful cultural symbol. Food, of course, is a basic human survival need, but food production, distribution, and consumption are also political, economic, and cultural activities. Food carries social, emotional, and spiritual meanings and embodies complex ideas about individual and group identity, justice, and ethics. The way in which food is marketed can either affirm or conflict with such ideas and values. Pragmatically, food is a high-volume, often perishable commodity that typically requires high turnover times on the retail market. Disruptions to this supply-and-demand chain, and the economic consequences for business, are felt very quickly. Food boycotts thus have both practical and symbolic value.

There are three main types of boycotts, each with differing goals and purposes. People may have multiple motivations for participating in boycotts, which are not mutually exclusive but generally include some sense of opposing unethical corporate or government behavior.

Instrumental boycotts are intended to change the status quo by applying pressure on the targeted business to change specific practices or policies, for example, to stop using child labor or to sign fair wage agreements with workers. An example of this is the California grape boycott of the 1960s. The United Farm Workers Organizing Committee, led by Cesar Chavez, brought public attention to the poor working conditions, low wages, and discrimination experienced by migrant grape pickers in California. By arousing the sympathy of community and church groups across America and mobilizing their support for *la causa*, as it became known, the organizers provoked a consumer boycott that resulted in a 30 percent reduction in grape sales. Eventually, the grape growers capitulated, and workers' contracts were significantly improved. More recently, a successful campaign by the Earth Island Institute against major tuna producers led to the adoption of dolphin-friendly fishing policies in 1990.

Expressive boycotts are less focused on specific goals, but signal general disapproval with the way a company or government conducts itself. Such boycotts' goals may be quite vague, for example, calling for "fair trade" practices—without specifics of what those practices are. Many large **multinational** food companies import raw foodstuffs from poor and developing countries. Such products as fruit, **coffee**, and cacao command far higher prices when they reach the American and European markets than are paid to the primary producers. On foreign-owned plantations, local workers may be paid poverty-line wages to grow and harvest crops that will make huge corporate profits abroad. By refusing to buy the products of particular companies, consumers in the affluent world can make their own protest against perceived exploitation and greed. Although they do not expect to be able to change the system, they can at least decline to participate in one part of it. The wide-scale boycott of South African food (and other) products in the 1970s as part of a protest against government policies of apartheid is another example. In this instance, the motivation was both to express moral disapproval and to effect practical political change through economic pressure. Companies that dealt with or sold the products of the apartheid regime themselves became targets of consumer boycotts, along with the government itself, and some British grocery chains did indeed stop stocking South African goods.

There can also be mixed expressive/instrumental boycotts. One, this time against a company, Nestlé, has been called the world's biggest boycott. In the early 1970s, the organization War on Want published a sweeping indictment of the role of marketing of baby milk formulas in developing countries, where poverty, illiteracy, and unsanitary conditions resulted in inappropriate product use and consequent infant malnutrition and death—a situation that was famously described by Derek Jelliffe as "commerciogenic malnutrition." In 1977 the Infant Formula Action Coalition organized a boycott against Nestlé, as the leading offender, to protest its unethical marketing practices. The boycott was suspended in 1984 after Nestlé made changes to its marketing practices, including signing the World Health Organization's International Code on the Marketing of Breastmilk Substitutes. However, the boycott was reinstated in 1988, as Nestlé was seen to be in breach of the code. It remains one of the most boycotted brands on the planet, with an extensive network of well-organized groups around the world that promote letter-writing campaigns, petitions, leafleting, and newsletters.

Self-enhancing boycotts invoke the "clean hands" concept. Though behaving virtuously in the marketplace, individuals are able to square their consciences and feel good about themselves as responsible consumers, without any realistic expectation of bringing about changes in market practices. Indeed, the boycott target may not even be aware it is being boycotted. Thus an individual makes a private decision to not buy a certain company's products, but neither lets the company know the reasons for this nor seeks to find support from like-minded people. It has been suggested that purchasing behavior as a form of self-expression is a substitute for more traditional forms of political participation. Nevertheless, such actions are ways for individual consumers to link themselves with global issues and may lead to more active social or political engagement in the long term.

Effectiveness *versus* Success

Boycotts are positioned to take the moral high ground. Whether they are effective or efficient tools for change is often a secondary consideration. It is possible to distinguish between the effectiveness of a boycott and its ultimate success. An *effective* boycott actually results in declining sales of the targeted product, as was the case with the California grape boycott. To be effective, a number of conditions must be fulfilled. First, there must be a significant body of consumers who are informed and concerned about an issue. Second, these consumers must be willing to use their purchasing power in a strategic way. Finally, there must be a substitute product or an alternate choice or source of supply; if not, the consumers must be willing to forgo the product altogether. *Success*, on the other hand, is gauged by the extent to which the boycott achieves its stated moral or sociopolitical goals.

Food boycotts persist largely because they are seen to work. Because the effectiveness and success of boycotts depend on mass consumer action, a degree of high-level organization is required to create and sustain public awareness and interest, ensure media coverage, and keep pressure on the target company through techniques such as petitions, letter-writing campaigns, and newsletters or websites. Where boycotts have been promoted by ad hoc committees and local volunteers, rather than large national or international groups or organizations, they have tended to be less successful.

Food Protests

Whereas boycotts typically target a readily available food commodity or the production relationships surrounding it, food protests or riots more commonly arise as a reaction to food shortages or high food prices. Such scarcity may be the result of environmental factors, such as weather or insect infestation leading to crop failure, or economic conditions or political decisions that result in a sharp decline in purchasing power, particularly of vulnerable groups. Actions may be directed against the actual food supplier or distributor or at the government whose policies are held to be the cause of the supply problem. Protests are usually focused on immediate and pressing needs caused by short-term emergency situations and dissipate once the crisis is over.

Food riots fall into three main categories. *Blockades* disrupt the transport of goods. *Price riots* involve the seizure of goods from shops, to be sold at "just prices" with the money being handed over to the merchant. *Market riots* are characterized by simple looting, without monetary reparation. Food dumping has also been used as a form of protest.

Food protests have a long history. They were particularly common between the 16th and 18th centuries; England and France, for example, both experienced Bread Riots in the 18th century. In England, the market economy that was replacing the feudal system abandoned the notion of "just food prices," giving rise to a sense of injustice as well as actual hunger. America had its own food protest in the form of the Boston Tea Party, when in 1773 colonists destroyed crates of tea in Boston Harbor as a protest against British taxation policies.

Although this form of protest declined during the 19th and 20th centuries, perhaps as the organization of **labor** began to allow for centralized and proactive rather than merely local and reactive measures, riots have continued sporadically during times of deprivation and social strife. For example, at the beginning of the 20th century, the United States experienced sometimes violent disturbances surrounding a meat boycott that was initiated in response to the setting up of the **Beef** Trust—an industry group that controlled prices in order to maximize profits. The actions of the boycotters resulted in a dramatic decline in meat sales, forcing many butchers to close their businesses. In New York, butcher's shops were the targets of break-ins, their products thrown onto the streets. Despite clashes with the police and arrests, the protests persisted until meat prices were eventually reduced.

The early part of the 20th century saw many examples of food protests, and historians have remarked on their similarities. Women played a prominent role in food riots in France in 1911, engaging in dumping of food and battles with authorities. In 1916 in the English county of Cumbria, housewives led riots when merchants tried to sell food above the government-set price. In New York in 1917, a working-class women's association led a boycott of chicken, fish, and vegetables to protest the high cost of living; they shut down markets for two weeks, provoking violent confrontations with shoppers, merchants, and police. Following World War I, when Barcelona suffered from crippling inflation, women from the radical republican movement attacked bread shops and took over a ship laden with fish. In Toronto in 1933, the Jewish Women's Labor League organized a boycott of kosher meat, forcing a reduction of prices. The prominent part played by women in such protests may be a consequence of their frontline role as family food providers and their frustration in being unable to fulfill this role, and it may be an expression of female community solidarity. It may also at least partially reflect the fact that women were often unable to effectively participate in formal political processes.

Food price protests are not always violent in nature. When price controls in the United States were lifted after World War II, there were some dramatic price rises that attracted organized consumer protests. The Washington Committee for Consumer Protection urged citizens to not buy meat for more than 60 cents a pound—and succeeded in getting prices reduced to 59 cents! A similar campaign was targeted at milk. Starting in Denver, in 1966 a nationwide series of protests against rising **supermarket** prices included boycotts and direct actions such as demonstrations, while the next decade brought, at various times, boycotts of coffee and staples including meat, milk, and **sugar**. While such protests may achieve short-term victories, they are not particularly effective in the long run, and prices inevitably creep back up. Contemporary examples include Mexican demonstrations against spiraling prices of tortillas and other staples in early 2007, blamed at least partially on increased U.S. **corn** costs due to the diversion of corn for bio-fuel usage.

Although boycotts offer a peaceable form of protest calling for fair food prices, violent food riots continue to be a human response to increases in food prices and food shortages, particularly in unstable economies. The Argentinean food riots of 1989 were provoked by soaring inflation and food shortages. Protestors demanded that supermarkets give food away, and there were episodes of looting as the protests spread. In 2003, riots erupted in Bulawayo, Zimbabwe, in protest against corruption in the distribution of food relief, and in 2006, hungry citizens in East Timor attacked government warehouses in search of desperately needed food. Such food protests are likely to continue to arise whenever human survival needs are threatened.

FURTHER READINGS: Friedman, M. *Consumer Boycotts.* New York: Routledge, 1999; Friedman, M. "Consumer Boycotts in the United States, 1970–1980: Contemporary Events in Historical Perspective." *Journal of Consumer Affairs* 19 (1985): 96–117; Klein, J. G., J. Andrew, and N. C. Smith. "Exploring Motivations for Participation in a Consumer Boycott." Centre for Marketing Working Paper, London Business School, 2001; Sikkink, K. "Codes for Conduct for Transnational Corporations: The Case of the WHO/UNICEF Code." *International Organization* Vol. 40, no. 4 (1986): 815–40; Smith, N. C. *Morality and the Market: Consumer Pressure for Corporate Accountability*. London: Routledge, 1990; Taylor, L. "Food Riots Revisited." *Journal of Social History*. Vol. 30, #2 (Winter 1996): 483–96; United Farm Workers of America. *The Wrath of Grapes*. Video. Wayne State University, 1986.

Paul Fieldhouse

Breakfast Cereals The invention of ready-to-eat breakfast cereal in the late 1880s changed the way Americans, and subsequently much of the rest of the world, ate breakfast. The radical shift in eating habits would not have taken place so rapidly, or been so widespread, without the **advertising** and promotions that were used so effectively to introduce them. As the early innovators persuaded people to buy an ever-expanding range of products, they also transformed their companies into major corporations by continuing to use increasingly sophisticated methods to sell their cereals. Sales continued to rise throughout the 20th century as cereal manufacturers effectively utilized the new technologies of radio and **television** to reach the public. The $6 billion ready-to-eat cereal industry began, however, because the protein-heavy diet of the late 19th-century American caused stomach problems that needed a cure.

Sanatoriums, run by religious-based organizations as part of the mid-19th-century health movement, were pivotal in the evolution of the cereal industry. James C. Jackson created the first breakfast cereal at his sanatorium in Dansville, New York, in 1863, although his version needed to be soaked in liquid before eating. Fourteen years later, the first ready-to-eat breakfast cereal was developed at another healing establishment, John Harvey Kellogg's (1852–1943) Battle Creek Sanatorium. Initially called "granula" (as was Jackson's version), the name was changed to granola in 1881, and within eight years Kellogg's Sanitas Food Company was selling two tons of the cereal per week.

Inventions flourished during the last decade of the century as inventors developed machinery that could turn assorted grains into different varieties of cereals. In 1895, Kellogg and his brother, W. K. (Will) Kellogg (1843–1906), created a machine that pressed boiled **wheat** through rollers to create flakes that crisped after they were baked, called Granose Flakes. Another inventor, Henry Perky (1843–1906), devised machinery that could form long strands of wheat by squeezing boiled grain between rollers with an incised groove; this was dubbed Shredded Wheat. Receiving several patents in 1892 and 1893, and after a meeting with Kellogg in 1894, Perky moved his company to Boston, where he began baking the cereal twice to create a long-lasting product. He also began heavily promoting the cereal, and by the next year he needed 11 machines to meet demand. Another inventor, Alexander P. Anderson, used a cannon to create puff rice kernels. Quaker Oats (until this time an oatmeal producer) bought his patent and released Puffed Rice in 1905.

Promotion, not machinery, was the forte of C. W. **Post**. Once a patient at Dr. Kellogg's sanatorium, Post later opened his own health clinic, where he produced a cereal-based **coffee** substitute, Postum, that he publicized through newspaper and magazine ads. It was so successful that he incorporated the Postum Cereal Company in 1896 with $100,000 in capital. In 1898, he introduced a whole-wheat and malted barley-flour nugget cereal, called Grape-Nuts, with a barrage of newspaper advertisements—the first national ad campaign. A year later, his Battle Creek factory was operating day and night to keep up with the demand. Three years later the factory was operating day and night, the company's capital had grown to $5 million, and its factories covered 20 acres and employed 2,500 workers.

By 1901, a *Washington Post* article proclaimed that "nearly everyone" was eating at least one of the three-year-old breakfast cereal industry's "countless brands." The industry's success also made Battle Creek, Michigan, a magnet for inventors, investors, and fledgling manufacturers; there were 40 breakfast cereal companies by the early 1900s, and within two years of the 1901 *Post* article, 30 of them were making wheat flakes. By 1911, there were 107 **corn** flake brands. However, taste alone could not create a successful brand, since most were quite similar—promotions and advertising were the key to increased sales, and the two most innovative and skillful manipulators were C. W. Post and W. K. Kellogg.

Kellogg had shocked his older brother, John, when he added sugarcane to their bland Sanitas Toasted Corn Flakes, and again when he suggested a national ad campaign. The cereal's success prompted him in 1906 to raise $35,000 to form the Battle Creek Toasted Corn Flake Company, which he then separated from the sanatorium. His successful advertising campaign included door-to-door and mailed samples and his signature on every box, plus newspaper ads. Within a year, the company employed 300 workers and was producing more than 4,000 cases of cereal a day.

By 1909, the firm, which changed its name to Kellogg Toasted Corn Flake Company, was selling more than a million cases of Corn Flakes. With a $1 million ad budget, Kellogg, one of the first to use outdoor advertising, erected the world's largest electric sign in 1912—106 feet wide by 50 feet high—in New York's Times Square. In 1922, the *Wall Street Journal* reported that the renamed Kellogg Company was the largest manufacturer of corn flakes in the country, its factories capable of producing a million boxes of cereal a day.

The same article also listed the C. W. Post Company's gross sales as over $17 million. The next year, the company, headed by Post's daughter, Marjorie Merriwether Post (1887–1973), became a publicly held corporation and began acquiring a wide variety of food companies, while continuing the extensive use of promotions, samples, coupons, advertising, and factory visits. After purchasing a **frozen food** company, **General Foods**, the corporation adopted its name in 1929.

To woo visitors and potential customers, Henry Perky moved the Shredded Wheat factory to Niagara Falls in 1901. Financiers helped him created a $10 million company, the first to mass-produce a breakfast cereal and the first to be nationally distributed. Perky's $2 million showplace factory, complete with visitor viewing areas and auditoriums, offered factory tours that brought more than 100,000 visitors from around the world, and each one left with a free sample of Shredded Wheat. Perky retired shortly after the plant opened, and in 1928 the company was sold to the National Biscuit Company, later **Nabisco**, for $35 million.

Washburn Crosby, the predecessor of General Mills, introduced Wheaties, a whole-grain flaked cereal, in 1924. Two years later, after buying a local radio station, it led cereal advertising in a new direction when the first singing commercial was performed on Christmas Eve, 1926, by the Wheaties Quartet. Sales soared, and by 1929 the company was using the singing ad nationally with similar success. Wheaties next sponsored the radio broadcast of local baseball in 1933, and its success was again repeated across the country. In 1939, it sponsored the first televised baseball game. Its sports theme included the "Breakfast of Champions" ad campaign, which used endorsements by major athletes. Expanding beyond sports, General Mills cereals also sponsored variety and children's shows and continued to introduce new brands, including Cheerioats in 1941, renamed Cheerios in 1946.

During the 1920s and '30s, demand continued to grow, even during the Depression, when Kellogg's 1930 sales exceeded those of all previous years. Kellogg made their largest ad expenditures to date in 1931, which was followed the next year by its largest campaign, which included all the country's major newspapers. Robust sales continued during World War II, but the number of companies producing cereals began to decline, solidifying the dominance of the four largest producers.

During the mid-1940s, Kellogg, General Mills, Post, and Quaker Oats strengthened their hold on the industry. With their huge budgets, they competed through advertisements and promotions, which built brand loyalty, and by introducing a wide variety of products. They did not, however, compete on price, since any action to lower prices by one producer would cause a similar reaction from its competitors. This strategy kept cereal prices high.

By the early 1950s, presweetened cereals, fortified with vitamins and minerals and targeted toward children, began to appear, as did advertising to children, a growing new market during the postwar baby boom. Throughout the next two decades, as Saturday morning television shows presenting cartoons and other fare geared toward young viewers became more prevalent, the cereal companies who sponsored the shows filled the airways with ads. Kellogg, which introduced several presweetened varieties, used cartoon characters, such as Tony the Tiger, introduced in 1953, as product pitchmen. These characters also began appearing in the **supermarket** aisles, on colorful new cartons designed to catch the eye of both the children and their parents.

Sales began to slow in the 1970s as the Baby Boomers matured, entering an age bracket that consumed less cereal. Also, critics also began voicing concerns about highly sweetened cereals and their ads targeted to small children. Additionally, in 1972 the Federal Trade Commission (FTC) began a lawsuit that charged Kellogg, General Mills, Quaker, and Post with monopolizing the industry (the four firms accounted for 80 percent of cereal sales). It charged that the cereal giants forced consumers to pay inflated prices and also brought charges of false advertising. Quaker was dropped from the suit in 1978, which dragged on for four more years.

The FTC dropped the suit in 1982, exonerating all the firms. Nonetheless, Kellogg experienced a difficult period as its market share sank to 37 percent in 1983, toppling it from its number-one position. During this period, the cereal companies began a barrage of product introductions; 60 new brands were introduced by mid-decade, rising to over 100 by 1989. Many were targeted to specific age groups, through either special ingredients or advertising; licensed characters pushed cereals to the under-9 group, while high-fiber cereals were marketed to those over 65.

By the mid-1990s, sales again slowed as consumers chose other types of breakfast fare and began to rebel against high prices. Shoppers turned to store brands, which were often as much as 50 percent less expensive than the national cereals. By 1994, the cereal companies, beginning with Post, then General Mills, and finally Kellogg, drastically lowered their prices. Even so, by 1996, more than 400 cereal brands were available in supermarkets, and the huge marketing budgets of the Big Four kept their boxes in the most coveted positions on the grocery shelves. During this time, Post was acquired by Nabisco (now **Kraft Foods**), and General Mills, maker of Cheerios and Wheaties, acquired of Ralcorp Holdings, with its Chex brand and private-label bagged cereals. Market share shifted, further lowering the once top-ranked Kellogg, as industry sales stagnated.

The first years of the 21st century have seen a turnaround in the cereal industry, which is adept at creating new products geared to consumer demand. Kellogg, Kraft, and General Mills have all introduced healthier or **organic** versions of their traditional varieties, selling for almost 15 percent more than the older brands, while coupons and special offers help introduce these variations to consumers. Kellogg has regained its market share, squeaking back into first place ahead of General Mills.

In 2001, Quaker Oats was acquired by PepsiCo for $13 billion, and in 2000, Kellogg acquired Kashi, a leading organic cereal company with triple-digit growth in the last decade. A handful of smaller organic cereal makers are making inroads into the cereal market, although their advertising budgets cannot compete with the major brands, who, according to a report by the **U.S. Department of Agriculture**, spend between 10 and 15 percent of the value of their sales in various mass-media advertising.

Although the cereal industry's sales have fluctuated in recent years, in 2006, 95 percent of Americans consumed breakfast cereal, purchasing a total of 2.7 billion boxes a year. Coupons continue to proliferate, and huge advertising budgets keep luring shoppers, as health claims multiply along with new cereal selections. Ready-to-eat cereals, an integral part of the American diet, continue to be one of the most profitable sectors in the food industry.

See also Marketing to Children.

FURTHER READINGS: Bruce, Scott, and Bill Crawford. *Cerealizing America: The Unsweetened Story of American Breakfast Cereal.* Boston: Faber & Faber, 1995; Price, Gregory K. "Cereal Sales Soggy Despite Price Cuts and Reduced Couponing." *Food Review* 23 (2000): 21–28.

Joy Santlofer

Burger King. *See* Fast Food Restaurants.

Bush's Baked Beans Bush Brothers & Company produces approximately 80 percent of the **canned** baked beans consumed in the United States, which represents estimated annual sales in excess of $400 million and the processing of more than 55 million pounds of beans per year. The company was started as a tomato cannery in 1908 in Chestnut Hill, Tennessee, by Andrew Jackson Bush and his sons Fred and Claude. It remains family owned to this day, with the fourth generation of the Bush family currently at the helm. Today, the company headquarters are in Knoxville, Tennessee, with plants located in Augusta, Wisconsin, and Chestnut Hill.

The company thrived during World War I, when the federal government became its largest customer and 90 percent of its canned tomatoes were allocated to the war effort. It became incorporated in 1922 and opened a second processing plant in Oak Grove, Tennessee, in 1928 and a third in Clinton, Tennessee, in 1931. In 1943, the Oak Grove land and plant were seized through eminent domain by the Tennessee Valley Authority, after which the company purchased the Blytheville Canning Company in Arkansas in 1944.

Bush Brothers & Company began to diversify after World War II and started to process other food products, including hominy, greens, and several varieties of peas and beans. The Bush's Best brand was developed in 1948, but it was the launch of Bush's Original Baked Beans under that label in 1969 that proved a key point in the company's history. The recipe is a closely guarded secret and is said to be a re-creation of the favorite family version made by the grandmother of the current owners. All that is revealed is via the obligatory ingredient list, which states that the product contains "prepared white beans, water, onions, brown sugar, sugar, bacon, salt, corn starch, mustard, onion powder, caramel color, spices, garlic powder, and natural flavor."

The popularity of Bush's Best baked beans can be attributed to a highly successful marketing campaign commenced in 1993 and centered around a **television** commercial featuring Jay Bush (great-grandson of the founder) and his "talking" dog Duke. The scripted dynamic between the two has Jay reminding buyers of the "darned good" taste of the beans, and the dog attempting to sabotage the secrecy of the recipe for the right price. As a result of the campaign, the pair became celebrities, and sales of Bush's Best beans rose from a 48 percent share of the national market to 80 percent.

Following on the success of what has become their signature product, Bush Brothers has since developed nine other varieties to cater to all preferences: Onion (1981), Vegetarian (1984), Home Style (1993), Boston Recipe (1995), Bold and Spicy (1997), Barbeque (1999), Maple Cured Bacon (2000), Country Style (2001), and Honey Baked (2006).

Janet Clarkson

C ❖ ─────────────────────────────

Cafeterias Cafeterias, reasonably priced, self-service **restaurants**, began as a way to feed hungry urban workers in the late 19th century. By the mid-20th century, they had become a popular style of regional restaurant, but cafeterias also never left the workplace, and self-service food operations were often found in hospital, school, corporate, and other institutional settings. Both commercial and institutional cafeterias have since faltered, and owners and managers have had to modify their formats, menus, and technology to meet changing tastes and needs.

The first of what might now be considered a cafeteria opened in 1885 in New York and was open only to men. Patrons selected their food, ate standing up, and paid on the honor system for what they ate. The idea of clean, economical self-service restaurants spread, helped along by a popular cafeteria exhibit at the Chicago World's Fair in 1893. Charitable and cooperative associations opened cafeterias in Chicago and New York to make sure workers, especially women, were able to get speedy and nutritious lunches. Commercial cafeterias began to open not long after, with the Childs brothers opening the first of their nine restaurants in New York City in 1898.

By 1903 the Childs chain had created what would become the classic cafeteria style: customers with trays choosing food from straight service lines on steam tables and cold stations, with payment made at the end of the service line. Classic cafeteria service was limited to employees serving hot items and clearing tables without traditional waiters or waitresses. One early variant was the Horn & Hardart automats. The now-defunct chain began in Philadelphia in 1902 by creating a restaurant of what were essentially **vending machines**. Employees put food into walls of open-backed small display cases. A patron would make a selection and insert the proper amount of change into the slot, the door would open, and the dish could be removed.

The Spread of Cafeterias

The first commercial cafeteria in Los Angeles opened in 1905 with signage offering customers food they could see being prepared and promising them they would not have to tip. Local YMCA and YWCA chapters then opened cafeterias there. San Francisco and Washington, D.C., were next. By 1917 the word *cafeteria* was officially in the dictionary, and cafeterias began to become urban fixtures. Philanthropic workplace restaurants were eventually taken over or replaced by employers, and by the 1920s, company cafeterias were widespread.

As America began its mid-century suburban sprawl, commercial cafeterias followed, providing regional food to families at reasonable prices, particularly in the South, Midwest, and California. At their height, there were so many cafeterias in the Los Angeles area, for example, that local telephone directories listed them separately from restaurants.

By the late 20th century, commercial cafeteria revenues were declining, while other forms of quick, casual dining chains were prospering. The public had begun to crave more **ethnic food** and a more changing variety, moving away from the typical cafeteria fare of a hot entrée with two vegetable side dishes. Concern about nutritious food choices also became an issue for consumers accustomed to cafeteria fare of gravies, fried foods, and mashed potatoes. An aging customer base and the traditional look of a cafeteria didn't help. Many potential customers associated the lines, trays, and general décor with institutional eating rather than family dining. Sales suffered, and many individual and chain cafeterias closed. Most of the Horn & Hardart automat chains saw their units converted to **fast food restaurants** in the 1980s and the last of the old automats closed in 1991. One chain that has survived posted sales in 2005 of $322.2 million, but the same chain had sales of $311 million in 1990.

In response to shrinking revenues, some cafeteria operators have begun to modify their concepts and menus and to promote healthy food choices in their restaurants and on their websites. One operator, the Plano, Texas–based Furr's, has converted some of its 54 units to buffet-style restaurants, with customers paying one fee for all they can eat (instead of the cafeteria-style policy of paying for the individual items) and with several food service stations instead of a straight cafeteria line.

Buffets, salad bar restaurants, and other self-service concepts are often included in the cafeteria category. Buffets and their variations are the most successful of the group, with four companies in *Restaurants and Institutions* magazine's Top 400 chains in 2006, having combined total sales of more than $4 billion and about 1,800 locations. There are another five traditional or mostly traditional cafeteria companies listed among the top chains, with total sales of more than $833 million and more than 370 locations. The top traditional cafeteria chain listed is Luby's of Houston, Texas, ranked at 101st place with 131 locations. Luby's, like a number of chains, had to close restaurants in the last few years to regain profitability. Another, Piccadilly Cafeteria, has gained revenue by running on-site institutional cafeterias for nonprofits and others. Most also offer meals-to-go or **takeout** to try to capitalize on the growing home meal replacement concept.

Unlike many restaurant chains, most cafeteria and buffet locations are company owned, although at least one large buffet chain has expanded rapidly through the use of **franchisees**. Cafeterias and buffets are a relatively small segment of what is expected to be a $537 billion restaurant industry in 2007.

Cafeterias at Work and School and in the Hospital

Corporate and institutional cafeterias are affected by some of the same trends as well. Many companies have slashed their corporate dining program budgets since 2002. Although the number of corporations that subsidize employee meals has been cut in half, some companies still look to workplace dining as a way to increase efficiency by reducing the amount of time an employee is away from work and to build employee loyalty despite the cost. A new cafeteria designed to serve 5,000 employees can cost as much as $5 million, but it can be a valuable investment for a company. An outstanding corporate cafeteria can also help promote a company's image. Google has found that its extensive **gourmet food** service adds to the company's allure and employee retention in the competitive Silicon Valley job market.

Most corporate food service patrons have other choices, and these consumers have the same concerns about taste, variety, and nutrition that other diners do. The food service operations that serve them now must at least cover their own costs or be outsourced. Institutions looking to trim costs have shifted operations as well as profit and loss to external caterers.

Compass Group, founded in 1941 to feed war workers, is now the world's largest food service company. A French firm, Sodexho Alliance, is the second largest, with Aramark third. These companies are replacing traditional cafeterias with food courts, marketplaces, and specialized food service stations instead of a straight cafeteria line. Environments have been made more inviting and entertaining. Food specials might range from tandoori chicken to sushi. They are also offering cooking lessons, guest chefs, **delivery** to offices and worker cubicles, and convenient take-home holiday dinners.

Colleges and universities have also outsourced and modernized their food service facilities along the same lines. One of the financial challenges these institutions face is that board plans that used to provide 95 percent of the food service revenues now provide only about 55 percent, as students have more choices. Their patrons are also demanding more **organic** and locally sourced food. The University of Massachusetts recently renovated a 25,000-square-foot, 800-seat straight-line cafeteria into one with multiple food service stations serving Asian noodles, sushi, pizza, pasta, and more in order to appeal to its students. The nine-month renovation cost more than $13 million.

Much like in the workplace, the first school cafeterias were set up by philanthropic organizations concerned about childhood nutrition, but it was the development of the suburbs that led to a boom in primary and secondary school cafeterias. Students could no longer walk home for lunch, so school lunchrooms, often with cafeterias, became the norm. With labor costs up and concerns about childhood **obesity** rising, school cafeterias face new demands to supply costlier healthy foods and to meet government nutrition regulations while their budgets are decreasing. Some school districts have responded by outsourcing their cafeteria operations. Others have switched to using a central kitchen and distributing cooked food to individual school cafeterias. Another approach has been to purchase processed food that needs less cooking, reducing labor and energy costs for the schools while ensuring nutrition guidelines are met.

The age-old concern of school food service is getting the children to eat what's good for them. Some operators are doing this by remaking school cafeterias into colorful spaces with music and special concepts such as a fat-free smoothie bar. Others are sneaking more nutrition into items kids like, for example, creating red potatoes by coloring them with beet juice and adding fiber to pizza crust. Some have embraced fresh foods and produce, often organic, combined with education about healthy eating, occasionally including having the children tend vegetable gardens. More than 400 schools have begun programs featuring fresh produce directly from local farms.

Cafeterias in hospitals and other health care facilities designed to serve visitors and workers are losing their institutional look, adding better seating and moving from serving lines to multistations and other renovations. More than a quarter of health care kitchens and cafeterias were upgraded in 2005–2006. The food has been revamped, too, to make it more flavorful, nutritious, and varied. One example is the Stony Brook University Hospital in Stony Brook, New York. The complete renovation of the hospital led to a rise in sales from $3.3 million in 2000 to $5.6 million in 2006. An emphasis was placed on food quality and variety (for example, the cafeteria now has doubled the number of soups in rotation). It also added serving stations and a brick-oven pizzeria, created a comfortable environment for patrons, and put a focus on customer satisfaction.

Sales of all food and beverages in 2005 for the institutional food service markets (not just including cafeterias) were $20.9 billion for business and industry, $14.5 billion in primary and secondary schools, $10.6 billion at colleges and universities, and $13.3 billion at health care facilities.

Both institutional and commercial cafeterias are looking to incorporate new technologies into the self-service experience. Many school and college cafeterias are already using prepaid cards that the students swipe through a reader to pay for their meals. Some primary schools are letting parents go online to block their children's cards from being able to purchase items such as **snack foods** or foods that cause an allergic reaction. Some schools use personal codes, and at least one school is using fingerprint scans for payment. At one cell phone manufacturer, employees scan their cell phones to charge cafeteria purchases to a preauthorized credit card. The technology for other forms of electronic self-service such as kiosk ordering and self-service payment are already in the marketplace.

FURTHER READINGS: Beern, Kate. "Hot Potato in the School Cafeteria: More Districts Outsource Their Food Services, But Some Raise Questions about Personnel Relations and Savings." *School Administrator*, September 1, 2004. Available at http://www.aasa.org/publications/saarticledetail.cfm?ItemNumber=1164&snItemNumber=950&tnItemNumber=1995; DiMassa, Cara Mia, and Pierson, David. "End of the Line for Cafeterias." *Los Angeles Times*, November 3, 2006; National Restaurant Association. "Restaurant Industry Facts." http://www.restaurant.org/research/ind_glance.cfm; Popp, Jamie. "Hospitals Build Better Business: Healthcare Operators Invest to Make Dining an Out-of-the Hospital Experience." *Restaurants and Institutions*, August 2006. http://www.rimag.com/archives/2006/08a/hospital-foodservice.asp; "2006 R&I Top 400." *Restaurants and Institutions*, July 2006. http://www.rimag.com/archives/2006/07a/top400/top-400.asp; Root, Waverly, and Richard de Rochemont. *Eating in America: A History.* New York: Ecco Press.

Faith J. Kramer

Campbell's Soup Joseph Campbell joined Abraham Anderson as a partner in a Camden, New Jersey, **canning** and preserving firm in 1869. Beginning with canned peas and asparagus, they added other canned and preserved products. In 1876 Campbell bought Anderson out and acquired new partners, one of whom was Arthur Dorrance. In 1891, Dorrance and Campbell incorporated in New Jersey under the name of the Joseph Campbell Preserve Company. By the 1890s, the company produced more than 200 products, including preserves, jellies, meats, fruits, sauces, vegetables, and soups.

Dorrance's son, John T. Dorrance, was a chemist trained in Germany who was hired at Campbell's Camden laboratory in 1896 to improve the quality of the company's soup. He concentrated on producing condensed soups. Within a few months of his arrival, he had created five condensed soups—tomato, chicken, oxtail, vegetable, and consomme—which were released in 1897. These were successful, and Dorrance expanded his work. As the soup division of the company expanded, the nonsoup sectors declined in importance and were phased out. In recognition of the importance of this product, the company changed its name in 1921 to the Campbell Soup Company.

Campbell's grew rapidly throughout the 20th century. The most important reason for its success was the company's promotional and marketing activities. It was newspaper and streetcar **advertising**, followed by magazines, that gave Campbell's broad exposure. Its major icon was the Campbell Kids, created by Grace Drayton in 1904. Campbell's was among the first food companies to advertise on radio. During the 1930s, it broadcast a jingle, "M'm! M'm! Good!" that is still used today.

The company exported its soup abroad for decades, but during the Depression, many countries put up protectionist barriers to help local manufacturers. Campbell responded by launching subsidiaries in other countries, including Canada and United Kingdom. The company expanded to other countries after World War II, and it has acquired firms in other countries, such as Liebig in France and Erasco in Germany.

The Campbell Soup Company's first major diversification was into tomato juice, which reversed its sole focus on soupmaking. Shortly after the World War II ended, the company made another logical addition when it purchased V8 juice from Standard Brands. Campbell's has been diversifying ever since. Its other American food brands include Pace Mexican sauces, Prego pasta sauces, Godiva **chocolates**, and Pepperidge Farm, which makes Gold Fish crackers and several lines of cookies. Soup nevertheless remains Campbell's flagship product, and the company remains the largest soup manufacturer in the world.

FURTHER READINGS: Collins, Douglas. *America's Favorite Food: The Story of Campbell Soup Company.* New York: Harry N. Abrams, 1994; Smith, Andrew F. *Souper Tomatoes: The Story of America's Favorite Food.* New Brunswick, NJ: Rutgers University Press, 2000.

Andrew F. Smith

Candy and Confections Candy and confections include any of a wide range of sweets, including preserved and candied fruits, taffies, hard candies, marzipans, licorices, toffees, marshmallows, and others.

Candy has a history stretching back at least 2,000 years, and one possible root of the word is the Sanskrit *khande*, which could mean that candy originated in India. The word *candy* has its earliest use in English in the phrase "sugar candy," which refers to crystallized **sugar**, and technically candies are only those sweets that are made by dissolving refined sugar in water, boiling it, and then recrystallizing it so that it sets as a solid mass. Sweets that are made by processes that do not involve the boiling and recrystallizing of refined sugar are, strictly speaking, not candies; however, both candies and noncandy sweets are *confections*.

The basic process of candymaking relies on the dissolving of sucrose, refined sugar, in water, which is then called *syrup*. Cooling syrup can be manipulated to form a variety of different types of candy. It passes through various stages as it cools, frequently called the thread, soft ball, hard ball, soft crack, hard crack, and caramel stages. These refer to a method of testing the syrup in which a small amount of syrup is dropped in cold water. Other methods of testing include the measurement of temperature with a candy thermometer or of syrup density using a saccharometer. The last method is most common in industrialized candy production. Common contemporary candies include fudge, rock candy, candied fruits and spices like candied ginger, and many of the cream and *fondant* fillings that are used in fancy **chocolates**.

The history of candy and confections has clear intersections with the history of sugar. Sugarcane is believed to have first been cultivated in prehistoric times, when it was in use in India and other parts of Asia. Refined sugar circulated through Europe and the rest of the world with traders from Muslim nations. Sugar at this time was a luxury, and confections of any kind would have been doubly luxurious due to the additional hours of labor required for their manufacture. The refining of sugar from sugar beets was developed in the mid-18th century. The process did not become commercially viable until near the end of that century, but Napoleon eventually pushed the further development of the process, as he saw the advantage of using sugar beets, which could be grown in Europe, over sugarcane. By the 19th century, sugar had become a common bulk commodity.

Historically, many candies and pulled-sugar confections such as taffy were used medicinally. In premodern times, sugar would help preserve herbs and other concoctions administered as medicine and would also help mask their bitterness. "Cough candies" and similar products were sold by both confectioners and herbalists in the 18th century. Although these uses date back to ancient Greece, they continue in the use of sweetened throat lozenges and cough syrups. In the 1950s, for example, Doreen Lofthouse, the head of Fisherman's Friend, introduced a Victorian-style medicinal lozenge that has proven incredibly successful. Although medicinal use of confectionery in general went into decline much earlier, concerns about the healthfulness of sugar and, by extension, candy and confectionery, did not develop until the 20th century.

Two Victorian-era instruments, the hydrometer, which measures the specific gravity of liquids, and the thermometer, which measures temperature, proved essential to the modernization of candymaking. The saccharometer, a specialized hydrometer specifically intended for use with sugar solutions, was developed by the end of the 18th century. Another important 18th-century development was Andreas Marggraf's discovery that glucose, a simple sugar, can be manufactured by boiling starch with dilute sulfuric acid. This discovery ultimately led to the discovery of methods for producing glucose syrup, which is one of many substances that can be used to manipulate the process of graining. These substances are frequently called "doctors" by those in the trade.

The modern candy and confection industry dates to the beginning of the 19th century, when semi-industrial makers packed sweets in jars and tins for distribution by the rail systems. By this time, not only sugar but also candy and confectionery were available even to the poor, owing to the relative cheapness of sugar as well as the increasing sophistication and reliability of instruments and machines. The technical component of candymaking become gradually more important as the production process shifted from a craft to an industry.

Significant 19th-century developments included the development of fondant, the proliferation of the starch-molding technique, the synthesis of artificial **flavors**, and the manufacture of drop rollers to cut candy into drops. In starch-molding, solid molds are pressed into dry starch; the indentations are then filled with warm syrup and left to set. Both fondant and artificial flavors were discovered near mid-century.

Although fondant is now commonplace, it was a craze through the beginning of the 20th century and helped usher in the contemporary candy bar, serving as filling. Drop rollers significantly cut the amount of **labor** necessary to produce candy drops and also reduced the difficulties of temperature control inherent to the process.

Candy and confection manufacture today is an industry much larger than that of steel. Manufacturers tend to depend on a delicate balance of brand loyalty and novelty, nurturing established products while developing new ones. In the United States alone, there are roughly 150 new sweets launched each year. Because of this endless pursuit of novelty, the secrecy of candy and confectionery manufacturers has become legendary, as manufacturers strive to protect not only the recipes of their candies but also the machines and manufacturing methods employed. Sweets manufacturing is highly dependent on technology, and most products can be made only by specific machines that have been modified in specific ways. Innovative use of machinery, like innovative recipes, is important for the success of candymakers.

In Great Britain, three major manufacturers, Fry, Cadbury, and Rowntree, had emerged as industry leaders by the mid-19th century. In the United States, Chicago is one of the most important hubs of candy manufacture. The first candy and cookie factory in the city was opened by John Mohr in 1837, and as candy companies proliferated, the National Confectioners' Association was founded there in 1884 by 69 sweetmakers. The large-scale candy retail trade also originated in Chicago; Brach's was founded there in 1904 and Fannie May sweets in 1920. However, Chicago was not unique in serving as a hotbed of candy manufacturing; Boston also had a high concentration of candy manufacturers, boasting 140 candy companies by 1950.

Two of the best-known American candy manufacturers, however, have their origins in less urban areas. Milton Snavely Hershey founded his first candy company, the Lancaster Caramel Company, in Pennsylvania around this time and began manufacturing plain chocolate bars in 1895. He went on to develop Hershey, Pennsylvania, as both a corporate center and tourist attraction. Frank Mars had begun selling butter-cream candies made by himself and his wife in Tacoma, Washington, in 1911. In 1924, Mars introduced the Mars bar, which marked the beginning of the Mars–Hershey candy rivalry, which continues to this day.

The peak of candy manufacturing in the United States, in terms of sheer number of companies, was the period between World War I and World War II, when some 6,000 companies were producing sweets. The 1960s marked the beginning of a period of consolidation, which continues today. Currently, the most widely distributed candies in the United States are produced by Hershey, Mars, and Wrigley, although as of 2001, there were a total of 2,381 confectionery wholesalers in the United States. The majority of these are small operations; only 97 have more than 100 employees. Among the most prominent independent companies are Tootside Roll Industries, founded in 1896, and PEZ Candy, founded in 1952.

In 2006, the worldwide candy and confectionery market totaled over $126 billion, with Western Europe leading the industry at $49.8 billion, followed by North America at $28.3 billion. In the United States, candy consumption totals roughly 7 billion pounds annually, with nonchocolate confectionery accounting for approximately half of this total. The pursuit of innovation remains a key component of industrial success, with 9,284 new candy products introduced between September 2005 and August 2006. **Supermarkets** generate roughly 40 percent of candy and confectionery sales, followed by mass merchandisers (15 percent), and convenience stores (14 percent).

Health-conscious adults have recently become key consumers, and in the late 1990s, reduced-fat, fat-free, and sugar-free candies become an area of growth, with the sugar-free candy market reaching a value of more than $50 million by the mid-1990s.

The candy industry has recovered from its steep declines of the early 1990s, and although market growth was slow for this industry through the 1990s, as of 1999, candy and confectionery remained the third largest consumer food category after **soft drinks** and milk. The international market is growing at a compound annual rate of 0.7 percent.

FURTHER READINGS: Almond, Steve. *Candyfreak: A Journey through the Chocolate Underbelly of America.* Chapel Hill, NC: Algonquin Books, 2004; Mason, Laura. *Sugar-Plums and Sherbet: The Prehistory of Sweets.* Totnes, Devon, England: Prospect Books, 2004; Richardson, Tim. *Sweets: A History of Candy.* New York: Bloomsbury, 2002.

Carly Kocurek

Canning From prehistoric times, humans have tackled the problem of how to preserve surplus foods in times of plenty for use in times of want. Numerous ways have been developed, from drying food in the sun to salting food in containers. A new process of preserving food was invented in 1795 when the French government offered a prize for an improved method of conserving food. Nicolas Appert concluded that the best method of preserving food was boiling and sealing it in a container without air. Appert packed fruits, vegetables, meats, and other foods into wide-mouthed glass bottles, heated them for various lengths of time in a bath of boiling water, and sealed the openings with cork stoppers tightly wired to the bottles. His experiments won the prize and launched the canning industry. The British built on Appert's methods, choosing tin for containers rather than glass, which was fragile and broke easily.

In the United States, commercial **bottling** operations did not commence until the arrival of experienced English canners. The first was William Underwood, an English pickler, who launched the firm later known as the William Underwood Company in 1819. Underwood canned luxury goods and ships' provisions, including oysters, lobsters, fish, meats, soups, fruits, and a few vegetables. During the next 30 years, many small canning factories were launched from Maryland to Maine. Canning techniques were not well understood, and problems emerged, including bursting cans and contamination, which all too often resulted in illness or death to consumers. Canning was limited to producing extremely expensive food for **restaurant** use and for use by sailing ships traveling long distances.

During the Civil War, the federal government purchased canned goods for the use of the military; this primed the pump for the American canning industry, and canneries sprang up across Northern states. The quality of these operations improved, as did their efficiency, which reduced costs. The result was that hundreds of thousands of American soldiers and sailors were exposed to canned goods. The demand for canned goods grew after the war, and the upward spiral continued. By the 1880s, canned foods were commonly available in most grocery stores throughout the nation.

Canning Revolutions

Canning technology took a major leap forward with the European invention of the "sanitary can" in the late 19th century. A thick rubber gasket, similar to those used on Mason jars, was placed between the end and body. It was crimped to the body by rollers. The rubber ring was cumbersome and costly. Charles M. Ams improved the design by lining just the top edge of the can with rubber cement and greatly simplifying the sealing process. Ams further improved the process and by 1903 had developed a line of commercial machines to make the cans. Ams's machines revolutionized the canning industry.

Challenges and Opportunities

Despite the spectacular success and rapid expansion of the bottling and canning industries, all was not well in the food-**packaging** world. Since the industry's inception, contamination and adulteration had been alarming problems. Fly-by-night manufacturers filled cans and bottles with low-quality products or toxic ingredients, and illness and death resulted. These abuses spurred on efforts to pass the Pure Food and Drug Act, which Congress did in 1906.

By 1900, most middle-size communities in America were home to one or more canners. However, the Pure Food and Drug Act required food processors engaged in interstate trade to strictly adhere to proper health and safety procedures. This made it more difficult for small and medium-size canners to survive, and many closed or were bought out. Slowly, the canning industry consolidated into large conglomerates, such as the H. J. **Heinz** Company, **Campbell's Soup**, **Del Monte**, and **Kraft Food**s. Larger canning operations had advantages of scale; they were able to invest in state-of-the-art equipment, ensuring maximum efficiency at the lowest possible price. Some large plants could manufacture millions of cans or bottles daily. Large canners were able to invest in developing national distribution networks and support extensive advertising campaigns, which greatly increased sales. Finally, large conglomerates could expand to markets in other countries.

Technology rapidly changed the industry throughout the 20th century. **Beer** cans became common during the 1930s, and canned carbonated beverages followed shortly thereafter. The invention of the aluminum can and its application to the beverage industry in 1965 created a low-cost and lightweight can that has been the industry standard ever since. Aluminum cans were also easier to manufacture. Today, one pound of aluminum yields 32 cans.

At the dawn of the 21st century, the Ball Corporation is the leading can manufacturer in the United States. Its Springdale, Arkansas, plant manufactures 2,000 cans a minute—more than 50 billion cans a year. In total, approximately 133 billion cans are manufactured annually in the United States. New innovations, such as the easy-open can, are under development. Other recent innovations include the self-heating can.

Since 1970, recycling of cans has become an important business in its own right. It is less expensive to recycle old cans than it is to mine minerals and manufacture cans, hence recycling reduces costs for the manufacturer. It also decreases waste and helps the environment. By the 1990s, Americans were recycling about 68 percent of all cans manufactured in the country. Since then, this has fallen, to about 50 percent as of 2004.

See also Bush's Baked Beans; Kraft Foods.

FURTHER READINGS: Collins, James H. *The Story of Canned Foods*. New York: E. P. Dutton, 1924; May, Earl Chapin. *The Canning Clan: A Pageant of Pioneering Americans*. New York: Macmillan, 1937; Sim, Mary B. *Commercial Canning in New Jersey: History and Early*

Development. Trenton: New Jersey Agricultural Society, 1951; Smith, Andrew F. *Souper Tomatoes: The Story of America's Favorite Food*. New Brunswick, NJ: Rutgers University Press, 2000.

Andrew F. Smith

Cargill. *See* Agribusiness; Corn; Multinationals; Poultry Industry.

Caviar. *See* Gourmet Foods.

Celebrity Chefs Modern celebrity chefs earn among the highest salaries in the food and entertainment industries. Because their celebrity relies on media exposure, celebrity chefs are famous not only for their food but also for their personality and public antics, often displayed on **television**, and their trademark phrases, behavior, or attire. Their celebrity status is closely related to advances in media and communications, particularly the rise of food TV. Like Hollywood stars, net worth and popularity make modern celebrity chefs powerful marketing tools for endorsing commodities, including their own brands, and give them considerable influence beyond cooking.

Criteria used to define a chef as a celebrity include a high media profile, high television ratings, best-selling cookbooks, one or more award-winning or highly rated **restaurants**, prestigious achievement awards, nonfood appearances, and other business ventures. Importantly, being a professionally trained chef is not a criterion for the modern celebrity chef. Formal, globally recognized systems that rank and generate celebrity status include Michelin, *Forbes* magazine's Celebrity 100, the *Time* 100, and *Restaurant* magazine's World's 50 Best Restaurants. Informal systems include political influence. The category "super chefs" designates a group of chef-entrepreneurs whose media profiles and business acumen supersede even the "normal" celebrity chefs.

The variance in criteria and in what celebrity chefs are famous for is illustrated by the number of chefs who have been designated the "first" celebrity chef.

The First Celebrity Chefs

Plato's dialogue *Gorgias* (4th century B.C.), in which he mentions the Sicilian baker Mithaikos, is one of the earliest written records of a celebrated cook. From a historical media perspective, Plato's text situates Mithaikos as the first celebrity chef.

Marie-Antoine Carême (1784–1833) is known as the founder of haute cuisine (classical "high" French cooking). Carême was one of the last chefs in service of the aristocracy and royalty. He was famous for his elaborate confectionary and for his clientele, including King George IV of England, Tsar Alexander I of Russia, and Napoleon.

Alexis Soyer (1809–1858), French by birth, was famed for his culinary and personal exhibitionism as head chef for the Reform Club in London. His enduring media profile is largely the result of philanthropic work such as writing cookbooks for the working classes, designing and setting up soup kitchens in Ireland during the potato famine, and working with Florence Nightingale in the Crimean War. He also invented kitchen gadgets, cooking implements, a campstove to be used by soldiers on campaign, and **condiments** such as Soyer's Relish, marketed under the Crosse & Blackwell brand.

Xavier Marcel Boulestin (1878–1943) was the first television chef proper. Boulestin hosted the BBC's earliest cooking series, *Cook's Night Out*, in 1937. He was already well known as the chef-proprietor of the top London restaurant Boulestin's (opened in 1927) and is remembered for his credo: "Good meals should be the rule, not the exception."

Cited by the BBC as the world's first celebrity chef, Philip Harben (1906–1970) hosted the first significant British food TV program (*Cookery*, 1946–1951) after World War II.

Fanny Cradock (1909–1994) was often referred to as the first TV celebrity chef. Cradock was famous for eccentricities such as cooking in elaborate evening wear. She hosted BBC cooking shows from 1955 to 1975. Cradock's career is depicted in the BBC drama *Fear of Fanny* (2006).

Julia Child (1912–2004) is widely recognized as America's first celebrity chef. Child's media prestige was first achieved with her best-selling cookbook *Mastering the Art of French Cooking* (1961), followed by her debut TV show *The French Chef* (1963). Her achievement awards include three Emmys (1966, 1996, 1997), the Ralph Lowell Award (1998), the French Légion d'Honneur (2000), and the Presidential Medal of Freedom (2003). She was on the cover of *Time* magazine (1966), cofounded the American Institute of Wine and Food (1981), and gives her name to the prestigious Julia Child Cookbook Awards.

Named "the original celebrity chef" by *Forbes*, Wolfgang Puck (1949–) enjoys a sphere of influence that qualifies him as a super chef. Based in California, Wolfgang Puck, Inc., includes a chain of restaurants; a range of food, drink, and cookware; book publishing; and media programming (TV, radio, **Internet**), as well as **franchising**, licensing, and merchandising ventures. Wolfgang Puck Catering oversees the annual Academy Awards Governor's Ball, and in addition to hosting *Wolfgang Puck's Cooking Class* on the Food Network, he has played himself in the popular TV drama series *Las Vegas*.

Frenchman Marie-Antoine Carême (1784–1833) was the first celebrity chef, but his notoriety could never compare with the sort of fame that today's chefs can attain—especially if they have shows on the Food Channel. Emeril Lagasse—a celebrity chef if there ever was one—had this to say about changes to the profession since the mid-1990s: "Chefs weren't really respected other than being in the kitchen. You rarely saw them in the dining room interacting with people. . . . Now all of a sudden, people have started looking at chefs and saying, 'Wow! That person really is a craftsman, is really a business person, they can do publicity'" (quoted in Ari Shapiro, "Americans' Insatiable Hunger for Celebrity Chefs," NPR, *All Things Considered*, March 5, 2005; http://www.npr.org/templates/story/story.php?storyId=4522975).

Rating Systems

Launched in 1900 (three-star ratings for cooking were added in the 1930s), the Michelin Guides are recognized as one of the most influential culinary rating systems in Europe. The launch of Michelin Guides for New York (2006) and San Francisco (2007) indicates its continued global influence.

Notable Michelin-rated celebrity chefs include Paul Bocuse (1926–), one of the fathers of nouvelle cuisine ("new" cooking, i.e., lighter than haute cuisine), founder of the prestigious Bocuse d'Or chef award, and the first chef to be sculpted for the

Grevin Museum in Paris; Alain Ducasse (1956-), the only chef to hold 14 stars for his restaurants in Monaco, New York, and Paris; and Bernard Loiseau (1951–2003), who rose to global media prominence posthumously when it was believed that a rumored retraction of one of his three stars caused him to commit suicide. Bocuse and Ducasse also qualify as super chefs.

Forbes's annual Celebrity 100 is a compilation of the "most powerful celebrities in the world," based on income and media prominence. Four chefs were ranked among these celebrities in 2006: Rachael Ray (81st), Wolfgang Puck (89th), Emeril Lagasse (94th), and Mario Batali (97th). Ray also featured on *Time*'s list of 100 "People Who Shape Our World" in 2006 and is notable as a celebrity chef whose fame is unrelated to restaurant experience. *Time* has previously listed Spaniard Ferran Adrià (1962–) under Innovators (2000) and Artists & Entertainers (2004).

Restaurant has twice named Adrià's El Bulli the best restaurant in the world (2002, 2006) in its World's 50 Best Restaurants listing. Despite numerous prior accolades (including three Michelin stars since 1997), the award considerably increased Adrià's global media presence. Adrià, also a super chef, is noteworthy as a modern celebrity chef whose fame is not primarily television-generated.

Political Influence

The political influence of celebrity chefs is exemplified by Jamie Oliver (1975–), whose campaign to improve school food resulted in revised government legislation. Oliver was voted the British Channel 4's "Most Inspiring Political Figure" in 2006. He has also received an MBE (membership in the Most Excellent Order of the British Empire) and is the first man since 1937 to appear on the cover of the British *Good Housekeeping*.

FURTHER READINGS: Cowen, Ruth. *Relish: The Extraordinary Life of Alexis Soyer, Victorian Celebrity Chef*. London: Wiedenfeld & Nicolson, 2006; Kelly, Ian. *Cooking for Kings: The Life of Antonin Carême, the First Celebrity Chef*. New York: Walker, 2004; Rossant, Juliette. *Super Chef: The Making of the Great Modern Restaurant Empires*. New York: Simon & Schuster, 2004; *Super Chef Blog* [online magazine]. http://www.superchefblog.com.

Signe Hansen

Chain Restaurants A **restaurant** chain is a group of two or more restaurants, usually sharing the same name or brand, under a central management structure. Chain restaurants, particularly in the fast-casual market, are the fastest-growing segment of the U.S. restaurant industry.

Industry Divisions

Chain restaurants are divided into two categories, casual dining and fine dining. Casual-dining restaurants offer family-oriented, moderately priced table service meals and generally do not have dress codes. Casual-dining menus feature a wide variety of meal options, alcoholic beverages are usually available, and the per-person check is generally $10 or less.

The casual-dining sector has recently seen the emergence of two profitable subdivisions: fast casual and upscale casual. Fast-casual restaurants, such as Panera Bread, do not feature table service, and the average per-person check is around $8.

Upscale-casual restaurants, such as the Cheesecake Factory, are usually anchored in malls or shopping centers and feature per-person checks of $15–17.

Not as prolific as casual-dining chains, fine-dining restaurant chains offer a more formal atmosphere and more complex meals, albeit with a smaller range of menu options. Meals cost upward of $20 per person, and alcoholic beverages are almost always available. Many fine-dining restaurants have a dress code, such as a jacket and tie for men, although the trend is away from such restrictions.

Management and Company Organization

Restaurant chains may operate under a central corporate organization, a **franchise** system, or a mixture of both. In a franchise system, individuals (franchisees) purchase the rights to a trademark and agree to a set of operating procedures from a larger entity (the franchiser). Franchisees usually pay the franchiser a recurring fee for use of the trademark, along with a continuing share of the franchisees' profits. As part of a restaurant franchise agreement, the franchiser may provide assets such as employee training techniques and **advertising**.

Chain restaurants may be local, regional, national, or international. In the United States, these restaurants are often situated in or near shopping centers or malls. Chain restaurants usually have similar building layouts and menu offerings, though menu prices may vary regionally in larger chains.

The National Council of Chain Restaurants (NCCR), which welcomes members from both the quick-service (**fast food**) and casual-dining segments of the industry, is the largest trade association for chain restaurant companies. In operation for more than 40 years, the NCCR is a division of the National Retail Federation. The National Restaurant Association (NRA), started in 1919, is the largest profession association for restaurant industry in the United States, with more than 300,000 restaurant company members.

Industry Leaders

Darden Restaurants, which owns brands such as Red Lobster and Olive Garden, is the world's top casual-dining chain restaurant operator, based on revenue. In fiscal year 2006, Darden earned more than $338 million and had a one-year net income growth rate over 16 percent; its restaurants had 157,300 employees and approximately 1,400 locations. Company founder Bill Darden (1918–1994) opened his first restaurant, the Green Frog, in the 1950s in Waycross, Georgia; Darden Restaurants went public, offering shares for public purchase, in 1995. Darden uses an exclusively company-owned and -operated business model and recently expanded its restaurant portfolio with the chains Bahama Breeze, Smokey Bones Barbeque and Grill, and Seasons 52. Its restaurants serve in excess of 300 million meals annually.

Brinker International, owner of Chili's Bar and Grill, is the world's second largest casual-dining chain restaurant operator. By 2006, the company's net earnings topped $212 million, with a one-year net income growth rate over 32 percent. Brinker operates 1,600 restaurants in approximately 20 countries, with more than 110,000 employees. The Chili's brand alone operates approximately 1,200 restaurants, making it second only to Applebee's in terms of individual restaurant units. Additional Brinker brands include Maggiano's Little Italy, Romano's Macaroni Grill, and On the Border Mexican Grill and Cantina. Brinker offers franchising for Chili's, Romano's, and On the Border. Norman E. Brinker founded the company in 1975, and it went public in 1983.

Applebee's International is the world's largest table service restaurant chain, with more than 1,900 casual-dining Applebee's Neighborhood Bar and Grill restaurants in 17 countries. As of 2005, Applebee's had a net income of more than $100 million, a one-year net income growth rate over 8 percent, and 32,360 employees. Bill and T. J. Palmer opened the first of their restaurants in 1980, under the name T. J. Applebee's Rx for Edibles & Elixirs. Most of the company's restaurants are franchised, with 25 percent owned and operated by the company, which went public in 1989.

Industry leaders among fine-dining chains are Ruth's Chris Steak House, Morton's Restaurant Group, and Palm Management Corporation. Ruth's Chris has the highest number of restaurants among the group, with 90 locations, both franchised and company owned, in 30 states and 6 countries. The company had a nearly $11 million net income in 2005. Morton's Restaurant Group owns around 70 Morton's Steakhouses in 30 states and had a 2005 net income of $700,000. Palm Management, a privately held company, operates approximately 30 Palm restaurants in the United States, Mexico, and Puerto Rico.

Industry Trends

The NRA predicts that chain restaurant growth will continue in upcoming years, although restaurant unit expansion is expected to be slower than in the boom decade of the 1980s. Local chain restaurants, which have the flexibility to adapt to consumer demand, are expected to have an advantage over national and international firms in the competitive chain restaurant market. Company expansion by merger and acquisition rather than internal growth is a growing trend.

Convenience is expected to be the driving factor in upcoming chain restaurant trends. Curbside takeaway service has emerged as a popular casual-dining trend in recent years. The concept allows customers to call in an order and pick it up at the restaurant, where the food is delivered to the car. Restaurants that offer the service, such as Outback Steakhouse and Applebee's, have seen curbside **takeout** sales account for up to 10 percent of total sales. The curbside takeaway phenomenon points to the incursion of casual-dining restaurants into the arena of convenience restaurants, which has been long dominated by fast food establishments.

The 21st-century development of "lifestyle centers"—shopping centers that may include a mall, a movie theater, and multiple chain stores—has positively affected the growth of chain restaurants, which often act as "anchors." Mall-based chain restaurants often use a "pad site" building concept that allows for both easy access for mall shoppers and high visibility from highways. Most mall-oriented chain restaurants, such as Applebee's, were started in the 1980s or later. The average cost for building and decorating a pad-site chain restaurant is $2 million.

Chain Restaurant History

The U.S. restaurant industry began a pattern of dramatic growth following World War II, largely due to a booming economy and population increase. Chain restaurants benefited from the growing popularity of the automobile. Individuals or families traveling long distances by car welcomed the site of familiar brand-name restaurants.

Howard Johnson's restaurants and motor lodges benefited from the increasingly mobile nature of the American public and became the first large-scale popular restaurant chain. Howard Deering Johnson had opened a drugstore in Wollasten, Massachusetts, in 1925 and expanded to a table-service restaurant in 1929. Despite the economic restrictions of the Great Depression, Johnson utilized the franchise system and operated 39 restaurants by the end of 1936. The number of franchised Howard Johnson restaurants nearly tripled by 1939. The company experienced continued exceptional growth in the following decades, including the addition of motor lodges in 1954. When the Howard Johnson Company went public in 1961, it operated 88 motor lodges and 605 restaurants, approximately half of which were franchises. The distinctive orange roof of Howard Johnson establishments became a pop culture icon in the 1940s, '50s, and '60s. The company's familiar slogans included "Host of the Highways" and "Landmark for Hungry Americans."

Facing increased competition from other chain restaurants and the emerging fast food industry, the Howard Johnson Company experimented with other restaurant chains in the 1960s and '70s, such as the Red Coach Inn and Ground Round brands. But despite these and other efforts, the failing company was ultimately sold to a British firm in 1979.

Theme Restaurants

Chain theme restaurants, which feature distinctive décor such as entertainment or sports memorabilia, blur the line between pop culture museums and food establishments. The most successful and long-lived theme restaurant chain is the Hard Rock Café, which first opened in London in 1971. The restaurant features the usual casual-dining fare, such as hamburgers and chicken dishes, served amid music memorabilia. The company began opening international locations in 1982 and expanded its portfolio to include hotels and casinos in 1995. The Hard Rock Café reached its highest popularity in the 1980s, but continues to thrive with 143 restaurants in 36 countries.

Planet Hollywood, a theme chain based on film memorabilia, opened in 1991 to great popularity, but went bankrupt twice during the 1990s. The chain once boasted nearly 100 restaurants, but approximately 70 were closed. The chain currently has six U.S. locations and 13 international locations.

One of the earliest theme restaurant chains was Trader Vic's, a Polynesian-themed restaurant opened in 1932 by Victor Jules Bergeron Jr. The restaurant features Polynesian décor, exotic cocktails, and foreign cuisine. During the 1950s and '60s, the company had approximately 25 restaurants worldwide. After a decline in popularity in the 1990s, the brand is experiencing a resurgence, and again had 23 restaurants open worldwide in 2006.

FURTHER READINGS: Brinker International. http://www.brinker.com; *Casual and Fine Dining*. Washington, DC: National Restaurant Association, 1990; Darden Restaurants. http://www.darden.com; Duecy, Erica. "Curbside Takeaway Service Grows Sales for Casual Sector." *Nation's Restaurant News* 39, no. 44 (2005): 22; "Evolving Tastes." *Retail Traffic* 35, no. 10 (2006): 80; Mariani, John F. *America Eats Out: An Illustrated History of Restaurants, Taverns, Coffee Shops, Speakeasies, and Other Establishments That Have Fed Us for 350 Years*. New York: Morrow, 1991; Misonzhnik, Elain. "Business Casual." *Retail Traffic* 35, no. 10 (2006): 37; National Council of Chain Restaurants. http://www.nccr.net; National Restaurant Association. http://www.restaurant.org; Pillsbury, Richard. *From Boarding House to Bistro: The American*

Restaurant Then and Now. Boston: Unwin Hyman, 1990; Wyckoff, D. Daryl, and W. Earl Sasser. *The Chain-Restaurant Industry.* New York: D. C. Heath, 1978.

Wendy W. Pickett

Chavez, Cesar. *See* Agricultural Unions; Boycotts and Consumer Protests; Labor and Labor Unions.

Chocolate All forms of chocolate are made from so-called beans embedded in fibrous white pulp contained in large almond-shaped pods of the tropical cacao tree (*Theobroma cacao*). Americans, of whom half nominate chocolate as their favorite flavor, eat approximately 12 pounds worth of chocolate **candy**, desserts, and drinks a year. Despite this, Americans consume less than residents of other countries; the Swiss are the most avid chocolate afficionados.

All lands within 20 degrees of the equator grow cocoa, but most of it, 70 percent, comes from West Africa. Forty to fifty million people worldwide depend on the cacao plant for their livelihoods, of which only five to six million, none in the United States, are cacao farmers.

Once harvested and roasted, cacao beans are "cooked" as chocolate liquor, which is then processed into baking chocolate, sweet or dark chocolate, semisweet milk chocolate, cocoa powder, Dutch-processed chocolate (another powder), and white chocolate (which is not really chocolate since it contains no solids but only cocoa butter).

Americans long thought that chocolate caused acne, tooth decay, and weight gain, but recent research has found these ideas to be exaggerated if not false. Instead, chocolate—at least dark (nonmilk) chocolate—has more recently been found to contain high levels of antioxidants, the same class of substances that make red wine and green tea helpful in lowering the risk of heart disease.

History

Chocolate is one of the Western Hemisphere foods first brought to Europe by Christopher Columbus, who came upon a dugout canoe full of local goods in the Caribbean Sea near Honduras in August 1502 on his fourth and last voyage to the West. He sent some beans back to Spain, where they made no impression. Twenty years later, Hernando Cortez sent three trunkfuls to Spain and introduced the bitter beverage made from the beans into Europe. Still, the flavor did not take.

Chocolate comes from a Mayan word for a bitter-tasting drink seasoned with unsweetened vanilla or chili peppers. The Aztec considered it an aphrodisiac and also a cure for both diarrhea and dysentery. They used seeds as an offering to the gods, and only rulers and aristocrats were allowed to drink the foamy bitter drink (made with water and laced with chilies). Throughout Central America, the seeds were also used as currency.

After about 1585, Europeans began to stir the bitter drink with **sugar**, and at last it became a favorite of the rich. Shortly thereafter, the European colonial powers began to grow cacao plants—and sugarcane—in their equatorial colonies, using African slaves or indigenous labor. More Englishmen drank chocolate at the new chocolate and **coffee** houses of London. The price kept falling throughout Europe, and more and more people could enjoy the beverage.

About 1828, a Dutch maker, Coenraad van Houten, patented a method for pressing the roasted beans to remove a proportion of the fat; the resultant cake, which was much lower in cocoa butter and could be pulverized to powder, was known as Dutch chocolate or Dutch-Process Cocoa. Adding alkali to the powder then made it easier to mix with water as a drink or with sugar and cocoa butter to form eating chocolate. Since then, the process has been used to make dark chocolate, milk chocolate, and also white chocolate. In 1849 various processes made it possible for an English chocolate maker, Cadbury, to produce an eating chocolate. Then, in the 1870s, Swiss chemist Henri Nestlé made chocolate paste with condensed milk and added more sugar to make a milk chocolate bar.

In 1893 Milton S. Hershey, a Philadelphia and Denver caramel candy manufacturer visiting the Chicago World's Columbian Exhibition, was fascinated by a 2,200-pound, 10-foot female statue, the symbol of a German chocolate manufacturer. Hershey added chocolate bars to his company repertoire, but using whole milk to make his chocolate bars. He sold the Hershey Bars for five cents each, a price that persisted through World War II.

From the three original chests of beans sent to Spain in 1519, a worldwide product and business has grown. The association of chocolate with romance, and possibly as an aphrodisiac, are probably responsible for the creation of boxes in the shape of hearts, filled with chocolates, being the gift of choice for lovers and suitors every Valentine's Day.

In other realms, chocolate is at the heart of the world-famous children's book *Charlie and the Chocolate Factory* (1964) by Roald Dahl, which was first made into a movie in 1971 and again in 2005. Other successful chocolate-related books and films include *Like Water for Chocolate* (1992) by Laura Esquivel, the Italian film *Bread and Chocolate* (1973), and most recently the Harry Potter series by J. K. Rowling, which employs chocolate as a remedy for the effects of exposure to evil.

FURTHER READINGS: Coe, Sophie D., and Michael D. Coe. *The True History of Chocolate.* London: Thames & Hudson, 1996; Lebowitz, Daniel. *The Great Book of Chocolate: The Chocolate Lover's Guide, with Recipes.* Berkeley, CA: Ten Speed Press, 2004.

Molly G. Schuchat

Ciba-Geigy The Ciba-Geigy Corporation's Ciba Seeds division (in collaboration with its research partner the Mycogen Corporation) produced the first **corn hybrid** with **genetically engineered** insect resistance in 1993, and by 1996 the variety was being planted in the United States. The Maximizer hybrid was modified with a total of three genes, one from *Bacillus thuringiensis* (Bt), one for resistance to the herbicide Basta, and a third, a "marker" gene that also confers resistance to the **antibiotic** ampicillin.

Bt is a **bacterium** normally found in the soil that is highly toxic to a wide range of insects, notably the European corn borer (*Ostrinia nubilalis*). The borer was introduced to the United States about 1915 and causes a billion dollars' worth of crop damage annually. Introduction of the crucial gene that enables the bacteria to produce the toxin confers that ability to the plant and has the potential to dramatically reduce crop losses due to the pest, as well as dramatically increase profits for the successful company.

Ciba-Geigy had been formed in 1970 by the amalgamation of two parent companies and was well placed to participate in the race for insect- and herbicide-resistant plants. It was combined with Sandoz in 1996 as Novartis, and subsequently merged with AstraZeneca to create Syngenta in 2000. The three original founding companies had more than 200 years' history in the production of industrial, agricultural, and pharmaceutical chemicals, and in their new incarnation, they were well situated to enter the 20th-century search to produce crops genetically engineered for a range of agriculturally advantageous features.

The intense competition for this potential profit has generated a proportional amount of litigation. When **Monsanto** received a patent for Bt-modified plants in 1996, it immediately instituted a claim of patent infringement against Ciba-Geigy. Eventually in 1998, this particular battle went to Ciba-Geigy (by then part of Novartis), but many other claims and counterclaims between companies that have a stake in producing genetically modified foods have been, and are still being, waged. The complexities of international law as it applies to this evolving science, in the context of the huge economic implications, seem set to ensure that the legal battles will continue for some time.

Another consequence of the development of genetically modified foods has been the increasing controversy about the environmental implications. There is concern that insects will develop resistance to the Bt toxin and also that the antibiotic resistance conferred incidentally on the plant via the marker gene may be transferred to bacteria pathogenic to humans. The **European Union** refused to authorize the use of Bt-modified corn in 1996 partly on these grounds. Again, the debate continues vigorously on all sides and seems most unlikely to fade away in the near future in view of the enormous economic, scientific, and technological investments already made by companies such as Ciba-Geigy as well as by various governments around the world.

Janet Clarkson

Cloning A clone is a duplicate of another organism that has the exact same DNA as the original organism. Cloning can be done on both animal and plant organisms. It has been used for a long time (especially in agriculture), but has only recently been brought to public attention, mainly through the success of Dolly, the first clone of a mammal. Cloning has the potential to become a key component of agriculture and herding in the future, but many scientific, economic, and ethical issues must be resolved before large-scale applications of this technology can be undertaken.

History of Cloning

Cloning is often perceived as a recent technology. It has come to the attention of the general public only since the cloning of a female sheep in 1997, but people have actually been cloning animals and plants for a long time; in fact, plants have been cloned for thousands of years, and a lot of our current agriculture is based on cloning. Vegetative propagation, which is an asexual reproductive process (a reproductive process where only one type of DNA is needed), has been used to reproduce crops with desirable qualities for centuries. It is also a naturally occurring phenomenon, found in nature in perennial plants (a perennial plant is one that lives for more than two years).

Modern cloning traces its roots to the mid-20th century. In 1952, Robert Briggs and Thomas King extracted the nucleus from the cell of one frog and inserted it into the egg cell of a second frog, resulting in a cloned frog. This experiment was slightly modified by John Gordon, when he cloned a frog with the nucleus taken from an adult skin cell of another frog. It was not until 1997 that cloning really came into the public eye, when a sheep was cloned at the Roslin Institute in Midlothian, Scotland. Dolly was the first mammal to have been successfully cloned from an adult cell. This event generated many ethical questions related to cloning, especially when the discussion turned to human cloning. Today, many mammals have been cloned, including mice and other rodents, cattle, sheep, cats, and mules.

The Basic Science behind Cloning

Cloning plants is a rather simple process, as plants can be cloned through grafting or planting cuttings. Animal cloning is much more complicated and must be done through a technique called *nuclear transfer*. As with the experiences mentioned above, cloning requires the presence of two cells: an adult cell that is used to obtain DNA; and an egg cell that is the recipient of the DNA. The main problem when cloning adult cells is that they are usually programmed for a specific function (for example, reproducing skin). Hence, the scientists at the Roslin Institute had to merge the two cells with a small burst of electricity, mimicking that natural burst of energy that accompanies the fertilization of an egg by a sperm cell. After that burst, the cell started to divide as a normal embryo; it was then implanted into the uterus of another sheep. The experience resulted in a newborn sheep, the world's first cloned mammal.

Cloned animals share the same genetic makeup, but do not necessarily act or look the same. Hence, the belief that a clone will be an exact duplicate, or at least an "identical twin" in appearance, is unfounded. In 2003, a physiological and behavioral study of cloned pigs was carried out at the North Carolina State University College of Veterinary Medicine. The behavioral study found that the cloned pigs had different temperaments and habits, as well as different preferences in food. The physiological study further found that there were physical variations between cloned pigs. Hence, the environment still plays an important role in the behavior and physical makeup of clones.

Cloning in Agriculture and Husbandry

Plants are able to clone themselves through *vegetative propagation*; this process occurs when plants reproduce themselves without the use of seeds or spores. For example, when you cut a plant and use the leaf cuttings to grow a new one, you are cloning the original plant through a part of the plant called the *callus*. Many common foods are cultivated through cloning or asexual reproduction because they reproduce asexually quite easily. Examples of "cloned" foodstuffs include sugarcane, bananas, potatoes, strawberries, and citrus. Hence, cloning has been a part of our agricultural system for thousands of years and is still frequently used today.

These days, we use bioengineering to enhance cloning techniques, creating plants with quicker growth rates, faster reproductive cycles, or even characteristics that are not native to the plant itself. Modified plants or animals in which the gene from another plant or animal has been transferred into it are called *transgenic*. One famous example is "golden rice," a betacarotene-enhanced rice. It was developed as a fortified food to be used in areas where there is a shortage of dietary **vitamin** A, but as with other cloned foods, it has generated a lot of controversy.

Bioengineered organisms are also used in a variety of fashions; for example, some biotechnology companies have used cloning to mass-produce pharmaceuticals through plants (such as alfalfa) and animals (chicken eggs). Replacing conventional bioreactors with transgenic livestock offers immense economic benefits, but also presents enormous risks. Alternative uses include modifying animals so they are more suited for farming or so they can be used in laboratories, as well as saving endangered species.

Advantages to cloning in agriculture and husbandry are numerous; for example, it can increase food production and as well as enabling the creation of healthier foods. Even with all the benefits that cloning presents, however, issues must be addressed before cloning can be used commercially on a large scale.

Scientific and Technical Issues

One problem with cloning is that it cuts down on biodiversity and may lead to the creation of new diseases. Cloning also reduces resistance to disease, meaning that cloned species are more susceptible to certain types of illness. Currently, animals that are the results of cloning often suffer from a variety of debilitating diseases associated with old age (such as arthritis) and seem to grow at an accelerated rate. These animals suffer from unusually high rates of birth defects, disabilities, and premature death. Nonetheless, a recent five-year study found that cloning created no qualitative risks beyond those encountered by all animals involved in modern agricultural practices, although the frequency of the risks appeared to be increased in cattle during the early portions of the life cycle of cattle clones.

The Food and Drug Administration's (FDA) Center for Veterinary Medicine recently issued "draft guidance" related to cloned foods. Following a comprehensive review, the agency did not observe anomalies in animals produced by cloning that have not also been observed in animals produced by other assisted reproductive technologies and natural mating. Also, the review did not identify any food-consumption hazards related to the meat and milk from cattle, swine, and goat clones and the progeny of cattle and sheep. Hence, the FDA concluded that food from these animals was as safe to eat as food from animals of those species derived by conventional means. FDA draft guidances are not definitive positions or decisions, but rather opinions and contain nonbinding statements; as such, cloning of animals remains a very sensitive scientific issue.

There also exist some technical issues that make cloning economically unviable at this time. First, the implantation of eggs in the uterus often results in an abortion, forcing scientists to perform several implantations to ensure the success of one. Also, cloned fetuses are usually much bigger at birth than their natural counterparts, resulting in a high number of cesarean operations; this makes it at present an unsafe and inefficient procedure for large-scale husbandry.

Ethical Issues

Until recently, the main limits surrounding cloning were technical; scientists were limited by what it was possible to do. Today, much more is possible, and stakeholders are now faced with ethical limits as well and must determine what is acceptable. For example, clones could be used to create organ banks for humans. Even without bringing up human cloning, **animal rights** issues surrounding the suffering of cloned animals have significantly impacted the subject. For some, only in cases where the usefulness of the technology can outweigh countervailing moral concerns (in sectors such as biomedical research) is cloning an acceptable alternative. For others, cloning is an acceptable technology that could be used in many different contexts. Debate is ongoing.

FURTHER READINGS: Archer, Gregory, & T. H. Friend. "Behavioral Variation among Cloned Pigs." *Applied Animal Behaviour Science* 82 (2003): 151–61; Archer, Gregory, Scott Dindot, Ted H. Friend, Bruce Lawhorn, Jorge A. Piedrahita, Shawn Walker, and Gretchen Zaunbrecher. "Hierarchical Phenotypic and Epigenetic Variation in Cloned Swine." *Biology of Reproduction* 69 (2003): 430–36; Borém, Aluizio, Fabrício R. Santos, and David E. Bowen. *Understanding Biotechnology*. Upper Saddle River, NJ: Prentice Hall, 2003; Food and Drug Administration, Center for Veterinary Medicine. "Guidance for Industry Use of Edible Products from Animal Clones or Their Progeny for Human Food or Animal Feed." Guideline No. 179, Draft Guidance, December 28, 2006; Lassen, J., M. Gjerris, and P. Sandøe. "After Dolly: Ethical Limits to the Use of Biotechnology on Farm Animals." *Theriogenology* 65, no. 5 (2006): 992–1004; Panarace, M., J. I. Agüero, M. Garrote, et al. "How Healthy Are Clones and Their Progeny? Five Years of Field Experience." *Theriogenology* 67, no. 1 (2007): 142–51; Rudenko, L., and J. C. Matheson. "The US FDA and Animal Cloning: Risk and Regulatory Approach." *Theriogenology* 67, no. 1 (2006): 198–206.

Jean-François Denault

Coca-Cola. *See* Soft Drinks.

Codex Alimentarius Commission International food standards are adopted by the Codex Alimentarius Commission (CAC), an international organization jointly run by the United Nations' Food and Agriculture Organization (FAO) and the World Health Organization (WHO). Its creation was prompted by increased concern in the 1940s and '50s among consumers over food technologies and associated health hazards, as well as a rise in trade barriers due to different food regulations across countries. Over the past 40 years, the CAC has adopted hundreds of food standards both to promote consumer safety and to facilitate **free trade** in food.

The output of the commission includes standards, guidelines, and codes of practice. *Commodity standards* address questions such as what constitutes **chocolate**, **sugar**, **canned** peaches, or corned **beef**. These standards are concerned with questions of fair labeling, consumer fraud, and unfair competition, as well as a safety benchmark expressed in the quantity and type of food **additives** or contaminants permitted. *General standards* cover issues such as labeling, food hygiene, and methods of analysis and sampling. Standards for pesticides and veterinary drugs are usually expressed in terms of a single number, a maximum residue limit (MRL) for the substance. A significant proportion of the CAC's output, however, takes the form of purely voluntary guidelines and codes of practice, which are not submitted to states for acceptance (they are passed on to the governments, but the governments are not requested to respond). Since 1963, the commission has analyzed more than 195 pesticides and 50 veterinary drugs; issued more than 200 commodity standards, 33 guidelines, and 43 recommended codes of practice; and adopted almost 3,000 MRLs and several dozen general standards.

Until the establishment of the World Trade Organization (WTO) in 1994, Codex Alimentarius standards, once adopted, were sent to governments for acceptance, which in theory meant that governments would integrate the standards into domestic regulations. In practice, however, there was no mechanism within the CAC to enforce acceptance of its standards.

CAC activities have been significantly affected by the founding of the WTO. When the Uruguay Round was signed in 1994 and the WTO was established, countries agreed to a set of procedures about how to resolve disputes over sanitary and phytosanitary (SPS) regulations. SPS regulations are a concern at the WTO because of their potential to serve as nontariff barriers to trade, that is, impediments that do not take the form of an official **tariff** or tax on imported goods. Instead, countries may and do use SPS regulations to protect domestic industries rather than promote health and safety as they are intended.

For instance, if a country refuses to import chicken parts from another country, citing high levels of **bacterial** contamination, and the exporter brought the ban to the WTO, the SPS Agreement would determine whether such a ban was for safety reasons or was disguised protectionism. It does this by referring to international standards in dispute resolution processes. The CAC, along with the International Office of Epizootics and the International Plant Protection Convention, are the international organizations mentioned in the SPS Agreement as sources of international standards. Thus, Codex Alimentarius food standards now serve as international benchmarks for resolution of disputes over SPS measures. This agreement has resulted in a tremendous increase in international attention to the CAC.

Management

The Codex Alimentarius Commission was established in 1963 as an intergovernmental body by FAO and WHO. Membership is open to all member states of FAO and WHO. There are currently 167 members, plus 149 international nongovernmental organizations (INGOs) with observer status, representing producers, industry, and civil society and 58 intergovernmental organizations. Standards are developed through 29 subsidiary bodies (of which 24 are active) consisting of regional, commodity, and general committees.

The work of the CAC, which meets in full body every year, and its subsidiary bodies is logistically, technically, and managerially supported by a small secretariat (known as the "Codex Secretariat"), which is housed within FAO and funded jointly by FAO and WHO. The cost of regional, commodity, and general committees is met in whole or in part by host countries, but also supported administratively by the Codex Secretariat. Members bear the costs of their own participation in meetings.

Expert scientific advice to inform Codex standard making is provided by two established Expert Committees financed and administered jointly by FAO and WHO. JECFA (Joint Expert Committee on Food Additives) is responsible for food additives, contaminants, and veterinary drug residues, and JMPR (Joint Meetings on Pesticide Residues) for pesticide residues. JEMRA (Joint Meetings on Microbiological Risk Assessment) is a new group, still termed a "joint expert consultation" rather than a formal committee, responsible for microbiological risk assessment. Other expert consultations may be set up as needed. Committees and expert consultations are administered and financed independently of the CAC by FAO and WHO. JECFA and JMPR each have a joint secretary in each organization.

Jerri A. Husch

Coffee There are many steps involved in bringing an average cup of coffee from the hills where the beans are grown to the cardboard cup passed over the counter at Starbucks. A **commodity food chain** analysis, which traces the route foods travel from beginning to end, might begin on a small mountainous plot in Kenya some 4,000 feet in elevation, now denuded of shade trees, where a poor farmer hand-picks ripe berries (or "cherries," as they are called and which they resemble) under the hot sun. Each bush yields about 5,000 berries or more, enough for about 50 good-sized cups of coffee. These berries are then crushed to separate them from the pulpy casing, dried in the sun, and packed in bags weighing more than 100 pounds. These bags are then sold to an exporter or cooperative agency, which puts them up for sale on the coffee exchange, in competition with coffee beans worldwide. The slightest change in temperature or weather conditions can alter the yield and ultimately affect the price for each bag, and in turn the profit for the farmer. This analysis would follow the bag of beans across the ocean to a roaster in the United States, where the beans are processed and packed in cans and shipped off to **supermarkets** across the nation, or directly to specialty coffee retail outlets, where the beans are carefully ground by a *barista*, tamped into a sophisticated espresso machine, brewed, and then ceremoniously slurped by an avid consumer eager for a morning jolt of caffeine.

This simplified picture of the complex steps involved in the coffee industry briefly illustrates how many people are involved in making a simple hot beverage. The coffee industry is a multibillion-dollar operation involving growers, brokers, exporters, roasters, distributors, and retailers—millions of people around the world. The **U.S. Department of Agriculture** (USDA) estimates that 128.6 million bags of coffee were grown worldwide in 2007. In sheer monetary value, coffee is the second most valuable natural product, trailing only behind oil.

There are two different coffee beans that are commercially viable: robusta (*Coffea canephora*), which accounts for about a third of production and is hearty, as the name suggests, though harsh and somewhat acrid in flavor; and *Coffea arabica*, which is said to be of superior flavor and aroma and accounts for most premium coffee. Although coffee originated in Ethiopia, it is today grown throughout the tropics in countries such as Brazil (the leading grower), Colombia, Mexico, and Indonesia (especially Java), as well as India and Vietnam, which have lately emerged among the top producers worldwide.

Ironically, the leading coffee consumers are not the countries that produce coffee. Scandinavians have long been the greatest coffee drinkers, with Finland, Sweden, Norway, and Denmark in a clear lead. Other Germanic countries trail slightly behind, with France and Italy, somewhat surprisingly, consuming less. Americans consume roughly the same amount as Italians, though consumption has been increasing lately. According to the USDA's Economic Research Service, the consumption of coffee in the United States increased between 1994 and 2004 by more than 20 percent.

The coffee industry has been the target of trenchant criticism in recent years, much of it concerning the cutting down of rain forests, particularly in the Amazon, to start new coffee plantations. Since trees in the Amazon produce much of the oxygen used on earth, such a process can have devastating long-term consequences. Such intensive farms also require significant use of **fertilizers** and pesticides. Because natural predators are wiped out the ecosystem is replaced by a monoculture export crop. Chemicals, which directly jeopardize the health of farmers, also run into water supplies and degrade the soil, which tends to wash away without the support of large trees. The plight of coffee farmers has been of concern, particularly because only a few cents per dollar of every bag of coffee are returned to the farmer as profit. This situation has been particularly grave in recent years as a glut of coffee due to overproduction has caused prices to drop, especially since price controls and quotas were abandoned in the 1990s.

To help ameliorate this situation, some coffee is sold today as fair trade and/or organic. This means that farmers are paid a price at which they can survive and use procedures that make their operations more sustainable in the long term. Some "shade-grown" coffee is even farmed under the canopy of larger trees, which yields less and is thus more expensive, but prevents soil erosion.

Most coffee processing has historically been controlled by large, now **multinationally** owned, companies such as Maxwell House, Folgers, and Chase and Sanborn. These produced a fairly standard, though mediocre, cup of coffee. Much the same can be said of decaffeinated versions and instant coffee, which was pioneered by Nestlé. With the rise of specialty coffee houses such as Peet's and Starbucks, Americans have become more discerning consumers and, in many cases, ardent fans of well-made coffee. In some U.S. cities, a Starbucks is never more than a few blocks away. Today there are more than 9,000 stores in over 30 countries, and more are opening in airports, as drive-throughs, and in every imaginable locale. Starbucks also sells beans in grocery stores and has launched a number of successful cold coffee beverages that are sold in stores and **vending machines**.

Coffee was once a simple commodity—something that came in a utilitarian cup, for a dime, something that just appeared on the lunch counter with no fanfare. Today, it is a huge business, and Seattle-based Starbucks is the biggest of them all. In the fiscal year that ended on October 1, 2006, the retailer's revenues were up by 22 percent over the previous year ($1.4 billion more than 2005's $6.4 billion). During the year, the company added 2,199 new Starbucks stores to bring the October 1, 2006, total to 12,440 Starbucks worldwide.

Source: "Starbucks Shares Soar in Advance of Earnings." Associated Press, October 16, 2006. Online at http://www.msnbc.msn.com/id/15133987/.

Darius Willoughby

Commodities Exchange A commodities exchange is a specialized form of trading goods or their derivatives that minimizes the risk of long-term transactions. Commodities exchanges specialize in trading in one of four products: agricultural goods (such as **wheat**, **sugar**, cotton, or **coffee**); metals (either precious such as gold or industrial like copper); energy (petroleum, electricity); and transport commodities. Transactions usually use futures contracts, although spot price and options on futures are also used. Commodities exchanges have the advantage of concentrating buyers and sellers into a single trading forum, hence reducing transaction costs. A recent United Nations Conference on Trade and Development (UNCTAD) study found that there are 17 commodities exchanges around the world that engage in trading of agricultural goods. The most important ones in terms of volume are the Dalian Commodity Exchange and the Chicago Mercantile Exchange.

Background

Exchanges are independent organizations that facilitate the orderly trade of equity products (such as shares or futures contracts). Different forms of exchanges specialize in different equity products; for example, a stock exchange facilitates the transaction of shares, while a commodities exchange facilitates the trading of goods. Exchanges can be a for-profit organization (even those listed on a different stock exchange), a mutual (owned by its members), or a nonprofit organization. A governing body of administrators oversees the management and regulation of the exchange. Exchanges offer services to their members, such as regulating listing of financial products, operating the settlement system for payment of transactions, and collecting and disseminating news relating to transactions and participants to media and other observers.

Commodities Traded on Exchanges

Commodities exchanges facilitate the trade of agricultural products, metals, energy, and transport. These commodities usually have the same basic characteristics that enable transactions; they can be stored for long amounts of time, the value of goods is highly dependent on measurable physical attributes, and goods must be fungible in nature (i.e., they do not depend on a specific individual or location; a futures contract on wheat is not tied to a specific farmer or field). Agricultural goods were customarily limited to cereals, but today a wide array of products is traded on exchanges. These include wheat, sugar, coffee, cotton, eggs, cattle, soybeans, ethanol, wood pulp, and orange juice.

Other commodities exchanges also engage in the trading of "virtual goods." For example, some exchanges facilitate the barter of emission permits (whereby companies may purchase and sell emissions allowances for greenhouse-related gases) or economic events (employment, fuel or housing prices, inflation, interest rates). In all these cases, commodities exchanges are used as tools to reduce the inherent risk of long-term transactions.

Financial Products Used on Commodities Exchanges

The majority of trades occurring on commodities exchanges use future contracts (often shortened to "futures"), which are contracts in which there is an obligation to buy or sell an underlying asset at a specific price at a specific time in the future. They are in a class of financial products called *derivatives*, as the value of the contract itself is derived from an underlying asset. They were originally used as a way to alleviate risk for agricultural products such as **corn** and cotton, but are now used in a variety of financial situations.

For example, a farmer cultivating wheat could sell a future contract for his wheat crop, which would be harvested in several months. This transaction would guarantee the selling price for the purchaser and the seller, reducing the risk of the transaction by protecting both actors from market variations. Speculators who attempt to profit by predicting upcoming market fluctuations also use futures; they purchase (or sell) goods with a futures contract and later fill the order with a lower (higher) price. For instance, a speculator might purchase a futures contract on wheat worth $100, then sell it six months later when it is worth $110, making $10 profit per contract.

Sometimes commodities are traded at "spot price"; this means that the product is sold at the price that is quoted for immediate delivery. For example, a purchaser buying a contract for the immediate delivery of corn would pay the spot price. Also, options on futures are used when the buyer purchases a "call option" (which, as it says, is an option, not an obligation) to purchase the underlying goods at the agreed price. Similarly, a "put option" is an option (and not an obligation) to sell a commodity at a future date. Both these derivatives differ from futures as they do not have any intrinsic value; for example, a put option to sell wheat at $100 per contract, when wheat is selling at a spot price of $120 per contract, would not be used and hence would be deemed worthless.

Major Commodities Exchanges for Agriculture Products

In 2004, the UNCTAD inventoried 17 commodities exchanges around the world that dealt in agricultural products. Two stood out as having the largest volumes of total transactions. The first is the Dalian Commodity Exchange, which was founded in February 1993 and had a volume of 240 million contracts in 2006. It is a self-regulated nonprofit organization located in Liaoning, China, and the main products being traded are soybeans, soy meals, and corn.

The other important agricultural commodities exchange is the Chicago Mercantile Exchange, a private, for-profit organization founded in 1898. It had a daily average of 78,000 contracts transactions in 2006. The main agricultural products traded there are cattle and hogs. Together, these two exchanges accounted for more than 50 percent of futures trades in agricultural products in 2004.

Three other exchanges had important daily volumes of agricultural products: the New York Board of Trade (NYBOT), the Tokyo Grain Exchange, and Zhengzhou Commodity Exchange. There are also many smaller commodities exchanges spread out around the world that specialize in local markets or specific products. Finally, the India commodities exchanges have recently opened up and started publishing their daily volumes; with the importance of the Indian agricultural market, it is expected that these exchanges will have major impacts on global trading volumes.

FURTHER READINGS: Levinson, Marc. *Guide to Financial Markets.* 3rd ed. Princeton, NJ: Bloomberg Press, 2003; Mobius, Mark. *Equities: An Introduction to the Core Concepts.* Singapore: Wiley, 2007; UNCTAD Secretariat. "Overview of the World's Commodity Exchanges." Geneva: UNCTAD, 2006. Available at http://www.unctad.org/en/docs/ditccom20058_en.pdf.

Jean-François Denault

Commodity Food Chain A commodity is any object that can be produced, transported from producer to seller, exchanged for money or like goods, and eventually consumed or used. Therefore, a commodity chain is the organizational series that coordinates the passage of goods from their place of production to the retailer and then finally to the consumer. The sequence of activities that follows the movement of goods from producer to buyer involves many people organized on a worldwide scale, an expanding network of **labor** and production processes. The businesses that are a part of a commodity chain are concerned with the exchange of money and various political regulations governing the process. Each step of the route is highly competitive and fiscally profitable and includes production and processing, **packaging**, transportation, marketing and **advertising** conditions, and **research** in development and innovation. This interconnected chain links different businesses and enterprises into a network of production concerned with "commodity" as a business proposition: namely, processing ease and innovation; product safety, quality, and consistency; fair competition in the marketplace; and financial profit.

Ensuring safe food sources and plentiful supplies to feed the world's population is one of the largest challenges of any society. The production of food products creates a chain that moves from the producers (including farming, fishing, ranching, and imports/exports) to store or **restaurant** retailers to the dining consumers. A properly functioning commodity food chain will provide the means to provide food cheaply, safely, and competently, while at the same time ensuring that already created markets will expand into new markets. This encourages a high rate of competition among businesses, creating better product quality and providing financial success for the business owners. Accordingly, the production and distribution of food throughout the world is one of the oldest commodity chains in economic history, with its origins in the Middle Ages during the period of vast global colonization.

In the past, societies ate locally grown and seasonally available foods, and the existent supply chain—usually directly from the producer to the consumer—moved items swiftly from the field to the plate. However, the population growth and resultant demand for staple foods (such as **wine**, oils, and grains, as well as nonedible supplies) and luxury items (such as spices, cured meats, and out-of-season items such as fruits and vegetables) in the Middle Ages encouraged the expansion of the trade of foods by merchants. The most lucrative of these commodity food chains was the spice trade, which featured the movement of such exotic ingredients as pepper, cinnamon, and cardamom from India into the Middle East. There, Venetian merchants would purchase the spices and bring them to European consumers. The trade of goods on a national and global scale resulted in the exploration of new lands and the growth of wealth for the countries and individuals that functioned as the importer and seller of the foreign food goods. The once simple act of food gathering was transformed into a profitable enterprise responsible for the distribution of food to a monied population eager to ingest commodities.

In the 19th and 20th centuries, the Industrial Revolution sparked the large-scale manufacture and distribution of food, aided by necessary innovations in the processing and packaging industries as well as the ability to transport perishable foods quickly and safely. Food products were no longer sold exclusively by local producers, instead becoming commodities to be sold internationally. These changes forged more links in the chain of food distribution, as producers and buyers encouraged retailers around the world. By the middle of the 19th century, South American meats and fruits could easily be shipped to Europe and America in **refrigerated** transports, a technological achievement that transformed consumers' expectations about the availability and quality of out-of-season products. This influx of foods from all over the world resulted in an abundance of available products, which in turn lowered food prices for staple goods while increasing profits for the manufacturers of foods in short supply.

Worldwide food exports, mostly of meats and grains, went from 4 million tons in the middle of the 19th century to 40 million tons by the beginning of World War I. However, with increased supplies and producer competition came a concern for food quality and safety. In the 1880s, the United States responded to chemists' concerns about the safety of food production and the commodity chain with the Pure Food and Drug Act, which was passed in 1906. This law enforced standards for inspection of meat production and banned the manufacture, sale, or transportation of impure food products. Government regulations became the norm in the commodity food chain as the mass production of food products was codified.

In the 20th century, commodity food chains continued to thrive as more producers entered the market. Today, food is seen as a business, a tool to be used by producers to gain favorable financial incentives and political gains in the global market. Large stores of food are the main asset of wealthy nations, which in turn ensures control of the commodity market. However, government regulations concerning quality and production practices have become more widespread, even to the point of producer subsidies in times of abundance. This governmental influence keeps producers in business while regulating the supply and raising the eventual final price of the commodity for the consumer. Developing countries are helped in the "food wars" by international groups (such as the World Trade Organization and the **European Union**) that attempt to maintain order in times of market and financial fluctuations, encouraging a free-flowing food chain. Many developed countries (such as the United States and France) produce and export basic staple goods to countries in need of food aid.

At the beginning of the 21st century, 2002 was a year of great anxiety over global food supplies, as harvests of raw materials declined throughout the world due to drought. Also, political instability worldwide increased the nutrition burden on even the wealthier countries, disrupting production and movement chains. The future of the commodity food chain is still in flux. The political influence of wealthy producers and the demand of high-income consumers currently occupies market precedence over the needs of developing countries with a genuine nutritional problem.

See also Food Laws and Regulations.

FURTHER READINGS: Gereffi, Gary, and Miguel Korzeniewicz, eds. *Commodity Chains and Global Capitalism.* Westport, CT: Greenwood Press, 1994; Higgins, Vaughn, and Geoffrey Lawrence, eds. *Agricultural Governance: Globalization and the New Politics of Regulation.* London: Routledge, 2005; Hughes, Alex, and Suzanne Reimer, eds. *Geographies of Commodity Chains.* London: Routledge, 2004; Lien, Marianne Elisabeth, and Brigitte Nerlich, eds. *The Politics of Food.* New York: Berg, 2004; Spedding, C. R. W., ed. *The Human Food Chain.* London: Elsevier Applied Science, 1989.

Margaret Coyle

ConAgra. *See* Agribusiness; Diet Foods; Hunt's; Poultry Industry; Swift.

Condiments Condiments enhance or alter **flavors** and often turn bland or unsatisfying foods into palatable and pleasurable ones. They usually appear on the table and are intended for individual use by the diner. Today, the term *condiment* is broadly applied to a variety of substances, including salt, spices, table sauces (ketchup, mustard, mayonnaise, etc.), salad dressing, **sugar** and other sweeteners, and **ethnic** sauces.

Condiments have been used by Americans since colonial times. Salt was the most important, as it also served as the primary food preservative. In early times, salt was imported into America; it was also extracted from salt water through evaporation along the coast. Later, major salt deposits were found in New York, West Virginia, and Louisiana; when production began at these sites, the price of salt declined. Other condiments, such as sugar, pepper, and spices, had to be imported, and cost was a major limiting factor in their early use: only the middle and upper classes could afford them. However, their price declined during the 19th century, and the use of these condiments became universal. At this time, table condiments, such as ketchup, mustard, and mayonnaise, also became common.

In the 20th century, American consumption of condiments expanded mainly due to the decrease in cost. The downside of the widespread dissemination of certain condiments has been standardization and the loss of diversity. This has been offset by the infusion of new condiments, occasionally based on immigrant food traditions. Gradually, ethnic condiments became part of the culinary mainstream. American condiments have greatly influenced the world, as many have been transported into other cuisines through American **fast food** establishments.

Salt and Spices

The two most common condiments in America are salt and pepper. Historically, salt was commonly used as a preservative and a seasoning on a wide range of foods. In early colonial times, domestic production did not meet demand, and salt was imported from England, France, Spain, and the West Indies. Then in the early 18th century, salt deposits were located in British North American colonies.

In 1848 a Chicago firm began supplying goods to the surrounding area, and salt became the most important product the company traded. In 1910, it was incorporated with the name Morton Salt Company. In 1924, it began producing iodized salt, which helped prevent goiters, a common health problem in America associated with iodine deficiency. Morton became America's largest salt company. In 1999, Morton Salt was acquired by the Rohm and Haas Company of Philadelphia.

Spices such as black pepper (*Piper nigrum*) have been used as condiments for millennia. They have also been used as ingredients in making condiments such as ketchups, sauces, and **pickles**. During colonial times, pepper was a luxury and was imported and sold by small specialty shops. In the 19th century, the price of pepper and other spices greatly declined. Spices were largely imported by small traders in cities throughout the United States. For instance, in 1881 August Schilling launched a **coffee**, spice, and extract house in San Francisco, while eight years later, Willoughby McCormick started a spice-trading company in Baltimore.

In 1907, spice-trading companies formed the American Spice Trade Association to promote the spice industry. During the past century, the spice industry has largely centralized. A. Schilling & Company expanded nationally, as did McCormick & Company. In 1947 McCormick acquired Shilling, and the combined company expanded abroad through acquisitions. Today McCormick and Company is the largest spice firm in America.

Table Sauces

Today, the major table condiments are ketchup, mustard, hot sauces, and mayonnaise. Mustard seeds arrived with European colonists. These seeds were converted into powdered form and sold in stores by the 18th century. Ketchup became an important condiment in America during the late 18th and early 19th centuries, but mayonnaise did not emerge until the last decade of the 19th century. All three increased their importance as they became interconnected with the rise of **fast foods**, particularly **hot dogs**, hamburgers, and French fries.

Small quantities of tomato ketchup were first bottled in the 1850s. After the Civil War, commercial production of ketchup rapidly increased. One commercial producer was the H. J. **Heinz** Company, which first sold tomato ketchup in 1873. At that time it was not among Heinz's important products. By 1890, Heinz hit upon the now world-famous combination of the keystone label, neck-band, screw cap, and octagonal-shaped ketchup bottle. This bottle has become a culinary icon throughout the world. Shortly after the turn of the century, the H. J. Heinz Company became the largest tomato ketchup producer, and it remains so today.

Another ketchup manufacturer was the **Del Monte** Corporation of San Francisco, which began bottling ketchup by 1915. It rapidly expanded production during the 1940s. Yet another manufacturer was the Hunt Brothers Packing Company, which began producing ketchup during the 1930s. Today, Heinz, Del Monte, and **Hunt's** are the three largest ketchup producers in the world, but many smaller companies produce designer ketchups, such as mushroom ketchup and cranberry ketchup.

Mustard is one of the most widely grown and used spices in the world. It was manufactured in Dijon, France, during the Middle Ages. Several mustard companies flourished in England, but it was the company launched in 1814 by Jeremiah Colman, a miller of flour in Norwich, that dominated English mustard production. Colman's Mustard was imported into the United States from a factory in Toronto, Canada.

Mustard had been manufactured in America since colonial times. America's most important manufacturer of mustard was the R. T. French Company of Rochester, New York. The business began manufacturing French's Cream Salad Mustard in the 1904. By 1915, French's mustard was America's largest-selling prepared mustard, outselling all other mustards combined. The R. T. French Company was purchased by Reckitt & Colman, the successor company to Jeremiah Colman's operation in England, and Reckitt & Colman expanded its mustard product line. In 1974 French's Squeeze package was introduced. Within 10 years, it introduced French's Bold 'n Spicy, followed by French's Dijon the following year. In 2000, Reckitt & Coleman merged with Benckiser to form Reckitt Benckiser. An estimated 80 percent of American households buy French's mustard annually. By 2002, the total mustard market in America was about $280 million, and French's remains America's largest-selling branded mustard, followed by private labels and **Kraft**'s Grey Poupon.

Mayonnaise, a thick sauce traditionally composed of egg yolk beaten up with oil, vinegar, and seasonings, was created in the late 18th century by French chefs. Mayonnaise separates and easily spoils and does not survive the **bottling** process, however. Commercial mayonnaise therefore differs greatly from that which is made fresh. The first known attempt to manufacture commercial mayonnaise occurred in 1907, when a **delicatessen** owner in Philadelphia named Schlorer marketed it as Mrs. Schlorer's Mayonnaise. Richard Hellmann, a delicatessen owner in New York City, began to sell mayonnaise in wooden containers in 1912. Later, he marketed two versions of mayonnaise in glass jars, one of which he put a blue ribbon around. There was such great demand that Hellmann designed a "Blue Ribbon" label, which was trademarked in 1926. In the same year, Hellmann produced his first advertising cookbooklet, which encouraged customers to incorporate his mayonnaise into various dishes.

About 1912, the Gold Medal Mayonnaise Company began producing mayonnaise in California. In 1923, it merged with Nucoa to form Best Foods. Richard Hellmann's firm was acquired by Best Foods in 1932, after which Hellmann's mayonnaise was sold east of the Rockies and Best Foods mayonnaise in the west. Best Foods and Hellmann's are now part of the Anglo-Dutch **multinational** Unilever.

The Kraft Cheese Company was begun in 1903 by James L. Kraft, who sold cheese in Chicago. By 1914 the company had begun manufacturing its own cheese. It began producing mayonnaise when it acquired the Miliani Company in 1925. Its first salad dressing was French dressing. Kraft introduced Miracle Whip at the 1933 Century of Progress World's Fair in Chicago. When Miracle Whip was introduced, Kraft launched a major food advertising campaign, including a weekly two-hour radio show. At the end of this introductory period, Miracle Whip outsold all brands of mayonnaise. In the late 1980s, Kraft introduced Miracle Whip Light and Miracle Whip Cholesterol Free. In 1991, Miracle Whip Free was launched with no fat at all.

Mayonnaise remains a major American condiment. Annually, Americans purchased more than 745 million bottles of mayonnaise. American mayonnaise is now increasingly sold in other countries as well. In part, this increase can be attributed to the global rise of American fast food.

Other popular table sauces include A.1 Steak Sauce, Harvey's Sauce, and Worcestershire sauce, introduced by Lea & Perrins, now part of Heinz. **Tabasco** sauce was produced after the Civil War by the McIlhenny family on Avery Island, Louisiana.

Barbecue sauces have been made at home at least since the late 18th century, but the first commercial product was released by Heinz in 1948. It was followed by a version from Kraft Foods in the 1950s. Today, hundreds of barbecue sauces are commercially available, but Kraft controls about 44 percent of the market.

Table Top Sweeteners

After salt and pepper, the most common condiment today is sugar. However, sugar was expensive in Colonial America, and honey and molasses were more commonly used. As sugar prices declined during the 19th century, it was used in greater quantity in a greater diversity of cookery, such as baking. As a condiment, sugar was particularly important added to bitter beverages, such as tea, coffee, and **chocolate**.

A sugar substitute, Sweet'N Low, was introduced in 1957. Other no-calorie sweeteners were subsequently marketed. Equal and NutraSweet, today manufactured by the Merisant Company, were introduced about 1982. Splenda was introduced into the United States in 1998 by the British multinational Tate & Lyle. Today, Sweet'N Low is manufactured and sold in the United States by Sugar Foods Corporation. The top artificial sweetener is Equal, followed by Splenda and Sweet'N Low.

Salad Dressings

In colonial times, the most important salad dressing was vinegar and oil. As salads became more important in the 19th century, salad dressings increased in diversity. By 1900, dozens of different dressings were employed on various salads. Beginning in the late 19th century, salad dressings were commercialized, and seven major salad dressings emerged: Russian, Italian, blue cheese, Thousand Island, French, Caesar, and ranch. The most significant 19th-century manufacturers were the E. R. Durkee Company of New York City and Curtice Brothers of Rochester, New York. Durkee began issuing advertising cookbooklets featuring its products by 1875, and other salad dressing manufacturers followed at a later date. Other important early salad dressing manufacturers included Chicago's Tildesley & Company, which manufactured Yacht Club salad dressing.

Hidden Valley Ranch dressing was invented by Steve Henson of Santa Barbara, California, in the 1950s. His company sold dry dressing mix and later bottled it. The brand was purchased by the Clorox Company in 1972. Competitors duplicated the recipe and today ranch dressings reign as one of America's favorite dressing flavors along with blue cheese. Other common salad dressings include Italian, creamy Italian, Thousand Island, French, Caesar, Green Goddess, vinaigrette, and Russian.

Ethnic Condiments

During the second half of the 20th century, ethnic sauces greatly changed the American condiment foodscape. These sauces have been purveyed by restaurants and cookbooks. Manufacturers and importers have also promoted them. By far the most important ethnic condiment in the United States today is salsa, an import from Mexico that is commonly sold in **supermarkets** and is available in many fast food outlets, such as Taco Bell. The first known manufacturer of salsa was Pace Foods of San Antonio. Dave Pace experimented with bottling salsa in 1947 and finally succeeded in getting the formula right the following year. Pace's initial market was regional. The fresh salsa market exploded during the 1980s and continued to increase during the following decade. By the 1990s, salsa outsold ketchup.

A short list of other popular ethnic condiments includes soy sauce, pickled ginger, oyster sauce, wasabi (*Eutrema wasabi*) paste, guacamole, chutney, curry sauce, garam masala, and fish sauces. Dozens of other ethnic condiments are now commonly manufacturered in the United States.

FURTHER READINGS: Cohen, Rich. *Sweet and Low: A Family Story.* New York: Farrar, Straus, & Giroux, 2006; Packaged Facts. *The Condiments Market.* New York: Packaged Facts, 1991; Rinzler, Carol Ann. *The New Complete Book of Herbs, Spices, and Condiments: A Nutritional, Medical and Culinary Guide.* New York: Checkmark Books, 2001; Smith, Andrew F. *Pure Ketchup: The History of America's National Condiment.* Columbia: University of South Carolina Press, 1996.

Andrew F. Smith

Consumerism The concept of consumerism signifies the belief that individuals and social groups create meaning through their purchase and use of goods and services. It further denotes the social tendencies of people to identify strongly with products or services they consume, especially those with commercial brand names or status-enhancing appeal (for example, clothing, cars, and **gourmet food** items), as well as a pejorative critique of the identification and meaning-creation rituals that accompany such goods and services. The term has also been used to designate the movement advocating greater protection of consumers' interests within market-based settings.

Consumerism is based on the notion that the act of consumption possesses symbolic properties that represent group affiliation, lifestyle, and identity and will allow a consumer entrée into that world, as well as providing social groups with inclusion- and exclusion-based venues. Yet, by creating areas and occasions for sociability and group association (or lack thereof), consumerism also sets up divisive inequalities among people and groups.

What drives contemporary consumerism? Is it corporate interests that, through their marketing and **advertising** campaigns, ultimately determine what consumers want? Or is it consumers, whom producers and the corporate world must satisfy in order to stay in business and maintain profitability? These questions remain at the heart of the scholarly and popular critiques of consumerism and the consumer society as a powerful and driving social, political, and economic force in contemporary Western culture.

History

In 18th-century Europe, a consumer-oriented boom proved a necessary analogue to mass-production systems of the Industrial Revolution, which was more than just a revolution in industrially based ideas and practices. Beginning at this historical juncture, more men and women than ever before enjoyed the ability and experience of acquiring material possessions beyond those necessary for survival. Previously, extravagant consuming served important social and political functions for the upper classes, hindering the emergence of a mass-consumer society among the general population. The consumer boom required popular changes in attitude and thought related to the worlds of leisure, of invention and creation, and of demand for what was new, exciting, and modern. Material possessions became increasingly desired for their fashionability and stylishness, as well as more readily available on a legitimate and regular basis.

At the same time, critiques of consumerism as the exaggerated use of consumption practices to display one's wealth or social status were embedded in the writings of 19th-century social thinkers, including Thorstein Veblen, author of *Theory of the Leisure Class* and well known for developing the expression "conspicuous consumption." Central to Veblen's analyses, in particular, were the ideas that visible spending was a tool of social communication or indicator of class and income differences and that valuations of specific goods are widely shared by members of a society or social group.

The concept of consumer society that emerged in the 20th-century United States was that of a consumer culture, characterized by material acquisition and the use of mass-produced goods by individuals and households. Such practices intertwined consumerism with critical discussions of the function of mass culture in American life. Consumer culture is also exemplified in this case by the separation of life interests (such as different identity positions in work versus home or leisure) and the different consumption needs attached to each (for example, owning and wearing suits versus owning a dishwasher). Consumption of goods and services today remains one of the more important methods of participating in social life, one that requires significant amounts of energy on both the supply and demand sides to maintain socioeconomic viability.

Scholars and critics of consumerism today often follow Veblen in recognizing that the modern consumer society demonstrates the dominance of market processes in creating shared social and political meanings. Participation in the consumer culture requires wage work, time, and effort. Today, trade-offs between participation in consumer culture and production systems order daily social and economic life. Consumerism also engages the notion that increasing consumption of goods is beneficial for a strong growth economy. Some scholars even argue that 20th-century consumerism has provided more dynamic and popular public selves than political belief systems. Many of the activities that contribute to the activities and culture of everyday life, as well as to special occasions, are dominated by the consumption of goods and experiences in a variety of destination-based locations, including shopping malls, **restaurants**, **supermarkets**, department stores, city centers, and tourist destinations. Further, this market-based system encourages consumers to covet the end product with little consideration for the full, social costs of production.

Consumer goods, then, are frequently used as resources by individuals and social groups to understand and classify the social world, as unstable and ambiguous as it may be. Consumers are additionally invited by marketers and advertisers to desire certain identity and lifestyle ideals associated with different modes of consumption. The wide range of imagery to make commodities even more enticing and exciting than they already are makes the act of purchasing a sought-after experience in and of itself. Consumerism, in this light, becomes a social norm where the means (i.e., consumers) have become the end, or the accomplishment, of the modern means of production.

Critiques of Consumerism

The core argument of the consumerist critique is twofold. The first issue is "overbuying," or purchasing goods and services that are not necessary for subsistence or basic living. The argument against overbuying is frequently associated with wastefulness and the exaggeration of trivial differences in the creation and promotion of various consumer products. Hence, part of the culture of consumption is to criticize it. In addition, the meaning of "necessary for subsistence" has also transformed dramatically, especially given rapid advancements in technology in the 20th century. Many Americans would argue that cars and telephones are necessary parts of their lives. There are also different types of need. Who gets to say that someone needs a meal more than a new shirt? Functional and psychological usages of a good or a service do not necessarily differ, if someone is willing to pay for it. Perhaps a trendy new shirt is a necessary item, if the buyer's main inclination is toward style instead of warmth, or a **fast food** meal is an essential one, if the eater's preference is one of personal taste and filling an empty stomach. Personal tastes, especially, are simply an added value to the economic worth of an item, and people reveal their consummatory tastes by purchasing. If a person desires to own and consume more than is deemed "necessary" by critics, it is his own will (and wallet) that allows him to do so.

Second, critics of consumerism hold that the development of the American consumer culture is premised upon the removal of regulatory restrictions, whether they be institutionally or culturally driven, on access to goods. This assumes that the ability to pay market price for an item is the sole arbiter of its use and that consumers value certain goods based on their willingness to pay for them. Yet, most critics also recognize that the world of commodities has changed so that these differences can sometimes make all the difference for a consumer seeking to make an active choice among the myriad goods and services available.

Scholars of consumer culture also increasingly recognize the role of the consumer and consumerist ideologies as they translate into venues not previously considered within the paradigm of consumption, such as education, politics, and health care. In a highly consumer-oriented culture, key social values, identities, and processes associated with such concerns are negotiated through the paradigm of the consumer rather than the citizen as a significant identifying characteristic. Various consumer-oriented movements, such as the environmental movement or the voluntary simplicity movement, likewise seek to alter forms of production, market competition and exchange practices, the cultural codes characterizing consumption identities, and institutional arrangements that serve the interests of existing economic elites.

Countercultural consumers who participate in such movements often define themselves through embodied opposition to dominant lifestyle norms and mainstream consumer practices. Supporters of anticonsumerism movements argue against mass-production and mass-consumption practices that sustain corporate capitalist and industrial profits. Instead, they seek production standards they deem socially responsible (which also raise the prices of related goods), claiming that when goods are cheap, social impact costs (such as the treatment of workers, negative environmental effects, or "food miles") are high. Anticonsumerist activism exists at the levels of individual purchases, **boycotts** and protests, and attempts at change from activist groups as well as at systemic change from industry players.

Relationship to the Business of Food

Given the numerous issues of complexity and uncertainty that exist in the marketplace of food, watchdogs of corporate and industry citizenship are to be found not in the ranks of consumers but among individuals and organizations that have the resources and political opportunities to act at an institutional level. For example, it was not consumers voting with their pocketbooks who fought back against initial federal guidelines that would have allowed genetically modified and **irradiated** foods to be classified as **organic** under the **U.S. Department of Agriculture** labeling process. Rather, an organized, grassroots political movement spearheaded by a network of activist organizations, including the Organic Consumers Association and Greenpeace, structured the effort.

Additionally, countercultural consumer resistance that permeates the marketplace is often considered a marker of upper-middle-class or upper-class lifestyles. Continuing with the above example, organic food, which exists in the broader realm of alternative agricultural products, is frequently not available or accessible to populations with exclusionary financial concerns. Attempts to promote certain consumption patterns and ideologies as championing a greater good often do not take into account the structural barriers that prevent such consumption, or related political dimensions of such activities, in the first place. This provides a partial explanation of why a nickname for the natural foods specialist **Whole Foods Market** (a market-based advocate of alternative consumption practices and organic food production) is "Whole Paycheck."

In sum, even those who critique the embodiment of mass and popular culture in marketplace choices affirm their identity and their urge to differentiate themselves within a consumerist realm, further powering the expression of self and identity through consumer choice. In other words, consumers of organic food are still consumers. As such, consumers do play a critical role in determining the type of food system and industries that will emerge over the course of the 21st century, and consumerism is generally an important theme for and within the food industry. Food costs and nutritional quality have always influenced consumer choices. For culinary commodities, price, appearance, taste, and perceived health benefits drive consumers' rational and utility-maximizing choices. Through their purchases, consumers send strong messages to producers, retailers, and others in the industry about what they think is important in terms of social costs and qualities. With regard to the consumption of food and the food industry, consumerism's codes translate into increased variability in choices of foods and venues in which food is available to consume (restaurants, supermarkets, shopping malls, etc.). Thus, the tenets of consumerism and consumer culture shape choices and issues that broaden consumer perspectives and are meaningful for food production, distribution, and consumption decisions.

FURTHER READINGS: Cohen, Lizabeth. *A Consumers' Republic: The Politics of Mass Consumption in Postwar America.* New York: Alfred A. Knopf, 2003; Cross, Gary. *An*

All-Consuming Century: Why Commercialism Won in Modern America. New York: Columbia University Press, 2000; Veblen, Thorstein. *The Theory of the Leisure Class: an Economic Study of Institutions.* New York: Macmillan, 1899. Reprint, New York: Oxford University Press, 2007.

Michaela DeSoucey

Cookbooks. *See* Publishing.

Cooking Schools More than 1,000 career and recreational cooking schools and programs in America vie for students who want to master the culinary arts, hone their home cooking skills, or train for new professions or who just want novel vacations. While there have been cooking schools in the United States since the early 19th century, it has only been since 1946 that career-oriented culinary arts training was available. Formal culinary training is in greater demand because of the availability of jobs and the increased visibility of the role of a chef. This popularization of **celebrity chefs** in the media and elsewhere, combined with enthusiasm for **gourmet** and **ethnic foods**, have contributed to the renewed success of recreational cooking schools.

The first American cooking school grew out of the pastry shop Elizabeth Goodfellow opened in 1808 in Philadelphia. She soon began giving lessons and then expanded to public classes. From the Civil War to the turn of the 20th century, the number of cooking schools began to rise. A few of these catered to the interests of the wealthy, such as the French cooking schools that opened in New York City in the 1860s. More often, though, cooking schools were aimed at teaching poor or working-class women a trade or educating immigrant women how to cook frugally and adapt to American food. Some of these schools specialized in instructing future cooking teachers, who would then open their own schools.

By the 1870s, curricula began to contain not just cooking skills but also lessons in nutrition and domestic science. Important schools included the New York Cooking School (founded by Juliet Corson, who aimed much of her work at feeding the poor); the Boston Cooking School (later to be led by Fanny Merritt Farmer), and the Philadelphia Cooking School (founded by Sarah Tyson Rorer, who became a popular author, editor, and lecturer on the art of scientific cooking). The leaders of these schools extended their impact on American society with their popular cookbooks and teacher training. Fanny Farmer, who left the Boston Cooking School in 1902 to open her own institution, was very influential in the development and acceptance of precise measurements and clear directions in recipe writing. She also focused on promoting what was then considered healthy eating to a wide audience, including instructing doctors on how to feed invalids. Farmer felt her audience was the middle-class household, which she described as having a family of six and one servant.

Settlement houses for new immigrants, schools for Native Americans, and charities serving the poor also set up culinary training programs. At the other end of the spectrum were degree programs set up at colleges and universities to accommodate the rising number of women students and their interest in professional education. Early programs focused either on applied chemistry surrounding the science of food or on a combination of cooking classes, dietetics, and scientific household management, which would eventually be called "home economics."

Cooking schools continued like this until after World War II, when both vocational and recreational cooking schools would undergo some big changes. Historically most fine chefs in America had come from Europe, but even before the war, **restaurant** owners and managers felt that there was a shortage of available trained chefs. During the war, the shortage intensified. In February 1946, the New Haven Restaurant Association in Connecticut sought to train professional cooks through formal education rather than the European model of apprenticeship. The restaurateurs lent the fledging New Haven Restaurant Institute startup money, located space, and chose the school's first director. By May of that year, the first class of 50, all returning GIs taking advantage of their educational benefits, was enrolled. The school thrived, soon paying back the association's loan. Renamed the Culinary Institute of America (CIA), in 1970 the school moved to Hyde Park, New York. The school remains one of the most distinguished in the country, with 2,700 full-time students, more than 125 faculty members, and a second campus in California's Napa Valley.

Two developments helped pave the way for the success of cooking schools—support for vocational schools and a changing view of the culinary trade as a profession. Both still have impact on cooking schools today. Until about 1925, there was not strong backing for formal vocational or trade education, but that began to change and such training became more accepted. In the 1960s and '70s, federal funding for vocational programs increased by 400 percent, and culinary programs boomed. Viewing a chef as a professional rather than a tradesman began with the creation of culinary unions in 1910s. These early unions offered professional training and support. Today's associations, such as the American Culinary Federation (ACF), which has continuing education classes and accredits culinary programs, continue to build on this professionalism.

Top-Ranked U.S. Culinary Schools

1. The Culinary Institute of America: Hyde Park, New York; St. Helena, California
2. Johnson and Wales University: Providence, Rhode Island; North Miami, Florida; Denver, Colorado; Charlotte, North Carolina
3. Texas Culinary Academy: Austin, Texas
4. Sullivan University: Louisville, Kentucky
5. New England Culinary Institute: Montpelier, Vermont
6. Schoolcraft College: Livonia, Michigan
7. Western Culinary Institute: Portland, Oregon
8. The Art Institutes: Houston, Texas, and other locations
9. Orlando Culinary Academy: Orlando, Florida

Source: Based on information from Chef2Chef.net

Professional Culinary Arts Programs Today

There are some 432 cooking schools aimed at producing professional chefs in the United States in the most recent edition of the ShawGuides' *Guide to Career Cooking and Wine Schools.* Every state has at least one cooking or food service program. California offers the most programs, 58, and New York State is second with 41. Depending on the curriculum, accreditation and course length, these programs may offer diplomas or certificates, associate degrees, or bachelor's degrees in cooking and culinary arts, pastry and baking, and other specialties. Some also offer ACF chef certification or an additional diploma from the classical French Cordon Bleu training program. The ACF has accredited 169 postsecondary culinary schools. Schools can also be accredited by regional educational associations. These associations evaluate whether a program meets standards of instruction, content, and facilities.

Class length can be 8 to 10 weeks for a diploma or certificate course, which might give a basic overview to a beginner or specialized training to an experienced chef. Bachelor's degrees take four years, and most associate degree programs are two years long. Postsecondary culinary schools range from small to large and may be public or private, nonprofit or for-profit. Tuition ranges from $1,000 to $55,000 per program, with the lower end for community college or other public courses. Most schools offer financial aid.

A basic culinary education provides training in the science, food-handling safety and sanitation, and cooking skills. Students learn how to use commercial kitchen equipment, explore new technologies, and prepare restaurant meals. Courses might also include nutrition, menu planning, and managing a commercial kitchen. Many programs now include externships at restaurants and other food service facilities and some schools have on-site public restaurants as part of their training experience. Degree programs also include core classes in English, mathematics, and other subjects. Some schools incorporate the culinary theme in nonfood classes, such as using actual restaurant ledgers in accounting classes.

Food service as a career has been made more visible with the rise of cable and broadcast **television** and now Web-based cooking programming, reality television shows, and celebrity chefs. Professional cooking school enrollment went from 35,000 students in 1996 to more than 90,000 in 2006. Despite this increase in students, more than 90 percent are placed after graduation. The food service and restaurant job market is growing. The National Restaurant Association projects there will be more than 14.8 million industry workers in 2017, a two million increase from 2006. According to the Bureau of Labor Statistics, the median hourly earnings of chefs and head cooks in 2004 were $14.75. The the average earnings of the top-paid 10 percent of all chefs is $26.75, the lowest 10 percent $8.28. Other positions in the industry earned less. Almost two-thirds of all chefs, cooks, and other food preparation workers are employed in restaurants and other food and drink establishments. About one-fifth of them work in institutions such as universities and hospitals. Grocery stores, hotels, and other outlets employed the remainder. Some go into **publishing**, television, food styling, consulting, food writing, or recipe development.

Supplying culinary training programs is also a growing business. *Chef Educator Today* is a magazine with more than 15,400 culinary educator and school administrator subscribers. The magazine quotes a 2006 survey that says America's cooking schools spent an average of almost $11,000 on food every month for student training and more than $33,000 a year on new or used equipment.

America's appetite for trained food service workers has created educational programs aimed at helping unemployed or struggling individuals learn a new career. Food banks associated with America's Second Harvest organization offer 8-to-10-week training programs to their clients, many of them homeless or on **food stamps**. In 2005 there were 30 of these no-fee programs, enrolling about 1,000 students. The $4,000-per-student costs were mostly covered by donations. About 70 percent of the 775 students who graduated were employed within one month.

High schools also run culinary career programs for their students. Two industry organizations work to support those efforts. The Careers through Culinary Arts Program (C-CAP) assists public schools with vocational cooking classes to prepare students for jobs and postsecondary programs. It has worked with more than 550 teachers and 100,000 students. C-CAP has the largest independent culinary scholarship program in the nation. The National Restaurant Association Education Foundation also supports high school students through its ProStart mentoring program and competitions. More than 54,000 students and 1,300 schools have participated in ProStart.

Recreational Cooking Schools Today

If, after World War II, veterans turned to vocational chef training, others, especially women, turned to cookbooks, television cooking programs, and recreational cooking schools to explore some of the foreign influences that increased globalization and later travel had brought to home cooking. By the 1960s, cooking had made the transformation from domestic duty to creative outlet.

In 1947, Dione Lucas's television show, restaurant, and cooking school in New York were popular. By 1955, James Beard had opened his school in New York, which also boasted a program aimed at brides and the country's first Chinese cooking classes, but it wasn't until the 1961 publication of *Mastering the Art of French Cooking* by Julia Child, Louisette Bertholle, and Simone Beck and Child's subsequent television programs beginning in 1963 that recreational cooking schools began to boom. By the end of that decade, there were 15 cooking schools in New York City; by 1984, some 1,200 schools nationwide were members of the Association of Cooking Schools (now the International Association of Culinary Professionals). In the late 1980s, numbers declined, but 10 years later, recreational cooking programs began a resurgence sparked by many of the same cultural factors that have pushed up enrollment at career culinary schools. The ShawGuides' *Guide to Recreational Cooking Schools* has listings from 503 recreational cooking schools or programs in the United States. There are 30 listings for cooking-for-fun programs in New York City alone, ranging from bread baking to the foods of Austria, Italy, France, Asia, and more.

Taking in a regional-foods cooking class while on vacation has also become popular. Cooking schools in New Orleans, Santa Fe, and elsewhere offer such programs. Disney World now has cooking lessons aimed at both adults and children. The Holland America cruise line's staff and guest chefs lead cooking demonstrations and teach hands-on cooking lessons on the line's 12 ships. ShawGuides lists about 600 **culinary tourism** opportunities in America or taught in English worldwide from France to Morocco to Vietnam to India.

Other types of recreational cooking programs include in-home instruction, cooking class parties, programs and camps aimed at children, and classes and culinary contests designed to promote corporate or group teambuilding. An increasingly popular segment is the in-store cooking school. Retailers from gourmet stores and culinary specialty stores to giant **supermarkets** are using the schools to attract and retain customers, to familiarize them with new products, and, in some cases, for additional revenue. One example of this is the Viking Cooking School, which has 11 locations in the South, New York, Ohio, and California. The school teaches a full line of classes to more than 67,000 adults and children a year. An important part of its curriculum is the free one-hour Viking Test Drive, which allows participants to experience Viking's line of ranges, cookware, and other products. The schools all have retail stores on premises with a variety of food specialty items and kitchenware for sale.

FURTHER READINGS: American Culinary Federation. http://www.acfchefs.net; Bureau of Labor Statistics, U.S. Department of Labor. "Chefs, Cooks, and Food Preparation Workers." *Occupational Outlook Handbook, 2006–07.* http://www.bls.gov/oco/ocos161.htm; Careers through Culinary Arts. http://www.ccapinc.org/about.html; *Chef Educator Today.* http://www.chefedtoday.com; Culinary Institute of America. http://www.ciachef.com; Leahy, Kate. "Epicurean Edge: As the Culinary Institute of America Turns 60, A New Era Dawns for Students of Culinary Education." *Restaurants and Institutions,* May 2006. http://www.rimag.com/archives/2006/05b/culinary-institute-america-cia.asp; National Restaurant Association. "Restaurant Industry Facts." http://www.restaurant.org/research/ind_glance.cfm; National Restaurant Association Education Foundation. "The ProStart Program. http://www.nraef.org/prostart/; "Peterson's Culinary Schools." http://www.petersons.com/culinary/; Schenone, Laura. *A Thousand Years over a Hot Stove: A History of American Women Told through Food, Recipes and Remembrances.* New York: W. W. Norton, 2003; Schremp, Gerry. *Kitchen Culture: Fifty Years of Food Fads.* New York: Pharos Books, 1991; Shapiro, Laura. *Perfection Salad: Women and Cooking at the Turn of the Century.* New York: Farrar, Straus, & Giroux, 1986; ShawGuides. http://www.shawguides.com; Thurow, Roger. "To Tackle Hunger, A Food Bank Tries Training Chefs." *Wall Street Journal,* November 28, 2006; Viking Cooking School. http://www.vikingcookingschool.com.

Faith J. Kramer

Cooking Technology Cooking technology, ancient and modern, stems from the need to transfer heat to food items in order to transform them in some way. While many foods are edible in a raw state, cooking transforms the food items in various ways. Some foods are more readily available to the body cooked than raw, others are impractical to eat in a raw state, some are preserved via cooking, and many taste better and are, therefore, more desirable in a cooked state.

It is commonly asserted that the first form of cooking technology used was roasting. The origins of this form of cooking technology are lost in prehistory, but given what is known about the prehistorical period, this may be an accurate assumption. The oldest reliably identified remains of a cooking "hearth" dates to nearly 2 million years ago, and the site contains evidence of roasted meats as well as vegetables and seeds. Spit-roasting was likely an early improvement to open-hearth roasting. Spit-roasted meats were certainly known to the Mesopotamians, the authors of the earliest recipes yet found, which still exist in their original form on clay tablets in the Yale Babylonian Tablets Collection. Spit-roasting is also mentioned in Homer's *Odyssey.* Moist-heat cooking was also possible in the prehistoric period by means of holes dug in clay soil that were filled with water heated by the addition of hot stones.

Transfer of heat to food happens by one or more of four methodologies: conduction, convection, radiation, or induction. *Conduction* is the direct transfer of heat from a warmer area to a colder area. Applying heat to molecules increases their kinetic energy, and their ability to transfer this heat to adjacent molecules is the basis of conduction. Conduction is affected by various factors, including the temperature difference between the areas, the material used as the conductor, and the amount of surface contact between the conductor and material to be heated. The best conductors of heat are metallic solids, while liquids and gases are much less efficient conductors. Copper is a quick conductor of heat, but transfers the heat so quickly that pans made only from copper often scorch food, so copper is often combined with a less efficient conductor in the manufacture of cookware. Dark, nonshiny metallic surfaces absorb heat readily and are frequently used in baking vessels to shorten the amount of cooking time. Transfer of heat to a pan via contact with the element on an electric stove is an example of the conduction of heat.

Convection works by transferring heat energy into or out of an object by circulating a heated fluid or heated air around it. Convection can occur naturally as a result of differences in temperature, because heat rises and cold sinks due to the principle that molecules of heated air or liquid become less dense when they are heated. Boiling water for pasta or hard-cooking eggs is an example of natural convection at work. However, this action is rarely uniform in a given space, causing heated environments such as ovens to heat erratically—with the resultant uneven cooking of the food enclosed therein. Creating more uniform convection currents in an oven can improve the evenness of the cooking process. In cookery, therefore, convection is usually aided by a mechanical device such as a fan, a process known as *forced* (or *mechanical*) *convection*.

Radiation is the transfer of heat energy in the form of electromagnetic waves moving through space. Heat is transferred via infrared waves to any object in their path. Radiation is used in a number of ways in cookery, including in warming lamps used in **restaurants** and microwave ovens. Heat sources from glowing elements or coals are forms of infrared radiation, while microwave radiation is generated from a tube contained within the oven itself.

Induction is another form of the transfer of heat energy via electromagnetic waves. In induction cooking, a high-frequency electromagnetic field is produced by a coil, which then transfers the energy to a ferrous cooking vessel by means of a circulating current between the coil and the cooking vessel. This circulating current produces heat in the ferrous cooking vessel, but does not generate extraneous heat outside the cooking vessel, so all areas immediately adjacent to the cooking vessel remain cool. The heat that is generated in the cooking vessel is transferred to the food to be cooked via conduction. If contact between the coil and the ferrous cooking vessel is broken (or the energy to the coil is discontinued), heat generation ceases immediately.

The primary fuel sources for cooking are electricity and some form of gas (natural, butane, or propane). Historical sources of heat such as wood, charcoal, or coal are still in use and are used when a characteristic **flavor** is desired. Smoke is a desirable flavor in some dishes, and certain woods such as hickory, fruit woods, and mesquite are in demand as heat sources that also impart distinctive flavors to the food item being cooked over them.

Cooking appliances are based on some form of heat transfer, and most use some combination of heat transfer methods. One of the most common forms of cooking technology is the kitchen range. This appliance comes in many forms, from the most basic household model to intricate commercial versions, but they are similar in terms of their basic functioning. The standard range comes in gas or electric versions and has a series of burners on the top and an oven underneath the burners. While most household versions include some type of broiling device, this is usually not the case in commercial versions, where broilers tend be a separate freestanding device. Some ranges today come with convection (fan-assisted) ovens. Ranges can be built-in or freestanding.

While ovens are frequent additions to cooktops, freestanding ovens are often used in commercial food service. While there are many examples of ovens using ordinary heated cavities, such as the deck oven and the carousel oven, there are also many specialized ovens in use in food service. One of the most common specialized ovens is the convection oven, a versatile piece of equipment found in many types of operations. It is useful because it eliminates warm and cold spots in ovens due to the forced convection provided by the built-in fan. This causes baked goods to cook more evenly with uniform browning, for example. The convection oven is also useful in the production of roasted meat items. Meats can be roasted at a lower temperature in a convection oven, thereby saving energy costs, and the finished product generally retains more of its natural moisture, resulting in a more desirable product.

An offshoot of the convection oven is the "combi-oven." The combi-oven is an oven that has the ability to inject steam into the oven cavity. This results in baked goods with a crisper crust. Most combi-ovens can be used in regular oven, steam oven, or convection oven modes, or in some combination thereof, hence the name. Combi-ovens are useful for rethermalizing prepared foods as well as cooking raw food products.

"Impinger ovens" are used for the rapid cooking of foods when quick browning is important. They use a conveyor to move food through a superheated cavity, where small jets direct the hot air over all surfaces of the food. Impinger ovens are commonly used in pizza operations, for example, to cook pizzas in about one-fourth the time required in a traditional deck oven.

Microwave ovens are in wide use in both foodservice operations and the home. Microwave ovens use a magnetron (a vacuum tube that generates microwaves) to cook food. The microwaves generated penetrate partway into the food and trigger the rotation of molecules more than two billion times a second, causing the food to cook from the heat of the friction buildup. Microwaves penetrate only about one to two inches into the food. The rest of the food product is heated via conduction from the areas where the microwaves penetrate and cause heat. Microwave ovens are popular due to the speed at which they heat food, which can be as little as one-tenth the time required in a regular oven or stovetop. Microwave ovens may be better for nutrient retention, too, as the food is subject to nutrient-destroying temperatures for shorter periods of time. Microwave ovens are best used for small amounts of food and are unsuited for baking and roasting, because browning does not occur during the cooking process. Uneven heating can be a problem in microwave cookery, although this can be alleviated by using a turntable in the microwave or manually turning the food as it heats.

Deep-fat fryers are used in nearly every genre of restaurant and in home kitchens as well. They are popular for the taste and texture of the foods prepared in them. Deep-fat fryers can use either gas or electricity as a fuel source. They have a well for oil, which is heated by some type of element or burner below the well; electric fryers use a heating element that is in contact with the fat itself. Deep-fat fryers come in two general varieties—open fryers and pressure fryers—although some specialty fryers exist as well. Open fryers are the most common of the two types and are used for a wide variety of products, including the ubiquitous French fry. Pressure fryers are less common and are used mostly for meat products, where they aid in moisture retention and reduce oil uptake in food products. Moisture loss is a problem in deep frying, because the high temperature of deep frying (often 350°F or more) tends to vaporize water in the product. Specialty fryers include donut fryers and chicken fryers.

There are a variety of steam-operated appliances for commercial kitchens. These generally can be divided into steamers and steam-heated kettles. Steamers are commercial versions of stovetop steam cookers and generally operate with pressurized steam, which cooks the food very quickly. Steamers are popular in commercial operations due to their ability to cook food rapidly without moisture and nutrient loss. They operate by injecting steam into a closed cavity, usually under a pressure of 10–15 psi. There are also pressureless versions available for use with more delicate foods. In either case, steam can be generated in a central boiler and delivered to the device via a plumbing network, or the steam can be generated within the appliance itself.

Steam-heated kettles, also known as steam-jacketed kettles, are used for the cooking and rethermalization of liquid foods and foods cooked in large amounts of liquid such as pasta. The steam is not introduced to the kettle, but circulates inside a cavity between the kettle's inner and outer walls. Steam kettles range in capacity from 1 quart to 200 gallons. As with steamers, the steam can be generated internally or delivered from an external source. Kettles may be stationary or tilting, the latter being useful for decanting of the product from the kettle. Due to the pressure of the steam being used, boiling temperatures can be achieved very quickly in a steam-heated kettle.

Sous vide, from the French for "under vacuum," is a method of cooking food in plastic bags at a lower temperature than those employed in conventional cooking methods. In the sous vide process, food is vacuum-packed in a form of reduced oxygen **packaging** (ROP), which creates an anaerobic environment for the food contained within. The food is cooked immersed in water at a low temperature (anywhere from 105°F to 190°F, depending on the producer) inside the ROP. This process takes anywhere from several minutes for vegetables to several hours for meats. Advocates of this method of cookery cite nutrient retention and improved flavor and texture as its benefits. However, the fact that some foods take so long to properly cook using this medium is of concern to public health agencies, including the Food and Drug Administration. The anaerobic environment created by the process is beneficial to the growth of certain foodborne illness-causing microorganisms, which may not be killed by the lower cooking temperatures. The method is in wide use in Europe and has been approved, with stipulations, in the United States, although some local health departments have not approved it for use in restaurants.

Induction cooktops are the newest type of cooking technology. As described above, the induction cooktop works by generating a powerful electromagnetic field that heats a ferrous pan in contact with the coil. Induction cooktops can be built into the top of a regular range, but are often portable. They are popular in commercial foodservice due to the fact that they can be safely used to generate high temperatures, yet are portable and do not have the attendant hazards of open flame.

There is some argument about the term *cooking* and whether it should include foods that do not involve some kind of change of state induced by the application of heat. Some argue that foods not transformed by heat should be referred to as *prepared*, not cooked. If change of state by some other means than the application of heat is included in the definition, then the category of cooking by chemical change must be added as a cooking technology. An example of this would be ceviche, where raw fish undergoes a change of state due to the application of a highly acidic liquid, usually some kind of lemon or lime juice. Under the broader definition, salted foods that dehydrate enough to be preserved and made edible would be included as well.

FURTHER READINGS: Bottéro, Jean. *The Oldest Cuisine in the World: Cooking in Mesopotamia.* Trans. Teresa Lavender Fagan. Chicago: University of Chicago Press, 2004; Brown, Amy C. *Understanding Food: Principles and Preparation.* Belmont, CA: Wadsworth/Thompson Learning, 2004; Drysdale, J. *Foodservice Equipment: Operation, Sanitation, and Maintenance.* Overland Park, KS: Hospitality Publishing, 2002; Elert, Glenn. *The Physics Hypertextbook.* Retrieved January 19, 2007, from http://hypertextbook.com/physics/; Fisher, Don. *Commercial Cooking Appliance Technology Assessment.* Food Service Technology Center Report No. 5011.02.26. San Ramon, CA: Fisher-Nickel. Retrieved January 30, 2007, from http://www.fishnick.com/publications/techassessment/; Wright, Clifford A. *A Mediterranean Feast: The Story of the Birth of the Celebrated Cuisines of the Mediterranean, from the Merchants of Venice to the Barbary Corsairs.* New York: Morrow, 1999.

Jeffrey Miller

Corn Maize (*Zea mays*) or corn was likely domesticated more than once from wild species of teosinte in central Mexico, Guatemala, or Honduras beginning about 8,000 years ago. It spread from Mesoamerica to North and South America in prehistoric times. All major pre-Columbian New World civilizations in Central America, North America, and to a lesser extent South America were based on the cultivation of maize. The Spanish were the first Europeans to encounter corn, and they introduced it into Europe. It quickly spread throughout the Mediterranean, where it was mainly employed as an animal feed grain, but its culinary usage was well established by the 18th century. In Italy, for instance, corn became the basis of the traditional dish polenta. Similar dishes appeared in southeastern and southwestern France about the same time. At an early date, corn was exported from the Mediterranean into the Ottoman Empire, eastern Europe, Asia, and Africa.

In North America, corn was a staple of many American Indian groups, who passed along the methods of growing and preparing it to European colonists. Beginning in the 17th century, farmers grew corn and used it for many purposes, including for bakery goods, livestock feed, and manufacturing alcohol. By the mid-nineteenth century, fresh corn began to be **canned**, and by the time of the Civil War, corn was one of the most important commercially processed foods in America.

Commodity Corn and Corn Products

Historically, corn sold for commercial purposes was stored and transported in burlap sacks. In 1856, the Chicago Board of Trade instituted a system of weighing, grading, and pricing corn. This meant that corn grown in one location was essentially the same as corn of the same grade grown elsewhere. Commodity corn became the basis for today's businesses related to corn.

By the mid-19th century, commodity corn was converted into various products, the most important of which was cornstarch. It was initially used in the laundry business, but cooks and early food processors soon began adding cornstarch to food. From cornstarch, refiners figured out how to make corn syrup, which became a cheap substitute for cane **sugar**.

As the 19th century progressed, corn was used for making other products. In the 1890s, John Harvey Kellogg rolled corn into flakes and served it as a **breakfast cereal** at his sanatorium in Battle Creek, Michigan. His brother, W. K. Kellogg, launched the Kellogg Toasted Corn Flake Company. Their efforts were duplicated by others, such as C. W. **Post**, who began manufacturing a vast array of cereals.

Corn sweeteners were initially based on glucose, which was less sweet than sucrose made from sugarcane. Chemists improved their products, and by the 1960s, they were making sweeteners that were sweeter than cane sugar, and high-fructose corn syrup (HFCS) became a major product used in many processed foods—particularly in the production of **soft drinks** such as Coca-Cola, Pepsi, and 7-Up.

Hybrids and Bioengineered Corn

Up to the mid-20th century, farmers alternated growing corn and legumes in their fields with raising cows. Legumes generated nitrogen in the soil for the corn, and the animals that fed on the corn produced fertilizer for the corn and the legumes. This began to change in the 1930s when corn **hybrids** were introduced commercially. With the vast expansion of chemical **fertilizers** in the 1950s, corn yields exploded. Using synthetic fertilizers, farmers could grow corn without the need to alternate with legumes or use the natural fertilizer produced by cows. Bioengineered corn was introduced during the 1990s. As of 2004, 45 percent of the corn planted in the United States was biotech. These changes lowered the cost of corn, making it profitable to fatten cattle in feedlots and use corn for making other products.

Price Supports

Until the 1930s, corn prices were controlled by normal market mechanisms. When supply was greater than demand, prices fell; when supply was less than demand, prices declined. During the Depression, however, the federal government created programs to limit the production of corn to help farmers avert overproduction. In the early 1970s, these programs were reversed, and farmers began receiving economic subsidies for growing more corn. At the beginning of the 21st century, the federal government gives about $5 billion of subsidies to farmers to produce low-cost corn. One reason for this program is that the price of corn greatly influences the price of other foods and products. Corn, for instance, is used to feed animals. Low-cost corn means lower-costing **beef** and chickens.

Corn Companies

The two largest companies in the corn business are Cargill and Archer Daniels Midland (ADM). Both companies make and sell pesticides and fertilizers to farmers, who grow corn; in turn, they buy about one-third of the total corn crop. This corn is used for animal feed, for export to other countries, and for making products such as HFCS, citric acid, sugars (glucose and fructose), starches, and alcohols (for alcoholic beverages as well as ethanol for use in cars). Neither company, however, sells products directly to consumers. Companies that use the products made by Cargill and ADM include Kellogg's and General Mills for cereal and PepsiCo and Coca-Cola for soda.

Corn Today

In 2004, the United States produces more than 11 billion bushels (more than 600 billion pounds) of corn, which was 43 percent of the world's total corn production. Of the American crop, 45 percent is used for animal feed, 13 percent is used for making ethanol and alcohol, and 8 percent goes into manufacturing HFCS and other sweeteners.

See also Agribusiness.

FURTHER READINGS: Fussell, Betty. *The Story of Corn: The Myths and History, the Culture and Agriculture, the Art and Science of America's Quintessential Crop.* New York: Alfred A. Knopf, 1992; Pollan, Michael. *The Omnivore's Dilemma: A Natural History of Four Meals.* New York: Penguin, 2006; Smith, Andrew F. *Popped Culture: A Social History of Popcorn in America.* Washington, DC: Smithsonian Institution Press, 2001; Smith, C. Wayne, Javier Betrán, and E. C. A. Runge. *Corn: Origin, History, Technology, and Production.* Hoboken, NJ: Wiley, 2004; Sprague, G. F., and J. W. Dudley, eds. *Corn and Corn Improvement.* 3rd ed. Madison, WI: American Society of Agronomy, 1988; Staller, John E., Robert H. Tykot, and Bruce F. Benz, eds. *Histories of Maize: Multidisciplinary Approaches to the Prehistory, Linguistics, Biogeography, Domestication, and Evolution of Maize.* Burlington, MA: Elsevier Academic Press, 2006.

Andrew F. Smith

Culinary Tourism Culinary tourism is both a recent trend within the tourism industry and a scholarly framework for exploring culture through food. It can be defined as traveling for food, traveling through food, eating out of curiosity, or integrating food into tourism. It can refer to specific tourism destination sites, such as **restaurants**, vineyards, and original homes of a particular food or to types of tourism that incorporate the intangible culture surrounding food, such as cooking classes, sharing of recipes, shopping in native markets, or uses of natural resources.

Although people have always traveled in order to obtain certain foods and have always eaten while traveling, such culinary tourism as a specific and systematic business trend has emerged in the tourism industry only since the beginning of the millennium. Several organizations promoting culinary tourism have developed, notably the Canadian Culinary Tourism Association, the Oregon Culinary Tourism Association, and the International Culinary Tourism Association (ICTA).

The ICTA is now taking the lead in establishing the goals and parameters of the field, stating its purpose as offering advice on "how to develop and market a new kind of visitor attraction—unique and memorable food and drink experiences." To that end, ICTA maintains a list of tour operators throughout the world (currently only in Italy, Australia, South Africa, and the United States), offers a website and publications, and holds an annual conference. The founder and president of ICTA, Erik Wolf, offers workshops promoting culinary tourism and **published** a book explaining this new industry, *Culinary Tourism: The Hidden Harvest.* Much of Wolf's work focuses on justifying culinary tourism as a profitable business (hence the title of his "white paper" publication in 2004, "Culinary Tourism: A Tasty Economic Proposition") and offering strategies for creating products and sites and developing markets. Wolf observes that "nearly 100% of tourists dine out when traveling and that dining is consistently one of the top three favorite tourist activities." He also notes correlations between the amounts spent by tourists on food and on other items: higher dinner bills generally represent higher amounts spent on other entertainments and **hospitality** services. Although conclusive numbers are not yet available in such a new industry, Wolf points out that the economic benefits of culinary tourism are tremendous.

Culinary tourism as an academic concept originated with folklorist Lucy Long, who first published on the topic in 1998. Her book, *Culinary Tourism: Eating and Otherness,* came out in 2004 and offers a framework for broadening our understanding of both tourism and food. This framework has been adapted by the tourism industry. Her definition of culinary tourism is "the intentional, exploratory participation in the foodways of another—participation including the consumption, preparation, and presentation of a food item, cuisine, meal system, or eating style considered to belong to a culinary system not one's own."

From this perspective, culinary tourism deals with the negotiation of both exotic and familiar foods. Foods have to be different enough to elicit curiosity, but familiar enough to be considered edible. Of course, exoticness or "Otherness" is a matter of perspective and can be based on factors other than culture. Region, time (past or future), ritual, ethos or religion, socioeconomic class, gender, and age can all offer foods that are different for an eater. For example, kosher foods might be exotic for non-Jews; alcohol for teenagers; stews cooked in a iron kettle over an open fire for modern-day eaters; **vegetarian** foods for an omnivore; and quiche for "real men." This approach to Otherness expands the possibilities of what foods can be available for tourism. Familiar foods can carry memories of the past and be reminders of people and places. Culinary tourism in one's own kitchen means looking differently at everyday, familiar foods as a possible adventure into one's own culture.

Culinary tourism looks beyond **gourmet** dishes to foodways, the total network of activities surrounding food and eating. This network includes procurement (obtaining food), preservation, preparation, presentation, consumption styles, contexts for eating, cleaning up, and symbolic performance. Individuals attach different meanings to foods because they have different memories associated with these components. For example, a fish caught in the local river during a family vacation might taste the same as one shipped in from a commercial distributor, but it carries memories of those people and events. This suggests then that venues for tourism can extend beyond the usual restaurants and **wine** tours to include cookbooks, cookware shops and catalogues, grocery stores, films, literature, **television** cooking shows, **advertising**, and **food festivals**. These venues are being used by the tourism industry to develop products, such as tours combining cooking classes and sightseeing, or weekend home-stays with families in another country in which the tourist assists with farming, shopping, and cooking in order to experience that culture through its foodways.

Historically, the two countries most associated with culinary tourism are Italy and France. Both have highly developed and respected cuisines, and both have native populations that are knowledgeable and willing to travel within their own countries for food experiences. Both also boast historical and contemporary cultures of wine consumption, often tied to strong family traditions of vineyards and vintners. Furthermore, Italy is home to the **Slow Food** movement, which advocates taking time to appreciate locally grown, well-prepared food. Started by Carlo Petrini, this movement is now international and tied to culinary tourism in that it promotes artisanal food production and leisurely, respectful consumption.

Canada, Australia, Great Britain, and the United States are at the forefront of culinary tourism as an industry trend. These countries are actively developing "destination restaurants," tours around food experiences, and foods that can be used as "brands" or symbols of a place. Wine tends to be the most common type of food for culinary tourism, lending easily to tours of vineyards and wineries, classes in wine tasting, and pairings of fine food and fine wines in restaurants. Also, wine historically is associated with fine dining and high-priced restaurants.

Other countries are becoming popular sites for culinary tours. These tend to have distinctive cuisines that appeal to Western tastes. Spain, Mexico, China, and Thailand are currently the most popular. However, more countries are being explored as such tourism proves successful. These countries also draw upon the complexity of regional cuisines within their own borders.

While tourism tends toward gourmet cuisines and dishes, any food associated with a place can become the focus of culinary tourism, for example, maple syrup in New England, beef in Argentina, lobster in Maine, crawfish in Louisiana, or grits in the Southern United States. Some cities become associated with particular foods—Cincinnati with chili; Kansas City or Memphis, barbecue; Boston, baked beans; Philadelphia, cheesesteak. Tourists often intentionally eat those foods in order to better "experience the place," and restaurants catering to tourists frequently market the foods that way. These iconic foods are also seen represented on tourist items, such as clothing, souvenirs, and gift items, and even on license plates and tourism brochures. In addition, groups of people may be associated with particular foods, such as the dishes of the Cajuns in Louisiana, the Amish in Ohio and Pennsylvania, Germans in the Midwest, and Native Americans throughout the country; food industries (restaurants and product producers) frequently develop specifically to offer those cuisines to tourists.

Culinary tourism is closely related to other varieties of tourism. It is frequently included in cultural tourism, in which tourists travel to a country to actively learn about and experience that culture. Food, in this case, is often presented as foodways and as a way to discover everyday life as well as to share a sense of community with members of that culture (or at least with the tour group). Many festivals, both at home and abroad, offer a site for cultural tourism, presenting specialty dishes intentionally selected to represent a cuisine.

Another related concept is agritourism. This usually consists of farm tours, observing or possibly participating in farm activities such as milking cows or harvesting crops, or tours of food-processing and manufacturing establishments, such as **canneries**, cheese-making facilities, or factories. For obvious reasons, agritourism tends to focus on rural areas, while culinary tourism is frequently urban with access to restaurants.

Heritage tourism can also be tied to culinary tourism. Living history museums often allow for the exploration of foodways of the past, with demonstrations of food preparation. Interpreters usually give explanations of such activities as cutting apples, baking bread, or working in the garden. In some venues, visitors are given the opportunity to participate, or at least to taste some of the results. Colonial Williamsburg in Virginia and Plimoth Plantation in Massachusetts are notable for developing displays of this sort.

Ecotourism, in which the focus is on exploring the natural environment without damaging it, many times also includes culinary tourism by including meals utilizing locally produced and **organic** foods.

A new type of tourism that can also be connected to culinary tourism is "extreme tourism," in which tourists test the boundaries of safety or social and cultural appropriateness. "Extreme cuisine" tests the boundaries of edibility and palatability, involving foods not usually considered "normal" or tasty in the tourist's home culture.

Issues within the culinary tourism industry involve the health safety of restaurants or tour sites, the authenticity of foods offered, and the ownership of traditions and recipes (food as intellectual property), as well as the cultural implications of culinary tourism. Food carries identity and reflects history and a specific group's adaptations of natural resources. By highlighting certain foods over others, inventing dishes, and constructing menus, tourism creates images of a place, cuisine, or culture. Since many people's understandings of a culture are through tourism, the industry needs to be aware of its possible impact.

FURTHER READINGS: Long, Lucy, ed. *Culinary Tourism: Eating and Otherness*. Lexington: University Press of Kentucky, 2004; Kirshenblatt-Gimblett, Barbara. *Destination Culture: Tourism, Museums, and Heritage*. Berkeley: University of California Press, 1998; Petrini, Carlo. *Slow Food: The Case for Taste*. New York: Columbia University Press, 2004; Sharples, Liz, Richard Mitchell, Nik Macionis, Brock Cambourne, and C. Michael Hall, eds. *Food Tourism around the World: Development, Management and Markets*. Oxford, U.K.: Butterworth-Heineman, 2003; Wolf, Erik. *Culinary Tourism: The Hidden Harvest*. Dubuque, IA: Kendall/Hunt, 2006.

Lucy M. Long

Cultural Imperialism Cultural imperialism is the practice whereby a culture, society, or nation imposes its cultural practices and institutions upon another culture, in the process weakening or destroying traditional elements of that other culture. Aspects of culture that may be the target of such imperialism include language, religion, dress, the arts (music, literature), and media (**television**, film). Food and cuisine—defining elements of many cultures worldwide—are often subject to cultural imperialism. In recent years, citizens of various nations have protested the infiltration of their nations' foodways by American **fast food** culture, a move that many regard to be culturally imperialistic, because the appeal of the American products erodes interest in local food traditions and undermines the continued viability of those traditions and the values that they embody.

Cultural imperialism may be carried out by governmental agencies, corporate entities, or less formally organized groups of individuals. Its mechanisms may range from rendering particular cultural practices illegal to more subtle, even benign, activities that may be welcomed by some members of the occupied culture (who regard them as signs of progress, development, or modernization).

Cultural imperialism historically has often both supported and been supported by other forms of imperialism, such as economic and political imperialism; it frequently has been employed in connection with these other forms of imperialism as a way to make them more resilient and resistant to dismantling. However, in the present era, in which instances of colonial occupation by a foreign government are less common than in the 19th and early 20th centuries, cultural imperialist relationships may exist even in the absence of other forms of imperialism; they are fueled by the actions of **multinational** corporations. The result is that cultural imperialist relations may exist even between two First World nations—the United States and France, for instance. A cultural imbalance of power exists even between these two nations, as illustrated by the fact that American-owned food **franchises** have exerted no small influence upon the venerable French food scene, much to the dismay of many in the French food industry.

Cultures experiencing cultural imperialism often experience the erosion as a violation—an erasure of their people's identity and a diminution of their culture's distinctiveness. Historically, such suppression of a culture has met with creative resistance, which may take myriad forms, ranging from official government edict to informal, ad hoc actions on the part of individuals.

Cultural imperialism is related to, yet distinct from, the less discussed phenomenon of cultural colonialism. The latter practice involves appropriating the social and cultural practices of a dominated culture and taking them up into one's own culture, whereas imperialism involves the imposition of one's culture upon another. Thus cultural colonialism might be seen manifested in Euro-American entrepreneurial efforts to create mass-market versions of "**ethnic foods**," while the worldwide popularization of American fast foods would exemplify cultural imperialism.

Cultural Imperialism in Support of Colonialism

Countries that have engaged in cultural imperialism have frequently done so as part of a larger campaign of political and economic imperialism. An invading nation may impose food, religion, or dress upon its colonized subjects, broadcasting the message that indigenous practices are "backward," "dirty," or "unsophisticated." Such impositions have the cumulative effect of eroding the morale of the colonized culture, leading at least some of its members to believe in their own cultural inferiority and thus the rightness of colonial rule.

In its most extreme forms, an occupying nation may use its official governmental institutions—the military, the education system, the court system—to suppress the cultural practices of the occupied nation, thereby weakening its identity and threatening its cultural cohesion. Cultural practices have been made illegal, subjected to fine or imprisonment, and expressly "taught against" in schools run by imperial powers. One notorious example of such culturally imperialistic practices in the United States involved forcible removal of Indian children to federally run boarding schools, at which they were forbidden to speak their own language, had their hair shorn and their clothing replaced with Euro-American dress, and were taught to embrace Euro-American occupations. The practice, colloquially termed "kill the Indian; save the man" (a statement allegedly made by Richard Henry Pratt, founder of the Carlisle Indian School), had as its explicit and intended goal the elimination of Indian nations as culturally distinct entities.

Many other, less draconian ways existed by which an imperial culture imposed itself upon another. Foods—including particular ingredients and styles of cooking—were among those aspects of culture that the colonizing nations of Europe used to illustrate their purported superiority over local populations. In British-occupied India, for instance, British colonials pointedly shunned the local cuisines and went to great lengths to ensure an uninterrupted access to traditional British foods. Clearly, this plan failed; various Indian culinary traditions came to exert considerable influence upon the traditional British diet, to the point that various "Indian-inspired" dishes such as curry are today regular features of British **restaurant** menus.

Cultural Imperialism in a Postcolonial World

In the contemporary era, often termed the "postcolonial era," literal, physical colonial occupation by foreign governments is relatively rare, but the residue of the European and American colonial activity remains both in the former colonizing nations and in the former colonies. Today, global economic and political power is often wielded by multinational corporations, whose incomes rival the gross national product of small nations. In the wake of these new global forces, cultural imperialism has assumed new shapes and purposes.

A multinational corporation interested in increasing its share of the world market for its product likely will not have, as an explicit goal, eliminating an indigenous culture per se. In this sense, cultural imperialism of this postcolonial sort differs from the imperial practices of earlier colonial governments, where such cultural erasure was sometimes stated government policy. Instead, a corporation may aim simply to create a market for its product in a new locale, by making the product appealing or alluring to the local population. Because these outside cultural influences are sometimes wholeheartedly embraced by members of a local culture, some would question the legitimacy of calling this a form of imperialism, a term that seems to presume force or coercion, not willing acquiescence. This more benign corporate aim may nevertheless produce the same net effect, because the desirability of the new imported product tends to make indigenous products and practices undesirable by comparison.

The products of multinational corporations, which usually have both a financial and a cultural base in the United States or another First World nation, can come to possess such popularity in a given region that local traditions and institutions may fall out of favor and wither away. The example of U.S.-based fast food corporations is often regarded as a paradigm of this form of cultural imperialism; "fast food culture" is being blamed worldwide for spreading the notion that "West is best."

As they make their presence felt in a culture, the American fast foods are welcomed by at least some members of the local culture as signs of modernization, of Westernization (Americanization), or of progress. Children and teens may be particularly inclined to regard these newcomers in a favorable light, both because children tend to be more vulnerable to the effects of **advertising** and because they may be inclined (or encouraged) to regard their parents' and grandparents' more traditional ideas as old-fashioned or out of step with the times. Local foods—and the cultural ways that surround them—fall out of favor, first with young people but often eventually with members of older generations as well. No military or political force is needed to effect this cultural transformation; a corporation uses the power of advertising to cultivate an image of the attractiveness of American culture and to link their particular products to this alluring image.

American-style fast food has come to have—or to be perceived as having—such popularity in nations as diverse and far flung as China, Mexico, and France that those who would protect the traditional foodways of these nations have expressed grave concerns about the future sustainability of those traditions and the values they represent. Critics of such corporate incursions point to the fact that the characters used to advertise fast food may be more well known to children than are images of worldwide religious figures, national politicians, or locally important personages. The terms "McDonaldization" and "Coca-Colonialism" illustrate these critics' beliefs that corporations such as **McDonald's** and Coca-Cola are having a homogenizing effect upon cultures worldwide, replacing local versions of quick meals and **soft drinks** with products that are highly sought after for their Western/American cachet.

Notably, corporations may wield such cultural power even in economically powerful First World nations. In a postcolonial world, cultural imperialism may go on even between countries that exhibit neither financial nor political dependencies upon each other; an imbalance of cultural power may still exist. American-style fast food is again a prime example; a "typical businessman's lunch" in First World industrial Japan is a Big Mac and a Coke, eaten standing up.

Resisting Cultural Imperialism

As the foregoing paragraphs have suggested, cultural imperialism is understood as a threat by persons who see their cultures being eroded by incursions from without.

If cultural imperialism is not resisted, the hegemonic culture—the culture that wields cultural power—will eventually replace all cultures of the world, transforming everywhere into "nowhere in particular." While global homogenization of cultures may seem an unlikely prospect, the possibility is very great that less powerful, localized ways of being will disappear in the face of competition from more powerful American-based ways.

Critics of cultural imperialism and advocates for local cultures have utilized a variety of methods for staving off this threat. The example of food is particularly illustrative; because of the importance food holds in many cultures, the efforts to protect it show considerable variety and ingenuity, ranging from official government policy to guerrilla action.

In the latter category, French farmer José Bové made world headlines when he rammed a bulldozer into a half-built McDonald's outlet to protest the fast food chain's contribution to *malbouffe*—bad food. In India, protesters burned chickens outside the first KFC outlet to open in the country. Across the globe, concerned—often deeply angry—local residents have turned out to protest the arrival of American fast food in their neighborhoods, using both peaceful and sometimes violent means to do so.

Other, more structural forms of resistance also abound. One organization that has emerged in part as a response to the spread of "fast food culture" is the Italian organization **Slow Food**, founded by Carlo Petrini, which is now spreading across the globe. Governmental policy has also been enlisted to stave off cultural imperialist threats to a country's food. The French Ministry of Culture in 1989 created a separate branch, dedicated to the culinary arts, partly to combat the dangerous threat the government perceived in the spread of fast food.

It is important to note that cultural exchange and interchange are inevitable and ongoing, and that cultures are always already composites of many influences. There are no "pure cultures," and the aim of eliminating cultural imperialism is not to protect a culture from all outside influences, which would be both impossible and undesirable. Not all cultural exchanges are culturally imperialistic. Furthermore, even when a culture has been the victim of cultural imperialist forces, that culture does not remain always or only a victim of those forces; creative forces from within a culture may work to incorporate the imperialist influences into the local culture, thereby making them their own and reclaiming the power to define their own culture in the process. The cuisine of Vietnam, for instance, illustrates an interesting example of such absorption and digestion of foreign elements. Various French foodstuffs and styles of food preparation—including some dairy products, coffee, and consommé-type soups—have become integral parts of Vietnamese cuisine. Thus have the dietary incursions of the former colonizer been taken up and made "local."

FURTHER READINGS: Said, Edward W. *Culture and Imperialism*. New York: Knopf, 1993. Reprint, New York: Vintage, 1994; Watson, James L., ed. *Golden Arches East: McDonald's in East Asia*. Stanford, CA: Stanford University Press, 1997.

Lisa Heldke

D ❖ —————————————————————————

Dairy Industry Over the past two centuries, the U.S. dairy industry has grown from a small-scale domestic enterprise to a large and influential industry that comprises about 10 percent of the total agricultural economy. Domesticated cows originally were brought to North America from Europe by Spanish friars and British settlers, and by the 18th century, dairy production was well established. But for the most part, dairy product production remained a largely local enterprise up through the mid-19th century, when growth in urban areas created a new market that necessitated changes in milk production and distribution.

With a rise in demand for milk among urbanites, large numbers of cows were penned in dairies just outside northeastern cities to minimize transportation time for milk. They were frequently fed swill, the remains of alcohol fermentation. Conditions were unhygienic, and "swill milk" was widely viewed as poor quality and often contaminated with microbes. Improvements in roads and railroads, especially those with ice-cooled cars, allowed for milk to be transported to cities from more distant rural farms, where milk was produced under cleaner conditions and was less likely to make its consumers ill.

The transport of milk over any distance requires some means of effective preservation, because fresh milk is extremely vulnerable to spoilage by **bacterial** contamination. In this way, the dairy industry is subject to constraints not faced by other kinds of food industries. Milk must be collected daily and swiftly moved to the market. Its quality deteriorates rapidly, and it requires continual **refrigeration**. It is more easily transported, however, if some of the liquid is removed, as in the production of butter, cheese, or dried milk.

One of the earliest efforts to solve some of milk's transport and shelf-life problems was a vacuum process of condensation/evaporation and **canning** of milk developed by Gail **Borden** in 1856. This was followed closely by Louis Pasteur's discovery of the benefits of pasteurization for killing bacteria. Pasteurization involves heating milk to a high temperature (over 145°F) for a short time (the higher the temperature, the less time required) and was the most significant innovation to allow for expansion of the dairy industry. It both prolonged the shelf life of fluid milk and reduced the likelihood that milk would spoil or spread infection. By the mid-20th century, technologies that could pasteurize faster were developed by using even higher temperatures, including those that could move the milk into containers directly, thus avoiding potential contamination in the **packaging** process. This is called UHT (ultrahigh temperature) milk; it has a much longer shelf life than traditionally pasteurized milk and does not require refrigeration.

Got Milk? A Dairy Timeline

1600s	Dairy cows are brought from Europe (to Jamestown Colony, 1611; to Plymouth Colony, 1624).
1800s	Cows are bred specifically for dairy purposes in the United States.
1841	Milk begins regular delivery to New York City from Orange County, New York, by rail.
1851	First dairy co-op is created in Rome, New York, to create a more efficient cheese plant.
1856	Frenchman Louis Pasteur begins experiments with milk. Gail Borden patents condensed milk in the United States.
1878	Swedish inventor Gustaf de Laval develops the continuous centrifugal cream separator.
1884	Hervey D. Thatcher invents the milk bottle in Potsdam, New York.
1886	Automatic bottle filling and capping machines are patented.
1890	Tuberculosis tests for dairy cows are begun. Tests of Babcock method for determining milk's fat and cream content are completed.
1892	Mehring milking machines patented.
1895	Pasteurizing machines are marketed for commercial use.
1908	Pasteurization is required by law in Chicago, except for milk from tuberculin-free cows.
1911	Rotary bottle filling and capping machines are patented.
1914	Milk begins being transported by tank trucks.
1917	Most U.S. cities require milk to be pasteurized.
1919	Homogenized milk goes on the market.
1922	Capper-Volstead Act, intended as an antitrust measure, encourages the formation of dairy co-ops (after 1950, consolidation results in the number of co-ops being reduced by 89 percent by 1998).
1930	Peak year for U.S. per-capita milk consumption (819 pounds, nearly twice that of current consumption).
1932	Vitamin D is added to milk in the United States. Plastic-coated paper milk cartons are introduced commercially.
1938	Milk cans begin to be replaced by bulk tanks on American farms.
1942	Because of World War II, milk delivery is reduced to every other day in the United States.
1944	Peak year for number of dairy cows in the United States (25.6 million, twice what it is today).
1946	Vacuum pasteurization of milk is introduced.
1948	Ultrahigh temperature (UHT) pasteurization of dairy products is developed in Europe.
1950	Vending machines for milk are introduced in the United States.
1964	Commercial plastic containers for milk are introduced in the United States.
1974	U.S. milk products get nutritional labeling.

1981	UHT milk is accepted by the American public.
1983	National Dairy Promotion and Research Board is created.
1984	American dairy farmers are required by law to contribute 15 cents per hundred pounds of milk to a fund for advertising of dairy products.
1988	Combined low-fat and skim milk sales exceed those of whole milk in the United States for the first time.
1993	Mandatory animal drug residue testing program is established in the United States.
1994	Artificial growth hormone rBST (recombinant bovine somatotrophin) is approved for use in U.S. dairy herds. Nutrition Labeling and Education Act takes effect.
1999	30% of all dairy cows in United States are in herds receiving rBST.
2000	Mozzarella consumption in the United States is triple that of 1980, largely due to increased popularity of pizza.

Sources: National Agricultural Library, "Early Developments in the American Dairy Industry," http://www.nal.usda.gov/speccoll/images1/dairy.htm; International Dairy Foods Association, "Milestones of Milk History in the U.S.," http://www.idfa.org/facts/milk/milkfact/milk4.pdf

Schlebecker, John T. "Agricultural Implements and Machines in the Collection of the National Museum of History and Technology." Washington, D.C.: Smithsonian Institution Press, 1972.

Pasteurization was slow to catch on among milk producers in the United States because of the costs it imposed on producers. But by 1924, based on the awareness that milk was a rich source of nutrients but also prone to bacterial contamination, the federal Public Health Service developed a model regulation, known as the Standard Milk Ordinance, for voluntary adoption by state and local milk control agencies. To provide for the uniform interpretation of this ordinance, an accompanying Code was published in 1927, which provided more details on what constituted satisfactory compliance. This regulation is known as the Grade "A" Pasteurized Milk Ordinance (PMO) and has been revised numerous times to accommodate changes in technologies, markets, and scientific advances. Grade "A" milk is the national standard for milk, and the criteria for this standard are outlined by the Food and Drug Administration.

Other changes in fluid milk production included separating the fat from the fluid milk. The continuous cream separator was developed in 1878, using a centrifugal process to skim the cream from the rest of milk. Cream could then be sold separately or made into butter, while the fluid milk was sent back to farmers to feed to animals or was used in making cheese products. Cream was much more efficiently transported, since it constituted a much smaller volume than fluid milk and did not require daily pickup.

The opposite of separation is *homogenization*, which was introduced in 1919 primarily for **ice cream** production. Homogenization breaks up the globules of fat and distributes them evenly throughout fluid milk, rendering a more uniform texture. Although there was initial consumer resistance to milk that didn't contain a visible "cream-line" at the top of the bottle, by 1950 most milk was homogenized, and large-scale dairies stopped production of "cream-line" milk entirely by 1970.

In the early days of urban distribution, milk was sold from pails and **delivered** door-to-door. In the 1880s, however, the glass **bottle** was developed as a means for reducing the opportunities for contamination of milk during the transfer from the pail to the customer's own container. Although an improvement from this perspective, bottles were quite expensive for the producer, as they had to be washed, rinsed, sterilized, sorted, and inspected in order to be reused. They were heavy, bulky, and awkward to transport. On the other hand, they did allow for some brand **advertisement** on the outside of the bottle.

This system prevailed throughout most of the era of home delivery, but after World War II, disposable waxed paper cartons became more common, especially as home delivery was gradually replaced by store sales. These were lighter-weight, non-returnable, and more easily transported across a wider geographic area. They also allowed more space for advertising and logos on the outside. The plastic-coated "gable-top" carton is still widely used, especially for school milk. At the **supermarket**, it remains in use for many half-gallon and smaller containers, but has been largely superseded by plastic "blow mold" jugs for gallons.

Dairy Products

The cream separator made possible more efficient production of butter, along with several other dairy products. The industry was able to expand further by processing milk into various dairy products, including cheese, dried milk, ice cream, cream, half-and-half, fat-reduced and skim milks, and baby formula.

Cottage cheese was one of the first widely produced cheeses, and its production is a simple separation of the milk's curds (solids) from the whey (liquid). By 1986 cheese production made use of more milk than went to fluid milk products and had increased almost 40-fold since 1950. Consumption has also increased dramatically, from less than 15 pounds per capita annually to almost 30 pounds in 2002. Cheddar, "American," Swiss, mozzarella, and cream cheeses have predominated in the American market. Processed cheese, which contains additives that prevent spoilage, was developed by **Kraft** and made famous by its trademark Velveeta cheese product.

Yogurt, a fermented milk product long known in other parts of the world, was not widely marketed in the United States until the 1960s. It is currently one of the fastest growing markets for dairy products.

Ice cream sales took off in the early decades of the 20th century, benefiting directly from mechanical refrigeration and then batch freezers in the 1920s. Initially served at drugstore counters, in ice cream parlors, and from bell-ringing trucks, its market expanded dramatically with mass marketing in supermarkets in the 1950s. Federal standards mandate that ice cream contain at least 10 percent butterfat (9 percent for flavored varieties). The ice cream industry in the United States is currently worth more than $5 billion, but accounts for only 7 percent of total dairy production.

The fluid milk left over from cream separation was considered to be of little value until the mid-1960s, when milk with varying amounts of fat began to be sold. These included milks that contained 1 or 2 percent fat and nonfat (skim) milk. Since taking out the fat removed some of flavor and texture of the milk, resulting in "watery" milk, other nonfat milk solids are often added to skim or low-fat (1%) milk. Nonfat milk is fortified with **vitamin** A, as this fat-soluble vitamin is lost when fat is removed. Commercial milk is also fortified with vitamin D, which facilitates calcium absorption and deposition in bone. This fortification is credited with ending a long-standing epidemic of rickets, a bone disease caused by vitamin D deficiency. Sweet acidophilus milk was first produced in the early 1980s, with added bacteria (*Lactobacillus acidophilus*) to facilitate digestibility. Flavored milk is another form in which fluid milk is available, with chocolate and strawberry predominating.

Whey, the watery by-product of cheese production, has long been considered a disposal problem, since it interferes with bacterial digestion of sewage in wastewater. The milk sugar lactose makes up 80 percent of the solids in whey, and it, along with whey proteins, can be extracted through a costly filtering process for other uses, such as in pharmaceuticals. Almost half of lactose extracted from whey is designated for export. The whey proteins are used in "health" bars or beverages.

Milk Processors and Pricing

As technologies for converting raw milk into a saleable product became more complex, and as markets and producers became more geographically distant, the dairy industry moved from a simple producer–consumer transaction to one that involved milk dealers. Initially these **middlemen** bought up milk from producers and delivered it to consumers, but subsequently the dealers evolved into processors, with further outsourcing of specialized tasks such as transportation and marketing. There is now a distinction between milk producers and milk processors, and the two are often at odds with one another over the pricing of raw milk or its products.

The equipment necessary for the production, transformation, and transportation of milk is expensive. The early requirement that milk be pasteurized placed new financial burdens on dairy producers, which led to the first period of dairy industry consolidation. Reduction in the number of dairy companies was a consistent trend throughout the 20th century, despite antitrust laws designed to encourage price competition and prevent monopolization of the dairy market. At first, there were numerous local dairy producer cooperatives, but their numbers diminished substantially over the course of the last century. The Dairy Farmers of America (DFA) is currently the largest cooperative, formed out of the merger of several regional cooperatives. In 2002 it had more than 14,000 member milk producers in 47 states; it controls over 28 percent of the milk in the United States. Dean Foods, which began in 1925 in Illinois, is the largest milk processor in the country. It was the first dairy to package milk in waxed paper cartons in the 1930s and then plastic jugs in the 1970s. Dean Foods acquired Land O'Lakes milk operations in 2000, and then in 2001 it merged with Suiza Foods, a Texas-based milk processor. Dean Foods now controls approximately 30 percent of the fluid milk sales in the United States and has more than 130 plants.

The pricing of milk follows a complex algorithm. Starting with the Agricultural Adjustment Act of 1933, the federal government designated milk as a commodity eligible for price supports. The government buys up surpluses to keep the market price above a certain floor. Surpluses are most easily stored as dried milk, but the government also buys milk for federally mandated feeding programs such as the School Lunch Program. Currently there is a federal regional order system in which milk processors pay producers a minimum price for different types of milk products. California maintains its own pricing program. There is also now in place the Dairy Export Incentive Program (DEIP), which provides subsidies to producers seeking international markets for their milk as a means to allow them to be more price competitive in the global market.

Dairy Marketing and Global Trends

With new mechanisms to ensure the safety and efficient transport of fluid milk in the early 20th century, efforts were made toward expanding the market for mass-produced milk. The National Dairy Council was formed in 1915 to promote and protect the various arms of the dairy industry. It later merged with the American Dairy Association and the U.S. Dairy Export Council to promote dairy products to the public. The Dairy Stabilization Act of 1983 created a "check-off" program in which individual producers pay a small amount per unit of milk to support dairy promotion, **research**, and education at the national and local levels, with the goal of increasing overall dairy consumption. Probably the best known of the dairy promotion efforts is that of the Milk Processor Education Program (MilkPEP), which together with Dairy Management, Inc., funded the "milk mustache" marketing campaign. The California Milk Processors Board initiated the "Got Milk?" slogan, which became one of the most successful food advertising campaigns, and it licenses the slogan to MilkPEP for use with the milk mustache promotions.

Despite these successes in the **marketing of milk**, per-capita milk consumption has been declining steadily in the United States over the past 30 years. Dairy industry analysts cite demographic trends, notably the aging of the population, as well as increased competition with other **soft drinks** such as soda, bottled water, and juice as important factors affecting milk consumption. Importantly, though, overall dairy product consumption has not declined, due to the surge in cheese and yogurt consumption.

Lackluster growth in Western countries has led to increased interest in international markets for dairy products. On a global scale, milk production has surged over the past 40 years, increasing by about 240 percent. Growth has been particularly high in developing countries, especially in Asia. There, milk production has more than doubled in the past 20 years, but consumption has surged such that imports are essential to meet market demand. China in particular has increased its production dramatically, but growth in consumption continues to outpace domestic production. Because of its large population, China is viewed as a key emerging market for milk and other dairy products. Younger populations, rising income and purchasing power, changing food preferences, and urbanization are seen as the keys to the boom in the dairy market in developing countries.

This trend has been accompanied by expanding trade networks for milk. The volume of the world dairy trade increased by 25 percent between 1995 and 2000. Countries that produce the majority of milk for the global market include those of the **European Union**, Australia, and New Zealand. The international dairy industry has become consolidated among fewer larger firms over the past decade. Between 1998 and 2000, there were 415 mergers and acquisitions of dairy companies worldwide. Nestlé is by far the largest dairy corporation, along with DFA, Dean Foods, Danone, Kraft, and Parmalat.

The future of the U.S. dairy industry is likely to be strongly influenced by the international market, as well as new domestic production and marketing opportunities. With the rise of interest in **organic** foods, organic dairy sales are increasing, especially in light of public controversy surrounding recombinant bovine somatotropin (rBST; also known as bovine growth hormone). Nor is rBST the only controversy in which the dairy industry is embroiled. People for the Ethical Treatment of Animals

(PETA) has repeatedly charged milk producers with inhumane treatment of cows and calves, while the Physicians Committee for Responsible Medicine (PCRM) has challenged the dairy industry's claims about the benefits of milk for health. PCRM has further argued that milk consumption may be associated with a number of negative health consequences (such as lactose intolerance, various cancers, etc.). Danone Group has launched a yogurt called Activia made with probiotics ("healthy" bacteria) designed to improve digestion; it is also developing a new line of "cosmetic yogurts" marketed as foods to enhance beauty. Thus the dairy industry is seeking new market opportunities, which are essential to its success in light of changes in the markets for milk and other dairy products.

FURTHER READINGS: Beghin, John C. "Evolving Dairy Markets in Asia: Recent Findings and Implications." *Food Policy* 31 (2006): 195–200; DuPuis, E. Melanie. *Nature's Perfect Food: How Milk Became America's Drink.* New York: New York University Press, 2002; Food and Drug Administration, Center for Food Safety and Applied Nutrition. "Grade 'A' Pasteurized Milk Ordinance, 2003 Revision." Available at http://www.cfsan.fda.gov/~ear/pmo03toc.html; Patton, Stuart. *Milk: Its Remarkable Contribution to Human Health and Well-being.* New Brunswick, NJ: Transaction, 2004; Physicians Committee for Responsible Medicine. http://www.pcrm.org; U.S. Department of Agriculture, Economic Research Service. "ERS Dairy Consumption Trends." http://www.ers.usda.gov/Data/FoodConsumption/spreadsheets/foodloss/Dairy.xls#'Total fluid milk'!A1; U.S. Department of Agriculture, Foreign Agricultural Service. "Production, Supply, and Distribution Online." http://www.fas.usda.gov/psdonline/psdhome.aspx; Zurborg, Carl E. *A History of Dairy Marketing in America.* Columbus, OH: National Dairy Shrine, 2005.

Andrea S. Wiley

Darden Restaurant Group. *See* Chain Restaurants.

Delicatessen The delicatessen might be considered the original **fast food** shop, preparing and wrapping made-to-order sandwiches, composed salads, and accompaniments for consumption either on site or to take home. Their provenance is urban, designed for people who can stop, by car or at the bus or subway entrance, to pick up a meal on the way home.

Although delis (as they are usually called) feature a wide variety of foods, they do not usually fry on the spot, more regularly catering with smoked meats and fish and, of course, desserts to go. The quintessential kosher Jewish deli as found in New York features highly stacked sandwiches of corned beef or pastrami on rye, **pickles**, and a variety of other **ethnic** specialties such as chopped liver, potato knishes, and stuffed *derma* (beef intestine). The concept of European delicatessens followed immigrants to the United States, at first from Germany but then predominantly among central European Jews arriving in New York City and up and down the East Coast. The term derives from the German "to eat delicacies," although now delis offer a wide variety of foods from many cultures around the world.

Originally found in cities, usually in ethnic enclaves, delis spread to the suburbs. Now urban and rural grocery **supermarkets** often have "deli counters," where the more or less fancy precooked cold cuts, cheeses, smoked, and otherwise prepared foods are dispensed, as do department stores and even some more formal **restaurants**, in separate **take-out** areas. Over time in the United States, delis added breakfast foods and counters and then tables; Italians added pizza to go, and other ethnic delis feature their own specialties—samosas or Chinese egg rolls, tabouleh or stuffed grape leaves. The original German and Eastern European concept of delicatessen has thus gradually expanded to include practially anything from Italian specialties to Korean takeout. Now delicatessens are doing brisk business in Tokyo; Ulan Bator, Mongolia; Cardiff, Wales; Phuket, Thailand; Cambodia; and Chad, where they most often cater to tourists from the United States and Europe.

Concurrently delicatessens have moved from the local corner to the **Internet**, providing national foods for local **delivery** in many cities throughout the United States. The concept has even spread beyond food: advertising online, Rebecca's Soap Delicatessen is a store featuring recipes for herb soups and balms, lotions, bath salts, and other items for health and beauty.

The influence of the deli has entered cultural realms beyond store-goods: *Delicatessen*, a French black comedy film of 1991 with Marc Caro, Jean-Pierre Jeunet, and Dominique Pinon, takes place above a butcher-shop deli where unpredicted events involving strange foods occurred with repercussions throughout the unspecified city. An American pop artist and photo realist, Wayne Thiebaud, painted "Delicatessen Counter." Much earlier, American poet Joyce Kilmer wrote the poem "Delicatessen" (1914), explaining, "here is a shop of Wonderment. / From every land has come a prize."

FURTHER READING: Brownstein, Bill. *Schwartz's Hebrew Delicatessen: The Story.* Montreal: Vehicule Press, 2006.

Molly G. Schuchat

Delivery Delivery is the process in which a business sends a shipment of goods (in this case, food) to a buyer. The buyer can be another business, but it often refers to the actual consumer of the goods. Pizza delivery is the most well-known form of food delivery today, although the service can range from mail-order smoked salmon to **Internet**-based grocery delivery. In the food industry, delivery enables products to reach a wider range of consumers than stores and **restaurants** can on their own. This garners more financial gain for food-based businesses and allows consumers to eat more globally. Food delivery is also a signpost for society's technological advancements; as our methods of transportation improved from the first step to the first flight, delivery of food has improved and increased with it. Finally, it stands as an indication of current societal trends, in an ever faster-paced society with little free time. Convenience services such as food delivery are paramount in such a culture.

When it comes to food delivery in the 21st century, there are several steps to complete the process. First, customers must choose a means of communication to place the order, such as by mail, phone, or Internet. Once they place the order, it is shipped via car, truck, train, or airplane. The most common type of delivery is restaurant delivery, which entails placing an order over the phone or Internet and having the restaurant deliver the food within a selected period of time (typically within an hour) to the chosen address. Pizza, naturally, must be delivered much more quickly, and many establishments pride themselves on the speed of delivery. The restaurant sets restrictions on the area to which it will deliver. Accepted forms of payment for delivery may include credit card, debit card, or cash.

Food delivery today has such variety that it is difficult to think of anything that cannot be delivered to your home. It is quite common now to have families in which both parents work or single-parent households, where convenience products and services are more than merely welcome but essential.

Food Delivery: The Early Years

In the past, food delivery was difficult because transportation was very limited, communication was restricted to mail, and storage was minimal at best. Only wealthy citizens could afford to have food sent from another land to their residence, typically by land (foot messengers, wagons) or through various waterways. Travel was difficult, and there was no means to prevent spoilage of food while traveling. Meats spoiled quickly, so animals were shipped alive.

The invention of the steamboat, the first railroad system, and the first gas-powered car in the 1800s helped improve transportation and increased the popularity of food delivery. It was around that time that grocery stores started offering deliveries to their customer's homes, which was an appreciated change. This was before individual product **packaging**, and grocers had to weigh out and package each order, making it a lengthy process. The invention of **refrigeration** in the 1870s allowed for the distribution of perishable food via the railroad system, which helped bring a wider range of foods to the masses. The shipment of butchered meat also helped speed up the delivery process. The year 1876 brought the invention of the telephone, which provided a quicker route of communicating delivery needs. Lhardy, a restaurant in Madrid, Spain, acquired a phone in 1885 that led to one of the first phone delivery systems involving freshly made food; it would send workers with a tray of food on their heads to deliver to local customers who phoned in their orders. This rapid improvement of transportation, storage, and communication in the 19th century paved the way for improved food delivery service.

Cooked-Food Delivery Services

From the late 1800s into the early 1900s, Americans used cooked-food delivery services to avoid the hassle of shopping, planning meals, and hiring a cook. This experimental catering service involved outside companies delivering fully cooked, ready-to-eat meals to a household based on how often they needed it. They relied on specially made wagons with the latest technology in refrigeration and heating to maintain their serving temperatures. Originally, galvanized tin boxes insulated with boiling water, kept on a stove in the wagon, provided the heat needed to deliver food. Other inventions included the "heat retainer," created by George Chamberlain of Massachusetts. It involved an insulated, galvanized iron bucket lined with aluminum. Hot soapstone went into the bucket, along with the plates of ready-to-eat food, followed by a lid. It was a cumbersome contraption, but successfully delivered hot food a hundred miles via train.

Prices ranged from 15 cents to one dollar per meal. One of the more popular companies, started by homemaker Bertha L. Grimes of Ohio, charged $2.75 a week for two meals a day. At her best, Grimes sold up to 175 meals per day. There was a stigma at the time of eating the same food as everyone else, but convenience won out in the end.

Toward the end of World War I, public kitchens with cooked-food delivery services opened for women and their servants doing wartime factory work. With fewer women and servants cooking for the family, convenience services like this became essential to survival. After the war, many women lost their factory jobs and had to return to domestic life, so the need lessened; then when inflation hit, the high cost of such services forced many out of business.

Rolling Stores

From the 1930s through the 1960s, the "rolling store," a traveling store made out of a vehicle to sell goods, became the next form of food delivery. These autos would travel set routes in rural towns whose residents did not have the means of getting to a grocery store. Constructed out of large trucks and old buses, the stores were simple in design and barely had room for the workers inside. Customers would purchase groceries, clothing, and tools from these stores, often paying on credit or trading farm goods for their purchase. For example, some rolling stores kept a chicken coop on board for those who wanted to trade live poultry for their week's groceries. Rolling storeowners had to pay taxes to the government for every county they sold in, which made it difficult to sell in multiple counties. Many of the mobile super marts died out by the late 1960s, but William King ran a successful rolling store from 1963 until 1994 in Russell and Macon counties in Alabama. There are a few surviving vestiges of the mobile stores today, the most common being the **ice cream** delivery truck.

Pizza Delivery

Pizza is the most popular kind of delivery in the American food industry and has significantly contributed to improvements in the field. The first official pizza delivery was made in 1889 by Rafaele Esposito of Pietro il Pizzaiolo (renamed Pizzeria Brandi) in Naples, Italy. Queen Margherita of Savoy requested a pizza from Esposito, but could not eat it among the lower class citizens in his establishment, so he delivered a tomato, basil, and mozzarella pizza that he later named after the queen.

Modern pizza delivery picked up after World War II, when pizzerias started popping up all over the United States due to the increased use of cars and the soldiers' newfound cravings. Domino's Pizza founder Tom Monaghan was the first person to focus on quality delivery in the 1960s, when no one thought it was profitable. Today, 93 percent of Americans eat pizza at least once a month, and pizza delivery continues to play a large part in it. A person delivering pizza transports the pizza via car in a bag (sometimes insulated or heated through the car's cigarette lighter). Most drivers in the United States make minimum wage and rely on customary tipping to make a decent living. In 2000, many companies began implementing a delivery charge to all orders.

Pizza delivery can be dangerous, especially when going to an unfamiliar house or neighborhood while carrying a lot of money. Robbery and even death can occur while on the job. The Bureau of Labor Statistics lists pizza delivery as the fifth most dangerous job in the country. Pizza delivery drivers have started their own union to protect their rights and wages. Jim Pohle, a Domino's Pizza delivery driver who felt all drivers deserve to make fair wages, started the American Union of Pizza Delivery Drivers in 2006.

Internet Delivery

Fast food establishments such as **McDonald's** or Taco Bell do not offer delivery services, but thanks to the Internet, even that is changing. VTLateNightFood.com is a new Internet-based food delivery service started at Virginia Polytechnic Institute and State University that allows students to place fast food orders on the Internet between

6 P.M. and 3 A.M. and have the food delivered via car to their dorm room for a small fee. This convenience service saves students a trip across town after dark, allowing them more time for studying.

Although grocery delivery has existed since the 1800s, it has had resurgence in popularity through the Internet. Customers simply pick the website of their choice, select the groceries they need, and wait for delivery. There is a difference in the quality of grocery-delivering websites. For example, NetGrocer.com offers only nonperishable goods and ships through express delivery services that can take up to a week to arrive. Others, like Peapod.com, will ship orders to a local grocery store and have the food delivered by someone who unloads the groceries directly in the customer's home. These services let the customer choose the time they would like their delivery, while the less flexible websites will ship the delivery whenever they can.

Another form of Internet delivery involves ordering specialty foods and **wines** off the Internet. These products are typically items that are not available in your local stores and can range from nostalgic (candy one ate as a child) to **gourmet** (a rare olive oil from Italy). This service typically ships all perishables, and most companies list on their websites their method for keeping the food fresh during transit. Many states' laws have restricted the shipment of alcohol from other states since the repeal of Prohibition in 1933, so wine deliveries are not available everywhere.

Charity Food Delivery

Many organizations use food delivery as a form of charity. Meals on Wheels, in 1954, expanded from England to America as a food delivery service for those in need, although its current focus is on senior citizen health. Moveable Feast is another organization that donates and delivers food to HIV/AIDS and breast cancer patients and their families. This service allows patients and their caretakers to focus on staying healthy and worry less about cooking nutritional, diet-specific meals. These charity, nonprofit food delivery services rely mainly on donations and volunteers to succeed.

FURTHER READINGS: Fernandez-Armesto, Felipe. "Feeding the Giants." In *Near a Thousand Tables: A History of Food*, pp. 190–221. New York: Free Press, 2002; Hayden, Dolores. "Gilman and Her Influence: Community Kitchens and Cooked Food Services." In *The Grand Domestic Revolution: A History of Feminist Designs for American Homes, Neighborhoods, and Cities*, pp. 215–27. Cambridge, MA: MIT Press, 1981; Hinson, Billy G. "Rolling Stores of Alabama." *Alabama Review*, July 2004. Available at http://www.findarticles.com/p/articles/mi_qa3880/is_200407/ai_n9439252; Miller, Hanna. "American Pie." *American Heritage* 57, no. 2 (April/May 2006); Pollack, Penny, and Jeff Ruby. *Everybody Loves Pizza: The Deep Dish on America's Favorite Food.* Cincinnati, OH: Emmis Books, 2005; Roberts, Lisa. "Daily Grind Can Grind You Down." *Baltimore Sun*, November 25, 2006, Arts/Life section.

Leena Trivedi-Grenier

Del Monte California-based Del Monte Corporation and its familiar Del Monte brand had their origins at the turn of the 20th century, at a time when California agriculture was rapidly expanding its presence in the national consumer market. Del Monte's founders understood, as did several other California food producers and processors, the importance of a well-recognized brand name to national marketing success. The business first organized in 1899 as the California Fruit Canners Association, a cooperative of 18 Northern California **canning** companies that pooled their resources to facilitate long-distance shipping and marketing. They choose Del Monte, the label of one of the firms, as the common brand of the association. The name was actually a local reference—an attempt to capture some of the prestige associated with the luxurious Hotel Del Monte in Monterey. The brand became the first nationally advertised one in the canning industry.

By 1916, the canning association had expanded to 28 firms, including plants in Oregon, Washington, Idaho, and Hawaii, and more than 50 products marketed under the Del Monte label—baked beans, jelly, and cranberry sauce, as well as a range of California fruits and vegetables. But the associational form of organization had become unwieldy, and the canners consolidated with a large Midwest-based grocery and packing concern, the Armsby Company, to form a corporation named Calpak. That remained the firm's name until 1967, when Calpak took the name of its brand and became Del Monte Foods.

In the meantime, Del Monte had placed its internationally recognized label on a wide range of food products. Although it occasionally referred to its products as "California's finest," it owned Hawaiian pineapple plantations and canning operations, and by the 1930s had expanded its pineapple operations to the Philippines. Florida citrus, New Jersey tomatoes, and Illinois peas were among the many products that were canned at various regional plants across the United States. Through an extensive series of post–World War II acquisitions and mergers, the company became a full-scale **multinational**, with banana plantations in the Caribbean, a tuna canning plant in Puerto Rico, tomato fields and canning plants in Mexico, pineapple operations in Thailand and Kenya, vegetable canning plants in Italy, and peach packing plants in South Africa.

In 1979, Del Monte was itself acquired by the huge conglomerate RJR Reynolds. The firm regained its independence 10 years later. Del Monte fresh produce was then spun off, although it still continues to display the Del Monte label, as do independent firms in Canada, Africa, Europe, and Asia. In 2002, Del Monte purchased several product lines from **Heinz**, including Starkist, Nature's Goodness **baby foods**, and a variety of **pet foods**. In addition to its Del Monte brand, it now owns Contadina and S&W. The company has shuttered many of its plants in California, and the Hotel Del Monte closed back in 1952, but the brand remains, a potent example of the power of labeling in food marketing.

FURTHER READINGS: *California's Finest: The History of Del Monte Corporation and the Del Monte Brand*. San Francisco: Del Monte Corporation, 1982; Del Monte Corporation. http://www.delmonte.com.

Jeffrey Charles

Diamond Walnuts Diamond Brand Walnuts originated in 1912 as the product of the California Walnut Growers Association (CWGA). This association was an early marketing cooperative, located in Los Angeles, modeled after the California Fruit Exchange, a citrus cooperative that marketed Sunkist oranges. In fact, Charles Teague, one of CWGA's founders and its president for its first 30 years, also served as president of the California Fruit Exchange for 30 years, in the process becoming one of the most powerful men in California agriculture. Like all cooperatives, growers within the walnut association worked together to set prices and establish product grades. They "taxed" their walnut proceeds to build a packing and shelling plant and to pay for **advertising** of the Diamond brand in magazines and newspapers across the country. Thus Diamond walnuts joined Sunkist oranges, Sun-Maid raisins, and Sunsweet prunes as familiar food brands, all products of California grower cooperatives.

Although the California walnut business had its ups and downs through the mid-20th century, the CWGA must be counted a success in sustaining California walnut growers and marketing the Diamond brand. Like other brand marketers, the CWGA handed out free recipe books, sponsored sales promotions in groceries, and experimented with **packaging**, including the use of a unique labeling machine that stamped each individual premium walnut shell with the Diamond label. From the latter part of the 20th century, however, major changes in walnut production and consumption required transformations in the CWGA and the Diamond brand. The pressures of Southern California real estate development shifted the geographical center of walnut growing to Northern California, and the CWGA moved its headquarters north, building a new packing plant in Stockton. In 1956, the CWGA renamed itself after its brand, becoming Diamond Walnut Growers. Increasing sales demands in the 1960s and '70s, coupled with an aggressive move into international markets, seemed to acquire additional financial resources and product diversification. In 1980 the walnut cooperative merged with two other pioneer cooperatives, Sunsweet Prunes and Sun-Maid Raisins, to create the Sun-Diamond Corporation. By 2005, the walnut growers had jettisoned their cooperative structure entirely, become an investor-owned corporation, Diamond Foods, and begun marketing a range of nuts and **snacks** under the Emerald label.

The move from successful cooperative to powerful corporation did not necessarily come smoothly. In 1991, workers at the Diamond Walnut plant in Stockton went on strike, and a drawn-out, 14-year battle between workers and management ensued, finally settled by a contract in 2005. In 1996, the Sun-Diamond Corporation was found guilty of bribing Agriculture Secretary Mike Espy. Although this conviction was overturned by the Supreme Court on the grounds that Sun-Diamond received no immediate quid pro quo, the taint of influence-buying persisted and made early marketing efforts seem innocent by comparison. Nonetheless, consumers can still purchase stamped Diamond Walnuts, and the brand remains one of the most recognizable in the food business.

FURTHER READINGS: Diamond Foods. http://www.diamondfoods.com; Hardesty, Shermain D. "The Bottom Line on the Conversion of Diamond Walnut Growers," *Agricultural and Resource Economics Update* 8, no. 6 (July/August 2006): 1–4, 11. Available at http://www.cooperatives.ucdavis.edu/reports/giannini_diamond.pdf; Scheuring, Ann Foley. *Eighty Years of Excellence: A History of Diamond Walnut Growers, 1912–1992*. Stockton, CA: Diamond Walnut Growers, 1997.

Jeffrey Charles

Diet Foods America's growing **obesity** problem has created a $63 billion market in diet, low-fat, low-calorie, or low-carbohydrate foods in the United States. Public fascination with fad diets can create rapid shifts in the diet food market. Products for dieters are available in almost every segment of the food industry. Looking to the future, nutritionally enhanced foods and products formulated for the South Beach and low-glycemic diets may be new trends, and children and Hispanic-American consumers may be new target markets.

The potential market for diet food in America is huge, literally. According to the U.S. Centers for Disease Control and Prevention (CDC), 66 percent of American adults are overweight or obese. Almost 33 percent of Americans are obese, which is more than double the number from a quarter-century ago. The hefty increase is blamed on many factors, including larger portion sizes and more sedentary lifestyles. Only 3 percent of Americans have an exercise and diet program that qualifies as healthy. Added to that is Americans' steadily rising appetite for snacks, a habit experts say is directly related to the rise in obesity.

Portion size has grown over time. Food businesses have found it effective to compete by enlarging the portion sizes of processed foods as production and ingredient costs have fallen over the last 30 years. With the general trend toward fewer home-cooked meals and more **restaurant**, **takeout**, precooked or ready-to-eat, and **frozen** meals has come weight gain and a taste for convenience.

Americans know they have a problem. Fifty-seven percent of Americans say they are trying to eat a healthy diet. Forty-two percent of American grocery shoppers say the desire to lose or maintain a healthy weight affects their purchase decisions. Thirty percent of the 55 percent who say they are overweight are trying to diet, with 59 percent of those counting calories or watching what they consume. Another 9 percent are following either the Weight Watchers or Jenny Craig commercial program, 11 percent are using a low-carbohydrate plan such as the South Beach Diet, and 6 percent are following low-fat diets. The desire to lose weight cuts across generations, with younger adults motivated more by appearance and older ones by specific health concerns. Another factor is the social importance placed on appearance and being thin, especially for women. A large number of American women worry about being overweight and continually diet, even if they are within the medically healthy weight range.

What Is in a Label

The result? Even when shopping for food not considered "diet," consumers are checking labels. Fifty-one percent of all shoppers and 64 percent of dieters say they check the fat content of items before they buy. For all shoppers, trans-fats rank second in the nutritional statistics checked, followed by **sugar**, cholesterol, salt/sodium, whole grains, calories, **vitamins** and minerals, fiber, chemical **additives**, and protein. For dieters, only fat, trans-fats, and sugar are regularly checked by more than 50 percent of shoppers.

Nutrition labeling and the descriptions used by food companies to market diet foods are regulated by the Food and Drug Administration and have very specific meanings. *Calorie free* refers to a product with less than five calories per serving. A *low-calorie* food has no more than 40 calories per serving. *Reduced-calorie* foods or one marketed as having "less calories" must have 25 percent fewer calories in the given amount than the food to which it is being compared. A *light* or *lite* food also has a specific definition: If 50 percent or more calories are from fat, fat must be reduced by at least 50 percent; if less than 50 percent, fat must be reduced at least 50 percent or calories must be reduced at least a third. A serving of a *fat-free* product has less than 0.5 gram of fat.

The diet foods that consumers buy include frozen entrees and meals, beverages, snacks, **candy**, and meal-replacement products. In the last five years, manufacturers have introduced about 10,000 new or reformulated food products or sizes featuring lower amounts of calories, saturated or other fat, sodium, or sugar or with other healthful benefits. Reduced-fat products make up the largest share of the diet food industry. Low-fat and fat-free products of all types had $35 billion in sales in 2005, including reduced-fat **dairy**, canned goods, and other products as well as items branded as diet foods.

Frozen entrees and meals are an important part of the diet food industry, with $1.4 billion spent on the category in 2004. The trend began in the 1970s when Weight Watchers began to license frozen food products bearing its name. Weight Watchers was sold to H. J. **Heinz** in 1978, which took over frozen food production and expanded the line. Heinz sold the diet plan and meeting sector of the business in 1999, but kept the diet frozen food business. In 1981, Stouffer's (a Nestlé unit) launched Lean Cuisine, and ConAgra's Healthy Choice came to market in 1988. Frozen food technology improvements in flavor, texture, and nutritional benefits and the widespread availability of microwave ovens helped fuel frozen food's use. These three companies remain leaders in the frozen dinner sector.

Low-calorie or calorie-free beverages are also an important market segment, with diet soda sales increasing 5.2 percent in 2005. Calorie-free sodas were one of the earliest diet foods. The regional No-Cal brand was developed by a Brooklyn, New York, hospital for diabetics and others in 1952. In 1962 Diet Rite Cola became the first sugar-free soft drink to be sold nationwide. The next year, Coca-Cola introduced Tab (Diet Coke came along in 1982) and Pepsi introduced Patio Cola (renamed Diet Pepsi in 1965). In 2006, four diet brands ranked in the top 10 carbonated **soft drinks**, with Diet Coke coming in as the third most popular soda in the nation and Diet Pepsi as the fifth.

Weight- and health-conscious consumers are also driving sales of bottled water sales, now the fastest growing segment of the liquid refreshment market, with an estimated market share of almost a third and rising. Bottled water brands owned by Coke and Pepsi are the top-selling brands of water. Dieting consumers have also had an impact on alcoholic beverages. Light **beer** now represents almost half of the beer sold in the United States, making it the largest segment of the market.

Meal-replacement shakes, bars, and other foods took a 16 percent slide between 2002 and 2004, but sales rebounded 6 percent in 2006. One factor was Unilever's Slim-Fast unit's 2005 introduction of its Optima brand, with $166 million in sales its first year.

Portion control has been one of the big successes of the **snack food** industry. **Kraft Foods' Nabisco** had a big success with its "100-calorie packs." The company developed reformulated versions of several of its cookie and snack products to make them healthier and lower in calories. The innovation generated more than $100 million in sales in 2004, its first year. Other companies have since introduced similar products.

Diet Foods, Fads, and Sales

Diet food sales and consumer preferences in weight-loss foods are cyclical. Diet food sales generally decline in the fourth quarter as consumers celebrate the winter holidays, then spike during New Year's week when resolutions are made. Many dieters do not follow a specific plan or program and may change the nature of their diet or even stop dieting when they grow bored or become unsatisfied with results. These shifts in consumer behavior in favored diets can create big changes in the marketplace.

One example is the low-carbohydrate diet boom of the early 2000s. Popularized by the Atkins Diet books and other plans that urged restricting consumption of carbohydrates, there was an onslaught of "low-carb" foods on the market, peaking in 2004 at $5 billion in sales with more than 1,500 products. At one time, about 30–40 million Americans were said to be following the diet and reducing their carbohydrate intake. The company formed to market foods with the Atkins name, Atkins Nutritional, had $2.6 billion in sales in 2004, but sales fell in 2005 and by July of that year had filed for bankruptcy (it has since come out of bankruptcy). The collapse of the low-carb market slowed the diet food industry growth to just 1 percent in 2005. A similar boom-and-bust pattern was observed in the 1990s with the low-fat and fat-free food craze.

These cycles show that people go to diets that promise results, but keeping people on such diets proves more challenging. The industry segments that meet with the most sustained success are those whose health benefits do not require a whole new way of eating. The **packaged** food industry is trying to help smooth out these cycles by creating or publicizing health and nutrition campaigns and funding community awareness programs. Still, marketers are already gearing up to meet the needs of American dieters who are embracing what are predicted to be the next major diets— South Beach and low glycemic.

The South Beach Diet was featured in a best-selling book and was developed by a cardiologist. It emphasizes eating slowly absorbed carbohydrates and polyunsaturated and monounsaturated fats. Kraft's new South Beach food products sold $210 million in their first year on the market (2001).

There are several "low-sugar" or low-glycemic diets gaining popularity. They generally rank foods, particularly carbohydrates, based on their effect on blood glucose levels within two hours of consumption. Diet candy is the fastest growing segment, with sales of about $20 million, an increase of more than 181 percent from 2005 to 2006. Low-glycemic foods and beverages had estimated 2006 sales of $350 million and could reach $1.8 billion by 2011 due to cross-marketing to dieters as well as diabetics, now thought to surpass 18 million in the United States, or about 6 percent of all Americans.

Adding additional nutritional elements to weight-loss products is also an emerging trend. Foods with added calcium, vitamins, omega-3 fatty acids, antioxidants, and other nutrients are becoming more popular. Called **functional foods**, or "phoods," the total market for these products is expected to reach $39 billion by 2011, and weight-loss food manufacturers are already beginning to include these ingredients in their products.

Two new consumer bases for diet foods might be children and Hispanic-Americans. According to the CDC, 17 percent of children between the ages of 2 and 19 are overweight. As government, business, and social forces focus on this problem, companies may well begin to market reduced-fat or low-calorie products for children to both them and their parents. Some snack food and low-calorie juice drinks aimed at youngsters are already on the market.

Obesity in the Hispanic community is another concern. According to the Latino Nutrition Coalition, after immigrants have been here for five or more years, their diet has changed and they are at greater risk for weight-related health problems. The nation's 41 million Hispanic-Americans are already experiencing a higher rate of diabetes than non-Hispanic whites. Companies trying to reach this market will have to develop weight-loss foods to replicate traditional Hispanic flavors and ingredients.

FURTHER READINGS: Centers for Disease Control and Prevention, National Center for Health Statistics. "Overweight." http://www.cdc.gov/nchs/fastats/overwt.htm; *Prevention* Magazine and Rodale, Inc. "Shopping for Health." Emmaus, PA: Research Department, *Prevention* Magazine, December 2006; Sansolo, Michael. "The Nutritional Dilemma." *Facts, Figures and the Future*, October 2006. http://www.factsfiguresfuture.com/archive/october_2006.htm; Siegel, Benjamin. "Sweet Nothing—The Triumph of Diet Soda." *American Heritage*, June/July 2006. Available at http://www.americanheritage.com/events/articles/web/20060619-soda-diet-tab-diet-coke-pepsi.shtml; U.S. Food and Drug Administration, Center for Food Safety and Applied Nutrition. "Definitions of Nutrient Content Claims." In *A Food Labeling Guide*, appendix A. College Park, MD: Center for Food Safety and Applied Nutrition, 1994. Available at http://vm.cfsan.fda.gov/~dms/flg-6a.html.

Faith J. Kramer

Diners From their humble beginnings as horse-drawn night lunch wagons in 1872, diners became synonymous with the American "everyman" urban and roadside food experience before industrial shifts and the increasing popularity of **fast food** and **chain restaurants** eroded their numbers. Today diners still play a role in the American food industry, but often as nostalgic design elements or **restaurant** concepts rather than the prefabricated, full-service, owner-operated diners of the past portrayed in movies, **television** shows, and commercials.

There is no official breakdown of diner operations in the United States. Government statistics include diners in the category of full-service restaurants. **Food service industry** groups also don't offer diner-specific information. Part of that lack of definitive statistical information could be because of the nature of what is considered a diner in the first place in the almost $500-billion-a-year commercial eating-place industry.

Defining what a diner is as a business is a combination of architecture, menu, and intent or concept. Classic diners were prefabricated off-site, or constructed on-site to look that way, and were freestanding buildings. (Diners adapted from trolley and rail cars are included in this category.) Diner styles and decoration varied through the years and by manufacturer, but generally all offered counter seating on swivel stools with a view of the food preparation area, booths, and sometimes tables. The streamlined art deco style with chrome or stainless-steel trim is probably how most Americans think of diners, but the look of a classic diner can vary depending on its cost, age, and manufacturer. Many diners also added on dining rooms with additional seating. At the height of diner popularity in the 1950s, there were an estimated 6,000 of these classic diners in America. Individuals working to preserve and restore the historic diners estimate there are about 2,000–2,500 of these food service icons still in existence, with perhaps two-thirds of them open for business. Some are listed on the National Register of Historic Places.

One example of a classic diner is the nine-seat Bay Way Diner in Linden, New Jersey. The Bay Way was prefabricated in the 1940s. Known as the White Crown, it was originally located near downtown but had been moved to service workers at a nearby oil-tank farm. Its new owners bought the building to knock it down and build a truck garage, but support for the diner was so strong that they decided to renovate instead. They took out one of the original 10 stools to make more room for **takeout** orders, which accounts for 80 percent of the little diner's business. Other changes kept the diner's retro feel but upgraded materials.

Another example, also from New Jersey, is the Mastoris Diner in Bordentown. The proprietors' family owned a series of diners dating back to 1927 when the father of one of the owners commissioned a prefabricated lunch wagon. In 1959 the owners opened a modern diner large enough to seat 350 people. That diner burned down and was replaced. Today's Mastoris Diner can serve from 1,200 to 2,800 people a day and has a crew of 160, including the owners' sons and grandchildren.

Bay Way Diner goes through about 1,000 eggs a week; the Mastoris's cooks can go through 3,600 in a weekend. But despite their difference in size, the owners of both restaurants take pride in their diners' heritage, the service they offer customers, and the quality and variety of food they serve.

Food is another way to define diners. In the beginning, diner fare was ordered from signs posted on the walls, but later diners were known for their expansive menus. The home-style food was served quickly, in generous proportions, and at reasonable prices. In addition to hamburgers, sandwiches, meatloaf, cakes, pies, and other American standbys, there would be regional variations to accommodate local **ethnic** favorites.

Many restaurants that feature this style of food and service and offer counter seating label themselves as diners regardless of architecture. One example is the Chicago Diner in Chicago: a narrow storefront restaurant, it offers diner food with a twist—everything is **vegetarian**. Its signage reflects the diners' chrome past and inside is a long counter with stools and a long row of wooden booths.

The third way to define a diner is by theme. Concept diners feature elements of classic diner styling, service, and menus but are used for design and nostalgia. The diner theme often serves as a backdrop. Menus may be very contemporary, but service is designed to be personal. Often a chain, this kind of diner is becoming more and more popular and is leading the resurgence of diners.

Development of the Classic Diner

Once imitators of Walter Scott's innovation of a horse-drawn wagon to serve quick meals to workers on the night shift in Providence, Rhode Island, began to park their mobile restaurants in permanent locations, the diner as we know it began to evolve. The diners were prefabricated (not just the building and its decorations but even the kitchen equipment and supplies down to the pots, pans, plates, and forks) and transported by rail, truck, or barge to their retail locations. They were designed to speedily serve working-class males during their meal breaks. Owners then and now could have them moved to new locations if needed. The diner's shape was influenced by its mobility, resulting in streamlined buildings and a shape much like a railroad car and probably contributing to the impression that they evolved from railroad dining cars.

Diner manufacture began in 1887 when Samuel Messer Jones began building a fleet of lunch wagons in Worcester, Massachusetts, including the innovation of indoor seating—a counter with stools. Eventually there were about two dozen manufacturers of diners, although most of the prefabricated diner manufacturers that sprung up in the 1920s–1950s "golden age" of diners have gone out of business. After years of declining prefabricated diner sales, Kullman Industries saw an increase in its diner business in the 1990s, and in 2001 it estimated food service would be 20–30 percent of its business. The trend did not continue, however, and Kullman delivered only one prefabricated diner in 2006; the firm is now focused on other forms of modular construction. With the cost of a prefabricated unit topping out at well over $1 million, traditional diner construction can be costly. Renovations of historic diners can be expensive, as well, since replacement equipment and decorations often must be custom made.

These diners were designed for efficient service and originally featured only counter seating in front of the food preparation area; later, they also offered booths and table service. The look of the diner could be customized by the owner, but overall the diners reflected the design choices offered by the manufacturer. The original diners' compact design allowed an owner to cook and serve from the open kitchen behind the counter. Smaller diners were one-person operations. As diners grew, the owners remained behind the counters, stoves, or cash registers, and they retained a reputation for interacting with their customers, adding to diners' local appeal. Diners began to hire waitresses and make other changes to help attract families and women. The restaurants gained even more of a home-away-from-home reputation, in some cases becoming community gathering places as well as reliable stops for travelers with quick, familiar meals, many open 24 hours a day.

Diners could be found throughout the country, but were especially popular in the Northeast and on the East Coast, often located near factories and highways where fast meals away from home were needed. In the late 1950s, diners began opening in the new suburbs and manufacturing communities to serve second- and third-generation Americans and blue-collar workers.

The decline of the diner can be traced to the shift of manufacturing plants to the south, west, or even overseas and the success of fast food and other chain restaurants. For example **McDonald's** had just 200 units in 1960; by the end of the decade, the company had 1,500 restaurants. The number of chain restaurants and bars almost doubled between 1958 and 1972, while owner-operated eating places such as diners declined by a third. Some diner owners tried to combat the trend in the 1960s and '70s by remodeling their businesses in Mediterranean, colonial, or contemporary styles in an attempt to appeal to customers lured away by the fast food and chain establishments.

Diner owners did not necessarily come from food service backgrounds. Owning a diner attracted proprietors from all walks of life. Diner manufacturers marketed the ease and success of owning a diner to returning veterans from both world wars. As ownership of many diners passed to new generations of immigrants, Greek, Middle Eastern, and other foreign flavors were added to the menus. This trend continues as these owners sell to the next wave of American immigrants, some of whom continue to adapt the look and menus of their diners to reflect their backgrounds and community needs.

The Diner as a Marketing Concept

Because diners play such a pivotal role in American popular culture as settings of commercials, television shows, and movies and because of the postmodern success of marketing nostalgia, a new kind of diner has gained popularity in the last 20 years or so. The menus of these style diners may be limited to just hamburgers or might reflect the breadth of the traditional diner. Some of these chains echo the roots of historic diners; others use the diner association to create an atmosphere or marketing difference for their establishments.

While some of these diners are freestanding restaurants, they can also be found in malls, on cruise ships, and in other nontraditional locations. They replicate decorative characteristics of their historic roots—perhaps offering stainless-steel facades, vintage signage, waitresses with personality and attitude, home-style foods, counters with swivel stools, revolving dessert cases, and vinyl-covered booths. Often chains, these diners go to great lengths to create the connection to America's expectations of diners, inventing colorful owners, scripting server interactions, and encrusting the walls with memorabilia.

Chain diners, whether privately owned or **franchised**, usually began as a successful local restaurant that expanded regionally. Some have a national market base.

Johnny Rockets is a California-based chain that recreates the American diner experience with tabletop jukeboxes and other retro details. The chain's menu focuses on hamburgers, sandwiches, and fries. The company serves more than 13 million hamburgers a year in its more than 200 restaurants in 29 states, 9 countries, and 8 cruise ships. The Johnny Rockets Group, a private company, is estimated to have almost $200 million in yearly sales.

Ruby's Diner started as a remodeled bait shop on a pier in Newport Beach, California, in 1982 and grew to include 37 diners and 2 dinettes, a self-service concept with a smaller menu designed for malls, airports, highway rest stops, and similar locations. The chain is named after one of the founder's mothers. Ruby's Diner is estimated to have $100 million in annual sales.

The Mesa, Arizona–based 5 & Diner chain started in 1989. Its first diners were modular, but now all are built on-site. The décor of its 18 locations features bright colors and a rock-'n'-roll theme. The 5 & Diner Franchise Corporation's annual estimated sales are $25 million.

One of the new diner chains that offers up a more classic experience is the Silver Diner, based in Rockville, Maryland. It was started by two men seeking the neighborhood spirit of a diner who wanted a family restaurant that offered more than fast food. The first restaurant, a gleaming prefabricated building by Kullman, opened in 1989. The chain's other 18 locations were built on-site to recreate the feel of a classic diner. The private company's estimated annual sales are $32 million.

Existing chain restaurants also saw value in the diner theme. In 2001 Denny's remodeled 20 percent of its then 1,822 restaurants in a diner style. Even McDonald's, one of the fast food competitors responsible for the diners' decline, has decorated outlets with diner elements.

The diner may never return to its former popularity, but it remains a beloved symbol of America's culinary and social heritage. With the proliferation of chain diners and the ongoing preservation of classic ones, going out to eat at a diner, or operating one, will remain part of the American way of life for years to come.

FURTHER READINGS: Gangemi, Jeffrey. "Coffee, Pie, and the Diner Guys." *Business Week Online*, July 6, 2006. http://www.businessweek.com/smallbiz/content/jul2006/sb20060706_763343.htm; Glenn, Sheldon. "'What's on Their Plates?' or Feeding the Hungry Mouths: Laborers, Families, and Food in the Late Twentieth Century." *Journal of Popular Culture*, Vol. 38, no. 3 (February 2005): 564; Gutman, Richard J. S. *American Diner Then and Now*. Baltimore: Johns Hopkins University Press, 2000; Hurley, Andrew. "From Hash House to Family

Restaurant: The Transformation of the Diner and Post–World War II Consumer Culture." *Journal of American History,* Vol. 83, no. 4 (March 1997): 1282; Jackson, Donald Dale. "The American Diner Is in Decline, Yet More Chic Than Ever." *Smithsonian*, Vol. 17, no. 8 (November 1986): 94–99; *Roadside Online*. http://www.roadsideonline.com.

Faith J. Kramer

Distilled Spirits A *distilled beverage* is a liquid preparation meant for consumption containing ethanol purified by distillation from a fermented substance such as fruit, vegetables, or grain. The word *spirits* usually refers to distilled drinks low in sugars and holding at least 35 percent alcohol by volume. Distilled spirits production also may include the production of secondary products such as distillers' dried grains used for livestock feed and other feed or food components.

Distilled spirits are divided into three major categories: "white," "brown," and "specialties." White spirits are colorless distilled spirits, including vodka, gin, rum, pisco, and tequila, although tequila and rum may also be dark or golden. Brown spirits are the whiskies and brandies. Specialties include brandies, liqueurs and cordials, and other spirituous beverages. Within these major categories, spirits can be further classified by fermentation base, distillation method, alcoholic strength, and country or region of origin.

Distilled spirits can be obtained by a variety of processes. They result most often from fermentation and distillation of grain (**corn**, **wheat**, rye, barley, etc.). However, spirits are also obtained from bases of fruits, roots, tubers, and other plants. For whiskies and some tequilas and rums, the distilled product is aged to provide flavor, color, and aroma.

In most countries, white spirits are becoming more popular than brown spirits. The suitability of white spirits as a base for mixing has been the main driver of their success, with younger consumers seeking an alternative to strongly flavored spirits such as whiskey. Also, brown spirits companies have been slow to add flavored brand extensions. A general shift from brown spirits such as whiskey and brandy has ensured that all the main white spirits (gin, vodka, and white rum) are on the rise. However, an identification of the white spirits with elements of the binge drinking culture could be a threat to the sector's development.

There are currently various "wars" for the recognition of both place and origins of spirits. The long-standing vodka-producing nations, in particular Finland, Poland, and Sweden, have taken measures to protect their national spirit. They were campaigning for legislation in the **European Union (EU)** that would mean only spirits made from potatoes and grain (wheat, barley, rice, etc.) could be labeled "vodka," but were unsuccessful. Vodka made from something else—apples, grapes, or sugar beets, for instance—could not. Vodkas made in Southern Europe favor citrus fruits and grapes, while in the United States most vodka is made from sugarcane. Even in Russia, the country synonymous with vodka, industrious and thirsty people have produced the spirit for centuries using just about anything that could be fermented.

The term "western-style" spirits refers to products made in accordance with internationally accepted industry standards (e.g., of the EU, World Trade Organization, etc.). Much of the whiskey produced in India, for example, does not qualify as "whiskey" under the EU standards, which specify that whiskey has to be made from cereals, contain at least 40 percent alcohol, and be aged for three years or more; Indian whiskey is derived from molasses (discussions are continuing for it to be marketed as "molasses whiskey" or "Indian whiskey").

Whiskey is produced in many countries, but the only significant whiskies on the U.S. market are those produced in Scotland, Ireland, Canada, and the United States. Scotch whisky (traditionally spelled without the *e*) is one of the United Kingdom's main export earners. In recent years, Scotch has been exported to many markets across the world and accounts for approximately 90 percent of the sales. The major markets are the European Union, the United States, Japan, and other Asian markets. The Scotch whisky industry is operating a two-pronged approach: targeting the increasingly wealthy urban professional with a sales pitch for sophisticated drinks and lobbying the governments with tax cuts.

Large emerging economies such as Brazil, Russia, India, and China also produce distilled spirits. With few exceptions, the domestic premium brands produced in these countries do not have an international focus. Local commercial distilled spirits producers dominate in most emerging markets and tend to be geographically fragmented due to the persistent popularity of traditional national specialties. Thus, in the Asia-Pacific region, Jinro produces *soju* for the large South Korean market, and San Miguel Corporation dominates the Filipino gin market. Similarly, in Latin America, the two leading companies, Companhia Muller de Bebidas and Pitú, make cachaça, a white spirit produced from sugarcane, in Brazil. In Africa, Distell ranks number one thanks to its lead in the region's dominant market, South Africa, where it is strong in the important local brandy segment.

India has some traditional whiskies. Major beverage companies such as the Edrington Group, Moet Hennessy, and Diageo are jockeying for position. However, they are currently priced out of the market because of **tariffs** of up to 525 percent, leaving Indian distillers with a tight grip on the mass market.

A few **multinational** companies dominate the whole sector, with strong global brands accounting for a large proportion of sales. The global distilled spirits industry has undergone consolidation since 2000, particularly through mergers and acquisitions operations and the geographic expansion of major multinational players. While the leading global spirits producers are getting bigger through such expansion, when compared with other beverage industries (e.g., **soft drinks**), the overall spirits industry remains highly fragmented with numerous, cheaper products available locally. Diageo, a British-based company, the maker of Smirnoff vodka and Johnie Walker Scotch, is number one, followed by Pernod Ricard (France), which purchased Allied Domecq (United Kingdom) in 2005.

The distilled spirits industry is highly regulated. In the United States, at the federal level, the Treasury Department's Bureau of Alcohol, Tobacco, and Firearms (BATF) enforces federal laws related to distilled spirits, while state governments (and some local jurisdictions) have regulatory control on distribution and sales within their borders. Furthermore, tax revenues from excise and other taxes on the production and sale of distilled spirits can be an important source of government revenue in many nations. In the United States, distilled spirits are one of the nation's most heavily taxed consumer products: taxes and fees make up more than half of the cost of an average bottle of distilled spirit.

Place of origin appears to be an increasingly important factor for a growing number of brands. By emphasizing a strong relationship with a particular country or region (e.g., tequila as a Mexican product), a distilled spirit can implicitly draw an association with the values that consumers associate with the place.

There are a number of factors behind the increasing interest in provenance—from surging **culinary tourism** and interest in far-flung destinations to a growing dissatisfaction with products and brands that are seen as artificial and meaningless.

The key objective for European producers is to secure enhanced certainty of legal protection for European spirits with geographical indications through the establishment of a multilateral Spirits Register. Counterfeiting remains a serious problem for the industry in many markets around the world. Indeed, in some key emerging markets, the problem is becoming significantly worse. The usurpation of spirits comes at a cost in terms of lost potential and the risk that poor quality counterfeit products might tarnish the genuine product's image in the eyes of consumers.

FURTHER READINGS: Lea, Andrew G. H., and John R. Piggott, eds. *Fermented Beverage Production*. 2nd ed. New York: Kluwer Academic/Plenum, 2003; Heijbroek, Arend. *The Fighting Spirits: In a Competitive Mood*. n.p.: Netherlands: Rabobank, 2004; McLaren, Charles. *Scotch Whisky*. London: Octopus, 2002.

Alfredo Manuel Coelho

Dole The Dole Food Company is the world's leading producer and marketer of fresh fruits, vegetables, and flowers. It is headquartered in Westlake Village, California, and had revenue of $5.3 billion in 2004.

In 1901, James Dole founded the Hawaiian Pineapple Company. Dole, who would be remembered as the "Pineapple King," established his first pineapple plantation on the island of Oahu. Eight years earlier, James Dole's cousin, Sanford Dole, along with other Americans, had helped to overthrow the Hawaiian monarchy in the name of the United States. Sanford Dole briefly served as president of the new Hawaiian Republic. When James Dole planted his first pineapples, Hawaii had only recently been annexed by the United States.

In 1961, Dole merged with Castle & Cooke, a company that had been involved in Hawaiian **agribusiness** since 1851. At the time, the Castle & Cooke brand name was kept, but in 1991 Castle & Cooke's shareholders chose to rebrand the company under the Dole name. In 1995, Dole was split up again. This time, the Dole Food Company would operate the food production and distribution parts of the corporation, while Castle & Cooke would take the real estate development and residential and commercial building segments.

Since 2002, American David Murdock has been the sole owner of Dole; he also serves as its chief executive officer. Dole is member of the SA8000 Social Accountability International (SAI) and maintains a strategic partnership with PepsiCo.

Eric Covey

Domino. *See* Sugar and Artificial Sweeteners.

Dunkin' Donuts. *See* Krispy Kreme.

Environmental Issues. *See* Animal Rights; Beef/Cattle Industry; Bottling Industry; Environmental Protection Agency; Organic Foods; Packaging; Poultry Industry.

Environmental Protection Agency (EPA) Located in Washington, D.C., the EPA is an organization of the U.S. federal government responsible for protecting human health and the natural environment. A general administrator, who is selected by the president to oversee the EPA's 10 regional offices and 17 laboratories located across the country, directs the agency. The EPA employs more than 18,000 highly educated and technically trained experts (engineers, scientists, environmental protection specialists, computer specialists, accountants, and lawyers) to lead the nation's research, assessment, and education programs, with the mandate of working toward a cleaner, healthier environment for the American people. With this intention in mind, the EPA develops and enforces regulations that implement environmental laws enacted by Congress; offers financial assistance to states, nonprofit organizations, and educational institutions in order to raise awareness about environmental pollution; carries out research to assess and identify emerging environmental issues; collaborates with more than 10,000 industries worldwide to create pollution prevention and energy conservation programs; and establishes the nation's maximums for contaminants in trading goods and food products.

Early History of the EPA

Established by President Richard Nixon on July 9, 1970, the EPA is the result of collaborative efforts between the White House and Congress to create an agency that would respond to possible attacks against human health and the environment (water, air, and land). The EPA became operative on December 2, 1970, under the leadership of William Ruckelshaus, who was appointed agency administrator. Ruckelshaus's first important, but controversial, decision was to support the passage of the Clear Air Act (CAA), by which Congress addressed public concern about air pollution after the recent Earth Day demonstrations. In a historical moment, Congress admitted to the flaws of the Air Quality Act of 1967, which delegated complete responsibility for adopting and enforcing pollution control standards to each region. The CAA imposed statutory deadlines for compliance with the national air quality standards. Although it did not achieve all of its objectives, the CAA can be said to have raised awareness about the dangers of environmental pollution.

Following this change of policy, in fall 1972 the EPA proposed the passage of the first legislation on the production and use of pesticides since the Federal Insecticide, Fungicide, and Rodenticide Act (FIFRA) of 1947. Like the CAA, the goal was to protect consumers and the general public by implementing the Federal Environmental Pesticide Control Act (FEPCA) or else to remove pesticides from the market. Under the new legislation, all pesticide products would be registered and classified. Those pesticides considered more harmful would be allowed for use only under the supervision of certified applicators. In addition to this, nearly all DDT pesticides (except for those needed for public health, quarantine, and a few minor crop uses) primarily affecting cotton, citrus fruits, certain vegetables, the aquatic life, and the avian populations were banned. Violators of FEPCA were subject to penalties that ranged up to $25,000 and a year in prison.

Harsh punishments were also established for water polluters by the enactment of the Federal Water Pollution Control Act (FWPCA) of 1972. In this case, anyone who endangered or degraded the quality or value of the water resources below national standards could be sentenced to pay $50,000 and/or to be sent to a year of imprisonment at a federal institution. The main objectives of the FWPCA were to prevent, control, and abate water pollution; to stop the discharge of all pollutants into the navigable waters of the United States by 1985; to protect fish, shellfish, and wildlife; and to monitor and restrict the amount of sludge waste and junk dumped into ocean waters, in combination with the Marine Protection, Research, and Sanctuaries Act (MPRSA). The EPA's work to guarantee the quality of the nation's water was continued with President Gerald Ford's approvals of the Safe Drinking Water Act (SDWA) of 1974, which ensured the purity of the water that we consume by reducing the authorized levels of drinking water contaminants (brine, wastewater, gases, or any other fluids), and the Resource Conservation and Recovery Act of 1976, which regulated the handling and disposal of hazardous wastes mainly generated by industries.

The EPA's Work against Environmental Disasters in the 1980s

Although the EPA continued developing more programs to safeguard the quality of American water, air, and land, in the 1980s a series of disasters challenged the agency's capacity to efficiently coordinate cleanup projects of contaminating industries. On April 4, 1980, for example, the EPA was commanded by the White House to monitor off-site radiation levels around the disabled reactor 2 of the Three Mile Island Nuclear Generation Station in the Susquehanna River in Dauphin County, Pennsylvania. This pressurized-water unit had suffered a partial core meltdown on March 28, 1979. Less than two months later, on May 21, 1980, the EPA was granted authority by President Jimmy Carter to relocate 700 families from the Love Canal area of Niagara Falls, New York, in response to the cumulative evidence that exposure to the toxic wastes deposited there by the Hooker Chemical Company was undermining people's health. In February 1983, history repeated itself: residents of Times Beach, Missouri, were forced to temporarily leave their homes after the Centers for Disease Control announced that the dioxin contamination of the soil in the area was a threat to the public health. DDT and fertilizers in Triana, Alabama, and the Chesapeake Bay area caused other cases of soil contamination in 1983 and 1984, respectively.

In response, the EPA lobbied for the immediate passage of the 1980 Superfund environmental program, by which funds would be made available to help clean up not only thousands of abandoned hazardous waste dump sites that could be a threat to nearby populations but also the hundreds of spills of oil and hazardous substances into American waterways that occur every year across the country. The Superfund received Carter's approval, but it was under the Reagan administration that the program was granted a trust fund of $1.6 billion to be spent over the next five years. The Superfund soon became the main source of income for emergency cleanup work; for example, $400,000 was spent in 1981 at the Valley of the Drums, Kentucky, and $7 million for the Love Canal cleanup.

Other legal achievements consisted of the passage of the Asbestos School Hazard Abatement Act of 1982 and the Hazardous and Solid Waste Amendments of 1984; the 1983 suspension of ethylene dibromide as a soil fumigant for agricultural crops; the 1985 reduction of lead content of gasoline to 0.10 gram per gallon; the 1985 expansion of the air toxics program to reduce the risk of air pollutants; and the 1985 approval of tests with two genetically altered strains of naturally occurring **bacteria** that could prevent frost damage to plants.

Focused on the control and abatement of pollution originating on U.S. soil, the EPA could not predict the nuclear disaster of 1986 at Chernobyl in the Soviet Union. Nevertheless, the agency assumed responsibility for informing the American people about the slight chance that dangerous radioactive fallout would head to the United States. The EPA also advised U.S. citizens traveling abroad and monitored of imported goods. The Chernobyl accident did not create any health problems for Americans, but it allowed people to realize that in case of nuclear emergency there was an effective domestic system in place to rely on.

On March 24, 1989, however, the EPA's credibility was seriously questioned. The 987-foot tanker vessel *Exxon Valdez* crashed against Bligh Reef in Prince William Sound, Alaska, and spilled oil over 3,000 square miles and onto more than 350 miles of beaches in one of the most pristine and magnificent natural areas of the country. It was the largest environmental disaster in American history. Overwhelmed by the magnitude of the incident, the EPA could not respond in time with the necessary equipment and personnel to prevent the spill of oil into ocean waters. Nevertheless, the EPA took responsibility for developing plans that would allow the agency to more effectively handle future accidents of this size, as well as proposing the creation of funds to compensate individuals and industries affected.

The EPA's Work on Food Legislation in the 1990s

In charge of the quality of air, land, and water resources since its foundation, the EPA has also played an important role in the enforcement of food legislation. One of the agency's major objectives has been to establish national standards for the breeding and handling of domestic cattle and the cultivation and treatment of vegetables and fruits. In 1989, for example, the EPA announced the cancellation of all food-use registrations of the pesticide daminozide, also known as Alar, and the prohibition of the sale, distribution, and use of its products domestically under the suspicion that exposure to the chemical could cause cancer in humans. In September of the same year, the EPA proposed to lower the allowable residue level of daminozide in imported fruits until the pesticide was finally removed from the marketplace.

An increasing interest in reducing the amount of chemicals ingested by people also prompted the limitation of the number of drinking water contaminants to 23, most rarely found in drinking water. After the passage of the Safe Water Drinking Act in 1992, the EPA took the lead in protecting groundwater from pollution and carcinogens. The EPA also committed to publishing the maximum contaminant levels allowed, renewing the promise it had made with the approval of the 1974 SDWA.

With the safety and health of children in mind, the Food Quality Protection Act (FQPA) was passed on August 3, 1996, to establish stricter safety standards and a complete reassessment of all existing pesticide tolerances for food. The FQPA amended FIFRA and the Federal Food, Drug, and Cosmetic Act. In 1997, a new plan to implement the FQPA was in order. It targeted the ways in which pesticides were regulated by proposing new standards for all pesticide residues in food, supporting thorough assessment and reevaluations of potential risks, and publicizing the dangers and benefits of pesticide use.

Accusations against the EPA

In spite of the EPA's great achievements, the agency's programs were not free of political obstacles. In 1974, for example, the EPA's resolutions to restrict the oil supply in order to minimize the environmental damage derived from its production and consumption were thought to be responsible for the nation's energy crisis. Although the EPA took accountability for some of the increased energy demand, the agency argued that this energy surge originated from low energy-pricing policies, lack of incentives to invest in domestic energy facilities, and depletion of the nation's oil and gas reserves. The EPA also stated that temporary relaxations of supply restrictions not only would fail to solve the crisis but would also exact an extraordinary cost to the public health. As valuable solutions, the EPA has proposed reducing the emission of gases, limiting the nation's dependency on foreign energy importations, developing energy conservation programs and more efficient auto propulsion systems, constructing mass transit systems, supporting resource recovery and recycling programs, and educating consumers on fuel-saving decisions that can improve and revolutionize Americans' lifestyle.

Not always obtaining the results they expected, the agency has become the target of politicians opposing the party in office. The EPA has been criticized in recent years for relying less and less on its scientists and more on personnel who lack scientific expertise. Harsh criticism has only spurred the EPA's directors to continue working hard today under the direction of Stephen L. Johnson. The agency has lobbied for new test methods to improve fuel economy and emission estimates in 2006 and revised on-highway heavy duty diesel engine emissions standards for 2007.

FURTHER READINGS: California Environmental Protection Agency. *Health Effects of Exposure to Environmental Tobacco Smoke: The Report of the California Environmental Protection Agency.* Bethesda, MD: U.S. Department of Health and Human Services, Public Health Service, National Institutes of Health and National Cancer Institute, 1999; Landy, Marc K., Marc J. Roberts, and Stephen R. Thomas. *The Environmental Protection Agency: Asking the Wrong Questions.* New York: Oxford University Press, 1990; Mintz, Joel A. *Enforcement at the EPA: High Stakes and Hard Choices.* Austin: University of Texas Press, 1995; Quarles, John. *Cleaning Up America: An Insider's View of the Environmental Protection Agency.* Boston: Houghton Mifflin, 1976; U.S. Environmental Protection Agency. *EPA Journal.* [Quarterly journal, 1975–1995].

Jorge Abril Sánchez

Ethnic Food Business In a vigorous commercial culture, many of America's immigrants naturally chose business—especially the food business—as their avenue of opportunity. Ethnic food enterprise was at once a means of holding onto vital cultural traditions in a strange society and a way of getting ahead. Throughout American history, newcomers worked in agriculture and as vendors, grocers, and **restaurant** proprietors.

Each successive wave of immigrants brought new arrivals who changed the food landscape. The Irish, Germans, French Canadians, and Scandinavians journeyed to the United States in the mid-19th century. In the most polyglot migration up to that time, Jews, Catholics, and Orthodox Christians poured in from Poland, Hungary, Russia, Greece, Italy, and other states in southern and eastern Europe between the last decades of the 19th century and the early decades of the 20th. Beginning in the 1970s, previously underrepresented groups from Africa, Asia, Latin America, and the Middle East started settling in.

Entrepreneurs in each wave staked out niches in the food business. Germans, for example, opened **delicatessens** selling knockwurst, bratwurst, mustards, and pumpernickel. Southern Italians started businesses purveying fresh ricotta and mozzarella cheeses and established salumerias to sell salami, prosciutto, and mortadella. Today, Salvadorans establish pupuserias, eateries that sell the *pupusa*—their country's version of the tortilla—tamales, and exotic drinks like the horchata and tamarindo.

Ethnics relied on family and Old Country ties in their ventures. Greeks, the archetypical food entrepreneurs, jumped ship, grabbed jobs as dishwashers or countermen, and began working long, laborious days. They scrimped and saved in hopes of accumulating enough money for their next move. After several years working for a kinsman, many opened their own lunch counter, coffee shop, or **diner**. They, in turn, brought in relatives from the "other side" to help out in their shops. Having learned the trade, brothers or cousins, in turn, embarked on a similar path. "Chain migration," as the social scientists call it, created an ever-expanding food business.

The Food Business: Courting Ethnics and Natives

The ethnic food venue served as a gathering place for "greenhorns," newcomers who felt lonely and adrift in anonymous cities. They congregated in eateries and cafés to recapture memories of pilaf and grape leaves or of samosas and biryanis. Nostalgic customers sought out these businesses to meet old friends and find new companions, to pick up gossip, and to debate homeland politics.

The pioneering food business in each community depended on a loyal ethnic customer base. In time and with greater financial success, merchants also began reaching out to strangers, worldly urbanites, and cosmopolitan eaters. As ethnic food over the decades became more familiar to natives, the enterprises became less insular.

The history of Sahadi's, a Brooklyn-based food giant that combines retailing, wholesaling, manufacturing, and importing, illustrates the steps in this evolution. Abraham Sahadi opened an "Oriental" grocery in the "Little Syria" district of Lower Manhattan in 1895. The merchant sold spices, nuts, olives, dried fruit, bulgur, and other grains to fellow Middle Easterners and imported sesame seeds—the basis for tahini paste, the flavoring for hummus—orange blossom water, lentils, and other goods.

Wade Sahadi, Abraham's nephew who worked in the store, eventually set out on his own. He soon bought his own shop on Atlantic Avenue in Brooklyn, which had replaced Washington Street in Manhattan as New York's Middle Eastern commercial hub. His son Charles, who took over the shop, catered to the special tastes of Syrian and Lebanese Christians during the 1950s and '60s. The Sahadi Importing Company stocked chickpeas, apricots, okra, and other Arabic staples. It also sold Turkish tea glasses, backgammon, and clay water pipes.

Today, the original small grocery has burgeoned into a vast emporium. Sahadi's now attracts both old and new immigrants—Moroccans, Yemenis, Egyptians, and Palestinians—as well as an affluent, sophisticated clientele of locals craving gourmet olive oil and **takeout** tabbouleh, the minty Lebanese salad.

Begun in 1888, by Rabbi Dov Behr Manischewitz in Cincinnati, Ohio, a simple matzoh bakery has grown into the largest American producer of processed kosher foods. In addition to the Manischewitz brand items, Manischewitz also sells prepared foods under the brand names "Horowitz Margareten," "Goodman's," and "Season." Since 1998, the company has been part of R.A.B. Holdings—and, in 2004, changed its name to R.A.B. Food Group, LLC.

The Manischewitz wine company is not related to the food company—but the Manischewitz name has been licensed from the food company since 1986. The wine company is currently a division of Constellation Wines U.S. Manischewitz wines are produced in Naples, New York, at Widmer Wine Cellars. All of its wines are sweet and kosher—and clearly labeled "Kosher" or "Kosher for Passover." All have blessings printed on the label, with different ones for fruit wines made from blackberries or cherries.

The Assimilation of Ethnic Food

Foods once considered peculiar and unpalatable have been absorbed into the culinary mainstream with the help of ethnic entrepreneurs. For example, yogurt (from the Turkish word for "to thicken") was at one time a mysterious item enjoyed mostly by Middle Easterners. Its later popularity is in large part due to the business prowess of the Colombosians, an Armenian family who owned a small farm in Andover, Massachusetts, during the Great Depression. They made old-country yogurt and peddled it in horse-drawn wagons to local Syrians, Lebanese, Greeks, and Armenians. The family named their product Colombo because many of their customers could not pronounce Colombosian. The merchants purchased a plant to manufacture the country's first commercial yogurt. Originally sold in glass **bottles** in ethnic stores, blue-and-white paper cups of Colombo yogurt began appearing in **supermarkets** in the 1960s.

Similarly, other ingredients, many now commonplace, were introduced to natives by newcomers. Like many Italian farmers and produce merchants, the D'Arrigo brothers, Sicilian immigrants, transformed U.S. agriculture. The young farmers transformed broccoli from an Italian vegetable into an American staple. The first shipments of broccoli grown in California were sent by the D'Arrigos to the East Coast in 1924. Innovators in advertising, they marketed bunches of broccoli with a pink label and a picture of the cherubic Andy, son of brother Stephen. Andy Boy broccoli was a groundbreaker in ethnic food branding.

Ethnic merchants have traveled from early jumping-off points on the East and West coasts to the hinterland. In the process, immigrant food has become more familiar. Greeks fanned out across the country opening diners, **candy** shops, pizzerias, and restaurants. The Thais have been equally intrepid; most substantial cities across the country can boast at least one eatery offering pad thai and satay.

Crossing Boundaries

Some entrepreneurs have not been satisfied with simply merchandising their own ethnic foods. William Gebhardt, a German café owner in New Braunfels, Texas, developed one of the earliest commercial chili powders during the late 19th century. Joseph Di Giorgio, the son of a lemon grower in Sicily, sold fruit in Baltimore during the early 20th century. When lemon imports slowed during the winter months, the Sicilian chartered steamships to bring in cargos of bananas from Cuba, Jamaica, and Honduras to the Maryland port.

Jeno Paulucci, the son of an Italian immigrant iron miner in Hibbing, Minnesota, popularized Chinese food in mainstream America. A natural huckster, the one-time grocery barker went from **canning** bean sprouts during World War II to manufacturing chow mein and chop suey under the Chun King brand name in the 1950s.

The Transformation of the Ethnic Food Enterprise

Ethnics have operated a wide range of food businesses, from small groceries and restaurants to wholesaling, manufacturing, and importing firms. Some of the most successful enterprises have developed into large corporations using modern technology and marketing.

The **Sara Lee** company, for example, sprang from a small chain of Chicago bakeries run by Jewish merchant Charles Lubin. Lubin, who named his signature cheesecake for his daughter because of its "wholesome and American" ring, devised an inventive production method. The aluminum foil pan in which the cake was baked was also used to freeze and package it. By 1954, the Kitchens of Sara Lee were marketing the cheesecake in 48 states. Lubin sold the business to the Consolidated Foods conglomerate in 1956.

The saga of Progresso Foods encapsulates the stages in the history of the ethnic food business. Its founder, Giuseppe Uddo, a Sicilian immigrant who arrived in New Orleans at the end of the 19th century, started out carrying olives, cheeses, and cans of imported tomato paste in a horse-drawn cart to nearby Italian truck farmers. The family firm expanded into importing and wholesaling items such as capers, chickpeas, anchovies, and pine nuts to ethnic groceries. During World War II, the company began processing domestically grown tomatoes, peppers, and eggplants. By the 1950s, Progresso's olive oil, roasted peppers, crushed tomatoes, and other wares were being sold in the chains. The products were grouped together in the first ethnic food section to be displayed in supermarkets. Looking for a year-round product, the family stumbled into the soup business. They launched their line with lentil, escarole, and other flavors made from old family recipes. The soups became the mainstay of the business. Today, the firm that started with a horse-drawn cart is owned by **Pillsbury**.

In the latest twist in the history of the business, firms have begun focusing on selling their products to second- and third-generation ethnics. Often too busy to prepare recipes from scratch, they are eager for quick and easy-to-prepare foods. Goya, the largest Hispanic food company, offers customers frozen yucca and packages of ready-to-make paella. Between 2000 and 2005, sales of ethnic foods in the United States grew by 4.9 percent per year, and by 2005 accounted for 11.8 percent of all retail food sales.

The ethnic food business mirrors the crazy quilt of American immigrant life. As Chun King titan Paulucci put it, "Only in America would it be possible for a man named Jeno Francesco Paulucci, son of poor Italian immigrants, to get rich selling Chinese food in a Scandinavian region"

FURTHER READINGS: Denker, Joel. *The World on a Plate: A Tour through the History of America's Ethnic Cuisine.* Boulder, CO: Westview Press, 2003; Gabaccia, Donna. "Immigration and American Diversity: Food for Thought." In Reed Ueeda, ed. *A Companion to American Immigration*, pp. 443–70. Malden, MA: Blackwell, 2006; Gabaccia, Donna. *We Are What We Eat: Ethnic Food and the Making of Americans.* Cambridge, MA: Harvard University Press, 1998; "Insights into Tomorrow's Ethnic Food and Drink Consumers." http://www.the-infoshop.com/study/dc32475-ethnic-food.html; Leipold, L. E. *Jeno F. Paulucci: Merchant Philanthropist.* Minneapolis, MN: T. S. Denison, 1968, 6; Rozin, Elisabeth. *Ethnic Cuisine: The Flavor-Principle Cookbook.* Lexington, MA: Stephen Greene Press, 1983; Shenton, James, ed. *American Cooking: The Melting Pot.* New York: Time-Life Books, 2003.

Joel S. Denker

European Union The European Union (EU) is an association of 25 countries that have yielded sections of their administrative, political, and economic sovereignty to enhance internal and regional security, to ensure economic growth in order to compete on the world stage with other major economies, and to achieve a stronger presence in world politics. It is the last development of an effort initiated in 1951 by the Treaty of Paris, which set up the European Coal and Steel Community. That organization became the European Economic Community (EEC) in 1957 and the EU in 1992.

To reach these goals, the Union actively operates in different sectors within its territory. The EU is relevant to the food industry with regard to four primary aspects: agricultural policies, the world market and interactions with the World Trade Organization (WTO), the determination of quality indications, and controls on **food safety**.

Common Agricultural Policy

As a response to the food security emergency following World War II, in 1958 the early member states outlined a Common Agricultural Policy (CAP), aimed at enhancing food productivity while ensuring stable supplies to consumers and economic viability to the producers. Its principles were implemented in 1962, offering subsidies and incentives, providing financial assistance, and guaranteeing prices of certain products to farmers. The CAP also acknowledged the disparities among the different agricultural regions and determined the appropriate adjustments, granting more financial aid to the needier areas. The policy, which absorbed an impressive two-thirds of the total budget, met its goals, but revealed flaws after two decades of implementation, such as continual surpluses of several commodities, large parts of which were sold with subsidies, stored, or, worse, disposed of. Consumers and taxpayers resented the measures, especially because of the new environmental sensitivity that found its expression in events like the 1992 UN Earth Summit in Rio.

In the 1990s the CAP underwent major reforms aimed at improved efficiency with minor costs for the Union. While in the past the subsidies to farmers were proportionally linked to the quantities produced, causing frequent overproduction gluts, in the future farmers are to receive direct payments that will ensure their income stability, independent from what and how much they produce. The goal is for the CAP to absorb less than a third of the total EU budget by 2015, to curb overproduction, and to stimulate farmers to meet consumers' expectations for quality, environmental protection, and food safety. Should farmers not respect these standards, their aid will be reduced. The overall goal is to make European farmers more competitive and market oriented, focusing on quality, diversity, and protection of local productions as key advantages on the world market. One of the most evident results of these policies is the establishment of the so-called quality logos.

Despite the ongoing reforms, the CAP still attracts heavy criticism from several quarters. Many developing countries argue that the subsidies amount to unfair competition on the world market, with oversupply preventing their products from reaching EU consumers. Within the EU itself, the CAP has been accused of keeping prices artificially high and of favoring certain countries whose agricultural sector is more relevant, and the whole system is said to be doomed to failure due to the enlargement process and the future accession of countries such as Bulgaria and Romania, whose agricultural sectors are in need of sweeping reforms.

The World Market

One of the goals of the EU is to develop common European policies on the world scene, including international trade. One of the first actions the organization took was to sign agreements with several countries in Africa, the Caribbean, and the Pacific (known as ACP countries) that had been part of European colonial empires. These actions were taken partly out of sense of responsibility, but also to reinforce commercial ties with the developing world and to ensure regular supplies of commodities and raw materials necessary to European markets and industries.

A first series of conventions began in Lomé, Togo, between 1975 and 1989 and led to the Cotonou (Benin) Agreement in 2000. While the first treaties were mainly based on the General System of Preferences (GSP), a system of **tariff** preferences and ad hoc funds that guarantee ACP countries access to the European market and price stability in agricultural and mining products, the new agreement aims to involve local authorities, trade unions, and civil society in upholding national strategies and implementing development programs. Some of the poorest ACP countries will basically enjoy full access to the EU, which on the contrary will establish regional trade agreements with the richer developing countries.

The close ties between the EU and the ACP countries led to clashes with the United States within the framework of the WTO and, in particular, its Doha Development Round, a series of negotiations started in Doha, Qatar, in 2001 aimed at lowering trade barriers to allow free commerce among all countries. The summits in Cancun, Mexico, in 2003 and Hong Kong in 2005 have not yet brought a solution. In 1994, the United States filed a complaint with the WTO, accusing the EU of discriminating against U.S. corporations and infringing on **free trade** by granting special treatment for the ACP commodities, among which were bananas. The legal controversy, which gave way to a series of retaliations on other products, was ruled in favor of the United States, but the issue of access to the EU market for developing countries is still open.

Quality Indications

Following the changes in food market and consumer preferences, the EU authorities have created a system that underlines the uniqueness of certain products and their connections with specific places and traditions. In 1992 the EU issued regulation 2081, which set up two quality indicators, the Protected Designation of Origin (PDO) and the Protected Geographical Indication (PGI). Regulation 2081 is now replaced by regulation 510, issued in 2006.

The PDO denomination contains the name of a specific place, region, or country to indicate that the qualities and other characteristics that make that product unique are essentially or exclusively due to a specific geographical environment. The regulation requires that all stages of production and transformation be carried out in that named geographical area.

The PGI denomination is less stringent, allowing fame and traditional notoriety to play some role. A product carrying the PGI logo has specific reputation or characteristics that associate it with the geographical environment of a given specific place, region, or country and its natural and human components. At least one phase in the production and transformation process must be carried out in the area mentioned in the geographical indication.

A third category, Traditional Specialty Guaranteed (TSG), is even less strict, being applied to products that have distinctive features referring not to a specific place but to traditional ingredients and methods of production.

For the EU authorities, the implementation of these quality indications offers guarantees for consumers, delivers clear and effective marketing messages, and protects farmers and producers against unfair imitation. The registered products can use the quality logos that immediately identify the PDO, PGI and TSG products for consumers.

These coveted registrations (there are already almost 700) cover mostly products from the southern countries of the Union, with France and Italy having the majority, followed by Portugal and Spain. The only Northern European country with a comparable number of protected products is Germany. The reason for this situation is that much of food production in the northern EU countries is industrial, with very few products connected to specific places and manufactured using traditional ingredients and methods. This tension transferred itself to food safety issues, with the Northern Europeans arguing that some of the traditional methods are not sanitary and do not meet the standards required by the Union. A cultural debate with very important economic ramifications has ensued.

These regulations and the reform of the CAP do not apply to **wine** production. In 1999, the EU issued regulation 1493 in an effort to reorganize the entire sector around the concept of "geographic indications," as is the case of other food products, and to adapt it to the WTO legal framework concerning the intellectual property rights. Nevertheless, various member states already have existing systems of wine classifications and different laws regarding vineyard planting, yields, and winemaking methods. Under the pressure of international competition, and to respond to the trend toward lower per-capita consumption, the EU has been trying to reform the wine sector.

Food Safety

From the late 1990s, events such as the **bovine spongiform encephalopathy** (BSE, or "mad cow") crisis stimulated a more widespread awareness among European citizens about what should make its way to their tables. The EU has implemented a series of regulations aimed at ensuring food safety "from farm to fork," as a slogan says. The legislation, known as General Food Law, whose general principles were laid out in 2002, imposes the traceability of all foodstuffs, animal feed, and feed ingredients—essentially the entire food chain. To ensure traceability, each business must be able to identify its suppliers and which businesses it supplied, according to the "one-step-backward, one-step-forward" approach.

In 2002 the EU established the European Food Safety Authority (EFSA). The EFSA offers an independent scientific point of reference in evaluating risks and guaranteeing the regular functioning of the internal market. It also formulates pronouncements about scientific matters that are objects of controversy and would help to manage any future emergency crisis at the Union level. The EFSA has no enforcement authority, but it passes its recommendations to the European Commission. Nevertheless, it is granted an autonomous right of communication to provide information directly to the public, although in case of emergency it has to coordinate its communication with the European Commission and member states. The internal organization, staff, and finance were all laid out in the 2002 regulations, and a December 2003 meeting of the heads of government of the EU member states held in Brussels assigned the offices of the newly created EFSA to the city of Parma, Italy.

The legislation set up an alert system that would allow the European Commission and EU national governments to react rapidly in the event of a food or feed safety scare. In managing the risk, the EU will apply the "precautionary principle." The commission will not necessarily need to wait for proof that there really is a risk: if, according to the EFSA, there are reasonable grounds for suspecting there is a problem, the commission will act to limit the risk.

Furthermore, since there is no definitive proof that genetically modified organisms (GMOs) are *not* harmful to humans, most Europeans tend to avoid anything that could be identified as **genetically engineered**. In July 2001, the EU adopted a legislative package that established a system to trace and label GMOs. It regulates the diffusion on the market of food and feed products derived from genetically modified elements when there is a content above 1 percent, which is considered a reasonable level of "accidental presence." The new regulation was implemented with the directive 18 of 2001 and the regulations 1829, 1830, and 1946 of 2003.

Organic farming, considered as part of the CAP effort toward sustainable agriculture, has become an important issue in the EU. In December 2005 the European Commission adopted a proposal for a new regulation on organic production, tentatively set to go into effect on January 1, 2009. The new rules will define the objectives and principles of organic production, clarify the GMO rules (notably the general GMO thresholds: 0.9 percent of GMO content through accidental contamination), render compulsory either the EU organic logo or a stylized indication "EU-Organic," and develop permanent import rules.

Fabio Parasecoli

F ❖

Famine Famine is a regional crisis of starvation or malnutrition caused by the practical scarcity of food. It is regional in the sense that it is in some respect confined to a clearly defined group of people (usually, though not necessarily, the inhabitants of a specific region). Famine is also regional in the sense that it is generally expressed in terms of a group's absolute number of starvation- or malnutrition-induced fatalities (e.g., "3,000 villagers died in 1516") or as a ratio of the affected population (e.g., "half of the sharecroppers now suffer from malnutrition"). Finally, famine is caused by the practical scarcity of food, meaning that the individuals affected by famine cannot, for any number of possible reasons, consume adequate quantities or qualities of food. In other words, famine is a statistically expressible crisis among a well-defined group of people who are unable to eat enough of the right kinds of food.

Historically, famines have generally been accompanied by political unrest and epidemic disease and have most often been caused by some combination of natural and man-made factors, including unfavorable weather, pestilence, misguided economic policies, widespread poverty, and war. Famine has generally been endemic to peasant and nonindustrial societies whose reliance on agriculture as both a supplier of food and a common employment makes failed harvests an economic crisis as well as an agricultural one; in such circumstances, a poor harvest means both rising food prices and increasing unemployment and wage depression in what is already likely to be an environment of widespread poverty and subsistence-level agriculture.

The demographic effects of famine are generally short-lived. In most cases and for perhaps obvious reasons, fatalities are concentrated among children, the infirm, and the elderly, and famines see reduced rates of fertility. Male mortality also consistently exceeds female mortality, although the reasons for this are not immediately clear—aside from biologically obvious gender differences, such as women's typically lower caloric needs and greater stores of body fat, the matter has not been satisfactorily explained. Regardless, famine tends to least affect the reproductive core of most populations (that is, healthy adult women), and postfamine periods are often characterized by a period of increased births, so even severe famines generally do not affect population growth for more than a decade. The famine-induced mortalities in Bengal (1943), China (1958–1961), and Ethiopia (1983–1985) were completely made up for by a growing population in substantially less time.

But famines' political effects often prove more durable; after the Irish Potato Famine that began in 1845, Ireland was largely depopulated by emigration rather than starvation-induced mortality, an effect of the famine that is still demographically visible in Ireland and elsewhere. Ireland's political memories of the Potato Famine also continue to complicate Anglo-Irish colonial relations—just as the memories of India's famines under British rule continue to complicate Anglo-Indian relations, and just as memories of the Holodomar, a famine induced in the Ukraine by Josef Stalin's economic policies (and by some considered a genocide) continue to complicate Russo-Ukrainian relations. Today's famines in Sub-Saharan Africa also in some respects define that region's political relationships with North America and Europe and will doubtless inform that region's relationships with the rest of the world for the foreseeable future.

Understandings of Famine

Famine has historically been understood as a geographically defined shortage of food, most famously in the work of the Reverend Thomas Malthus, whose 1798 *Essay on the Principle of Population* argues that there is a natural tendency for any region's population to increase more quickly than its food supply, with the result that population growth would be periodically checked directly (e.g., through starvation) or indirectly (e.g., through war over arable land). This Malthusian portrait of populations periodically pruned by famine and war has often been married to the language of supply and demand, and analyses of contemporary and historical famines often suggest that an increasing demand for food in the form of an increasing population makes societies more susceptible to famine, either through the reduction of the food supply by inclement weather and the depredations of war or by the growing population's needs eventually overtaking its ability to feed itself.

Though this Malthusian understanding of famine is statistically convenient and in some circles remains widely used, it has over the past three decades given way to Amartya Sen's more sophisticated and useful "entitlement theory" of famine, which considers famine in terms of any individual's or group's access to food rather than solely in terms of abstracted supply and demand. In Sen's model, any individual might be said to have any number of entitlements to food, through either production (food she grows herself), ownership (food she purchases at market or receives as compensation for labor), social security benefits (food distributed by a state system to, for instance, the poor, invalids, or children), charity (food distributed by, for instance, a humanitarian relief agency), or any number of similar mechanisms. Famine, according to Sen, represents the failure of one or more of these entitlement systems. For instance, a civil war might cripple the state's ability to distribute food to the needy through a social security system and might also compromise the charitable distribution of food through conventional channels (perhaps by causing relief agencies to relocate or flee the country); in such a case, famine (or at least an increased starvation or malnutrition mortality) is likely even if both the population and the absolute supply of food remain relatively constant.

Sen's approach is of exceptional use in explaining why famines often occur in the face of only modest agricultural shortfalls or even in years of robust food production; the Irish Potato Famine occurred while Ireland was exporting food to England (where it could command higher prices), a policy that either induced or worsened the famine in Ireland. Likewise, the Ethiopian famine of 1973 saw its highest mortality rates in the Wollo region, although food was being shipped out of Wollo to the capital city of Addis Ababa, where it could be more easily and profitably sold. In these cases, as in many others, market entitlements rather than food production seem to have principally determined the geography of famine mortality. These examples suggest a point that bears repeating: regardless of the amount or quality of food a region produces, those with the weakest entitlements to food may be led into famine through political, economic, and social changes unrelated to agriculture, and they are at the greatest risk of starvation in the face of failed harvests or other agricultural panics.

Responses to Famine

Nearly every modern society has experienced famine or the threat of famine at some point in its history, and most societies have had formal or practical measures for relieving them. As early as the 14th century, cities then as small as London had established municipal granaries from which the needy might be fed during times of scarcity, and similar measures have been in place in cities large and small for most of recorded history. In short, most societies have historically had some provision for collectively storing food for relief in times of need.

Modern approaches to famine relief add to this some mechanism for anticipating agricultural failures. One of the earliest of these modern approaches was the Indian Famine Codes implemented by the colonial British in the late 19th century, which defined three stages of food-related crisis—near-scarcity, scarcity, and famine—and provided for each level a set of indicators and administrative countermeasures. Many later famine codes have been derived from the general principles set forth in the Indian Famine Codes and similarly classify different famine-related conditions by severity and provide a set of measures that may be used to anticipate the nature and locations of famine crises (such as rainfall measurements, food prices, and migrant populations). Perhaps the most effective of these is northwest Kenya's Turkana District's Early Warning System, which considers rainfall levels, market prices of staple foods, the condition of livestock (including the conditions of their rangeland), and enrollment in social security programs and has preplanned responses for famine-related crises ranging from "alarm" to "emergency."

Aside from their anticipation of famines, modern systems differ from their predecessors in responding to famine as an economic crisis as well as a humanitarian one. Famines often find individuals and families obtaining food at the cost of long-term hardship (for instance, by mortgaging land and selling or consuming their farms' breeding stock or seed corn); intervention before these types of irreversible coping strategies are widely used can both save lives and prevent famine crises from impoverishing affected populations.

Medieval and Early Modern Famine

Famines were a frequent occurrence throughout early and medieval Europe, but they were generally the geographically isolated effects of failed harvests or warfare. There was throughout most of Europe a string of failed harvests from 1315 to 1317, during which there was widespread and severe criminal unrest that extended to infanticide and cannibalism. In some estimations, the Black Death (1347–1350) relieved some of the population pressures that contributed to earlier food scarcity, but it is more likely (in light of Sen's entitlement theory) that the less famine-prone conditions of the 15th century had more to do with the surviving workers' ability to demand better payment for their labor and, consequently, gain improved access to market grain.

The 16th century was relatively famine free, save for a string of failed harvests from 1593 to 1597. These led to crises in most of western Europe except the Netherlands, which had established a thriving Baltic trade and was able to import enough grain to avoid disaster; the Netherlands in this sense became the first European state to slip the shadow of famine, although southern England (and particularly London) was able to import Baltic grain and effectively (by the standards of the day) administer a set of orders, including extensive market regulation, that blunted the famine's worst effects. Both the Netherlands and London seem to have ridden out the crisis of the 1620s, which affected most of continental Europe as well as northern England, Ireland, and Scotland. There was a severe famine in Finland in 1696, which may have killed as much as a third of the population, and the droughts of 1740–1743 led to famine for some areas and increased grain prices in most of Europe. Imperial Russia, meanwhile, experienced periodic droughts and famines approximately every decade. These continued until the middle of the 20th century.

> Famine has always been a threat to human populations, and the Irish Potato Famine of the late 1840s is only one example from modern memory. Currently, famines are raging in many parts of the world—in Afghanistan, Angola, Burundi, Cote d'Ivoire, Democratic Republic of Congo, Eritrea, Ethiopia, Iraq, Kenya, Liberia, Madagascar, Malawi, Mozambique, North Korea, Rwanda, Sierra Leone, Somalia, Sudan, Tajikistan, Zambia, and Zimbabwe.

The Recent History of Famine

Today, famine remains a threat in much of Africa. The early 21st century has seen the Famine Early Warning System (which was created as a response to the Ethiopian crisis of the 1980s) alert the rest of the world to potential crises in Chad, Ethiopia, Niger, southern Sudan, Somalia, and Zimbabwe; it has also seen the United Nations' Food and Agriculture Organization warn of possible crises in Djibouti, Ethiopia, Somalia, and Kenya (caused by a combination of drought and military conflicts), as well as a serious humanitarian crisis in Darfur. The 20th century saw about 70 million deaths from famine, nearly half of which resulted from China's famine of 1958–1961 during the Great Leap Forward; China also saw famines in 1928 and 1942. Other significant 20th-century famines occurred in the Soviet Union (throughout the 1930s), Bengal (1942–1945), Cambodia (throughout the 1970s), Ethiopia (1983–1985, but to a lesser degree throughout the late 1970s and early 1980s), and North Korea (throughout the 1990s).

The 19th and earlier 20th centuries saw the famines and agricultural crises that would shape much modern famine policy. India experienced at least a dozen severe famines (that is, famines that killed more than 200,000 people) throughout the 19th century, during which as many as 30 million Indians may have died of starvation or malnutrition. This situation prompted the British (then the colonial power in India) to author the aforementioned Indian Famine Codes during the 1880s.

Africa's colonial experience also led to frequent and widespread famines. These became more severe during and after 1888, the year the introduction of Europe's epizootic rinderpest killed much of Africa's cattle—a crisis not only because it devastated this part of the food supply but also because it impoverished even the wealthiest ranchers and herders and so hamstrung an economy and source of charitable relief on which many depended. Aside from leading to (even more) widespread poverty, it also helped institute a colonial agricultural economy that produced little food for domestic consumption and instead largely relied on selling cash crops in order to import food from other regions. This practice created, and continues to create, an especially famine-susceptible peasant society in Africa, not only because cotton-farm laborers are poorer than livestock herders or ranchers (both in terms of money and in terms of direct access to food) but also because fluctuating commodity prices or problems with transport (either of food or of commodities to be exchanged for it) can lead to immediate crises. And the situation continues to worsen. In short, a combination of the effects of this colonial cash-crop economy, political instability (including armed conflict and all-out civil war), local and international corruption, mismanagement of food and commodity transport, and trade policies that continue to harm Africa's agriculture has led to widespread famine susceptibility for a continent that was not, in the estimation of many agriculturalists, famine prone for much of the late 19th and early 20th centuries.

China throughout the early 19th century had an exceptionally robust and effective system of food subsidies and famine countermeasures in place, since the famously apt Qing dynasty bureaucracy devoted extensive attention to minimizing the number and severity of famines. But as the Qing weakened through the mid-19th century and abandoned the traditional relief techniques (which included a legal requirement that the wealthy distribute food to the poor, an extensive regulation of food prices, and shipments of food to affected regions), failed harvests posed an ever greater danger. The 1877 droughts throughout northern China were an unmitigated disaster, killing 9–13 million and depopulating the northern province of Shangxi.

In Europe, France saw occasional 19th-century famines. It remained the last European region to experience peacetime famines until the 20th century, when Eastern Europe saw localized, periodic crises (especially under Stalin) and World War II starved 30,000 in the Netherlands during what is now known as the Hongerwinter. Most famously, Ireland's Great Famine (also known as the Irish Potato Famine, since one of its causes was potato blight) killed as many as a million people between 1845 and 1849 and led to widespread emigration. The combined effects of these reduced Ireland's population by a fifth (between 1841 and 1851).

It is worth noting that all of these countries were either colonies, dictatorships, or practical dictatorships when these famines occurred, and that no functioning democracy or republic has in modern times suffered a peacetime famine; this suggests that (at least so far as the last two centuries are concerned) while famine might not always have political causes, it is nonetheless politically preventable. During the Ethiopian famines of the late 20th century, dictatorships such as Ethiopia and the Sudan experienced famines while nearby democracies such as Botswana and Zimbabwe, even though they had more severe drops in food production, were able to avoid catastrophe by creating temporary employment for their most endangered populations.

Nate Eastman

Farmers' Markets Farmers' markets are designated public areas, facilities, or events, typically held outdoors or in a large, covered space, where farmers and food producers can market and sell their products directly to the public. They are a traditional way of selling agricultural, crafts, and homemade products, as evidenced by markets and market days in cities and towns throughout the world. Some venues, such as New York City, also call it a *greenmarket*.

Farmers' markets are urban phenomena worldwide, established for the benefit of the urban consumer who values quality, variety, and freshness in food. They assume characteristics determined by the cultural norms, the regional environment, and local forms of government particular to their locales.

In the United States, farmers' markets are often limited to particular days and hours of operation, for example, on a weekly or biweekly schedule, usually during the growing season of summer and autumn months. Some locales have year-round markets. The number of farmers' markets in the United States has grown considerably, from about 340 in 1970 to more than 3,700 operational markets as of 2004, with an increase of 111 percent between 1994 and 2004, according to the 2004 *National Farmers' Markets Directory* and the **U.S. Department of Agriculture** (USDA). The Farmer-to-Consumer Direct Marketing Act of 1976 encouraged the creation of many new markets in the late 1970s and 1980s. Recent increases in the popularity of farmers' markets have been attributed to growing consumer interest in fresh, local, and **organic** foods and the changing economics of agriculture.

Though these criteria differ from market to market, the most important general principle of farmers' markets is that goods be locally produced and that vendors sell their own products, including meat and **dairy** products. Farmers' markets often feature produce and products that are seasonal, grown with natural or organic methods, grown locally, and very fresh. A typical farmers' market sells in-season fruits, vegetables, flowers, fresh and dried herbs, honey, and value-added foodstuffs such as jams, preserves, and baked goods. Many farmers' markets also sell meat, eggs, and dairy products from animals that are humanely treated, free-range, and free of **antibiotics** and hormones.

Proponents of farmers' markets note that since farmers' market produce is picked and sold when ripe, **flavor** is at its best. Also, they argue that locally grown produce does not have to travel as far as the produce available in conventional **supermarkets**, saving fossil fuel expenditure from transportation costs, as well as that the markets help small farms stay in business. The farmers' market, then, possesses a special status within the larger food system.

Farmers who participate in these markets are more likely to be small-scale farmers and producers. These markets therefore appeal to those who find it difficult, impossible, or personally objectionable to participate in food markets or production at the commercial level. Many do not have farming backgrounds, arriving at farming via other career routes. Some are retired from other occupations or farm part-time and have other sources of household income. Farmers and producers who sell directly to consumers avoid having to use a **middleman** or distributor, meaning that consumers get a better price for the food and more money goes directly to the farmer. This increases the economic viability of small farms and family farms, as well as marketing and retailing options for these farms.

By participating in direct relationships with their customers, farmers' markets purposefully promote the virtues of quality, community, and authenticity in the food products they make available to the public. First, the farmers' market plays a cultural role as either preserving or newly creating a sense of nostalgia for the existence of family farms. Second, these farmers use the proliferation of popularly available discourse surrounding the language of organic food, providing a generalized conceptual framework to consumers of how the food system ought to work. Growth in the organic food industry has paralleled the rise in the popularity of farmers' markets. Until recently, farmers' markets were the most publicly visible source of organically grown products. Some farmers who sell at these markets have begun calling their products "locally grown," "pesticide free," and, increasingly, "beyond organic" to avoid needing the USDA's certification process to market their food to consumers as well as to differentiate themselves from larger-scale organic food producers. This rhetoric emphasizes the importance of these foods, and their producers, in order to counter the broad idea that the **agribusiness** version of food has the same virtues.

Additionally, farmers' markets can be a social event for consumers. Customers can easily talk with farmers about how the produce was grown and how it can be prepared. Many markets have a festive atmosphere. Some of the larger markets include regular presentations by local musicians or demonstrations by local chefs.

Though farmers' markets play a marginal role in overall food distribution networks and consumption patterns, their popularity and growing presence in urban and suburban communities allows consumers and producers to develop direct market-based relationships. According to the USDA, in 2000 more than 19,000 farmers reported selling their produce only at farmers' markets, and 82 percent of markets were considered self-sustaining. Farmers' markets often convene on public property and are sponsored by nongovernmental entities, which may be farmers' associations, chambers of commerce, cooperatives, or other community organizations, although they may also be managed by local governments. More than half of farmers' markets participate in state and federal nutrition programs for low-income individuals, including accepting WIC (Women, Infants, and Children) coupons and **food stamps**. Such programs and local support systems demonstrate that farmers' markets provide opportunities for social interaction, both formal and informal, to engage communities and neighborhoods and educate people about local food and agricultural concerns.

FURTHER READINGS: Brown, Allison. "Farmers' Market Research, 1940–2000: An Inventory and Review." *American Journal of Alternative Agriculture* 17, no. 4 (2002).

Michaela DeSoucey

Fast Food Restaurants Fast food **restaurants**, also known as quick service restaurants, are characterized by a limited menu, minimal service, and inexpensive food served quickly to customers. To ensure speedy service, food is often prepared in advance and shipped from a central **franchise** location, then reheated or assembled to order. As part of a growing multibillion-dollar industry, fast food restaurants have experienced considerable growth, both domestically and worldwide. However, this growth has not occurred without criticism. In recent years, fast food restaurants have come under fire for contributing to the **obesity** epidemic and for reportedly poor **labor** practices. These restaurants have also been the ongoing targets of criticism by environmentalists, animal welfare advocates, and antiglobalization activists.

History, Franchises, and Growth

Fast food restaurants, as they currently exist, were invented in the United States during the post–World War II era. The White Castle hamburger chain is credited with inventing fast food. Early founders like Richard and Maurice McDonald, of the famous Golden Arches, began in the drive-in food business that was fueled by Americans' newfound love of cars and convenience. However, by the end of the 1940s, the McDonald brothers grew dissatisfied with the constant need to replace not only staff like carhops and short-order cooks but also items such as the dishes and silverware that teenage clientele would steal. Instead, the brothers decided to try something new. They developed and implemented an innovative assembly-line system of food preparation designed specifically to increase volume. The use of disposable serving items, along with a specialized division of labor where employees performed a single task, resulted in the efficient fast food production system with which society has grown familiar. The success of **McDonald's** soon led others to mimic the model. The 1950s thus witnessed the birth of new **chain restaurants** such as Burger King, Wendy's, and Kentucky Fried Chicken (KFC). A fast food war soon erupted, particularly in Southern California; some chains flourished, others quickly faded. This intense competition remains prevalent in the industry today.

Several large corporations that operate multiple chains compete today for consumer dollars. The two leading industry giants are Yum! Brands (which owns KFC, Pizza Hut, Long John Silver's, Taco Bell, and A&W) and the McDonald's Corporation (which owns Boston Market and until 2006 controlled Chipotle Mexican Grill). Operations for these giants are extensive and global. For example, with about 33,000 restaurants in more than 100 countries, Yum! Brands is considered the world's largest restaurant company, employing a workforce of about 272,000 employees and recording revenues of $9.9 billion. Yum! Brands competes directly with the McDonald's Corporation, which operates 31,000 restaurants in 119 countries, employs 447,000 people, and has revenues of $20 billion.

Given the intense competition, fast food restaurants must market aggressively not only to attract new customers but also to retain old ones. While polls suggest that consumers are not necessarily loyal to a single fast food brand, millions of dollars are spent on **advertising**. Fast food corporations have sponsored an array of athletic events, including NASCAR races, the FIFA World Cup, and the Olympic Games. Widespread marketing campaigns with catchy jingles and entertaining characters have also been used to instill brand-name recognition, often among children. For example, children can enjoy a McDonald's Happy Meal that includes a toy featuring their favorite Disney or Pixar film character. Athlete and celebrity endorsements ranging from Michael Jordan to Paris Hilton are another common marketing strategy.

The U.S. fast food market continues to grow. The market value of the industry is currently $51 billion and is forecast to increase. The amount consumers spend at fast food restaurants has grown at an annual rate faster than at table-service businesses. Sales continue to rise as consumers want convenient, inexpensive, and quick meals. Trends toward longer workdays, combined with the growing number of dual-income families, make fast food an extremely attractive food option. Many Americans simply no longer have time to dine in restaurants or prepare elaborate meals at home.

Particularly high rates of fast food consumption are seen in certain populations. Nonwhite and low-income groups are susceptible to increased fast food consumption, especially since it is readily available in these neighborhoods. In areas without local parks, fast food restaurants with playgrounds offer even greater appeal to families with children.

Growth of U.S. fast food chains has been mirrored abroad. Today, U.S. companies make up more than half of the global fast food market. As Western European and North American markets become saturated, fast food chains are expanding into high-growth regions such as Eastern Europe and Asia. To survive in these new environments, companies entering foreign markets need to adapt their menus to local tastes. For example, KFC restaurants have proliferated in China by offering fare such as "duck soup." They also offer "Old Beijing Twister"—a wrap made of fried chicken that is modeled after the way Peking duck, a Chinese specialty, is served. Interestingly, while domestic fast food is targeted to lower-income clientele, food at **multinational** chains, especially in the developing world, is often more expensive than local fare. As such, it is targeted toward a higher-income population.

Fast Food, Food Quality, and Obesity

Despite phenomenal industry growth, fast food restaurants have been the target of ongoing criticism. Nutritionists charge that fast food fare is poor quality food because it is high in fat, sodium, **sugar**, and calories, while being low in fiber, **vitamins**, and nutrients. For example, McDonald's limited-time-only Bigger Big Mac was 40 percent larger than the original Big Mac and contained an entire day's recommended allowance of saturated fat.

Since the well-known Jack in the Box deaths in the early 1990s, along with other cases in well-known chains, the mass production and distribution of food has also raised concerns over *E. coli* **bacterial** contamination in hamburger meat. Such cases have led to industry-wide changes and the implementation of more stringent quality control and **food safety** standards.

Public interest groups have also criticized the industry for misleading the public about the nutritional value of its products, directing **marketing to children**, and offering "super-sized" portions that encourage excess consumption. Critics have been quick to point out that two-thirds of Americans are overweight and a third are obese and that eating fast food has been linked to weight gain. Weight gain, in turn, has been connected to a long list of health maladies, including diabetes, heart disease, and stroke.

The concern over fast food and obesity was brought to the public's attention when the parents of two teenage girls in New York sued McDonald's for making their daughters "fat and unhealthy" (*Pelman v. McDonald's*). Even though the case was dismissed, it nevertheless drew attention to the industry's questionable practices. Filmmaker Morgan Spurlock used this case as a backdrop to his 2004 film *Super Size Me!* that explored the dangers of consuming excessive amounts of fast food.

In general, directly and indirectly through industry lobby groups, the fast food industry has expressed disapproval of proposals that attempt to regulate the industry. Lawsuits are vehemently condemned as frivolous by industry representatives. The National Restaurant Association has been especially vocal in the campaign to pass "commonsense consumption laws" that restrict lawsuits from customers seeking personal injury damages related to obesity and fast food consumption. Commonsense consumption laws are now enacted in more than 20 states. At the federal level, the

Personal Responsibility in Food Consumption Act, also known affectionately as the Cheeseburger Bill, has received House approval and awaits consideration in the Senate.

Public interest groups have attempted to put checks on the fast food industry by using strategies similar to those used against the tobacco industry. Groups such as the Center for Science in the Public Interest have called for special taxes and subsidies on unhealthy foods. The so-called fat tax or "Twinkie tax" would provide incentives to fast food restaurants, along with other food producers, to revise the nutritional content of food. Proponents of these taxes also argue that the revenues generated from these could be used to sponsor nutrition and other health promotion programs. Such taxes are now implemented in several U.S. states and Canadian provinces. In light of increasing rates of childhood obesity, public interest groups have also called for the stricter regulation of fast food marketing to children.

Fast food restaurants have been somewhat responsive to the demands of both public health officials and consumers. McDonald's, an industry leader, has now phased out super-sized products, while other leading companies such as Burger King, Wendy's, and Jack in the Box are now offering an array of lower- or low-fat items such as salads, grilled chicken sandwiches, and baked potatoes. Most major chains have now switched from cooking their French fries in animal fat or tallow to vegetable oil, a change that has resulted in food containing significantly less saturated fats. There is also a recent move by companies to remove trans-fats, which have been linked to heart disease, from menus. As health-consciousness rises, fast food chains such as Subway are becoming more visible, marketing their products as fresh and healthy alternatives to the standard, arguably less healthy, burger.

Fast food chains are directly promoting balanced, healthy, and active lifestyles in their advertising and making nutritional information accessible to consumers, both in restaurants and on company websites. Indeed, in this highly competitive market, many fast food companies are feeling strong pressure to adjust their products to health-conscious consumers. More and more consumers are demanding not only healthier foods but also **organic** and ethical foods that are free from genetic modification.

Despite industry responsiveness and industry changes adapting to consumer needs, the overall industry position still remains that fast food restaurants are merely providing what customers want. In a quick-paced society, fast food restaurants offer convenient, inexpensive, and tasty food to busy consumers. From the industry perspective, supply and demand should regulate the free market, and regulations should be kept to a minimum. The fast food industry emphasizes individual choice and personal responsibility. The Center for Consumer Freedom, a vocal nonprofit food industry group that represents more than 30,000 restaurants and taverns in the United States, argues that adult consumers are sensible enough to make their own decisions about what to eat and drink. In their view, if customers want to eat fast food, then it is their own personal choice.

Labor Practices

Fast food restaurants have also been accused of questionable labor practices—from the undocumented immigrant farm laborers who harvest the tomatoes that wind up on burgers to the factory workers in developing countries who manufacture the toys included in children's meals. An outspoken critic of the fast food industry and the author of the best-selling book now turned Hollywood film, *Fast Food Nation* (2001),

Eric Schlosser points to the unethical practices in American **beef** slaughterhouses. These factories, which provide the meat for the fast food industry, employ a large number of nonunion (and often illegal) immigrant workers who work under physically dangerous conditions. Foremen and supervisors push workers to maximize plant production at the cost of life and limb. In these plants, hourly wages are about a third lower than other production employees.

Low wages are also paid to those who work directly in fast food restaurants. Studies show that fast food wages are closely tied to the minimum wage and that fast food workers are among the lowest paid in the United States. Employees are predominantly young teenagers, although a growing number are recent immigrants, elderly, or handicapped. Little skill is required to perform tasks and employees receive limited job skills training. Overtime pay is rarely compensated as employee hours are strategically kept below the requisite number of qualifying hours. Most employees also do not receive benefits, which are restricted to a handful of salaried employees. The anti-union approach of many fast food corporate headquarters has further limited the power of employees to organize.

In addition to unfavorable working conditions, many fast food restaurants have become dangerous places of employment. Their proximity to highways has made them suitable targets of armed robberies.

Given these conditions, it is not unexpected that fast food restaurants experience high turnover. Most fast food workers occupy their job for less than a year. Indeed, the typical fast food restaurant worker quits or is fired in three to six months.

Environmentalism, Animal Welfare, and Globalization

The visibility of fast food restaurants, both domestically and worldwide, has made them targets of criticism by a range of social activists. The growth of fast food restaurants has effectively changed the landscape of American agriculture. The ownership of large farms by a few multinational corporations has resulted in the demise of traditional small-scale farming and the concentrated control of a large portion of American's food supply. Factory farming is widespread and has been criticized by animal welfare advocates for its inhumane treatment of animals. Environmentalists have also been critical of the excessive **packaging** used in many fast food restaurants and the use of genetically modified products.

Activists have targeted fast food restaurants, in both violent and peaceful protests. Animal rights groups have been in a constant battle with chains such as KFC over its treatment of farm animals. The counterculture has made activists like José Bové, who in 1999 destroyed a McDonald's in France, a global symbol and hero of the anticonsumerism, antiglobalization, anti-imperialism movement. In 1990, British protestors who were distributing leaflets that exposed McDonald's allegedly problematic practices, including the exploitation of its labor force, cruelty to animals, and the wasting of resources, were slapped with a libel suit. The high-profile "McLibel" Case resulted in damages being awarded to the company, although the court did rule in favor of a number of the defendants' claims.

The expansion of fast food into the global market is also seen as a symbol of U.S. dominance and **cultural imperialism** that contributes to the continued so-called Americanization of the world. Fast food is considered a potential threat to local and national identity in that it imports not only American tastes but also American culture. Even while (or because) American-owned fast food restaurants adapt superficially to local tastes, activists claim that they threaten local businesses and bring the world closer to cultural homogeneity. The **Slow Food** movement emerged specifically to counteract this force and is a direct attempt to preserve local culture, cuisine, and foodways.

See also Takeout.

FURTHER READINGS: Block, Jason, Richard A. Scribner, and Karen B. DeSalvo. "Fast Food, Race/Ethnicity, and Income." *American Journal of Preventive Medicine* 27 (2004): 211–17; Datamonitor USA. *Fast Food in the United States: Industry Profile*. New York: Datamonitor USA, 2006; Jekanowski, Mark D. "Causes and Consequences of Fast Food Sales Growth." *Food Review* January–April, Vol. 21 (1999): 11–16; Leidner, Robin. *Fast Food, Fast Talk: Service Work and Routinization of Everyday Life*. Berkeley: University of California Press, 1993; Ritzer, George. *The McDonaldization of Society*. Thousand Oaks, CA: Pine Forge Press, 2004; Schlosser, Eric. *Fast Food Nation: The Dark Side of the All-American Meal*. New York: Perennial, 2002.

Samantha Kwan

Fertilizers A fertilizer is an agricultural additive used to enhance the growth of a vegetal organism. Fertilizers can be either organic or inorganic in nature and are usually applied via the soil for uptake through the plant roots or through the foliage for uptake through the leaves. Fertilizers can be naturally occurring (such as peat or mineral deposits) or manufactured through natural (composting) or chemical processes.

The largest consumer countries of fertilizers are those with the largest populations, such as the United States, China, India, Russia, and Brazil. While current demand has remained stable globally for the last few years, strong growth rates were observed in Asia and northeast Africa, while offsetting reductions were experienced in Central Africa, Latin America, North America, and western Europe.

History of Fertilizers

Organic fertilizers are thought to have been in use since plant cultivation began, close to 10,000 years ago. At the time, farmers used basic organic elements, such as cow manure or seaweed, to enhance crop growth. Chemical fertilizer made its debut in the 19th century following the discovery of nitrogen, phosphorus, and potassium.

Description of Fertilizer

Fertilizers supply three main macronutrients to plants (in various levels) that are essential to food production: *Nitrogen* plays a major role in boosting crop yields and is a key component of chlorophyll (making the plants greener). *Potassium* helps plants grow strong stalks, in the same way that calcium gives people strong bones. As for *phosphorus*, it enhances early rooting, general health, and larger yields.

When purchasing a fertilizer, the buyer will see that it has three grade numbers, listing the percentages of nitrogen, phosphorus, and potassium content, respectively. As an example, a fertilizer described as a "5-10-15" will be composed of 5% nitrogen, 10% phosphorus, and 15% potassium; the rest of the fertilizer will be micronutrients and filler. As each soil is different, farmers using fertilizers must carefully select the balance of main components in the fertilizers they will use.

Organic versus Chemical Fertilizers

Some organic fertilizers are naturally occurring, as in the case of manure, peat, seaweed, and guano, while others are man-made, such as compost. Organic fertilizers have some advantages over their chemical counterpart. First, organic fertilizers can be produced on-site by the farmer, lowering the farming operating costs. It is also believed that organics avoid some of the long-term effects of chemical fertilizers, such as an oversupply of some nutrients, or reduce the necessity of reapplying artificial fertilizers regularly. On the other hand, the composition of organic fertilizers is inexact, making it difficult to use with precision when handling larger crops; generally speaking, large-scale agriculture relies on chemical fertilizers (which can precisely explain their composition), while smaller-scale projects can successfully use organic fertilizers.

Objections to Use of Fertilizers

Overuse of fertilizers, especially chemical fertilizers, can lead to many problems such as surface runoff (fertilizers being washed into streams), or they can seep into the groundwater. Excessive application, especially of nitrogen fertilizers, has also been known to lead to pest problems. Hence, farmers have started to use a process called "nutrient processing," balancing the nutrients coming into the farming system against those leaving.

FURTHER READINGS: Fertilizer Institute. "About Fertilizer." http://www.tfi.org/factsandstats/fertilizer.cfm; Heffer, Patrick, and Prud'homme, Michel. *World Agriculture and Fertilizer Demand, Global Fertilizer Supply and Trade, 2006–2007, Summary Report.* International Fertilizer Industry Association. Paris, 2007; Kraus, J., et al. "Effects of Fertilizer, Fungal Endophytes and Plant Cultivar on the Performance of Insect Herbivores and Their Natural Enemies." *Functional Biology* 21, no. 1 (2007) 107–16; Lewis, Jerre, and Leslie Renn. *How to Start and Manage a Fertilizer and Pesticide Business.* Interlochen, MI: Lewis and Renn Associates, 2004.

Jean-François Denault

Financialization Over the last 30 years, the food and beverage industries have been progressively consolidating. The development of **multinational** firms across the world food and beverage industries has been driven by external growth strategies (i.e., mergers and acquisitions). The problem with mergers and acquisitions is that firms are required to search for alternative sources of financing (self-financing, banking, stock market) to finance their restructuring operations. "Financialization" could be described as a process in which financial value (shareholder value maximization) becomes the leading institutional and organization criterion for firms listed on stock markets. The main principles of these finance-driven strategies are the minimization of costs and risks and the maximization of liquidity and capital returns. Usually, and as a result, financialization leads to tensions between shareholders and stakeholders.

During the 1990s, researchers were particularly interested in the study of the effectiveness of excessive concentration and market power of the food and beverage industries. At the end of the decade, new issues emerged. The wave of mergers and acquisitions in the food and beverage industries and the simultaneous internationalization of shareholdings of the leading food and beverage firms changed the agency relationships between owners and managers and particularly contributed to the establishment of new managerial practices across the industry, supported by complex and integrated information technology systems (SAP, Efficiency Resource Planning). Most particularly, publicly listed companies started to buy their own shares, commonly known as "share buyback" plans. These companies include heterogeneous industries such as alcohol (Diageo, Lion Nathan Pernod Ricard, Louis-Vuitton Möet-Hennessy), **soft drinks** (Pepsi Bottling Group), tobacco (British American Tobacco, Japan Tobacco, Imperial Tobacco), and **dairy** products (Danone, Robert Wiseman Dairies). This phenomenon is essentially driven by the leading firms in every subindustry.

Diageo is the company that announced the most significant share buyback plans in the food and beverages industries. Why are some subindustries more affected than others? The first explanation is that food and beverage is a "defensive" industry. However, in times of crisis or slow growth, investors prefer to invest in this industry as a means of protecting investments.

The main targets for share buybacks are the alcoholic beverages and tobacco industries. Both face difficulties in growth, such as significant taxes and lobbies against alcohol and tobacco consumption. In the case of the tobacco industry, the companies also face many expensive court trials, particularly in the United States. Furthermore, a growing number of European countries made tobacco purchase and consumption restrictive, and it became increasingly expensive. The consequence is that European countries are becoming less attractive for firms and increasingly difficult for those companies to run their businesses. From an investor's perspective, alcohol and tobacco are forbidden investments to most ethical or socially responsible investors.

Share buybacks are probably the most important driver of financialization. It became an important method for companies to pay out cash to shareholders. Traditionally, dividends were the most significant way of distributing money. Currently, firms need to anticipate the evolution of their stocks in the financial markets and find new ways of attracting shareholders. Dividends depend on performance achievements; share buybacks depend on managers' will.

A growing number of studies document the reasons for share buybacks. The most common explanation is signaling managers' intentions. These studies report that on the announcement date of a share buyback plan, share prices increase significantly. The signaling hypothesis is based on the premise that managers are better informed and launch a share buyback program to tell the market that the shares of the company are undervalued. However, the signaling hypothesis is controversial, because repurchasing shares in the stock exchange is not a costly signal, as it does not commit the firm to actually buy back its own shares. Another explanation is based on the assumption that investors and analysts use a company's financial decisions as a window into what managers really think about the company's prospects. The announcement of a share buyback program indicates that managers are so confident of their company's prospects that they believe the best investment they can make is in its own shares.

The financialization of firms' strategies can raise some legitimacy fears: Do investor claims put at risk the possibilities of growth of food and beverage firms? The value of a firm is based on its future prospects of growth, and long-term investments should be focused on the maximization of shareholder value. However, the pressure over (short-term) performance achievements may lead to excessive prudence in terms of managerial behavior; managers themselves may be interested in avoiding risk-taking.

Financialization may lead to tensions and conflicts between shareholders and stakeholders. The focus on shareholder value leads generally to cut costs and relocation of assets and facilities. Job cuts are generally the most effective way of cutting costs and of improving results. In this perspective, stakeholders (employees, customers, suppliers) are only a means used to achieve shareholders' financial goals. The stakeholders' approach maintains that long-term sustainability is only possible if both shareholders' and stakeholders' interests are taken into account. Financialization puts emphasis on the shareholder view and as a result is subject to the same criticism.

From a broader perspective, it is possible to say that financialization depends on the particulars of corporate governance systems. For example, cooperative and family firms are usually more stakeholder-oriented than firms controlled by financial investors (banks, insurance companies, institutional investors).

Share buybacks affect value in two ways. First, the announcement of a buyback program, its terms, and the way it is implemented all convey signals about the company's prospects and plans, even though few managers publicly acknowledge this. Second, when financed by a debt issue, a buyback can significantly change a company's capital structure, increasing its reliance on debt and decreasing its reliance on equity.

The principle is that share buybacks are not good if the company pays too much for its own stock. Even though buybacks can be huge sources of long-term profit for investors, they are actually harmful if a company pays more for its stock than it is worth. Also, a share buyback can send a negative signal, because other information can contradict and sometimes swamp the expected buyback signal. In a growing industry, a share buyback program can also indicate that the company has few important new opportunities on which to otherwise spend its money. In such cases, long-term investors may respond to a buyback announcement by selling the company's shares.

How does financialization relate with the ongoing consolidation trends in the food and beverage industries? The intensification of industrial and commercial concentration (brands, distribution networks) has led to a progressive reduction of profit margins of firms across the global food and beverage industries. The overall food and beverage chain has been particularly impacted by the rise of prices in commodities and energy costs. As a result, many of these firms operating upwards (suppliers) and downwards (customers) are also themselves consolidating. On the suppliers' side, there are many examples of industrial concentration in raw materials, such as **packaging**, **bottling**, and machinery.

Consolidation contributes to increasing levels of negotiation power between suppliers and customers. Thus, the food and beverage firms are required to reconstitute their margins to keep the same level of performance and to find new financing sources. Initial public offerings (IPOs) are one of the main financing sources to finance investments in the food and beverage industries. Over the last 30 years, many firms entered the stock market.

Share buybacks and mergers and acquisitions are alternative ways for food firms to create value. The wave of mergers and acquisitions in the food industry fostered concentration in the industry but simultaneously created a gap between the "head" of the food and beverage oligopoly and the "fringe" of small players. Under these circumstances, and by keeping in mind the difficulties faced by some large players to grow and expand their businesses, share buybacks emerge as the most attractive and rapid way to create shareholder value. With the exception of food and beverage firms established in Brazil, Russia, India, and China, the number of IPOs by food and beverage firms decreased considerably. On the other hand, the number of publicly listed firms in Western stock exchanges decreased. Several firms exited the stock exchange because of the financial crisis of 2001–2002, as they became an easy target for hostile takeovers and needed to preserve their independence. The average market values of food and beverage firms decreased considerably after this period.

One of the consequences of this process was a progressive reduction of mergers and acquisitions among the top world food and beverage firms (the "head"). This meant that mergers and acquisitions became a less attractive way of creating shareholder value.

That said, to some extent mergers and acquisitions are an alternative way of financialization. When food and beverage firms are not able to create value either through endogenous growth or through mergers and acquisitions, financialization becomes a logical response to shareholder value creation.

Is the transformation of the world market for wine through financialization sustainable in the long run? With respect to this question, several comments seem to be appropriate: The supply side of the food and beverage industries is much less concentrated than that in other industries. Thus, it seems that the ongoing moves of mergers and acquisitions will continue, at least in the near future, but not necessarily among the large players. On the other hand, mergers and acquisitions are becoming more and more difficult as a result of the reduced number of targets available in the financial markets, as mentioned above.

It is also important to highlight that share buybacks are not a specific issue of publicly listed companies. Customers and suppliers of the food and beverage industries are also consolidating themselves and are subject to the same performance criteria of shareholder value creation. Those practices impact the food industry in terms of prices and margins requirements. Consequently, share buybacks are driving the strategies of private players as well. The financial risks after undertaking this type of operation may spread across the whole food chain.

This framework is particularly rich and combines different streams of research, particularly the corporate governance approach and those inspired from the knowledge-based approaches. The structures of governance are used not only as a means of aligning transactions and the characteristics of transactions but also as a goal to reach as a means of creating and transferring knowledge. Moreover, as a goal to learn, firms need to enlarge their potential targets.

Share buybacks are only one of the main elements of finance-driven strategies. A broad view on financialization should also include the rise of financial investors in the ownership of food and beverage firms and the creation of new specialist funds in the food industry.

A new type of financial investor is emerging, driven by logic other than industrial production. For example, in France, the Crédit Agricole bank became one of the main owners of **wine**-related assets. In Australia, the International Wine Investment Fund is one of the main shareholders involved in the wine industry and also owns shareholdings in the French companies Gabriel Meffre and Laroche. The new investors come essentially from the financial sector and include banks, insurance companies, venture capitalists, institutional investors, and hedge funds. CVC Capital Partners is one of the main venture capital firms, being very active in the European food industry. The California pension fund CalPers is also an important investor. Since early 2000, these investors have become prominent across the food and beverage industries.

Financial Institutions and Specialized Food and Beverage Funds

Specialized food and beverage funds and financial investors have brought a new financial discipline to the industry. Their influence operates through board representatives in the target companies. In some cases, they act as "greenfield" investors. These new types of shareholders modify the governance structures and strategic configuration of food firms. In this context, food firms are less and less considered as traditional food producers and more like "value-seekers." The adoption of proactive financial strategies by the new investors allows the minimization of the cost of capital and the maximization of value creation in comparison to direct competitors in domestic and international markets.

The three factors highlighted above make part of an international convention requiring an *ex-ante* definition of profit rates—generally above 15 percent. Top managers are required to adjust their goals by considering this ex-ante rule. The evaluation of the general achievements will not be based in the growth potential of firms (*ex-post* criteria) but more on the *standard (shareholder) convention* in the industry. From this perspective, shareholder value creation becomes the main criterion for judging management performance. This is consistent with the spread of the Anglo-American corporate governance practices.

We should, however, highlight some of the main risks, particularly the risk of excessive gearing ratios and of borrowing money from banks to finance share repurchases (nonindustrial investments). After all, it is legitimate to ask if the food business is a means of developing sustainable business models by effectively investing in food production (commodities and industrial assets), brands, and distribution networks or in a technical artifact (share buybacks). There are probably some differences here between different corporate governance systems.

Financialization leads to a dissociation between industrial and financial strategies. Excessive financialization also entails some risks in the food and beverage industries, as most products are biological in nature and by not integrating this issue into the process of creating value for shareholders many food crises can arise (food security, traceability, health and environmental issues).

In order to reduce the risks associated with excessive financialization of industries and countries, some alternative roads could include more stakeholder-oriented firms such as socially responsible investing, employee-ownership, and family ownership.

FURTHER READINGS: Coelho, Alfredo, and Jean-Louis Rastoin. "Financial Strategies in the World Wine Industry: An Assessment." *Agribusiness* 22, no. 3 (2006): 417–29; Coelho, Alfredo Manuel and Victor Manuel Castillo-Giron. "Multinational Corporations, Collective Action Problems and the Tequila Cluster." Online at http://www.fscpo.unict.it/catania_workshop2005/pdf/Coelho&Castillo-Giron(paper).pdf.

Alfredo Manuel Coelho

Fishing, Commercial In 1602, Cape Cod, Massachusetts, was so-named for the immense schools of cod swimming in its Atlantic waters. Flounders, grouper, halibut, herring, shad, menhaden, striped bass, and salmon, as well as lobsters, scallops, oysters, and other shellfish, were equally abundant. Economically and politically, cod was the most important: when salted and dried, it lasted for a long time. Salting, as well as smoking and brining, reduced spoilage and allowed the fish to be transported, before **refrigeration**. As a result, it became a dietary staple that fueled migration westward and provided income to the new colony through exports to Europe. Spanish and Portuguese fishing fleets were already present when colonists arrived in Gloucester, New Bedford, and Boston to join a thriving and profitable fishing industry. Even by 1650, however, concerns about variability in fish harvests were being voiced.

Fisheries in the Pacific took longer to evolve, although Native Americans had long had dried salmon industries on the Columbia River. Cod, hake, halibut, mackerel, and pollock and many kinds of shellfish were fished commercially after settlers arrived in Seattle, San Francisco, Monterey, and San Diego. **Canning** and refrigeration became dominant methods of preservation; marine territories were starting to be defined. The U.S. population increased from 4 million in 1790 to 56 million in 1890, 250 million in 1990, and 300 million in 2006. Today, an increasing worldwide population of six billion puts intense pressure on commercial fisheries, while consumption of fish, in fresh and processed forms, is increasing annually.

Populations of Atlantic cod and haddock, Gulf of Mexico red snapper and wild shrimp, Pacific salmon and some species of tuna and herring have diminished to record low levels. Other depleted fish populations (swordfish, Chilean sea bass, Louisiana redfish) have partially rebounded only to drop again, to the point where the likelihood of full and long-term recovery of these species is unknown at present.

Variability in fish populations occurs for many reasons, including seasonal weather fluctuations and storm disruptions. Nevertheless, overfishing and pollution, to name only two contributors to fish population reduction, are human-made problems that can be managed. In the 21st century, a systemic approach to marine resource management is taking hold. Marine biology, aquatic reproductive strategies, habitat renewal, currents and temperature fluctuations (El Niño and global warming), migratory habits, differences between carnivorous and other fish, the nature of coastal waters, intertidal zones and estuaries, salinity and oxygen levels, and bycatch—unwanted species of fish and shellfish inadvertently taken—are all threads in the fabric of marine conservation. Determining sustainability levels for fisheries and wild fish populations is an ongoing process, and some progress has been made, despite the knowledge that these goals may not be achievable for all species. Huge harvests, made possible through the use of such advanced fish-finding technology as purse seines, dredges (which often rake up the ocean bottom and destroy coral reefs), trawl nets, sonar, and airborne spotters, are still the norm. The use of highly efficient factory trawlers has resulted in smaller catches of younger fish for many species. The implication that the fish may not live long enough to reproduce and replace themselves, much less increase in numbers, is clear. Other influences on the decline of larger fish at the top of the food chain include faster food-processing technology, creation of value-added fish products, changing eating habits, increasing popularity of fish as a source of healthy protein, and the use of fish products in other industries (animal feed, **pet food**, and industrial oils).

Aquaculture, also called fish farming, has been practiced for centuries and is an important and expanding industry. Shrimp, salmon, tilapia, catfish, and mussels are commonly farmed fish and shellfish. Aquaculture has problems of its own, however, including the use of **antibiotics** in fish feed, accumulation of fish waste in densely crowded pens, and escape of farmed fish into the oceans where the fish are thought to breed with wild stocks, with unknown results. The use of wild-caught fish (sometimes as bycatch) to make fish pellets is controversial: three pounds of wild fish are needed to raise one pound of farmed salmon.

Freshwater fishing in the United States contributes a small amount to commercial fishing; this category does not include fish that live in the ocean but spawn in fresh water, such as salmon, shad, and sturgeon. The problems of freshwater fishing, from the Great Lakes to the Mississippi and other rivers, echo those of ocean fisheries. Overfishing, the unwitting introduction of foreign species (e.g., the zebra mussel in 1988 in the Great Lakes), and water pollution are similarly important problems that have yet to be resolved.

Commerical Fishing and Government Regulation

In 1871 President Ulysses S. Grant authorized creation of the U.S. Commission on Fish and Fisheries to monitor fish stocks and maintain commercial fishing at high levels. States' rights, Native American rights, and interstate commerce made enforcing governmental policies difficult. The Bureau of Fisheries, as it was later named, was shifted several times, coming under the Department of Commerce in 1903 and the Department of the Interior in 1939. In 1940, the Bureau of Fisheries and the Bureau of Biological Surveys merged and were renamed the Fish and Wildlife Service. Sportfishing and commercial fishing were separated categorically from each other only in 1956: sport- and freshwater fishing remained under the auspices of the Department of the Interior.

Today, commercial fisheries are regulated by the National Marine Fisheries Service (NMFS), created in 1970, part of the National Oceanic and Atmospheric Administration (NOAA). In 1972, Congress passed the Marine Protection, Research, and Sanctuaries Act, which created marine sanctuaries in the Great Lakes and extended protected areas from the continental shelf into the oceans, for restoration and conservation. Further legislation to protect endangered species were passed, ranging from increasing taxes for fish restoration to the broad Endangered Species Act passed in 1973, which covered all living species. The Lacey Act of 1900 was updated in 1981 in order to further regulate interstate and foreign shipments of fish, which were not already prohibited by federal, state, or tribal law. The Lacey Act empowered the secretary of commerce, as well as the national marine fisheries service, to assess penalties and otherwise impose more stringent controls on violators.

In 1976, when the Magnuson Stevens Act passed, the local territorial limit was extended to 12 miles (and signed onto by 60 countries), with a conservation zone extending 200 miles into the ocean. Renamed the Sustainable Fisheries Act (SFA) when amended in 1996, the Act established a protected fishing radius around U.S. coasts. Eight regional fishery councils were created to manage the living marine resources within their areas: New England, South Atlantic, Mid-Atlantic, North Pacific, Gulf of Mexico, Pacific Fishery, Western Pacific, and Caribbean Fishery. Although they have only an advisory role and are controversial, they are nevertheless influential. While maximum sustainable yields are the goal for each region, the SFA addressed three major concerns: overfishing, bycatch, and habitat destruction. Fish quotas were developed based on the biology of fished species. Rebuilding overfished species within a specified timetable and minimizing bycatch were two other goals of SFA. "Essential fish habitats" were defined—areas that fish use throughout their lifecycles that need to be protected from fishing impacts. The Supreme Court gave precedence to the federal government in matters of fish management, and laws were passed to allow Native Americans to maintain their customs and fishing traditions.

The Food and Drug Administration (FDA) Office of Seafood monitors antibiotic and pesticide levels, while the **Environmental Protection Agency** monitors heavy metals.

The legal history of commercial fishing is full of contradictions. Only recently has there been some contentious agreement as to which methods are best suited to maintain particular fish stocks within U.S. jurisdiction, especially with foreign trawlers just outside the 200-mile limit. While federal efforts to protect fish stocks started as early as 1871, fish-finding technology and harvest size far outpaced conservation efforts in the 20th century. Recovery of depleted fisheries and ecologically acceptable harvesting methods, as lawfully mandated goals, characterize some fisheries today, but there are continuing conflicts about definitions of sustainability, fish survival rates, and most other issues associated with commercial fishing.

Ocean Fisheries

The United States has more than 100,000 miles of coastline. Marine fisheries were fairly independent until 1970 when fisheries management was taken over by NMFS. Regional offices of NMFS oversee commercial fishing in the United States, and its jurisdiction extends out to legally mandated "borders." International and Native tribes laws were passed, and conservation zones were created: these efforts were intended to ensure that contiguous waters for each state or country would be sufficiently abundant to keep fishing fleets localized and maintain the fisheries involved. Agreements with other nations regarding tuna, New England groundfish, halibut, herring, and salmon were difficult to enforce, as the concept of borders in ocean waters and the migratory habits of many fish made implementation difficult. Furthermore, fishing vessel locations were difficult to pinpoint. International factory trawlers, a constant presence just outside U.S. jurisdiction off the fisheries of Alaska and New England, fillet and freeze thousands of tons of fish on board.

The relationship between Native Americans and individual states has varied, and the Supreme Court has mediated some disputes. Salmon, for example, return to their natal waters to spawn, where they congregate in huge numbers. This fact makes their spawning location highly valued for fishing. In 1906, in *United States v. Winans*, the Court ruled that in the Pacific Northwest many Indian tribes could still fish in their traditional locations, even if the land on which they fished was owned by others.

The Food and Agriculture Organization (FAO) of the United Nations began collecting global fish-catch statistics in 1950. The total global catch increased by as much as 6 percent per year until 1969, tripling from 18 million to 56 million tons caught during that period. Total global catch rates increased by just 2 percent each year throughout the 1970s and 1980s, and leveled off in the 1990s, as cod and herring stocks off New England collapsed. The FAO has warned that two-thirds of major commercial fish in the world are near or below sustainable levels.

Fishery Catches, Consumption, Imports, Exports, and Trends

Per-capita consumption of seafood (all fish and shellfish: fresh, **frozen**, canned, and processed) in 2004 was 16.6 pounds per person (edible weight), compared to 14.6 pounds in 1997. Shrimp and tilapia top the list. World fish and shellfish supplies have increased from 50 million tons in 1965 to 130 million tons in 2003.

The largest fishery in the United States is the Alaska Pollock Fishery in the Gulf of Alaska and Bering Sea, with much of the fish catch there exported to China for processing. With import/export agreements in place and lower **labor** costs abroad, fish are exported, processed, and reimported into the United States. While China exported 825 million pounds of seafood products to the United States in 2004, for example, this type of import/export relationship exists with other countries and highlights the seesaw nature of commercial fishing agreements. The Department of Commerce estimates that all edible fishery products imported into the U.S. for 2005 weigh in at 5.1 billion pounds (valued at $12.1 billion dollars), while exports from the U.S. total 2.9 billion pounds (valued at $4.1 billion dollars).

Many fisheries are working to achieve good fishing practices and oversight. Certification by the Marine Stewardship Council for continuing efforts to become and remain sustainable were awarded to the West Coast Rock Lobster Fishery in 2003 and the Alaska Pollock Fishery in 2006, two examples of commercial fisheries that are using a whole-ecosystem approach to maintaining fish at sustainable levels. Other fisheries are altering their philosophy from a short-term, species-specific approach to a long-term, whole-ecosystem view, as a more enlightened form of marine resource management evolves; even though there are those who believe that a "seal of approval" from the Marine Stewardship Council is a form of ecological marketing, it is still a step in the right direction. Fisheries targeting Pacific cod, Pacific halibut, Alaska salmon, and sablefish have also won recognition for sustainable management.

Domestic Alaskan pollock catch in 2004 ranked fourth in pounds per capita of edible weight: it is a major American export as roe, fillets, and *surimi* (popularly known as "imitation crab legs"). In terms of quantity (the catch in whole-fish weight), Alaskan pollock ranks first with 2.5 billions pounds, representing 25 percent of fishery landings in the United States. This list continues with menhaden (originally used for **fertilizer**, this oily fish is an industrial giant that is used to make fish meal, margarine, supplements, and pharmaceuticals), cod, salmon, flounder, hake, crab, and shrimp.

The U.S. salmon supply from 1995 through 2004 increased domestically, with decreased imports. Less than 10 percent of this is farmed salmon. Yet, of the world supply of salmon in 2004, farmed salmon represented 64 percent of the total. Occasional reports of PCB contaminants in farmed salmon, U.S. **tariffs** on Norwegian salmon, and **European Union** trade restrictions on Norwegian salmon have all reduced salmon sales and consumption in the United States. Some of these factors have made retailers cognizant of the need to sell salmon that is farmed in an environmentally friendly way. Wal-Mart and **Whole Foods Market** are two U.S. retailers that use third-party certification to assure customers of fish safety and good farming practices. At present, use of the word *organic* is highly contentious and unclearly defined, despite a federal definition for land-based products (which is, in and of itself, controversial).

World Fish and Shellfish supplies have increased from 50 million tons in 1965 to 130 million tons in 2003. For comparison's sake, Japan imports more fish and fish products than does the United States, while China, Thailand, and Norway export more fish and fish products than does the United States. World aquaculture production rose from 12 million tons (live weight) in 1994 to 22 million tons in 2003.

Even though American fisheries supply the home market, import/export agreements exist with many other countries. China supplies part of each of the top 10 seafoods consumed in the United States (2004). This includes shrimp (peeled, breaded, and shell-on), crabmeat, pollock (fish sticks), salmon (frozen), tilapia, scallops, and catfish. Shrimp consumption per capita has doubled from 1990 to 2004. The top 10 states in commercial landings (whole fish/shellfish) are Alaska, Louisiana, Virginia, Washington, California, Massachusetts, Oregon, Maine, New Jersey, and Mississippi.

Leading U.S. seafood exports in 2004 were fresh and frozen salmon (this includes imported and reexported fish), surimi, lobster, crab and crabmeat, pollock roe, canned salmon, flatfish, pollock fillets, salmon roe, and fresh/frozen shrimp. The leading U.S. seafood import in 2004 was frozen shrimp—shrimp consumption per capita has doubled from 1990 to 2004—followed by lobster, whole tuna, salmon fillets, groundfish fillets, whole salmon, canned tuna, scallops, fish blocks, and flatfish fillets.

Canned Tuna, an American Staple

Canned tuna is perhaps the most familiar fish product in American culture. More than one billion cans of tuna are eaten in the United States every year. The first canned seafood products in the country appeared in the early 19th century and included oysters, lobster, salmon, and sardines. The Civil War accelerated acceptance of canned fish as a source of safe protein. From oyster canneries in Maine to menhaden canneries in Long Island, use of canned fish spread, with the addition of mackerel, crab, clams, carp, sturgeon, and shark. The canned sardine industry moved to California, and as demand exceeded supply, other fish were canned.

Canned albacore tuna was launched in 1903 by three Italian fishermen. From 2,000 cases in 1909 to 237,000 cases in 1915, canned tuna rapidly became an American staple, along with canned sardines and salmon. To meet increasing demand, new fishing techniques were developed, including the use of giant nets that can haul in 150 tons of fish. The harvests included large amounts of bycatch, including dolphins. Dolphins, mammals that surface to breathe, are often found swimming on top of schools of tuna, making them a "miner's canary" for finding tuna, but also putting them at high risk of being caught in nets and drowning. Albacore catches dropped in the 1920s, and other species of tuna were used to replace albacore (yellowfin, marketed as light-meat tuna). Sardine catches also dwindled, and tuna fishers moved further out into the ocean, with even larger nets that could haul 200-ton catches. Increasing dolphin mortality and escalating criticism led to passage of the Marine Mammal Protection Act of 1972, which banned importation of fish and fish products that were caught or processed in ways that increased risks to ocean mammals. Most tuna fishing in the United States became dolphin-safe after passage of the Boxer-Biden Dolphin Protection Consumer Information Act of 1991. Star-Kist (owned by **Del Monte**), Bumble Bee Seafoods LLC (owned by Connors Bros.), and Chicken-of-the-Sea (Tri-Union Seafoods LLC) can albacore tuna, which is caught on long lines.

The finding of methylmercury at different concentration levels in tuna species has been and remains a politically charged issue. Methylmercury in small amounts causes neurological damage. How tuna acquire methylmercury is not fully understood, although industrial pollution is thought to be a source. While the FDA has issued guidelines about consumption of canned tuna, including advisories for high-risk populations such as children and pregnant women, some think that this chemical should not be eaten under any circumstances.

FURTHER READINGS: Food and Drug Administration, Center for Food Safety and Applied Nutrition. "What You Need to Know about Mercury in Fish and Shellfish." http://www.cfsan.fda.gov/~dms/admehg3.html; Grainger, Richard. "Recent Trends in Global Fishery Production." http://www.fao.org/docrep/field/006/ad743e/ad743e00.htm; Johnson, H. M., ed. *2005 Annual*

Report on the United States Seafood Industry. Jacksonville, OR: Howard M. Johnson Publishing, 2005; Martin, Roy E., and George Flick, ed. *The Seafood Industry*. New York: Van Nostrand Reinhold, 1990; McGee, Harold. *On Food and Cooking*. 2nd ed. New York: Scribner, 2004. National Marine Fisheries Service. http://www.nmfs.noaa.gov. U.S. Department of Commerce, National Oceanic and Atmospheric Administration, National Marine Fisheries Service. *Fisheries of the United States, 1997*. Washington, DC: GPO, 1998; Woods, Fronda. "Who's in Charge of Fishing?" *Oregon Historical Quarterly* 106, no. 3 (Fall 2005): 412–41. Available at http://www.historycooperative.org/journals/ohq/106.3/woods.html.

Renee Marton

Flavors and Fragrances Artificial flavors and fragrances are a major component of the food industry whose products are included as **additives** in a wide variety of ingredient lists, although more often they are hidden under the vague and misleading term "natural and artificial flavors." These companies essentially manufacture and mix chemical compounds that replicate natural ingredients or enhance the taste and aroma of processed foods. Sometimes these substances are chemically exactly the same as those extracted from so-called natural sources, which may in fact require more energy and processing to extract.

Though consumers, especially in the wake of recurrent surges of enthusiasm for "natural foods," generally suspect frightening-sounding polysyllabic chemicals, it is important to remember that every substance ultimately comes from nature, including poisons. On the other hand, there is justified suspicion that people's taste buds are being so overwhelmed by enhanced flavorings (both natural and artificial) that they are becoming unable to appreciate the qualities of foods in their unprocessed state. A case in point is the souped-up Chicken McNugget, carefully and chemically designed to arouse the perfect mouthfeel, the right balance of crunch and soft yielding processed chicken flesh, and just the right punch of enhanced chicken flavor. Arguably, it is difficult to taste real chicken while eating a nugget. In the long run, such chemical enhancement, which is used in most processed foods, is degrading our gastronomic capacities and making us ever more dependent on processed food for satisfaction.

The flavor and fragrance industry gained widespread public attention thanks to a section in Eric Schlosser's exposé *Fast Food Nation* (2001), which features a visit to the leader in the industry: International Flavors and Fragrances. Many of its competitors are also located nearby, in a corridor along the New Jersey Turnpike. Within these companies, expert tasters—and expert smellers, too, since much of what people think of as taste is actually perceived through the nose—carefully craft complex admixtures of chemicals that make their way into practically every **snack food**, **soft drink**, **breakfast cereal**, **candy**, **ice cream**, and indeed any food that is processed. In the contemporary industrial food system, the only way to avoid such additives is to eat only unprocessed **whole foods** as they come directly from nature.

Darius Willoughby

Food Fads Fads are crazes or trends that enter popular culture rather quickly but then fade away, usually just as quickly, although in some cases, fads may evolve into long-term trends. These fads may be related to any aspect of popular culture, including language (e.g., "rad" in the United States in the 1980s), fashion (e.g., poodle skirts in the 1950s), or music and dance (e.g., the "Macarena" in the 1990s). Food fads are those fads that concern cooking, eating, food, and drink. For the food business, such fads are exceedingly important to anticipate—or generate—because anticipating or developing a fad such as the low-carbohydrate craze in the United States or bubble tea in China can be very profitable.

While fads are by no means limited to the area of food, food fads are especially noticeable due to the prominence of food in our lives, with most of us eating and drinking many times daily; the multibillion-dollar food business in wholesale and retail marketplaces, in both ingredient and prepared form; the intimate connection between diet and health; and the powerful cultural and symbolic aspects of food (consider, as examples, the symbolic power of the communion wafer, wedding cake, or oversized ribeye steak).

Food fads have been present for millennia, especially among leisured classes who have the luxury not to worry about subsisting, but rather can develop a food culture around which intricate meanings, traditions, taboos, and habits are ascribed. But even in subsistence cultures, where there is food, there can be fads.

In Western culture through the ages, one can find food fads among the leisure class of Rome, including vomiting during banquets to allow for additional eating, animals stuffed one inside the other and then roasted (the predecessor of the present-day "turducken"), and the consumption of exotic fish. In medieval Europe, royalty subscribed to a fad of live birds hidden inside a crust and then released at table (familiar from the nursery rhyme as "four-and-twenty blackbirds baked in a pie") as well as the heavy use of exotic spices from around the world. The Industrial Revolution gave rise to many historic food faddists, including Horace Fletcher, a proponent of mastication, that is, chewing food many times until it is complete mush before swallowing. Fletcher was a contemporary of the Kellogg brothers, John Harvey and William K., more familiar names who were advocates of high-fiber diets and health foods of their invention. Even modern American food faddists like Rachel Ray have managed to enter EVOO (extra-virgin olive oil) into the vernacular and the dictionary; similarly, home cooks may be caught shouting "Bam!" when seasoning food at home, in imitation of Emeril Lagasse.

The essential features of most fads are that they spread throughout a significant portion of society and are not long-lasting. Some fads die down but remain integral to culture. **Ice cream**, for example, took America by storm when it became consistently available in the 1800s. But even today, while no longer a fad, it is part of food culture in the United States.

Although there is no formal categorization of the types of fads, for the purposes of this entry it may be helpful to classify food fads as follows: culinary fads, health food fads, **ethnic food** fads, aesthetic food fads, and technological food fads.

Culinary Fads

Many food fads are developed by chefs on the cutting edge of fine dining. Many of these then travel through other high-end restaurants down to casual dining and ultimately into home kitchens. One current fad in fine dining is "foams," as in "carpaccio of beef with parmesan foam." This foaming technique, typically using a nitrogen-powered whipped-cream maker, was developed by **celebrity chef** Ferran Adrià of El Bulli restaurant in Spain and quickly traveled throughout the fine dining world and even into home kitchens. Other recent culinary fads include plate presentations of towering height; the widespread use (or overuse) of specialty ingredients such as sun-dried tomatoes, miso, purple potatoes, or pesto; cappuccino, a traditional breakfast drink in Italy served after dinner worldwide; and squeeze-bottle plate decorations, including mayonnaise lattice-work throughout restaurants in Asia and patterns made with reduced balsamic vinegar in North America.

Culinary fads are by no means limited to modern times. Centuries ago, frozen and gelled desserts were considered culinary masterpieces limited to the elite. As technology and access to food products improved, such desserts became common.

Many culinary fads become institutionalized by casual dining or quick-serve restaurants, signaling widespread acceptance and often the end of the fad. Dunkin' Donuts serving lattes, **McDonald's** serving premium **coffee**, KFC serving wrap sandwiches, and Sonic a breakfast sandwich on focaccia bread all serve to designate the fading of a culinary fad.

Health Food Fads

Perhaps the largest category of food fads, and indeed the connotation of the term *food faddist*, is in the realm of health and nutrition. The connection between eating and health was noted early in our history—after all, someone who does not eat, dies. But the complexities of this relationship are still not fully understood. Even with the benefit of a scientific understanding of food and nutrition, fad diets are pervasive. The macrobiotic diet, the Atkins Diet, the South Beach Diet, the grapefruit diet, Weight Watchers, and Jenny Craig all represent contemporary fad diets—and a multibillion dollar industry—of varying degrees of departure from traditional food habits. Some preach a standard diet with moderate portions. Others propose the elimination or severe restriction of specific foods (carbohydrates in Atkins, for example), while still others propose heavy reliance on a so-called miracle food (e.g., grapefruit in the grapefruit diet). There is even a diet and spiritual path called Breatharianism, the idea that one does not need to eat to live.

Health food fads often fall into one of two categories: fads that emphasize the curative benefits of a particular food item, and those that propose to eliminate or reduce the consumption of a common but allegedly unhealthy food item. In the first category, foods whose miraculous benefits have been cited include dark **chocolate**, red **wine**, cod liver oil and fatty fish in general, blueberries, raw eggs, whole grains, yogurt, greens, miso, green tea, pomegranate, almonds, milk, and soybeans and soy products. Food industry interests are often closely bound with these fads. From the second category, food fads that advocate the elimination or decreased consumption of various food items have variously targeted alcohol, **sugar** and other carbohydrates, milk and other forms of **dairy**, meat, fish and **poultry**, **wheat** flour, and fats and oils.

Health food faddists are known throughout history, not only for their colorful characters but also for the entrepreneurial aspects of the fads, resulting in some of our largest food businesses today. Both the Kellogg and C. W. **Post** cereal companies developed from the Kellogg brothers' health fad invention of **corn** flakes—a fibrous, precooked, ready-to-eat cereal that was a strong departure from the oatmeal and other long-cooked hot cereals of the day. Post was a patient and early competitor of Kellogg. Sylvester Graham, an earlier advocate of whole grains and a **vegetarian** diet, is commemorated in the form of the eponymous graham cracker. More recent food faddists include Dr. Robert Atkins, founder of the Atkins low-carbohydrate diet, and George Osawa, founder of the zen macrobiotic diet.

Ethnic Food Fads

Tourism, politics, and immigration have long generated interest in other cultures. Throughout history, people have been drawn to learn about others, and engaging with the food of other cultures has resulted in many food fads and trends. In the United States, as immigrants from around the world came to the country, ethnic enclaves generated food fads that spread throughout mainstream American culture. For example, chop suey, unknown in China, became a common dish throughout the United States in the mid-20th century. Similarly, the British occupation of India resulted in an initial fad and ongoing resonance of curry and chutney in the British Isles, again in a form unknown on the subcontinent. Ethnic food fads are often attributed to merchant marines and returning veterans from wars overseas. At other times, these fads gain ground by also being consistent with another fad. For example, the explosion of specialty coffee and sushi in the United States coincided with the low-fat/no-fat craze, into which they seemed to fit.

Aesthetic Food Fads

Some food fads are part of a larger aesthetic movement. Often these aesthetics are tied to entertaining in the home or textural novelties. For example, the 1950s in the United States gave rise to many foods based around the ideas of gelatin, aspic, and gelling. These were often special-occasion dishes used to show off the artistic skills of the cook by molding fruit in an ornate gelatin mold, for example, or slicing into a white-frosted cake with a sweet gelatin filling. An example from today is the fad of bubble tea that originated in Taiwan: iced teas where largely flavorless colorful tapioca balls are sipped through a large straw for the visual and textural novelty.

Technological Food Fads

Many food fads are generated by a technological advancement and its concomitant excitement. In the 1960s, following the excitement of manned space expeditions and the moon landing, children across the United States were eating "astronaut ice cream," freeze-dried blocks of ice cream. Similarly, ice cream cones, soft-serve ice cream, home-brewed cappuccino, bread baked in a home bread machine, homemade ice cream, and microwave popcorn became fads immediately following the technological advances that made these foods widely available. The advent of the microwave prompted microwave-only cookbooks where a complete meal, including bread, meat, vegetable, starch, and dessert, could be made entirely in the microwave. While this is still possible, now that the fad has ended, microwaves may be used only to reheat a beverage or make popcorn in a typical day. In the early to mid-20th century, **canned** and **frozen** vegetables, **TV dinners**, and sliced white bread were prominent fads, largely due to their new availability, thanks to technology.

See also Culinary Tourism; Diet Foods.

FURTHER READINGS: Ellis, Alice Thomas. *Fish, Flesh and Good Red Herring.* New York: Virago, 2006; Lovegren, Sylvia. *Fashionable Food: Seven Decades of Food Fads.* Chicago: University of Chicago Press, 2005.

Jonathan M. Deutsch

Food Festivals From Kodiak, Alaska, to Marathon, Florida, Americans attend food festivals to be entertained, to celebrate history and culture, and most of all, to eat food iconic of a group or a place. A food festival is a recurring public event that has food as its primary focus. It is a demarcated space and time for the celebration and consumption of food.

There are many possible organizing themes for food festivals, among them:

- a specific cultural, **ethnic**, or religious heritage, as typified by the Greek Food Festival organized each year by the Annunciation Greek Orthodox Church in Little Rock, Arkansas
- an identifiably regional food such as grits, which are celebrated in St. George, South Carolina, at the yearly World Grits Festival
- a food associated with a particular place, like chicken wings with Buffalo, New York, an association commemorated at the annual National Buffalo Wing Festival in Buffalo
- a specific ingredient or crop, such as artichokes, which are venerated at the annual Castroville, California, Artichoke Festival
- different preparations of the same dish, exemplified by the plethora of local and regional chili cookoffs and epitomized by the Terlingua, Texas, International Chili Championship.

The last quarter of the 20th century witnessed a rise in the number of food and wine or "Taste of . . ." festivals, many featuring restaurant chefs and their food. While such epicurean food events qualify as food festivals, the term typically is applied to community-based events coordinated by not-for-profit organizations featuring food prepared by nonprofessional cooks.

Contemporary American food festivals are modern articulations of traditional harvest festivals that celebrated a local crop. As the national economy shifted from agrarian to industrial, so too did the format of community festivals. Most modern food festivals only implicate the agricultural process through which the eponymous food goes from farm to table. Like traditional harvest festivals, modern festivals are about **consumerism** and consumption. Rather than focus on food as sustenance, however, contemporary food festivals commodify food as symbolic currency in the service of attracting attention to and generating income for the host town or group.

Community leaders and planners regard festivals as a strategy for economic development and local boosterism. Business leaders, chambers of commerce, and heads of civic organizations capitalize on the economic potential of festivals and the allure of food for attracting visitors. As such, recurring food festivals have become ubiquitous on community calendars throughout the country. Often with assistance from corporate sponsors who underwrite some of the production expenses, food festivals become fundraising efforts for school groups and civic organizations, while also generating favorable exposure for organizers and sponsors. Financial recompense may come from increased tourism and associated spending by residents and visitors in the locale that hosts the festival as well as from festival-goers who pay an entry fee to the festival grounds. When an admission fee is charged, those funds generally offset festival production costs, with any profits donated to local charities. In addition to economic benefits, food festivals offer intangible rewards such as increased civic engagement through volunteerism and a bolstered sense of group or place identity.

Food festivals exploit the communicative capacity of food: food is a tangible symbol of a group or a place. Eating food that symbolizes identity is an accessible and usually appealing way to learn, albeit superficially, about the culture, history, and traditions of others. Especially when incorporated into the jovial format of a festival, food can be a medium through which potentially divisive cultural or political issues might be—at least temporarily—suspended. Within the spirited frame of a festival, sampling unfamiliar food is a safe way to experience the cultural "Other," for example, with minimal investment of energy, time, or money.

The highlight of all food festivals is the fêted food, most often presented in various forms prepared and sold by local charities or businesses. Most contemporary food festivals are moveable feasts: attendees can buy snacks from multiple vendors who offer traditional and esoteric preparations of the celebrated food. For example, visitors to the Gilroy, California, Garlic Festival wander the grounds savoring garlic-laden foods ranging from garlic bread to garlic **ice cream**. In contrast to an eclectic menu of perambulatory refreshments, a few food-themed festivals culminate in a sit-down meal, like the Allen's Neck, Massachusetts, Friends Clambake.

Food festivals often involve food-centric competitions such as recipe, cooking, eating, or tossing contests that feature the iconic food. For example, area residents submit homemade peach pies and other baked goods for judging at the annual Stonewall, Texas, Peach Jamboree and Rodeo. Additionally, food festivals typically incorporate other traditional elements of festivals, including queen or beauty pageants, parades, and displays of occupational skills. Food festivals vary in duration from a few hours to several days and take place indoors or outside, depending on the host organizations, climate, and festival events.

Usually these festivals are family events and include multigenerational activities such as games and contests, historical displays, arts and crafts activities and sales, and informational displays on health concerns or local civic organizations. Often there is at least one stage for musical performances and/or cooking demonstrations, and at larger festivals, there might be a midway with carnival rides and additional amusements. There may be ancillary events sanctioned by the festival organizers, such as a foot race, that generate additional interest in and attendance to the actual festival.

Community-based food festivals and epicurean festivals are part of the burgeoning business of **culinary tourism**. Their ubiquity on community calendars across the country suggests the popularity of food as an organizational theme among organizers, who recognize that food and beverage attract people willing to spend money, and also among consumers, who are attracted to the idea of eating and drinking within the celebratory festival frame.

Pauline Adema

Food Laws and Regulations Because food production is work that must be performed safely but nevertheless habitually is shared among various persons, most if not all communities have taken steps to monitor and regulate the chain of production, preservation, and service. This has been accomplished through such means as obliging bakers to place identifying brands on their bread (as in ancient Rome) or instituting an computerized identification database for **beef** and veal, complete with cattle passports (as in the modern **European Union**).

The key variables to food laws and regulations are their scope, the types of foods to which they apply, and the changing balances of power that determine them. Power and scope in food law have been contested by individual consumers, producers, governments, kings, and companies, with accordingly disparate outcomes: the battle for control over food labeling of genetically modified products is one modern example of this struggle and the range of potential outcomes resulting from legislation. There remains one constant in different cultures and times—the strictest controls and most intense interest are almost uniformly reserved for those foods upon which a given culture bases its cuisine, or foods whose production threatens those basic foodstuffs. In Western societies, this basic foodstuff has most often meant bread: French law has prescribed four acceptable ingredients in a plain baguette and enforced a low price for centuries, while in England the Assize of Bread under King Henry III, which regulated price and quality, was merely the first in a series that would continue to adapt and change in England and its colonies. Secondary staples of the day such as meat, **beer**, and milk would later be added to regulation.

These and counterpart staples in other cultures—rice, for instance, or **corn**—still retain their importance in food laws in that, unlike many modern foods, they are still widely expected to be "pure"—that is, free of any other ingredient. Although breads (for example) now routinely contain preservatives, and milk has added vitamins, many contemporary food laws and regulations still refer to this premodern concept of purity, which has a signification for consumers and legislators no less powerful for its ambiguity. The concern stems from diverse early food laws calling for purity in production and purity of company when eating.

If "purity" was a relatively achievable goal for the first consumers and legislators, the concept was complicated to the point of impossibility with the advent of an industrialized food industry. Three distinct steps have been identified in the industrial development of the food industry and the increasingly governmental regulation of foods in America—steps that have been closely matched in other industrial and post-industrial nations. The first step manifested the demand for "purity" as legal injunctions against certain additions to food: pioneering food laws in the late 19th century prohibited additions to bread and milk. The second step, provision of information about foods to the public, first appeared as labeling legislation in a 1938 Act that becomes more precise each decade and today usually requires full disclosure of ingredients and nutritional index, including the possible trace presence of numerous allergens. The third and most recent development remains the most difficult to define and accordingly to regulate in the public interest: legislating to change the traditional characteristics of a given food to make it more nutritious. In its earliest incarnations, this meant legislation to require salt packers to add iodine against the threat of goiter; more recently, government legislators have been forced to monitor and legislate in cases where manufacturers hope to add health benefits to foods such as **chocolate** and fried foods, which have more general appeal than "healthy" equivalents.

Early History of Food Regulation

Government or royal regulations are in fact relative newcomers to food law: before them came religious injunctions and prohibitions, most of which were originally linked to food hygiene, sustainability of the food supply, and maintenance of communities. Observances of shared food laws give a sense of devotion, strength (such as through fasting), and shared identity that is especially vital for minority religions. Many religions thus require purity not only of foodstuffs (such as vegan, **vegetarian**, kosher, or halal foods) but also of commensality, that is, that the believer eat only with members of the same religion. The rapid rise of early Christianity has been partly attributed by some historians to its lack of food injunctions or fears of pollution by commensality: although the idea of "purity" remains strong in the Christian consciousness, mainstream Christianity interprets literally certain New Testament passages that declare all foods and company clean and rejects the Pentateuchal food law that characterizes the elder Judaism.

Early Greek and Roman writers, on the other hand, expressed a comparable concern for purity, but thought that individual responsibility for health (dissociated from community or religion) was the key. They saw it as important to guard one's internal homeostasis (internal state of equilibrium) through self-regulation. Theophrastus warned of the pollution of the food supply by adulteration, as did Pliny and Galen, and Pythagoras recommended pure and simple food not far removed from its natural state. Of course, individual concern resulted in common laws: Roman civil law, for example, prohibited the adulteration of foods such as bread and **wine**, and contravention could mean hard labor or temporary exile.

The Christian lack of interest in purity of company and in differentiation between foods on a religious basis, comfortably united with a literary tradition that drew on Greek attention to individual states and balances, ruled the development of Western civil food regulation well into the Renaissance. The important point for early modern regulators was that food production be good for trade and not actively poisonous: a healthy diet, as such, remained an individual matter. Sumptuary law was symptomatic of this attitude: although the foods proscribed to the poor were thought to be unhealthy for their constitutions (under Greek theory), the laws existed in large part for social and economic imperatives such as limiting consumption of imported foods. The development of government or royal food legislation relating to supply and consumption increased dramatically as wider, and hence more anonymous, systems of trade for staple food evolved. These regulations, extending as they did to drugs and cosmetics, provided a model for the landmark laws made in the Industrial Revolution and provided a blueprint for the scope of the Food and Drug Administration (FDA).

The Industrial Revolution

The concept of personal responsibility for a healthy diet was born when staple foods had few ingredients and little processing. Moreover, small-scale production and limited opportunity for transport meant that poisonous products could usually be sourced to a culprit: a butcher who sold tainted meat could be reasonably easily identified and held to account. This state of affairs changed radically with the advent of the Industrial Revolution. The federal Pure Food and Drug Act of 1906, prompted by consumer concern over meat and milk, was one of a chain of new initiatives that reflected the second basic change to food law: a shift toward consumer information, accompanied by increased government control (for instance, the creation of the FDA). Processing methods had begun to surpass the comprehension of the everyday consumer, so science and government inspections took a more active and more informative role.

In the new factory-led food market, many types of food could be **canned** or otherwise **packaged** and sold far from their place of origin: even fresh milk could be transported longer distances than ever before. These products began to pass through many hands on their way to market and could be hard to source to a particular farmer or butcher: they could be tainted, thinned, or colored by one or several handlers with a degree of anonymity. A number of health crises resulted: deaths from tainted tinned meat were not uncommon, especially among soldiers. At first, these industries were self-regulating, but as public anxiety increased, government regulators were forced to increase the scope of the law to develop means to deal with these products and with entirely new foods (such as oleomargarine and glucose) that were made possible only by large-scale factory processing and for which "purity" had lost much of its original meaning.

Milk was, famously, the test case for this kind of food law in the United States. Drawn from cows kept in unsanitary conditions and fed tainted food, and subsequently thinned, adulterated, colored with such products as annatto, and transported over increasingly long distances, the final product provoked outrage in a population accustomed to thinking of milk (with all its religious and cultural baggage) as the very purest of foods. In 1862 a swill-milk bill forbade selling or exchanging adulterated or otherwise unsanitary milk and required milk dealers to mark cans with their names and districts.

Contemporary Food Law and Regulation

Prevention of food adulteration and provision of information about foods to the public have been largely systematized under governmental control in the modern West. Food manufacturers as well as **restaurants**—in fact, all those involved at each point in the food chain—must open their premises to public health inspectors and be open regarding the nutritional content of foods. The third major stage in food law—regulation of changes to food to increase its health benefits—is now the major site of struggle between consumers, government regulators, and producers. The struggle is further complicated by increasingly holistic notions of health and purity and increased consumer knowledge of the food chain as a whole. Modern consumers still desire purity, especially in basic foodstuffs, but the concept has taken on a variety of new meanings. Food has since premodern times been treated under the same laws as medicines and drugs, but the modern era offers new products such as the lipid replacement Olestra that claim not only nutritive but also pharmaceutical benefits, and in foods traditionally thought of as better-tasting rather than healthy: "purity" can be sought in an artificially cholesterol-free diet or one in which unnaturally high doses of **vitamins** are taken from altered foods. Calcium can be had from orange juice, folic acid from **breakfast cereal**, omega-3 fatty acids from eggs.

Organic food production is increasingly in demand, and organic, biodynamic, local, and free-range foods partly fall under the same set of concerns as the genetically modified foods that have numerous beneficial possibilities but also pose concern over such issues as rising need for **fertilizers** and insecticides and the threat to biological diversity. Food regulators in the postmodern food market thus face not only conflict between consumer and producer but constantly changing theoretical challenges in this transformative stage as well.

The food market has also undergone significant change in recent years as a number of high-profile lawsuits have modified public and industry perception of just who is responsible for keeping food safe and freely available. Perhaps the best-known example, and one which has impacted on **advertising** and food packaging world-wide, is *Liebeck v. McDonald's Restaurants*, in which Stella Liebeck successfully sued **McDonald's** for negligence after spilling and being burned by a hot coffee: McDonald's was able to prove only that Liebeck was partially responsible for control of the hot beverage. McDonald's high-profile and significant role in the global diet means that the results of cases against the **chain** are frequently employed as precedents, and that mere attention brought by an unsuccessful case can prompt change: a 2003 ruling acquitted the company of causing childhood **obesity**, but extensive menu changes made by the company nevertheless have been copied throughout the food industry.

Another McDonald's case, popularly known as the "McLibel" case, saw defendants Helen Steel and David Morris contesting allegations of libel and of prompting consumer panic brought against them by McDonald's. It renewed debate about the degree to which a producer is ethically responsible for its product. Libel is an increasingly visible aspect of the contemporary food market: talk show host Oprah Winfrey was similarly targeted by representatives of the beef industry when, on her influential television program, she expressed fear of contracting **bovine spongiform encephalopathy** from hamburgers.

Food law is also increasingly acquiring elements of intellectual copyright law (chefs may sue if a photograph or replica of their edible creation, or even a copy of their menu, appears outside their restaurant without permission) and of branding and trademarks (a recipe is considered individual property and can be sold as such). Although KFC advertising, for instance, sustains the folkloric idea that the company keeps its "secret recipe" under lock and key, any replica offered for sale would infringe intellectual copyright as well as property law. Whether or not companies like KFC are responsible for their customers' health, or for the welfare of the chickens in question, is still a matter of contention.

See also Environmental Protection Agency; Food Safety; Genetic Engineering; Marketing of Milk; Marketing to Children; Monsanto; North American Free Trade Agreement; Nutrition Education; Nutrition Labeling; U.S. Department of Agriculture.

FURTHER READINGS: DuBoff, Leonard D., and Christy O. King. *The Law (in Plain English) for Restaurants and Others in the Food Industry.* Naperville, IL: Sphinx, 2006; French, Michael, and Jim Phillips. *Cheated Not Poisoned? Food Regulation in the United Kingdom, 1875–1938.* New York: St. Martin's Press, 2000; Hutt, Peter Barton. "Government Regulation of the Integrity of the Food Supply." *Annual Review of Nutrition* 4 (1984): 1–20; Levenson, Barry M. *Habeas Codfish: Reflections on Food and the Law.* Madison: University of Wisconsin Press, 2001; Okun, Mitchell. *Fair Play in the Marketplace: The First Battle for Pure Food and Drugs.* Dekalb: Northern Illinois University Press, 1986; Simoons, Frederick J. *Eat Not This Flesh: Food Avoidances from Prehistory to the Present.* Madison: University of Wisconsin Press, 1994; Young, James Harvey. *Pure Food: Securing the Federal Food and Drugs Act of 1906.* Princeton, NJ: Princeton University Press, 1989.

Anne Brumley

Food Poisoning An estimated 76 million cases of foodborne illness (FBI) occur annually in the United States. Of these, 325,000 people are hospitalized and 5,000 people die. *Food poisoning* refers to any illness resulting from eating or drinking contaminated foods or beverages. Before discovery of microorganisms, the link between food poisoning and foods was unknown, although food spoilage was understood. After the germ theory of disease was accepted, treatment of FBI, including preventive measures, became possible. In the mid-20th century, and particularly after 1970, some trends led to increased numbers of FBI. These include the demise of small family farms and rise of **agribusiness** and factory farms; consolidation of the **beef**, **poultry**, and pork industries, with attendant increases in speed of processing carcasses and other kinds of assembly lines; an increase in consumption of fresh produce; and improved reporting of FBI statistics. Prevention became the basis for maintaining and monitoring food and drink safety.

Most cases of FBI occur as a result of microorganisms on or in foods or beverages consumed, or as pathogenic toxins produced by microorganisms once they are ingested. They usually cannot be seen, tasted, or smelled. Physical response time to pathogenic microorganisms varies from immediate to delayed by as much as eight weeks. Smoking, drying, salting, and brining are preservation methods that retard food spoilage. Cooking also decreases the likelihood of food poisoning because heat kills many microorganisms. **Refrigeration** and freezing also delay food spoilage by creating conditions that limit pathogenic growth for a time for many, but not all, pathogens.

Conventionally known foodborne diseases, such as typhoid fever, tuberculosis, and cholera, are more common in the developing world; in industrialized countries, with municipal water treatment plants, vaccines, and legally mandated **food safety** measures, these FBI have almost been eradicated. In developed countries, including the United States, pathogens such as *Campylobacter* and *Salmonella* species and *E. coli* are the more likely cause of foodborne illnesses in the late 20th and early 21st centuries. The increasing size of farms and feedlots led, as the population also increased, to consolidation of food-processing industries, where oversight was more difficult. Processing was sped up from harvest or slaughter to storage, **packaging**, and transport, and each step provided opportunities for pathogens to develop and spread rapidly when conditions were suitable. Also, new pathogens have evolved.

Invention of the high-powered microscope by Dutch scientist Anton van Leeuwenhoek in 1677 allowed scientists to see "little animals"—pathogens could be seen through the lens. In 1850, Hungarian surgeon Ignaz Semmelweis began advocating thorough hand washing as a means to halt the spread of puerperal fever in obstetric patients. French scientist Louis Pasteur discovered that heating food (and milk) for the purpose of killing harmful organisms such as **bacteria**, viruses, protozoa, molds, and yeasts was possible. The process, completed in 1862, is named after him. Unlike sterilization, not all pathogens were killed by pasteurization. Nevertheless, pasteurization achieves a logarithmic reduction in the number of pathogens, reducing their number so they are less likely to cause illness.

The germ theory of disease took hold and was further elaborated upon by German bacteriologist Robert Koch in 1876, through his work on anthrax and cholera (among other diseases). The science of microbiology had been born. These discoveries led to new methods of harvesting, transporting, preparing, and preserving foods, as well as to new treatments of FBI. A good example is **antibiotic** treatment for infections. However, increasing resistance to antibiotics in humans continues to be a problem, especially for certain infections, including salmonellosis and campylobacteriosis.

In 1810, French innovator Nicolas Appert invented a successful means of **canning** to preserve food safely for long periods (he won a contest sponsored by Napoleon

Bonaparte to find a way to increase the shelf life of foods for the military). Once sealed, cans are heat treated.

Since 1960, a Hazard Analysis and Critical Control Points (HACCP) system has been used to identify points of potential contamination at all stages of food production and consumption. Checkpoints built into the farm-to-plate process try to ensure that the highest possible safety standards are maintained. This preventive approach is what characterizes food poisoning control programs today.

In the 20th century, food safety and shelf life became linked concepts, as consumption of fresh, processed, and ready-to-eat foods increased, while the distance foods travel from farm to final destination increased. Storing and serving foods came under the purview of food safety screening. *Sous vide* cooking, modified atmosphere packaging, and flash pasteurization, to mention a few examples, are processing advances that maintain flavor while providing safe technology with which to produce, package, and ship enormous quantities of foods and drinks.

Just as pathogens evolve, so do eating habits. Canned and **frozen foods** are industries where safeguards for foods produced in quantity are well established. Foodborne illnesses are often associated with fresh fruits, raw vegetables, and meat. The speed of assembly lines in food-processing factories (beef, pork, and chicken) makes monitoring food safety procedures difficult, if not impossible. The consolidation of small farms into national conglomerates that use long-distance haulers (trucks, planes, ships) for distribution means that oversight is critical to maintain food safety. Salad bars and food courts with reheated or ready-to-eat foods can be problematic if oversight is not maintained. The rise of **chain restaurants** that purchase nationally distributed, partially prepared ingredients has influenced the way safeguards are implemented. From its possible origin on the farm to the dinner plate, the impact of a FBI on our health is magnified because national distribution systems are efficient: an episode of FBI can start in one state and become national in a matter of days—witness the scare over California spinach in 2006, linked to distributors on the East Coast.

Larger discrete populations, including day-care centers, nursing homes, cruise ships, and the military, have made prevention of FBI a priority because of the speed with which an outbreak can and does spread. International travel across borders by people and foodstuffs is the norm. Globalization of the food supply (Mexican cantaloupes in New York in February) has made oversight more and more difficult.

The U.S. population is changing, and higher risk groups (people who are more likely to become ill than others) are increasing numerically: an aging population with weaker immune systems, people who take medications for chronic diseases, people with organ transplants who take immunosuppressive drugs, and so on. Food allergies are also increasing, although the definitive causes of this trend remain speculative at present. The traditional group of high-risk populations remains: infants and children, the elderly, and pregnant women.

Sources of Foodborne Illnesses

Major causes of FBI and FBI outbreaks (defined as illnesses that result when two or more people become ill after eating the same food) result primarily from bacteria, viruses, parasites, and fungal contamination. In addition to pathogenic microorganisms, foodborne illnesses may result from physical and chemical causes.

Physical contaminants, such as broken glass or metal staples, while regrettable, do not usually cause gastrointestinal problems. Chemical toxins, such as metals, pesticides, and cleaning products, are more problematic and may cause physical and neurological problems. However, the main culprits in most cases of FBI are microorganisms. Conditions that minimize growth of pathogens are critical to achieving acceptable levels of food safety. Personal hygiene (primarily oral-fecal contamination through improper hand washing), time and temperature limits, acidity and moisture controls, the presence or absence of oxygen, and cross-contamination are some of the concepts incorporated into food safety systems.

Bacteria

The most common source of FBI is bacterial contamination. In healthy adults, bacterial pathogens, if ingested in sufficient quantity, generally cause abdominal cramps, diarrhea, and occasionally vomiting and fever and can be fatal to high-risk individuals. A stool or blood sample tested in a lab is the only sure way to know which pathogen is involved in a case of FBI. Traceability (and transparency) through monitoring procedures can help discover causes of FBI and is required for certain foods. For example, bivalves such as mussels and oysters that are served in restaurants must have their tags kept on file for 90 days, precisely in order to be able to trace pathogens back to the place of harvest.

Campylobacter jejuni, found in the intestines of healthy poultry, is the most common source of FBI in the world. Transmission comes by eating undercooked poultry, or ready-to-eat foods that will not be cooked, contaminated either through direct contact between foods, on the hands of the preparer, or on cooking utensils.

Salmonella species live in the intestines of birds, mammals, and reptiles. Salmonella bacteria are usually found in poultry, beef, dairy products, eggs, fresh produce (from contaminated water), and ready-to-eat foods. Poor personal hygiene practices; cross-contamination between foods or with other foods, persons, or food contact surfaces; and improper time/temperature controls are the main transmission routes for salmonella species to humans.

Shigella species are found in feces of humans who have become ill by eating foods or water contaminated with these bacteria. Ready-to-eat foods, fresh produce, and flies are sources; improper personal hygiene is a common method of transmission.

Listeria monocytogenes is found in water, soil, and plants. This pathogen, particularly dangerous for pregnant women, is associated with ready-to-eat foods, including cold buffets, salad bars, unpasteurized milk, and raw meat.

Vibrio parahaemolyticus and *Vibrio vulnificus* types 1 and 2 are found in warm tropical waters and are associated with raw or undercooked shellfish.

Bacillus cereus is associated with cooked cereal plants and starches, such as rice, **corn**, and potatoes, but can also be found in meat products and cooked vegetables. It is a spore-forming bacterium: when conditions for reproduction are not optimal, the bacterium goes into a state of suspended animation by cloaking itself in a thick wall of protective material that is tolerant of extreme heat and cold. It sheds its coat when conditions improve.

Staphylococcus aureus is associated with human hair, nose, throat, and sores and is normally found in one-third of the population. Cooking does not destroy this pathogen: good hygiene and food-handling techniques are essential to prevent contamination.

Clostridium botulinum, the cause of botulism, is an anaerobic (i.e., lives without oxygen), spore-forming bacterium. It can be found in almost any food, but is associated with produce grown in soil, such as potatoes, onions, and carrots, as well as vacuum-sealed packages (such as smoked salmon) and damaged cans. Nausea and vomiting may be followed by weakness, difficulty speaking and swallowing, and double vision. Vigilant time and temperature controls for foods that typically sit on the counter for a number of hours, such as baked potatoes or garlic in oil mixtures (the garlic and oil mixtures in the **supermarket** have been pasteurized) are necessary to maintain food safety.

Clostridium perfringens is a spore-forming bacterium found in soil. Cooking, serving, cooling, and reheating foods to temperatures that kill this pathogen are needed for food safety. *C. perfringens* is often found in stews and gravies, as well as meat and poultry dishes made at home (it is rare in commercial foodservice).

Hemorraghic colitis is usually associated with undercooked ground beef. The most well known and sometimes deadly variant is caused by *E. coli* O157:H7. These bacteria live in the intestines of healthy cattle and other herding animals. Fecal contamination is the usual route of transmission, either through water (groundwater contamination from manure waste or during slaughter from intestinal leakage onto muscle tissue) or through personal hygiene, food contact, or food contact surfaces. In its most severe form, it causes hemolytic kidney failure and death. Proper cooking kills the pathogen.

Viruses

Viruses are the smallest microbial contaminants. Unlike bacteria, they do not reproduce on food, but once on a food will cause the person eating it to become ill. Their presence can be minimized by practicing good personal hygiene, especially that involving ready-to-eat foods and bare hand contact with such foods.

Hepatitis A and E are linked with ready-to-eat foods and with raw or partially cooked shellfish taken from contaminated waters. Cooking does not kill these viruses, which if left untreated can lead to jaundice. There is now a vaccine for hepatitis A.

Norovirus and its variants are found in shellfish from contaminated waters and in ready-to-eat foods. These viruses pass easily from person to person and are highly contagious. Minute amounts can rapidly cause illness.

Parasites

Parasites are living organisms that need a host to survive, and they can be found in food and water. They live in and on many animals and can be microscopic or visible. *Anisakis simplex* is a wormlike parasite associated with fish and shellfish. Proper cooking or freezing will destroy this parasite. If left untended, the parasite will penetrate the lining of the stomach. *Cyclospora cayetanensis* and *Cryptosporidium parvum* are found in sewage (from humans and animals) and in contaminated water that is used to irrigate fruit and vegetables. *Giardia duodenalis* is also found in contaminated water or in feces of those who have the parasite. Proper food handling, hand washing, and good personal hygiene, as well as properly treated water, are essential to halt the spread of this parasite.

Biological Toxins: Shellfish

Common sources of fish toxicity include histamine, found in the scombroid species (tuna, bonito, mackerel, and mahi mahi), and ciguatoxin, found in predatory reef fish that eat marine algae which produce this toxin naturally (e.g., barracuda, grouper, jacks, and snapper). Other shellfish toxins may cause paralysis, amnesia, and neurological problems. Saxitoxin, brevetoxin, and domoic acid are three toxins associated with clams, mussels, scallops, and oysters; they are not destroyed by cooking or freezing.

Plant Toxins

Certain plants naturally produce chemicals that may cause illness in some people. Examples include mushrooms (toadstools), rhubarb leaves, fava beans (raw), red kidney beans (raw), jimsonweed, and water hemlock.

Nonfood Chemicals

Cracked or chipped pots and tableware may contain lead, antimony, and other metals that are harmful and could be ingested with food. Other chemicals used in manufacturing, such as Teflon, are known to be dangerous when used at high temperatures. Mercury levels in canned tuna, for instance, are legally tolerable below certain limits, despite warnings from the federal government on consumption of canned tuna for pregnant women and children. Cleaning products and pesticides are other sources of potential contamination.

Allergens

An allergy is the body's negative reaction to a food, usually a food protein. Seven million people in the United States have food allergies. Common allergens are peanuts, **wheat**, strawberries, milk and dairy products, eggs and egg products, fish, shellfish, soybeans and soy products, and tree nuts. For unknown reasons, food allergies are increasing.

Bioterrorism

The Bioterrorism Act of 2002 was signed into law after the terrorist attacks of September 11, 2001. Reinforcement of food security for foodstuffs arriving in and distributed throughout the United States is the Act's primary goal. While the Food and Drug Administration (FDA) is responsible for carrying out certain provisions of the Bioterrorism Act, food safety regulations are spread among the FDA, the **U.S. Department of Agriculture**, and the National Marine Fisheries Service. In addition, the Centers for Disease Control and Prevention tracks epidemiological information and statistics and assesses prevention efforts.

FURTHER READINGS: Centers for Disease Control and Prevention, National Antimicrobial Resistance Monitoring System. "Frequently Asked Questions (FAQ) about Antibiotic Resistance: Why Is Antibiotic Resistance a Food Safety Problem?" http://www.cdc.gov/narms/faq_-pages/5.htm; Food and Drug Administration, Center for Food Safety and Applied Nutrition. "*Anisakis simplex* and Related Worms." http://vm.cfsan.fda.gov/~mow/chap25.html; National Restaurant Association Educational Foundation. *Servsafe Essentials.* 4th ed. Chicago: National Restaurant Association Educational Foundation, 2006; Partnership for Food Safety Education.

FightBAC! http://www.fightbac.org; Ray, Bibek. *Fundamental Food Microbiology.* 2nd ed. New York: CRC Press, 2001.

Renee Marton

Food Safety The United States food supply is touted as the safest in the world. Regulatory oversight is a complex system comprising more than 30 **food laws** administered by 12 agencies—and cooperating state agencies—charged with ensuring the safety, wholesomeness, and proper labeling of all foods. Despite great strides in food safety, foodborne illness and **food poisoning** still present a serious public health problem. The Centers for Disease Control and Prevention (CDC) estimates that each year 76 million people get sick, 325,000 are hospitalized, and 5,000 die from food-related illnesses in the United States. The federal government spends upwards of $1.3 billion a year on food safety that encompasses both domestic and imported foods. Yet costs associated with foodborne illness surpass this sum; medical costs and lost productivity are calculated at $7 billion.

Food-related sickness outbreaks shake consumer confidence and adversely affect the food industry. While advanced technology is useful in controlling organisms that cause illness, increased industrialization and concentration of the food supply may be creating new and virulent pathogens and incidents of widespread infection. It is widely agreed that the nation's overlapping food safety system is in need of modernization to address accidental and deliberate threats to the food supply. It is in the best interests of business, government, and consumers to enhance safety for domestic and imported foods, provide safe food at a reasonable price, and reduce the frequency of food-related illness.

The Impetus for Food Safety Legislation

Adulteration of food by unscrupulous merchants is an ancient problem; Roman laws prohibited the dilution of wine, and Henry III issued the Assize of Bread in 1266, which pilloried bakers who adulterated the staff of life by adding indigestible substances that increased the weight of the loaf but sickened consumers. Today, adulteration occurs in myriad ways; typically a harmful substance either winds up in food accidentally as part of the manufacturing or transportation process or is inserted by intentional tampering, or a substance might be added to food that has not been approved for use by regulatory agencies.

When food production was primarily local, farmers and merchants were under close scrutiny by the consuming public. As the population increased and shifted from the countryside to cities, the distance between production and consumption widened. Food safety practices deteriorated as food industries created nationwide distribution networks. By the turn of the 19th century, unsubstantiated health claims for foods and beverages were rampant; mislabeling and adulteration of foods, including milk laced with formaldehyde, were commonplace; and filthy meatpacking plant conditions, as detailed in Upton Sinclair's *The Jungle*, outraged the public. In response, Congress enacted the Pure Food and Drug Act of 1906 and the Federal Meat Inspection Act of 1906. The **U.S. Department of Agriculture**'s (USDA) Bureau of Chemistry—the predecessor of the Food and Drug Administration (FDA)—soon gained fame under the guidance of Harvey Wiley and his "poison squad," comprised of young men who tested questionable foodstuffs by consuming them, and set about cleaning up the food supply. For its part, the USDA began to inspect the slaughter of all cattle, sheep, pigs, goats, and horses—a federal inspector still must be present daily while meat is processed for human consumption. Inspection of **poultry** wasn't required until the enactment in 1957 of the Poultry Products Inspection Act. The Egg Products Inspection Act followed in 1970.

Advances in food preservation techniques, nutritional science, and agriculture increased the use of chemicals, the number of **additives** such as **vitamins** and minerals, and the amount of pesticide residue in foods. This led to the passage in 1938 of the Federal Food, Drug, and Cosmetic Act (FDCA). New regulatory developments under the Act, still in effect, included the creation of standards of identity that define the specific ingredient composition of certain foods and nutrient fortification for staples, such as cereals and milk. Continued concern about the use of chemical additives led to the Food Additives and Color Additives amendments in 1958 and 1960, respectively. Under the Federal Insecticide, Fungicide, and Rodenticide Act, first passed in 1947 and extensively amended in 1972, the **Environmental Protection Agency** (EPA) regulates the sale and use of pesticides and set limits or "tolerances" for pesticide residues in or on foods.

The development of safety oversight for seafood is a complex interaction of state and federal laws dating from the 1920s. Outbreaks of typhoid fever and other illnesses tied to the consumption of raw shellfish and fish from contaminated waters led to a series of regulations and voluntary cooperative agreements between state agencies and the Federal Bureau of Commercial Fisheries (the predecessor of the National Marine Fisheries Service), the Public Health Service, and the USDA Bureau of Chemistry. The FDA took federal responsibility for the program in 1968.

Due to severe funding restraints, beginning in the 1990s the FDA and USDA phased in the Hazard Analysis and Critical Control Points (HACCP) system as a requirement for virtually all food production. First implemented by NASA to eliminate the risk of foodborne illness for astronauts, HACCP requires food companies, including seafood operations, to inspect their food production procedures, identify areas where contaminants could enter the production process, and proactively lower those risks. Critics of universal HACCP implementation complained it was an abdication of federal oversight responsibility in favor of industry self-monitoring.

After the September 11, 2001, attacks, fears of deliberate contamination of the food supply or targeting of food production facilities by terrorists led to passage of the Public Health Security and Bioterrorism Preparedness and Response Act of 2002. This legislation and subsequent regulations require the FDA to register food processors, ensure the safety of imported foods, receive prior notice of all food imports, inspect records, and detain adulterated food. The Act also contains appropriations for the USDA to increase border inspections and augment biosecurity research.

The Current Food Safety and Security System

The current food safety and security network was created primarily in response to periodic health emergencies, technological developments, and economic crises, rather than strategic design. A congressionally mandated review conducted in 2004 by the Government Accountability Office (GAO) describes a "fragmented legal and organizational structure" that provides food oversight responsibilities to different agencies with "significantly different authorities and responsibilities."

Governing jurisdictions have evolved according to the type of food, food-processing techniques or technology, and even the type of adulterant in specific foods. Essentially, the USDA regulates meat, poultry, and certain egg products, while the FDA, now part of the Department of Health and Human Services (DHHS), enforces safety standards for all other domestic and imported foods, including whole eggs in the shell, seafood, milk, grain products, and fruits and vegetables. However, there is significant overlap that wastes resources and confounds coordination of safety efforts. For example, differing regulations result in daily inspection of USDA-regulated facilities by Food Safety Inspection Service (FSIS) inspectors, while the FDA inspects most domestic food-producing facilities only once every three to five years. Depending on the food ingredient, a processing plant might be subject to inspection by both USDA and FDA. Pizza inspection famously depended on whether there was meat topping. While that specific anomaly has been remedied by a change in regulations, multiple other problems have not.

In general, foods regulated by the USDA must be approved prior to marketing, while FDA-regulated foods can be marketed without prior approval. Both the USDA and FDA issue warning letters, can generate adverse publicity for industry members, and seek judicial assistance to obtain injunctions, initiate criminal prosecutions, seize food, and order recalls. Although recall is critical to the enforcement of food safety laws, they are voluntary; neither the USDA nor FDA has the statutory authority necessary to mandate a recall. In addition, neither agency will immediately identify the stores affected by a recall or notify individual consumers despite the fact that many purchases are tracked through store loyalty programs. The USDA does, however, have the ability to remove its inspectors from a processing plant; that action will effectively cease operations. Fortunately, the threat of regulatory action, adverse publicity, and legal liability are powerful incentives for voluntary action. Legislation to grant the agencies recall authority has been unsuccessful. Opponents of agency mandatory recall authority fear the government could cause unwarranted economic injury to companies if recalls are ordered without sufficient basis. Thus, the USDA and FDA mostly provide guidance to industry and primarily monitor the food industry for adherence to regulations governing safe food production.

State and Local Food Safety and Security

State public health and agriculture departments, multiple other state bodies, and literally thousands of local agencies license and inspect millions of retail food establishments, including markets, **restaurants**, schools, and hospitals under state laws and regulations. The FDA publishes a model food safety manual, the Food Code, whose guidelines have been adopted by most state and local officials. For example, the code establishes safe temperatures for commercial food preparation, service, and storage. There is lack of uniformity, however, since each agency can adopt varying versions of the Food Code, which is modified approximately every four years. Such discrepancies can create problems in enforcement and coordination for both food safety and food security issues. Certain localities may also be using obsolete or incorrect safety guidelines.

Progress Measured by Past and Emerging Threats

In 2005 the CDC announced progress toward foodborne illness reduction goals established in Healthy People 2010, the nationwide health promotion and disease prevention agenda issued by DHHS. The CDC credited USDA's science-based policies and enforcement for declines in illnesses caused by the consumption of **beef**, poultry, and eggs contaminated with pathogens such as *E. coli*, *Listeria monocytogenes*, and *Campylobacter*. The FSIS also reported a drop in voluntary recalls of foods that tested positive for infectious agents.

Despite the significant decline of food safety threats such as trichinosis, changes in agricultural practices, industrialized food processing with swift and wide distribution channels, and globalization have all contributed to the emergence and spread of new and equally dangerous pathogens. **Bovine spongiform encephalopathy**, a variant of Creutzfeldt-Jakob disease commonly known as "mad cow disease," is believed to stem from a change in animal feeding practices. Contaminants in fish, primarily methylmercury, and the threat of an avian flu pandemic are emerging food safety issues. Other concerns are raised by **antibiotic** resistance in humans due to overuse in animals, regulation of genetically modified organisms, food from the offspring of **cloned** animals, and the safety of fresh produce. Larger populations with immune weaknesses, increased consumption of meals outside the home, and ironically growth in the consumption of fresh fruits and vegetables have all been fraught with food safety concerns.

Recommendations for Improvement

Myriad government and some industry groups have pointed to specific problems with the current system that would be remedied if food safety and security were under the umbrella of one agency. These problems include that the frequency of inspections is not based on risk, agency budgets are not based on the volume of foods regulated or consumed, and expenditures are not proportionate to incidence of illness caused by a particular food. The GAO report cited above calls for a single food safety agency with the enforcement powers to implement a uniform, risk-based inspection system. Short of complete integration, the GAO urges Congress to modify existing laws so that one agency takes the lead for all inspections. No legislation has been successful to date. Industry opposition is based on the need to focus on science to advance food safety goals, rather than more regulations. Federal officials assert that unification is unnecessary since cooperation and formal memorandums of understanding among agencies have reduced most duplication of efforts.

See also Bacteria.

FURTHER READINGS: Congressional Research Service. *Food Safety Issues in the 109th Congress.* Washington, DC: GPO. Available through http://opencrs.com/document/RL31853; Food-safety.gov: Gateway to Government Food Safety Information. http://www.foodsafety.gov; Nestle, Marion. *Safe Food: Bacteria, Biotechnology, and Bioterrorism.* Berkeley: University of California Press, 2003.

Ellen J. Fried

Food Service Industry The food service industry encompasses those organizations and institutions responsible for feeding individuals away from home. Food service includes a wide variety of **restaurants, cafeterias, supermarkets**, school lunch programs, and other commercial establishments that ensure food is readily available whenever a consumer wants to consume. With more than 12 million workers, this industry employs more Americans than any other industry. Moreover, food service accounts for more than $400 billion in annual sales for the U.S. market.

At the same time, the rise of the food service industry is not a phenomenon exclusive to the United States. As with most major advancements in modern cuisine, the development of the food service industry, restaurants in particular, is credited to the French. The first restaurants emerged in 18th-century France as a space where one could consume a *restaurant*, otherwise known as a bouillon-based medicinal broth. Additionally, the standard brigade system used by most large kitchens was developed in 19th-century France by Auguste Escoffier. Although the French initiated the trends that gave rise to the industry, Americans have made their share of contributions to the growth and magnitude of food service, most notably the creation of **fast food** and roadside restaurants.

The reach of the food service industry extends far beyond commercial sites such as restaurants. Institutions including schools, hospitals, prisons, nursing homes, and community outreach programs also provide important nutritional resources to individuals in need. For example, the Meals on Wheels program has provided home-**delivered** meals for vulnerable and elderly individuals since 1939. Moreover, starting in the late 1990s, several schools on the National School Lunch Program (NSLP) began renegotiating their contracts with vendors to provide healthier options for students during lunch. Ultimately, the food service industry, with its commercial and community interests, has a significant influence on the ways in which we eat on local, national, and global levels.

Commercial Food Service

The first restaurant is believed to have opened in 1765 by Monsieur Boulanger, a French vendor of the aforementioned medicinal broths. In all actuality, the first restaurant most likely resembled a modern-day soup kitchen. A restorative broth or *restaurant* was usually consumed by an individual too weak to eat a full evening meal. As such, poor, elderly, or sick individuals frequented the first restaurants. Over the next 240 years, restaurants developed and diversified into a sophisticated network of **gourmet** dining, **takeout** meals, and specialty food preparation. By the 1820s, Paris was smattered with eateries and cafés that closely resemble the restaurants of today, with written menus, set prices, and table service. By the 1990s, there were almost 200,000 fast food or takeout restaurants in the United States alone.

Restaurants represent only one aspect of the commercial food industry, although they do make up a significant part of food service. Aside from restaurants, commercial food service is also characterized by both grocery stores and specialty service shops such as bakeries and caterers. First, grocery stores, convenience stores, and local markets increasingly serve as sites for food service. Descended from old general stores, modern-day markets are now points of service for food sales. For example, **Whole Foods Market** has the elements of a specialty grocery store, including **organic** foods. The store also has a café area where patrons can sit to eat items such as sandwiches or salads purchased at the deli counter. Additionally, convenience marts such as QuikTrip serve hot breakfast sandwiches in the morning and **hot dogs** and hamburgers throughout the day, making them a significant and speedy contributor to the food service industry. Other, more specialized points of service include bakeries, butchers, **wineries**, and caterers, each of which adds different dimensions to commercial food service. For example, the demand for wedding cakes alone often keeps many local, small bakeries in business even in the face of larger competitors.

Institutional Food Service

The other side of food service involves a complex network of federal, state, and local government agencies, for-profit and not-for-profit organizations, and consumers, many of whom come from underserved populations. Institutional food service primarily includes educational and medical food service. Perhaps the most expansive system of educational food service involves school meal programs. For both K–12 schools as well as major colleges and universities, the feeding of students, faculty, and staff has taken up a secure niche within the industry. For example, the National School Lunch Program was established in 1946 under the National School Lunch Act. This program is a federally assisted meal service for all K–12 public and nonprofit private schools who wish to participate. Schools can receive reimbursements from the federal government depending on how many full-priced, reduced, and free meals they serve.

The NSLP is an interesting example of institutional food service in an educational setting, because it demonstrates how schools must negotiate with both government officials and commercial vendors to ensure service. To participate in this federal program, schools must first document how many students qualify for free or reduced-price meals. Then schools must structure their meals according to guidelines from the **U.S. Department of Agriculture** and provide documentation for all of their recipes and other foods sold on campus. Moreover, schools are reviewed on a semiannual basis. If a school violates any of the rules set forth, it risks losing its reimbursements for the day. For example, schools must turn off their soda machines during the lunch hour, because sodas are not allowed to compete with the NSLP; if a reviewer finds that a machine has been left on during lunch, the school will lose its reimbursements for that day.

Not only must schools comply with government standards in order to participate, but they must also negotiate with commercial vendors to stock their shelves. While some schools do receive commodities from the federal government, other schools must get everything through vendors, from the raw materials used to cook from scratch all the way to full meals catered every day. Many schools also have expansive à la carte menus and fully stocked **vending machines** with pizza, pretzels, **candy**, and chips from familiar companies such as Pizza Hut or Lay's. These negotiations can often be tricky, because commercial vendors see children as willing consumers. As such, many vendors want to stock their machines with foods that kids want, while at the same time the NSLP is trying to teach them what they need.

There are a variety of other forms of institutional food service. The cafeteria structure is the most popular among these institutions, particularly at colleges and universities, hospitals, nursing homes, mental health facilities, and prisons. Unlike the National School Lunch Program, there are few unifying standards across these different institutions, and many of them have rules and procedures that are unique to their specific location. But there are some similarities: As with commercial and educational food service, these types of institutions still have to work with vendors, consumers, and other stakeholders in order to keep their doors open.

Food Service Innovations

As the food service has developed over the decades, the industry has been a driving force of several innovations. Most notably, the sheer organization of eating practices is a monumental feat. The breadth and depth to which the food service industry has grown is a testament to modern forms of organization. For example, when Ray Kroc bought the first McDonald's from the McDonald brothers, he was the man selling milkshake machines. However, his ideas on technology, simplified work, and mechanization transformed a family business into the largest global restaurant **chain**. Modern restaurants are now dependent on new forms of technology to communicate orders from the "front of the house" to the "back of the house," fill cups with beverages and ice, and even process and assemble certain entrees.

These advancements in technology have also given rise to another innovation—anti–fast food movements. Food criticism has always been a part of modern cuisine; however, the tone of the criticism is taking a much more sociological form. With the publication of Eric Schlosser's *Fast Food Nation* in 2001 and the release of Morgan Spurlock's documentary *Super Size Me!* in 2004, the **labor** practices, food quality, and general health states surrounding the fast food industry have been called into question. These media have served to complement the **Slow Food** movement started by Carlo Petrini in Italy during the late 20th century. This movement emerged as a response to fast food restaurants, which Petrini believed were undermining the quality and community associated with eating. By 2006, Slow Food organizations had formed in more than 100 countries and had nearly 100,000 members.

Finally, institutional food service is looking to innovate, particularly in the school service sector. Across the nation, schools are looking for more innovative ways to serve healthy foods that students want to buy. For example, starting in 2004, several schools in Arizona initiated a redesign of their school meal programs to look more like a commercial food court. However, they did not simply invite Taco Bell and Pizza Hut into their schools. Rather, schools designed their own Asian, Mexican, Italian, and All-American cuisines. These lunch lines attempt to combine healthier food options in a setting that students find engaging and familiar. Ultimately, these innovations suggest that the food service industry will continue to shape the ways in which we eat in new and creative ways.

See also Airline Food; Delicatessens.

FURTHER READINGS: Fischer, John W. *At Your Service: A Hands-on Guide to the Professional Dining Room.* Hoboken, NJ: Wiley, 2005; Schlosser, Eric. *Fast Food Nation: The Dark Side of the All-American Meal.* New York: Perennial, 2002; Spang, Rebecca L. *The Restaurant: Paris and Modern Gastronomic Culture.* Cambridge, MA: Harvard University Press, 2001.

Marianne LeGreco

Food Stamps Food stamps are a means of providing low-income Americans with access to enough food to meet their basic nutritional needs. They are named for the original orange and blue stamps used to purchase regular and surplus food commodities, respectively. The Food Stamp Program (FSP) developed historically as a mechanism for combating hunger and food insecurity in the United States while promoting American agriculture. It was initiated by the federal government as a way of delivering direct aid to the poor for purchasing food.

The concept of using food stamps had its origin in the 1939–1943 period as a Depression-era New Deal relief program to promote the use of agricultural surplus. After an 18-year hiatus, the idea was revisited as a pilot project in 1961 by way of an

Executive Order from President John F. Kennedy. As part of the Johnson administration's "war on poverty," a more formalized program was given congressional approval in 1964 as the Food Stamp Act. In addition to a number of eligibility requirements, the Act required the purchase of food stamps on a sliding scale based on household income. State and local participation in the program was initially on a voluntary basis.

Over the next 10 years, eligibility requirements were continually reformulated with new amendments. The program became mandatory in all states in 1974. Some of the most sweeping reforms in the program took place with the Food Stamp Act of 1977. While trying to target those most in need of aid, the Act eliminated the purchase conditions, attempted to standardize eligibility requirements, and sought to define the household unit. However, by the early 1980s, eligibility criteria were reformulated and legislated with increased restrictions. With hunger in America on the rise during this period, incremental changes to the program that counterbalanced these restrictions and favored easier access were implemented by the late 1980s.

Further change came with the Personal Responsibility and Work Opportunities Reconciliation Act of 1996, commonly known as the Welfare Reform Act. It reduced the number of eligible people by placing time limits on benefits and requiring specific work requirements. In addition, eligibility for most legal immigrants was eliminated. Most of the immigrant benefits were eventually restored in the 2002 Farm Bill. The FSP will be reauthorized through the 2007 Farm Bill.

Even though the federal government pays for the program benefits, administrative costs are shared with states. Federal oversight of the program is performed by the Food and Nutrition Service (FNS) of the **U.S. Department of Agriculture** (USDA), but state and local agencies are still responsible for determining food stamp eligibility and distribution. Households can also be temporarily enrolled in the FSP as part of disaster relief, as was the case following Hurricane Katrina in 2005. Other targeted FNS programs not mutually exclusive of food stamp benefits include Special Supplemental Program for Women, Infants, and Children (WIC); the Nutrition Program for the Elderly (NPE), incorporating the "Meals on Wheels" **delivery** program; the Child and Adult Care Food Program; and the National School Lunch and Breakfast programs.

As a means of providing direct support to low-income people, food stamp recipients may purchase such items as bread, cereals, **dairy** products, meat, fish, **poultry**, fruits, and vegetables, but are restricted from nonfood items such as alcohol and tobacco. For nearly 40 years, food stamps were traditionally paper vouchers or coupons that were cashed in when purchasing food items at an approved retailer. Today, Electronic Benefit Transfer (EBT) cards are primarily used. EBT is an electronic system that authorizes the transfer of one's benefits from a federal account to a food vendor's account. Currently, 99.8 percent of food stamp benefits are issued by this means.

The FSP provides a monthly allotment that is determined by various factors. It is based primarily on the number of individuals in a household, their gross and net incomes, and assets. Criteria translate to having less than $2,000 in disposable assets ($3,000 if a household member is age 60 or older or disabled) and, depending on the household size, a gross income below 130 percent of the poverty line and a net income of less than 100 percent of the poverty line. High-cost areas such as Alaska and Hawaii have exceptions to these criteria. The USDA has an online Pre-Screening

Tool that can be used to determine food stamp eligibility (www.foodstamps-step1.usda.gov).

Actual maximum food stamp allotments are standardized and determined by using the USDA's Thrifty Food Plan (TFP). This amount is the estimated purchasing power needed to buy items in a "market basket" so that a household can obtain an economical and nutritious diet. The TFP is standardized and adjusted for inflation, yet it is clear that food costs vary widely across the country and in urban versus rural areas. In addition, the TFP assumes that households will be purchasing food with other income they receive.

In fiscal year 2005, the FNS reported that the $28.6 billion food stamp benefit program served on average 25.7 million people living in 11.2 million households. It also noted that most food stamp recipients were either children (50%) or elderly (8%). Overall, the average food stamp household was small in size, had little income, possessed few resources, received an average monthly benefit of $209, did not receive cash welfare benefits through Temporary Assistance to Needy Families (85%), and had earnings from work (29%).

Complaints about fraud and abuse have long plagued public perceptions of the FSP. Although the incidence was not high given the scale of the program, media stories of individuals selling their food stamp coupons for cash and then using the proceeds to buy alcohol or drugs or gamble were widely circulated. This has led to political attempts to tighten eligibility and reduce the program's budget and thus the number of participants. The reality is that there is only a small percentage of fraud currently associated with the program, especially since the widescale implementation of the EBT system.

An additional criticism of the program has been the low rate of participation, given the estimated number of households that could qualify for the program. Research grants and outreach programs have been supported by the FNS to increase enrollments, but there are still obstacles that prevent greater involvement. These include a lack of education about federal eligibility and state administrative requirements, barriers to signing up for the programs, and a continued stigma and shame associated with participation. The EBT system has reduced some of this stigma at the point of purchase because it is less conspicuous than the old coupon method.

Research has shown that although hunger in America has not been eliminated by the FSP, it has been a great benefit to needy households through increasing the availability and awareness of nutritious foods along with wise food choices. Criticisms that fault the program for contributing to the **obesity** epidemic in the United States have not been substantiated. There is still, however, a great deal of variation in intra-household food distribution and regional food purchasing power.

Overall, the program was intended from its inception to be America's temporary nutrition assistance safety net and was never meant to be a permanent solution to ending hunger. That goal will come about only through improved poverty reduction policies that address the larger issue of structural inequality in the country.

FURTHER READINGS: U.S. Department of Agriculture, Food and Nutrition Service. "Food Stamp Program." http://www.fns.usda.gov/fsp; U.S. Department of Agriculture, Office of Analysis, Nutrition, and Evaluation. *Characteristics of Food Stamp Households: Fiscal Year 2005*, by Allison Barrett. FSP-06-CHAR. Alexandria, VA: USDA, 2006. Available at http://www.fns.usda.gov/oane/menu/published/fsp/files/participation/2005characteristics.pdf.

Barrett P. Brenton

Franchises In the late 19th century, American manufacturers such as the Singer Sewing Machine Company, expanded their retail operations by licensing individuals to sell their products. This process, called franchising, benefited the manufacturer, which did not have to expend its own capital to establish and maintain retail operations, and also benefited the franchisees by permitting them to start their own business without risking everything on a new venture.

The first food franchisers were A&W Root Beer in Lodi, California, and the Pig Stand in Dallas, Texas. Both franchised their first outlets in 1924. Both sold territorial franchises, in which a franchisee was given a territory, such as a city, state, or a group of states. *Franchisees* could then franchise others within their authorized territories.

Another early franchiser was Howard Johnson, who bought a drugstore with a soda fountain in Wollasten, Massachusetts, in 1925. He invented his own "28 flavors" of **ice cream** and began franchising ice cream stands that proved very popular during the summer. Beginning in 1935, he launched roadside coffee shops and required franchisees to have a similar orange-roofed appearance and serve the same menu. Johnson also required franchisees to buy their products exclusively from him. This maintained the quality of products, which was crucial for the success of the **chain**.

Franchising after World War II

Following World War II, franchises initially catered to the rapidly growing suburbs and small towns. Dairy Queen began franchising soft-serve ice cream parlors, and other franchise chains quickly followed. Dunkin' Donuts, Baskin-Robbins, Chicken Delight, Burger King, Jack in the Box, and Kentucky Fried Chicken all began franchising in the early 1950s.

Richard and Maurice McDonald started to franchise their **McDonald's restaurant** in 1952. Ray Kroc saw their advertisements and visited the brothers in San Bernardino, California. Kroc was impressed with what he saw. In 1954 he signed an agreement to franchise the McDonalds' operation nationally. In 1955 Kroc sold his first franchise to himself and opened an outlet in Des Plaines, Illinois.

At the time, chains typically demanded large franchise fees, sold off rights to entire territories, and earned their money by selling supplies directly to their franchisees. This caused numerous problems—the most important being that if franchisees disobeyed the contract, there was little the franchiser could do. Kroc changed this franchising formula: his company purchased or leased the property, and then leased the property to franchisees at a hefty profit. If franchisees refused to obey the franchise contract, McDonald's could easily evict them. This control greatly assisted the growth of McDonald's.

Franchising Opportunities and Challenges

The relationship between franchiser and franchisee evolved into a lengthy contractual relationship. The franchiser often developed business plans for the franchisee; created specific building requirements; supplied expertise, equipment, and supplies; and engaged in **advertising** that increased sales of the product. The franchiser, in turn, created strict regulations that were imposed upon franchisees. Franchisers made money on selling the license to distributors and also received a portion of the profits when the products or services were sold. Franchisees were often small investors. As many franchisees lack proper credentials to acquire loans from banks, the franchisers sometimes put up a portion of the funds necessary to launch the business.

When profits rolled in, both franchisers and franchisees were happy; when things went wrong, the franchisers usually came out ahead. **Fast food** is considered a mature business in the United States. For most fast food chains, the American market is saturated. Franchisers have allowed franchisees to open ever closer to existing franchises, which was called *encroachment*. Sales and profits decline when new franchises open near existing outlets. Another problem relates to product sourcing, where franchisers required franchisees to purchase products only from them or their designated suppliers, often at inflated prices. Many franchisee chains have formed organizations to protect themselves.

Typical contracts today call for franchiser to assist with site selection, furnishings, training, promotions, operating instructions, and recordkeeping and accounting systems, as well as building designs and equipment layouts. These are covered by licensee fees and assessments to support chain advertising. In addition, a franchisee might be required to lease equipment and buy food products and supplies from the parent company.

FURTHER READINGS: Birkeland, Peter M. *Franchising Dreams: The Lure of Entrepreneurship in America.* Chicago: University of Chicago Press, 2002; Dicke, Thomas S. *Franchising in America: The Development of a Business Method, 1840–1980.* Chapel Hill: University of North Carolina Press, 1992; McDonald, Ronald L. *Ronald McDonald's Franchise Buyers Guide: How to Buy a Fast Food Franchise.* Philadelphia: Xlibris, 2003; Parsa, H. G., and Francis A. Kwansa, eds. *Quick Service Restaurants, Franchising, and Multi-unit Chain Management.* New York: Haworth Hospitality Press, 2002; Thomas, R. David, and Michael Seid. *Franchising for Dummies.* Foster City, CA: IDG Books Worldwide, 2000.

Andrew F. Smith

Free Trade Free trade refers to economic policies and ideologies aimed at reducing government and societal intervention in the economy. Proponents of free trade argue that regulation is necessary only to ensure open markets. Thus free trade advocates call for the elimination of national **tariffs** and subsidies for national industries. The philosophical underpinnings of free trade are found in the writings of 18th-century Scottish economist Adam Smith, who argued against the protectionist policies that characterized **mercantilism** between the 16th and 19th centuries. Britain moved quickly to embrace free trade policies during the early 19th century, and the repeal of the British Corn Laws in 1846 signifies many the beginning of free trade in food.

The current global regime of free trade dates generally from the signing of the General Agreement on Tariffs and Trade (GATT) in 1947. Trade liberalization, or the opening of markets for free trade, has characterized capitalist globalization especially since the 1980s. The contemporary framework for free trade in agriculture is shaped by the Uruguay Round of the GATT negotiations launched in the 1980s. The Uruguay Round Agreement on Agriculture brought agriculture within the purview of multilateral trade rules as of 1994. It impelled the opening of markets and the reduction of policies protecting local production. Significantly, it also imposed penalties on support of domestic industries.

Much of contemporary trade liberalization has occurred through regional trade agreements such as the **North American Free Trade Agreement** (NAFTA), the Asia-Pacific Economic Cooperation (APEC) forum, the Association of Southeast Asian Nations (ASEAN), and the **European Union** (EU). In addition, the EU developed a large number of so-called preferential trade agreements with poorer countries in Africa, the Caribbean, and the Pacific, allowing those countries increased market access. The development of regional trade blocs has reduced the costs of trade liberalization between blocs, thus propelling further liberalization.

In reality, as many critics suggest, free trade is not actually free. Rather it is a system of corporate management of trade in which policies that favor larger **multinational** corporations are developed against the interests of poorer countries, small-scale producers, and the environment. Under free trade rules sanctioned by the World Trade Organization (WTO), poorer countries are compelled to open agricultural markets to products from wealthier countries. WTO rules have required countries in Africa and Asia, for example, to import at least 4 percent of their production. Even if the country produces as much as it needs, it is required to bring in foodstuffs from abroad. In Asia, this has led to the oversupply of rice and a disastrous decline in prices for local producers. Through trade rules and structural adjustment programs tied to loan programs, poorer countries are also required to cease support for local farmers. In addition, free trade agreements undermine ecological concerns, as well as the rights of workers and consumers, since environmental protection policies and social programs can be considered impediments to trade liable to the imposition of penalties through the WTO.

Free trade has contributed to the growing monopolization of the world food industry. With the move of multinational corporations into growing numbers of markets, mergers and acquisitions have left control of the industry concentrated within the hands of a very small group of companies. A recent report by the organization ActionAid gives a picture of the extent of monopolization. According to the report, five companies control three-quarters of the global trade in grain, while just three companies trade 85 percent of the tea trade and only two companies account for sales of half of the world's bananas. A single company, **Monsanto**, controls over 90 percent of the global market in genetically modified seeds. Approximately 30 companies now account for one-third of the world's processed food. Since the signing of NAFTA, one company, Wal-Mart, has gained control over 40 percent of the retail food sector in Mexico.

Companies such as Nestlé, Monsanto, Unilever, Cargill, Bayer, and Wal-Mart have all expanded their reach and global influence as a direct result of trade liberalization policies developed and promoted by governments in the wealthiest countries since the 1980s. Indeed, critics argue that global trade rules have been designed by Western governments and their corporate sponsors primarily, or even exclusively, to benefit Western-based corporations. One result has been that multinational food companies are often more economically powerful than the countries in which they operate. Unilever enjoys profits larger than those of the national economy of Mozambique, while Nestlé has recorded profits larger than for the gross domestic product of Ghana.

This monopolization of the food market by global agricultural powerhouses has exacerbated poverty in poorer countries by driving down the prices local producers can get for goods that are sold to global purchasers, and upon which local economies are based, such as tea, **coffee**, bananas, and grains. Prices for coffee, cocoa, rice, **sugar**, and palm oil have fallen by more than half during the free trade era. At the same time, local companies are pushed out of local markets. Global food companies, because trade liberalization has increased their domination of local markets, are able to charge local consumers more for staple goods.

Despite the claims of free trade advocates that the market should be allowed to determine prices, food companies in wealthier countries benefit greatly from government subsidies. This allows large producers to dump food on world markets at prices substantially lower than the cost to grow it. The U.S. government subsidizes American farmers at levels exceeding $55 billion per year. This number is greater than the total of all rural-sector funding sources in Mexico combined. Sugar processors in the EU receive guaranteed prices at three times world market rates, which allows them to set export prices that are a mere fraction of production costs. Using preferential trade agreements with former colonies allows the EU to develop large surpluses for export. The result is that poorer sugar producers, such as those in Mozambique, can no longer compete in their traditional export markets, including Nigeria and Algeria. Subsidized food from wealthier countries forces down global commodity prices, while also shutting local producers out of domestic markets in poorer countries. At the same time, the subsidies do little to assist small producers in the EU or the United States, for example, since most of the funding goes to larger producers, processors, traders, and retailers. Thus subsidies to multinational **agribusinesses** have led to the bankruptcy of thousands of small-scale or family farmers, not only in poorer countries but even in the United States itself.

Despite increased trade liberalization, poorer countries have not captured a larger share of agricultural trade, a fact that speaks to the unequal nature of free trade. Between 1980 and 2000, the proportion of global agricultural exports among poorer countries remained almost constant at a little over one-third.

In response to these issues, groups such as Via Campesina, led by French farmer José Bové, have mobilized opposition to free trade in agricultural products and food. Against free trade policies, Via Campesina argues for what it calls "food sovereignty," the idea that each population should be able to eat from its own locally produced food. This is not opposition to trade itself, but rather a call for local control over local and regional markets and prices. It is an attempt to protect local agriculture from dumping and to remove the WTO from issues of food and agriculture.

FURTHER READINGS: "Power Hungry: Six Reasons to Regulate Global Food Corporations." n.p.: ActionAid, 2005.

Jeff Shantz

Freeze-dried Foods. *See* Frozen Foods.

Frieda's Frieda's, Inc., began in 1962 as a small produce distribution business and has grown to be a force in the specialty fruits and vegetables industry on the West Coast. The company is known for innovative marketing. It helped pioneer the branding, labeling, and **packaging** of produce and has developed a reputation for being able to introduce American consumers to new and unusual foods from around the world.

The company was started in Los Angeles by produce specialist Frieda Caplan to market fresh mushrooms, and it took off after a buyer asked for help locating the fruit then known as a Chinese gooseberry for a missionary recently returned from New Zealand. Caplan found the fruit for him, helped dub it "kiwifruit," and then went on to be a factor in changing how fresh produce was marketed in the United States.

The Caplans (daughter Karen took over the presidency in 1986) and their company became known for working with small growers of lesser-known fruits and vegetables. The elder Caplan credited traditional produce distributors' focus on high-volume items for creating a niche for her fledging specialty-produce firm. Over the years, Frieda's became known in the press and the produce market for finding the oddest, ugliest, or weirdest fruits and vegetables and finding ways to promote them to American retailers and consumers alike. In-store consumer education programs, trade seminars, newsletters, image makeovers for unfamiliar produce (including name changes), recipe distribution, development of local resources for formerly imported exotics, appearances on popular late night **television** shows, and a website that averages 250,000 hits a year are just some of the techniques Frieda's has used to peddle its produce to the media, produce buyers, and consumers.

The company's influence goes beyond its $38 million share of the almost $36-billion-a-year U.S. wholesale fresh produce distribution market. According to Frieda's, some of the world's produce that the company brought to America's tables include brown mushrooms, alfalfa sprouts, spaghetti squash, jicama, mangos, and a number of Latin and Asian specialties. About 25 percent of the more than 500 products the company distributes are not fresh fruits or vegetables, including ready-made crepes and dried chili wreaths.

Besides mainstreaming **ethnic** trends and unfamiliar produce, the company, now based in Los Alamitos, California, led in branding and packaging. Frieda's adopted purple as its signature color and used it in its logo (a purple heart with green leaves) to distinguish its produce, a practice then uncommon in the industry. The labels often contained preparation instructions and recipes, making it easier for consumers to experiment with unfamiliar fruits or vegetables.

Frieda's is no longer relatively alone in discovering and promoting new products; the specialty produce segment has grown. Other firms are increasingly competitive and innovative. The branded and packaged segment of the produce aisles has also grown, now accounting for about 13 percent of all produce bought at retail outlets.

See also Middlemen.

FURTHER READINGS: Caplan, Frieda. "Marketing New Crops to the American Consumer." In *Progress in New Crops*, 122–26. Alexandria, VA: ASHS Press, 1996; El Sawy, Nada. "Fruitful Enterprise: L.A. Company Sowed the Seeds of Specialty Produce." *San Diego Union-Tribune*, August 28, 2003, C3; Frieda's, Inc. http://www.friedas.com; Hamilton, Martha McNeil. "Ripe Dreams; How Produce-Aisle Exotica Becomes Everyday Fare." *Washington Post*, August 12, 2003, E1.

Faith J. Kramer

Frito-Lay. *See* Snack Foods.

Frozen Foods Frozen foods offer the consumer many advantages: the year-round availability of seasonal produce, product consistency, reduced preparation time, portion control, ease of storage, price stability, and lowered costs. Modern technologies have resulted in a product that, with proper handling, is often indistinguishable from fresh. Today, frozen foods are used by over 99 percent of American households and represent approximately one-third of food service sales.

Early Freezing Methods

All fresh foods contain water and a small population of microorganisms. Spoilage occurs when these microorganisms, such as **bacteria**, feed on matter and decompose it, releasing chemicals in the process that can cause disease or that simply render food unappealing. When the water in food is converted to ice, however, microbes become inactive, making freezing a highly effective method of food preservation.

Freezing has long been used by populations living in Arctic and other naturally cold environments, even though effective technologies for freezing and storing food in warmer climates were not perfected until well into the 20th century. As early as 1000 B.C., the Chinese used ice cellars to preserve foods, while the ancient Greeks and Romans employed a similar technique, housing food in insulated chambers filled with compressed snow. The Inca made a practice of storing foodstuffs in the frigid temperatures of the Andes Mountains, where reduced atmospheric pressure allowed moisture to dissipate more quickly than it would at sea level.

In 1861, Enoch Piper of Camden, Maine, patented a technique for freezing whole fish, using a combination of ice and salt. Once frozen, the fish were then kept in an insulated cabinet that was kept cold with chilled brine. The quality of food preserved by these early methods was poor, however, as temperatures were inconsistent and freezing occurred over too long a period of time.

The Birth of the Industry: Clarence Birdseye

Frozen food as we know it today was first invented and brought to the national retail marketplace by American naturalist and entrepreneur Clarence Birdseye. In 1917, while on a fishing trip to Labrador, Birdseye observed the Eskimo technique for preserving their catch. When fish was caught in extremely cold temperatures, it would begin to freeze almost immediately after removal from the water. Fish that was preserved by this natural "flash-freezing" or quick-freezing method, Birdseye noted, maintained much of its original flavor and texture when subsequently defrosted.

Flash-freezing, however, could not be achieved through any of the existing commercial methods of the day, so in 1923, with a modest initial investment of $7 for an electric fan, buckets of brine, and slabs of ice, Birdseye set about developing a new process. In 1924, Birdseye formed a company called General Seafoods Corporation—later renamed **General Foods**—and developed an effective technique whereby fresh food was packed in individually portioned waxed cardboard boxes before freezing. The product was then quickly frozen using a heavyweight double-belt machine and was ready to be sold to the consumer, complete with its **packaging**.

Together with a team of 22 chemists employed by General Foods, Birdseye worked to develop more than a hundred types of processed foods that could be sold frozen. This new product line, now marketed as **Birds Eye**, was first launched in Springfield, Massachusetts, on March 6, 1930. It included 26 different fruit, vegetable, fish, and meat products, which were test marketed in 18 retail stores.

In order to enable cash-strapped retailers to carry his products during the Depression, Birdseye contracted the American Radiator Corporation to develop an inexpensive retail freezer display case, which could then be leased to merchants directly. In 1944, Birdseye began leasing insulated railway cars, facilitating nationwide distribution.

World War II Expansion

Food scarcity and the restrictions imposed on purchased goods during World War II were the key to the growth of the frozen food industry. After Japan gained control of a large segment of the world's tin resources, the U.S. government limited **canners'** production in order to conserve metal. Frozen foods, however, which required only paperboard, waxed paper, and cellophane to produce, were not subject to such restrictions. Consumers were given strong incentives to purchase frozen goods, as they required fewer ration points.

Seizing upon this new opportunity, many new, inexperienced processors quickly entered the field. By the end of the war, there were 45 American companies processing and marketing frozen foods, but standards for quality had dropped.

Postwar Decline

The years immediately following the war saw an abrupt fall in frozen food sales. After the Allies declared victory, the U.S. military canceled all frozen food contracts, and surpluses began to accumulate in processor plants. The quality of frozen food, along with its reputation, had declined during the war years, and so, with the reappearance of canned goods on store shelves, consumers were eager to return to their prewar buying habits. Between 1946 and 1947, production of frozen food plummeted by 87 percent.

Industry Standards: The Time-Temperature Tolerance Studies

In 1948, at the request of a group of industry leaders represented by Helmut C. Diehl of the Refrigeration Research Foundation, the **U.S. Department of Agriculture** (USDA) commenced a thorough scientific investigation of the factors affecting frozen food quality. Until this time, most commercially frozen food contained large ice-crystal formations, and flavor, texture, and nutritional value suffered as a result. **Food safety** was also a serious issue to be addressed; while freezing significantly retards microbial activity, the process itself does not act to sterilize food.

From 1948 to 1965, the USDA's Western Regional Research Center (WRRC) in Albany, California, conducted an extensive **research** effort known as the Time-Temperature Tolerance (T-TT) Studies. Scientists observed the ways in which frozen foods reacted to fluctuations from their ideal temperature of 0°F over varying lengths of time. The team also developed techniques to detect and measure the chemical compounds linked to off-flavors and rancidity. The T-TT Studies' findings were ultimately used to establish guidelines for handling frozen food through all the stages of its manufacture and distribution.

TV Dinners

In 1954, C. A. **Swanson** & Sons launched a product that was to revolutionize the frozen food industry: the **TV dinner**—a complete, frozen meal that could be both heated and served in its own segmented tray. The product was originally created as a use for some 260 tons of frozen turkey that remained unsold after the 1953 Thanksgiving season. Swanson had insufficient warehouse space to house the surplus product and resorted to storing it in **refrigerated** railroad cars, which had to remain in motion to stay cold.

Inspired by the aluminum trays he saw used in the food kitchens of Pan American Airways, Gerry Thomas, a salesman for Swanson, designed a three-compartment tray, which, when filled with turkey and side dishes, was to become the prototype for the TV dinner. Capitalizing on the current popularity of **television** and consumers' growing appetite for novelty and convenience, Thomas suggested designing packaging to resemble TV screens, complete with volume controls.

The first TV dinners were priced at 98 cents apiece and included turkey, cornbread stuffing, buttered peas, and sweet potatoes. They could be heated in the oven and served in front of the television. More than 70 million dinners were sold by Swanson and other manufacturers during 1955. In subsequent years, as demand increased, new meals such as Salisbury steak, meatloaf, and fried chicken were added to the product line. In 1960, desserts such as cherry cobbler and brownies were also introduced. Subsequent innovations included the introduction of the microwaveable plastic-crystallized polyetheylne tray in 1986, which was often designed to resemble china.

Health-conscious Meals and Microwave Technology

The 1960s saw a new demand for **diet foods** and health-conscious foods. Brands such as Lean Cuisine and Weight Watchers were launched during this era, and the market for such products continued to grow until slowed by the economic recession of the 1970s.

The frozen food industry enjoyed a resurgence in the 1980s, however, with the introduction of new technology. As more and more households acquired microwave ovens, there was a new demand for convenience foods that could be prepared in minutes using this new household appliance. Single frozen entrees began to replace traditional multicourse TV dinners. In 1990, 651 new frozen entrees entered the market, while manufacturers introduced only 55 new frozen dinners.

New regulations in the 1990s requiring full disclosure of ingredients in packaged foods coincided with consumers' appetite for low-fat, low-sodium, and low-cholesterol meals. Manufacturers struggled to balance the often-contradictory requirements of nutritional value, taste, and convenience.

Trade Associations

Several trade associations have established themselves in the United States to promote frozen food to consumers and other groups. The largest of these are the American Frozen Food Institute (AFFI) and the National Frozen and Refrigerated Foods Association (NFRA).

The AFFI is a national trade association representing all aspects of the frozen food industry supply chain. Headquartered in Washington, D.C., it serves to represent the interests of the industry to lawmakers shaping public policy. A not-for-profit trade association based in Harrisburg, Pennsylvania, the NFRA provides programs and services in industry market research, education and training, and promotion. It organizes a National Frozen and Refrigerated Foods Convention each year in October. In September 2006, it was announced that AFFI and NFRA would embark on a joint venture with a shared logo and tagline, which each association would present to its respective audiences.

Frozen Food Day

In 1984, to commemorate the 54th anniversary of frozen foods, President Ronald Reagan proclaimed March 6 to be Frozen Food Day "in recognition of the significant contribution which the frozen food industry has made to the nutritional well-being of the American people" (Proclamation 5157). The president cited the international frozen food industry's American roots, frozen food's heightened profile in America during World War II, and the use of frozen foods in the U.S. space program.

The U.S. frozen food industry now recognizes March as National Frozen Food Month, staging annual media campaigns and offering promotions to consumers and awards to merchandisers.

The Industry Today

The frozen food industry continues to grow into the 21st century, employing a workforce of over two million and accounting for approximately $5 billion in export sales. According to the AFFI, total retail sales of frozen foods in the United States topped $26.6 billion in 2001. Frozen dinners and entrees represent the largest category in this market, with more than $5.9 billion in annual supermarket sales. Other recent growth areas include Mexican and other **ethnic** frozen entrees, as well as frozen appetizers and snacks.

Sixty percent of total U.S. frozen food sales today are in the food service market. Improved frozen food technology has allowed **restaurant** owners to incorporate more frozen ingredients and prepared foods into their menus. Further technological developments may eventually render frozen foods virtually indistinguishable from fresh when cooked and served to the customer.

FURTHER READINGS: American Chemical Society. "Frozen Food Research Begins at WRRC." *National Historic Chemical Landmarks.* http://acswebcontent.acs.org/landmarks/landmarks/frozen/fro6.html; American Frozen Food Institute (AFFI). http://www.affi.com; Lebeau, Mary Dixon. "At 50, TV Dinner Is Still Cookin'." *Christian Science Monitor*, November 10, 2004; National Frozen and Refrigerated Foods Association (NFRA). http://www.nrfaweb.org; "Post-War Bust and Blossoming of the Brands." *Frozen Food Age* 46, December 2002, 46–47; Volti, Rudi. "How We Got Frozen Food." *American Heritage Invention & Technology* 9 (Spring 1994): 46–56; "The War Years—and Boom," *Frozen Food Age*, August 1997.

Nora Maynard

Fruit Juice and Sports and Health Drinks Fruit juices were once relegated to the breakfast table or were only **marketed to children**, but that has changed dramatically. Beginning in 1917, pure orange juice was sold in cans—but that product was virtually eliminated from the market after frozen concentrate was developed in the late 1940s. Freezing had been tried earlier, but the results were unpalatable until scientists C. D. Atkins, L. G. MacDowell, and E. L. Moore discovered that adding 7 percent fresh juice to the concentrate improved its flavor. Minute Maid (which was later acquired by Coca-Cola) built the first orange juice concentrate plant in Plymouth, Florida, 1946.

Today, frozen concentrate is being driven out by "premium" orange juice—marketed to upscale consumers as "not from concentrate." These juices were first sold by Tropicana (found in the **refrigerated** sections of **supermarkets** in the same kind of containers as milk) in 1953 but did not really take off until the 1980s. By the late

1990s consumers could also choose "shelf-stable" containers of orange juice, further eroding the frozen concentrate market.

Perhaps the best-known juice, marketed directly to children, is **Welch's** Grape Juice. Thomas Bramwell Welch first pasteurized Concord grape juice in 1869 (Concord grapes had been developed 16 years earlier). His son, Charles E. Welch, created the company and promoted it to national fame at Chicago's 1893 World's Fair. Welch's juice became even better known after Secretary of State William Jennings Bryan served it to the British ambassador in 1913. Welch's Frozen Grape Juice Concentrate was introduced in 1949, just as orange juice concentrate was coming to market. The National Grape Cooperative Association acquired Welch's in 1952. "JuiceMakers," a shelf-stable concentrate, was introduced in 1996.

Libby's Juicy Juice was marketed as "100% juice" in the 1970s and sold in cans (just as orange juice first appeared). In a curious repetition of historical pattern, Juicy Juice introduced its concentrate (shelf-stable, not frozen) in 1998. Nestlé currently owns the company, but the juice is produced in plants owned by Ocean Spray (makers of cranberry products, including juice). Juicy Juice's marketing "hook"—that it was a good source of **vitamin** C and lacked added **sugars** or artificial **flavors**—helped to distinguish it from other juice drinks intended for children and foreshadowed the later development of healthy drinks for all age groups.

Juices for adults—other than breakfast juices (which included grapefruit and prune juices)—began to appear in the early 1960s. They were, however, neither canned nor frozen, but rather prepared fresh in health food stores, using electric juicers and blenders. "Juice bars" grew in popularity in the 1990s, eventually creating an entirely new market for healthy juice drinks.

Smoothies

Smoothie bars—outside of health food stores—began to appear in malls and other popular "mainstream" locations at the end of the 20th century. Two companies, Juice Club (later Jamba Juice) and Smoothie King, pioneered the commercial smoothie industry. In addition to smoothies, they sold snacks (i.e., healthy alternatives to the **snack foods** sold elsewhere) and fresh juices. Jamba Juice expanded by acquiring Zuka Juice in 1999.

Sports Drinks

While juices and smoothies had their origins in the counterculture movement of the 1960s (as did Juicy Juice, which was sold to baby boomers who were then becoming parents themselves), "healthy drinks" were sprinting along another track as well. The University of Florida football team was often troubled with illness caused by excessive heat. In 1965, one of the coaches approached another kind of team—four scientists—to come up with a solution to the problem. Their answer actually was a "solution": a mixture of water, carbohydrates, and electrolytes (sodium and potassium salts) that was intended to replace the key ingredients players lost through exercise and subsequent perspiration. They added a citrus-like flavor, to make it easier for players to drink in sufficient quantities, and named it after the university's team. Gatorade was born. By 1983, it was the official drink of the National Football League (and many other sports franchises).

Robert Cade, who had obtained a patent for the greenish-yellow drink, agreed to have it produced and marketed by Stokely-Van Camp. However, the university sued Cade in 1973, claiming it owned the rights to Gatorade; as a result of the settlement, it currently receives royalties on the drink's sales. Stokely-Van Camp was sold to Quaker Oats in 1983, which in turn licensed the Gatorade line to PepsiCo. In 2001, PepsiCo bought out Quaker.

Powerade, an early Gatorade competitor, began distribution, by Coca-Cola, in 1992. Within two years it added several fruit flavors, and in 1996 (to add to its appeal to aspiring—and perspiring—athletes), it began to be sold in plastic sports bottles. Powerade distinguished itself from Gatorade by adding vitamins B_3, B_6, and B_{12}, which were said to be involved in the metabolism of carbohydrates into energy.

In 1980 in Japan, Otsuka Pharmaceutical developed another sports drink (Pocari Sweat). Originally a chemical company, Otsuka had been in the pharmaceuticals business since 1946, and Pocari Sweat was an extension of its nutraceuticals line. Related products include Amino-Value and Calorie Mate. Pocari Sweat is sold mostly to Asian customers (and, interestingly, in the United Arab Emirates), but, like Powerade, its added vitamin content signals the arrival of another class of "health drink."

Vitamin Water

Polar (a company that had begun in 1882 as a seller of seltzer and liquor, then later ginger ale) began to diversify in the 1960s. It acquired the brands Clear 'n' Natural and Waist Watcher in 1996, and in 1999, the distributor of Nantucket Nectars and Arizona Tea (both of which were marketed to health-conscious young people). In 2004 Polar bought Snapple of Boston, a company that had begun by selling bottled iced teas and natural fruit-flavored soft drinks. This meant that they now had control of Glaceau's Vitaminwater. Coca-Cola bought Glaceau in 2007.

Glaceau's Vitaminwater, like Powerade, contains B vitamins—but has much more sugar (which it hides by describing its 24-ounce bottle as containing 2.5 servings). Coca-Cola, interested in making up for reduced sales of its carbonated beverages, also acquired Glaceau's Fruitwater, Smartwater, and Vitaminenergy beverages. Smartwater is simply distilled water with added electrolytes—a simpler, almost ascetic version of Gatorade. Vitaminenergy is similar, but with added flavor, vitamin C, and caffeine.

PepsiCo's Propel Fitness Water and Propel Fitness Water with Calcium are direct competitors to Coca-Cola's Glaceau acquisitions. They were developed by the Gatorade Sports Science Institute and contain B vitamins and flavoring to induce greater consumption. The PepsiCo brands outsold the Glaceau brands in 2006 by 23 percent.

Another player in the vitamin water arena is SoBe Life Water. It is a similar drink, but contains—in addition to vitamin C and the B vitamins found in other drinks—vitamin E (which is touted for its antioxidant properties). SoBe's first beverage, in 1996, was SoBe Black Tea 3G. The three "G's" were gingko, ginseng, and guarana (a Brazilian plant that contains several times as much caffeine as coffee beans). It was followed by SoBe Cranberry Grapefruit Elixir, SoBe Energy, SoBe Green Tea, SoBe Oolong Tea, and SoBe Orange Carrot Elixir.

The healthy beverage market seems to be moving away from its counterculture origins and toward a perception of healthiness that is actually the enhanced "energy" that results from the ingestion of stimulants.

Herbal Teas, Chai, Green Tea

The move toward stimulants is very different from the approach originally used by Celestial Seasonings, a company founded in 1968 by Mo Siegel and a small group of Colorado hippies. They created an herbal tea (Mo's 36 Herb Tea) that became the first of many caffeine-free teas. In 1970, their Sleepytime Herb Tea was released, followed by Red Zinger in 1972 (the year that Celestial Seasonings was incorporated). Within two years, their sales exceeded a million dollars.

In 1984, the company was sold to **Kraft**. Two years later, company founder Siegel retired, and Celestial Seasonings began selling Gourmet Black Tea, its first caffeinated product. Within a year, Kraft tried to sell the company to Thomas J. Lipton. The sale was challenged in court, however, on antitrust grounds. Instead, a consortium consisting of Vestar Capital Partners and the management of Celestial Seasonings repurchased the company. In 1991, Siegel came out of retirement to become CEO and chairman of the Board of Directors of the company he had founded.

Celestial Seasonings began in 1997 to market medicinal teas that more closely resembled the products that were once sold only in health food stores: Detox A.M., Diet Partner, Echinacea, GingerEase, GinkgoSharp, Green Tea, LaxaTea, and Melatonin P.M. In a move that might have been intended to return to the company's roots, these beverages actually were sold in health food stores—as opposed to Celestial Seasonings' other products (which were available in ordinary supermarkets everywhere).

In 1998, the company purchased Mountain Chai, the manufacturer of concentrated tea used in making the newly popular chai drinks. Celestial Seasonings shortly thereafter released six new flavors of chai.

Chai had become in the 1990s a healthier alternative to the very popular lattes, which are made with strong, sweetened coffee and milk. "Chai" is short for *masala chai*, an Indian iced tea that is flavored with spices (cardamom, cinnamon, clove, pepper) plus milk and sugar. Chai drinks rapidly developed into dozens of flavor combinations in the United States.

In the same year as its chais, Celestial Seasonings launched six green teas (Authentic, Decaffeinated, Emerald Gardens, Honey Lemon Ginseng, Misty Jasmine, and Total Antioxidant). Green teas are considered to be more healthful than black teas. Their caffeine content are identical, but green teas contain an antioxidant (EGCG, epigallocatechin gallate) that is missing in black teas and discourages the spread of cancer cells. Green teas are also supposed to lower LDL (bad cholesterol) and reduce the occurrence of blood clots.

In 2000, Celestial Seasonings began selling organic teas (Black Tea, Chamomile, Green Tea, and Peppermint). It also partnered with Arizona Tea to produce bottled iced tea. The first "Cool Brew Iced Teas" appeared two years later (Lemon Ice, Summer Ice, and Raspberry Ice).

Celestial Seasonings is the prototype for companies that began in the counterculture of the 1960s and grew into large mainstream corporations (or were acquired by such corporations when they began to become successful). Unlike most of them, Celestial Seasonings has been actively involved in supporting the causes of the 1960s, both financially and in its day-to-day operations and its treatment of its employees. It has frequently been awarded for its socially responsible practices.

See also Functional Foods and Nutraceuticals; Raw Foods; Soft Drinks; Whole Food.

FURTHER READINGS: Belasco, Warren James. *Appetite for Change: How the Counterculture Took on the Food Industry, 1966–1988.* New York: Pantheon, 1989; Belasco, Warren James. "History/Timeline." http://www.celestialseasonings.com/about/history-timeline.html; Belasco, Warren James. "Tea Drinks: Chai, Thai Iced Tea and More." http://www.teaclass.com/lesson_0109.html; Celestial Seasonings. "Green Tea: History and Health." http://www.teaclass.com/lesson_0209.html; Gatorade. "The History of Gatorade." http://www.gatorade.com/history/proven_on_the_field; Juice and Smoothie Bar Consulting. "History of the Smoothie Industry." http://www.juiceconsult.com/why_a_juicebar/history_of_industry.html; McPhee, John. *Oranges.* New York: Farrar, Strauss, & Giroux, 1966. Reprint, New York: Noonday Press, 1994; Smith, Andrew F., ed. *The Oxford Companion to American Food and Drink.* New York: Oxford University Press, 2007; University of Florida, Citrus Research and Education Center. "Brief History of Frozen Concentrate." http://www.lal.ufl.edu/about/History/frozenconcentrate.htm; Welch's. "Company History." http://www.welchs.com/company/company_history.html.

Gary Allen

Functional Foods and Nutraceuticals Food and medicine have always been intimately linked. Hippocrates in 400 B.C. declared, "Let food be your medicine and medicine be your food," and for many centuries, physicians from Greek, Indo-Aryan, Arabic, Chinese, and other indigenous traditions treated patients predominantly through diet. With the rise of Western scientific medicine, the concept of health foods was largely marginalized, but continued to exist mainly as part of a counterculture.

Toward the end of the 20th century, a renewed interest in traditional systems of healing and alternate medical therapies emerged, along with, and perhaps stimulated by, increasing dissatisfaction with costly iatrogenic health care based on drugs and heroic surgical interventions. In addition, as consumer understanding and awareness of the relationship between diet and chronic disease have grown, the concept of healthy living has gathered force, including increased emphasis on individual responsibility for personal health behaviors.

Diet, ever a matter of popular concern, is now at the forefront of public consciousness as a means to promote well-being and avoid or mitigate the health challenges that come with aging in an affluent society. In this context, the rise of nutraceuticals and functional foods in the past 25 years has been aptly described as a revolution that swept through the food system, engaging the attention of producers, manufacturers, retailers and consumers, researchers and governments alike, and offering a wide range of scientific, health, and commercial opportunities.

Definitions

Foods contain a range of essential nutrients (proteins, fats, carbohydrates, **vitamins**, and minerals) that are necessary for human health. Both deficiencies and excesses of nutrients are linked to health and disease. Since the 1980s, it has become increasingly apparent that other food components also have a role in health and disease. These include a range of bioactive compounds such as probiotics, omega-3 fatty acids, beta glucans, carotenoids, flavonoids, tannins, and others, which are naturally occurring chemical compounds contained in, or derived from, plant, animal, or marine sources and that provide health benefits. They differ from traditional nutrients in that they are not essential for normal metabolism, and their absence will not result in a deficiency disease.

The term *functional foods* was invented in Japan in the 1980s and gained currency around the world in the 1990s. It is used to describe the concept that foods may provide physical or mental health benefits beyond what are considered to be their basic nutritional functions. Fibe Mini is a Japanese **soft drink** with added dietary fiber that was launched in 1988 and is regarded as the world's first functional food.

The term *nutraceutical* is a portmanteau word coined in 1989 by Stephen DeFelice of the Foundation for Innovation in Medicine, combining *nutrition* and *pharmaceutical*. It refers to a food or part of a food that has medical benefits including prevention and treatment of a disease. However, in contrast to functional foods, which are consumed as part of a normal diet, nutraceuticals are formulated products, isolated or purified from foods, but generally sold in medicinal forms not associated with food.

The term *functional foods* is now commonly used to include all of these products, and consists of four major categories:

1. Basic foodstuffs that contain naturally occurring health-enhancing ingredients, such as oat bran, which contains naturally high levels of beta glucan, or carrots, which contain high amounts of beta carotene, an antioxidant. They are portrayed as functional foods even though they have not been modified in any way.
2. Processed foods that have health-promoting ingredients added—for example, orange juice with added calcium, or yogurts and drinks with added **bacterial** cultures—or that are formulated to have specific health benefits, such as cholesterol-reducing margarines.
3. Enhanced foods that have levels of bioactive compounds increased through conventional breeding or **genetic engineering**: tomatoes with higher levels of lycopene, eggs with increased omega-3 fatty acids, and so forth.
4. Purified preparations of active food ingredients in the form of pills, powders, or liquids. These might include omega-3 capsules or cod liver oil.

Functional foods and nutraceuticals blur the line between food and drugs, giving rise to novel regulatory challenges as well as concerns about the medicalization of the food supply.

What They Do

Functional foods may protect against chronic disease by combating degenerative metabolic processes. Some examples include:

- Flavonoids and carotenoids in fruits and vegetables may reduce the risk of cancer by neutralizing free radicals that may cause cell damage.
- Omega-3 fatty acids in fatty fish may reduce cardiovascular risk, as may dietary fibers such as beta glucan in oats.
- Conjugated linoleic acid in meat and cheese products may have a positive effect on immune function.
- Plant sterols, from **corn**, **wheat**, and soy, lower blood cholesterol.
- Probiotics in yogurt and other **dairy** products may improve gastrointestinal health.
- Saponins from soy products may lower LDL cholesterol, while soy protein may reduce cardiovascular risk.

A long list of other bioactive compounds includes tannins, sulfides, phytoestrogens, phenols, and glucosinolates.

The regulatory environment for functional foods is challenging and evolving. Regulators must attempt to balance considerations of public health, consumer safety, and veracity of claims with private-sector interests in innovation and investment. The Food and Drug Administration (FDA) currently regulates food products according to their intended use and the nature of claims made on the package. Five types of health-related statements or claims are allowed on food and dietary supplement labels:

- *Health claims* confirm a relationship between components in the diet and risk of disease or health condition, as approved by the FDA and supported by significant scientific agreement.
- *Qualified health claims* convey a developing relationship between components in the diet and risk of disease, as reviewed by the FDA and supported by the weight of credible scientific evidence available.
- *Dietary guidance claims* describe the health benefits of broad categories of foods. Dietary guidance statements used on food labels must be truthful and not misleading, but unlike health claims, they are not subject to FDA review and authorization.
- *Nutrient content claims* indicate the presence of a specific nutrient at a certain level.
- *Structure and function claims* describe the role of a nutrient or dietary ingredient intended to affect normal structure or function in humans, for example, "Calcium builds strong bones." In addition, they may characterize the means by which a nutrient or dietary ingredient acts to maintain such structure or function, for example, "Fiber maintains bowel regularity." The manufacturer is responsible for ensuring the accuracy and truthfulness of these claims; they are not preapproved by the FDA but must be truthful and not misleading. If a dietary supplement label includes such a claim, it must state in a "disclaimer" that the FDA has not evaluated the claim.

Producers

The functional food movement offers partnerships to advance mutual interests of university researchers, agricultural producers, and food manufacturers. Researchers can identify what food components have health benefits and how they act in the body. Agricultural producers can diversify and grow different, or new, varieties of crops with desirable health profiles. Food manufacturers can formulate and sell these products in the marketplace. The government also contributes to the growth and development of the functional food sector through the support of primary research, provision of advice and technical assistance to farmers, and support to producers and entrepreneurs in developing new products and bringing them to market. Certainly, the advent of functional foods has led to a new relationship between the health and agriculture sectors.

Size and Value of Industry

Functional foods and nutraceuticals are a small sector of the current food market, but are tremendously significant for the future, as most major food companies have invested in this area, anticipating that it is a development that is here to stay. According to Euromonitor International, the U.S. **packaged** functional or fortified foods market was worth $6.3 billion at retail in 2005 and is expected to grow to $7.6 billion by 2010. One of the reasons for this anticipated growth is the potential that functional foods offer to food manufacturers to sell "value-added" products to niche markets and with a high profit margin. While the general market for food and beverages is relatively stable—people can only consume so much food—functional foods offer a way to expand the market.

There are two distinctive markets for functional foods. One is the group of consumers with existing health problems and chronic conditions, to whom functional foods are presented as a way of treating, ameliorating, or even curing health problems. The other group consists of consumers who are in good health, but who can be persuaded that functional foods offer significant benefits in further enhancing health and preventing disease. Implicit in both of these is the notion that normal diets do not or cannot supply adequate levels of dietary components. In effect, the advent of functional foods has shifted the emphasis in food marketing to gaining positive benefits from intrinsically healthy foods rather than downplaying the negative consequences of the high fat and **sugar** levels commonly associated with processed foods.

Issues and Controversies

While there is credible scientific evidence to back the health benefits of certain food components, there are also many instances where such evidence is lacking. Some see the functional food movement as a new form of food quackery, making claims that cannot be substantiated. The focus on marginal health benefits for individual consumers is also seen as being fundamentally irrelevant to public health nutrition issues such as **obesity** and food security. Functional foods may cater to the more affluent and health-conscious segments of society, but are likely to exclude those at the low economic end of the spectrum. Others see the movement as a marriage of convenience between the **research** and industry sectors, simply providing a scientific rationale for traditional wisdom and effectively co-opting or taking over of that tradition in the name of profit making.

The rise of functional foods points toward a possible future of "designer foods" formulated to meet individual requirements and desires, an emerging field known as *nutrigenomics*. However, there are also misgivings about this movement to individualized, medicalized approaches to nutritional health. Several decades of nutritional science research has led to much consensus worldwide on basic guidelines for healthy eating that focus on restriction of fats and sugars and promotion of dietary fiber in the context of a varied balanced diet chosen from the general food supply. Making healthy choices into easy choices has become something of a slogan for the promotion of healthy eating. This is achieved through public health measures such as fortification of the food supply, creation of healthy food choice environments in schools and other institutions, and public nutrition education that emphasizes total diet. In contrast, functional foods and nutraceuticals shift the emphasis back to individuals discerning the need for, and taking action to select, specific foods and dietary components, based on a narrower medicalized approach to nutrition.

FURTHER READINGS: Food and Drug Administration. "Claims That Can Be Made for Conventional Foods and Dietary Supplements." Center for Food Safety and Applied Nutrition./

Office of Nutritional Products, Labeling, and Dietary Supplements. September 2003. Online at http://cfsan.fda.gov/~dms/hclaims.html; Heasman, Michael, and Mellentin, Julian. *The Functional Foods Revolution: Healthy People, Healthy Profits?* London: Earthscan, 2001; Wildman, Robert E. C., ed. *Handbook of Nutraceuticals and Functional Foods.* 2nd ed. Boca Raton, FL: CRC/Taylor & Francis, 2007.

Paul Fieldhouse

Futures Markets. *See* Commodities Exchange.

G

General Foods For most of the 20th century, the General Foods Company was a recognizable national brand name along with General Mills and General Electric. Because of repeated corporate mergers and acquisitions over the years, the brand name is not so easily identified by today's consumers. The name exists today as General Foods International, a manufacturer of flavored **coffee** and noncoffee beverages.

In 1895 C. W. **Post** created the Postum Cereal Company to market a coffee substitute made from wheat bran and molasses. He called his health drink Postum. In 1897 Post marketed a **breakfast cereal** called Grape-Nuts, and in 1904 this was followed with a **corn**-based cereal that was originally called Elijah's Manna, but was not a hit with consumers until it was renamed Post Toasties. Upon his death in 1914, Post's daughter Marjorie Merriwether Post took over the company. In 1920, she married E. F. Hutton, an investment broker, who became chairman of the Postum Cereal Company in 1923.

The company soon acquired the Jell-O Company, along with Swans Down Cake Flour, Minute Tapioca, Baker's Coconut, Baker's Chocolate, and Log Cabin syrup. Maxwell House Coffee was added in 1928. The following year, Postum purchased the General Foods Company from Clarence Birdseye, the man who perfected a commercial method for quick-freezing food. To reflect its diverse mix of packaged consumer food products, the name of the company was changed to General Foods.

Over the next 30 years, more brand names were added, including Gaines Dog Food and Yuban coffee. Shortly after World War II ended, Maxwell House instant coffee was introduced. Other successful products included Kool-Aid, Tang, Crystal Light, 4 Seasons salad dressing, Oscar Mayer meat products, and Open Pit barbecue sauce. General Foods is recognized as a case study of how large companies acquire and assimilate smaller companies under one management.

The tobacco giant Philip Morris bought General Foods in 1985. General Foods and **Kraft** (which Philip Morris had bought the year before) were combined in 1989 to form a food products division called Kraft General Foods. In 1995 the management of these two separate organizations merged to form a single North American entity called Kraft Foods. The change was intended to give senior management direct access to 12 business divisions and improve decision making.

See also Birds Eye.

FURTHER READINGS: Paulakepos, Paula, ed. *International Directory of Company Histories.* Vol. 7. Detroit: St. James Press, 1993.

Joseph M. Carlin

Genetic Engineering Genetic engineering, also called gene modification, is the manipulation and modification of the genetic material of a living organism by technical intervention. Hence, the procedures end up modifying organisms in ways that are not possible with classical breeding techniques or natural recombination. Genetically modified (GM) foods are usually altered to increase productivity, nutritional values, and safety profiles. GM foods have generated a lot of debate on the safety of modified organisms, and studies have found that the general public commonly distrusts and misunderstands genetic engineering. The process used in the United States to approve GM foods has also been criticized. Nonetheless, GM foods have steadily increased in terms of production and consumption.

Background

GM foods were first invented in the 1960s, when a team of Belgian scientists managed to insert **bacterial** DNA into barley. Although they were met with skepticism, the Belgium team in 1970 produced a crop of *Arabidopsis* flowers that could produce vitamin B. This invention led companies to invest heavily in this technology; **Monsanto** was a front-runner in this field and is still today responsible for many of the large-scale, commercially viable GM crops.

The cultivation of GM crops has increased dramatically in the last few years. Globally, the production of GM crops has grown from 4.2 million acres in 1997 to 169 million acres in 2003. The main crops being cultivated are **corn**, rape (canola), potatoes, and soybeans. Also, it is estimated that 70 percent of foods sold in the United States have some genetically modified ingredient.

When modifying food products, there are two key differences between classical breeding and genetic engineering. First, genetic engineering enables the transfer of a specific number of genes into an organism, while conventional techniques usually result in the change of undefined parts of the genome. Furthermore, the species barrier does not limit genetic engineering, while breeding is possible only within an organism's species.

Benefits of Genetic Engineering in Food Products

Genetic engineering has presented many benefits, which has generated a lot of excitement over its development; for example, it is possible to genetically engineer plants to increase crop yield or enhance nutritional value. One of the best examples of modifying nutritional value is the Golden Rice story. This product was produced to alleviate the worldwide shortage of **vitamin** A, a lack of which can lead to retinal deficiency and blindness, particularly in children. To alleviate this problem, scientists created a strain of rice, dubbed Golden Rice, that is beta carotene enhanced. Due to intellectual property issues, the distribution of this product has been limited, but it has continued to be profiled as a typical benefit of GM food.

Animals have also been subject to genetic modifications. One of the major pathways of modification is **cloning**. Also, some animals are genetically modified so they produce different products. One famous example is spider silk. In the early 2000s, a biotechnology company transferred spider-silk genes into mammals; sure enough, the GM cells (grown in a culture) secreted soluble cells that the scientists could harvest and transform into BioSteel, a fiber which is stronger than Kevlar yet lighter than nylon. Animals are also used as living bioreactors for farming specific proteins. AviGenics, Origen Therapeutics, and Viragen are three examples of companies that genetically modify chickens so that their eggs produce pharmaceutical proteins.

Concerns and Constraints on Genetic Processes

There is a great deal of concern over genetically modified organisms and their impact on our ecology. Although contamination would require the combination of several highly improbable events to occur, the potential for harm does exist. Also, as our consumption increases, a number of fundamental questions relating to harmful immunological responses (including allergic hypersensitivity) have been raised. In addition, the unchecked spread of GM crops has raised a number of legal questions, such as the case of *Monsanto Canada Inc. vs. Schmeiser*, in which genetically modified and patented seeds were accidentally scattered in the farmer's field, for which he was sued. Other doubts that have been expressed include vertical and horizontal gene transfer and biodiversity concerns.

No case of significant harm to humans or the environment due to genetically modified cells currently exists. Nonetheless, there has been huge consumer backlash to GM food, especially in Europe and New Zealand. This is a paradox, as these countries usually exhibit elevated levels of acceptance of genetic modification for products with industrial or medical applications.

The five main indicators on which consumer acceptance varies are awareness of food technology, perceived consumption benefits, sociodemographic profile, social/moral consciousness, and perceived food quality and trust. Awareness is often mentioned as the main indicator, because consumers have a very limited exposure to genetic engineering, rendering perception very vulnerable to preexisting beliefs. Two recent studies (one in Greece, the other in New Zealand) demonstrated that consumers are generally uninformed about genetic engineering, which was directly correlated to consumer acceptance.

Concerns over the U.S. Process Surrounding GM Foods

As a rule, GM foods are required to exhibit high levels of purity, but requirements are far less stringent than modified organisms used in therapeutic contexts. Nonetheless, the United States, using a "substantial equivalence" principle to assess the safety of GM food products, has been criticized for its lax approach. This has led to friction with the **European Union**, which possesses a far more stringent approach to GM foods that requires considerably more analysis and labeling.

The U.S. system for approving GM food is based on the principle that if a novel or modified food product can be shown to be substantially equivalent in composition to an existing food product, it can be assumed to be safe. The approach thus focuses on the final product, rather than the production process, and safety is demonstrated by the absence of differences in a range of characteristics. If the product exhibits traits that make it substantially different from the approved product, then additional tests are required.

GM Foods: Future Direction

With increased use of GM foods, there has been a growing public concern for strengthening the data requirements for approval. Also, obligation of postlaunch surveillance (akin to phase IV studies in the pharmaceutical industry) has been proposed to evaluate allergenic trends. Traceability and better labeling are often mentioned as solutions to GM concerns. All of these issues require significant developments in the form of new analytical detection tools, which have yet to be commercialized.

See also Agribusiness; Ciba-Geigy; Environmental Protection Agency; Food Laws and Regulations; Research and Development.

FURTHER READINGS: Arvanitoyannis, Ioannis, and Athanasios Krystallis. "Consumers' Beliefs, Attitudes and Intentions towards Genetically Modified Foods, Based on the 'Perceived Safety vs. Benefits' Perspective." *International Journal of Food Science and Technology* 40 (2005): 343–60; Arvanitoyannis, Ioannis S., Persefoni Tserkezou, and Theodoros Varzakas. "An Update of US Food Safety, Food Technology, GM Food and Water Protection and Management Legislation." *International Journal of Food Science and Technology* 41, suppl. 1 (August 2006): 130–59; Avise, John. *The Hope, Hype and Reality of Genetic Engineering.* New York: Oxford University Press, 2004; Prescott, Vanessa, and Simon Hogan. "Genetically Modified Plants and Food Hypersensitivity Diseases: Usage and Implications of Experimental Models for Risk Assessment." *Pharmacology & Therapeutics* 111 (2006): 374–83; Schilter, Benoit, and Anne Constable. "Regulatory Control of Genetically Modified (GM) Foods: Likely Developments. *Toxicology Letters* 127 (2002): 341–49; Shuler, Michael, and Fikret Kargi. *Bioprocess Engineering: Basic Concepts.* 2nd ed. Upper Saddle River, NJ: Prentice Hall, 2002.

Jean-François Denault

Gerber The Gerber Products Company dominates the American **baby food** industry, with an 80 percent share of the $890 million market. According to company legend, the idea for a baby food product line came about as a result of a comment by Dorothy Gerber, the wife of Daniel Gerber of the Fremont Canning Company, in Fremont, Michigan, who found that straining food for their infant daughter was a chore. By the end of 1928, five products (strained peas, carrots, prunes, spinach, and a beef and vegetable soup) were on the shelves, and a widespread national **advertising** campaign was under way in a range of publications. The advertisements featured the now famous "Gerber Baby," which proved instantly popular and recognizable and was trademarked in 1931. The company moved into the life insurance market in 1967 and has since broadened its product base to include infant toys, skin care, health care, breast therapy products, and children's clothing. Gerber merged with Sandoz Ltd. in 1994, which became part of the Novartis group in 1996.

The company has suffered a number of scandals over the last few decades. Glass fragments were discovered in jars of baby food in 1984, 1986, and 1993, and although the company was exonerated from responsibility, the publicity was damaging and sales suffered dramatically. There were three issues in 1995: several thousand cases of apple juice were declared unfit due to a sour taste and were recalled; the company was accused of reducing nutritional value by using fillers and starches in its foods; and it was claimed that unacceptable levels of pesticide residues had been found in some products. In 1997 there were two further controversies: in September, more than two million jars of carrots were recalled due to high levels of arsenic; and the company was accused of deceptive advertising (in suggesting that its product was recommended by four out of five pediatricians) and was ordered to cease such statements. Also in 1997, Gerber ceased production of several products (e.g., pacifiers, nipples) containing polyvinyl chloride (PVC), in light of public fears that ingestion might be harmful to infants. Finally, in 1999 the company came under fire when genetically modified **corn** was identified in its mixed-grain cereal.

Gerber has weathered these controversies and continues to grow. Almost 200 Gerber products are now sold in 80 countries, with the most recent addition being the Gerber **Organic** range. As for the future, Gerber has clearly decided to position itself as a responsible authority on matters of parenting and pediatric nutrition. The company launched its "Start Healthy, Stay Healthy" **nutrition education** campaign in 2002 and provides a wide range of parental resources and information leaflets via its website.

FURTHER READING: Bentley, Amy. "Inventing Babyfood: Gerber and the Discourse of Infancy in the United States." In Belasco, Warren, and Phillip Scranton, Eds. *Food Nations: Selling Taste in Consumer Societies.* New York: Routledge, 2001.

Janet Clarkson

Globalization. *See* Agribusiness; Cultural Imperialism; Free Trade; Multinationals; Tariffs.

Gourmet Foods Gourmet foods are characterized by high-quality or exotic ingredients and typically require fancy, specialized, or highly skilled preparation. Gourmet foods often, but not always, necessitate a **restaurant**'s specialized cooking facilities. Such foods are typically more expensive and less readily available in either restaurants, **supermarkets**, or both, than other, more conventional types of foods. Gourmet food distribution companies typically supply restaurants and specialty food stores. For example, D'Artagnan, a distribution company based in Newark, New Jersey, is the leading purveyor of foie gras, pâtés, charcuterie, smoked meat delicacies, **organic** game, and wild **poultry** in the nation, specifically targeting restaurants in the New York City metropolitan area. Many such distributors and marketers also allow consumers to buy through catalogs or over the **Internet**.

People who take pride and pleasure in eating gourmet foods are known as gourmets, epicures, gourmands, or foodies. Such people claim to distinguish themselves by their discriminating palates and their knowledge about the world of fine dining, food, and drink. *Foodie* is a more recently adopted term, often used in the media or conversationally, for a person who has a special interest in all types of foods, including gourmet foods, and turns eating and discovering new foods into a hobby or pastime.

Gourmet food preparations have transitioned over time according to their political and economic contexts as well as due to the availability of certain ingredients and to changes in cooking styles. Marie-Antoine Carême, a French chef and author who lived from 1784 to 1833, is considered the originator of the culinary movement known as *haute cuisine*, the "chef of kings and king of chefs," and the first **celebrity chef**. The great French chef and culinary writer Auguste Escoffier, who wrote *Le Guide Culinaire* in 1903, followed Carême's lead and gained enormous fame as an important culinary figure in the world of haute cuisine, popularizing and elaborating upon traditional French dishes as well as inventing new classics, such as Peach Melba, named after singer Nellie Melba.

Haute cuisine is characterized by elaborate preparations and presentations, large meals of small but rich courses, and extensive **wine** lists and cellars. The restaurant Le Pavillon, begun by Henri Soulé in New York City at the 1939 World's Fair, is viewed by food historians as the embodiment of haute cuisine's prominence in the United States. Many disagreements have since occurred within the American restaurant scene between purveyors of haute cuisine and those with newer ideals of fresh ingredients, the embracing of **ethnic** cuisines, and bringing out food's natural flavors. These new culinary ideas, called *nouvelle cuisine*, became popular in the late 1970s and '80s in Europe and the United States.

The popularity of foods considered "gourmet" expanded in the United States throughout the second half of the 20th century, and the American fine-dining restaurant has since mutated into a populist combination of New Californian, ethnic, and domesticated French and Italian cooking. Julia Child, one of the most significant **television** personalities and author of *Mastering the Art of French Cooking*, pioneered the art of teaching audiences about gourmet cuisine through the medium of television. She became a cultural icon for her willingness to make fun of herself and her mishaps at the stove, demonstrating that gourmet food was indeed within the middle class's reach.

Gourmet foods continue to be celebrated in the media through magazines, television programs and networks, and restaurant popularity. The growth of the idea of the celebrity chef, created through television programming, cookbook **publishing**, and restaurant ownership, has expedited the growth and popularity of gourmet foods within the middle class. It is now possible for chefs to reach millions of people through a multimedia empire—with books, restaurants, TV shows, specialty cooking items or tools, and even commercial endorsements. The term "celebrity chef" is sometimes used in a slightly derogatory way, referring to those who have "sold out," and such celebrities may be considered inferior by traditional restaurant chefs, even though many restaurant chefs (such as Charlie Trotter, Thomas Keller, and Todd English) are frequently featured in all the major media.

Gourmet American cooking was partially popularized by James Beard, a food writer and chef, whose name today is used for a set of awards for excellence in food and cooking. The work of foundations, including the James Beard Foundation in New York City, offers prestige and celebrity to the culinary world. Other well-known food celebrities who prepare gourmet foods include Jacques Pepin, Paul Bocuse, Paul Prudhomme, Wolfgang Puck, Emeril Lagasse, Alice Waters, Rick Bayless, Anthony Bourdain, and Gordon Ramsay.

In the 1990s, cable television's Food Network encouraged the public's interest in the gourmet foods, professional tools and cooking techniques, and designer ingredients, contributing to the growth of stores selling cooking equipment and vocational cooking schools. Through these chefs and their techniques, recipes that use ingredients such as goat cheese, balsamic vinegar, aioli, beurre blanc, and green peppercorns, among others, which have become trendy pantry staples. Magazines such as *Gourmet* and *Bon Appetit* and websites such as Epicurious.com continue to connect readers with gourmet food ideas, preparations, and ingredients.

Chefs and nonchefs alike sometimes argue that gourmet cooking has little to do with the quality of basic materials, the artistry of the cook, or a discriminating palate. However, certain ingredients are more easily categorized as gourmet than others. Typical examples of gourmet food ingredients include, but are not limited to, caviar, cheese, foie gras and pâté, gourmet **chocolates**, oils and vinegars, smoked salmon, specialty meats, truffles, and wines. Foods such as game meats, once ubiquitous in Western diets, are currently favored by modern gourmet food aficionados and have become a rarity in urban society. Companies like D'Artagnan specialize in game meats for this reason.

The price of gourmet food items can be inflated, due to marketing techniques or campaigns, rarity, or having a relatively short growing season. The last is exemplified by the case of hard-to-find white truffles, which cannot be farmed and are in season for only three months out of the year. Foods that are less available because of their place of origin or growing season make them more likely to be classified as special or gourmet due to their rare status. The following three foods, which have long been considered the ultimate indulgence, illustrate the characteristics of gourmet foods and how they attain this status.

Caviar

Caviar is the processed, salted roe (eggs) of sturgeon and other species of fish, eaten primarily as a garnish or hors d'oeuvre. Today, the finest caviar comes from large sturgeon that are fished in the Caspian Sea, though decades of overfishing have dwindled available numbers; the population of Beluga sturgeon, for example, has dropped by more than 90 percent in the past 20 years. The collapse of the Soviet Union in the late 20th century further weakened control over fisheries in the Caspian Sea and Volga River, raising illegal poaching to the estimated level of 10 times that of legal catch. Due to this decline, less costly alternatives, processed from the roe of whitefish, lumpfish, and North Atlantic salmon, have grown in popularity due to their availability.

Caviar is known as a food of the elite, identified with affluence and luxury items more broadly. Demand in the **European Union**, the United States, and Japan together accounts for 95 percent of the world's total consumption. Sturgeon caviar sells for around $100 an ounce at U.S. food retailers. It also remains expensive in Russia, its place of origin, and is typically eaten only at holidays and other celebrations.

Foie Gras

Considered by some as one of the greatest delicacies of French cuisine and frequently noted for its silky, buttery texture, foie gras is the fattened liver of a duck or goose that has been force-fed in the last few weeks of its life. It has enjoyed status as a gourmet food item for centuries, with historical roots reaching back to Roman-occupied Egypt. Ninety percent of foie gras production and consumption today occurs in France, primarily centered in regions in the east and the southwest, where **culinary tourism** around its production plays an important economic role.

Traditional techniques of force-feeding by hand have been substantially modified during the past few decades to industrialize foie gras production and increase profitability. Today, the feed typically is administered using a funnel fitted with a long tube that uses a long screw-shaped tool moved either by hand or an electric motor where food delivery time in most cases takes between 45 and 60 seconds per feeding. The feed, usually soaked or boiled **corn** and grain, builds fat deposits in the liver, thereby producing the buttery consistency sought by the gourmet eater. In France, though it is more readily available than ever before in history, foie gras is still a luxury or special-occasion food, often consumed at the holidays or during special events.

Animal rights organizations regard foie gras's production process as cruel because of the force-feeding process and the health consequences resultant from the birds' enlarged livers. Foie gras production and consumption is illegal in several countries and in several U.S. jurisdictions, including California and the city of Chicago.

Truffles

These edible fungi, known for their earthy flavor, are held in high esteem in traditional French and northern Italian cooking, as well as in international haute cuisine. They are nicknamed "black diamonds" due to the combination of the pebbly skin and high prices and can be found in either white or black varieties, selling for upwards of thousands of dollars each.

Collecting truffles requires training and experience, making the collection process difficult. They grow below ground in the root systems of certain broad-leafed trees, primarily oaks, hazelnuts, and poplars. Since they cannot be seen, truffles are "hunted" not harvested, using pigs or dogs that are specially trained to detect truffles' strong smell underneath the ground. Truffles are used sparingly in gourmet cooking due to their high cost and powerful flavor. They are typically used in meat dishes, oils, specialty cheeses, and pâtés.

FURTHER READINGS: Child, Julia, Louisette Bertholle, and Simone Beck. *Mastering the Art of French Cooking.* New York: Knopf, 1961; Kamp, David. *The United States of Arugula: How We Became a Gourmet Nation.* New York: Broadway, 2006; Kuh, Patric. *The Last Days of Haute Cuisine.* New York: Viking Press, 2001; Saffron, Inge. *Caviar: The Strange History and Uncertain Future of the World's Most Coveted Delicacy.* New York: Broadway, 2003.

Michaela DeSoucey

Goya. *See* Ethnic Food Business.

Grocery Stores. *See* Supermarkets.

Health Foods. *See* Food Fads; Functional Foods and Nutraceuticals; Whole Food.

Heinz The H. J. Heinz Company's founder, Henry John Heinz, was born to German immigrants in 1843 and grew up on a farm along the banks of the Allegheny River in Sharpsburg, Pennsylvania. As a young man, he began processing horseradish to sell to neighbors and local grocers out of the basement of his family home. By 1869, Heinz and L. C. Noble had started Heinz, Noble, & Company and produced a variety of **condiments** under the Anchor Brand label. In 1872, Heinz opened a larger factory on Pittsburgh's North Side, but the next year, the small company went bankrupt, largely because of the 1873 economic depression and monetary crisis. Heinz, in conjunction with his brother John, his cousin Frederick, and his wife Sallie, re-formed the business in 1876. By the turn of the 20th century, the H. J. Heinz Company was one of the largest condiment producers in the country.

Heinz used innovative marketing techniques to sell his products. Not only did he use exclusive salesmen to sell his goods, but he also employed female product demonstrators to distribute samples of **pickles**, preserves, relishes, soups, ketchups, and sauces at industrial expositions, World's Fairs, local grocery stores, and even the homes of middle-class women across the country. In addition to product tastings, Heinz's marketing included an electric sign on the Flatiron Building in New York City, cookbooks featuring Heinz products, "pickle pins," and elaborate window displays made from Heinz products, such as a scale model of a battleship.

With growth and shifting partners, the company was incorporated in 1905 to create stability as well as take advantage of this new legal entity. Based on his religious convictions, H. J. Heinz was one of the leaders of welfare capitalism, providing workers with an array of services, including changing rooms, showers, lectures, plays, and death benefits. Although Heinz was generous to his workers, his largely female workforce regularly left the company because of the hard and often unpleasant work of cleaning fruits and vegetables or filling jars and **bottles**.

H. J. Heinz controlled the company until the early 1910s, when his son Howard took over. Howard had a different vision of the company than his father. He transformed food production at the company from an artisanal to a scientific ethos. Howard began employing **bacteriologists** and engineers to redesign production and ensure product consistency. He also created a **research and development** department to develop and test new products.

After his death in 1941, Howard's son H. J. Heinz II continued expanding the company, but shifted the corporate vision abroad. By the 1950s, the company grew through acquisition rather than new startup ventures. When R. Burt Gookin assumed the presidency of the company in 1966, the Heinz Company shifted from a family-run business to an international conglomerate. Star-Kist Foods and Ore-Ida were acquired in 1963 and 1965, respectively. This trend continued with Anthony J. F. O'Reilly into the 1980s with the acquisition of Weight Watchers International in 1978, Olivine Industries (Zimbabwe) in 1982, and Win-Chance Foods (Thailand) in 1987. Under O'Reilly, the company shifted to a cost-cutting strategy to maintain its position in the competitive global food market and currently faces an increasingly competitive global food market.

See also Advertising; Del Monte; Diet Foods; Peanut Butter.

Gabriella M. Petrick

Hershey. *See* Candy and Confections; Chocolate; Snack Foods.

Hines, Duncan Duncan Hines (1880–1959) is usually identified today with the bakery products that bear his name, but for the first 33 years of his working life he was a travelling salesman, and for the next 10 a food critic and writer. Hines loved to eat, and while he was working on the road, he recorded his dining experiences in a journal. For Christmas 1935, in lieu of cards, he sent to his friends a list of 167 recommended "harbors of refreshment" from across 30 states. Interest in the list spread beyond his personal circle, so in 1936 (at age 56) he published *Adventures in Good Eating* and almost immediately gave up his sales job. Six more books followed: *Lodging for the Night* (1938), *Adventures in Good Cooking* (1939), *The Art of Carving in the Home* (1939), *Duncan Hines Vacation Guide* (1948), *Duncan Hines Food Odyssey* (1955), and *Duncan Hines Dessert Book* (1955). His popular guidebooks were regularly reprinted until 1962, and establishments approved by him were entitled to display a sign saying "Recommended by Duncan Hines."

Hines was the right man in the right place at the right time. Travel was becoming more popular due to the increase in automobile ownership and the expansion of the U.S. highway system, and he was considered trustworthy. He developed a huge following via his books, his syndicated weekly newspaper column (which reached an estimated 20 million readers), and his daily featured spot on the Mutual Radio Network. In the early 1950s, he was said to be better known than the vice president of the United States, Alben Barkley. His reputation was founded on his rigorous independence, his insistence on high standards of quality of food and cleanliness of premises, and his scrupulous fairness.

Hines's association with bakery products began in 1948 when he was approached by businessman Roy Park from North Carolina and was asked to lend his name to a range of **packaged** food. In 1950, the first product to bear his name (a vanilla **ice cream**) reached the shelves. In 1953 he sold the rights to his name to Hines-Park Foods, which then licensed its use to Nebraska Consolidated Mills (NCM) of Omaha for the cake mix that soon became its flagship product. NCM sold the highly successful brand to Procter & Gamble in 1956, which sold it to Aurora Foods in 1998 for a reported $445 million.

Today there are 60 baking mixes in the Duncan Hines product line, and the success of the brand name has all but overwhelmed what must surely be his most significant legacy—the enormous influence he indirectly affected on the **hospitality industry** by increasing customer awareness and hence expectations.

Janet Clarkson

Hormel The Hormel Foods Corporation is a **multinational** manufacturer and marketer of meat and food products, based in Austin, Minnesota. The company's roots go back to 1891, when George Hormel, a former Chicago slaughterhouse worker and wool and hide buyer, started his own pork **meatpacking** operation under the name George A. Hormel and Co.

The company expanded rapidly, and Hormel pursued an early and aggressive export business that soon represented a third of the company's sales. Several key events occurred in the 1920s: in 1926 Hormel produced Hormel Flavor-Sealed Ham—the world's first **canned** ham; in 1927 an innovative distribution system of "sausage trucks" driven by salesmen on specific routes was established; in 1928 the first manufacturing facility outside of Austin was set up in Los Angeles; and Hormel became a public company the same year.

In the 1930s, in order to maintain market share in the face of an increasing number of canned ham producers, Jay Hormel, George's son, developed a "spiced" canned meat that also made use of the shoulder meat from the hogs left over from ham processing. The new product could not be labeled "ham," and Jay wanted a catchy name, so he ran an in-house competition for ideas. **Spam** was launched on May 31, 1937, and it would be an underestimate of monumental proportions to say it never looked back. What was promoted by the company as "Miracle Meat," and referred to disparagingly by others as "mystery meat," is now produced in Hickory Smoked Flavored, Hot & Spicy, Less Sodium, Lite, and Oven Roasted Turkey varieties in order to cater for a larger range of religious, dietary, and taste preferences.

The Hormel facility at Austin was the center of a bitter industrial dispute in 1985 when more than a thousand workers protesting wage cuts and safety issues took part in what came to be called the "strike of the decade." The workers were not supported by the national office of their union, and after 10 months the strike ultimately failed when the company brought in nonunion labor.

Hormel Foods Corporation currently operates in five segments: Grocery Products (shelf-stable products), Refrigerated Foods (pork products), Jennie-O Turkey Store, Specialty Foods, and All Other (beef products). Hormel was named to *Forbes* magazine's "400 Best Big Companies in America" in 2001, 2002, and 2003. Its annual revenue in 2006 was reported as $5.41 billion. There has been no interruption to the quarterly dividend since company publicly listed in 1928, and the company (at the discretion of the board of directors) distributes a share of its profits each year to its 17,000 employees.

Janet Clarkson

Hospitality Industry The hospitality industry is concerned with food, shelter, or entertainment for people away from their homes. The term *hospitality* is derived from the word *hospice*, which was a place of rest for travelers in the medieval period. The range of businesses encompassed by the hospitality industry is large, traditionally including hotels, **restaurants**, casinos, microbreweries, **cafeterias**, cruise ships, quick-service restaurants, theme parks, resorts, private clubs, sports arenas, and the corner tavern, among others. The hospitality industry can roughly be divided into three overarching categories: operations based in the **food service industry**, operations based in lodging, and operations based in recreational activities such as gaming and theme parks. Of course, in many cases, there is a great deal of overlap across the categories. For instance, a casino in Las Vegas may exist for the purpose of gaming, but the revenues from lodging and food service are important components as well.

Food Service

The modern restaurant is usually credited to M. Boulanger, a French tavern keeper sued in 1765 for serving prepared sheep's feet in infringement of the rights of one of the numerous culinary guilds of Paris, although some scholars place the first operations that would be analogous to the modern restaurant in 13th-century China during the Song dynasty. During and after the French Revolution, numerous cooks who had worked for the nobility found themselves without work as the noble households were dispersed. Many of these cooks went into business for themselves, establishing the restaurant as a common part of society. French chefs were in demand in other countries due to the reputation of French cuisine, and the trend spread across Europe. The term *restaurant* derives from the French *restaurer* (to restore), a reference to the purported restorative powers of soup.

Restaurants, or food and beverage operations as they are more precisely known, generally are placed into one of three general classifications: full-service restaurants, casual-dining operations, and quick-service restaurants.

The full-service restaurant generally offers an extensive menu, cooked-to-order food, and a specialized atmosphere. While the classification "full service" implies a certain minimum of service and quality of surroundings, the level of service offered varies widely, usually based on the operation's pricing structure. Service at full-service restaurants ranges from simple delivery of traditionally plated food to full tableside cookery from carts. Full-service restaurants at the high end of the price spectrum tend to be independently owned, while there is more **chain** and **franchise** ownership in the middle and lower parts of the segment.

Casual-dining operations tend to be mid-scale operations with an emphasis on liquor service and a "fun" atmosphere. Dining is less serious than in full-service restaurants, and menus rely on easily recognizable menu items and some degree of unity with the operational theme of the restaurant. While there are numerous independent operators in this segment, the majority of operations are national brand-name stores that are company owned and operated. Examples of this market segment in the United States include Chili's, Olive Garden, Bennigan's, and Outback Steakhouse.

Quick-service restaurants feature menus that are limited in scope, easily and quickly prepared, and do not require table service. Most offer self-service from counters or drive-through windows. These **fast food restaurants** are targeted to an audience who perceive themselves to be in a hurry and who are cost conscious. The perception of value (amount of food received for money spent) is an important consideration in the quick-service segment, and marketing campaigns target value as frequently as, if not more so, than quality or variety. The independently run fast food restaurant is a shrinking part of the segment in the United States, and most are run as franchises. Examples of quick-service restaurants in the United States include **McDonald's**, Wendy's, Taco Bell, and KFC.

Ownership of restaurants can be independent, chain, or franchise. Independently owned and operated restaurants are still common in most countries, as it can be a business with low threshold financial entry requirements. Chains are very common in the casual segment because the location, build-out, and startup requirements for successful operations are often beyond the means of the individual investor. The quick-service restaurant is often a franchise run by an operating company that specializes in running multiple outlets of a certain brand, although some franchises are targeted at the entry-level individual operator. Franchising in the restaurant industry is more than the right to sell a brand name. In order to be awarded a franchise, the operator must agree to strict adherence to rules in areas such as dress, recipe/food production, and marketing.

Lodging

Modern lodging practices likely originated in the practice of innkeeping in the Middle Ages in Europe. Innkeeping was well established by the time of Chaucer's *Canterbury Tales* (c. 1400), in which much of the action occurs in one, and inns were critical to the act of religious pilgrimage, a common reason for travel in the era. Medieval inns served many functions for the traveler—eating place, tavern, stable, and so on—and are, in some ways, analogous to the modern full-service hotel that offers many services in addition to just a bed for the night.

While food service establishments cater to both the local resident and the tourist, lodging establishments are primarily connected to the traveler. Travel occurs for both leisure and business reasons, and lodging establishments are segmented to cater to both types of travelers. Lodging establishments for business travelers tend to be concentrated in business locales, both in city centers and in business-related fringe locations such as airports and business parks. Lodging for the leisure traveler tends to be clustered either along major motor routes or in recreational destinations.

Beyond the categorization of lodging for leisure or business is classification by price and range of amenities offered. There is a broad range of classification by price. At the lowest end of the price spectrum are limited-service hotels, and at the high end are luxurious resorts with an ever-increasing variety of services. Limited-service hotels usually offer only guest rooms, have limited public space (lobbies, pools, etc.), and rarely offer food service outside of the increasingly common free continental breakfast. The market for limited-service hotels tends to be the economy-minded leisure traveler. In contrast, full-service hotels generally cater to business travelers and usually include much more public space, including meeting rooms and food and beverage facilities. Resort hotels tend to be at the middle and upper parts of the price continuum. "Destination resorts" are those in specialized vacation locales such as at the beach or in the mountains. Resorts used to be seasonal operations, but most now operate on a year-round basis. There are many specialty lodging operations catering to specific desires and tastes. Examples include bed and breakfasts, suite hotels, and numerous types of boutique and specialty hotels.

Recreation

The fastest-growing segment of the hospitality industry is the recreational activity segment, especially the casino business. *Casino* originally meant a music hall, but the term has since come to refer to a hospitality operation where gambling is the primary attraction, along with food and drinks. Other institutions in the recreation segment include theme parks, operations associated with natural attractions (e.g., national parks) or festivals, cruise lines, various types of private clubs, and resorts.

The cruise ship has changed from a luxurious method of transportation to a destination in its own right. Today, cruise ships often have as many passengers and crew as a medium-size town. Cruise ships offer a plethora of entertainment and dining options and function as floating resorts.

Traditionally only businesses that were in the commercial or for-profit sector of the business arena were considered hospitality businesses, but usage of the term is rapidly expanding into the noncommercial, traditionally nonprofit, sector as well. Today, organizations such as hospitals, jails, military kitchens, nursing homes, K–12 school food service, college and university food service, and retirement communities are considered to be hospitality operations with increasing expectations regarding food quality and service.

Organizations

Trade and industry organizations in the hospitality industry tend to be organized by primary business interest and nationality—food, lodging, health care, education, and so forth. Examples in the United States include the National Restaurant Association for food service, the American Hotel and Lodging Association for lodging, the National Society for Healthcare Foodservice Management in health care, and the Council on Hotel, Restaurant, and Institutional Education in education. International linkage among national groups is common.

FURTHER READINGS: Angelo, Rocco M., and Andrew N. Vladimir. *Hospitality Today: An Introduction.* 5th ed. Lansing, Michigan: American Hotel & Lodging Association Educational Institute, 2004; Ninemeier, Jack D., and Joe Perdue. *Hospitality Operations: Careers in the World's Greatest Industry.* Upper Saddle River, NJ: Pearson Prentice Hall, 2005; Powers, Tom, and Clayton W. Barrows. *Introduction to Management in the Hospitality Industry.* 8th ed. Hoboken, NJ: Wiley, 2006; Walker, John R. *Introduction to Hospitality.* 4th ed. Upper Saddle River, NJ: Pearson Prentice Hall, 2006; Walker, John R. *The Restaurant: From Concept to Operation.* 5th ed. Hoboken, NJ: Wiley, 2007.

Jeffrey Miller

Hostess. *See* Snack Foods.

Hot Dogs Although it was a $4 billion retail industry in 2006, people in the hot dog business often say that theirs is a "pennies business." The phrase means that economic health often boils down to pennies per pound of product at all levels of the industry: sourcing of raw ingredients, manufacturing, and retailing. The nature of the final product itself more or less forces this reality upon all.

Most hot dogs are made of meat and most are highly processed, mass-produced products meant to be sold as low-cost commodities. Nevertheless, hot dogs can be categorized by quality of ingredients and taste profiles. These range from artisanal types that replicate products made in local shops (companies such as Usinger's or Aidell's) to midlevel manufacturers whose sausages are often made from one meat and no fillers (Vienna Beef, Boar's Head, Sabrett, and the kosher Hebrew National) to large-scale producers whose products are often found in retail market and many large foodservice operations (Oscar Mayer, Ballpark, **Armour**, and others). The midlevel companies such as Vienna Beef, with sales of about $100 million per year, tend to be regional and are usually the kinds found in places where hot dog stands are important parts of local culture.

Sourcing

Historically, for meat producers, the farmers who raise food animals, small price rises have always meant the difference between economic life and death. That much is seen in American newspapers that have printed agricultural commodity prices since the early 19th century. Small-scale meat production became industrialized during that century as characterized by such figures as Gustavus **Swift** and Philip Armour, both of whom came to Chicago and began huge meat-processing plants. Based on accumulating large herds from the west, they and other Midwest meat barons created a new economy of scale. By the late 19th century, beef sold at 1840s prices, as did pork, both the traditional main ingredients of hot dogs (before the rise of chicken and turkey varieties). Without this scale of industry, the modern hot dog would not exist.

Processing

Doubts about what goes into hot dogs originated with the earliest sausages—maybe even the butcher's dog, so the joke went. Economies of scale in hot dogs that rose at the end of the 19th century involved acquiring not just cheap ingredients but also new machinery. Heavy-duty, steam-driven meat choppers, grinders, and emulsifiers appeared from midcentury on, in ever more efficient versions. This allowed companies to process most of the scraps from meat cutting—fats, ears, lips, lungs, and other unsaleable parts—into sausages. By the 20th century, processors were using milk solids, powdered bone, mechanically separated meats (an even newer technology that allows recovery of virtually all meat from bone), and cereals as extenders. The apogee of such mechanization is the "continuous flow" process, the famous "wiener tunnel" invented by the Oscar Mayer Company in the late 1950s and early 1960s. Seventy-five percent of today's cheap "**supermarket**" hot dogs, a $1.5 billion business, are made by this technique, with products often selling at less than a dollar per 12- or 16-ounce package.

Better grades of hot dogs naturally cost more to make. With beef prices at least double those of pork, without benefit of fillers, and with costs added for natural casing, when used, wholesale prices for all-beef hot dogs are higher. They represent a much smaller, but culinarily significant, market segment.

Retailing

Roughly 800 million packages of hot dogs were sold by retail food markets, not counting Wal-Mart, which does not report its sales. Since food marketers' profit margins are small, little more than 3 percent on average, wholesale price per unit is important if for no other reason than that customer preferences are often based on low prices. With considerable **advertising** budgets and imaginative marketing, national brands—Ballpark, Armour, Oscar Mayer, and others—have dominated the food market business. However local brands, such as John Morrell's Hunter Brand in the St. Louis area, also hold customer loyalty.

It is in the **restaurant** segment of the hot dog business that the "pennies" doctrine holds sway. Hot dog stand and cart operators stand at the lower end of the restaurant economic spectrum. Theirs is usually a cash business, sometimes unreported to tax authorities, with generally low overhead. Expected to serve low-price food by their customers—their historic function—low food costs for ingredients are of paramount importance. Operators regularly haggle with suppliers over a penny or two per pound, especially if serving higher-cost products. Several kinds of economic behaviors are on display in bargaining. Suppliers must constantly watch and adjust their prices because, with competition always at hand, stand operators will change for pennies per pound. To hold their customers, manufacturers often offer other incentives such as signage, common advertising, and reinforcement of their own reputation for high quality. And hot dog stand owners often display true open marketplace mentality—they watch very single penny that comes in and goes out.

There is a reason for this attitude. As common lore and number of websites have it, a good deal of money can be made from peddling hot dogs—to the tune of $2,000–3,000 per day. Hot dogs are a pennies business, but a lucrative one.

FURTHER READINGS: Horowitz, Roger. *Putting Meat on the American Table: Taste, Technology, and Transformation.* Baltimore: Johns Hopkins University Press, 2006.

Bruce Kraig

Hunt's In 1888, Joseph and William Hunt launched a small preserving business in Santa Rosa, California. Two years later, their business was incorporated as the Hunt Brothers Fruit Packing Company. They expanded their operation in the following years, and in 1896 moved their operation to Hayward, California. By the turn of the century, the company was producing an extensive line of fruit and vegetable products.

Hunt Foods

In the early 1940s, Hunt Brothers was a regional canner known mainly in the West. In 1943, they sold their operation to Norton Simon. At the time, Simon owned Val Vita Food Products, a small orange juice **canning** factory in Fullerton, California. Through **advertising**, he had increased Val Vita's sales dramatically within a few years, and he hoped to do the same with Hunt Brothers. In 1945, Simon merged Hunt Brothers with Val Vita to form Hunt Foods.

Simon targeted tomato sauce as a major product worthy of national promotion. In 1946 he launched a major advertising campaign around the slogan, "Hunt—for the best." In national women's magazines, Hunt Foods placed advertisements with color illustrations of Hunt's Tomato Sauce. Ads also featured recipes for dishes using Hunt's tomato sauce as the key ingredient. Simon also printed similar recipes inside millions of matchbook covers. This campaign propelled Hunt Foods from a regional business into a national brand.

Hunt Foods acquired the E. Prichard Company in Bridgeton, New Jersey, which had manufactured "Pride of the Farm" ketchup. Hunt Foods began an extremely aggressive campaign on behalf of its ketchup during the 1950s. In addition, Simon introduced new lines of convenience foods, including Manwich, Skillet dinners, and snack packs. By the 1950s, the company claimed to be the largest processor of tomato-based products in the world. It later increased its tomato product line to include spaghetti sauce and barbecue sauce.

Simon merged Hunt Foods with the Wesson Oil & Snowdrift Company to create Hunt-Wesson Foods in 1960. Eight years later, Hunt-Wesson became a major group of Norton Simon, Inc., which in turn was acquired by ConAgra, a **multinational** corporation based in St. Louis and the second largest U.S. food conglomerate behind **Kraft Foods**. Today, the Hunt Foods brand manufactures only tomato products, such as barbecue sauce, ketchup, sauce, and puree, as well as diced, stewed, and crushed tomatoes.

See also Condiments.

FURTHER READINGS: Mahoney, David J. *Growth and Social Responsibility: The Story of Norton Simon Inc.* New York: Newcomen Society in North America, 1973; Smith, Andrew F. *Pure Ketchup: The History of America's National Condiment.* Columbia: University of South Carolina Press, 1996.

Andrew F. Smith

Hybridization Hybridization is the biological process of producing offspring from two different organisms to create a new variety called a *hybrid*. A hybrid can be of two separate species (two different plants or animals) or can be from two plants from the same species (as often happens in the process of breeding). The advantages in creating hybrid plants include a stronger organism profile and higher production rate.

From the perspective of the company selling hybrid plants, there are two main commercial advantages to hybridization: proprietary control over the seeds they develop, and the fact that the enhanced vigor of the seed is not always passed on to the offspring, therefore requiring farmers to buy new seeds every other year.

Although traditional breeding was at first used to create hybrids, today's use of biotechnology and **genetic engineering** has increased the productivity of hybrids, while also generating controversy.

History

Hybridization for agriculture goes back at least 150 years, but the first systematic use of hybridization in crop culture was recorded in the 1930s. The crop used was **corn**, and the hybrid seed proved a much better alternative than open-pollinated crops (those pollinated by pollen blowing in the wind). Today, more than 80 percent of corn grown in North America is a single-cross hybrid of this nature, while the remaining 20 percent consists of double, three-way, and modified (related-line parent) crosses. Many other vegetable crops also rely on hybrids; for example, sorghum is now mostly grown from hybrid seed, as are onions, spinach, tomatoes, and cabbage.

Plant Hybrids versus Animal Hybrids

The main distinction between creating plant and animal hybrids is that the former often does not lose the capacity to reproduce, while animal hybrids such as the mule (offspring of a female horse and a male donkey) are sterile; this is due to the different number of chromosomes in each species. Although sterility is not a side effect that is sought after, some fruit producers use hybridization sterility to create seedless fruits (such as seedless bananas). Some other producers create hybrids with plants that have natural resistance to pesticides; **wheat** is one of these plants that have a natural profile of pesticide resistance.

The Process of Hybridization

Most hybrids are created by human intervention, but hybridization is a process that can also be found in the wild; these are called *hybrid zones*, an area where two species are known to coexist. Some scientists believe that hybridization is a part of our evolutionary process, rather than a fully artificial process. Successful hybrids can evolve into new species within 50 to 60 generations.

The process for hybridization of plants is quite complex. First, researchers must identify the appropriate germplasm (genetic resource package of the plant). Following this, they must develop superior inbreeds from the parental population and evaluate these inbreeds. Afterward, they must identify the superior hybrid combination and test the precommercial hybrid. Once developed, the research must enter an extensive seed production phase, as well as a marketing campaign to commercialize the new product.

Hybrid seeds are developed by different **research and development** efforts; for example, the corn seed market is developed essentially by the private sector, while wheat is developed by public sector research.

Critics of Hybrid Plants

Hybrid plants have come under scrutiny for the potential dependency they create. As hybrid plants seeds are usually weaker (or altogether sterile), it has been suggested that these types of seeds encourage dependency in farmers, requiring them to purchase seeds every year. The most famous example of this is the "terminator technology"; this was developed by the **U.S. Department of Agriculture** and was the first attempt to create sterile seeds. Due to controversy, companies such as **Monsanto** have vowed not to commercialize this type of technology.

FURTHER READINGS: Fernandez-Cornejo, Jorge. *The Seed Industry in U.S. Agriculture: An Exploration of Data and Information on Crop Seed Markets, Regulation, Industry Structure, and Research and Development.* Agriculture Information Bulletin No. 786. Washington, D.C.: USDA Economic Research Service, 2004. Available at http://www.ers.usda.gov/publications/aib786; Loureiro, Inigo, M. Cristina Chueca, M. Concepción Escorial, and José Maria Garcia-Baudin. "Hybridization between Wheat (*Triticum aestivum*) and the Wild Species *Aegilops geniculata* and *A. biuncialis* under Experimental Field Conditions." *Agriculture, Ecosystems and Environment* 120 (2007): 384–90.

Jean-François Denault

Ice Cream Today, ice cream is a $20-billion-a-year-plus business in the United States, according to the International Dairy Foods Association. Yet until the middle of the 19th century, it was hardly a business at all. Ice cream then was an elegant indulgence for the privileged few. But the vision of several remarkable entrepreneurs, the increased availability and affordability of ingredients, and improvements in ice cream–making equipment transformed ice cream into a significant industry. In 1900, per-capita consumption was less than one quart; at the dawn of the 21st century, it is more than 21 quarts.

From the time scientists discovered how to freeze substances in 16th-century Italy using ice and saltpeter, cooks began making ices and ice creams. These were made in small quantities by individual confectioners. It was time-consuming, hands-on work. First, they made the mixture that would become the ice cream. They poured it into a small canister called a *sorbetière*, and placed that in a larger bucket filled with ice and salt. They turned the sorbetière continuously and opened it from time to time to stir the mixture. The constant movement was necessary to keep the mixture from freezing into a solid block. The desired consistency was of snow rather than ice.

Despite the difficulties of producing ices and ice creams, early confectioners made them in every conceivable flavor, from such familiar ones as vanilla, lemon, and **chocolate** to exotic ones like saffron, Parmesan cheese, and truffle. They molded them into the shape of fruits, vegetables, and fish; painted them to reproduce their natural colors; and presented them to their noble patrons with great fanfare. Everything about ice cream making was extravagant, from the **labor**-intensive process to the cost of the ingredients.

In 1806, Boston-area entrepreneur Frederic Tudor began to transform ice harvesting from a local trade into an international business with his first shipment of ice from Boston to Martinique. At its peak, in 1886, the annual ice harvest was estimated at 25 million tons. The ice industry transformed many food products, none more so than ice cream.

Nancy Johnson, a Philadelphian, invented an ice cream maker with an inner dasher connected to an outer crank in 1843. It allowed the ice cream to be churned without opening the container, saving time and effort. Others improved on the model and, in the 1870s, steam-powered ice cream makers increased production still further.

At about the same time, the cost of **sugar** fell as a result of agricultural expansion, processing improvements, and government policies.

In the summer of 1851, **dairy** businessman Jacob Fussell found himself with a surplus of cream. Fussell made his living by buying milk and cream from Pennsylvania dairies and selling it to city dwellers in nearby Baltimore. Faced with too many lemons, one is enjoined to make lemonade; faced with too much cream, Fussell decided to make ice cream. He sold it for 25 cents a quart at a time when confectioners were charging 60 cents, and the wholesale ice cream business was born. Fussell began by cranking out a few quarts of ice cream by hand, but soon he expanded the business and opened factories in several cities. Others followed his lead. In 1859, national ice cream production was estimated at 4,000 gallons; by 1899 it was more than five million, according to the International Association of Ice Cream Vendors.

Elite confectioners complained that wholesalers sold second-rate ice cream, but to little avail. Ice cream had become a democratic treat. At the turn of the 20th century, street vendors were selling ice cream sandwiches, soda fountain operators were dishing out ice cream sodas and sundaes, and ice cream cones had made ice cream a treat fit for a kid. Per-capita consumption was up to a gallon by 1915.

Technology continued to improve. Factories were built and equipped with brine freezers, which sped up the process. A new method produced ice cream in a continuous stream rather than separate batches. **Packaging** was mechanized. Soon afterward, **delivery** trucks replaced the horse and buggy. But the industry continued to be dependent on ice and salt until the early 1920s. Then, at a convention, the Nizer Cabinet Company, later to become the Kelvinator Company, introduced an electric **refrigeration** cabinet. Refrigeration made possible increased production with fewer employees, as well as lower delivery and distribution costs.

The Temperance movement and Prohibition gave the ice cream industry a boost, as corner saloons were transformed into ice cream parlors, and breweries became ice cream manufacturers. Novelties such as Eskimo pies, Good Humor Bars, and Popsicles were created, and ice cream became one of the nation's fastest-growing industries. Although Repeal and the Depression brought on a slump in ice cream consumption, the industry recovered by the late 1930s, thanks largely to five-cent novelty ice creams.

Americans still ate most of their ice cream outside the home. It was not until after World War II that the average family had a refrigerator with a freezing compartment large enough to store ice cream. When gas rationing ended and Americans took to the road again after the war, companies such as such as Howard Johnson's, Baskin-Robbins, Dairy Queen, and Carvel prospered. In the 1950s, **supermarket** sales soared as consumers stocked up on half-gallon packages.

Supermarket ice cream was affordable, but some manufacturers compromised quality for low cost. As a result, many consumers yearned for good, old-fashioned ice cream. The market responded with high-butterfat, superpremium ice creams, including Häagen-Dazs and Ben & Jerry's. In many towns, young entrepreneurs opened small ice cream shops where they made and sold high-quality ice cream.

Today, the marketplace includes everything from superpremium to low-fat, no-sugar-added offerings, packaged ice cream cones, and frozen yogurt and cereal bars. There is even a space-age, freeze-dried ice cream for would-be astronauts—no refrigeration required.

FURTHER READINGS: David, Elizabeth. *Harvest of the Cold Months*. New York: Viking Penguin, 1995; Funderburg, Anne Cooper. *Chocolate, Strawberry, and Vanilla*. Bowling Green, OH: Bowling Green State University Popular Press, 1995; International Association of Ice Cream Vendors. http://www.iaicv.org; International Dairy Foods Association. http://www.idfa.org.

Jeri Quinzio

Internet As Internet use becomes more and more part of everyday life, opinion formation, and purchase-decision making, many food-related businesses are finding ways to communicate, market, sell, inform, share, and generally transact business using the World Wide Web. This is accomplished by producing compelling websites, integrating the online environment with other marketing efforts, developing e-commerce capabilities, understanding how consumers use the Internet, and using the Internet to understand, influence, or respond to customers.

Most company and corporate presence on the Internet is in the form of **advertising**, sponsorships, and most importantly websites, which can vary from static to interactive. All these activities might be in pursuit of building brand awareness and loyalty, corporate image or relations, or sales directly from the Internet encounter. Major firms tend to have established distribution channels and are not using their Web endeavors to gain direct revenue. Retailers, whether a traditional store owner with a Web-commerce extension of a "bricks-and-mortar" outlet or an exclusively online vendor, are more likely looking to the Web for direct sales as are artisanal, regional, or small food manufacturers, specialty food makers, and others who otherwise would have only a limited distribution area or would find using traditional distribution channels expensive or ineffective.

The food industry is the leading buyer of advertising in the United States, so it makes sense that it has a strong presence on the Web. Corporations such as **Kraft Foods** sponsor video webcasts of three-minute cooking shows on the Microsoft Network portal. Other companies have banners and other ads on websites that attract their target market to their products or websites. On their own websites, or on third-party sites such as iVillage, Epicurious, Yahoo, and America Online, companies are increasingly integrating advertising and website content to create dynamic and interactive environments that try to snag viewers of all ages and have them become repeat visitors. The ultimate goal is to convert website loyalty to immediate or future purchases either from the websites directly or traditional distribution channels and dealers. Because the websites offer more detailed information and interaction, their addresses are often referred to in other advertising and programming. Websites are also cross-promoted on **packaging** and other marketing efforts.

Making Websites Compelling

Much food promotion is in the form of **marketing to children**. Almost all major food companies that target children have created their own websites for them or offer a direct link to one. Interactive programming built on product characteristics are an important component of such websites, even for preschoolers. Games, screensavers, and other activities mix advertising with interactivity. In a study of 40 food and beverage websites (representing the top five brands in eight categories) that market to youngsters, 63 percent featured gaming. The sites were also entertaining, with more than half having cartoon or other characters for the child to relate to as a main feature of the website.

Depending on the product and company image, some websites geared for adults also feature games. Developers work directly with marketers and companies to create a game that reinforces the brand message. For example, Launchpad created websites for several food manufacturers incorporating games to increase the number of people visiting the sites as well as to attract repeat visitors. While for Pinnacle Foods' Mrs. Paul's Fish Sticks Launchpad designed a game to engage children, for Pinnacle's Hungry Man brand of frozen dinners, the agency designed retro arcade-style games that would appeal to the products' target market: men between 18 and 35 years old.

Games aren't suitable for every website, product, or consumer, so some sites offer a free members-only area that provides value to the user. According to website designers, marketing professionals, and consumer behavior studies, other tactics to keep users engaged and clicking back include content that is updated regularly, in-site search engines, an easy-to-understand and -navigate format, responsive customer service, links to other sites of value, design and graphic updates, recipes, meal planning, online menus or other helpful information, ask-the-expert columns, and special merchandise or deals only available on the website.

Recipes or other information on how to use a product will pull a consumer to a food-related website and add to its perceived value. For example, recipes were the number-one reason clients of **nutritional education** professionals used their agencies' sites. Yahoo cited users' desire for recipes as a reason it recently began offer a Yahoo food component to attract and keep users on its site. In fact, the desire to share or discover recipes was an early use of the Internet. Today RecipeSource.com (www.recipesource.com) has more than 70,000 online recipes.

How Food Shoppers Use the Internet

Shopping for food on the Internet is growing, and understanding how and why consumers use the Internet to shop for food and related products can help Web merchants maximize their Web presence. Repeated studies have shown that consumers consider certain products as being suitable for purchase over the Internet and others not. Generally, items they need to experience by sight, touch, or taste; ones that are bought often and have a relatively low cost; and ones that are either unbranded or are perceived as having few differences among brands are less likely to be purchased over the Internet by consumers. There is little need to gather information or research alternatives or trusted opinions to make the purchasing decision. Lack of immediate **delivery** or shipping costs are also factors. Most everyday food products fall into this category. But if a company can create value for this kind of service, it can be very successful.

Grocery shopping is time and energy consuming. Websites that create interactive shopping lists and reduce the time it takes to shop every week, for example, may cause a consumer to perceive a favorable difference. Providing photographs and detailed information about products on the website helps shoppers overcome the lack of actual experience with the product. Discounted or free shipping, quick delivery, and other benefits can also help drive these purchases. Offering hard-to-find items and regional brands helps. Another key is to make the actual purchase as familiar to customers as possible by recreating in-store or other online checkout experiences.

Despite the failure of earlier Internet grocers such as Webvan, there is increasing corporate commitment to the concept, and the category appears to be growing.

Online grocery sales grew 29 percent in 2005. Five percent of Americans shopped the Internet for groceries in 2005, an increase of 2 percent from the year before.

Now joining Safeway, Peapod, Sam's Club, and other regional and national online grocers is Amazon.com. Consumers who spent more than $250 online in the past three months purchased more than $800 at grocery stores in that same time period. Individuals who spent under $250 online spent $660 for groceries. With its strong Web retailing advantage, Amazon could be in a position to capture some of these sales and a piece of the $500-billion-a-year market. The e-commerce retailer opened its virtual store, its 34th product category, in 2006. It stocks about 14,000 different items. Amazon had already been selling **gourmet food** and similar items three years before its grocery store opened, allowing the company time to build a customer base and develop relationships with vendors. It hopes to avoid some of the known pitfalls of the business by not selling perishable items and by packaging items in bulk to make product handling more economical.

Food-related products that offer a higher sense of intangibles, need more explanation, and are more unique are probably an easier sell on the Internet. Specialty products that appeal to enthusiasts, regional tastes, or nostalgia are easier purchase decisions for online shoppers. For example, Groovycandies.com carries old-fashioned **candy** and sweets. The company began with one kind of candy box in 1999 and by 2005 had grown to a $2.3 million company. Products that offer a special health, quality, environmental, or other claim such as fat-free, **organic**, or "green" are also well suited to Internet sales. Another category is products that allow the buyer to identify with a social group or aspiration. An example would be buying **ethnic foods** or having French bread shipped from France. The Internet works well for these shoppers, allowing them to search, evaluate, become informed, and collect opinions. Websites for these products benefit from having links and other referrals to other sources that consumers trust, which lend credibility to them and aid consumers in the decision-making process.

Food Blogs: A Growing Resource

Consumers don't only visit food-related websites on the Internet; they also create them through blogs, personal websites, and social networking groups. A *blog*, or Web log, is a personal website presented in a diary or journal format. It can be written by one person or a group. Blogs usually invite feedback in the form of comments, and blogs within the same category often link or refer to each other. Readership can be in the tens or the tens of thousands or more a day. Blogs can react quickly to changing events and are frequently updated. Seven percent of adult Internet users have created a blog of some kind. Thirty-two million Americans read them, many checking on their favorites regularly. The blogs bring together people who are related by ideas or enthusiasms rather than proximity. Fourteen million of them are using the Web's interactivity to take the time to post a comment on what they have read about.

The boom in blogging is partly responsible for the mostly free or low-cost programming, site-design templates, and hosting provided by Google's Blogger, Wordpress, Typepad, and other services. One of the best-known and most popular food blogs is "Chocolate and Zucchini" (www.chocolateandzucchini.com). Its founder, a Frenchwoman who lived and worked in California for a time, writes about food and life in Paris, and its success led to a cookbook contract.

Food blogs are becoming an important factor in new product introductions, **restaurant** patronage, and other areas, with many bloggers reporting that they are receiving public relations inquiries, news releases, and offers of free products for review of cookbooks, **chocolate**, kitchen gadgets, and many other categories. Services such as Google advertising programs have made it easy for companies to purchase ads on groups of blogs that best suit the their needs, providing an extremely targeted and motivated audience. However, most food blogs are not businesses looking to make money, but rather are idiosyncratic personal expressions of the author's particular interests, and many—even some of the very influential ones—refuse advertising. For most of the bloggers that do accept advertising (which is mostly food related), it is not a significant revenue source.

Some blogging industry watchers contend that blogs' value to companies is not for click-through sales but for building community and public awareness. Food companies and others are now sponsoring their own blogs, sometimes hosted on their websites, sometimes appearing elsewhere. It remains to be seen if the corporate blogs can engender the same sense of community the independent bloggers do. Food blogs and other independent food websites such as Chowhound.com (www.chowhound.com), eGullet (www.egullet.org), and Leite's Culinaria (http://leitesculinaria.com) often serve as informal information channels for businesses, giving them feedback and insight. Companies are using syndicated feeds, sophisticated search techniques, and other technologies to scan blogs, websites, and portals for references not only for marketing purposes but also to gain feedback for new food product development.

There are many other ways in which food-related concerns are using the Web. Some vendors and distributors are using private networks to facilitate sales and distribution. Other companies are using the Web to help train chefs and other food service workers. Examples include downloadable video broadcasts on basic kitchen preparation and service tips and techniques, food safety courses, and online **wine** training programs. The **food service industry** is working with third-party online reservation services and is looking to the near future to deliver menus to handheld devices such as Apple's iPod or to take orders from mobile communication devices such as BlackBerries. Scientists are working on ways to use the Internet to trace food production from field to table to help track health and environmental concerns. The Internet also has a wealth of food-related organization, association, and other sites for industry, consumer **research**, and other use.

FURTHER READINGS: Allen, Gary. *Resource Guide for Food Writers*. New York: Routledge, 1999; Popp, Jamie. "Taming the Techies: Foodservice Gears Up for Blogs, Webcasting and Other Interactive Media." *Restaurants and Institutions*, May 2005. http://www.rimag.com/archives/2005/05b/internet-marketing2.asp; Ramus, Kim Bjarne, and Klaus G. Grunert. "Consumers' Willingness to Buy Food via the Internet: A Review of the Literature and a Model for Future Research." MAPP Working Papers, no. 84, Aarhus School of Business, University of Aarhus, Denmark, September 2004. Available at http://ebslgwp.hhs.se/aarmap/abs/aarmap 0084.htm; Story, Mary, and Simone French. "Food Advertising and Marketing Directed at Children and Adolescents in the U.S." *International Journal of Behavioral Nutrition and Physical Activity* 1, no. 3 (February 10, 2004). Available at http://www.ijbnpa.org/content/1/1/3; Tedeschi, Bob. "After Delving into 33 Other Lines, Amazon Finally Gets Around to Food." *New York Times*, July 24, 2006.

Faith J. Kramer

Irradiation Irradiation, also known as electronic or cold pasteurization, is a process by which foods are exposed to a source of radiation (such as gamma rays or high-energy electrons) for the purpose of killing microbial pathogenic organisms, deinfesting (especially spices), and extending shelf life by retarding spoilage. Irradiation is a controversial subject; although industry and government agencies, both domestic and international, endorse food irradiation as a safe and beneficial **food safety** tool, non-governmental food advocacy and consumer groups disagree and have consistently challenged all forms of food irradiation as unsafe for the consumer and unnecessary for a clean food supply.

Renewed interest in food safety technologies including irradiation has most recently been driven by large foodborne disease outbreaks, only to be dampened by consumer failure to embrace the technology or unwillingness to pay for its increased cost. Despite the periodic postoutbreak increase in support for irradiation, consumer awareness and demand for irradiated products remain low; supply is accordingly limited by processors. Nevertheless, food irradiation facilities continue to irradiate foods, which are consumed by a public often unaware that the product has been irradiated. The food industry maintains confidence in the utility of irradiation; it most often compares the expected eventual consumer acceptance of the technique to the virtually universal acceptance of the pasteurization of milk and milk products.

History of Irradiation

The century-long history of irradiation weaves its way through several government agencies and the military, prior to the more recent integration of private industry into the process. Following the path of development and the appearance of irradiated foods into the food supply provides an explanation for the source of some of the fierce opposition to irradiated foods.

The first U.S. patent to treat food with ionizing radiation to kill **bacteria** was granted in 1905. Other than the approval in 1921 of an x-ray process to kill *Trichinella spiralis* in meat, irradiation received scant attention until the atomic age was ushered in under President Dwight D. Eisenhower. In 1947, interest in food irradiation was boosted when **researchers** discovered that meat and other foods "sterilized" by the application of high energy could safely preserve foods destined for troops in distant locales. Thus, treating foods by irradiation became another addition to the long list of advances in food technology that had its genesis in the need for a nation to feed its troops.

With a dual focus on employing nuclear technology for peacetime and improving the safety and shelf life of military and consumer food supplies, the National Food Irradiation Program, in conjunction with the U.S. Army and Atomic Energy Commission, sponsored research projects spanning several decades from 1953 to 1980. Ever since Congress gave the Food and Drug Administration (FDA) authority over food irradiation and amended the Food, Drug, and Cosmetic Act in 1958 to define sources of radiation as a new food **additive**, there has been a slow yet steady trajectory of approval for treating foods with irradiation. Initial specific purposes included the control of insects in **wheat** and flour, inhibition of sprouting in white potatoes, and sterilization of **packaging** materials. In the 1960s, additional approvals were sought by the Army and the **U.S. Department of Agriculture** (USDA)—the government agency primarily responsible for inspection of **beef**, pork, and **poultry**—from the FDA to approve the irradiation of ham.

In 1976, the Army entered into contracts with commercial companies to study the wholesomeness of irradiated ham, pork, and chicken. The regulatory authority over irradiated foods shifted in 1980, when the USDA took over the Army's food irradiation program. As the list of foods approved for irradiation grew, private processors sought approval for the irradiation process to be applied to their products as well. Approvals have been granted for spices and dry vegetables (1983); pork carcasses (1985); certain fresh foods, including fruits and vegetables (1986); fresh and **frozen** uncooked poultry (1990 and 1992); **refrigerated** and frozen uncooked beef, lamb, goat, and pork (1997 and 2000); and fresh eggs (2000). There is currently joint and overlapping governmental authority exercised over certain irradiated foods. The FDA is the agency primarily responsible for ensuring the safe use of irradiation of all foods. Concurrently, the USDA's Food Safety and Inspection Service is responsible for meat, poultry, and shelled egg products, including the irradiation of such products.

Additional government agencies involved in the irradiation process are the Nuclear Regulatory Commission, the Occupational Safety and Health Administration, and the Department of Transportation. These agencies oversee a range of irradiation-related issues, including approval of permissible processes, the safe use of radiation, and the safety of the workers in irradiation facilities, as well as the safe transportation of radioactive materials.

Process and Technologies

Food irradiation exposes food to ionizing radiation—often compared to the type of energy in radio and television or microwaves—which penetrates foods at energy levels high enough to kill microorganisms yet not significantly raise the food's temperature (thus the promotion of the term "cold pasteurization"). Three types of ionizing radiation have been approved for irradiating food in the United States: gamma rays, high-energy electrons (sometimes referred to as electron beams), and x-rays. Gamma rays produced by cobalt-60 were the exclusive technology used to irradiate foods in the United States until electron beam processing facilities—which use electricity, not radioactive isotopes—became a primary process for the irradiation of ground beef. Electron beams cannot penetrate as far into food as gamma rays or x-rays. Supporters of the safety of irradiation technologies point out that facilities have been used for other purposes for many years, such as sterilizing medical and consumer products like bandages, juice containers, and baby bottle nipples. Opponents point to the potential hazards to workers that can endanger workers in any nuclear facility (as well as contamination of local resources) and the as-yet unknown effects potentially caused by consumption of irradiated products.

Labeling Issues

The international symbol for foods that have been treated by irradiation is the Radura. Irradiated foods sold at retail must bear the Radura symbol and a statement that they are "treated with radiation" or "treated by irradiation." Thus, unprocessed foods such as irradiated raw ground beef would carry the Radura symbol and a statement. Consumers are not always aware, however, that they are purchasing or consuming foods that have been treated with irradiation, because *processed* foods that contain a small percentage of irradiated ingredients need not be labeled. **Restaurants** and hospitals that serve irradiated food need not post a Radura symbol or statement that irradiated foods are being used in the facility. **Organic** foods may not be irradiated.

Taste, Wholesomeness, and Safety Factors

Since taste varies by individual and is highly subjective, it is difficult to establish whether changes in taste created by the irradiation of food are significant enough to turn consumers away from irradiated products. The question of changes in taste from irradiation also varies depending on the food that has been irradiated. The most often-heard taste-related complaints about irradiated foods are that they develop a "wet-dog" odor or become mushy in texture.

Despite several years of testing, controversy continues over the issue of changes in nutrient content after irradiation. While some deterioration of nutrients does occur, proponents consider it insignificant when compared to the harm that can be caused by microbial pathogens. Opponents of irradiation, however, argue that treatment of the food by radiation fundamentally changes healthful nutritional composition of those foods and potentially introduces harmful elements that do not otherwise naturally occur. Critics also cite to potential nuclear pollution from some processing plants.

Economics

Irradiated foods are purchased primarily by facilities that must feed a population with weakened immune systems. Thus, nursing homes and hospitals are major purchasers of irradiated foods, which they serve in order to reduce the risk of foodborne illness. Since foodborne illness or **food poisoning** outbreaks also occur with some degree of frequency in schools, irradiated foods were also viewed as a useful tool for protecting children, whose immature immune systems increase their risk of illness. However, legislation that permitted the purchase of irradiated beef by school systems for use in ground meat recipes has met with much resistance from parents and little success in the nation's schools. Specifically, the 2002 Farm Bill authorized the service of irradiated foods in the National School Lunch Program and allows the USDA to include irradiated food in its commodity distribution. The WIC Reauthorization Act of 2004 provided that irradiated foods could be served in schools, but only at the request of states and school food authorities. School food service managers reported in a 2005 survey that the higher cost of irradiated foods, coupled with lack of demand or even awareness of availability, made it unlikely they would introduce irradiated foods into their menus. The need to educate parents and children about irradiated foods was also cited as a reason to shy away from irradiated foods; school food service managers felt it was not within their purview to undertake a consumer education campaign about irradiated foods within the school context.

Ideological issues aside, economic considerations drive the availability of irradiated foods. Facilities are costly to build and require that a premium be charged for irradiated products such as meats. Consumers, who are reluctant to purchase irradiated food to begin with, are even less likely to purchase irradiated products that cost more than untreated foods. A highly promoted roll-out of premium irradiated beef into **supermarkets** was met with a tepid reception by consumers. Ground beef patties are available by mail order from one premium retailer, but sales of irradiated beef do not constitute a significant amount of sales for any processor or producer.

Future of Irradiated Foods

At least one legislator has unsuccessfully sought to ban the sale of irradiated foods. Some processing plants have gone bankrupt, although industry entrepreneurs confident of the future need for irradiated foods in a highly industrialized food system prone to large foodborne outbreaks have continued to build new facilities and revive bankrupt ones. FDA officials and consumer groups caution that irradiation should not been seen as a substitute for good industrial practices; it must be seen as but one part of a comprehensive food safety program. Moreover, consumers must still be aware of potentially hazardous food-handling practices that could recontaminate irradiated foods; poor handling and storage practices could still result in foodborne illness.

FURTHER READINGS: "Irradiation." Foodsafety.gov: Gateway to Government Safety Information. http://www.foodsafety.gov/~fsg/irradiat.html; Public Citizen, Critical Mass Energy and Environment Program. "Food Irradiation and Global Trade: What Irradiation Means for Farmers and Ranchers in the United States and throughout the World." Washington, D.C.: Public Citizen, 2003. Available at http://www.citizen.org/documents/tradereport.pdf.

Ellen J. Fried

K

Keebler In 1853, Godfrey Keebler opened a neighborhood bakery in Philadelphia. It grew quickly, and he brought his sons into the business. By the early 20th century, Keebler bakery products were distributed regionally. The company's main competition was the National Biscuit Company (**Nabisco**). To compete with Nabisco, in 1926 Keebler joined the United Biscuit Company of America, which was a federation of cracker and cookie manufacturers, including Strietmann of Cincinnati and Herkmann of Grand Rapids. By 1944, United Biscuit was headquartered in Elmhurst, Illinois, and consisted of 16 bakeries from Philadelphia to Salt Lake City.

Each United Biscuit Company bakery produced its own line of products under various brand names. In 1966, Keebler Company became the official corporate name and the brand name for all products. This shift permitted the company to **advertise** nationally. In 1968 Ernie Keebler and the elves who baked with a magic oven in a hollow tree were developed by the Leo Burnet Company of Chicago and became the company's advertising icons. The famous Keebler jingle was: "Man, you never would believe where the Keebler Cookies come from. They're baked by little elves in a hollow tree. And what do you think makes these cookies so uncommon? They're baked in magic ovens, and there's no factory. Hey!" The Elves, known for making "uncommonly good" products, are among the best-recognized advertising characters in America. The ads paid off.

By the 1990s, Keebler was the second largest manufacturer of cookies and crackers in America, the largest manufacturer of private label cookies, and the number-one manufacturer of cookies and crackers for the food service market. It produced 8 of the 25 best-selling cookies and 10 of the 25 best-selling crackers. It also manufactured pie crusts and **ice cream** cones for retail sale. The company's products were sold in 30,000 retail locations throughout the United States.

In 1996, Keebler acquired the Sunshine brand, makers of Hydrox cookies. Keebler decided to change Hydrox's flavor and rename the cookie Keebler Droxies. Through its Little Brownie Bakers subsidiary, Keebler is also a leading licensed supplier of Girl Scout cookies.

In 2001 Keebler was acquired by the Kellogg Company for $4.56 billion, the largest acquisition in Kellogg's history. Today, the Keebler brand remains the second largest branded manufacturer of cookies and crackers in the country and the largest manufacturer of private label cookies and crackers. Its products include Animals cookies, E. L. Fudge cookies, Keebler Grahams and Graham Cracker Crumbs, Famous Amos cookies, Sunshine Krispy crackers, Murray crackers, and Zesta crackers. Its annual sales are estimated at $2.8 billion.

FURTHER READINGS: Manley, Duncan J. R. *Technology of Biscuits, Crackers, and Cookies.* 3rd ed. Boca Raton, FL: CRC Press/Woodhead, 2000; Panschar, William G. *Baking in America.* Evanston, IL: Northwestern University Press, 1956; Smith, W. H. *Biscuits, Crackers and Cookies.* London: Applied Science, 1972.

Andrew F. Smith

Kellogg. *See* Breakfast Cereals.

Kentucky Fried Chicken. *See* Fast Food Restaurants; Poultry Industry.

KFC. *See* Fast Food Restaurants; Poultry Industry.

Kosher Foods. *See* Ethnic Food Business.

Kraft Foods Kraft Foods is the second largest food and beverage company in the world, with net revenues of more than $34 billion in 2005. Chicago businessman James L. Kraft started the company in 1903 by pioneering innovations in the wholesale distribution of cheese. His four brothers joined him in 1909, and they incorporated the fledgling business as J. L. Kraft & Bros. Kraft used innovative and aggressive **advertising** techniques to promote his line of 31 varieties of cheese, becoming one of the first food companies to use color advertisements in national magazines. The company opened its first cheese factory in 1914.

Until Kraft entered the business, cheese was produced in large wheels and had a tendency to spoil quickly when cut because most grocers and consumers had no access to **refrigeration**. This problem inspired Kraft in 1915 to produce a blended, pasteurized cheese that he marketed in metal containers as "process cheese." The sale of six million pounds of cheese to the U.S. Army during World War I insured the fortunes of the company.

The company changed its name to Kraft Cheese Company in the 1900s soon after merging with the Phenix Cheese Corporation, the maker of Philadelphia Brand Cream Cheese (introduced in the United States in 1872). In 1928 the company introduced Velveeta pasteurized processed cheese spread and Miracle Whip salad dressing, adding Kraft caramels in 1933. Kraft's now famous macaroni and cheese dinner was introduced in 1937, and Parkay margarine entered the limelight in 1940. Once again, the company benefited when it became a major food supplier to the Army during World War II.

To market its growing list of products, the company sponsored the *Kraft Musical Review* in 1933, which evolved into the *Kraft Music Hall*, hosted by Bing Crosby. In 1947 the company created *Kraft Television Theatre*, the first network program on **television**.

Cheez Whiz was launched in 1952, individually wrapped cheese slices in 1965, and Light n' Lively yogurt in 1969.

Because of a shrinking tobacco market, the Philip Morris Company purchased **General Foods** in 1985. Kraft was added to its corporate holdings in 1988 followed by the purchase of **Nabisco** in 2000.

Because Kraft Foods is the world's second largest food and beverage company, there is probably not a refrigerator or cupboard in America that does not have at least one product made by the company. Some of these brands include **Post** cereals, Oscar Mayer meat products, Maxwell House **coffee**, Velveeta, Life Savers, Kool-Aid, Jell-O desserts, Planters nuts, Ritz crackers, and Snackwells low-fat cookies and crackers.

Despite being the country's largest **packaged** food company, with hundreds of brands, analysts say that Kraft has failed in recent years to introduce innovative and successful products. To reduce the bureaucracy and streamline the company, Kraft has eliminated thousands of jobs and closed numerous plants, and it is divesting itself of brands such as Life Savers, Altoids mints, and Milk-Bone Dog Snacks. In 2006 Irene B. Rosenfeld, chairwoman and chief executive of Frito-Lay North America, was hired as chief executive. Rosenfeld is one of only 12 women leading a Fortune 500 company. Upon assuming her position, she announced a new executive team to build a Kraft that is more aggressive, agile, and imaginative and that will focus more intensely on consumers' evolving food and beverage needs. The **Altria Group**, which had an 85 percent holding in Kraft, had been preparing the company for a spin-off once it resolves its nagging tobacco litigation cases, which happened in 2007.

See also Altria Group.

FURTHER READINGS: Mirabile, Lisa, ed. "Kraft General Foods Inc." *International Directory of Company Histories*. Vol. 2, 530–34. Chicago: St. James Press, 1990; Pederson, Jay P., ed. "Kraft Foods Inc." *International Directory of Company Histories*. Vol. 45, 235–243. Chicago: St. James Press, 2002.

Joseph M. Carlin

Krispy Kreme A red-glazed brick building with the familiar green roof and distinctive sign "Hot Doughnuts Now" marks the location of a Krispy Kreme Doughnut retail factory shop. When the sign is lit, committed customers know that hot, freshly made doughnuts are moving along an overhead conveyor belt.

Joe LeBeau, a French chef in New Orleans, is credited with developing this light and fluffy, yeast-raised doughnut sometime during the first quarter of the 20th century. Vernon Rudolph purchased the business in 1935 and set up his operation in Winston-Salem, North Carolina. The Beatrice Foods Company bought the company in 1970, but operated the company without success. Krispy Kreme's largest **franchisees** then purchased the company from Beatrice in the 1980s.

Once largely confined to the South, Krispy Kreme moved into New York City and invaded Dunkin' Donuts' home territory in New England in the 1990s. During the first part of the 21st century the companies lost market share because of overbuilding their large and expensive factory stores and being dependent on one product in an increasingly health-conscious world. A federal investigation of accounting practices and lawsuits by shareholders and franchisees compounded the company's problems. Unlike other food **chains** such as Dunkin' Donuts and Honey Dew Donuts, Krispy Kreme sells mostly doughnuts. In contrast, 63 percent of Dunkin' Donuts sales come from **coffee**. Many of Dunkin's regular customers never buy doughnuts at all, perhaps making a health-conscious decision to buy bagels with low-fat cream cheese or a high-fiber bran muffin.

Some analysts believe that Krispy Kreme made a strategic mistake by wholesaling fresh doughnuts to **supermarkets**, gas stations, and convenience stores in the vicinity of their distinctive stores. For consumers, the novelty of standing in line to see their hot doughnuts being made took a back seat to the convenience of getting their Krispy Kreme doughnuts with their groceries or at the gas pump.

By 2006 the company had 334 stores, including 293 factory stores. Krispy Kreme is still ranked among the Top 100 Chains by *Nation's Restaurant News*, but its 26th rating in 2005 dropped to the 65th position a year later. In 2006 the company entered into a joint venture with the Lotte Company to open 40 stores in Tokyo. This decision was based upon the successful introduction of nine Krispy Kreme stores in South Korea. The food conglomerate Americana Group, based in Kuwait, has also been awarded franchise rights to open as many as 100 Krispy Kreme outlets in the Middle East. While Krispy Kreme has seen its bottom line dipped in red ink, their doughnuts are still, as the sign says, hot.

FURTHER READING: Grant, Tina, and Jay P. Pederson, eds. "Krispy Kreme Doughnut Corporation." In *International Directory of Company Histories*, 21: 322–24. Detroit: St. James Press, 1998.

Joseph M. Carlin

Labor and Labor Unions Labor issues have perennially shaken the food industry since its inception in the 19th century, as workers in agriculture, food processing, and transportation have always been among the lowest paid in the U.S. workforce. Better working conditions, minimum wages and pensions, and equal opportunity without discrimination on the basis of race or sex were merely a few of the great labor battles waged in the 20th century. Food industry workers have been central players in all the major labor disputes. The majority of food-oriented unions have until very recently been part of the AFL-CIO (American Federation of Labor and the Congress of Industrial Organizations, the two most powerful U.S. unions, which merged in 1955). This organization has concentrated the collective bargaining power of workers who would otherwise have been separated into distinct unions—the Teamsters for transport, the United Farm Workers (UFW) for agriculture, and the United Food and Commercial Workers International Union (UFCW), which in 2005 withdrew from the larger organization.

The situation has also been complicated by the dependence on inexpensive migrant labor, especially in fruit and vegetable harvesting and meat processing. Because they are not U.S. citizens, such workers are invited as guests (originally through the Bracero program), largely from Mexico. They are not subject therefore to U.S. labor standards and have often been ruthlessly exploited. The same, of course, applies to illegal immigrants, who have found work in various sectors of the food industry, especially meat processing. Interestingly, labor movements such as the UFW, the descendant of Cesar Chavez's historic union efforts to gain rights for farmworkers in the 1960s through **boycotts** on grapes, have also been supporters for stiff legislation against illegal immigrants.

Certain sectors of the food industry, most notably **fast food** operations and grocery outlets such as Wal-Mart, have been the target of trenchant criticism. These businesses depend largely on part-time workers who receive no health care benefits or overtime pay. Because the work has been highly mechanized, in the case of fast food **franchises**, it is essentially deskilled. Practically anyone, by and large teenagers, can operate the essentially foolproof machinery. Understandably, the turnover of employees is extremely high, and thus workers have had little incentive to collectively bargain. The corporations themselves have also been overtly hostile toward unions.

They recognize that higher wages, better working conditions, and health care coverage would all cut into their profits. It has been easier to make labor as cheap and expendable as possible.

Labor issues are likely to be among the most pressing problems facing the food industry in coming decades. It is becoming increasingly difficult to find affordable labor in the United States, especially in agriculture and food processing. The solution traditionally has been to mechanize, getting machines to do work for which one would otherwise have had to pay a human, and to produce everything on a larger scale. In the long run, however, it is increasingly cost-effective to have food grown and processed abroad, where labor is still inexpensive. What will happen when so-called developing nations themselves achieve higher living standards and greater expectations remains to be seen.

See also Agricultural Unions.

Darius Willoughby

Laws and Legal Issues. *See* Food Laws and Regulations.

Libby's From the Civil War until the 1920s, Chicago was the nation's slaughtering and **meatpacking** center. One of the firms contributing to the city's meaty reputation was Libby, McNeill, and Libby, created in 1868 by brothers Arthur and Charles Libby with Archibald McNeill. Although the company no longer exists, their Libby's-brand **canned** food products continue to grace American pantries.

The history of Libby's is emblematic of American corporate history. What began as a family company producing a single food grew into an industry leader whose brand became a household name. For years, the company succeeded amid changes in consumption patterns, technological developments, and shifts within corporate culture. Eventually, however, the increasingly powerful corporate conglomerates overpowered the small company, which filed for bankruptcy. Other industry leaders acquired the successful brand and assumed production of the goods.

The first Libby's-brand product was canned corned **beef**, introduced in 1868. In 1875, the company began canning the meat in a distinctive, trapezoidal metal container, a shape still used today. This popular meat product was easily distributed to consumers nationwide, thanks to the extensive network of railroads that passed through Chicago, the same rail lines that brought the animals to the city for slaughter and propelled the city's reputation as a manufacturing center. By the late 1880s, Libby's packed 35 million cans annually, filling the bellies of American and European consumers. By 1918, Libby's was the second largest meat canner in the United States.

As the meatpacking industry grew, so did Libby's product line early in the 20th century, to include canned vegetables and fruits. By the 1940s, annual sales of Libby's canned foods exceeded $100 million. Libby's influence on the consumer landscape was both gustatory and economic. As the company expanded its product line, its impact on food retailing, **advertising**, and agricultural communities throughout the country grew. From building a fruit-packing plant in Sunnyvale, California (1906), and **pickle** factories in Columbia and Willard, Wisconsin (around 1910), to establishing lemon orchards in Babson Park, Florida (1948), Libby's contributed to the livelihood and the meals of many Americans.

Despite its products' popularity, the company struggled to compete against global conglomerates and, in the late 1970s, declared bankruptcy. As part of the bankruptcy settlement, Nestlé USA (a division of Switzerland-based Nestlé S.A., the world's largest food company) acquired the Libby's brand. Nestlé retained some of the Libby's line and licensed out production of other Libby's canned goods.

Production of Libby's fruit cocktail typifies the transition of ownership some branded foods go through, changing hands as many times as there are types of fruit in the canned medley. Libby's created its fruit cocktail around 1906. Upon acquiring the Libby's brand, Nestlé licensed the fruit canning division to Tri-Valley Growers cooperative. When Tri-Valley went into bankruptcy in 2001, the canneries producing Libby's fruit cocktail went to one of their creditors, Signature Fruit, a company held by the John Hancock Life Insurance Company. In 2006, New York State–based Seneca Foods, a major canned foods producer that already had the license to produce Libby's canned vegetables, acquired Signature Fruit and the license to make Libby's fruit cocktail. By this time, Corlib Brand Holding owned the Libby's brand: all companies producing Libby's-brand products must pay royalties to Corlib for use of the name. In little more than a century, Libby's evolved from a family business to a globally recognized brand of canned foods produced by multiple international conglomerates.

Pauline Adema

Liquor. *See* Distilled Beverages.

M

Marketing of Milk The marketing and sale of milk is controlled by federal milk marketing orders (FMMO), a complex set of rules that aim to maintain orderly market conditions; benefit producers, processors, and consumers by establishing and maintaining orderly marketing conditions; and assure consumers of adequate supplies of a safe, quality product at all times. **Dairy** farmers are therefore assured of a reasonable minimum price for their milk, while consumers are provided with an adequate supply of milk to meet their needs and are shielded from wild fluctuations in price during periods of heavy and light milk production. To this end, each FFMO establishes a classified price plan, system of minimum prices, terms of the order, and provisions for administering the order. Currently, federal milk marketing orders are in existence for nine regions of the United States: Northeast, Appalachian, Southeast Florida, Mideast, Central, Upper Midwest, Southwest, Pacific Northwest, and Arizona.

Many states exert control over milk marketing within their borders with their own sets of marketing orders, as well. Like the federal orders, state milk marketing orders emerged in the 1930s as a means to bring order to the chaos of the Great Depression. The extant classified pricing system broke down under the new economic conditions. Caught in the downward spiral, consumer purchasing power fell, and demand for milk dropped. In the meantime, farmers exacerbated the situation by increasing milk production, hoping to make up for the lost income brought on by lack of demand and lowered prices. Seeing that neither farmers nor consumers would benefit from this situation, many states took steps to intervene. In fact, while both state and federal milk marketing orders were established at roughly the same time and for similar reasons, the state efforts enjoyed earlier acceptance. FMMOs did not see widespread support for another two decades, in part because the fluid milk markets at the time were purely local (transportation and storage technology not being what it is today), making it more practical to manage them at the state level.

Wisconsin was the first state to pass milk control legislation, in 1932, and within the next year its example was followed by almost two dozen more states. Prior to the Depression, cooperatives had played a strong role in milk marketing by helping farmers negotiate prices with processors and dealers, and it was here that the classified pricing plan came into existence. Milk was to be priced according to usage, being for either bottled (for fluid usage) or storable dairy products such as cheese and butter.

Higher value was placed on fluid-use milk in these schemes, a fact that remains to this day.

As it was believed that excessive competition was the cause of the Great Depression, many marketing orders were geared toward controlling competition. Since then, state milk control has declined due to legal challenges to the anticompetitive nature of these rules, but state milk marketing orders still exist in nine states: Virginia, Pennsylvania, New York, New Jersey, Nevada, North Dakota, Maine, Montana, and California.

The oldest and largest state milk marketing order in terms of pooled milk is California's, which was passed in 1935 after it was determined that federal orders could not be enforced in the state due to the local nature of the market. An order establishes a "uniform price" for all producers that contribute their milk. This ensures that all producers receive the same price regardless of whether their individual contributions are sold for fluid or other uses. As the former commands higher prices, this system allows all producers to participate and benefit from the higher-valued market.

The Pennsylvania marketing orders also predate congressional legislation that enacted the FMMOs, but they operate in conjunction with two federal orders (numbers 4 and 36). The state maintains a separate agency, the Pennsylvania Milk Marketing Board, which operates as a legal cartel and regulates prices at the farm, wholesale, and retail levels among six marketing areas in the state. Fluid milk prices maintained by Pennsylvania have been consistently higher than federal rates since 1988.

Milk marketing is unlike almost any other food-product marketing because the goal of milk pricing is to ensure a flow of a continuously produced product. Cows cannot start and stop production on demand, and milk's high perishability means that sanitary conditions must be observed at every step, from udder to milk carton. In contrast, other food commodities are priced in batches according to set criteria, with prices varying for each batch. Neither can milk producers store their products in warehouses, like **wheat** or potato farmers do, to wait for a better price; once obtained from the cow, milk must be processed and delivered to the consumer within a matter of days. When considering how milk came to involve such complicated marketing practices, it is useful to bear these unique characteristics in mind and reflect upon the challenges they present to the mass-production and commoditization of this age-old basic food.

FURTHER READINGS: Bailey, Kenneth W. *Marketing and Pricing of Milk and Dairy Products in the United States.* Ames: Iowa State University Press, 1997; Manchester, Alden Coe. *Issues in Milk Pricing and Marketing.* Agricultural Economic Report no. 393, USDA, 1–19. Washington, D.C.: Economic Research Service, U.S. Dept. of Agriculture, 1977.

Karen Y. Lau

Marketing to Children The direct marketing of foods (including beverages) to children constitutes a distinct enterprise, one that encompasses businesses engaged in **research**, **advertising**, and public relations that meet in annual conventions and operate under an industry-wide code of ethics. Recently, as concerns about the influence of food marketing on childhood **obesity** have intensified, this enterprise has expanded to include law and lobbying firms retained to protect food companies' First Amendment rights to market to children and to defend the industry against lawsuits and regulations. Because most firms engaged in marketing to children also market to adults, it is difficult to estimate the size of this enterprise, but marketers are believed to spend about $10 billion annually in the United States to promote sales of foods and food products to children.

Marketing to children is not a new phenomenon. Vance Packard's 1957 exposé of the advertising industry, *The Hidden Persuaders*, described the research methods then used by companies to discover how to entice young children to request products at the grocery store. Since then, the food industry's interest in attracting children's purchases has expanded. In the early 1980s, changes in U.S. policies encouraged farmers to produce more food, and the number of calories in the food supply (production plus imports less exports) rose from 3,200 calories per capita per day to 3,900 in the early 2000s, an amount roughly twice average need. Rates of obesity rose in parallel. The early 1980s also marked the advent of the shareholder value movement; its demands for higher immediate returns on investment forced companies to increase sales to meet quarterly growth targets. To meet growth goals, food companies developed new products and ways of selling them, and children became increasingly important targets of such efforts.

Business Rationale

From a business standpoint, marketing to children makes sense. Although children usually have only small amounts of money from allowances, gifts, and jobs, together they spend an estimated $30 billion annually on food purchases and control much larger amounts through their influence on family purchasing decisions. Their influence is attributed to changes in society. Today's families are smaller and headed by older, wealthier, and often more indulgent parents. Working and single parents tend to delegate more responsibility to children. Perceptions of danger keep children indoors under "house arrest" watching **television**, playing video games, or surfing the **Internet**, where they are exposed to advertisements for purchasable products. Busy families often view children's requests for food products as benign, easy to satisfy, and rarely worth a struggle.

Beyond the amounts spent, companies cite three purposes in marketing to children: brand loyalty, the "pester factor," and "kid cuisine." Early habits establish brand preferences, and children especially want to buy sweets, **soft drinks**, **snack foods**, and **fast food**. In particular, they influence purchases of a substantial proportion of the sales of certain foods: 25 percent of the total amount of salty snacks, 30 percent of soft drinks, 40 percent of frozen pizza, and 50 percent of cold **breakfast cereals**, for example. For the companies that make such products, marketing to children is an essential part of normal business practice.

In addition to fostering brand loyalty, food marketers promote the pester factor and kid cuisine. Marketing campaigns encourage children to ask their parents for foods by sight and by brand name and encourage children to request foods designed specifically for their age group. Such foods are readily identified by illustrations of cartoon characters or celebrities on the packages and by their attractive colors and shapes. Thus, food marketing aims to place children, rather than adults, in charge of decisions about what they and their families eat.

None of this would raise questions if the advertised foods were healthier, but most marketing efforts are directed toward "junk foods," the pejorative term for foods that are highly processed, relatively high in calories, depleted in nutrients, and made with inexpensive ingredients. Children today eat large amounts of such foods. In contrast to their diets in the 1950s, the diets of up to 80 percent of young children today are considered poor or in need of improvement. Societal trends foster such patterns. Children are eating fewer organized meals at home, but more fast food, snacks, and soft drinks. On average, children derive nearly one-third of their calories from such foods.

Companies introduce many new products every year to tap this market, three-fourths of them **candy**, gum, other sweets, or salty snacks. Companies spend substantial sums to market these products and receive substantial returns on those investments. In 2005, for example, **McDonald's** spent $742 million on direct media advertising (radio, television, print, Internet) and perhaps twice as much on other marketing methods to generate nearly $7 billion in sales in the United States. On a smaller scale, in 2004 **Campbell's Soup** spent about $9 million on direct media to generate $168 million in sales of Goldfish snacks, Kellogg spent $22 million to sell $140 million of Cheez-Its, and Domino's Pizza spent $131 million to generate $3.2 billion in sales.

Food companies make and market such foods as harmless amusements. They say they are just offering choices and that the parents—not food companies—are responsible for what children eat. Marketing to children, they say, is an expression of free speech and an education in "street smarts." This rationale, however, has come under scrutiny as children's poor diets and obesity have emerged as significant health problems. Since the early 1980s, rates of obesity have doubled among children ages 6–11 and tripled among children ages 12–19. Food marketing is increasingly viewed as contributing to these trends.

Food Marketing Research

Research on marketing to children involves interviews, focus groups, and direct observations of children's food preferences and behavior. Studies demonstrate that even very young children are aware of advertised brands, establish strong preferences for them, and respond to messages that appeal to their desires for sensual gratification, play, fun, friends, and nurturance. By age 2, most children can recognize products in **supermarkets** and ask for them by name. By age 7 or 8, they can shop independently. But only after the age of 9 or 10 do children begin to distinguish the purpose and content of commercial messages. Even some high school students have difficulty identifying sales messages cloaked as entertainment or information.

Today's marketing methods are more intensive and pervasive than those in the past. Television remains the dominant method for reaching children, but the balance is shifting to product placements in toys, games, clothing, educational materials, songs, and movies; cartoon licensing and celebrity endorsements; and stealth methods such as "advergames" and "viral" campaigns involving word-of-mouth, cellular-telephone text messages, and the Internet. Many food companies reach children in schools through label redemption programs, teaching materials, advertising at sports events, coupon campaigns, and giveaways. In the late 1990s, soft drink companies initiated contracts with school districts for exclusive sales of their products in **vending machines** and at sports events. Because these contracts rewarded schools for purchases, they appeared to promote consumption of soft drinks and brought attention to the idea that sweetened beverages contribute to childhood obesity.

How effective is food marketing to children? Studies of this question invariably conclude that marketing profoundly influences children's preferences for brands and food categories, particularly for the most heavily advertised breakfast cereals, soft drinks, candy, snacks, and fast foods. Studies in the 1970s showed that television commercials influenced children's food choices and demands, and later studies have repeatedly correlated children's caloric intake and obesity with hours spent watching television.

The Challenge of Obesity

In seeking to reverse rising rates of overweight, especially among children, health advocates as well as investment bankers, lawyers, and legislators have singled out food marketing as an important influence on food choice. By 2003, three British investment banking firms had warned food industry clients that obesity posed a threat to company profits and urged them to produce healthier foods and market them more responsibly or face lawsuits and regulations.

Concerns about childhood obesity prompted Congress to commission the Institute of Medicine (IOM) to review nearly 125 research studies on the effects of food marketing on children's health. The IOM's 2005 report noted that food marketing pervades children's lives, targets children too young to distinguish advertising from truth, and induces them to eat high-calorie, low-nutrient foods. The report called on food companies to develop and enforce higher standards for food marketing and warned them that if they failed to do so, they would bring on regulations such as those in effect in 50 other countries. In 2006, the American Academy of Pediatrics called for laws to ban junk food advertising in schools and on television as well as for a 50 percent decrease in the time permitted for commercials during children's television.

By 2006, advocacy groups were threatening to sue Kellogg and the Nickelodeon network to stop them from marketing junk food to children, dozens of state legislatures had introduced bills to curb such marketing, and parent and advocacy groups had demanded bans on food marketing in schools. In the United States, the First Amendment protects commercial speech, and attempts to regulate television advertising to children since the 1970s have failed on this basis. In recent years, however, Congress has introduced bills that would permit regulation of marketing directed at children. Although these have not passed, advocacy groups are exploring ways to use legislative and legal strategies to restrict marketing of junk foods to children.

Self-Regulation versus Regulation

Obesity poses difficult challenges for food companies caught between the demands of children's health advocates and those of stockholders and Wall Street analysts. Companies deal with this dilemma through self-regulation of marketing practices, developing "better-for-you" products and pressing for legislation that protects them against legal liability.

Food companies participate in the Children's Advertising Review Unit (CARU) of the Better Business Bureau, which sets voluntary guidelines for self-regulation. CARU guidelines say that advertisements to children should be truthful and not misleading and should not induce children to pester their parents, should encourage good nutritional practices, and should depict products within the context of a balanced diet. Analyses by advocacy groups, however, cite many examples of violations of CARU guidelines.

In July 2003, **Kraft Foods** promised to set standards for marketing practices and to eliminate all in-school marketing. Two years later, the company said it would only advertise its Sensible Solution (healthier) products to children ages 6–11. Other food companies viewed these actions as an admission of guilt that would encourage regulation. Yet Kraft also said it would not reduce its annual $80 million annual expenditure on advertising to children, and it joined General Mills, Kellogg, and other companies in creating the Alliance for American Advertising aimed at protecting the industry's First Amendment right to market to children.

Nevertheless, most major food companies are reformulating existing products for children or creating new products with health attributes that can be used as sales incentives. For example, PepsiCo produces snack foods with "0 grams trans fat," General Mills adds whole grains to its cereals, and Kraft has reduced the **sugars** in some of its cereals and added polydextrose to increase the fiber content. This strategy is based on the as-yet untested assumption that small improvements in nutritional values will produce a large health benefits across the entire population.

Companies also establish their own criteria for evaluating the nutritional quality of their products. PepsiCo identifies its "better-for-you" products with green Smart Spots. General Mills cereals have Goodness Corners. Kellogg cereals have flags, and Kraft's healthier options are designated as Sensible Solutions. The companies' nutritional criteria permit many of their own products to qualify. In 2006, Hannaford, a supermarket chain in the Northeast, developed independent criteria for a "Guiding Stars" program that awards one, two, or three stars to foods based on nutritional values. By Hannaford's criteria, fewer than 25 percent of the store's 27,000 products—and hardly any of the food companies' self-endorsed products—qualify for even one star.

In 2006, a foundation headed by former president Bill Clinton and the American Heart Association induced the American Beverage Association to agree to phase out sweetened beverages in schools and also induced five leading food manufacturers to set nutritional standards for snacks sold in schools. Ten of the world's largest food companies voluntarily announced formation of a new Children's Food and Beverage Advertising Initiative to limit the marketing of foods of poor nutritional quality. The initiative called for half of television advertising to promote healthier foods or lifestyles, for cessation of advertising in elementary schools, and for reduction of use of licensed cartoon characters in advertising for foods that do not meet nutritional standards. A 2006 federal report on food industry self-regulation viewed such actions as favorable, but said that companies needed to do much more to set higher nutrition standards for foods marketed to children.

In 2002, McDonald's was sued on behalf of two teenagers who claimed they had become overweight and chronically ill as a result of eating at its restaurants. Although such suits might appear frivolous, they are taken seriously by the courts. Food companies responded by pressing state legislatures to pass "Commonsense Consumption" laws to exempt them from civil liability for obesity and its health consequences. By 2006, 23 states had passed such legislation. The House proposed a federal act in 2005 that would force dismissal of all anti-obesity court cases, new and pending, but the bill failed to pass in 2006. States remain the focus of such attempts; in 2005, 26 states considered such legislation and another 16 did so in 2006.

Such events indicate that food companies need to change business practices in response to childhood obesity or are likely to be forced to change them through lawsuits and regulations. By 2007, industry publications ranked campaigns for regulation of food marketing to children as among the top legal issues facing food companies in the years to come.

FURTHER READINGS: American Academy of Pediatrics. "Children, Adolescents, and Advertising." *Pediatrics* 118, no. 6 (December 2006): 2563–69. Available at http://pediatrics.aappubli cations.org/cgi/content/full/118/6/2563; California Pan-Ethnic Health Network and Consumers Union. "Out of Balance: Marketing of Soda, Candy, Snacks and Fast Foods Drowns Out Healthful Messages." September 2005. Available at http://www.consumersunion.org/pdf/Outof Balance.pdf; Federal Trade Commission and Department of Health and Human Services. *Perspectives on Marketing Self-Regulation and Childhood Obesity.* Washington, D.C.: GPO, 2006; Gardner, Stephen. "Litigation as a Tool in Food Advertising: A Consumer Advocacy Viewpoint." *Loyola (Los Angeles) Law Review* 39 (2006): 101–20; Institute of Medicine. *Food Marketing to Children and Youth: Threat or Opportunity?* Washington, D.C.: National Academies Press, 2005; Moore, Elizabeth S. *It's Child's Play: Advergaming and the Online Marketing of Food to Children.* Menlo Park, CA: Kaiser Family Foundation, 2006. Available at http://www.kff.org/entmedia/upload/7536.pdf; Nestle, Marion. *Food Politics: How the Food Industry Influences Nutrition and Health.* 2nd ed. Berkeley: University of California Press, 2007.

Marion Nestle

McDonald's

> "The two most important requirements for major success are: first, being in the right place at the right time, and second, doing something about it."—Ray Kroc, founder of McDonald's
>
> *Source:* http://www.brainyquote.com

In 1930, Richard and Maurice McDonald, born in New Hampshire, moved to Los Angeles attracted by potential employment in the movie industry. They bought a small movie theater, but it was not successful. To make ends meet in 1937, they opened an orange juice and **hot dog** stand near the Santa Anita racetrack in Arcadia, a suburb of Los Angeles. Their stand grew, but they found that their customers were more interested in purchasing barbecue and hamburgers. In 1940, they opened the McDonald Brothers Drive-in on E Street in San Bernardino, California. It featured 20 female carhops picking up and delivering barbecue and hamburgers. The brothers then noted that 80 percent of their sales were hamburgers, and so they dropped the barbecue, which also took too long to make.

Assembly-Line Hamburgers

After World War II, the McDonald brothers decided upon a radical change to reduce expenses and increase profits by increasing efficiency. A central feature of their operation was an industrial assembly-line model popularized by Henry Ford, whose techniques had previously been adapted for use in food service by **cafeterias** and automats, on railway dining cars, and at the Howard Johnson's **restaurant chain**. The model included a division of labor into simple tasks that could be performed with a minimum of training. This meant that their employees were essentially interchangeable and could easily be shifted from one task to another. The brothers redesigned the kitchen, making room for larger grills and **labor**-saving equipment, and created an efficient assembly line to make hamburgers and French fries. This assembly-line model provided customers with fast, reliable, and inexpensive food; in return, customers were expected stand in line and pick up their own food, eat quickly, clean up their own waste, and leave without delay, thereby making room for others.

The McDonald brothers were convinced that their target audience was families, so they tried to create an environment that would attract them. They concluded that their new operation needed to discourage teenagers, who bought little but littered and broke or stole cups, glasses, plates, silverware, and trays. The main reason teenage boys visited drive-ins, the brothers reasoned, was to flirt with the carhops. Hence, the brothers did away with carhops, who the brothers believed were more interested in socializing than selling burgers anyway. They also did away with the plates, glasses, and tableware, replacing them with paper and plastic utensils.

To implement these ideas, the McDonalds closed their restaurant, installed larger grills, and purchased Multimixers, which made many milkshakes simultaneously. Eighty or more shakes were prepared in advance and placed in a refrigerated holding case, thus speeding up the process of fulfilling orders with milkshakes.

They also developed a militarized production system that was based on teenage boys, who were responsible for simple tasks—some heated the hamburgers, others packaged the food or poured the **soft drinks** and the shakes, and still others placed the orders into paper bags. This division of labor meant that workers needed to be trained to perform only a single task. Their new restaurant did away with indoor seating and greatly reduced the menu to a few low-cost items: 15-cent hamburgers, 19-cent cheeseburgers, 10-cent fries, 20-cent shakes, and large and small sodas. The hamburger patties weighed only 1.5 ounces and all burgers came with the same **condiments**: ketchup, chopped onion, and two **pickle** slices. In their new "self-service" restaurant, customers placed their orders at a window and ate in their cars. All food was placed in disposable paper wrappers and paper cups, so there was no breakage or loss due to theft. The service was speedy: the McDonald brothers claimed that their employees could serve a customer who ordered everything that they had—hamburger, fries, and a beverage—in 20 seconds.

Increased volume led to greater profits. Reports of their phenomenal success spread around the nation and *American Restaurant* ran a cover story on the "McDonald's New Self-Service System" in July 1952. The brothers used their national visibility to advertise for franchisees. Unlike previous food-service **franchises**, the brothers demanded that every franchise be constructed in the same way as their model and that each outlet sell the exact same food prepared in the exact same way. This model promised consistency, predictability, and safety. By the end of 1953, the brothers had 10 operating franchises in the Los Angeles area and Phoenix.

The McDonald's restaurant in San Bernardino attracted large crowds, and many future **fast food** entrepreneurs visited the site. Ray Kroc, an owner of the Chicago company that sold Multimixers, visited the McDonalds' operation in 1954 and was astounded by the crowds. Kroc met with the brothers and signed an agreement allowing him to sell McDonald's franchises nationwide. In 1955 Kroc created McDonald's System, Inc., and sold himself the first franchise in Des Plaines, Illinois, which he opened in 1955. He intended it to be a model operation that would attract potential franchisees.

By the end of 1959, there were more than a hundred McDonald's operations. The early success of McDonald's rested in part on the managers selected to oversee operations. Kroc's mantra was "Quality, Service, Cleanliness, and Value," which he tried to instill in every franchisee. Kroc bought out the McDonald brothers in 1961 for $2.7 million. By 1963 McDonald's was selling a million burgers a day, and this was only the beginning. The company began **advertising** nationally in 1966, the same year that McDonald's was first listed on the New York Stock Exchange. When Kroc died in 1984, there were 7,500 McDonald's outlets worldwide.

Promotion and Children

McDonald's national promotional campaigns have been a significant reason for its success. Its slogans, such as "You deserve a break today," which *Advertising Age* rated as the top advertising campaign in the 20th century, and its "Two all-**beef** patties, special sauce, lettuce, cheese, pickles, onions on a sesame seed bun" became national hits. According to Eric Schlosser, author of *Fast Food Nation*, McDonald's expends more on advertising and promotion than does any other hamburger operation.

Kroc initially targeted middle-class families with children in the suburbs. Children had "pester power," and studies indicated that children determined where many families ate. And children liked fast food establishments. McDonald's was a place where they could choose what they wanted to eat. Kroc set out to make visits to its outlets "fun experiences" for children. Ronald McDonald was selected as the company's national spokesperson in 1966. The McDonald's outlet in Chula Vista, near San Diego, opened the first McDonaldland Park in 1972. This proved to be such a success that McDonald's began opening bright-colored Playlands for children complete with playgrounds and mythical characters. McDonald's Happy Meal, inaugurated in 1979, packages its food with toys, and as a result, McDonald's became the world's largest toy distributor. By 1980 the millions of dollars expended on child-oriented television advertising and local promotions had succeeded: 96 percent of American children recognized Ronald McDonald, rating second only to Santa Claus.

New Product Development

To keep ahead of the competition, McDonald's regularly develops new products. It diversified its menu beginning in the 1960s. The Big Mac, with its two patties, originated with a Pittsburgh franchisee who was trying to create a product to compete with Burger King's "Big Whopper." It was released nationally in 1968. The Egg McMuffin debuted in 1973. By 1977 McDonald's were serving a complete line of breakfast sandwiches and biscuits for eating on the run. Other innovations include the Quarter Pounder, the McDLT, and the McLean Deluxe, a 90-percent fat-free hamburger that failed. In 1983 McDonald's introduced Chicken McNuggets, consisting of reconstituted chicken delivered frozen and then reheated before serving.

Globalization

McDonald's opened its first Canadian outlet in 1967. Its success convinced Kroc that McDonald's should aggressively expand to other countries. It has continued to expand abroad ever since. The company opened in Tokyo in 1971, followed by Australia and European countries. By 1988 McDonald's had established itself as one of France's most popular fast food operators. As of 1994, McDonald's counted more than 4,500 restaurants in 73 foreign countries. Today, McDonald's has more than 30,000 restaurants in 121 countries. It operates more than a thousand restaurants in Japan alone.

Challenges and Issues

Despite this success, McDonald's, along with other large fast food chains, faced numerous problems. The most serious problems identified by managers at McDonald's were rising labor costs, the high employee turnover rate, and the lack of reliable workers. In addition, in part because of McDonald's success, the company has been criticized on a variety of issues, and it has frequently responded positively to meet the criticism. In the 1960s, for example, the company was criticized for a lack of African American managers in its restaurants, and McDonald's made an effort to recruit more black franchisees. When it was charged with promoting junk food, the company began selling salads, reduced the fat content of its hamburgers, and changed the way it made its French fries.

Critics charged McDonald's with causing harm to the environment, specifically for its use of polystyrene foam for its **coffee** cups and food containers for Big Macs and Quarter Pounders. polystyrene, a plastic, is not easily biodegradable, and McDonald's was the world's largest purchaser of it. The company responded by creating an alliance with the Environmental Defense Fund to make McDonald's more environmentally friendly. It company changed from polystyrene to paper products and began encouraging recycling. The Environmental Defense Fund has estimated that since 1989, McDonald's has saved 150,000 tons of waste due to the improved packaging it has required of its suppliers. In addition, the company has purchased more than $4 billion of recycled materials for its own operations. As a result of these environmentally friendly programs, McDonald's has received a good deal of positive press coverage.

McDonald's has also been charged with causing adverse affects on local cultures and businesses around the world. In other countries, McDonald's is viewed as an American symbol, and it has both gained and suffered as a consequence. McDonald's outlets have been trashed, bombed, and boycotted due to policies of the U.S. government. Some believe that McDonald's expansion threatens local culinary traditions. In France, José Bové demolished a McDonald's restaurant that was nearing completion. Similar actions have occurred in other European countries. At other times and places, McDonald's has been considered a modernizing force that has improved culinary conditions. McDonald's has pointed out that many of its foreign operations are locally owned and most products used in McDonald's are produced in-country.

McDonald's Today

Studying McDonald's has also become a hot academic topic, and many popular works have tried to dissect its success and examine the company's influence. Among the more famous studies are George Ritzer's *The McDonaldization of Society* (1993), which examined the social effects of McDonald's in the United States, and Benjamin Barber's *Jihad vs. McWorld* (1995), which used the fast food giant as a global symbol for modernization. Dozens of other works have examined McDonald's worldwide impact.

Today, one out of every eight American workers has at some point been employed by McDonald's. Studies proclaim that 96 percent of Americans have visited McDonald's at least once, and McDonald's serves an estimated 22 million Americans every day. It has expanded even more rapidly abroad. In 1994 McDonald's operating revenues from non-U.S. sales passed the 50 percent mark.

McDonald's is one of the world's most famous brand names. The company is an icon for efficient and successful business and is ingrained in popular culture throughout the world. McDonald's is the largest purchaser of beef, pork, and potatoes and the second largest purchaser of chicken. It is the largest owner of retail estate in the world, and it earns the majority of its profits not from selling food, but from collecting rent.

See also Cultural Imperialism; Marketing to Children; Multinationals; Poultry Industry.

FURTHER READINGS: Boas, Max, and Steve Chain. *Big Mac: The Unauthorized Story of McDonald's.* New York: New American Library, 1977; Cartensen, Laurence W. "The Burger Kingdom: Growth and Diffusion of McDonald's Restaurants in the United States, 1955–1978." In George O. Carney, ed., *Fast Food, Stock Cars, and Rock 'n' Roll: Place and Space in American Pop Culture.* Lanham, MD: Rowman & Littlefield, 1995; Fishwick, Marshall, ed. *Ronald Revisited: The World of Ronald McDonald.* Bowling Green, OH: Bowling Green University Popular Press, 1983; Kroc, Ray, with Robert Anderson. *Grinding It Out: The Making of McDonald's.* Chicago: Regnery, 1977; Love, John F. *McDonald's: Behind the Arches.* Rev. ed. New York: Bantam Books, 1995; Ritzer, George. *The McDonaldization of Society.* Rev. ed. Thousand Oaks, CA: Pine Forge Press, 1993; Royle, Tony. *Working for McDonald's in Europe: The Unequal Struggle?* New York: Routledge, 2001; Schlosser, Eric. *Fast Food Nation: The Dark Side of the All-American Meal.* New York: Perennial, 2002; Watson, James L., ed. *Golden Arches East: McDonald's in East Asia.* Stanford, CA: Stanford University Press, 1997.

Andrew F. Smith

Meat Packing Since its origins in the 19th century, the meatpacking industry has used the technologies of mass production and **refrigerated** transport to increase popular access to animal protein. Nevertheless, the variability of live animals and their rapid deterioration after slaughter slowed the application of industrial techniques and led ultimately to significant changes in the taste and healthfulness of meat.

Humans have salted and smoked meats to slow decay since ancient times, and rules governing the industry have been a focus of religious and civic authorities. Medieval butchers guilds, for example, regulated the preparation of a wide range of sausage, hams, and fresh meats. Early modern urbanization in Europe encouraged a continental trade in livestock, which expanded further in the 19th century with railroad and steamship transport. Bringing live animals to market, however, posed significant pollution problems and also spread diseases such as pleuropneumonia, bovine tuberculosis, and foot-and-mouth disease.

The growth of industrial packing in stock-raising regions promised to increase urban meat supplies while avoiding these drawbacks. The transformation began in Cincinnati about 1830 with the large-scale slaughter of hogs from throughout the Ohio River Valley. Packers devised an efficient division of **labor**, employing teams of specialized workers, each of whom performed a single, repetitive task, cutting away a ham or a side of bacon, until the hog vanished completely at the end of this "disassembly line." Once packed in barrels of brine, the meat was shipped east by barge. At first, the industry functioned only in winter months, when freezing temperatures slowed the process of decay, but by the 1850s the arrival of railroads and ice harvesting extended production year-round. During the Civil War, access to hogs fattened on **corn** from Iowa and Nebraska allowed Chicago to replace Cincinnati as the meatpacking capital, "Porkopolis."

Mechanical refrigeration was another critical breakthrough, giving urban consumers greater access to fresh **beef**. Unlike pork, which took well to curing, corned and jerked beef were less palatable. The 1867 opening of the Chisholm Trail, driving Texas longhorns north to the railhead at Abilene, Kansas, replaced declining local supplies for eastern markets. Yet live cattle transport had barely begun when George Hammond first shipped beef by railroad icebox, and within a decade, refrigerated rail cars had become economical. Applying the same industrial techniques used for hogs, the Chicago meatpacking firms of Hammond, **Swift**, and **Armour** dominated the beef trade as well by the turn of the 20th century.

Horizontally integrated packinghouses processing all manner of livestock facilitated industrial concentration. These multistory factories benefited from economies of scale by making continuous use of facilities, unlike local butchers who slaughtered at most for a few hours a day, and by replacing skilled tradesmen with a relatively untrained industrial workforce. The logistics of shipping offered further advantages, since only half the animal's weight comprised edible meat, and much of that was lost through wastage during the long trip east. Industrial packers also profited from the sale of by-products such as blood, bones, hooves, and horns, which were processed into a wide range of goods, including **fertilizer**, glue, and buttons. Local butchers could not withstand relentless price competition by the Big Five, later Four, who gained an oligopolistic grip on national markets, excepting only the specialized demand of the kosher meat trade.

Industrial meatpacking practices raised concerns over the health of both workers and consumers. Profit-minded executives constantly worked to speed up the pace of production, which led to countless debilitating injuries among exhausted workers. Moreover, to convey meats to distant markets without apparent rotting, firms routinely employed borax and boracic acid, antiseptic compounds originally used to treat wounded soldiers in the Civil War. Upton Sinclair's muckraking novel *The Jungle* (1906), which graphically depicted dangerous, unsanitary conditions in Chicago packinghouses, finally assured action by Congress to require the inspection of foods sold in interstate commerce. Sinclair's primary goal of improving workplace conditions was achieved only through decades of union organizing and strikes.

Long before there was *Fast Food Nation*, there was *The Jungle*. Upton Sinclair wrote it for a socialist magazine in 1905, and it was published in book form in 1906. It was intended to be an exposé of working conditions in Chicago's meatpacking plants, but its descriptions of sanitary conditions in the plants so affected the American public that meat sales fell by 50 percent, forcing the government to enact the first Pure Food and Drug Act.

Sinclair later famously remarked that it was ironic that he had "aimed at the public's heart, and by accident hit it in the stomach."

Source: Leon Harris, *Upton Sinclair: American Rebel*. New York: Thomas Y. Crowell, 1975.

Beginning in the 1960s, however, these labor gains were lost as a new generation of meatpackers such as Iowa Beef Processors transformed the industry once again. These vertically integrated firms specialized in a single type of animal, while operating, ironically, in single-story buildings located near feedlots in rural areas. Slashing production costs, particularly wages and safety measures, they replaced established firms in the 1970s and 1980s. Their enormous plants operated production lines at extremely high speeds, increasing the risk both of injury to predominantly migrant workers as well as of food contamination.

The modern **poultry industry** likewise emerged in the postwar era when breeders developed broiler chickens with uniformly plump breast meat and rapid weight gain, a goal facilitated by **antibiotics**. The industry originated in Delaware to supply the New York market, but the dominant firms Perdue and Tyson later moved to lower-cost production sites in the South. Selling individually wrapped parts instead of whole chickens further increased profits, culminating in the creation of the boneless chicken nugget. By the end of the century, **fast food** sales had helped catapult chicken past beef and pork as the nation's leading meat.

The consolidation of feedlots and slaughter facilities for cattle, hogs, and poultry has raised public fears over nationwide epidemics of antibiotic-resistant *E. coli*, salmonella, and other infectious diseases. Most terrifying of all was the outbreak of **bovine spongiform encephalopathy** (BSE) in the United Kingdom in the 1980s. The so-called mad cow disease, initially caused by feeding cattle sheep tissue, has been linked to more than 150 human deaths in Britain alone. In the following two decades, cases of BSE also appeared in cattle in continental Europe, North America, and Japan. Nevertheless, growing health concerns have prompted an emerging trend back to local, sustainable production and perhaps someday to more moderate consumption as well.

See also Food Poisoning; Food Safety.

FURTHER READINGS: Horowitz, Roger. *Putting Meat on the American Table: Technology, Taste, Transformation.* Baltimore: Johns Hopkins University Press, 2006; Perren, Richard. *Taste, Trade and Technology: The Development of the International Meat Industry since 1840.* Aldershot, England: Ashgate, 2006; Pilcher, Jeffrey M. "Empire of the 'Jungle': The Rise of an Atlantic Refrigerated Beef Industry, 1880–1920." *Food, Culture & Society* 7, no. 1 (Fall 2004): 63–78; Stull, Donald, and Michael Broadway. *Slaughterhouse Blues: The Meat and Poultry Industry in North America.* Belmont, CA: Wadsworth, 2004.

Jeffrey M. Pilcher

Mercantilism Mercantilism refers to a diverse set of perspectives that claimed hegemony over economic thought for almost three centuries, between the early 1500s and the early 1800s. Mercantilism held that a country's wealth was best measured by the supply of capital held in its treasury. In particular, a country's level of prosperity was reflected in its stores of bullion, gold or silver, the quantity of which was best increased through a positive balance of trade (the proportion of exports over imports).

Mercantilist ideologies were especially concerned with state policies designed to ensure the export of manufactured and processed goods and the import of raw materials. At the same time, the state was expected to set policies that limited the loss of domestic raw materials while restricting the importation of finished goods. Foreign trade was privileged above domestic trade especially because of its capacity for bringing bullion into the country. Similarly industrial production was privileged above agriculture because the former provided the most desirable goods for foreign trade.

The term *mercantilism* was applied because the system primarily benefited the interests of merchants and producers, as opposed to the agricultural system espoused by the French physiocrats. Mercantilist policies expressed a symbiotic relationship between rent-seeking merchants, who benefited from bans on foreign competition and monopolization, and governments that benefited from the payments made by merchants. Monopolies such as the British East India Company, whose activities were sustained through the active intervention of the state, stand as enduring symbols of mercantilism.

Because wealth was viewed as a zero-sum competition, an active state was viewed as a necessary factor in securing a favorable balance of trade. Indeed, within mercantilist ideologies, state making was viewed as synonymous with nation making. Thus, the government had an important part to play within a mercantilist framework. Government protectionism and the use of tariffs were crucial for discouraging imports and encouraging exports.

Not coincidentally, mercantilism was the dominant school of economic thought throughout the period, from the early 16th to late 18th centuries, that saw the rise and entrenchment of the modern nation-state as the locus of political power domestically as well as internationally. Mercantilist economic perspectives, especially the view of life as a zero-sum game in which each side in a violent competition attempts to vanquish its opponent, found expression in the political writings of Thomas Hobbes and his call for a state "leviathan" to quell nature's struggle of all against all. In Europe, this period saw the replacement of the network of feudal estates by the centralized authority of the nation-state. Notably this was also the period during which much of the economic system of capitalism was established. Thus many commentators point, against the ideology of neoliberal **free traders**, to statist intervention as a necessary feature of capitalist development.

A crucial force propelling these developments was the fact of European contact with the Americas. The capturing of new sources of natural resources, especially minerals, along with the development of new markets, drove the development of foreign trade to unprecedented levels. The need for colonial possessions as suppliers of raw materials, especially minerals, fueled the ongoing violence that marked the mercantilist era. Violent conflict regularly broke out between the colonial powers as well as between the colonizers and their colonies. The need for a large supply of inexpensive **labor** drove the development and expansion of slavery under mercantilism.

The status of the working classes was one issue upon which advocates of mercantilism found agreement. For mercantilists, economic exploitation was necessary for the maximization of profit and, thus, there was little concern for the living conditions of workers and farmers beyond maintaining them at a level of bare subsistence that would allow them to keep producing. Calls for decreased work time and increased income for working people and the poor, as some reformers raised, were viewed as recipes for vice and avarice. Little attention was given to possible economic gains to be made from working-class consumption. Not limited to economic spheres, such positions would actually find expression in early manifestations of British sociology such as the writings of Herbert Spencer.

By the end of the 18th century, most of the economic ideas, if not the social ideas, associated with mercantilism had fallen from favor. Critics noted that government quotas and price controls encouraged the development of informal economies and "black markets."

The death knell of mercantilist economics was sounded by Adam Smith, who directed much of his 1776 masterwork *The Wealth of Nations* toward a sustained dismantling of mercantilism. The mercantilists' emphasis on bullion came under heavy fire from Smith, who argued that gold and silver, apart from being in limited supply, were simply commodities like any other.

David Hume argued against mercantilist notions of wealth by suggesting that a country's bullion reserves were related to the size of the economy rather than government trade policies. By the early 1800s David Ricardo's notions of comparative advantage suggested that trade need not be a zero-sum game or winner-take-all competition. By allowing for local efficiencies in production and specialization, Ricardo suggested, both states could benefit from exchange. In comparison, the imposition of import restrictions and **tariffs** could leave both sides less well off.

The Wealth of Nations had a tremendous impact on economic decision making and was uncritically accepted as the framework for economic policy throughout the British Empire. By the 19th century, the British government had fully taken on Smith's laissez-faire perspective and free trade became the order of the day. Monopolies and tariffs were removed and industrial regulation withdrawn.

The end of mercantilism came much later in Germany, where the historical school of economics, an advocacy of mercantilist ideology, held sway through the first decades of the 20th century. Notably, the United States did not adopt Smithian economics following independence but instead maintained a protectionist system of neo-mercantilism, as expressed in the policies of Alexander Hamilton and Abraham Lincoln.

Whatever its economic claims, however, the real legacies of mercantilism were colonial plunder, violence, and international warfare. During this period, armies and navies became professional standing institutions rather than temporary forces raised to address specific challenges.

Mercantilism has enjoyed something of a revival since the economic depression of the 1930s. Especially important in this regard has been the work of John Maynard Keynes, whose work is sometimes referred to as neo-mercantilist. Keynes was especially concerned with the positive role that government intervention in the economy might play.

Others argue, against contemporary proponents of free trade and neoliberal ideology, that some form of mercantilism is essential for the economies of poorer nations that need to protect infant industries. Countries like the United States and Britain, which attempt to coerce poorer nations into accepting the rule of free trade, as in structural adjustment programs, are condemned for prohibiting poorer countries from following the very economic practices that allowed the Western economies to become economic powerhouses (at the expense of their former colonies) in the first place.

Jeff Shantz

Middlemen The term *middlemen* is a purely colloquial expression referring to numerous segments of the food industry that neither grow or process food nor sell it directly to the customer in retail. They are therefore largely invisible to the consumer, even though their services ultimately account for a large percentage of the final cost of most food products. Middlemen include such occupations such as food brokers, wholesalers, warehousers, transporters, and distributors, though these various functions may overlap within a single company.

A *food broker* is essentially an independent firm that negotiates sales of products and ingredients on behalf of the manufacturers on a commission basis and then markets them to wholesalers or retail outlets. The *wholesaler* is a company that buys food in bulk and maintains centralized warehouses, enabling the coordinated distribution of food, which is then resold to **supermarkets**, convenience stores, and other retail outlets. There may in turn be another independent distributor, although these three functions are increasingly controlled by single companies for the sake of efficiency.

While there have always been many small independent regional food brokers in the United States, the general trend in the past decade has been toward the concentration of food brokerage and marketing firms into fewer hands on a national scale through mergers and acquisitions. Acosta, Advantage Sales and Marketing, and Crossmark are the three largest such companies, which essentially control the majority of food sold to the major grocery chains. Because negotiations take place between the large processors and big brokers and then in turn with big retailers, it is very difficult for small manufacturers to sell their products, since it is easier for everyone involved to go through the middlemen and grocers prefer to deal with the largest players who carry a wide range of products and can keep their shelves consistently stocked.

This system has, of course, only increased the number of "food miles" the average item travels, using more fuel in transportation and ultimately costing much more for the consumer. It is arguably more efficient to centralize such operations, but the cost to the environment and local economies is incalculable. When one considers, for example, that a tomato grown in the Central Valley of California may be purchased from the farmer by a broker, then shipped to a centralized warehouse in Los Angeles, only to return to grocery shelves a few miles from where it was actually grown, the true inefficiencies of this system become apparent. Furthermore, merely to facilitate this distribution system, the tomato is normally picked hard, green, and unripe and is then gassed to turn red before appearing in the supermarket. This also means the farmer only earns the merest fraction of the retail price; the majority is earned by the middlemen and retailers.

Many of the largest supermarkets and wholesale chains, however, have begun managing their own warehouses and distribution, controlling more of the transfer of food from field to fork, thus cutting out these independent middlemen. In few cases has this had any positive impact on the scale of warehousing or the distance food travels in distribution networks. It does mean that the largest companies, such as Wal-Mart, by far the largest retailer of food in the United States, can demand the lowest possible prices from manufacturers, since they have few other options when the entire system is controlled by large corporations.

Darius Willoughby

Monsanto Monsanto is a **multinational** agricultural company headquartered in St. Louis, Missouri. In 2006, the company was present in 47 countries and employed more than 17,000 people worldwide. Monsanto activities are concentrated in two major divisions: Seeds & Genomics and Agricultural Productivity. The company concentrates **research and development** (R&D) efforts on two core platforms: breeding and biotechnology.

Company History

The current Monsanto Company was founded in 2002, but traces its history to as early as the beginning of the 20th century. In 1901, John F. Queeny founded the original Monsanto; the company's first product was saccharin, an artificial sweetener. In 1975, the company started to focus on biotechnology and established its first cell biology research program; the first version of Roundup, the brand name for its herbicide products, was commercialized in 1976. The original Monsanto then merged with Pharmacia and UpJohn, and the new combined company kept the name Pharmacia Corporation. The agricultural division of Pharmacia was later spun off into an independent company in 2002, which is the current Monsanto.

Monsanto Divisions

The Seeds & Genomics Division at Monsanto is responsible for the seeds, biotechnology traits, and plant genomic technology projects. It is gradually generating the majority of Monsanto revenues. The division produces seeds for many different large-area crops such as **corn**, cotton, and some oilseeds (e.g., soybeans and canola), as well as small-area crops (vegetables). Research focuses on topics such as drought tolerance and yield enhancements for farmers.

The Agricultural Productivity Division focuses primarily on herbicides and other crop protection products as well as animal agriculture. Its main herbicide, Roundup, is a nonselective, glyphosate-based herbicide that is used in more than 130 countries. It is also used in the industrial, lawn-and-garden, and turf and ornamental markets.

The Animal Agriculture Division is focused on products used in **dairy** cow productivity and swine genetics.

Monsanto invests on average $500 million each year on R&D efforts. Two core platforms are at the heart of R&D at the company: breeding and biotechnology. *Breeding* is defined as the variety of processes used while cross-pollinating plants with desirable qualities; the final objective is to combine all favorable traits into a single crop plant. As for *biotechnology*, it is defined as "any technological application that uses biological systems, living organisms, or derivatives thereof, to make or modify products or processes for specific use," according to the Convention of Biological Diversity (CBO) of the U.N. Biotechnology often results in entirely new products that are not available in nature.

Legal and Public Controversy

As a company at the forefront of agro-biotechnology, Monsanto has been the target of many lawsuits. Most of its innovations are related to food, and hence it is targeted more often than its pharmaceutical counterparts. Monsanto is also subject to a lot of criticism from lobbying groups and activists. Many of its technologies are divisive, making it an easy target for activists; nicknames such as "MonSatan" and "Frankenfoods" for its **genetically engineered** products are often used when criticizing the company. One such controversial project was the merger with another company (Delta & Pine Land Company) that was developing a seed technology nicknamed "Terminator"; the project consisted of creating sterile seeds. This drew criticism from environmental groups and farmers alike, as it would encourage dependency (having to buy crops year after year). Although the merger was never completed, Monsanto still draws condemnation for having expressed an interest in the technology.

Monsanto trials often set precedents in the legal system. Throughout 2004 and 2005, Monsanto engaged in a series of lawsuits with farmers in the United States and Canada over their alleged misuse of Roundup Ready seed; these cases have been viewed as test cases for patent laws. The most famous of these was *Monsanto Canada Inc. v. Schmeiser*. In 1997, Monsanto discovered that a farmer (Schmeiser) had some areas of crops that were resistant to the Roundup herbicide, even though he had never purchased any of the patented seeds. He contended that the resistant crops' presence was accidental, the result of seeds that had flown onto his field from a passing truck; he said he had not purposely cultivated the seeds and had never acquired them. Monsanto sued for patent infringement because he had kept the Roundup seeds and failed to obtain a license. Monsanto argued that the farmer promoted the growth of the Roundup seeds; in 1998, Monsanto alleged that more than 95 percent of the farmer's canola crop was identified as the Roundup Ready variety. Schmeiser claimed that independent experts put contamination at less than 8 percent, with a ditch having a 60 percent contamination rate.

The court ruled in favor of Monsanto and determined that the protection of a patented gene or cell extends to its presence in a whole plant, even though the plant itself, as a higher life form, cannot be patented. Hence, the court ruled that the farmer deprived Monsanto of its monopoly on the special canola plant by storing and planting the Roundup Ready canola seeds and had profited from his use of Roundup seeds. The court only ruled on the planting and storing of seeds, but took great pains to not address the accidental contamination of fields; this question is still unanswered.

FURTHER READINGS: Monsanto Canada Inc. v. Schmeiser (2004), Supreme Court of Canada. http://scc.lexum.umontreal.ca/en/2004/2004scc34/2004scc34.html; Monsanto Corporation. http://www.monsanto.com.

Jean-François Denault

Multinationals A multinational corporation is an organization with office or distribution operations in two or more countries. Multinationals are sometimes integrated vertically, sometimes horizontally, or they may possess diversified structures. Reasons for a firm to adopt a multinational structure might be to meet offensive or defensive objectives. Multinationals face distinctive problems when moving into foreign markets, such as cultural diversity and import restrictions. Most of the largest multinationals, in terms of revenue, are American or Japanese.

The emergence of multinational companies has led to regional specialization. For example, India is now renowned as an information technology hub, while China has a reputation as a manufacturing center. Manufacturing was a sector that was traditionally vulnerable to globalization, but the service industry is increasingly subject to this trend as well.

Organizational models

Multinational companies use different integration models. *Horizontally integrated* companies use the same production model from one country to the next to produce similar products; for example, **McDonald's** has the same organizational model everywhere it operates. *Vertically integrated* corporations distribute different functions of their production chain to different countries. For example, Adidas might produce its products in one country and then distribute and sell them in other countries. The food industry is less likely to use this model, due to the high transportation costs and perishable nature of food goods.

Although strategic considerations for becoming a multinational are usually very complex, companies which do so usually have offensive or defensive objectives. *Offensive* objectives might include increasing long-term growth, maximizing total sales revenues, or taking advantage of economies of scale. *Defensive* reasons include taking advantage of technological innovations that are available in other countries, utilizing operating-cost differentials between countries, and pre-empting competitors' global moves.

Furthermore, multinational companies can be organized in either a global or a multidomestic model. The *multidomestic model* enables each national component to pursue different local strategies, while in the *global model*, a corporation will have one integrated strategy that it will pursue worldwide. Examples of companies using a multidomestic model include Honeywell and **General Foods**, while Caterpillar and General Electric are two examples of global corporations.

Potential Roadblocks

Companies entering foreign countries that are unfamiliar with the local environment face many obstacles. These include cultural misunderstandings, political uncertainties, import limits, and ownership restrictions. Cultural differences include those linked to languages, religion, and local customs, which must be integrated into marketing and sales components. Import and ownership restrictions are reflected through international agreements such as the **North American Free Trade Agreement** (NAFTA) and influence the organizational strategy (such as partnering with local companies). As for political uncertainty, this is a risk companies operating outside their current borders must contend with, as changes in local or national governments could significantly impact international subsidiaries.

Multinationals and the Agribusiness Sector

Multinationals in the **agribusiness** sector are also called multinational food processing enterprises (MNE); they face distinct challenges related to distribution due to the perishable nature of food, as well as cultural adaptation of their products to domestic markets. Recent studies of the top MNEs has shown that as these firms grow larger due to international expansion; they are also specializing into specific food segments to establish dominant positions. In addition, the large companies, especially in the Western world, have been hit with many downsizing events related to the wave of mergers and acquisitions that have led to many duplications and redundancies in large corporations. Globalization of MNEs has also led to their participation in nontraditional sectors of investment such as biotechnology, specialized services, and microbiological products.

The Growing Role of the Multinational Corporation

As there is a growing trend toward globalization, the corporate and social responsibility of multinationals is increasingly called into play. For example, multinationals are more and more asked to participate in the enforcement of international norms and human rights. For example, multinationals are pressured to apply norms to subsidiaries or national offices in other countries, which might not have the same stringent laws as the head office. Some companies are criticized for their perceived mistreatment of workers in other countries. Yet multinationals have an opportunity to play a positive role in their environment, and the idea of a multinational's role as a social actor is slowly making progress.

FURTHER READINGS: Davis, Gerald F., Marina v. N. Whitman, and Mayer N. Zald. "The Responsibility Paradox: Multinational Firms and Global Corporate Social Responsibility." Ross School of Business Working Paper No. 1031, University of Michigan, April 2006. Available at http://deepblue.lib.umich.edu/bitstream/2027.42/41221/1/1031.pdf; Farrell, Diana. "Beyond Offshoring: Assess Your Company's Global Potential." *Harvard Business Review* (December 2004), 12: 82–90; Rama, Ruth. *Multinational Agribusinesses*. New York: Food Product Press, 2005.

Jean-François Denault

N ❖ ───────────────────────────────

Nabisco Nabisco, once a mighty cookie and cracker company, today exists today only as a brand name, part of global conglomerate **Kraft Foods**. The company's path, from its origins as the first U.S. food corporation, then known as the New York Biscuit Company, to its present position, has been the trajectory that many American businesses have traveled as **multinational** corporations grow in size and scope.

New York Biscuit, the forerunner of Nabisco, was created when eight of the largest New York–area bakeries consolidated in 1890. The company's sizable capitalization allowed it to include 23 bakeries in 10 states when it began operations and to build the largest, most modern bakery in the world located in New York City. Competitors quickly formed, and in 1898 an even larger merger occurred, combining New York Biscuit with its two rivals, regional bakers American Biscuit Company and United States Baking Company. The new entity, the National Biscuit Company, dominated the cracker and cookie industry.

What set National Biscuit Company apart, beyond its massive size, were the marketing and **advertising** campaigns devised by the N. W. Ayers & Sons advertising agency. A several-month-long national advertising campaign introduced to the public to the Uneeda Biscuit, the company's signature soda cracker, which was the first national cracker brand. Ads also promoted the innovative package, which was made of moisture-proof cardboard with an air-tight, waxed-paper inner seal devised for freshness. The biscuits became an immediate success, and a succession of new products followed throughout the first half of the 20th century.

By the early 1940s, the company had 59 manufacturing facilities across the country producing some 200 products. By the post–World War II era, the company was ready for revitalization. In a multimillion-dollar modernization, it refurbished older bakeries and built sprawling new cracker and bread factories, including a 40-acre site in Fair Lawn, New Jersey. Changing its name to Nabisco in 1971, the company merged 10 years later with Standard Brands to become Nabisco Brands, adding a wide variety of biscuits, **snack foods**, and premium grocery products.

Nabisco Brands next merged with R. J. Reynolds, the second largest American tobacco company, in 1985, creating the largest consumer goods company in the United States. Originally called RJR Nabisco, the company was purchased for $25 billion in 1989 by Kolhberg, Kravis, Roberts (KKR) in the largest leveraged buyout of the time. The tobacco business was spun off into a separate company to protect the renamed Nabisco Group Holdings, from tobacco-related lawsuits. Once again becoming a publicly traded company in 1991, four years later KKR divested its remaining holdings. In 2000, Nabisco Holdings was sold to Phillip Morris (**Altria**) for $18.9 billion, which combined it with its Kraft Foods division. Eventually, Kraft Foods was also spun off into a separate company, where Nabisco lives on as a brand name.

FURTHER READINGS: Burrough, Bryan, and John Helyar. *Barbarians at the Gate: The Fall of RJR Nabisco.* New York: Harper & Row, 1990; Cahn, William. *Out of the Cracker Barrel: From Animal Crackers to ZuZu's.* New York: Simon & Schuster, 1969.

Joy Santlofer

Nanotechnology Nanotechnology is a broad term that encompasses multiple sciences and technologies in which development is being made at the nanoscale. The *nanoscale* refers to items smaller than 100 nanometers (nm): for comparison, a human hair is about 80,000 nm wide, while a DNA strand has a width of 2 nm. Nanotechnology is an interdisciplinary field, mixing material science, chemistry, biology, physics, and engineering and is applied in many fields such as medicine and computers. Its applications are steadily increasing in the food industry as well: some examples of use include better **packaging**, improved **food safety**, and better nutritional content.

Nanotechnology is usually developed following either a "top-down" or "bottom-up" model. In a top-down model, researchers start from a larger object and continually reduce its size; this form of development is mostly used in nanoelectronics. In a bottom-up model, researchers strive to understand the basic blocks and build upon them; in nanotechnology, processes that use chemical properties usually resort to a bottom-up approach.

Some of the potential uses for nanotechnology in food packaging include increasing security in the manufacturing process and shipping by using biosensors to react to pathogens. Also, nanofibers (fibers having diameters of less than 100 nm) could be used to build and reinforce elements in food packaging.

Food safety will also benefit from improvements in nanotechnology. Nanolaminates (laminated films about 2 nm thick) can be used as edible coatings for food or can even have textural properties. Other tools, such as nanofilters, can be used to remove viruses and **bacteria** from milk, improving its safety and giving the product a longer shelf life.

Nanocapsules and nanodispersion will play key roles in potential delivery systems. These can be used in many functional ingredients such as vitamins, **flavoring**, and preservatives. For example, encapsulating nutrients in nanoscale spheres could enhance biological activities of some dietary supplements by delivering them directly into cells.

Like genetically modified foods, some people are concerned about the safety of nanomodified food and have demanded that modified food add a "nanohazard" label. When a material is sufficiently shrunk, it can have different physical, chemical, and biological properties than its regular-size counterparts; hence, a key concern is potential unanticipated effects, including greater absorption or altered uptake of nutrients. A handful of products are already sold in the United States containing nanoscale **additives** without a regulatory context to govern nanofoods. **Research** is currently under way.

FURTHER READINGS: Parry, Viviane. "Food Fight on a Tiny Scale" Times Online (2006); Sargent, Ted. *The Dance of Molecules: How Nanotechnology Is Changing Our Lives.* New York: Penguin, 2005; Weiss, Jochen, Paul Takhistov, and D. Julian McClements. "Functional Materials in Food Nanotechnology." *Journal of Food Science* 71, no. 9 (2006): R107–16.

Jean-François Denault

North American Free Trade Agreement (NAFTA) The North American Free Trade Agreement, an international treaty among Canada, Mexico, and the United States, came into effect in January 1994, creating the largest **free trade** area in the world. The main objectives of the agreement are to eliminate trade barriers, promote conditions of fair competition in commerce, and increase investment opportunities. Although the treaty is generally beneficial to participating countries, there are challenges for the future that remain to be addressed.

History of NAFTA

NAFTA was preceded by the Canada–U.S. Free Trade Agreement, which entered into force on January 1, 1989. The deal was beneficial to both countries, but especially to Canada, as Canadian goods gained access to the U.S. market and could benefit from economies of scale. A few years later, Mexico approached the United States asking to enter a similar bilateral agreement, and Canada expressed an interest in participating. Major roadblocks to the trilateral negotiations existed in several industrial sectors such as agriculture, automobiles, energy, and textiles. Agriculture was removed from the general NAFTA negotiations and was subject to separate bilateral negotiations. The final NAFTA agreement came into effect on January 1, 1994.

NAFTA and Agriculture

NAFTA's provisions relating to agriculture include the replacement of major nontariff barriers in the agricultural sector with "harmonized equivalents" and the commitment to reduce these equivalents. Nonetheless, agriculture is subject to bilateral treaties between each participating country, rather than a global trilateral treaty like other industrial sectors. Some food commodities were seen as politically sensitive, and hence were excluded from free trade status. For Canada, the exclusions include **dairy** and feather products (**poultry**, eggs, turkeys, and hatching eggs), while U.S. exceptions included **sugar**, sugar products, dairy, cotton, and peanuts.

NAFTA and Agricultural Trade Patterns

Mexico is the United States' second leading agricultural trading partner, accounting for about 10 percent of U.S. agricultural imports and receiving 14 percent of U.S. exports. Conversely, the United States is Mexico's main agricultural trading partner. Over 80 percent of Mexico's agricultural exports go to the United States, while two-thirds of its agricultural imports come from the United States. This bilateral trade relationship was estimated to be worth close to $23 billion in 2006, with Mexico having a slight trading deficit. Major exported products from Mexico to the United States include fresh vegetables, **wine** and **beer**, fresh fruits, live animals, and processed fruits and vegetables. Mexico has the climate to supply out-of-season commodities to its northern neighbors, which is clearly reflected in trading patterns. U.S. exports to

Mexico include **corn**, red meat, soybeans, cotton, processed fruits and vegetables, and poultry meat. However, trading between the United States and Mexico remains strained by the continued interference of American lobbying groups and politics in its commitment to free trade. Many of the major trade disputes (transportation, emigration of migrant workers, and sugar) specifically concern these two trade partners and have yet to be resolved.

Agricultural goods being traded across the Canadian-U.S. border were estimated to have reached a value of $28 billion in 2005. Canada's agricultural trade surplus with the United States has more than tripled since 1993, reaching $3.5 billion in 2005. Foods being moved to Canada from the United States include fresh fruits and vegetables, **snack foods**, processed fruits and vegetables, and fresh and frozen red meats. Of these exports, 72 percent are consumer-oriented food goods. Exports from Canada to the United States include red meats, live animals, snack foods, processed fruits and vegetables, and fresh vegetables.

Agricultural trade between Canada and Mexico is much smaller by comparison. Nevertheless, it has increased exponentially, reaching nearly $2 billion in 2005, relatively balanced between both partners. Canadian exports to Mexico revolve around oilseeds, meat, and meat products, while Mexican exports are concentrated in fruits, vegetables, and beer. Therefore, trade between these two partners, although geographically distanced, is still possible and profitable to both partners. Since the establishment of NAFTA, Canadian companies have continually made considerable investments in the Mexican economy, forging a favorable position in many industries.

Changes in Domestic Agricultural Patterns

The introduction of NAFTA has led to distinctive changes in domestic agricultural specialization. For example, Mexico has access to a large, relatively unskilled **labor** pool, leading to production and exportation of goods that require labor-intensive production methods (such as fruits and vegetables). Given the wage disparities among Mexico, the United States, and Canada, this trend is expected to continue. Canada and the United States, with greater access to investment capital, have moved to capital-intensive cultures such as grains and livestock. Distortions still exist in heavily protected industrial sectors (such as sugar in the United States).

Challenges for the Future

Many problems currently exist when applying the terms of NAFTA. These include cross-border trade-dispute resolution, current restrictions in the transportation of agricultural products, and the relationship between human resources and agricultural cultivation.

Increased trading invariably leads to tension between trading partners. In the case of NAFTA, this mainly affects the smaller trading partners (Canada and Mexico), as U.S. special-interest groups often call for countervailing and antidumping procedures. Other frictions arise when dealing with specially protected products such as sugar and meat. Sugar remains one of the thorniest issues related to agriculture in NAFTA. Both the U.S. and Mexican governments persist in subsidizing the sugar industry, to the point that consumers continue to pay inflated prices for this product. While the United States subsidizes sugar and restricts imports for political, rather than economic reasons, Mexico has continued to subsidize antiquated refineries (some being close to 100 years old), resulting in oversupplies there.

Instead of a simple unified conflict resolution process, several mechanisms exist in NAFTA for the settlement of disputes between trading partners. These include the World Bank International Center for the Settlement of Investment Disputes (in case of investment disputes), the host country's domestic courts, and panel arbitration by individuals appointed by all participating countries. This web of different measures and appeal processes slows down attempts to resolve conflicts. The lack of a unified structure has led to inefficiencies in the trading process and is seen as a limit to future growth. However, others believe that if one takes into account the size of trade among the three participating countries, there are relatively few important trade disputes.

Transportation bottlenecks also impede the application of NAFTA. Increased border security and insufficient border infrastructure create delays, especially in the southern regions. Crossing the border can take up to 20 hours, in effect becoming a tax on cross-border trade and having a detrimental affect on products being shipped to northern destinations. This is especially a concern in the case of perishable goods. Increased security following the 9/11 terrorist attacks led to increased concerns and amplified efforts to harmonize transnational border procedures. Recent procedures to require passports at the Canadian-U.S. border (which were not mandatory in the past) have also raised concerns. Nonetheless, member countries have moved to comply with NAFTA provisions on transportation issues. For example, in February 2007, the U.S. Chamber of Commerce endorsed a pilot program that would allow cross-border trucking between U.S. and Mexican terminals.

While also increasing trade of goods, NAFTA provisions have also allowed for freer movement of agricultural workers. Farm workers are hired seasonally from Mexico for work in the United States and Canada. Canada operates the Seasonal Agricultural Workers Program (SAWP) to regulate the movement of these laborers. Mexican workers under this program have wages comparable to domestic Canadian workers. There are talks to extend SAWP and to develop a similar program in the United States. Yet the persistent poverty and labor and environmenal concerns in Mexico remains one of the major challenges to establishing a stable environment in NAFTA.

FURTHER READINGS: NAFTA Secretariat. http://www.nafta-sec-alena.org/DefaultSite/index.html; Neaver, Louis E. V. *NAFTA's Second Decade: Assessing Opportunities in the Mexican and Canadian Markets.* Mason, OH: Thomson/South-Western, 2004; Robert, Maryse. *Negotiating NAFTA: Explaining the Outcome in Culture, Textiles, Autos, and Pharmaceuticals.* Toronto: University of Toronto Press, 2000; Veeman, Michel, Terrence S. Veeman, and Ryan Hoskins. "NAFTA and Agriculture: Challenges for Trade and Policy," 305–43. In Edward J. Chambers and Peter H. Smith, eds. *NAFTA in the New Millennium.* La Jolla: Center for U.S.-Mexican Studies, University of California, San Diego, 2002.

Jean-François Denault

Nutraceuticals. *See* Functional Foods and Nutraceuticals.

Nutrition Education Nutrition education involves both formal and informal instruction regarding how food affects the human body. There are two general philosophies that drive most nutrition education. The first, supported by most federal agencies, including the **U.S. Department of Agriculture** (USDA), theorizes that there is no such thing as a bad food. Rather, all foods, if used in a balanced and informed way, can be used to construct a healthy diet. The second approach suggests that some foods are better than others; moreover, some foods should be strictly limited in a healthy diet. For example, many nutritionists and health professionals argue that **fast food** should be reduced if not avoided altogether. These contrasting philosophies are often the source of controversy regarding nutrition education, particularly when it comes to educating children.

Nutrition education occurs across several levels, including public, private, and professional education. Moreover, because good nutrition practices often vary according to age, sex, and other cultural factors, nutrition education is sometimes tailored to specific populations within these public, private, and professional realms. For example, Pima Indians living in the United States have one of the highest rates of type 2 diabetes in the world. With rates on some reservations reaching nearly 60 percent, the Food Distribution Program on Indian Reservations, a subsidiary of the USDA, has published nutrition information specifically for the Pima in order to reduce cases of diabetes. At the same time, organizations such as Tohono O'odham Community Action (TOCA) have also started nutrition education about type 2 diabetes, advocating that Native Americans return to more ancestral ways of eating.

Considering the different approaches to nutrition education and the factors that can vary across groups, stakeholders continue to look for ways to transform nutrition education to make it easier to understand and apply. Government agencies such as the USDA, the Food and Drug Administration (FDA), and the Department of Education inform policy that can transform how nutrition should be taught in schools and other public institutions. Nonprofit organizations and national associations such as TOCA and the School Nutrition Association work to translate complex nutrition information into educational materials that help change nutritional behaviors. Finally, individual consumers of all ages, sizes, genders, and races often seek out innovative nutritional advice and share their experiences of transformation and change in order to promote better education.

Public Education

Public health education in the United States is informed largely by the USDA, FDA, Department of Education, and Department of Health and Human Services (DHHS). With regard to nutrition education specifically, the USDA and DHHS set the tone for all educational materials with the publication of *Dietary Guidelines for Americans*. Since 1980, the USDA and DHHS have jointly updated nutrition recommendations every five years. With suggestions about caloric intake, daily recommended values for **vitamins** and minerals, and official positions on different fats and carbohydrates, the dietary guidelines were created as a way to educate the general public about good nutrition. Furthermore, the guidelines provide the foundation for two of the most highly recognizable nutritional tools: My Pyramid and the **nutrition labeling** provided by products' Nutrition Facts labels. Thus, *Dietary Guidelines for Americans* is the starting point for most nutrition education in the United States.

Perhaps the most identifiable symbol for nutrition education is the USDA's My Pyramid. Formerly known the USDA Food Guide Pyramid, My Pyramid was released in 2005 as a pictorial representation of the dietary guidelines. The pyramid shows daily recommendations for grains, vegetables, fruits, oils, milk, and meat and beans, as well as suggestions for physical activity. My Pyramid is the first revision of the USDA Food Guide Pyramid, which was released in 1992 and hailed as a breakthrough in educating the public about nutrition. However, since its release, the original pyramid failed to meet expectations. In 2000 and 2002, Dr. Walter Willett and his **research** team from the Harvard School of Public Health published several reports with longitudinal data about people who ate according to the Food Guide Pyramid. The research team found little if any benefit from sticking to a diet communicated by the pyramid. These results, alongside criticisms that few Americans actually ate according to the pyramid, prompted the redesign of the Food Guide Pyramid. Thus, in 2005, My Pyramid was released. In addition to updating information regarding whole grains, healthy fats, and complex carbohydrates, My Pyramid also makes explicit connections between food and physical activity. Moreover, the USDA also released educational materials, including computer games, to help children learn how to use the pyramid.

Other public efforts at nutrition education include the National School Lunch Program (NSLP). Started in 1946 under the National School Lunch Act, the NSLP is one of the most direct ways in which *Dietary Guidelines for Americans* is translated into nutrition education. Meals served at schools that participate in the NSLP must comply with guidelines established by the USDA. For example, "foods of minimal nutritional value" may not be served during the lunch hour. Accordingly, beverages such as Coca-Cola or Pepsi and **candies** like Skittles or Starburst may not be sold during lunch, because it is unlawful for them to compete with the NSLP. Should a school fail to comply with these standards, it risks losing financial support from the USDA. Although some schools do have a specific nutrition curriculum built in to their health education courses, many schools treat their lunch programs as the primary method of teaching children how to eat.

Private Education

While public health education communicates general health information to many groups, individuals also seek out nutrition education from more private sources, including dieticians and nutritionists as well as weight-loss and nutritional support groups. Dieticians and nutritionists have several outlets through which to share their knowledge about nutrition. In traditional settings, registered dieticians (RDs) and some nutritionists often work in hospitals, nursing homes, or other medical institutions where meals need careful planning and preparation. Clients can seek private consultations in these settings in order learn more about good nutrition. More contemporary approaches to private nutrition education emphasize accessibility. For example, many fitness centers have developed nutrition programs as a complement to their physical training programs. As such, individuals can seek nutritional education outside of a traditional hospital setting.

In the spirit of accessibility, several organizations have emerged to help individuals who are interested in losing weight and improving their nutritional knowledge. The most well-recognized of these organizations is Weight Watchers. Starting in the 1960s, Weight Watchers has consistently provided nutrition education and social support for individuals who join the organization. It has developed specific programs, most notably their Weight Watchers Points System, to help individuals monitor their nutritional health. Other organizations, including Jenny Craig and Overeaters Anonymous, have also found success providing both nutritional and social support for individuals in a more private atmosphere than public nutrition education.

Professional Education

Public and private approaches to nutrition education are aimed generally at educating an individual on how to make better food choices. At the same time, there are a number of professions that often require additional training, instruction, and accreditation on a more professional level: dieticians and nutritionists, chefs, and doctors and nurses.

Initially, RDs require a college degree, as do most nutritionists. The primary difference is that the RD must hold an internship and pass an additional exam after his or her undergraduate degree is completed. Once these requirements have been met, the Commission on Dietetic Registration of the American Dietetic Association (ADA), the major accrediting institution for dieticians, can award the RD credential. Although this credential is not required to practice nutrition counseling, many clinical settings prefer an RD over a nutritionist. Moreover, of the 46 states that have laws about dietetic education, 31 require a license and 14 call for certificates. Most major colleges and universities offer a bachelor of science degree in nutrition or a related field; some of the top programs include those of the Harvard School of Public Health and the University of California Berkeley School of Public Health.

Although RDs and nutritionists require the most professional education in order to educate others about nutrition, there are other professions that require some nutrition education. Most graduates of culinary schools are required to pass at least one nutrition course before they receive their degree. Although their primary education is in food conceptualization and preparation, nutrition education is still an important part of instruction and practice for most chefs. Top programs that provide culinary education include the Culinary Institute of America, Johnson & Wales, Kendall College, and the Scottsdale Culinary Institute. While there is no accreditation for nutrition education in the culinary world, the American Culinary Federation Foundation Accrediting Commission does take nutrition education into consideration when awarding credentials to **cooking schools**.

Finally, both doctors and nurses will receive nutrition education as part of their medical training. The degree requirements and credentials for this type of education vary by institution, and there is no accrediting association apart from the ADA.

Transforming Education

Even though very structured systems of nutrition education are in place across public, private, and professional levels, there always remains room for transformation and innovation. Because nutrition information is both complex and ever-changing, consumers of all ages and cultures need increasingly sophisticated tools to put nutrition rules into practice. The most sophisticated advancements in nutrition education have been aimed primarily at children. For example, as part of the No Child Left Behind policy, all K–12 schools in the United States are required to have a wellness policy on file. This mandate does not specify what the policy has to advocate, but it requires schools to address nutrition education in several places. Although No Child Left Behind stopped short of requiring schools to actually implement the wellness policies that they designed, some schools took their policies as an opportunity to institute real changes. For example, some school districts in Arizona used their wellness policies in conjunction with a statewide policy passed in 2005 to strengthen their nutrition curriculum and remove sodas and certain **snack foods** from their **vending machines**.

The early part of the 21st century has also witnessed some interesting social movements involving nutrition education. These social movements, along with nonprofit organizations aimed at improving children's health, advocate better nutrition education that will help children become more involved with the production and consumption of their food. For example, Alice Waters, chef of Berkeley, California's famed Chez Panisse **restaurant**, started the Edible Schoolyard in 1994. The Edible Schoolyard outfits public schools in urban areas with a one-acre organic garden and 'a kitchen classroom. The purpose behind this program is to teach children about nutrition, sustainability, and the fun involved with good food.

Additionally, nonprofit organizations like the Oakland-based Sports-4-Kids recognize that nutrition education should be a part of K–12 education but that many schools are too financially strained to ensure that their students receive adequate instruction. As such, this nonprofit offers supplemental education during recess, as well as before and after school regarding physical and nutritional health. Ultimately, nutrition education is a primary concern for organizations and individuals, as we all search for better ways to learn how to eat.

FURTHER READINGS: Bijlefeld, Marjolijn, and Sharon K. Zoumbaris. *Food and You: A Guide to Healthy Habits for Teens.* Westport, CT: Greenwood Press, 2001; Nestle, Marion. *What to Eat: An Aisle-by-Aisle Guide to Savvy Food Choices and Great Eating.* New York: North Point Press, 2006; Planck, Nina. *Real Food: What to Eat and Why.* New York: Bloomsbury USA, 2006.

Marianne LeGreco

Nutrition Labeling Nutrition labeling encompasses a wide array of rules and institutions used to translate complex nutrition information for consumers. Both government agencies and commercial organizations play important roles in labeling food products for personal consumption. Organizations such as the United Nations' Food and Agricultural Organization (FAO), the World Health Organization (WHO), and the **U.S. Department of Agriculture** (USDA) have established international standards for food production, fair trade practices, and labeling of nutritional content. At the same time, commercial food services use nutritional labels to make health claims about their products. Labels such as "low-fat" or "low-carb" provide consumers with useful information about their food and producers with a nice selling point.

The motivation behind these standards is that consumers need better **nutrition education** resources to make informed decisions about their nutritional health. More informed consumers understand how food affects their bodies, know where their food comes from, and participate more fully in making their food choices. In order to execute the standards involving nutrition labeling, public health officials have developed a number of useful tools. For example, both the Nutrition Facts label (see below) and the USDA's My Pyramid (*see* Nutrition Education entry) are symbols for communicating nutrition information in the United States. Moreover, institutions such as the **Codex Alimentarius Commission** regularly update international standards on labeling food for consumers. The struggle many of these institutions face is finding the most effective ways to disseminate nutrition information in a form that consumers can actually put into practice. Thus, nutrition labeling is really the process of translating complex rules about food production and consumption into simple messages that consumers can use to make nutritional health decisions.

Policy Provisions

Modern practices of labeling food to better communicate nutrition content started in 1963 with the creation of the Codex Alimentarius Commission. The FAO and WHO established the commission to coordinate food standards and ensure fair **packaging** and labeling of food. At the time of publication, the Codex Alimentarius publication included 253 official standards, 61 codes of practice, and 60 general guidelines that lay the foundation for how food should be talked about, and therefore, how food should be labeled. For example, the Codex Standard for Instant Noodles, established in 2006, lays out provisions for which types of instant noodles can use the term *halal*, designating food approved under Islamic law, on their labels. Some 160 nations now belong to the commission, making it one of the most comprehensive and coordinated efforts to create standards for food handling and labeling.

In the United States, the policy provisions that guide nutrition labeling stem from the Fair Packaging and Labeling Act of 1966. This act created specific requirements for the labeling of foods with regard to placement of labels, form, and content, as well as portion size and quantity. For example, a food label must identify the commodity and provide a business contact for the manufacturer. The Act also outlines which foods are exempt from such labeling requirements, for example, food sold for immediate consumption, like a **hot dog** sold on a street corner during the lunch hour. Finally, this policy also takes a position on misleading and false information within labels, claiming that the intentional misdirection of consumers through nutrition labels is unlawful.

The Fair Packaging and Labeling Act was complemented in 1990 with the Nutrition Labeling and Education Act. This act gave the Food and Drug Administration (FDA) authority to require nutrition labeling of most foods. Moreover, the act allowed the FDA to begin regulation of health claims made on food labels such as "high fiber" or "heart healthy." Probably the most significant change in nutrition labeling practices introduced by this Act was the inclusion of the Nutrition Facts label. In short, both the 1966 and 1990 policies made significant advances in communicating nutrition information to consumers.

In addition to the policies specific to labeling, there are other provisions that describe how nutrition in the United States should be labeled. *Dietary Guidelines for Americans*, published every five years by the Department of Health and Human Services and the USDA, has provided the foundation for nutritional advice since 1980. With recommendations on caloric intake, balance of nutrients, and general eating habits, the dietary guidelines were designed to promote good health and reduce the risk for disease through better nutrition information. Nutrition Facts labels and My Pyramid both take their cues from *Dietary Guidelines*; therefore, nutrition labeling is influenced directly by the suggestions outlined in this document. Considering the formal rules in *Dietary Guidelines*, as well as other nutrition policies, it is apparent that comprehensive labeling of food and nutrition commodities is a primary concern for government institutions, producers, and consumers.

Nutrition Facts Labels

The single most identifiable nutrition label in the United States is the Nutrition Facts label or panel. Starting in 1990 with the Nutrition Labeling and Education Act, food manufacturers were required to disclose the nutritional content of their products. The nutrition facts are published directly on the package, in a box offset from other labeling. To ensure maximum readability, there are specific requirements regarding positioning, font size, format, and color contrast. For example, all nutrients listed in the Nutrition Facts label must use at least an eight-point font.

Within the Nutrition Facts label, food manufacturers must communicate specific nutrition information in a specific order. All labels must start with the recommended serving size for the product, followed by the number of servings per container. Following these numbers, the label must declare the following nutrients in the product in the "Amount Per Serving" section: Total Fat, Saturated Fat, Trans Fat, Cholesterol, Sodium, Total Carbohydrates, Dietary Fiber, Sugars, and Proteins. Next, the label needs a declaration of **vitamins** and minerals for the following: Vitamin D, Vitamin E, Thiamin, Riboflavin, Niacin, Vitamin B_6, Folate, Vitamin B_{12}, Biotin, Pantothenic Acid, Phosphorus, Iodine, Magnesium, Zinc, and Copper. However, producers must declare these vitamins and minerals only when they are an added nutrient or are present as part of a health claim. Only the aforementioned vitamins and minerals can be declared, and they must appear in the order listed.

There are two key features of the Nutrition Facts label that communicate information regarding recommended daily values. Along the right side of the panel, consumers will find a "% Daily Value" figure for each nutrient, vitamin, or mineral listed on the label. Additionally, these percentages are connected to a footnote that tells consumers how to interpret them. Simply, the percentages shown in the Nutrition Facts are based on a 2,000-calorie diet. The footnote tells the consumer the maximum amounts of fat, saturated fat, cholesterol, and sodium, as well as the minimum amounts of total carbohydrates and dietary fiber, an individual should have in a 2,000- or 2,500-calorie diet.

The presence of Nutrition Facts labels reinforces the responsibility that both producer and consumer have in communicating nutrition information. Because many consumers do not have the same nutritional knowledge as a registered dietician or other expert, they are dependent upon producers to be forthcoming about the calories and nutrients per serving in a product. On the other hand, producers depend on consumers to use the nutrition information translated through the Nutrition Facts to ensure the safe and continued use of a food product. Unfortunately, many consumers still face difficulty realizing how to put these nutrition facts into practice. As such, there is still room for developing even more effective ways of explaining good nutrition habits to consumers.

Commercial Health Claims

Not only did the Nutrition Labeling and Education Act of 1990 require the use of a Nutrition Facts label for the majority of food products, but it also created uniform definitions for health claims that are often used to label foods. Before 1990, there was little regulation for health claims like "low sodium" or "reduced calorie." For example, **ice cream** could have been called "light" simply because its packaging was a lighter color than normal. With the passage of this law, however, these types of statements would be considered unlawful.

Terms used to make a health claim on a food product generally use the word *free* or *low*. *Free* claims mean that the product contains none, or only a trivial amount, of an item. For example, according to the FDA standards, *calorie-free* means that a food has five or fewer calories per serving. *Low* claims are applied to foods that can be eaten often without exceeding dietary guidelines. For example, *low-fat* foods have three grams of fat or less, while *low-sodium* foods have no more than 140 mg of sodium. Other terms defined by the FDA include:

- *Lean* and *extra lean* describe the fat content in meat. According to the FDA, "lean" has to have less than 10 grams of fat, 4.5 grams of saturated fat, and 95 milligrams cholesterol per 100 grams; "extra lean" has to have less than 5 grams of fat, 2 grams of saturated fat, and 95 milligrams cholesterol per 100 grams.
- *High* means that the food contains at least 20 percent of the daily recommended value of a nutrient
- *Good source* indicates that the food contains 10–19 percent of the daily recommended value
- *Reduced* applies to a nutritionally altered product that contains 25 percent less of an item than the original product
- *Less* applies to foods, altered or not, that have 25 percent less than the original product
- *More* means that a food has at least 10 percent more of a nutrient than the original product

Finally, while *light* cannot be used to describe the color of a package, it can still be used to talk about color and texture of the food. For example, C&H can still call its brown sugar "light" as long as the packaging clearly illustrates that it is talking about color, not calories. Of course, *light* also refers to the health claim that a product has one-third fewer calories, 50 percent fewer calories from fat, or 50 percent less sodium.

Some food manufacturers and marketers have become very clever in their application of these rules regarding health claims, often to the mystification of consumers. Examples of cloudy claims abound in food **advertising** and labeling. The bread that claims to have 25 percent fewer calories might simply be sliced 25 percent thinner. The can of Pam that claims to be fat free actually has a high proportion of fat, but with a $1/3$-second spray serving size, the amount per serving is less than 0.5 gram, technically qualifying it for *fat-free* status; at the same time, few consumers use only a $1/3$-second spray when cooking with Pam.

Other manufacturers use terms not defined by the FDA, such as "natural," to make their health claims. Close inspection of foods claiming to be "100% Natural" reveals that, while some of the products are indeed natural, others are not. Because there is no standard for how terms like this should be applied, consumers cannot tell which parts of a product are being hailed as natural. As such, many consumers might think that they are making better health decisions, when in fact they might not be.

Global Labeling Standards

Nutrition labeling has become an international concern over the past few decades. As government agencies attempt to institute standardized practices of food production, fair trade, and packaging, new practices of nutrition labeling have begun to emerge. Perhaps the most recent global movement regarding food labeling involves the production and consumption of **coffee**. International coffee production has begun to experience problems such as questionable trade practices and encroachment on rain forests. Consequently, labels encouraging the purchase of "Fair Trade Certified,"

"Shade Grown," and "Bird Friendly" coffees have made these products a popular commodity. Advocates claim that these coffees promote not only consumer responsibility but also consumer health because these coffees are produced more naturally.

Another example of global label standards is illustrated in the international practice of "eco-labeling." Ecolabels are placed on products to communicate that they were produced using sustainable, environmentally friendly methods. As part of its regulatory powers, the FAO certifies products and distributes ecolabels; however, most of the regulations remain voluntary. In 2005, the FAO established new standards for fish caught in the world's oceans in order to ensure their sustainability. In doing so, the FAO claims to support responsible food production.

These examples suggest that nutrition labels and health claims have begun to move beyond the realm of communicating simple nutrition messages to include messages that encourage social and consumer responsibility.

FURTHER READINGS: Hawkes, Corinna. *Nutrition Labels and Health Claims: The Global Regulatory Environment*. Geneva: World Health Organization, 2004; Nestle, Marion. *Food Politics: How the Food Industry Influences Nutrition and Health*. 2nd ed. Berkeley: University of California Press, 2007.

Marianne LeGreco

Obesity Historically, *obese* has been defined as weighing more than 100 pounds over the ideal body weight. This definition has been replaced by the use of the body mass index (BMI), which is calculated by dividing the body weight by the square of a person's height, yielding a number that is usually between 20 and 70. Today, *overweight* is defined as a BMI between 25 and 30, *obesity* as more than 30, and *morbid obesity* as more than 40.

During the past 50 years, the number of people suffering from obesity has been increasing throughout the world, but nowhere is it more acute than in the United States, where the statistics are staggering. Today, an estimated 61 percent of Americans have been judged overweight, and obesity rates have risen from 12 percent of the population in 1991 to 20 percent today. An ominous statistic indicating that this may get worse is that the percentage of children and adolescents who are obese has doubled during the last 20 years.

Obesity has been linked to high blood pressure, arthritis, infertility, heart disease, type 2 diabetes, strokes, birth defects, gallbladder disease, gout, impaired immune system, liver disease, and breast, prostate, and colon cancers. In addition to physical illness, obese people are victims of social discrimination. Fashion holds up skinny models as the ideal and obesity as a stigmatized condition. Also, many Americans hold the individual responsible for his or her own obesity and consider obese individuals to have a lack of control or a moral defect. Psychologically, many obese people believe the same and feel badly about themselves.

Health Care

The Centers for Disease Control and Prevention has estimated that 248,000 Americans die prematurely annually due to obesity; others believe that the figure is closer to 400,000. The difficulty of determining the exact figure relates to the fact that people die not due to obesity itself but from complications such as heart disease, diabetes, or cancer, which also affect nonobese individuals.

Estimates of added health care expenses due to obesity vary, but they hover between $80 billion and $250 billion annually. Obesity is considered the number-two cause of preventable death in the United States (the number-one cause is smoking). Health officials from the surgeon general to medical practitioners have identified obesity as a disease of epidemic proportions in the United States. Treating obesity and illnesses related to obesity has become a major business in the United States and is likely to grow in the future.

Dieting

In the late 19th century, chemist Wilbur O. Atwater began measuring the caloric values of food, which became a building block of many subsequent diets. Russell Chittenden, a chemist at Yale University, applied the idea of calories to the amount of energy burned in exercise. Lulu Hunt Peters then built on these two ideas in *Diet and Health, with Key to the Calories* (1917), which advocated calorie counting as a method of weight reduction. This principle has been part of many subsequent diets. In the 1930s, a variety of diets became popular. "Dr. Stoll's Diet-Aid, the Natural Reducing Food," was a liquid diet consisting of milk **chocolate**, starch, whole **wheat**, and bran in one cup of water to be consumed at breakfast and lunch; it was promoted through beauty parlors. Since then, numerous diet drinks have been offered, including Metracal (1959) and Slim-Fast (1977).

Another 1930s diet was proposed by William H. Hay, who believed that starches, proteins, and fruits should be consumed separately. His diet called for a few select vegetables, protein sources, and grapefruits, which Hay claimed had a special fat-burning enzyme. The grapefruit diet re-emerged in the 1970s. It was then based on the unproven idea that the fruit's low "glycemic index" helped the body's metabolism burn fat. It was rejected by experts as a crash diet that deprived the body of essential nutrients.

After World War II, individual stories of weight loss were published in women's magazines. Alternatively, it became commonplace to believe that individuals who were unable to control their weight lacked discipline or self-control. Being overweight became a sign of moral or psychological weakness.

Entrepreneurs cashed in on these views toward fat. In 1951, "Tasti-Diet," the first **diet food** line, was launched by Tillie Lewis, who sweetened her food products with saccharin. Likewise, physical fitness guru Jack La Lanne went on **television** to promote weight loss through exercise; he generated additional profits through sales of exercise equipment, vitamins, diet foods, and books. Others, such as Richard Simmons, have followed La Lanne's example.

Borrowing a technique from Alcoholics Anonymous, Jean Nidetch, a housewife from Queens, New York, started a self-help peer group to help her lose weight. Albert Lippert and his wife, who lost 50 pounds, were members of the group. In 1963 Nidetch with Lippert as the business manager started Weight Watchers. Other weight-loss programs, such as Weight Losers Institute (1968), Nutri/System Weight Loss (1971), and Jenny Craig (1982), followed Weight Watchers' example.

Do-it-yourself diets also proliferated. Robert C. Atkins's *Dr. Atkins' Diet Revolution* (1972) and Herman Tarnower's *The Complete Scarsdale Medical Diet* (1978) were based on the theory that too many carbohydrates prevent the body from burning fat; hence, dieters could consume protein in unrestricted quantities, while pasta, bread, and foods with **sugar** were to be eliminated. High-protein diets such as Barry Sears's *The Zone* (1995) and Michael R. Eades's *Protein Power* (1996) are variations on Atkins's theme. Sears's diet permits "low-carb" vegetables, such as broccoli, green beans, and fruit; Eades's diet avoids most fruit. Critics proclaimed that these diets included too much saturated fat and cholesterol, which can increase the risk of heart disease. In 1979 Nathan Pritikin in his *Pritikin Program for Diet and Exercise* (1979) proposed a very low-fat diet combined with exercise. Like Pritikin, Dean Ornish's book *Eat More, Weigh Less* (1993) proposed reducing fat to less than 10 percent of calories consumed along with exercise and meditation.

In 2002, Gary Taubes's article "What If It's All Been a Big Fat Lie?" in the *New York Times Magazine* questioned the view that fat consumption is the main cause for overweight. Taubes pointed to carbohydrates as a major culprit. His article gave new life to the Atkins Diet. Critics pointed out that calories did matter in dieting: fat contains twice as many calories as either protein or carbohydrates. Just as interest in the Atkins Diet began to wane, Miami cardiologist Arthur Agatston recommended reducing carbohydrates (bread, rice, pastas, and fruits) and increasing high-fiber foods, lean proteins, and healthy fats. His book, *The South Beach Diet: The Delicious, Doctor-Designed, Foolproof Plan for Fast and Healthy Weight Loss* (2003), was a best-seller, and his diet plan has swept the nation.

Most diets do work in the short run, but over the long term, most dieters gain their weight back. There are many reasons for this. Some work because of loss of water in the first few days of the diet. Most diets are based on the drastic reduction of calories. A normal-size person has 30–35 billion fat cells. When a person gains weight, these fat cells increase first in size and later in number. When a person starts losing weight, the cells decrease in size, but the number of fat cells stays the same. When the body is starved of calories, the metabolism slows down to conserve energy, and weight loss stops. The body compensates for decreased caloric intake by lowering energy expenditure, which is why it is easier to lose weight at the beginning of a diet and less so as the diet continues. When dieters go off their regimen, their metabolism is still working at a high efficiency and consequently continues to store carbohydrates to make up for the loss of weight.

Many diets deprive bodies of essential nutrients, and they may trigger overeating and make it more difficult to lose weight in the long run. There is not much evidence that sustained weight loss is possible for most people through fad diets, while there is some evidence that trying to lose weight repeatedly can cause harm.

Today, dieting is a ubiquitous business in United States. In 2005, the American diet industry had $40 billion in overall revenue, and it is projected to increase substantially in the near future. Despite extensive dieting, diet programs, diet books, and diet products, as a nation, Americans have continued to gain weight. As of 2005, it was estimated that 6 out of 10 people in the United States were overweight. As a result, it is believed that obesity will soon lead to 300,000 premature deaths annually, and the financial costs for health care and lost wages are estimated at $117 billion.

The increase in obesity is correlated with the growth of the **fast food** and junk food industries. Junk food manufacturers and fast food operators have been particularly targeted as being responsible for the obesity epidemic. Both industries have made inexpensive high-caloric and high-fat foods widely available and have promoted them through billions of dollars of **advertising**, much of which is **marketed to children** watching television.

Weight-Loss Products and Drugs

To support weight-loss programs and do-it-yourself diets, manufacturers have produced tens of thousands of weight-loss foods. In 1969, Nidetch introduced frozen, low-calorie dinners. Nutri/System and Jenny Craig followed with a complete line of prepackaged foods with the right portion and proper nutrition for participants. Commercial spinoffs included Stouffer's Lean Cuisine and **Heinz**'s Weight Watchers line. In addition to diet products produced by weight-loss programs, in the 1970s, hospitals began offering liquid diets to obese patients. Slim-Fast and Nestlé Sweet Success are commercial versions that replace two meals with convenient 200–calorie, nutritionally balanced shakes made from skim milk.

Thousands of food products that purport to be diet foods are now on the market. An estimated 50 percent of all food products on the market include such claims as "diet," "low-calorie," "reduced fat," or "no fat." Even premium **ice cream** manufacturer Häagen-Dazs has introduced low-fat ice cream. Lay's produces Baked Potato Chips, and Pringles offers a fat-free version, while Frito-Lay has introduced its Wow! line of low-fat chips. Fast-food purveyors also developed low-fat foods. Not all commercial low-fat or low-calorie foods have been successful, however. **McDonald's**, for instance, tried a low-fat burger called the McLean, which was discontinued due to lack of interest by customers. Salads, carrot sticks, and other products were more successful.

In the 1890s, weight-loss products with ingredients such as laxatives, purgatives, and Epsom salts began to be marketed. Numerous pills and drugs have been offered for sale since. Recently, PPA (phenylpropanolamine) was employed in a variety of over-the-counter drugs such as "Dexatrim." In 1993 Fen-phen, a combination of two diet drugs, fenfluramine and phentermine, appeared. It was proven to cause heart valve problems and possibly brain damage and was withdrawn by the Food and Drug Administration (FDA) in 1997. Ephedrine-based herbal supplements have alos become popular. Olestra (using the trade name Olean), a fat molecule that is too big to be digested, was introduced in 1996 after approval by the FDA. Other weight-loss drugs have been sold over the counter, but have little scientific evidence for success.

Physical Exercise

Strongly opposed to pill pushers was Bernarr Macfadden, who advocated physical exercise to avoid obesity and promote weight control. Often called the "father of the physical culture movement," Macfadden published magazines and books to promote exercise and a diet strong in raw milk, fruits, vegetables, and whole grains. Macfadden was followed by other exercise gurus, including Jack La Lanne, who opened up a chain of health clubs in 1938. Others followed in La Lanne's footsteps, including Ray Wilson, who invented the Lifecycle and opened his American Health Silhouette Clubs in the 1950s and later the Family Fitness Centers in the late 1970s. Perhaps the most famous exercise franchise is Gold's Gym, launched in 1965 by Joe Gold in Venice, California. It attracted the likes of Arnold Schwarzenegger and spread to more than 500 gyms. In 1968, Kenneth H. Cooper coined the term *aerobics* and founded the Cooper Aerobic Center in Dallas. Two years later, Arthur Jones established Nautilus Sports/Medical Industries, which sold equipment to Nautilus Fitness Centers around the country. Many new franchises have subsequently opened up.

Other exercise gurus have appeared and created successful businesses based on television programs, videos, products, and books. Among the more successful and popular fitness gurus is Richard Simmons, who began his weight-loss exercise program in 1973. In addition to diet and exercise, Simmons created a number of products, including 50 fitness videos, which have sold more than 20 million copies, and nine books, of which *Never Say Diet* was a best-seller.

Surgery

Surgery has been recommended for morbid obesity, which is defined as BMI of 40 or more. The most common procedure is gastric bypass surgery, which removes much of the stomach, creating a smaller pouch to which the small intestine is attached. With a smaller stomach, the patient eats less, and thus over time weight is decreased. In 2005, an estimated 140,000 gastric bypass operations were performed in the United States at a cost of about $25,000 per operation.

Weight losses of up to 80 percent have been reported as a result of surgery. However, all surgery is a risk, and the mortality rate for gastric bypass surgery is estimated at 0.5 percent of the operations performed. Fatalities are often a result of complications related to obesity, such as heart disease. What the health effects of gastric bypass surgery might be in the long run is unknown.

Prevention

As obesity is extremely difficult to cure, health professionals have concluded that prevention, not treatment, offers the best long-term solution. Of particular concern has been the increase in obesity of youth. Over the past three decades, the rate of obesity has more than doubled among preschool children and adolescents and tripled among all school-age children. The causes for this increase are twofold: a lack of exercise and the increased consumption of junk food. Solutions that have been offered include better **nutrition education** for children and their parents; increased exercise for youth; a decrease in the availability of junk food, particularly in schools; and banning the advertising of junk food on children's programs.

Congressional representatives have proposed national legislation to restrict marketing and sales of **snack foods** and **soft drinks** in schools. In 2005, Sen. Edward M. Kennedy, for instance, introduced a bill entitled the Prevention of Childhood Obesity Act. In support of the bill, Kennedy stated: "Prevention is the cornerstone of good health and long, productive lives for all Americans. Childhood obesity is preventable, but we have to work together to stop this worsening epidemic and protect our children's future."

FURTHER READINGS: Acs, Zoltan J., and Alan Lyles, eds. *Obesity, Business and Public Policy.* Northampton, MA: Edward Elgar, 2007; Beller, Anne Scott. *Fat and Thin: A Natural History of Obesity.* New York: Farrar, Straus, & Giroux, 1977; Bray, George A. *The Battle of the Bulge: A History of Obesity.* Pittsburgh, PA: Dorrance, 2006; Campos, Paul. *The Obesity Myth: Why America's Obsession with Weight Is Hazardous to Your Health.* New York: Gotham Books, 2004; Chase, Chria. *The Great American Waistline: Putting It On and Taking It Off.* New York: Coward, McCann & Geoghegan, 1981; Critser, Greg. *Fat Land: How Americans Became the Fattest People in the World.* New York: Houghton Mifflin, 2003; Fraser, Laura. *Losing It: America's Obsession with Weight and the Industry That Feeds on It.* New York: Dutton, 1997; Gardner, Gary. *Underfed and Overfed: The Global Epidemic of Malnutrition.* Washington, D.C.: World Watch, 2000; Kushner, Robert F., and Daniel H. Bessesen. *Treatment of the Obese Patient.* Totowa, NJ: Humana Press, 2007; Oliver, J. Eric. *Fat Politics: The Real Story behind America's Obesity Epidemic.* New York: Oxford University Press, 2005; Schwartz, Hillel. *Never Satisfied: A Cultural History of Diets, Fantasies and Fat.* New York: Free Press, 1986.

Andrew F. Smith

Organic Foods *Organic food* refers to food produced without using the conventional inputs of modern, industrial agriculture: pesticides, synthetic **fertilizers**, sewage sludge, genetically modified organisms (GMOs), **irradiation**, or food **additives**. It is marketed as being healthy for both the body and the environment. It is also portrayed as being natural, implying a connection between the human body and Nature as inherently pure, complete, clean, and friendly. Organic production, in this vein, resists a human-made system of production that suffers from pollution as a result of attempts by human intervention to manage and manipulate Nature.

Characteristically, organic food producers and advocates emphasize conservation of soil, water, and renewable resources to protect and enhance overall environmental quality. Animal-based organic food, such as meat, eggs, and **dairy** products, necessarily come from animals that are not given any **antibiotics** or hormones throughout their entire lives. Livestock must also have outdoor access and be fed 100 percent organic feed.

Historically, organic food has been produced on small, family-run independent farms that rejected the use of conventional farming practices and sold their food products locally. Organic food and farming's social presence began as a countercultural movement in the 1960s and '70s, mirroring grassroots concerns about environmental issues and the use of chemicals in food production. Organic food was available mainly at small specialty stores, **farmers' markets**, and roadside stands. Its supporters were frequently dismissed as backward, nonproductive, and nostalgic back-to-the-landers. It symbolized an ideological antithesis to large-scale **agribusiness** and the corporate marketing of processed foods.

Today, the organic food market has mobilized support on local, regional, national, and international levels and has been somewhat assimilated into the corporate mainstream. While organic food accounts for only 1–2 percent of total food sales in the United States today, it is the only area of the food market that is currently growing; organic farmers have evolved into an industry in terms of their collective production capacity. Large natural-foods **supermarkets** began opening in the late 1980s, and by the mid-1990s retail sales of organic food totaled about $4 billion. In 2002, it was an $11 billion industry, and it has been growing at a rate of 20 percent per year since then.

Organic foods are typically thought to belong to the market segment of the cultural creative and professional classes (based on prices, availability, and consumer ideologies associated with the 1960s counterculture). Its growth is perceived as a response to conventional farming and production standards that have threatened the environment and the methods by which food is grown, handled, and processed. Organizations such as the Organic Consumers Association monitor organic foods' development and related legislation as an important player in the agriculture industry.

Legal Definition and National Standards

The U.S. legal definition of organic food was formally institutionalized in October 2002 as the National Organic Program (NOP) by a set of certification standards, created and implemented by the **U.S. Department of Agriculture** (USDA) with recommendations from the National Organic Standards Board (NOSB), that speak to the methods used in producing and handling organically produced foods and food products. A voluntary green-and-white seal on foods' **packaging** denotes that a product is at least 95 percent organic. Before these national standards were instituted, certification standards varied by state, region, and certifying agency. Introducing a federally consistent definition of organic has given producers an incentive to undertake the certification process and allows them to compete in this national and international growth market. Formal certification procedures at the governmental level also exist in other countries.

The national organic standards also deal with issues of processing, food handling, and manufacturing. The NOSB maintains the National List of Allowed and Prohibited Substances, which identifies synthetic materials permissible for inclusion in the production and handling of organics; for example, baking soda is an allowable synthetic material in organic food production. Under the NOP and USDA organic certification label, food products can be called "100 percent organic" only if every ingredient and all processing aids were produced through the methods described above. They can be "organic" if they contain 95 percent organic ingredients, with the remaining 5 percent from the National List, and "made with organic ingredients" if 70 percent of their makeup is organic materials. The USDA seal may not be used on packaging with 95 percent or less organic ingredients. Any product labeled "organic" must have been manufactured, processed, and handled according to specific rules and requirements. For products that contain between 70 and 95 percent organic ingredients, the packaging may say "made with organic ingredients" on the front, but may not depict the seal. Products with less than 70 percent of organic ingredients may list these ingredients on the side of the packaging, but may not tout organic claims on the front of the package. Organic food can be sold as either fresh or processed items, depending on production methods, similar to conventionally produced food.

For a food production or distribution entity to become certified as organic, a government-approved agent inspects the farm or production facility to make sure the producer is following the USDA's relevant rules and regulations. Under these rules, land used for organic production may not have had any of the regulation's prohibited substances applied to it for at least three years before the harvesting of food labeled "organic." The land is required to be maintained through practices that encourage natural methods of cultivation, including crop rotation and the use of cover crops to improve the content and quality of soil matter, instead of using artificial materials such as synthetic fertilizers and pesticides. Fruit and vegetable producers are required to use organically grown seeds, annual seedlings, or planting stock, although they may substitute untreated nonorganic seeds and planting stock when equivalent organic varieties are not commercially available. The organic label is also federally required to show the country of origin, and companies that handle or process organic food must also be certified. As of 2006, there were almost 7,000 certified organic farms in the United States.

Not all organic farmers have taken the path of NOP certification. A production or handling operation that has $5,000 or less in gross annual income from organic sales is exempt from certification. This exemption is primarily designed for those producers who market their product directly to consumers, but it also permits such producers to market their products direct to retail food establishments for resale to consumers. Many community-supported agricultural groups, local sustainable farms, and individual producers maintain the standards and modes of production they have participated in for years. Now that legislation and regulation exist at the national level, farmers' markets and farms earning more than the $5,000 income limit have begun calling their products "locally grown," "pesticide-free," and increasingly, "beyond organic" to indicate their foods' qualities without undergoing the USDA's certification process.

These standards are much stricter than the USDA's initial proposals, which would have permitted the use of genetically modified foods, irradiation, and sewage-based fertilizers. However, 275,000 angry letters from the public forced the USDA to redraft the standards to the more stringent current level. Additionally, as some small organic farmers note, the standards do not differentiate between foods produced by small-scale farms and those produced by huge factory-style farms that require large environmental inputs, whether or not they use organic growing methods.

In the **European Union**, organic food production is regulated by the EU Eco-regulation, created in 1991, and has since become a widely accepted sector of agricultural and food **research**. Publicly funded research, particularly in Northern Europe, has shifted toward organic farming, while research funding for conventional farming has been cut considerably. The EU has funded several coordinating actions, such as the European Network for Scientific Research Coordination in Organic Farming, Documentation of Ecological Agriculture, and the Network for Animal Health and Welfare in Organic Agriculture. Japan also possesses comprehensive organic legislation. In countries without government legislation, organic certification is typically handled by private organizations.

The Environment and Health

Organic food is positioned as an environmental issue and has firm links to environmental groups and movements that emphasize the use of renewable resources and soil and water conservation. The social problem these supporters aim to address is the long-term endangerment of the Earth's production capacity due to the application of pesticides, additives of hormones, antibiotics, and other such substances to crops—all of which cause soil depletion; pollute the land, water, and air; and raise health concerns. Such groups include the Sierra Club and the Nature Conservancy. Additionally, support for organic food production has sociological links to globalization, sustainable development, the fair trade movement, community issues, and other nutritional and agricultural movements based on the principles that social and environmental sustainability are interdependent.

Organic food is also farmed and marketed as a health issue. Heavy reliance on pesticides by conventional farmers is suspected of leading to increased rates of cancer and reproductive problems. More than 80 percent of the most commonly used pesticides today have been classified by National Academy of Sciences researchers as potentially carcinogenic. Choosing organic foods allows consumers to choose to buy and eat foods grown without pesticides.

The Growing Organic Food Industry

Well-known organic food producers include Niman Ranch and Amy's Organic. Organic dairies Organic Valley and Stonyfield Farms operate cooperative programs to offer subsidies to dairy farmers who desire to convert their production methods from conventional to organic. **Whole Foods Market** is important to the organic food trade as a result of its status as the only "certified organic" grocer, its acquisition of other natural-foods stores around the country, and its ability to capitalize on widely used (conventional) distribution channels for organically produced and natural foods.

Many organic brands are now owned by or partnered with major conventional food companies. These include Stonyfield Farm, owned by Groupe Danone; Cascadian Farms, owned by General Mills; Seeds of Change, owned by M&M-Mars; Celestial Seasonings, Imagine Foods, Garden of Eatin', Terra Chips, and Yves Veggie Cuisine, owned by Hain Celestial; Odwalla, owned by Coca-Cola; and Boca Foods, owned by **Kraft**. Horizon Organic, owned by Dean, has been called "the Microsoft of milk." It purchases smaller dairy farms around the country and controls 70 percent of the retail market for organic milk. **Gerber**, **Heinz**, **Campbell's Soup**, Kellogg's, **Dole**, ConAgra, Pepsi, and Archer Daniels Midland, among others, have all created or acquired organic brands.

Wal-Mart, the largest U.S. grocery retailer, declared in 2006 that it plans to double its offerings of organic products, including produce, dairy, and dry goods, under its store brand, which will be available at a lower price than equivalents on the market. Wal-Mart's move into this market, among others, dismays organic activist groups, as well as some organic food retailers and dairies, who contend that big food retailers, while conforming to legal definitions of organic, are diluting the larger principles of organic agriculture, such as keeping food production geographically close to the point of sale. The international purchase of organic ingredients can be more affordable, and so more lucrative, for these types of large organic food companies. Some organic ingredients, like conventional food ingredients, travel 1,500 to 2,500 miles "from farm to plate," belying the original intent of organic food's early advocates. Yet, increasing concerns about **food safety** continue to position "organic food" as an important phrase, and phase, in the contemporary food industry.

FURTHER READING: Fromartz, Samuel. *Organic, Inc.: Natural Foods and How They Grew.* New York: Harvest Books, 2007.

Michaela DeSoucey

P ❖ ───────────────────────────────

Packaging Packaging plays an integral role within the food production, distribution, and marketing systems. It is a complex process that must integrate the needs and limitations imposed by technological, legal, environmental, and marketing requirements. Over time, advancements in food packaging have affected the food industry as a whole by increasing the market's competitiveness, lowering the cost of many foods through effective processing techniques, and realigning the entire retail and display system. Innovations in food packaging have also led to revolutions not simply in the area of food storage but also in grocery store configurations, display systems, manufacturing, and transport and in the way we prepare and consume food.

A food's package is integral to its success, impacting profitability through areas such as brand recognition and loyalty, cost-effective product distribution, and more appealing product appearance. Packages must meet the needs and expectations of the customer and fit within the industry's existing distribution chain. There must be a seamless union between suppliers and retail outlets. Also innate within the food packaging process are critically important safety and regulatory standards. Developments in food science, processing, and preservation techniques over time have begun to ensure the safety of the consumer while retaining the quality of the product. As packaging technologies increase and greater numbers of packaged products come to market, consumers' concern regarding the environmental impacts of food packaging has increased. Packaging designers must now, more than ever, take these consumer pressures and expectations into account.

Key Features of Packaging Design

Packaging design is an intricate and strategic process. Alongside preservation, product protection, and containment, there are many other things to consider in designing a package. Packages should appear unique on a grocery store shelf, create and identify brand, describe the product, display the product attractively, and be easy to manipulate. In keeping with shipping and display standards, designers must consider size, shape, structure, imagery, text, color, and font.

Every aspect of the package communicates something about the product to the consumer. For instance, **ice cream** in a one-pint paperboard container suggests a different quality than ice cream in a two-liter tub. Size, shape, and material used impact a shopper's decision. As well, the package is a canvas that must express information and evoke an emotional response in the consumer.

In the recent redesign of its soup can, **Campbell's** began printing recipes on the cans, accompanied by full-color images of the finished meal. Campbell's move to incorporate recipes on their packages was made to imply that canned soup could be used in everyday meals and that cans were not simply to be stockpiled. The images insinuated that busy families could easily incorporate these quick, convenient, and simple recipes into their lives. In its overall form, the Campbell's soup can has not changed for decades, but its exterior has been modified countless times in order to stay current and relate to the needs of modern consumers.

Advances and Innovations in Packaging Technologies

Packaging, in the form of containers, has been in use for thousands of years. One of the earliest examples of such packaging was a container found in the Zagros Mountains of western Iran that dates back some 5,000 years. The chemical traces left within the unearthed vessel indicate that it contained a **beer**-like substance. Although such early containers are not comparable to modern packages, they did serve similar functions such as preservation, containment, distribution, and even labeling, characteristics that continue to be central to today's package. In these ways, they act as an important precursor to the modern package.

The Industrial Revolution inevitably played an immense role in the advancement of technologies and processes that enabled food packaging and the growth of the food industry. It was during this time that widespread mechanization allowed for the cost-effective production of packaged products such as canned and paper-packed goods. However, the existence of the technological capacity to produce a package is not the sole reason for its adoption. A food's packaging must also promote sales of the product it contains. The first modern example of packaging was seen in London around the turn of the 17th century. Often hand-blown and covered with handmade paper, glass **bottles** containing so-called medicinal herbal and alcoholic elixirs were hawked by traveling salesmen. The paper wrappers that covered these early packages would often fold out to poster size and display physician and patient testimonials, as well as scientific reasoning (often false) upholding the product's benefits. These paper pamphlets and the salesmen who carried them played a greater role in the success of the product than the contents of the packages. Such packages sold a concept through imagery, story, and brand confidence, rather than product. These instances of early advertising through packaging highlight the importance of packaging to the success and adoption of a product.

Throughout the years, modern packaging developments have also been driven by advances, requirements, limitations, and restrictions caused by the circumstances of war. For instance, **canning** was invented in response to a contest initiated by the French government in 1795. A prize of 12,000 francs was offered to the individual who could produce a method for preserving military food supplies. After a testing period of 14 years, Nicolas Appert was awarded the prize for canning meats and vegetables in glass jars and supplying Napoleon's army with a steady source of rations. This canning technology quickly made its way to Great Britain, where tinplate was implemented in place of glass.

Although the use of cans was taken up quickly by the military, mass production of cans for the consumer market was slow to occur. This changed with the invention of the Bessemer steelmaking process in 1856–1857. This procedure allowed tinplate to be produced in thinner and more malleable sheets ideal for the production of cans. However, it was not solely technological innovation that propelled the production and widespread adoption of canned goods. As they originally did and continue to, marketing and sales played an important and influential role. For example, American inventor Gail **Borden** marketed his canned milk products as being fresher and more sanitary than milk sold in bulk. Directing his product at the large New York City market, he couched the canned milk in a vision of pastoral freshness, implying that unpackaged milk was contaminated and unhygienic. The successful marketing techniques that Borden implemented were not new, yet his application of technological innovation in conjunction with deliberate and targeted promotion continues to embody today's packaging process and strategy.

The impact of the war shortages was also seen during World War I, when tinplate, necessary for steel cans, became scarce. It was due to this shortage that paper packaging was more widely distributed. Paper bags had already become a cheap and efficient way of packaging and carrying foodstuffs such as **sugar** and rice. However, they did not provide protection and stability.

It was the folded paper box, invented in 1879 by Robert Gair, that paved the way for the affordable mass marketing of paper-packaged goods. Quaker Oats was the first to adopt the paper box for its **breakfast cereal** products in 1884. As a packaging vessel, the box provided freshness, while also acting as an **advertising** space for the product. Items such as sugar, flour, salt, and a myriad of other products are still packaged in paper. Today, paperboard remains one of the most commonly used forms of packaging, amounting to 45 percent of the value of all packaging.

Further innovations and an immense increase in the demand for packaged foods occurred during and after World War II. Like paper during the First World War, the plastic industry saw many advances during World War II. Although it had been in use since the turn of the century, innovations stemming from restrictions on steel induced plastic manufacturers such as DuPont to adapt plastics to different uses and increase its durability and strength. Since the war, the growing use of plastic packaging has been steady and continuous. The flexibility of plastic enabled food producers to step outside of the box and create an environment within which a variety of products might be contained. Unlike canning, the packaging environment did not dictate the contents of the package.

The postwar era also saw the prevalence of frozen foods, particularly the packaged frozen dinner. In 1923, before freezers were even widely available to the ordinary consumer, food was packaged and frozen for retail by Clarence Birdseye of General Seafood. It was not until after World War II that the freezer became a popular household item, growing in size and capacity. In this case, it was the availability of affordable new appliances both at home and throughout retail outlets that allowed for the adoption of quick-frozen packaged meals by grocery stores and consumers.

The greatest innovation in packaging to come out of the **frozen food** industry was the **TV dinner**. Frozen-food manufacturers soon realized that foods could take any form, and packages such as the compartmentalized tray emerged. These trays, as we continue to know them today, could hold a portion of meat, potatoes, vegetables, and even a dessert. The introduction of frozen TV dinners meant that packaged, prepared foods did not have to mimic canned food. It opened the door to entirely new opportunities within the food market.

Another major postwar innovation in food packaging was the aseptic package. Aseptic packaging allows the package and the product to be sterilized separately, creating a sterile environment for the product. Using this technique, products that could not otherwise withstand the canning process, such as milk and eggs, could now be stored without **refrigeration**. Popular individually packaged items such as puddings and juice boxes all employ this form of packaging. Aseptic packaging allowed a huge array of products to move out of the refrigerator and into the pantry, both in the home and within the food industry.

Environmental Impact, Concerns, and Benefits

In recent years there has been increasing pressure from consumers to reduce the negative impact food packaging has had on the environment. Items such as aerosol cans, which were embraced after World War II, fell out of favor due to the damaging effects of their emissions. However, the surplus of waste produced by excessive packaging has become an even more contentious issue. Consumers' perceptions of packaging as excessively wasteful have become a major factor within the packaging and food manufacturing industry. Images of landfills littered with plastic bottles and **fast food** wrappers create an emotional response in consumers, and this outcry has forced manufacturers to respond.

The fast food industry often receives much attention because of the amount of packaging necessary to create portable and standardized wrappers that preserve the corporate identity. After polling suggested that consumers viewed its industry as one of the most wasteful, **McDonald's** responded with a packaging redesign. Plastic-coated wrappers replaced polystyrene foam hamburger packages. These new wrappers were not recyclable, but because they were less bulky, the amount of landfill waste was estimated to decrease by 70 percent.

Today, more and more packages advertise their use of recycled materials or their overall reduced use of packaging materials. In the evolving world of package design, production and innovation are now being shaped by anxieties concerning environmental impact.

While perceived as creating waste, packaging also plays an enormous part in eliminating food spoilage. It allows for the preservation worldwide of food resources and the prevention of waste. As stated, the chief functions of the package are to contain, protect, inform, and preserve. By effectively achieving these goals, food packaging reduces financial loss and damage to the environment due to waste, increases shelf life and accessibility, and ensures safety and convenience for the consumer.

See also Birds Eye.

FURTHER READINGS: Coles, R., D. McDowell, and M. Kirwan, eds. *Food Packaging Technology*. London: Blackwell, 2003; Hine, Thomas. *The Total Package: The Evolution and Secret Meanings of Boxes, Bottles, Cans and Tubes*. Boston: Little, Brown, 1995; Meyers, Herbert M., and Murray J. Lubliner. *The Marketer's Guide to Successful Package Design*. Chicago: NTC Business Books, 1998; Richardson, Gordon L. *Food Packaging: Principles and Practice*. New York: Marcel Dekker, 1993; Sacharow, Stanley, and Roger C. Griffin Jr. *Principles of Food Packaging*. 2nd ed. Westport, CT: AVI, 1980.

Sarah Kornik

Peanut Butter In the early 1890s John Harvey Kellogg, a **vegetarian** entrepreneur in Battle Creek, Michigan, sought a replacement for "cow's butter." He crushed various nuts between two rollers and claimed the results to be "nut butters." At the time, peanuts were less expensive than tree nuts, and they soon became the most significant of his vegetarian nut butters. To commercialize his discovery, Kellogg created the Sanitas Nut Food Company and placed his brother, Will K. Kellogg, in charge. Nut butters quickly became a fad among other health-food manufacturers in America. By 1900, peanut butter manufacturing spread throughout the United States. Ten years later, peanut butter was being manufactured in virtually every large and medium-size city in the United States.

Beech-Nut and Heinz

The two most important early peanut butter manufacturers were the **Beech-Nut** Packing Company of Canajoharie, New York, and the H. J. **Heinz** Company of Pittsburgh, Pennsylvania. Beech-Nut began making peanut butter in 1905. Around 1912, it began **advertising** its product, and the advertising paid off. By 1915, Beech-Nut was the largest peanut butter manufacturer in the country. The H. J. Heinz Company first manufactured peanut butter during the early 1900s. It followed Beech-Nut's lead and began advertising its peanut butter in 1913.

Both the Heinz and Beech-Nut peanut butters were premium products. Many competitors turned to inferior raw materials. Others failed to keep their machinery clean and frequently added mineral oil to cover up defects or lower the cost. These lower-cost goods flooded the market and gave peanut butter manufacturers a bad name. At the time, there were no standards on peanut butter contents and no uniform standard for **packaging**. As a result, in June 1922 the major producers banded together and created the National Peanut Butter Manufacturers Association to help set standards and improve the quality of peanut butter in America.

Skippy and Peter Pan

In early commercial peanut butters, oil separated from the butter, creating an oily pool at the top of the jar. In 1922, Joseph L. Rosefield of the Rosefield Packing Company of Alameda, California, developed a process to prevent oil separation and spoilage in peanut butter. He removed 18 percent of the liquid oil and replaced it with an equal amount of hydrogenated oil, which was solid at room temperature. The result was a semisolid peanut butter; no oil rose to the surface. The peanut butter was thick and creamy and did not stick to the roof of the mouth as much as previous products. Hydrogenated oil also permitted a finer grinding of peanuts, which prevented the salt from separating from the peanut butter.

Rosefield continued his experiments and found several different ways of making peanut butter. He patented a process for a "malted peanut butter," in which the peanut was allowed to germinate and then roasted, blanched, and ground into peanut butter. Rosefield asserted that this yielded a product with a higher content of **vitamins** and a richer, nutty flavor. Rosefield selected the name Skippy for his new peanut butter. Most likely, the name was derived from a children's comic strip called "Skippy," launched by Percy L. Crosby in 1923. This presumed origin generated several lawsuits. Undeterred, Rosefield introduced creamy and chunky-style peanut butters in 1932. Three years later, Rosefield inaugurated its first wide-mouth peanut butter jar, which has remained the industry standard ever since.

Another early peanut butter manufacturer was the E. K Pond Company, a subsidiary of **Swift** Co., which began producing peanut butter in 1920. Lackluster sales encouraged the company to change the name of its product to Peter Pan—the popular fantasy character popularized in film and in books. As soon as Pond changed the name, sales took off.

Jif

Of the major pre–World War II peanut butter manufacturers, Beech-Nut and Heinz discontinued producing peanut butter during the 1950s. While the reasons for these decisions remain obscure, surely one reason was the competition from three major peanut butter manufacturers: Skippy, Peter Pan, and a new rival, Procter & Gamble's Jif, which was introduced in 1958. Jif was sweetened with honey and was an immediate success. However, its competitors complained that peanut butter with honey was not consistent with the **U.S. Department of Agriculture** definition of peanut butter, which requires at least 90 percent peanuts, with the remaining 10 percent restricted to salt, sweeteners, and stabilizers. By the time the ruling was made, Procter & Gamble was already committed to manufacturing peanut butter, so it removed the honey and increased advertising.

Procter & Gamble later diversified its peanut butter products, adding Creamy Jif and Extra Crunchy Jif, which made its debut in 1974. According to Procter & Gamble, a 28-ounce jar of Jif contains about 1,218 peanuts. It takes approximately 120 billion peanuts to make all the Jif peanut butter produced in one year. The Jif plant in Lexington, Kentucky, is the largest peanut butter–producing facility in the world.

Peanut Butter Today

The peanut butter industry has been in a process of change. Peter Pan Peanut Butter was sold to Beatrice/**Hunt**-Wesson in 1984, which, in turn, was acquired by ConAgra in 1988. Peter Pan is currently manufactured at plants in Sylvester, Georgia, and Dallas. In 1955 Best Foods purchased Rosefield Packing Company, makers of Skippy Peanut Butter. Best Foods is today a subsidiary of Unilever.

Americans annually consume about 857 million pounds of peanut butter, which works out to about $3^1/_3$ pounds per person. The top seller in the $800 million peanut butter category is Jif, with sales of $272 million, compared with $159 million for Skippy and $154 million for private-label brands.

FURTHER READING: Smith, Andrew F. *Peanuts: The Illustrious History of the Goober Pea.* Urbana: University of Illinois Press, 2002.

Andrew F. Smith

PepsiCo. *See* Soft Drinks.

Perdue. *See* Poultry Industry.

Pet Food Many Americans live with companion animals of one kind or another, and the animals need to be fed. A lively industry has emerged to help with this task, with its own trade associations, annual meetings, and **Internet** sites. The strength of this industry depends on the number of people with pets. The American Pet Product Manufacturers Association (APPMA), one such trade association, estimates that 63 percent of American households have one or more pets, most of them dogs and cats. Nearly 40 percent of American households have at least one dog, and 34 percent have at least one cat, for a total of about 74 million dogs and 90 million cats. Horses, donkeys, a variety of small mammals, and numerous birds, fish, and reptiles make up a much smaller proportion of the pet population. All must be fed foods appropriate to their species, but this entry focuses on dog and cat food.

The Pet Food Marketplace

Businesses involved in pet care are a small but growing industry in the United States, one that sold $38.4 billion worth of products in 2006, an increase of $9 billion since 2001. Nearly half this amount—$15.2 billion—is spent on food, 95 percent for dogs and cats. This amount exceeds expenditures on veterinary care and pet supplies (including over-the-counter medicines), which amount to about $9 billion each.

People tend to buy food for their pets in the same places they buy their own food. In 2005, they purchased nearly 34 percent of their pet food at **supermarkets** and another 33 percent at mass-market stores such as Wal-Mart and Target. Dedicated pet stores such as PETCO and Pet Smart accounted for just 17 percent of pet food sales, but this percentage is expected to grow. Less than 5 percent of pet foods are bought at warehouse clubs such as Costco and Sam's Club, and even smaller percentages at farm stores or from veterinarians, kennels, and dollar stores or over the Internet. APPMA estimates that annual expenditures for pet food amount to about $1,500 per dog and $900 per cat.

Six companies dominate the pet food market and collectively control more than 70 percent of sales. Nestlé is the largest, with a market share of 33 percent; it owns at least 30 brands of dog and cat foods. Nestlé's share of the cat food market is exceptionally high; it holds a 57 percent share of canned cat food and a 47 percent share of the dry varieties. Nestlé supports such sales with impressive **advertising** budgets. In 2005, its expenditures for **television**, radio, and print advertising included $123.1 million for Purina products, $67.3 million for Friskies, and $21 million for Fancy Feast.

The next largest companies—Mars, Procter & Gamble, **Del Monte**, Colgate, and Doane—hold market shares of between 6 and 10 percent each. Mars spent $67.3 million to advertise Pedigree brand foods in 2005, and $16.1 million on Whiskas, while Procter & Gamble devoted $57.9 million to advertising Iams. These expenditures are similar to those for nationally advertised products for people. Doane, a company unknown to most Americans, is the largest manufacturer of private-label pet foods; for example, it supplies Wal-Mart's Ol' Roy brand. A large number of smaller brands share the remaining sales, among them Newman's and other makers of organic and specialty pet foods.

Composition of Pet Foods

Today's pet foods result from decades of **research**. Following World War II, scientists were engaged in two lines of research that eventually led to improvements in pet feeding: studies of human nutritional requirements intended to improve human health; and studies of the nutritional requirements of farm animals intended to improve food production. Because animal and human nutrition are similar, much of the early research on human requirements was conducted on dogs. These studies produced useful information about the nutritional requirements of dogs as well as of humans.

Research results from studies on farm animals also often apply to cats and dogs. This meant that companies developing feed for cows, pigs, and sheep were in a position to produce foods to meet the requirements of cats and dogs as well. What initially began as a sideline to feeding farm animals grew into today's sophisticated and profitable pet food industry.

The composition of commercial pet foods might surprise anyone familiar with the evolution of dogs and cats. Although the wild ancestors of these animals are considered to be primarily carnivores—meat eaters—modern pet foods supply nutrients from cereals and other plant by-products commonly used to feed farm animals. A typical mainstream dry dog or cat food, for example, lists yellow **corn** as its first ingredient, followed by meat or **poultry** by-products that include parts of food animals considered unfit for human consumption, followed by other plant sources of protein such as soybean meal. These ingredients are supplemented with animal fats, vitamins, and minerals. Cat foods, for example, contain taurine, an amino acid required for their growth and reproduction, as well as certain fatty acids that are not generally required in the diet of humans or other animals.

Dry foods represent about 55 percent of the dog food market and about 48 percent of the cat food market. These are typically made by passing the ingredients through an extruder and spraying the extruded particles with animal fat and flavorings. Canned foods make up about 24 percent of the dog food market and 46 percent of foods for cats. Canned foods are moist, contain water, and may contain more meat than dry foods, although they sometimes contain cereals and animal or plant by-products. Foods considered "treats" make up more than 20 percent of the market for dog foods and 6 percent of the cat food market.

Regulation of Pet Foods

Pet foods are regulated by the Food and Drug Administration (FDA) under the Federal Food Drug and Cosmetic Act, as well as by feed laws passed by specific states. The federal Act requires pet foods, like human foods, to "be pure and wholesome, contain no harmful or deleterious substances and be truthfully labeled." The FDA Center for Veterinary Medicine (CVM) is in charge of pet foods and feed for farm animals.

The FDA does not require pet food manufacturers to obtain premarket approval of new products, but does regulate food **additives** in these foods. It requires the additives to be safe and effective for their intended use. For new additives, companies must submit extensive data to demonstrate safety and efficacy. Such data are not required for substances that are obviously safe; the FDA considers these as "generally recognized as safe" (GRAS).

In 1994, Congress passed the Dietary Supplement and Health Education Act, which effectively deregulated products marketed to humans as dietary supplements. This Act, however, does not apply to pet foods. Thus, dietary supplements added to pet foods are regulated under the more stringent requirements of food additives (requiring proof of safety and efficacy) rather than the relaxed regulations that apply to dietary supplements for humans. In practice, however, this distinction is largely ignored.

To regulate pet foods, the FDA works closely with the Association of American Feed Control Officials (AAFCO), an organization of state and federal officials who oversee the production and labeling of feed for farm animals. AAFCO develops model laws and regulations, uniform feed ingredient definitions, and appropriate labeling requirements to ensure the safe and effective use of animal feed. These model laws form the basis of most state feed regulation legislation.

Pet food ingredients were shown to be a weak link in food safety early in 2007 when the industry discovered that the **wheat** gluten it had been importing from China was actually wheat flour mixed with melamine, a nitrogen-rich compound that makes substances appear to have more protein than they actually do. The adulterated product, incorporated into a large number of brands of pet food, was in part responsible for the death of untold numbers of cats and dogs, leading to the largest recall of pet foods in history. The incident revealed that a single manufacturer was producing foods sold under brand names ranging from commonplace to premium. It also revealed that recalled pet foods were fed to pigs, chickens, and farmed fish, potentially exposing the human food supply to risk. Finally, it exposed weaknesses in **food safety** regulations in developing countries such as China, as well as in the United States. Thus, "mere" pet foods were shown to be key indicators of issues as important as food safety, international trade, and globalization.

Federal regulations, enforced by the CVM, establish labeling standards that apply to all animal feeds: proper identification of the type and weight, the manufacturer's address, and the ingredients in order of quantity by weight. In addition to the federal rules, AAFCO has developed nutrient standards for pet food and specific rules for label claims. For example, a cat food labeled "chicken" must contain at least 95 percent chicken, excluding the water used for processing. One marketed as "chicken dinner" must contain at least 25 percent chicken, but one "with chicken" need only be 3 percent chicken. A product can be labeled "chicken flavor" as long as it contains a detectable amount of that flavor component.

When pet foods are labeled "complete" or "balanced," it means that they meet nutrient profiles established by AAFCO for animals at stages of life from infancy to old age, as demonstrated by feeding tests carried out under specific AAFCO protocols. In practice, these regulations ensure that the nutrient profiles of pet foods marketed for specific life stages are much the same across brands. Manufacturers must work within these regulations to distinguish one brand from another.

Marketing Trends

The market for pet foods is driven by what this industry refers to as the "humanification" of pets—their treatment as members of the family rather than as property. In June 2006, for example, *USA Today* reported that 69 percent of people considered their companion animal to be a family member, whereas only 19 percent considered them possessions. Some surveys have found that more than 80 percent of people think of themselves as their animal's mom or dad and that more than 60 percent say "I love you" to their dog at least once a day. In contrast, just 57 percent of people say they rely on their spouse or partner for companionship, and only 4 percent say they rely on their children.

Pet humanification has business implications. It has led to the development of premium foods and snacks that appeal to peoples' interests in feeding their animals healthfully and pleasing their animals through food. The gourmet market provides pet foods made with food-grade meat and fish, excluding ingredients that humans would not eat. Some specialty products are designed specifically for animals that have health problems such as allergies or urinary, joint, or dental disorders. Others are labeled as designed for specific market segments: puppies, kittens, older pets, pregnant and lactating pets, big dogs, small dogs, obese dogs and cats, and particular breeds. In 2006, manufacturers introduced 175 new food products for cats and dogs.

Natural and **organic** pet foods represent a rapidly growing segment of this market, reflecting similar trends in human food. The Organic Trade Association estimated sales of organic pet foods as $30 million in 2005, a 46 percent increase from just the previous year. Manufacturers produce kosher, **vegetarian**, and **raw foods** for specialty markets, along with bottled water, vitamin water, and bakery-style treats.

The Obesity Dilemma

The most important challenge to today's pet food market is the same as that affecting the market for human foods: **obesity**. One-third or more of household pets in the United States weigh more than is good for their health. As with humans, pet obesity is more than a cosmetic problem; it raises risks for diabetes, kidney disease, and joint problems, and it affects longevity. Thinner dogs and cats live longer. To prevent obesity, pets should be fed enough—but not too much (and, of course, should be given plenty of exercise). But for reasons of humanification, people often are reluctant to withhold food from an apparently hungry dog or cat, even if doing so would help the animal live longer.

Obesity creates the same dilemma for pet food companies that it does for companies producing foods for humans: Pet food companies are in business to sell more food, not less. If they care about pet health, they should be advising people to feed pets less food, less often. Even if they make special formulas designed for weight control, they will be trying to sell more such products, not less. In this regard, the pet food business mirrors trends in the human food industry. Such trends are likely to include further consolidation of the pet food business, increased emphasis on health, and increasing interest in the source and quality of pet food ingredients.

FURTHER READINGS: American Pet Products Manufacturing Association. "Industry Statistics and Trends." http://www.appma.org/press_industrytrends.asp; Association of American Feed Control Officials. *AAFCO Pet Food and Specialty Pet Food Labeling Guide, 2004.* Available at http://www.aafco.org; Banasiak, Karen. "Pampering Your Pet." *Food Technology* 60, no. 11 (2006): 35–41; Benz, Sharon. "FDA's Regulation of Pet Food." http://www.fda.gov/cvm/petfoodflier.html; National Research Council. *Nutrient Requirements of Dogs and Cats.* Washington, D.C.: National Academies Press, 2006.

Malden C. Nesheim and Marion Nestle

Pickles Production of pickles in America began with the early colonists, and the country's appetite for them is still strong. Fermented, brined, or otherwise cured cucumbers are what Americans generally refer to as "pickles," and they eat an average of nine pounds of them a year per person.

The history of pickle making goes back to ancient Mesopotamia. Christopher Columbus brought pickles to the New World, growing cucumbers in Haiti to turn into pickles, a common ship's store. Dutch settlers in what is now New York City brought pickles with them in the 16th century. In 1606 English colonists in Virginia produced pickles both at home and commercially. By 1659 Dutch colonists in New York were growing cucumbers for dealers who would cure them in brine; these pickles were sold in market stalls in lower Manhattan.

In the 19th century, commercial pickle **packaging** came into its own, helped by the 1858 invention of the glass Mason jar and the 1881 invention of the metal canning lid. In 1871 pickles were the second product offered by H. J. **Heinz**'s new company (the first was horseradish). A small, green, pickle-shaped plaster charm giveaway at the Chicago World's Fair in 1893 proved to be so popular that Heinz still distributes a plastic pin version of it. That year saw the establishment of Pickle Packers International, a pickle processors trade group. Pickle popularity only increased as waves of Jewish, Eastern European, and other immigrants came to America in the late 19th and early 20th centuries and brought their tastes for pickles with them.

More than 36 different styles and varieties of pickled cucumbers are produced in the United States. They range it style from sweet to sour, with different seasonings, fermentation and brining methods, and regional and **ethnic** popularities. They can be found in the **refrigerator** case or in shelf-stable jars or cans. One popular style of pickle, the dill or kosher dill pickle, is made by putting cucumbers in large wooden barrels and covering them with salt, dill, spices, and water. The pickles are kept like this until the desired sourness, crispness, and color are reached. Selling these pickles from barrels on the street was a popular enterprise among new immigrants. At one time, more than 80 pickle stalls were in business on the Lower East Side of Manhattan. One such pickle stand remains in business there today.

While most pickles are not bought out of pickle barrels today, they are still popularly eaten as a snack, alongside or on sandwiches, hamburgers, or other foods in more than 67 percent of American households. Annual consumption of pickles is 5.2 million pounds. Between 100,000 and 120,000 acres of cucumbers are grown in the country every year specifically for pickles. Pickle sales are tracked as part of the fermented vegetables category that includes pickles, olives, and relishes. Sales of the category were almost $2.6 billion in 2006.

FURTHER READINGS: Alberts, Robert C. *The Good Provider: H. J. Heinz and His 57 Varieties.* Boston: Houghton Mifflin, 1973; Lower East Side Tenement Museum. "From the Brine: Pickles in New York." http://www.tenement.org/pickle; Martinez, Lourdes, Suzanne Thornsbury, and Tomokazu Nagai. "National and International Factors in the Pickle Market." Agricultural Economic Report No. 628. East Lansing: Michigan State University, Department of Agricultural Economics, 2006. Available at http://ageconsearch.umn.edu/bitstream/123456789/25373/1/aer628.pdf; Mt. Olive Pickle Company. http://www.mtolivepickles.com; Pickle Packers International. http://www.ilovepickles.org.

Faith J. Kramer

Pillsbury Charles A. Pillsbury (1842–1899) joined his uncle, John Sargent Pillsbury, in Minneapolis in 1869 and purchased a flour mill. Charles's marketing and managing skills made the company flourish. By 1872, in league with his uncle and father, he formed C. A. Pillsbury & Co. At the end of 10 years, the company had expanded to seven mills and was the largest flour enterprise in the world. The company was active in establishing favorable freight rates for dealers who brought their grain into Minneapolis. Later as senator, 1878–1885, Pillsbury was instrumental in the development of the Minneapolis, Saulte Sainte Marie & Atlantic Railway.

At a time when the best flours were graded XXX, Pillsbury took it upon himself to classify his flour as "Pillsbury XXXX," a greater superlative. As time went by, the company developed many Pillsbury-branded products, including breads, pizzas, **frozen** sweet treats, cookie doughs, pie crusts, and bread, cake, frosting, muffin, and roll mixes.

The Pillsbury Company was sold to an English syndicate (Pillsbury-Washburn Company, Ltd.) in 1889, and Pillsbury stayed on as managing director. Though he lost much through speculating in the **wheat** market, Pillsbury was also known to be charitable to his employees and other organizations.

Charles Pillsbury's uncle John was a state senator when he and his nephew founded their company. John later became Minnesota's governor (1876–1882) and was credited with government reorganization, straightening out railroad bonds that brought an end to much corruption. He later returned to the flour business, joining his nephew in contributing to many charities.

The Pillsbury Company has remained prominent in the public eye due to its innovative promotion and marketing practices. Over the years, as it increased its product line, Pillsbury issued memorabilia, including numerous booklets, pamphlets, and a vast amount of **advertising** items. Many are collectibles today. The company was also a major cookbook **publisher** for more than 100 years, producing a wide range of titles ranging from the general all-purpose *Pillsbury Complete Cookbook* to specifically themed books.

Poppin' Fresh, the famed Pillsbury Doughboy mascot, was created in 1965 by a Leo Burnett Agency ad copywriter. In each television ad, an anonymous finger touches Poppin' Fresh's dough belly causing him to emit his signature squealing giggle. The Doughboy is considered one of Pillsbury's biggest assets.

The Pillsbury Bake-Off competition started in 1949 as a showplace to demonstrate how amateur cooks set trends in American cooking. Over the years, more than 4,000 finalists have competed. Originally, prize awards were $50,000; more recent purses have been $1 million. To honor the recipes—and their creators who have most touched Americans' lives—the company established the Bake-Off Hall of Fame as part of the contest's 50th anniversary celebration in 1999. Chosen based on consumer popularity throughout the years, the 14 Hall of Fame recipes represent a slice of American cooking history.

In 2001, the Pillsbury Company and General Mills (maker of Gold Medal Flour) merged. Each company brought many products to the merger.

FURTHER READINGS: Pillsbury Bake-Off. http://food.yahoo.com/pillsbury-bakeoff; Pillsbury Company. http://www.pillsbury.com; Pohl, Kathy, ed. *Pillsbury Annual Recipes, 2006.* Minneapolis, MN: Taste of Home Books, 2006.

Marty Martindale

Popcorn. *See* Snack Foods.

Post Post is the brand name of a line of **breakfast cereals** and cereal bars currently owned by **Kraft General Foods**. Originally created by the Postum Company in the early 1900s, the "Post" name was given to some of the very first ready-to-eat cold cereals to enter the American marketplace, and the brand still maintains a significant market presence today.

The Postum Company was founded in 1895 by C. W. (Charles William) Post in Battle Creek, Michigan. Several years before, Post had been a patient at a sanitarium run by John Harvey Kellogg and had developed an interest in the market potential of the new health foods he sampled there. Inspired by the chicory-based **coffee** substitutes Post recalled from childhood, the entrepreneur soon formulated a caffeine-free beverage of his own—Postum Food Coffee—a "cereal beverage" blended from **wheat**, bran, and molasses.

Product **advertising** during this period was strictly regional, and mostly limited to soaps, medicines, and household cleaners. Post, however, became the first to launch a national campaign for a branded food product, and his efforts proved to be a remarkable success. While sales of Postum were only $5,000 during the first year, they exceeded $260,000 in 1896.

In 1897, Post introduced a new product made of wheat and malted barley: Grape-Nuts cereal. Named for its nutty flavor and the "grape sugar" Post said was formed during the baking process, it was one of the first ready-to-eat cold cereals on the market. It was soon followed by Post Toasties (originally introduced as Elijah's Manna) in 1904.

After C. W. Post's death in 1912, the Postum Company continued to expand its market reach, acquiring more than a dozen companies and major brands, such as Jell-O gelatin in 1925, Baker's **chocolate** in 1927, and Maxwell House coffee in 1928. In 1929, in an intricate deal partnered with Goldman Sachs, the company also acquired the **Birds Eye** line of **frozen foods**, along with the company's patented freezing process and the rights to the name General Foods. The Postum Company soon adopted the name for itself and began operating as the General Foods Corporation in 1929. Its earnings were over $19 million that year.

In 1989, Kraft and General Foods merged to form Kraft General Foods, the largest food company in the United States. Today, the Post line of breakfast foods includes Grape-Nuts, Raisin Bran, Golden Crisp, Alpha-Bits, Honeycomb, Fruity Pebbles, Cocoa Pebbles, Fruit & Fibre, Frosted Shredded Wheat, and Honey Bunches of Oats, among others.

FURTHER READINGS: Caprock Cultural Association. "Mr. Charles William Post, Founder of Post, Texas (1907)." http://www.posttexas.com/CWPostHHistory.htm; Kraft General Foods. "Post Heritage." http://www.kraftfoods.com/postcereals/heritage.htm; Volti, Rudi. "How We Got Frozen Food." *American Heritage Invention & Technology* 9 (Spring 1994): 46–56.

Nora Maynard

Poultry Industry By far the most important commercial fowl is the chicken, followed by the turkey, which is a distant second. Chickens lay more eggs than do hens of other fowl, and they provide a mild-flavored steady source of meat throughout the year. They are easily and inexpensively raised, and their eggs and meat can be eaten in a wide variety of ways.

The American poultry industry dates to the late 19th century, when chickens were raised on a large scale for city markets. In Petaluma, California, Christopher Nisson began manufacturing incubators in the 1880s. His sales were brisk and hatcheries were established around Petaluma. Area farmers began to specialize in raising chickens and acquired henhouses to increase their production. Other companies started producing high-quality feed for the chickens, and still others specialized in processing them. The resulting eggs and meat were sent to feed the rapidly growing population in the San Francisco area. By 1910, Petaluma was the largest poultry-producing area in the country. Other communities, such as Hunterdon County and Vineland, both in New Jersey, followed a similar path, producing chicken eggs and meat for the New York area market.

A similar pattern, though much smaller in numbers, occurred in turkey raising during the early decades of the 20th century. Turkey eggs, however, were never a major commercial item, as virtually all were employed to produce chicks. Turkeys were mainly sold in the fall for the holidays: Christmas, New Year's, and especially Thanksgiving.

During World War I, poultry businesses rapidly increased production, and the industry thrived, sending eggs and chickens to the armed forces and abroad to America's allies. When the war ended, the poultry business weathered storms due to the increase in productivity. During the Depression, the poultry industry continued to expand, and during World War II, it expanded even further.

Scientific Improvements

The post–World War II era saw a fundamental transition within the poultry industry. Important scientific discoveries before the war began to change the industry after the war. For instance, in 1934 John Kimber started Kimber Farms, a chicken hatchery, in Fremont, California. He began breeding chickens for specific purposes, such as egg laying or meat. The **hybrid** chickens that resulted revolutionized the poultry industry. By the 1950s, Kimber Farms had produced hybrids that laid 250 eggs per year. Hybrid chickens were less resistant to diseases, so Kimber Farms developed vaccines to inoculate its chicks before they were sold.

Likewise, turkey breeding started before the war. In 1939, George and Johnny Nicholas purchased a farm near Vineburg, California. Their Nicholas Turkey Breeding Farm specialized in breeding turkeys. In the 1950s, the company developed the first commercially successful, white-feathered turkey that became the industry standard.

Scientific studies produced by agricultural schools improved the genetic characteristics of the birds and greatly increased the productivity of chickens and turkeys. Uncontrolled production meant a decreasing price for eggs and meat. The results made it difficult for farmers to raise chickens unless they used expensive high-technology equipment, which required large amounts of capital.

The poultry industry has attempted to maximize profits through improved efficiency. A major way to reduce costs was through vertical integration—combining all aspects of poultry farming into one operation, thus eliminating **middlemen**. Hatcheries and feed operations were a logical marriage, so mills producing feed were built next to hatcheries. The industrial poultry assembly line made it possible for birds to be raised in warehouses near hatcheries, and slaughterhouses could be built on or near the same site. These changes saved on expenses related to transportation, management, marketing, and record keeping. The changing industry also required extensive **research**; new discoveries, particularly in genetics, led to even greater efficiency.

Poultry processors had to cut costs to survive. Narrow profit margins drove many small farms out of the turkey business, concentrating the industry in fewer hands. Turkey raising and processing had evolved from a collection of regional businesses to a handful of highly centralized, integrated, national companies, such as Perdue on the Delmarva Peninsula, Tyson in Arkansas, Pilgrim's Pride in Texas, the Butterball Turkey Company in Indiana, Carolina Turkeys in North Carolina, and the Jennie-O Turkey Store in Wisconsin.

Chicken Processors

In 1920, Arthur Perdue started an egg-laying operation in Salisbury, Maryland. It slowly expanded. In the 1940s, the company, later named Perdue Farms, shifted from egg production to raising broiler chickens. Arthur's son, Frank Perdue, took over the operation in the 1950s,. He contracted with local farmers on the Delmarva Peninsula to raise chickens and opened another plant in North Carolina. The following decade, the company began operating grain and processing facilities, and it later launched breeding and research programs. By the late 1960s, Perdue was the largest broiler producer in the United States, even though its operation was still regional. To expand its operation to other regions of the country, Perdue began a major national **advertising** campaign. In the 1980s, the company diversified its operations to include turkeys. It also opened many new facilities around the country, including a poultry-processing plant in Perry, Georgia, that is one of America's largest. The company remains controlled by the Perdue family.

In 1946, Lonnie and Aubrey Pilgrim opened a feed store in Pittsburg, Texas, and began selling chickens. They purchased a hatchery in 1958 and opened additional processing plants. Pilgrim's Pride is a supplier of KFC (formerly Kentucky Fried Chicken) and was named its "supplier of the year" in 1997. Other customers include Wal-Mart, Wendy's, and many more. Pilgrim's Pride acquired ConAgra's chicken division in 2003. Today, Pilgrim's Pride is the second largest poultry producer in the United States.

During the 1930s, John Tyson began transporting chickens from Springdale, Arkansas, to Chicago and other Midwestern and Southern cities. During World War II, Tyson sold the U.S. Armed Forces Commissary on precooked, portion-controlled chicken. Even before the war, Tyson began to expand his operation. He acquired a hatchery in 1936 and a processing plant in 1957. In 1963, the company went public and began to acquire other poultry companies. Tyson is the largest supplier of Chicken McNuggets to **McDonald's** and also supplies chicken patties to Burger King. By 1986, Tyson had surpassed its largest competitor, ConAgra, and became the largest poultry-producing company. Tyson Foods acquired Holly Farms, the nation's third largest poultry firm, in 1989; in 1995, it acquired McCarty Farms and Cargill's broiler operations, and in 1999, Hudson Foods. Today, the company is the world's largest poultry producer.

Turkey Processors

Peter Eckrich, an immigrant from Germany, opened a meat market in Fort Wayne, Indiana, in 1894. He opened a second store and then began selling products at wholesale. In 1925 the company was incorporated as Peter Eckrich and Sons, and it established branches in 17 states. In 1954, Eckrich introduced Butterball turkeys, which were sold with a device called a "bar strap" to keep the drumsticks tucked neatly against the bird. This device makes skewering or trussing unnecessary. In the 1970s Butterball pioneered the turkey lifter, making it easier to lift a hot bird from the roasting pan. The company launched the "Butterball Turkey Talk-Line" in 1981 to answer questions about cooking turkeys. Butterball was also among the first companies to produce "self-basting" or "enhanced" turkeys. Self-basting is a technique that injects chemical solutions of approved **additives** into turkey flesh to increase flavor and juiciness; it can also increase the weight of the turkey. In 1990 ConAgra Foods acquired the company and merged it with its Refrigerated Foods Group. In addition to Butterball turkeys, the company sells dozens of turkey products. Butterball is America's third largest turkey producer.

In 1865, William Wallace Cargill set up a grain storage facility in Conover, Iowa. Subsequently, Cargill expanded its operations. In the 1950s, it acquired turkey companies. Today, Cargill Turkey Products includes brand names such as Honeysuckle White, Plantation Fiesta, and Black Forest Turkey Ham. It is the second largest turkey producer in the country.

Earl B. Olson launched Farmer's Produce Company in Minnesota in 1949. It operated a small creamery and raised turkeys on the side. In 1953, the company named its eviscerated turkey the "Jennie-O," after Earl and Dorothy Olson's daughter, Jennifer. In 1971, the company changed its name to Jennie-O Foods and began expanding its operations and product line. Jennie-O in 1986 became part of **Hormel** Foods Corporation, which also acquired the Turkey Store in 2001. Hormel changed the name for the two brands to the Jennie-O Turkey Store, which is now America's largest turkey producer.

Poultry Products

Chicken producers also diversified their products, such as segmenting the chicken into legs, thighs, wings, and breasts, as well as producing chicken pot pies, **frozen** chicken meals, chicken soup, chicken dogs, and numerous other products. Logs of raw chicken and turkey meat compressed in molds, frozen, and then wrapped in aluminum foil were just what **delicatessens**, **cafeterias**, and small **restaurants** needed. It was easier to prepare turkey and chicken sandwiches, salads, and dinners from logs than dealing with a whole bird. Carl **Swanson** sold frozen pot pies in the late 1940s, and in 1953 he began to market frozen **TV dinners**.

Other poultry products were developed and marketed, as well. Chicken products included chicken dogs. Turkey products included ground turkey; turkey steaks; cooked, roasted, and smoked deli turkey breasts; turkey sausages; turkey ham; turkey bacon; sliced turkey for sandwiches; turkey pastrami; Cajun turkey; and a host of other products.

Chicken Retail Operations

The major reason chicken production became so successful during the latter part of the 20th century was the rapid rise of **fast food** operations such as Kentucky Fried Chicken, Chicken Delight, Popeye's, Church's Chicken, and McDonald's.

In the 1930s, Harland Sanders devised a secret recipe for making fried chicken at his restaurant in Corbin, Kentucky. By the early 1950s, he believed that he had a successful formula that could be **franchised**. He attended a food service seminar in Chicago, where he met Pete Harmon, a hamburger restaurateur in Salt Lake City. Harmon became the first franchisee for what would become Kentucky Fried Chicken. Sanders's chicken was the most successful item on Harmon's menu, and he urged Sanders to sell his recipe and methods for frying it nationwide. When Sanders's own restaurant failed in 1955, he went on the road selling franchises. Lacking money to promote his company, he dressed in a distinctive white suit, with his white hair, goatee, and a black string necktie. He charged no fee, but franchisees paid him a few cents on each chicken sold. Franchisees were required to display KFC signs and his likeness. It was a good formula for success. By 1963 Sanders had 600 restaurants under license, many of which were existing restaurants that sold his chicken, but had little else in common.

Sanders sold KFC to John Y. Brown and Jack Massey for about $2 million in 1964, plus an additional salary for life to act as a spokesperson for the company. Brown and Massy thereafter required a uniform structure for every franchise. They changed the franchising agreement so that royalties were based on a percentage of sales, and franchisees were required to purchase some goods and seasonings from the parent company. In addition, franchisees were charged an annual advertising fee, and the company launched a major advertising blitz that cultivated a family image. Brown and Massey quickly expanded franchises. By the late 1960s, its sales exceeded that of McDonald's. In 1970 KFC had more than 6,000 franchise agreements. It dominated the fast food chicken market and during the early 1970s became the nation's largest commercial food service operation. KFC next began opening outlets in other countries. As of 2005, KFC had outlets in 45 countries, with more restaurants outside the United States than inside.

In 1952 George W. Church Sr., a retired incubator salesman, launched "Church's Fried Chicken to Go" in downtown San Antonio. It was a low-overhead operation that sold only **takeout**, but what was distinctive about Church's was that it served larger chickens than did its competitors. The company eventually began an expansion beyond San Antonio. Between 1969 and 1974, Church's grew by an additional 387 restaurants. International expansion began in 1979. As of 2005, Church's had 1,334 outlets—100 in Mexico and the rest in the United States, where it is the third largest chicken franchise **chain**.

In 1972 Al Copeland opened a fast food restaurant in New Orleans that sold spicy fried chicken. He named it Popeye's. It proved a success, and Copeland began to franchise the chain. By 1981, there were more than 300 Popeye's outlets open. It opened its first international restaurant in 1991. As of 2005, there were more than 1,800 Popeye's restaurants in the United States and 27 international markets, including Puerto Rico, Japan, Germany, Korea, and the United Kingdom. Popeye's is the second largest chicken-franchise chain.

McDonald's McNuggets

In 1979 McDonald's chairman Fred Turner wanted to sell a chicken product that could easily be eaten while a customer was behind the steering wheel of a car, so he requested that a chicken processor create a finger food without bones. It took six months to produce McNuggets—small pieces of reconstituted chicken held together by stabilizers that were breaded, fried, frozen, and shipped to the outlet, where they were reheated. When Chicken McNuggets debuted in 1983, they were an immediate success. Other fast food chains came up with their own McNugget's-type clones, such as Burger King's Chicken Tenders and KFC's Chicken Fingers.

McNuggets helped change not only the American diet but also the system of raising and processing poultry. In 1980, most chickens were sold whole; today about 90 percent of those sold in the United States have been cut into pieces to produce cutlets or nuggets. Due to the McNuggets, McDonald's is the nation's second largest chicken seller, behind only KFC.

McNuggets originally contained ground skin in addition to chicken meat and were fried in oil. When the McNuggets were tested by McDonald's technicians, six McNuggets were found to have twice as much as fat as a Big Mac hamburger. The skins were removed, and the improved McNuggets weighed in at 16.3 grams fat compared to 32.4 grams for the Big Mac.

Poultry Industry Today

Today, chicken remains the dominant poultry in America and the world. Chickens are eaten by practitioners of most religions (except those that practice **vegetarianism**). Americans eat an average of 67 pounds of chicken per year. For 2004, the broiler industry sold more than $22 billion in poultry meat and by-products; eggs added more than $7 billion.

Today, virtually all commercial poultry are raised under conditions of intensive confinement in windowless barns that are illuminated 24 hours a day to encourage the birds to eat more food. Factory-like warehouses hold thousands of birds. The birds are fed high-nutrient food automatically via feeder chains, which convey the feed along small troughs throughout the houses. Poultry frequently break legs and wings and often die because they are unable to reach water containers.

The high concentration of animals and the conditions in which they live on factory farms weakened their immune systems and created unsanitary conditions. The **U.S. Department of Agriculture** estimates that salmonella is present in 35 percent of turkeys and 11 percent of chickens. It can easily be spread to other foods by improper handling. The Centers for Disease Control and Prevention estimates that at least 180 people die from salmonella annually. Most people so infected are often unaware of its cause, placing the blame on the flu or other ailment. Several salmonella outbreaks have been traced to fast food outlets.

Centralized factory farms cause untold damage to the environment and destroy local communities. As factory farms have spread around the world, this system is particularly harmful to communities in the developing world. In addition, critics believe that factory farms are contributing to the loss of the diversity of gene pools, as they focus their attention on higher-producing industrial breeds. This has led to the demise of many indigenous poultry breeds. For the past century, chickens and turkeys have been bred for large size of their breast and quick maturation.

FURTHER READINGS: American Poultry Historical Society. *American Poultry History, 1823–1973.* Madison, WI: American Poultry Historical Society, 1974; Davis, Karen. *More than a Meal: The Turkey in History, Myth, Ritual and Reality.* New York: Lantern Books, 2001; Davis, Karen. *Prisoned Chickens, Poisoned Eggs: An Inside Look at the Modern Poultry Industry.* Summertown, TN: Book Publishing Company, 1996; Horowitz, Roger. *Putting Meat on the American Table; Taste, Technology, Transformation.* Baltimore: Johns Hopkins University Press, 2006; Pearce, John, ed. *The Colonel: The Captivating Biography of the Dynamic Founder of a Fast-Food Empire.* Garden City, NY: Doubleday, 1982; Sanders, Harland. *Life as I Have Known It Has Been Finger Lickin' Good.* Carol Stream, IL: Creation House, 1974; Sawyer, Gordon. *The Agribusiness Poultry Industry: A History of Its Development.* New York: Exposition Press, 1971; Schwartz, Marvin. *Tyson from Farm to Market: The Remarkable Story of Tyson Foods.* Fayetteville: University of Arkansas Press, 1991; Smith, Andrew F. *The Turkey: An American Story.*

Urbana: University of Illinois Press, 2006; Smith, Page, and Charles Daniel. *The Chicken Book.* San Francisco: North Point Press, 1982.

Andrew F. Smith

Produce. *See* Labor and Unions; Middlemen.

Publishing

Food Magazine Monthly Circulation Figures, 2003

Cooking Light: 1,603,680
Bon Appetit: 1,322,577
Food & Wine: 957,838
Gourmet: 934,778
Weight Watchers: 745,384
Cooking Pleasures: 647,611
Saveur: 381,585
Wine Spectator: 346,781
Vegetarian Times: 242,774
Fine Cooking: 221,108

Source: Data from Media Distribution Services, http://www.mdsconnect.com/topcirculation.htm

---

Americans have always written about food. Even precolonization, stories about the bounty of the North American continent caused some to give up settled life elsewhere and journey to this unknown cornucopia where the waters were rumored to be so thick with fish that an able bodied soul could skip from one to another and in this way cross an inlet, bay, river, or lake. That sort of sacrifice alone would prompt many words, and write they did: a steady stream of food information, opinion, advice, and celebration appeared in journals, letters, novels, travelogues, autobiographies, histories, and ethnographic studies from the New World.

It was not, however, until the 1840s that stories about food began to appear in newspapers and magazines. One hundred years later, in 1941, *Gourmet*, was introduced. The magazine, however, was originally imagined as a lifestyle book, not a food book, and it was not until March 12, 1950 that the term "food writer" finally appeared in a newspaper. The term made its debut in *The New York Times*, appearing in a story by Jane Nickerson about a press trip to the manufacturing plant of Tabasco sauce in Louisiana. Today, "food writer" is almost right up there with "rock star" as the fantasy career and there has, over the past quarter century, been an explosion of food magazines, food stories in newspapers, and food-centric websites and blogs.

Just under 150 food magazines, quarterlies, and newsletters were produced in the United States in 2006 and, if the circulations that each claims are accurate, a total of 19.7 million people read regularly about food. No one has reliably calculated the number of websites dedicated to food—there are lots and their number changes on a daily basis—but one executive of America Online did acknowledge that recipes and porn are the most popular searches on the Internet. Meanwhile, the number of books about food and wine sold each year continues to climb from the 530 million that *Publisher's Weekly* reported in 2000.

In the midst of this explosion, interest in food itself has remained steady at three meals per day for most Americans. Therefore, one can only assume that interest in food quality, in food as medicine, in food as a public health issue, in food as a moral arbiter, and in food as a cultural indicator has soared. Like food itself, the issues surrounding its growing, cooking, and eating are not new to the American psyche. The tug-of-war between Puritan restraint and hedonistic indulgence is as American as apple pie; in fact, the first editor to include food in his newspaper—Horace Greeley—was an abolitionist who supported dietary reform and had dreams of Utopian communities. A founder of the Republican Party and an acolyte of Sylvester Graham, Greeley was neither a meat-eating nor a whiskey-drinking man; food coverage was, to him, a serious moral and social issue and he brought to it the same muscle and enterprise that made his the newspaper of choice among the thoughtful just after the Civil War.

Greeley's motivation was, however, not solely philosophical. In the heyday of his paper, from the 1840s to the 1870s, a huge wave of immigration brought thousands of foreigners a day into his home town of New York, all of them looking to become Americans. Food stories served as cultural primers in How to Live Like Americans. Female literacy was also on the rise and food stories were a way of growing a female audience. In fact, writing about food, primarily in the form of "household manuals" and instructional books such as *The Boston Cooking-School Cookbook*, were among the earliest ways for women to get published. As the Victorian ideal progressed and women were increasingly charged with setting a table that ensured both the physical and spiritual well-being of their families, female reformers like Katherine Beecher and her sister Harriet Beecher Stowe supplemented their income by writing about food.

Traditionally, there were several schools of American food writing. In the gentlemanly tradition of gastronomic prose, the food writer was a sort of everyman's "Jeeves," a high-class know-it-all. The domestic science branch of food writing was the voice of a finger-wagging, über-Mother. Both were social arbiters and each approach created guide books for upward mobility. The merging of these two sensibilities contributed to the food-writer chic in the final years of the twentieth century.

Another social and economic change—the shift from making everything in the home to factory-based mass production—had been an incentive to publish food stories in 1840. Today, as an increasing amount of food is prepared outside the home and simply reheated and more and more meals are taken in restaurants, the appeal of food stories is similarly pronounced. The rise of the dual-income household has also contributed to the growth of interest in food. More men are reaching for culinary inspiration and instruction and already, both men and women of the "latch key" generation are turning to books and television to give them the cooking lessons that got lost when grandma and mom went to work outside the home.

All of these socioeconomic shifts have resulted in an altered perception. Food has gone from being drudgery (and largely, women's work) to a spectator sport, an entertainment (and often a showcase for male talent). TV's Food Network claims that over 80 million households subscribe, and rare indeed is the television network that does not offer at least one food show. Feature-length foodie films are popping up and, in both the movies and television, food has become a way to create context or character or both. What began as a small and rather exclusive club—Le Tout Societé du Gourmet—that was served by a handful of tony magazines has become a mass-market phenomenon in need of newspaper food stories, big general food magazines, and tiny single-subject food magazines, as well as newsletters, blogs, and websites.

From its beginning, writing about food has been charged with multiple and sometimes contradictory purpose. Food writing educates and inspires and entertains. More than any other sort of journalism, food writing is personal. Opening a window into others' lives, food writing can be a voyeur's delight. Because it is a potent source of advertising and editorial identity, food writing is also highly aspirational—it creates an appetite for the good life, or at least some little slice of such life as can be purchased or confected. Food writing is also the liberal arts of journalism. To write about food well, one needs knowledge of nutrition, economics, restaurants, fashion, architecture, etiquette, gender, travel, multiculturalism, and the history of private life. History, politics, current events, culinary skills, food science, and a few languages also help. The precise measure of each of these qualities shifts constantly, generally in direct proportion to advertising dollars. Close study of any given year in food writing is a way of measuring the sorrows and joys of the culture as well as the demographics, economics, and ambient anxieties of the culture.

Each food publication has a personality, and its readership consists of those who feel a kinship with that personality. Once the exclusive province of the very wealthy, the very white, and the very rich, *Gourmet* has, in recent years, become younger and more hip. Like a once-restricted country club that is now eagerly courting diversity, the magazine maintains an exclusive air—it is for smart people with good taste who either have, or will have, or will always want and will work very hard to appear to have, independent means. Of all the food magazines, *Gourmet* serves the most balanced diet of travel, home cooking, and restaurant news.

Bon Appetit also balances well, although it emphasizes home cooking over chef-idolatry and tends to feature travel in United States more frequently than to far-flung destinations. If *Gourmet* is Ivy, *Bon Appetit* is State College—more practical than poetic, more educational than inspirational.

Food & Wine Magazine tends to rest somewhere between the previous two on the high-brow/low-brow scale and, tends toward trend-watching and chef-worship and to feature more short, declarative essays, and articles than it does evocative or provocative ones.

With its stunning visuals and writerly text, *Saveur* magazine is designed to promote the romance of food and the food-centric lifestyle. It tilts toward travel and, in its bid to fill the void left as its predecessor scrambled toward the mass market, is attempting to add more muscle to it reportage as well.

If the magazines were dissected by a fashion writer today, *Gourmet* would wear basic black, *Bon Appetit* would be dressed for the Junior League lunch, *Saveur* would be in Armani, and *Food & Wine* would be sporting whatever is "in" at the moment. *Martha Stewart Living*, on the other hand, would always look like Martha. If food was once part of "conspicuous consumption," it is now more of an exercise in conspicuous competence—and *Martha Stewart Living* is the Bible of cheerful can-do-ism. Both those aspiring toward the middle class—and those struggling to organize and make sense of the chaos of middle class life—are well served by this steady diet of How to Make a Perfect Life. Readers who wish to focus more exclusively on the cooking part might reach instead for *Cook's Illustrated*, with its obsessional (and really clear) instructions or, for even more detail, *Fine Cooking*. Healthy life-stylers might prefer *Cooking Light, Simple Living,* or *Vegetarian Times*.

The more widespread foodism becomes, the more publishers see potential specialty or niche markets. Examples include *Cucina Italiana*, for Italophiles, or regional magazines such as *Midwest Living* or *Southern Living*, with substantial food sections. Rare indeed is the significant city lacking a local food magazine, and whether it is raw foodists or chile-lovers, it is also the rare special interest group that does not publish some food screed. Chocolate magazines have come and gone and although there is certainly an audience, *Bacon Living* has not yet appeared. But in the rush to distinguish—and at its core food is a way of distinguishing between people, regions, and social strata—a pork magazine, a coffee chronicle, and *The Dew-Kissed Baby Vegetable Quarterly* seem imminent.

Likewise, as food becomes more of a mass-market special interest and less a special special-interest, there is great interest in "inside" information and this might help explain the growing circulation of industry titles such as *Nation's Restaurant News, Culinary Trends, Food Arts, Restaurant Business, Restaurants and Institutions,* and *Wine Spectator*.

Interest in food has waxed and waned throughout American history, generally in tandem with the economy. There has, however, never been such democracy in a taste for fine food and its origins and practitioners as there is today. Advertising in the epicurean magazine category has increased by 25 percent since the mid-1990s, but as more and more magazines, newsletters, and food web pages have appeared, the circulation of individual magazines has begun to dip. In 1994 *Gourmet's* circulation was 916,800; by 1998, it had shrunk 3 percent to 885,600. And in 1994, *Bon Appetit's* circulation was 1.2 million; by 1998, it had shrunk 16 percent to 1 million. An article by Rachel Weissman in the June 1999 issue of *American Demographics* suggests that the shrinkage has to do with an aging readership. Quoting Ed Papazian, president of Media Dynamics, the article stated: "When readers get to be past 50, you start losing them as they convert to other issues like health or retirement."

Perhaps the top selling magazine today—*Cooking Light*, with a circulation of 1,603,680—is further evidence that an aging population will begin to aspire toward health and longevity. Or perhaps the nexus of health and food remains irresistible to the American mind. So irresistible that nearly two million people will pay to hold in their hands information, images, and recipes that they could as easily download for free from the internet. The internet is probably the home of the next generation of food magazines. But as long as cooking is not being taught at home or at school, there will be a need for culinary education and enough Americans whose personal Don't-Tread-on-Me is focused on dinner to keep the food prose flowing.

The flavors will change—French will give way to Asian and then suddenly-American cooking will be the media darling once again (and again). One era will feature folksy fare and cheap, easy recipes; the next will define itself by fine dining and impossibly complicated and expensive recipes. The health-obsessed decades will be followed by generations of sybarites. The food prose will be personal, then clinical and detached, and then memoiristic once again. And, eventually, the mania for food may subside and all food magazines will shrink and some will fold. Those that remain, however, will likely continue to do what food writing has always done: tell the stories of our lives, meal by meal.

FURTHER READINGS: Allen, Gary. *The Resource Guide for Food Writers*. New York: Routledge, 1999; Mendelson, Anne. "Introduction: The Forties," "Introduction: The Fifties," "Introduction: The Sixties," "Introduction: The Seventies," "Introduction: The Eighties,"
"Introduction: The Nineties." *Gourmet Magazine*. September, 2001; O'Neill, Molly. "Food
Porn." *Columbia Journalism Review*, September/October 2003. http://cjrarchives.org/issues/
2003/5/foodporn-oneill.asp; O'Neill, Molly. *American Food Writing: An Anthology: With Classic Recipes*. New York: Library of America, 2007; "Top Circulation Magazines." *Media Distribution Services*, 2003. http://www.mdsconnect.com/topcirculation.htm' Weissman Rachel X.
"Guess Who's Not Coming to Dinner." *American Demographics*, June, 1999. http://findarti-
cles.com/p/articles/mi_m4021/is_ISSN_0163-4089/ai_54933575)

Molly O'Neill

R

Raw Food The Raw Food Movement, which promotes a diet of uncooked **organic** foods, has undergone tremendous growth in the past decade. While all uncooked foods, including meat and fish, can be classified as raw food, strict raw foodists reject flesh from their diet entirely. Like vegans, of which they are a subgroup, pure raw foodists eschew meat, fish, **dairy**, eggs, and all animal by-products. Driven by the belief that cooking kills enzymes vital to digestion, along with **vitamins** and minerals important for the body's general welfare, raw food vegans consume organic fruits, vegetables, nuts, seeds, sprouted grains, and legumes, none of which ever reach a temperature above 118 degrees. Methods commonly used to prepare raw foods include pickling, dehydrating, soaking, sprouting, juicing, and fermenting. Raw food "cheeses" are fashioned from soaked nuts, such as cashews and almonds. Pastas are made from such ingredients as coconut, zucchini, and turnips. Breads include base ingredients such as sprouted and dehydrated grains, ground seeds and nuts, and dehydrated fruits. A well-stocked raw food kitchen might include a juicer, an automatic sprouting machine, a food processor, a mandolin, a dehydrator, and a mill.

Few Americans eat raw 365 days a year—approximately 4 percent of the U.S. population identifies itself as **vegetarian** and roughly 5 percent of vegetarians identify themselves as vegan; only a small percentage of vegans follow a strict raw food diet. Increasing numbers, however, have begun eating raw on a temporary basis to cleanse the body, fight disease, boost energy, or lose weight.

Average Americans were first introduced to the link between good health and raw food in the mid-19th century, when Sylvester Graham began promoting a diet of whole grains and raw fruits and vegetables. Toward the end of the century, Arnold Hills wrote *Vital Foods* (1892), which delineated the benefits of raw food. More recently, Anne Wigmore popularized the Living Foods Program or raw nutrition, which calls for a diet of wheatgrass juice, sprouted beans, and raw fruits and vegetables. Such a diet, Wigmore believed, works to detoxify the body and strengthen its immune system, alleviating allergies, digestive disorders, and arthritis, among other ailments. She founded the Hippocrates Health Institute in 1963 and the Anne Wigmore Foundation in 1985. A more recent addition to the raw food movement and likely its best-known contemporary advocate, David Wolfe, devotes himself full-time to promoting the benefits of eating raw through books, videos, lectures, an online raw food store, and raw retreats.

Because organic ingredients are an essential part of eating raw, individuals with the space and time to grow their own gardens or urban professionals in cities housing cooperatives or chains such as Wild Oats or **Whole Foods Market** have a far easier time gathering ingredients for daily raw meals than the average American. In addition to offering many of the specialty food items needed to prepare tasty "uncooked dishes," the aforementioned grocery stores have recently begun to include raw bars or raw selections in their deli section and to offer raw "cooking" classes. They also offer a variety of commercial prepared foods such as chips, cookies, jerky, and snack bars.

For those farther from urban centers without such raw-friendly stores or without access to the soil and climate needed to grow their own vegetables and fruits, raw websites have entered the market, selling dried goods, prepared foods, kitchen equipment, vegan cosmetics, supplements, and specialty foods over the **Internet**. Just a few of the snack and energy bar brands available online include Eat Raw, Go Raw, Jake's Unbaked, Lärabar, Lydia's Organics, Organic Food Bar, Perfect 10 Bars, One Lucky Duck, Raw Indulgence, Vega, and Virta. The specialty foods available online include raw organic products such as agar, a plant-based jelling agent; agave juice, a sweetener used in lieu of honey or sugar; cacao beans; coconut butter-oil; rejuvelac, a fermented liquid made from sprouted grains; a variety of seaweeds; and sprouting beans.

The Raw Food Movement has spread beyond the fringe into select segments of the American mainstream, gaining popularity among those Americans wealthy enough to hire personal chefs, including celebrities such as actor Woody Harrelson, fashion designer Donna Karan, and model Carol Alt. Public access to prepared raw foods has likewise expanded beyond juice bars, health food stores, and the occasional community pot luck to include high-end **restaurants**. For professional chefs, creating raw food dishes has provided an aesthetic challenge that several have embraced by opening raw food restaurants, including Quintessence and Pure Food and Wine in New York City; Juliano's Raw in Santa Monica, California; Ecopolitan in Minneapolis; and Karyn's Raw Vegan Gourmet in Chicago. Other chefs have begun to include raw dishes on their daily menu as well. In addition to its modest showing on restaurant menus across the nation, raw food has also begun to appear on spa menus, and personal chefs have begun offering raw food cleanses to their clientele.

The **publishing** industry has likewise seen an upswing in raw food books. A small sample of recent publications includes cookbooks by professional chefs (including *Raw*, 2003, by Roxanne Klein and Charlie Trotter, and *Raw Food/Real World*, 2005, by Matthew Kenney and Sarma Melngailis), books on how and why to live and eat as a raw food vegan (including *Living Cuisine*, 2003, by Renée Loux Underkoffler, and *Eating in the Raw*, 2004, by Carol Alt), testimonials on raw food living (*The Live Food Factor*, 2006, by Susan E. Schenck), and diet books (including *The Great American Detox Diet*, 2005, by Alex Jamieson).

Long before cooked foods, there were raw foods. Since the 1990s, raw foods have become trendy among health-conscious individuals. The main idea behind the movement is that essential nutrients, especially enzymes, are destroyed in the cooking process. To obtain the health benefits of unheated, unprocessed, and organic foods, uncooked "cookery" often requires the use of equipment such as blenders, dehydrators, food processors, juicers, and, of course, refrigerators and freezers.

FURTHER READINGS: Iacobbo, Karen, and Michael Iacobbo. *Vegetarians and Vegans in America Today.* Westport, CT: Praeger, 2006.

Alice McLean

Refrigeration When the temperature of food is lowered, **bacterial** growth slows and spoilage is reduced. For millennia, humankind has intuitively understood this and has stored foods in cold caves or in snow. American colonists stored food in cool underground cellars. By the late 18th century, ice was placed in the cellars to cool food even further. By 1830, blocks of ice were being harvested in New England during the winter and spring and were shipped along the nation's coasts and navigable rivers. The blocks were stored in insulated icehouses and was available in large cities year-round.

Ice cooling was also used in transporting food. By the 1840s, ice-cooled railroad cars transported milk and butter. Seafood was subsequently shipped in a similar manner. Ice cooling made it possible to ship food short distances with minimal spoilage. In 1867, J. B. Sutherland of Detroit designed a much more efficient insulated railroad car with ice bunkers at each end. Gustav **Swift** improved upon Sutherland's design, and his refrigerated rail car made it possible to ship **beef** and other butchered meat hundreds of miles, provided that ice was replenished en route.

Despite its success, ice cooling had many limitations. It was bulky and required costly transportation, large insulated storage facilities, and a massive distribution system consisting of ships and wagons. Natural ice taken from lakes often contained impurities and toward the end of the 19th century, natural ice became increasingly polluted due to sewage dumped into the lakes where the ice was harvested. Even when machines were developed to manufacture pure ice, problems persisted. When the ice melted, the moisture frequently promoted the growth of mold and bacteria, creating unhealthy conditions within the icebox, rail car, or room. Even in the best conditions, ice had great difficulty in greatly lowering the temperature of enclosed places.

Artificial Refrigeration

Mechanical refrigeration systems had been under development since 1748, but little practical use was made of them until 1842, when American physician John Gorrie designed and built an air-cooling apparatus. His system compressed gas, cooled it, and then expanded it to lower the temperature of an enclosure. After conducting experiments, Gorrie submitted his plans to the U.S. Patent Office, and in 1851, he was granted the first U.S. patent for a refrigerator.

An Australian named James Harrison examined the plans used by Gorrie, improved upon them, and introduced a vapor compression refrigeration that was used by the brewing industry beginning in 1870. Within 30 years, nearly every brewery was equipped with refrigeration machines.

The **meatpacking** industry was slower to adopt refrigeration. Nevertheless, by 1900 the packinghouses began to adopt the ammonia compression system, and by 1914 almost all U.S. packing plants were refrigerated. This change permitted livestock to be slaughtered and butchered closer to where it was raised and then shipped to cities hundreds or thousands of miles away. As this system required large amounts of capital, it also brought about the centralization of the livestock industry, and major meatpacking companies such as **Armour**, Cudahy, Morris, Wilson, and Swift emerged during this period.

Despite their widespread adoption, early refrigeration systems had problems. The refrigerants, such as sulfur dioxide and ammonia, were toxic and/or flammable. When they leaked out of cooling systems, fatalities often resulted. Engineers searched for substitutes, and in the 1920s, chlorofluorocarbons (CFCs) and hydrochlorofluorocarbons were substituted for the previous toxic refrigerants. Beginning in the 1930s, nonflamable and nontoxic Freon, along with other synthetic refrigerants, were commonly used in refrigerators and other cooling systems.

Advantages and Disadvantages

The development of refrigerators and freezers offered a variety of advantages. It encouraged regional specialization: fruits and vegetables could be grown in the best climate and soil and then frozen and shipped great distances. As foods could be more easily stored, farmers and distributors could sell their products when they would obtain the highest price. For the consumer, freezing expanded year-round food choices because the availability of produce was no longer limited to its growing season. **Frozen food** tended to stabilize prices. By eliminating waste at the point of origin, it saved on transportation and storage. Frozen foods were particularly useful for **restaurants**, where small kitchens could supply a diverse menu.

Freezers and refrigerators kept meat and dairy products cool, which meant that Americans could buy in bulk and store foods more easily. It also meant that Americans had to shop for groceries less frequently.

The major drawbacks to frozen foods were that they required expensive freezing plants and special **packaging**, transportation, warehouses, and retail stores. Frozen food companies also had to educate the public about their products, for there was extensive opposition to frozen food. Many people believed that frozen foods were unhealthful; others did not like the taste or smell of thawed food, and still others complained about its expense. There was some justification for these complaints during the early years, when the process of freezing was in its infancy. Some companies froze inferior-quality food since it was impossible for consumers to tell the difference between good and bad food at the point of sale. Some retailers thawed or refroze foods before sale, thus speeding its deterioration.

Corporate laboratories and the **U.S. Department of Agriculture** began experimentation on frozen food and made recommendations on matters such as the rapidity with which foods needed to be frozen, methods of freezing, storage temperature, dehydration, and the length of time frozen foods could be held without spoilage. However, hostility did not disappear entirely, and the industry engaged in mass promotional efforts to win over skeptical consumers. Package design was important both to prevent dehydration during storage and to attract consumers. Some of the frozen food problems declined after 1911, and they greatly decreased in the 1920s when the cost of frozen foods declined and the use of the home refrigerator became more common.

Building on these efforts, Clarence Birdseye, perhaps the best-known name in the industry, began quick-freezing food in 1923. His major contribution was not in the process of freezing, but rather in the invention of moisture-proof packaging, which permitted food to be frozen faster and kept it from disintegrating when thawed. Birdseye also championed the use of the freshest possible food. Birdseye sold his company to **General Foods**. Under the brand name **Birds Eye**, General Foods invested the capital necessary to promote and market frozen food. Other companies began to compete, but sales were insignificant until the late 1930s, largely because of the

Depression and the unwillingness of grocery stores to invest the $1,000 for a freezer that held relatively little product.

Electric Refrigerators and Freezers

Refrigeration in the home lagged behind industrial applications. By 1884, ice-boxes were common in all but the poorest tenements. Electric refrigerators had been marketed since the 1890s, but none was successful until General Electric released the Guardian unit in 1915. The following year, it was followed by the Frigidaire, manufactured by the Guardian Frigerator Company, which was acquired by General Motors Corporation. GM began to mass-produce refrigerators, promoting them through national **advertising** and wide distribution. The Frigidaire's small freezer section held ice trays and had room for little else. By 1920, more than 200 different kinds of refrigerators were being sold by other companies, including Kelvinator and Servel.

Despite the large number of models, a total of only 5,000 electric refrigerators was sold in 1921, and it wasn't until 1930 that refrigerators outsold iceboxes. In 1940, however, more than four million refrigerators were sold. During World War II, home refrigerators were not manufactured. After the war, refrigerators steadily increased the size of the freezer section as commercial frozen foods became common. It was not until the 1950s that refrigerators became common in most American kitchens.

Freestanding freezers were not marketed during the 1920s, but they were beyond the reach of most Americans. Ice cube trays appeared in the 1920s. Small deep freezers became fixtures in grocery stores by the late 1930s. Just before World War II, new open self-service freezers were introduced into grocery stores, and customers responded by buying more frozen foods. After the war, home freezers became more common as their price declined and the number of frozen foods available in grocery stores grew. During the 1950s, freezers, like refrigerators, became common in American homes. The 1950s and '60s saw technical advances like automatic defrosting and automatic ice making.

Industrial refrigerators were developed for restaurants and **supermarkets**. Cooling and freezing compartments offered consumers and workers convenient access to everything from frozen peas to **ice cream**.

Frozen Food

Perhaps the most significant influence of refrigeration was in the production of frozen food. Prior to World War II, the main frozen foods were peas, beans, **corn**, spinach, berries, cherries, apples, and peaches. During the early 1940s, canned goods were needed for the war effort and were in short supply at home. Frozen foods containing meat were rationed, but frozen fruits and vegetables, became more prevalent during wartime. Consequently, many Americans tried frozen foods for the first time. When the war ended, sales of frozen foods increased greatly, which encouraged the frozen food industry to invest in a major expansion.

Frozen prepared foods, such as chicken à la king, came on the market in 1939, but did not become popular until after the war. Breyers Ice Cream manufactured frozen chow mein and chop suey under the brand name Golden Pagoda. Following the war, an avalanche of new frozen foods hit the market, including **Sara Lee** cakes, Quaker Oat waffles, **Swanson** chicken pot pies, and Birds Eye fish sticks. The first successful frozen meal, consisting of meat, potatoes, and vegetables, was marketed by the W. L. Maxson Company of New York; the meals were sold to Pan American Airways.

The most successful of all postwar frozen foods was orange juice, which had been first marketed unsuccessfully during the 1930s. Experiments demonstrated that removing water from the orange juice before freezing improved the taste. Orange juice concentrate was sold after the war; by the early 1950s, orange juice accounted for 20 percent of the frozen food market.

As the volume of sales of frozen foods increased, the price declined. A landmark in frozen food history was the **TV Dinner**, first produced by Swanson in 1953. These were complete meals in a covered foil tray with meat, vegetables, and potatoes in separate compartments. As **television** was just becoming popular in America, many assumed that this dinner was supposed to be consumed in front of the television set.

The success of frozen food manufacturers encouraged centralization: Coca-Cola purchased Minute Maid, and H. J. **Heinz** purchased Ore-Ida, a maker of frozen potatoes. In 1955 **Campbell's Soup** purchased C. A. Swanson and expanded its line of frozen foods to 65 items.

Microwave and Frozen Food

The wedding of the microwave and frozen food was the next major leap forward. The microwave made it possible for frozen foods to be cooked in minutes, which was particularly useful in restaurants. However, food processors needed to change their products for microwave use by reducing the moisture content of food and replacing metal foil—which blocked microwaves and damaged ovens—with other materials.

At first, the market was not big enough to encourage food processors to cater to the needs of microwave oven users. However, this had changed by the 1970s, as more Americans acquired microwave ovens. In addition, a large number of restaurants began preparing food in a central commissary, freezing it, and shipping it to their outlets, which would microwave it when ordered by customers. This process also lowered the costs of the food.

Environmental Problems

CFCs turned out to also have problems. Beginning in 1973, scientists reported that trace amounts of these gases had been located in the upper atmosphere and concluded that they would deplete the Earth's ozone layer. While researchers explore coolant alternatives to CFCs, manufacturers have taken steps to minimize CFC emission from refrigerators and cooling systems. Improved efficiency has reduced the amount of Freon needed, and leak detection systems have been installed. Today, refrigerant is recovered and recycled whenever possible. Despite problems with coolants, sales have continued to expand for refrigerators, freezers, and frozen foods.

FURTHER READINGS: Anderson, Oscar Edward. *Refrigeration in America: A History of a New Technology and Its Impact.* Princeton, NJ: University of Cincinnati by Princeton University Press, 1972; Cummings, Richard O. *The American Ice Harvests: A Historical Study in Technology, 1800–1918.* Berkeley: University of California Press, 1949; Thévenot, R. *A History of Refrigeration throughout the World.* Trans. J. C. Fidler. Paris: International Institute of Refrigeration, 1979; Williams, E. W. *Frozen Food: Biography of an Industry.* Boston: Cahners, 1963; Woolrich, Willis Raymond. *The Men Who Created Cold: A History of Refrigeration.* New York: Exposition Press, 1967.

Andrew F. Smith

Research and Development (R&D) Research and development are the activities a corporation (either private or public) dedicates to product innovation. R&D activities can be fundamental (scientific) or applied (technical), depending on the corporation developing it. As a whole, there are important R&D investments in the traditional food industry, while agro-biotech companies focus on matters of **food safety** and increasing the food supply. Ethical and safety questions are regularly raised when dealing with R&D and food.

Global Overview

Research and development is usually described as a two-step process. Research activities are related to the discovery of new knowledge centered on objects, processes, and services, while development is related to the application of that research to create new and improved objects, processes, and services to fill market needs. Private R&D activities are geared toward commercialization, to generate income through the invested capital. In contrast, R&D projects developed by universities and state agencies are typically fundamental and less commercial in nature; basic scientific applications are developed in these contexts, which can then be applied to further research. For example, a university's R&D might develop the basic science behind an ultra-performing filtration system, while a private company's R&D department would develop different ways to use these filters in river, dam, or household products.

R&D can be funded by private investors or government programs and is a key activity companies must engage in to maintain their competitiveness. R&D activities are usually found in specialized units composed of scientists and technicians. In the public sector, to ensure that the innovation developed is used, many universities and state agencies have offices of technology transfer, which are dedicated to the commercialization of fundamental technologies with commercial partners. Different indicators on the success of R&D activities exist, such as budgets allocated, number of patents (filed or obtained), or number of peer-reviewed publications.

The customary R&D budget investment for a private company is about 3.5 percent of the total revenues. Innovative companies may invest anywhere from 7 percent of their budget, in the case of computer-related companies, up to 40 percent or more for biotechnology companies. Some early-phase biotechnology companies may spend upwards of 70 percent of their total spending in R&D, as it is their most important commercial activity. When a company dedicates more than 15 percent of its budget to R&D, it is usually referred to as a "high-tech" company. R&D spending usually gives the company access to local and federal tax credits, so spending is usually encouraged as a tax-deductible activity.

In 2004, the Americas accounted for 43 percent of the world's R&D, followed by Europe with 33 percent and Asia with 24 percent. By itself, the United States accounted for 41 percent of global R&D, followed by Japan with 20 percent and Germany with 10 percent. The high level of risks that these companies shoulder is somewhat offset by the high margins of return successful companies enjoy; it is not rare for a high-tech company to have gross profits of anywhere from 60 to 90 percent of revenues (most industrial companies get only 40 percent of gross profits on revenues).

R&D in the Food Sector

Companies engage in food-related R&D activities for a number of reasons. First, food brands have life cycles and, like all things, they eventually die; through consumer apathy or new paradigms, the popular products of yesteryear must eventually make way for new products. Changing needs also play a role in our evolving food market; the increased focus on health-related products, for example, has led to the birth of a whole industry of health food companies, which requires some measure of investment and research. New technologies also enable companies to create new products for the consumer. Finally, changes in legislation and regulations can render some types of food obsolete and require the development of replacement products.

Hence, the general characteristics of new food products being developed from traditional companies go from line extension and repositioning existing products to developing new forms, sizes, or formulas of existing products or entirely new and innovative products.

A company engages in *line extension* when a variant of an existing line of products is developed, for instance, a new flavor or a different type of coating. Hence, when a company develops a cherry-flavored cola, it is engaging in line extension R&D. *Repositioning existing products* happens when a company finds that a current product is being used in an alternative medium; for example, if there is evidence that a drink reduces cholesterol, the company might do research as to market it as a "health drink." Companies also do research to modify the form, size, or formula of its products, developing faster-cooking foods, or making the product spicier or higher in fiber. Hence, traditional products, which we have been using for years, can sometimes be redeveloped through R&D efforts.

Another segment of companies that do food-related R&D is the agro-biotech sector (or agro-bio companies). These companies develop technologies that can be used in multiple contexts, such as plant seeds, feedstock, and even growth technologies. Some companies have R&D activities related to animals, either therapeutic (healing animals) or enhancements (developing animals). Most of their R&D is less focused on the consumer products. There is significant debate about biotechnology innovations entering the food supply chain.

Many different technologies are developed by R&D activities of the agro-biotech sector, from developing novel processes to reduce **bacterial** levels in foods or developing new **packaging** technologies to innovating new **flavors**, aromas, and ingredients and extending shelf life. Several of these advances promote better **food safety**, reduce costs, increase food supplies, and respond to current food trends (such as **obesity** and weight-control issues).

Increasing demand for food supplies is one of the main concerns relating to food R&D. As the world's population increases, it is estimated that the demand for grains will increase by 40 percent by 2020. This is combined with the increasing demand for crops to be processed into ethanol fuel. Making foods that grow faster, in greater quantities, and that last longer are all priorities in the food technology sector.

Although large sums of capital are invested each year in food-related R&D, the amounts are relatively small when compared with other sectors of the industry. Food R&D is ranked 15th worldwide (in terms of money invested), and accounts for just 1 percent of the global R&D budget. Top investing countries in this category include the United Kingdom and Switzerland. Still, the sector is enjoying some growth, as total R&D investments increased by 2.4 percent from 2005 to 2006. R&D activities in food products usually have slightly higher profitability than the average of other business sectors, while requiring slightly less investment intensity.

Ethics and Controversies in Food and R&D

Advances in R&D in the food sector have led to the creation of genetically modified (GM) foods. These are developed from a genetically modified organism such as a crop plant or an animal; soybean, **corn**, canola, and cottonseed oil are among the most important GM crops. In 2005, it was estimated that 222 million acres was dedicated to growing GM foods.

Some countries, like the **European Union** nations and Japan, express doubts on the safety of these foods. Hence, they require that GM foods be labeled as such before being sold to the public (a practice not replicated in the United States). Concerns have been raised that genetic modifications in plants might be passed on to humans; other scientists have expressed concerns that **genetic engineering** can potentially introduce hazards such as allergens or toxins. Hence they need to be evaluated on a case-by-case basis, rather than being presumed to be globally safe.

FURTHER READINGS: Alston, Julian. *Agricultural R&D, Technological Change, and Food Security.* Department of Agricultural and Resource Economics, University of California, Davis. Seminar, spring 2001. Online at http://aic.ucdavis,edu/research1/FSROTC-paper.pdf; Arvanitoyannis, Ioannis S., Persefoni Tserkezou, and Theodoros Varzakas. "An Update of US Food Safety, Food Technology, GM Food and Water Protection and Management Legislation." *International Journal of Food Science & Technology* 41, suppl. 1 (August 2006): 130–59; Fuller, Gordon. *New Food Product Development: From Concept to Marketplace.* Boca Raton, FL: CRC Press, 2005; GreenFacts. "Scientific Facts on Genetically Modified Crops." http://www.greenfacts.org/en/gmo/index.htm; United Kingdom, Department of Trade and Industry. "The R&D Scoreboard (Executive Summary)." http://www.innovation.gov.uk/rd_scoreboard/executive.asp.

Jean-François Denault

Restaurants Any facility that prepares individual meals for consumption on or off the premises falls under the rubric "restaurant." Restaurants range from formal temples of gastronomy, where highly trained chefs in multimillion-dollar kitchens cosset the palates of affluent gourmands with exotic delicacies, to ephemeral, open-air cookstands, where inexpensive, hearty meals or quick snacks are prepared on rudimentary cooking equipment with simple ingredients.

Brief History

Throughout history, residents of the world's cities and towns have depended on taverns, inns, and cookshops to supply many of their daily meals. Poor and middle-class urbanites often lived in housing that lacked decent cooking facilities, due to the danger of fire in cities built of wood and the historically high cost of fuel and cookwares. Cookshops or bakeries marketed precooked meals that could be brought home, while the ubiquitous taverns and inns offered camaraderie while eating and drinking publicly.

It was not until the mid-18th century that the term *restaurant* was applied to certain eating establishments in France that served, among other things, "restorative" meat broths ("restorative" being the literal translation of *restaurant*). What quickly came to distinguish these restaurants from their predecessor institutions were elegant surroundings, extensive menus that gave the diner a choice among comestibles, and flexible dining hours. Restaurants became fashionable entertainment for the well-to-do and spread in the late 18th and early 19th centuries to urban centers in Europe and America.

As the 19th century progressed, restaurants emerged to serve a broader clientele. Urban laborers, recent immigrants, and adventurous Americans flocked to cheaper eateries, especially those presenting **ethnic** cuisines from the home country of the diner or proprietor. Unlike the haute-cuisine dining palaces, these restaurants used smaller staffs and menus, less expensive ingredients, and informal table accoutrements; their profit depended on multiple seatings over the course of a meal period. By the late 19th century, diverse restaurants served working-, middle-, and upper-class diners with different needs, purses, and social agendas.

Prohibition and the Great Depression interrupted American fine dining by eliminating the lucrative alcohol sales that often made the difference between profit and loss. The problem was exacerbated when diners chose to eat and drink at home, rather than dine out in a "dry" establishment. The repeal of Prohibition in 1933 came too late, as the stock market crash of 1929 had ended the free-spending excesses of the Gilded Age. High-end restaurant dining would reemerge as a major social activity only after World War II.

By contrast, lower-end and middle-market restaurants flourished during the 1920s, '30s, and '40s. This period saw the birth of **fast food**, notably the White Castle and **McDonald's** franchises, and family-style restaurants, such as the now nearly defunct Howard Johnson's. These enterprises relied on limited menus and centralized commissaries to reduce food costs and the need for skilled kitchen staffs. Volume, rather than price, made these establishments profitable.

Contemporary Restaurants

The restaurant industry divides dining establishments into three broad categories according to the lavishness of the food and surroundings, the target audience, and the speed and elegance of service. Seventy-two percent of restaurants in the United States are independently owned or are small, usually local, **chains**, with the remaining locales owned by large chains. The Southeast has the greatest proportion of large chains and the fewest independents, while the Northeast has the greatest proportion of independents and small chains.

The fanciest restaurants, with refined table service and the highest per-person checks, are called "white tablecloth" establishments. It used to be easy to identify such places by the presence of crisp linens on the tables; in recent years, however, many trendy upscale restaurants have dispensed with tablecloths altogether in favor of highly striking décor and unique tablewares. White tablecloth foods are frequently expensive and are prepared to order from extensive or creative menus that bespeak **gourmet** or elite aspirations. For much of their history, white tablecloth restaurants have been standalone ventures dependent on an omnipresent chef laboring in the kitchen; recently, however, certain **celebrity chefs** have opened branches of their successful white tablecloth restaurants in multiple cities, sometimes even on different continents, delegating to well-trained subordinates the quotidian kitchen duties.

Casual or family dining restaurants are the second major group and offer full menus and table service, although the menus are less elaborate and the service is less formal than at a white tablecloth places. These spots include items appealing to children and offer copious meals prepared to order in comfortable surroundings. Casual and family restaurants may be independent or part of a chain or **franchise**, such as Applebee's and the Olive Garden. In both white tablecloth and casual or family restaurants, patrons typically pay after they finish their meal.

"Fast food" and **takeout** operations are the last category of restaurants and function much like the historical cookshop. Known for their limited menus, self- or very limited service, and modest amenities, these establishments offer speed, relatively low cost, and predictable menus. Patrons pay for their meals before consuming them. The White Castle hamburger chain relied on a clean environment and low prices to attract a large working-class audience. The key to its success was volume: by abolishing chairs or offering spartan seating, diners purchased meals to be eaten off premises, allowing greater sales. Fast food restaurants rely on inexpensive foodstuffs prepared in advance of orders and kept warm under a heat lamp or quickly rewarmed in a oven or microwave by low-skilled employees.

In recent years, the fast food industry developed a negative image among some consumers because of lower-class associations and nutritional concerns. The industry has reacted by trying to rebrand these establishments as "quick service," by increasing the amenities and menu offerings at the traditional burger and chicken joints, and by developing more upscale versions of fast food. The Prêt à Manger and 'wichcraft chains, the latter founded by a white tablecloth chef, are prime examples and are perceived to offer healthier food with a gourmet flair. A variation on the quick-service theme are places that can rapidly assemble dishes from prepared ingredients, such as the array of burritos and tacos at Chipotle Mexican Grill or wood-fired ciabatta sandwiches at Così.

While individual checks at casual and family dining and quick-service restaurants are much lower than those at white tablecloth establishments, these two sectors account for most of the spending on food away from home in the late 20th century and are projected to continue to be the largest segments of the restaurant industry in the early 21st century. Americans still typically spend a bit more money on food prepared in the home, but this gap is predicted to close within the decade, the result of convenience in the face of accumulating time pressures, successful **advertising**, increased discretionary spending, and, according to some experts, a lack of cooking skills in Americans under the age of 40.

The Size of the Restaurant Industry

The American restaurant industry is huge. The most detailed information comes from the National Restaurant Association (NRA), founded in 1919 to "represent, educate and promote the restaurant industry." Starting in 1976, the NRA, with the assistance of major accounting firms such as Deloitte, began reporting annually on U.S. restaurant operations. According to the NRA, in 2006, direct sales by restaurants of all types accounted for approximately 4 percent of the gross domestic product and nearly 9 percent of jobs in the United States, making the restaurant sector the largest employer outside of the government, with more than 12.5 million people employed. Industry experts calculate that the average American ate 83 meals in restaurants in 2004 and purchased another 100 or so additional meals for off-premises consumption (Fleming and Miller, 5).

As of 2005, there were more than 900,000 restaurants in the United States, with sales approaching approximately $475 billion. The foregoing numbers must be regarded cautiously, however: the 2002 Economic Census prepared by the U.S. Department of Commerce identifies slightly more than 504,000 "food service establishments," with sales in excess of $322 billion and more than 8.3 million employees, and the difference in numbers is not attributable exclusively to the different years in question. The government figures will be updated after the 2007 business census, but the disparity between government and industry figures suggests differences in definitions and data collection methodology in a very large and complex industry.

The restaurant industry grew steadily during the later 20th century, but not without small bumps along the way. For example, after adjusting for inflation, there was a small decline in dollars spent on food away from home (FAFH) in the period from 1990 to 1999, compared with the 1980s; inflation-adjusted growth resumed in 2000. Nonetheless, the NRA predicts that, by 2010, Americans will spend more than 53 percent of their food dollars on FAFH, a significant increase over the 46.4 percent of food dollars spent on FAFH in 2004. This does not mean, however, that more than half of all meals will be made outside the home, because the cost of restaurant or takeout meals is greater than cooking in the home; industry experts estimate that, as of 2004, about 77 percent of meals were still prepared in the home.

Restaurant Patrons

Age, income, gender, ethnicity, marital status, and employment status all influence who is dining out, which meals are eaten in restaurants, and what sort of restaurant is patronized. Conventional wisdom holds that, as income and educational level rise, the number of meals eaten in restaurants also rises, in part because of the increased discretionary income but also because restaurant meals may be work-related, as an adjunct to business travel, business meetings, or other business functions. Few workers return home for lunch anymore, and the homemade brown bag lunch, too, is beginning to become an endangered species: families with two or more workers devote approximately 70 percent of their lunchtime expenditures to FAFH. Convenience and social status play important roles in encouraging these restaurant-prepared meals.

Recent analysts have suggested that other factors must now be weighed in forecasting restaurant patronage. Among them is a perceived lack of cooking skills in Americans born after the Baby Boom, although there is little empirical evidence to support this assertion. According to one 2004 survey, the demographic group that frequents restaurants most are young adults: members of "Generation Y" (between the ages of 16 and 27 in 2005) ate restaurant meals most often, averaging 24 meals out per month, followed closely by "Generation X" (those aged 28–39), who averaged 21 restaurant meals per month (Fleming and Miller, 62). The decrease in restaurant dining was attributed to marriage and children. A report by another market research group confirmed the overall trend and predicted that, through 2010, Gen Y would continue to patronize its favored quick-service and take-out restaurants on the grounds of convenience, while their slightly older Gen X siblings would gravitate toward full-service restaurants (Fleming and Miller, 61).

Trends in Restaurant Dining

All levels of the highly competitive restaurant industry demand constant innovation to attract patrons and grow. Quick-service restaurants are looking to exploit the previously underdeveloped late-night and breakfast markets. Fueled by the demands of the 24/7 society, well-trafficked spots now keep their doors open past midnight: in 2004, 90 percent of Wendy's outlets were open until midnight or later, while McDonald's reported that 12 percent of its restaurants remain open around the clock. Even Starbuck's, originally geared to the daytime consumption of **coffee**, pastries, and cold refreshments, has some all-night units. Breakfast has also become a significant

part of the quick-service sector. McDonald's pioneered rapid breakfast with the introduction of the Egg McMuffin in 1973, a sandwich emulated by many competitors.
Most recently, Starbuck's has begun introducing ovens to certain locales to reheat its
gourmet version of the egg sandwich, spurred by the fact that 25 percent of all American who eat breakfast do so away from home. Other quick-service amenities, such as
wireless **Internet** access and on-site ATMs, encourage patronage, as do "frequent
diner" programs that offer free or discounted foods after multiple purchases, encouraging repeat customers.

The white tablecloth sector has its own version of these loyalty-building promotions.
In major cities, "Restaurant Week" promotions lure customers into these normally expensive locales by offering limited fixed menus at greatly reduced prices. On-line reservation services make booking a table fast and convenient. But the most important
trends set in white tablecloth restaurants involve the introduction of new ingredients
and preparations to the fine dining public, which often trickle down to the general public. Among the most notable examples are the current fetish for balsamic vinegar and
extra virgin olive oil; these ingredients became the rage of many white tablecloth restaurants in the 1980s and early '90s, only to become ubiquitous in the casual and quick-
service sectors, albeit in slightly different form, by the dawn of the 21st century.

Restaurants of all varieties can become lightning rods for political activism, both
grassroots and governmentally imposed. Some promote serving **organic** foodstuffs
and purchasing from farms practicing sustainable agriculture. Most often, independent white tablecloth establishments make these claims, but chains such as Starbuck's
boast "fair trade" coffees in an effort to distinguish their beverages. Certain high-end
restaurateurs have voluntarily stopped serving foie gras in response to protests that
the geese are fattened inhumanely; going even further, the city of Chicago banned restaurants from selling foie gras. In a more paternalistic mode, New York City restaurants have been forced to eliminate trans fats from their kitchens on health grounds,
as well as to list calorie contents on standardized items in a effort to assist diners to
make informed choices.

See also Cafeterias; Diners.

FURTHER READINGS: Fleming, Ciji A., and Richard K. Miller. *The 2005 Restaurant and
Foodservice Market Research Handbook.* 6th ed. Loganville, GA: Richard K. Miller & Associates,
2005; Hogan, Dave. "White Castle: How Billy Ingram Made Hamburger 'the America's Choice.'"
Journal of Restaurant & Foodservice Marketing 4, no. 3 (2001): 123–35; Hurley, Andrew. "From
Hash House to Family Restaurant: The Transformation of the Diner and Post–World War II
Consumer Culture." *Journal of American History* 83 (1997): 1282–1308; Moskin, Julia. "The
Breakfast Wars." *New York Times,* January 10, 2007, F1; National Restaurant Association. "Res-
taurant Industry Facts." http://www.restaurant.org/research/ind_glance.cfm; Olsen, Michael D.,
and Jinlin Zhao. "The Restaurant Revolution—Growth, Change and Strategy in the International
Foodservice Industry." *Journal of Restaurant & Foodservice Marketing* 4, no. 3 (2001): 1–34; Pau-
lin, Geoffrey D. "Let's Do Lunch: Expenditures on Meals Away from Home." *Monthly Labor
Review* (May 2000): 36–45; Russell, Cheryl. *Best Customers: Demographics of Consumer
Demand.* 2nd ed. Ithaca, NY: New Strategist Publications, 2004; Spang, Rebecca L. *The Inven-
tion of the Restaurant.* Cambridge, MA: Harvard University Press, 2000; U.S. Department of
Commerce, U.S. Census Bureau. "2002 Economic Census, Food Services and Drinking Places."
EC02-721-02. Available at http://www.census.gov/prod/eco2/ec0272i02.pdf; *Who's Buying at
Restaurants and Carry-Outs.* Ithaca, NY: New Strategist Publications, 2004.

Cathy K. Kaufman

S ❖ ─────────────────────────────────

Sara Lee In 1935, Charles Lubin and his brother-in-law, Arthur Gordon, bought a small chain of Chicago neighborhood bakeries called Community Bake Shops. They sold fresh products throughout the city, and their business slowly expanded. Fourteen years later, Lubin acquired the company in its entirety and named it after his daughter—the Kitchens of Sara Lee. Its most famous products were its All Butter Pound Cake and All Butter Pecan Coffee Cake, which were introduced in 1952.

During the early 1950s, the company began experimenting with **frozen** products that could be shipped outside of the Chicago area. Two years later, Sara Lee had developed a process for freezing baked goods that retained their quality. The company also launched a revolutionary foil pan in which the company's products could be baked, frozen, and distributed. By 1955, Sara Lee was distributing its frozen products nationally. The following year, Consolidated Foods Corporation (a Canadian company that had entered the U.S. market in 1939) acquired the company. Beginning in 1960, the Sara Lee brand began **advertising** on national television. Its famous jingle and slogan, "Nobody doesn't like Sara Lee," was launched in 1968. Consolidated Foods eventually concluded that its most famous brand name was Sara Lee and consequently changed the name of the company to Sara Lee in 1985.

Sara Lee has regularly opened facilities in other countries, beginning with Canada in 1963. It has also continually expanded through aggressive acquisition of other companies, such as Endust, Hanes apparel, and Kiwi shoe polish. It acquired a number of nonbakery food brands, including Healthy Choice, Hillshire Farms, Ball Park, Jimmy Dean, Bryan, Best's Kosher, Superior Coffee, Senseo **coffee**, and Trail's Best. However, its main business remained bakery goods. Sara Lee purchased Chef Pierre in 1988, the International Bakery Company in 1992, and the Earthgrains Company of St. Louis in 2001. The company's food service products include bagels, bread, buns, cakes, cheesecakes, muffins, rolls and other desserts, **hot dogs**, breakfast sausages, sandwiches, luncheon meats, bacon, meat snacks, and ham.

In February 2005, Sara Lee decided to consolidate its operations and focus on its food, beverage, household, and body care businesses. In 2006, the company therefore spun off its Branded Apparel Americas/Asia businesses into an independent public company called Hanesbrands, which makes Hanes, L'eggs, Playtex, and Wonderbra.

In the same year, Sara Lee expanded its food focus by acquiring Butter-Krust Baking Company. Sara Lee is the nation's leader in **refrigerated** and frozen bakery goods.

FURTHER READINGS: Brinson, Carroll. *A Tradition of Looking Ahead: The Story of Bryan Foods.* Jackson, MS: Oakdale Press, 1986.

Andrew F. Smith

Saran Saran is the proprietary name for polyvinylidine chloride (PVDC), a thermoplastic synthetic resin derived from vinylidene chloride. Since its development in the 1930s, PVDC has had a wide range of industrial, military, and domestic applications due to its ability to form a barrier to water, oxygen, solvents, and other chemicals. The name Saran is now primarily used to refer to a thin film of the material used for wrapping food.

PVDC was discovered accidentally in 1933, when an employee of the Dow Chemical Company, a college student named Ralph Wiley, was unable to remove a greenish deposit from some laboratory glassware. He named the material "eonite" after the imaginary indestructible material featured in the "Little Orphan Annie" comic strip. Later it was officially named Saran (supposedly after Wiley's daughers, Sarah and Ann), and the name was trademarked in 1940.

Initially Saran was manufactured for military use to provide a protective coating for equipment being transported and used overseas during World War II. When the war ended, the (by then) huge plastics industry set to convert its products to peacetime use. A thin, transparent, odor-free film of Saran was produced and sanctioned for commercial use in food packaging in 1949, and for domestic use in 1953.

Dow Chemical had developed its consumer arm on the strength of the success of Saran Wrap, but in 1997 made a decision to return to its core business of industrial and agricultural chemical manufacture. To this end, Dow sold its Dowbrands subsidiary (which produced Saran Wrap) to S. C. Johnson & Son for $1.12 billion.

All substances that come into contact with food, including food **packaging** materials, are subject to the Federal Food, Drug, and Cosmetic Act of 1938. In 1956 in anticipation of the Food Additives Amendment (enacted in 1958), Saran was one of about 200 substances "prior sanctioned," i.e., exempted from the requirement to provide scientific evidence of safety on the grounds that they were "generally recognized as safe." This assumption has been aggressively debated over recent decades amid concerns of environmental and **food safety** issues. There are concerns about possible transfer of plasticizers (plastic additives that increase flexibility) to food, particularly when heated, as when plastic food wrap is used on food being heated in a microwave. There is also concern about the environmental impact resulting from the highly toxic dioxins known to be emitted when chlorinated plastics are burned at high temperatures, as they are when waste is incinerated. In response to consumer anxiety on these issues, in 2004 S. C. Johnson changed the formula of Saran Original to a chlorine-free low-density polyethylene and renamed it Saran Premium.

In spite of these concerns, in view of the cheapness and convenience of plastic films such as Saran, it seems highly unlikely that their popularity in either domestic or commercial use will wane in the near future.

Janet Clarkson

Seed Banks Agricultural curators collect germplasms in seed banks (also called *gene-banks*) to ensure biodiversity and conservation of agricultural resources before they disappear. Seeds are the first link in the food chain. Their integrity and regeneration directly influence the world's food security. Seed is collected to stave off potential agricultural collapse due to predators, changes in the environment, pollution, natural disaster, or political unrest. The **U.S. Department of Agriculture** (USDA) houses the largest collection of seeds in several **refrigerated** vaults scattered across the country, and seed banks number nearly 1,400 globally.

The first recorded instance of seed collecting was initiated by Egypt's Queen Hatshepsut around 1500 B.C., but exploration and colonization of the Western Hemisphere in more recent times drove the gathering and exchange of seeds. The indigenous crops of North America included blueberries, cranberries, and **corn**, an inadequate diet for settlers or the economic and agricultural growth of the young United States. Thus an imperative to import agricultural resources was born.

Three of the Founding Fathers—Benjamin Franklin, Thomas Jefferson, and George Washington—were directly involved in the conservation and trade of seeds. In fact, Jefferson smuggled rice seed from Italy and, while posted to France, sent a steady stream of seeds to botanists and farmers in the United States. Franklin also arranged seed exchanges between horticulturalists in France and America.

In 1819 the secretary of treasury, William H. Crawford, directed diplomats to collect seeds and plants to send home for cultivation. In the late 1830s Henry Ellsworth, commissioner of patents, expanded the U.S. Patent Office's charge to include the collection and distribution of seeds to farmers via the Post Office. In an effort to increase the nation's crop variety and supply, Congress allocated $1,000 in 1839 for the Congressional Seed Distribution Program, a precursor to the USDA. By 1849 the Patent Office was shipping more than 60,000 packets of seeds annually. The USDA was formed in 1862 and charged to collect new and valuable seeds and distribute them to farmers. Around the turn of the 20th century, the department was sending 22 million packets each year. However, 1924 saw the program terminated when lobbyists representing private seed companies prevailed.

Formal seed banks were established in the United States and Russia in the 1890s, but nearly a century passed before the National Seed Storage Laboratory (NSSL) was built at Fort Collins, Colorado, in 1958. Its assemblage of germplasms served as backup to that of regional seed banks located at Ames, Iowa; Geneva, New York; Griffin, Georgia; and Pullman, Washington. In 2001 the NSSL expanded its mission beyond preservation of plant genetics to include animal genetics, as reflected in its new name, the National Center for Genetic Resources Preservation. Seed bank genetic material is used by plant breeders and researchers, who improve the raw material to produce, for example, drought- and pest-resistant crops.

The Norwegian government's Svalbard Global Seed Vault in Longyearbyen, Svalbard, is slated for completion in September 2007. Once it is fully operational, it will be the largest seed bank in the world. Its location and climate ensure that seeds will remain frozen regardless of electricity availability.

Nongovernmental seed banks exist in several countries. The Global Crop Diversity Trust, formed in 2004 and located in Rome, Italy, conserves nearly three million seeds to guarantee that farmers worldwide have access to raw materials from which they can generate our food supply. Six states in India host community seed banks established by the Navdanya movement to save seeds and keep their availability equitable.

The Millennium Seed Bank Project located at Surrey, England, opened in 2000 and stores thousands of seeds in underground vaults.

Grassroots-level seed banks have been established by individuals whose objectives are counter to those of plant breeders and researchers. For instance, Diane Ott Whealy and Kent Whealy founded Seed Savers Exchange in 1975 in an effort to preserve heirloom seeds and share them with future generations. Commercially available seed produces a uniform and high-yield product with minimal **flavor** that is easily harvested by machines. Heirloom seeds appeal to gardeners and hobbyists who relish crop variety and flavor.

Seed banks are threatened by several factors, the greatest of which is funding. They are often undervalued in governmental budgets and do not receive adequate funding for trained staff or physical expansion. Lack of staff prevents banks from processing seeds in a timely manner. Untrained staff poorly catalog and sometimes inadvertently dispose of seeds that may hold the answer to future agricultural questions. Proper humidity and temperature must be maintained in seed banks. Seed must be regenerated on a regular schedule to ensure its viability; old seed must be replanted to secure a younger supply. Their numbers prevent seeds from being germinated adequately and may lead to extinction.

War, famine, political unrest, and economic collapse threaten the existence of seed banks. In 2002, looters discarded seeds hidden for safekeeping in Ghazni and Jalalabad, Afghanistan.

The importance and value of seed availability are immeasurable to global food security. Controlling germplasms is a major issue pitting farmers against plant breeders and seed companies. Seeds are freely available, yet once they are enhanced (i.e., genetically altered or bred to create a new variety), they belong to seed companies that consider the new seed intellectual property. Third World countries object to the use and removal of their native germplasms without fair compensation. Additionally, many **hybrid** or genetically modified seeds cannot be saved and replanted year after year, because seed companies developed a seed technology that produces sterile seed; thus, farmers must purchase new seed each year.

FURTHER READINGS: Kennedy, Donald. "Save the Seeds." *Washington Post*, January 3, 2003; Kloppenburg, Jack Ralph, Jr. *First the Seed: The Political Economy of Plant Biotechnology, 1492–2000*. 2nd ed. Madison: University of Wisconsin Press, 2006; Lustgarden, Steve. "Draining the Gene Pool." *Vegetarian Times* 194 (October 1993): 88–94; Raeburn, Paul. *The Last Harvest: The Genetic Gamble That Threatens to Destroy American Agriculture*. New York: Simon & Schuster, 1995; Raloff, Janet. "The Ultimate Crop Insurance: A New Treaty Strives to Save 10,000 Years of Plant Breeding." *Science News* 166 (September 11, 2004): 170–73; Service, Robert F. "Plant Biotechnology: Seed-Sterilizing 'Terminator Technology' Sows Discord." *Science* 30 (October 1998): 850–51.

Rebecca Tolley-Stokes

Slow Food Slow Food is an international nonprofit organization based in Italy that promotes the enjoyment of wholesome and tasty food as a way to ensure pleasure and quality in everyday life, considering the kitchen and the table as places to reaffirm authenticity, tradition, and community. It has around 80,000 members worldwide, organized into more than 800 local chapters in 50 countries. Slow Food has helped to establish a cultural trend that not only considers food through fashions, market trends, and economics but also focuses on collective enjoyment and sharing. Inviting its members to transform daily consumption into "agricultural acts," the association makes food into a means of active political resistance, sociality, and redis-covery of vital traditions. Aiming at a slower, more harmonious rhythm of life, Slow Food operates to educate large audiences about "eco-gastronomy," touching on issues such as cultural and biological diversity, sustainability in food production, and the protection of the global environment.

Early Years

The movement started in 1986 in Bra, a small town in the Langhe **wine** area in the northern Italian region of Piedmont, under the name ArciGola. ARCI was the acronym for the Recreation Association of Italian Communists, while in Italian the word *gola* means both "food" and "gluttony," referring to the pleasure of food. *La Gola* was also the name of a short-lived though groundbreaking magazine where several relevant left-ist intellectuals wrote about the pleasures of the table, food history, and various issues connected with food and wine. ArciGola was founded by Carlo Petrini, a union mili-tant from Piedmont who had moved from Catholic charity work to more political endeavors. Its first arena was *Gambero Rosso*, a monthly supplement to the leftist daily newspaper *Manifesto*, which also started in 1986. ArciGola and Slow Food scandalized the mainstream leftist organization by affirming the social, cultural, and political value of pleasure, as experienced in the convivial consumption of good quality food.

Because both *Gambero Rosso* and Arcigola believed that the world of wine was not properly presented in Italy, in 1988 they initiated the *Italian Wines Guide*, which within a few years became a very authoritative voice and a trend-setter in the Italian wine market.

Prompted by the arrival of **fast food** in Rome as illustrated by the opening of Italy's first **McDonald's** just beside the historic Spanish Steps, ArciGola became Slow Food, an international organization that marked its official birth on November 9, 1989, at the Opéra Comique in Paris, when representatives from many countries signed its manifesto. The document stated that only a staunch defense of quiet mate-rial pleasure and its long-lasting and slow enjoyment could resist the widespread madness of Fast Life, which forces human beings to consume Fast Foods. The first line of defense, according to Slow Food, was right at the table, where consumers should develop their taste in order to appreciate and defend local and artisanal foods and to protect the environment, which is threatened by industrial food production. Far from being a relapse toward pure hedonism to avoid engagement in the public arena, the defense of pleasure was to become a weapon to bring citizens back to social and political action. The movement immediately adopted a little snail as its insignia.

In 1994, during its yearly convention in Palermo, Slow Food acknowledged its international potential and voted to promote its associative model abroad. It was the birth of Slow Food International, which found its voice in the magazine *Slow*, launched in 1996 in Italian, English, and German, and two years later also in French and Spanish.

Structure

Slow Food can be described as an umbrella organization formed by many entities, including nonprofit associations and commercial businesses. Its main components are

Slow Food International, the various national associations, the Foundation for Biodiversity, a publishing house, and the so-called Pollenzo Agency, which hosts the University of Gastronomic Science, a hotel, a restaurant, and the Banca del Vino (Wine Bank), conceived as an archive of Italian wine production, where already more than 300 producers have stocked bottles. Slow Food Italy Promotion is the business arm of the organization, in charge of organizing all the events, and obtaining grants, **advertising**, and sponsorships.

The international organization is quite decentralized. Its main functional structures are local chapters called *convivia* (about half of the chapters are in Italy, where they are called *condotte*). These are the local associations of members interested in the Slow Food philosophy and its activities, which include gatherings such as subscription dinners to enlarge the member basis, tastings, fundraisers, visits to food and wine producers, and other cultural and educational activities. Each *convivium* has its own leader, often helped by a committee; the leaders, or *fiduciaries*, who are the legal representatives for the convivium, work on a voluntary basis, but can receive subsidies to participate in national and international meetings, such as the International Congress, which is held every four years and elects the International Council. This body, from which a president and his six-member committee are chosen, determines the general policies for Slow Food International, establishes rules and regulations, and approves the committees for the national branches.

So far, besides Italy, there are formal national associations in Switzerland (founded in 1995), Germany (1998), the United States (2000), France (2003), and Japan (2005). Their function is to supervise the operations and activities of the local convivia and to coordinate them with the international movement. Despite its fast international growth and the increasingly complex and formalized organization, president and founder Petrini is still a major figure, being both a charismatic leader and an apt, world-famous spokesperson for the movement.

Main Activities

Besides the local actions and gatherings set up by the convivia all over the world, Slow Food organizes national and international events to further its cause, expand its member basis, and raise funds for its operations. The largest and most relevant is Salone del Gusto, a vast food and wine fair first held in 1996, It has become the world's largest exhibition of quality food and wine and is held every two years at the Lingotto Exhibition Center, a former car factory, in Turin. Here, many small producers have the opportunity to showcase their best goods for a paying audience. The goal of the event is to increase public awareness about the rising food homogenization and the need to defend disappearing species of plants and animals and to sustain small manufacturers of traditional foodstuffs that are risking total oblivion. The Salone del Gusto introduced a new form of cultural marketing that was more effective than the average, purely commercial food show. Slow Food also organizes Cheese, a cheese fair that takes place in Bra, and Slowfish, an exhibition in Genoa that promotes sustainable **fishing**.

In its goal to uphold slow life through slow eating and appreciation of high-quality products, as well as the traditions and knowledge connected to them, Slow Food gives importance to education at all levels. In 1996, the movement began to experiment with educational endeavors and organized the first Laboratori del Gusto (Taste Workshops) during the Vinitaly wine fair in Verona. These workshops aimed to give a growing audience of passionate food lovers a better knowledge of specific products or wines, learning about their origin and history, their social value, and above all their **flavors**.

Besides stressing the relevance of food education for children, the organization has created the Master of Food program to introduce adults to food culture and sensory appreciation in a more structured way than the occasional Laboratorio del Gusto. The Master of Food consists of 20 four-lecture courses on 18 subjects, organized at the convivium level. The participants, who can take the courses offered by their own convivium or by neighboring ones, are able to complete the curriculum in an average of three years. The project, managed by Slow Food Italy Promotion, works well in Italy, where a high number of convivia can share the burden of organizing the courses.

The University of Gastronomic Sciences is located in Pollenzo, Piedmont, near the Bra headquarters, in a former residence of the Savoys, former kings of Piedmont. It was officially founded in 2003 and started its activities in 2004. The institution offers a three-year undergraduate degree in gastronomic sciences, recognized by the Italian government, and two master's degrees (in quality products and food culture) held at the Colorno campus, near Parma.

Following Slow Food's growing engagement in conserving biodiversity and safeguarding products at risk of extinction, the movement created a nonprofit organization, the Slow Food Foundation for Biodiversity, which manages the projects dealing with environment, sustainability, and the defense of gastronomic traditions all over the world. The main initiatives supported by the foundation are the Ark of Taste, the *presidia*, and the Slow Food Awards.

Launched at the 1996 Salone del Gusto, the Ark of Taste discovers, catalogues, protects, and promotes endangered food products on all continents that have actual economic and commercial viability. Responding to the interest in disappearing food-stuffs, in 1997 the movement published the *Manifesto of the Ark of Taste*, a document that set up a methodology to identify products and crops in danger of extinction and proposed policies to defend them. In 1999, a scientific commission determined the specific principles to select the products for the Ark, among which are high levels of quality, connection to a specific territory and the social and historical practices of its inhabitants, manufacture in limited quantities carried out by small producers, and potential or actual risk of disappearance. For instance, the list of U.S. products admitted to the Ark includes Roman taffy **candy** from Louisiana, Olympia oysters from Washington State, and the Crane melon from California.

With the realization that the identification and cataloguing of products was not enough to maintain their existence, in 1999 Slow Food created the presidia, the actual working arm of the Ark of Taste. Presidia are small-scale projects aimed at assisting artisans and producers of items admitted to the Ark to establish stricter standards, buy equipment, create the necessary infrastructures, and promote and market their production. Presidia are not limited to individual products, but can protect communities, traditions, and specific areas in order to ensure local biodiversity.

In 2000, Slow Food also created the Award for the Defense of Biodiversity. Every year an international commission of experts evaluates hundreds of candidates (individuals and associations) from all over the world that have distinguished themselves in defending the biological heritage and the technical know-how connected with their gastronomic and cultural traditions. With this same goal, Slow Food in 2004 organized the first Terra Madre convention, defined as a "world meeting of food communities," where thousands of farmers can meet with experts, chefs, and cultural institutions to discuss methods to promote agriculture models that ensure biodiversity, defend the environment, and respect the health and the culture of local communities.

Slow Food founded its own **publishing** house in 1990. Its first book, *Osterie d'Italia*, introduced terms such as *territory, tradition, straightforwardness, hospitality,* and *conviviality* into the language of **restaurant** reviewers.

Debates

Although Slow Food is widely acknowledged for returning food to social and political debates through its large membership, the immediacy of its concerns, and its media-savvy public relations activities, critics of the organization have accused it of elitism, since its members are usually middle to middle-upper class, its initiatives and activities require a certain amount of disposable income, and the products it protects and promotes through the presidia are often expensive. Many quote the cases of the Zolfini beans and the Colonnata *lardo* (cured pork fat) in Tuscany, which have now become hard to get for the local communities that in the past had easy access to them, beyond their financial means, and often copied by less-than-scrupulous producers who just want to cash in on their names.

Other critics have attributed to Slow Food what has been defined as "culinary luddism," whose goal would be to stop the industrialization process of food worldwide in order to protect traditional ethnic foodways and products. This criticism points to the possibility that the rediscovery of traditions gets captured within a conceptual framework of ahistorical geographies that helps in reconstructing the ideological myth of a time that knew neither disruptions nor crises.

FURTHER READINGS: Chrzan, Janet. "Slow Food: What, Why, and to Where?" *Food, Culture & Society* 7, no. 2 (2004): 117–32; Gaytàn, Narie Sarita. "Globalizing Resistance: Slow Food and New Local Imaginaries." *Food, Culture & Society* 7, no. 2 (2004): 97–116; Kummer, Corby. *The Pleasures of Slow Food: Celebrating Authentic Traditions, Flavors, and Recipes.* San Francisco: Chronicle Books, 2002; Labelle, Julie. "A Recipe for Connectedness: Bringing Production and Consumption with Slow Food." *Food, Culture & Society* 7, no. 2 (2004): 81–96; Laudan, Rachel. "Slow Food: The French Terroir Strategy, and Culinary Modernism." *Food Culture & Society* 7, no. 2 (2004): 133–44; Parasecoli, Fabio. "Postrevolutionary Chowhounds: Food, Globalization, and the Italian Left." *Gastronomica* 3, no. 3 (2003): 29–39; Parasecoli, Fabio. *Food Culture in Italy.* Westport, CT: Greenwood Press, 2004; Paxon, Heather. "Slow Food in a Fat Society: Satisfying Ethical Appetites." *Gastronomica* 5, no. 2 (2005): 14–18; Petrini, Carlo, ed. *Slow Food: Collected Thoughts on Taste, Tradition, and the Honest Pleasures of Food.* White River Junction, VT: Chelsea Green, 2001; Petrini, Carlo. *Slow Food: The Case of Taste.* New York: Columbia University Press, 2003; Petrini, Carlo, and Gigi Padovani. *Slow Food Revolution.* New York: Rizzoli, 2006; Wilk, Rick, ed. *Fast Food/Slow Food: The Cultural Economy of the Global Food System.* Lanham, MD: Altamira Press, 2006.

Fabio Parasecoli

Snack Foods Snacking—eating foods between meals—has always been a part of America's diet. Until the mid-19th century, snacks mainly consisted of natural foods: fruits such as apples, peaches, pears, and when available, bananas and citrus; and nuts such as walnuts, chestnuts, peanuts, and pecans. These foods were often prepared and consumed in the home.

This changed after the Civil War, when **candy** makers began manufacturing candies such as jawbreakers, lollipops, lemon drops, licorice, taffy, and caramels. As **sugar** prices declined in the late 19th century, America's craving for sugar blossomed. Hundreds of manufacturers throughout the United States mass-produced penny candies. Other snack foods, such as pretzels, peanuts, and popcorn balls, were commonly sold by vendors at fairs, circuses, sporting contests, and amusement parks.

Cracker Jack, a combination of popcorn, peanuts, and molasses, was formulated in Chicago and first marketed in 1896. Mainly due to **advertising**, Cracker Jack became the largest-selling snack food during the first half of the 20th century. Many other snack food companies were subsequently launched, such as Hershey's, which began manufacturing **chocolate** bars in 1900, and Planters Peanuts, which began selling packaged peanuts in 1906.

During World War I, the U.S. government sent chocolate to the American armed forces overseas. After the war, returning soldiers wanted more, and sales of chocolate bars and other chocolate products soared during the 1920s. During World War II, consumption of sweets and chocolates by the American public greatly decreased due to rationing of sugar and chocolate. But this created an opportunity for salty snacks. Potato chips had been manufactured in America in the late 19th century, but it wasn't until the 1930s that they became an important snack food. During the war, potato chips, Fritos, and other salty snacks became popular. After the war, both sweets and salty snacks continued their relentless drive to stardom. During the second half of the 20th century, snack foods—particularly candy—became imbedded in holidays, especially Halloween, Christmas, Valentine's Day, and Easter.

Junk and Fast Foods by the Decade in Which They First Appeared

1870s	Blackjack chewing gum
1880s	Coca-Cola
1890s	Cracker Jack, Fig Newton, Good & Plenty, Jell-O, Juicy Fruit gum, Nabisco graham crackers, Tootsie Roll, Triscuits
1900s	Banana split, Barnum's Animal Crackers, Canada Dry ginger ale, Chiclets gum, cotton candy, Dr Pepper, Epsicle (later Popsicle), Hershey's chocolate bar, Hershey's Kisses, Pepsi-Cola, popcorn, Royal Crown cola, Sunshine crackers
1910s	Clark Bar, Doublemint gum, fortune cookie, Konabar (Peter Paul), Life Savers, Lorna Doone cookies, Mr. Peanut, Moon Pie, Orange Crush, Oreo, Peppermint Life Savers, Whitman's Sampler
1920s	A&W Root Beer, Almond Roca, Baby Ruth, Bit-O-Honey, Butterfinger, Charleston Chew, Dum Dum sucker, Eskimo Pie, Good Humor, Karmel-korn, Klondike bar, Kool-Aid, Life Savers (fruit-flavored), Lithiated Lemon (later 7Up), Mike & Ike, Milk Duds, Milky Way, Mr. Goodbar, Mounds, Oh Henry!, Orange Julius, Reese's Peanut Butter Cup, Welch-ade, Wrigley's gum
1930s	Corn chips, Cryst-O-Mint Life Savers, Fifth Avenue bar, Friendly ice cream, Girl Scout cookies, Heath bar, Hershey Krackle bar, Jell-O chocolate pudding, Kit Kat bar, Lay's potato chips, Life Savers (five-flavor), Lime Jell-O, Mars Bar, Nestlé chocolate chip cookies, Nestlé Crunch bar, Reed's Butterscotch, Ritz crackers, Rolo, Sara Lee cheese cake, Smarties, Snickers, Sugar Babies, Sugar Daddy, Three Musketeers, Toll House cookies, Tootsie Pop, Twinkies

1940s	Almond Joy, Baskin-Robbins ice cream, Dairy Queen, Jolly Rancher candy, Junior Mints, M&Ms (violet replaced with tan), M&M's Plain chocolate candies, Nestlé's Quik, Rain-Blo gumball, Reddi wip, Whoppers malted milk balls, York Peppermint Patty
1950s	Ball-O-Fire gumball, Burger King hamburgers and fries, Danny's Donuts (later became Denny's), Dunkin' Donuts, Häagen-Dazs ice cream, International House of Pancakes, M&M's peanut candies, McDonald's fast food, No-cal Ginger Ale (first sugar-free soft drink), Pez (comes to the United States), Pizza Hut, Shakey's pizza, Sweet'N Low sugar substitute
1960s	Bac-Os Bits, Bugles, Chips Ahoy!, Cool Whip, Diet-Rite cola, Diet 7-Up, Domino's pizza, Fresca, Froot Loops, Kellogg's Pop-Tarts, McDonald's Big Mac, M&M's (red, green, and yellow), nachos, Sprite, sugarless gum, Tab cola, Taco Bell, Tang
1970s	A&W Root Beer in cans, Egg McMuffin, Honey Maid cinnamon grahams, Jell-O pudding treat, Jelly Belly, M&M's (orange), McDonald's Happy Meal, Reese's Pieces, Starbucks
1980s	Ben & Jerry's ice cream, Cherry Coke, Cherry 7-Up, Classic Coke, Diet Coke, Equal, Nestlé Alpine White chocolate bar, New Coke, Nutrasweet, Pop Secret microwave popcorn, Symphony bar
1990s	Benecol, Crystal Pepsi, Hershey's Bites, Hershey's Hugs, Hershey's Kisses with almonds, Incredibles (push-up food), Jamba Juice, M&Ms (blue), M&M's Crispy Chocolate Candies, Olestra, Pepsi One, Wow! potato chips
2000s	Boston Market Homestyle Meals, Heinz green ketchup, Heinz purple ketchup, Hershey's Kisses (rich dark chocolate), M&Ms (black and white)

Sources "Twentieth Century Timeline; Edibles and Quaffables." http://www.geocities.com/Foodedge/Timeline.htm

Chocolate Industries

All chocolates were made by hand until Milton S. Hershey, a caramel maker in Lancaster, Pennsylvania, began producing chocolate bars in 1900. Since then, the Hershey Company has dominated chocolate candy production in the United States, and it remains the largest American chocolate producer today.

Chocolate makers duplicated Hershey's mode of operating and began producing chocolate bars of their own. The Standard Candy Company of Nashville, Tennessee, produced the first combination candy, called the Goo Coo Cluster, in 1912. The Clark Bar was the first nationally marketed combination candy bar, and the Butterfinger candy bar was released in 1926. Mars, Inc., released many candies, including the Milky Way bar, followed by Snickers, Three Musketeers, and M&Ms. Thousands of candy bars have been manufactured since then.

Many chocolate candy companies were launched during the 19th and early 20th centuries. In Denver, candy salesman Russell C. Stover opened a candy store in 1921. Stover began manufacturing candy and slowly expanded its manufacturing and retail operations, eventually opening stores in most states. Subsequently, Russell Stover Candies bought out its major competitor, Whitman Chocolates, which produced a "Sampler" consisting of various chocolate-coated candies. In Tacoma, Washington, Harry L. Brown, owner of a small candy store, went into business with J. C. Haley in 1912 to manufacture candy. Their signature product, Almond Roca, was invented in

1923. Today, Russell Stover and Brown & Haley are among America's largest sellers of chocolate candies.

Salty Snack Industries

The popcorn industry began in the latter part of the 19th century. Hundreds of companies were launched, such as the American Pop Corn Company, founded in 1914 by Cloid Smith in Sioux City, Iowa. Popcorn kernels were usually sold in cardboard containers, which exposed the kernels to changing levels of moisture, thus affecting their ability to pop. Smith sealed the popcorn in glass jars in 1920. The kernels in the airtight package did not lose or gain moisture until opened; however, glass was expensive and breakage was high. Smith's second solution was to pack popcorn in hermetically sealed cans, causing a revolution in popcorn packaging. The new techniques were soon applied to other salty snack foods.

Popcorn was not sold in movie theaters until the Great Depression, when owners found that they could make more money on popcorn and other snack food sales than they did on theater admissions. The selling of ready-to-eat popcorn in large bags began before World War II, and sales have increased ever since. When **television** became important during the 1950s, Americans began watching movies in their homes, and they wanted popcorn in their homes as well. Popcorn sales expanded rapidly. The invention of the microwave oven and the release of **hybrid** kernels with tremendous popping volume increased popcorn sales and profits to even greater heights. By the early 21st century, popcorn snack food markets were producing about $1.8 billion per year. More than 60 percent of popcorn is microwaved, and 70 percent is consumed in the home.

When Prohibition ended in 1933 and the bars reopened, salty snacks were given free to customers to increase drink orders. The interest in salty snacks increased even more during World War II, as rationing caused a severe shortage of sugar, sweets, and chocolates, making many familiar candies unavailable. Salty snacks based on corn, potatoes, and peanuts were abundant in America during the war. Other salty snack foods include extruded snacks.

Before World War II, two companies were formed that would revolutionize the snack food industry. Herman W. Lay of Nashville was hired in 1932 by Barrett Foods, an Atlanta snack food firm, to sell **peanut butter** sandwiches in southern Kentucky and Tennessee. He was an aggressive businessman and began acquiring distributorships. When Barrett's founder died in 1937, Lay bought the company, which included plants in Atlanta and Memphis. Lay began manufacturing potato chips in 1938. During World War II, the sale of potato chips increased in part because of the absence of competitive sweet snack foods. By the end of the war, the firm had become a major regional producer of snack foods. After the war, Lay automated his potato chip manufacturing business and diversified its products.

In 1945, Lay met Elmer Doolin, who had been manufacturing corn chips in San Antonio since 1932. Doolin licensed Herman Lay to distribute Fritos in the Southeast, and this was expanded nationally in 1949. The two companies cooperated on other ventures. In 1949 Chee-tos were invented by the Frito Company and were marketed by Lay in 1948. In 1958, Lay acquired the rights to the new type of potato chip, called Ruffles, a thick chip with ridges made especially for dipping.

Doolin died in 1959, and two years later his company merged with Lay's, creating Frito-Lay, with headquarters in Dallas. The merged company continued to grow. Six years later, Frito-Lay merged with the Pepsi-Cola Company, creating PepsiCo. Frito-Lay continued to innovate and develop new products. In 1966, it released Doritos, which became popular nationwide. Rold Gold–brand pretzels were introduced in 1989. Frito-Lay has acquired other food companies, such as Grandma's brand cookies in 1980 and Cracker Jack in 1997. Frito-Lay is the largest snack food conglomerate in the world.

Bakery Snack Industries

Many bakery snacks were sold commercially on the local level, including Moon Pies, which were invented in 1917 in Chattanooga, Tennessee, and TastyKakes, invented about 1914 in Philadelphia. Relatively few of these snacks made it to national prominence. The first that did was Chocolate Cup Cakes, which was reportedly invented by the Indianapolis-based Taggart Bakery in 1919. The Continental Baking Company purchased Taggart in 1925 and looked for a brand name for its cake products. It settled on the name Hostess. The Hostess Chocolate Cupcakes did not add the familiar white creme filling until after World War II. In 1930, the Continental Baking Company produced Twinkies, and subsequently launched coconut-covered Sno Balls in 1947. Its Ding Dongs, a flat chocolate cake first marketed in 1967, were similar to Ring Dings, produced by Drake's Cakes.

Newman E. Drake baked pound cakes in Brooklyn in 1888. He expanded his operations to reach New York, New England, and Florida. Drake's Cakes produced Yodels, a chocolate-frosted and creme-filled Swiss roll, and Ring Dings, a chocolate-covered, creme-filled chocolate cake. When Hostess released its Ding Dongs, Drake's sued for copyright infringement and Hostess was required to change its name.

The Interstate Brands Corporation (IBC) released its Dolly Madison line of commercial pastries in 1937. The Dolly Madison brand also includes Zingers (creme-filled cakes), Gems (miniature donuts), angel food and pound cakes, and a variety of breakfast items, such as Sweet Rolls, Dunkin Stix, and Pecan Rollers. In 1995, IBC acquired the Continental Baking Company, maker of Hostess, and changed its name to Interstate Bakeries Corporation, keeping its initials. IBC acquired Drake's in 1998.

McKee Bakery Company of Chattanooga launched the Little Debbie brand in 1960. The largest-selling Little Debbie products include Swiss Cake Rolls, Nutty Bars Wafer Bars, Oatmeal Creme Pies, and Fudge Brownies. As of 2005, Little Debbie cakes manufactured by McKee Foods were the largest-selling cakes in America, followed by Hostess ($165 million).

William Entenmann opened his first bakery in Brooklyn in 1898. He made small cakes, breads, and rolls. His business flourished, and in the 1950s, the company began to expand throughout the East Coast, selling its goods through grocery stores as well as through the bakeries. In 1961, the company moved to Bay Shore, Long Island. The company discontinued making bread and concentrated on pastries. Today, Entenmann's is one of America's largest pastry makers and the nation's second largest donut maker. **Krispy Kreme** donuts are the largest-selling donut in grocery stores.

Cheese-flavored Snack Industries

The first commercial cheese-based snacks were Cheez-It crackers, which were introduced in 1921 by the Sunshine Biscuit Company of Kansas City. It has been a very successful brand ever since, so much so that many other companies have tried to make similar crackers.

During the 1930s, extruded snacks were invented by an animal feed technician, Edward Wilson. His commercial product, Korn Kurls, became popular after World War II. During the 1940s, the Frito Company began experimenting with extruded snacks, and in 1948 it released Chee-tos, a corn snack covered with an artificially colored powdered cheddar cheese. Other companies began manufacturing cheese puffs, a generic name for extruded snacks with a cheese covering. Yet another cheese-based snack, Goldfish, a small orange-colored cheese-flavored cracker shaped like a fish, was released by Pepperidge Farm, a subsidiary of **Campbell's Soup**.

Frito-Lay increased its promotion for Chee-tos, which acquired a mascot named Chester Cheetah. Today, the Chee-tos product line has been extended. In the 1980s, Frito-Lay also introduced other cheese-flavored products, such as "Puffed Balls." Although similar products are manufactured by other companies, Frito-Lay's Chee-tos dominate the puffed snack market with sales twice as high as the other top 15 competitors combined.

Nuts and Peanut Industries

Roasted chestnuts and other nuts have been sold on America's streets since colonial times. Nuts require little preparation and can easily be transported. They are relatively inexpensive and generally nutritious. The most commercially important nuts sold in America are almonds, walnuts, and pecans, followed by chestnuts, pistachios, and macadamias. All are grown extensively in California with the exception of macadamias, which are grown mainly in Hawaii. In addition, other nuts, such as cashews, are imported.

In the 19th century, nuts were roasted and salted by vendors and homemakers, but the commercial processes of salting nuts so that the salt remains on the nut after packaging was not learned until the early 20th century. Salted nuts were commercially packaged and sold in the United States thereafter.

The most important snack nut, however, is technically a legume. Peanuts were relatively unimportant as a snack food until after the Civil War, when vendors began selling them on streets in cities. One peanut vendor was Amedeo Obici, an Italian-born immigrant who lived in Wilkes-Barre, PA. In 1906 Obici formed a partnership with another Italian immigrant to form the Planters' Peanut Company (later changed to Planters, without the apostrophe). Their products then went through a **packaging** revolution, permitting Planters to sell fresh peanuts to a larger clientele. Planters also emphasized advertising and marketing, and "Mr. Peanut" quickly became an American culinary icon. The company went from a small vendor operation to a national snack food company in less than two decades. As of 2004, Planters is the largest-selling nut brand.

Challenges Facing the Snack Food Industry

During the 1950s the term "junk foods" was used to describe foods that were high in sugar, fat, salt, and calories but low in nutritional value. The vast increase in snack food consumption in the following decades alarmed nutritionists even more. Studies reported that about 30 percent of the average American's diet was made up of junk foods. The increase in consumption of the junk foods correlates with an increase in heart disease, high blood pressure, cancer, **obesity**, and other diseases. Also, as junk food consumption has increased, the consumption of healthier foods, such as milk, fruit, and vegetables, has decreased, thus reducing nutrients in the diet of many Americans, particularly of children.

Snack Food Industry Today

For many people, snacking has become a continuous process indulged in throughout the day. Snacking has replaced meals for many Americans. By the beginning of the 21st century, Americans annually consumed almost $45 billion worth of snack food. While nutritionists properly complain about the consumption of snack foods, there is no sign that Americans are decreasing their consumption of them.

Despite the wealth of snack foods, the industry is today dominated by relatively few large conglomerates, especially Frito-Lay, Hershey, Nestlé, Mars, Interstate Bakeries Corporation, and the Kellogg Company.

FURTHER READINGS: Brenner, Joël Glenn. *The Emperors of Chocolate: Inside the Secret World of Hershey and Mars.* New York: Broadway Books, 2000; Jacobson, Michael F., and Bruce Maxwell. *What Are We Feeding Our Kids?* New York: Workman, 1994; Matz, Samuel A. *Snack Food Technology.* 3rd ed. New York: AVI Van Nostrand Reinhold, 1993; Richardson, Tim. *Sweets: A History of Candy.* New York: Bloomsbury, 2002; Smith, Andrew F. *Peanuts: The Illustrious History of the Goober Pea.* Urbana: University of Illinois Press, 2002; Smith, Andrew F. *Popped Culture: A Social History of Popcorn in America.* Columbia: University of South Carolina Press, 1999; Snack Food Association. *Fifty Years: A Foundation for the Future.* Alexandria, VA: Snack Food Association, 1987.

Andrew F. Smith

Soft Drinks In early America, sanitation was not well understood, and drinking water was often contaminated, particularly in cities. As a result, most Americans drank "hard" beverages, such as hard cider, rum, **beer**, and ale, rather than water. The high consumption of liquor led to alcoholism and other serious societal problems. To combat these evils, the Temperance Movement emerged during the early 19th century. It encouraged the consumption of alternative nonalcoholic beverages, such as root beer, made from sassafras roots, leaves, and other parts of aromatic plants and trees. By the 1840, hundreds of root beers were manufactured locally, and many were combined with carbonated soda.

Other commercial soft drinks were launched after the Civil War. A nonalcoholic ginger ale was first marketed in 1866 by James Vernor, a Detroit pharmacist. Tonic water, consisting of quinine and ginger ale, was marketed by Schweppes, an English soda manufacturer, beginning in 1870. An itinerant pharmacist, Augustin Thompson, concocted "Moxie Nerve Food" in Lowell, Massachusetts, in 1876; carbonated water was later added and the medicine was converted into Moxie, a soft drink.

Manufacturing carbon dioxide for carbonation was a difficult and dangerous business. It wasn't until the mid-19th century that safer and easier mechanisms were developed. This new technology was demonstrated at the Centennial Exposition held in Philadelphia in 1876, when James W. Tufts and Charles Lippincott constructed a building with a 30-foot soda fountain and dozens of soda dispensers ready to refresh thirsty fair-goers. Alcoholic beverages had been banned at the exposition, and the summer proved to be extremely hot, so large numbers of fair-goers were introduced to carbonated beverages for the first time. After the exposition closed, Tufts and Lippincott made a fortune selling soda fountains to drugstores around the nation. One soda advertised at the exposition was Hires Root Beer, developed by Philadelphia drugstore operator Charles E. Hires. Hires Root Beer became America's first successful national soft drink. Hires sold the concentrate to druggists, who then combined it with carbonation.

Many other drugstore operators began manufacturing carbonated beverages. Charles Alderton, an employee of Morrison's Old Corner Drug Store in Waco, Texas, began to experiment with carbonated beverages served at a store's soda fountain. The owner of the store, Wade Morrison, is credited with naming one of Alderton's popular soft drinks "Dr Pepper" in 1885. Robert S. Lazenby, who owned the Circle "A" Ginger Ale Company in Waco, went into business with Morrison. They formed the Artesian Manufacturing and Bottling Company. Dr Pepper quickly became a favorite in the Southwest. In 1904 it was marketed at the St. Louis Exposition. When the beverage was a tremendous success, the company's name was changed to the Dr Pepper Company. Lazenby moved the company from Waco to Dallas in 1923.

Cola-based Soft Drinks

Soft drinks based on the kola nut were first tried in 1881, but these were unsuccessful until the arrival of Coca-Cola. It was invented by Atlanta druggist John Stith Pemberton in 1886 and consisted of kola nut extract, **sugar**, and other ingredients. The original formula also contained coca derivatives, which at the time was neither illegal nor unusual. Pemberton considered his new beverage a cure for headaches and morphine addiction, and he sold the syrup as a medicine in drugstores, which added the carbonation when customers ordered the beverage. Pemberton sold out to Asa Chandler, who rapidly expanded the business by expert marketing. Chandler plowed most of his profits back into his business, and his efforts paid off. **Bottling** of the beverage began in 1894. By 1900 Coca-Cola's revenues topped $400,000. Four years later, Coca-Cola was one of the most recognized brand names in America.

Coca-Cola was enormously popular, and many other druggists began to imitate its success. In 1905 Claud A. Hatcher, a pharmacist, launched the Union Bottling Works in the basement of his family's grocery store in Columbus, Georgia. "Chero-Cola" was the first of his Royal Crown line of beverages, and it was followed by ginger ale, strawberry, and root beer-flavored sodas. In 1912, Hatcher changed the name of the company to the Chero-Cola Company. The company struggled through World War I, when sugar was difficult to obtain, and continued to have financial difficulties during the early 1920s. In 1924, the company was strong enough to bring out a new line, called Nehi, of fruit-flavored sodas, such as orange and grape. Hatcher died in 1933, and his successor reformulated Chero-Cola and shortened the brand name to RC Cola.

Yet another early cola manufacturer was Caleb Bradham, a pharmacist in New Bern, North Carolina, who named one of his kola nut beverages "Brad's Drink." In 1898, he rechristened it "Pepsi-Cola." It was successful, and this encouraged Bradham to incorporate the Pepsi-Cola Company in 1902. Bradham began to rapidly expand his sales. By 1907 the company had 40 bottling plants across the United States, and three years later, Bradham had **franchised** more than 300 bottlers in 24 states to produce Pepsi-Cola. Nevertheless, Bradham ran into financial problems and the company went into bankruptcy in 1922. It was resurrected by a Wall Street broker, Roy C. Megarel, who controlled the company until 1931, when the company again went bankrupt. It was saved by Charles Guth, the president of the Loft Candy Company. The formula for Pepsi was changed at this time. The new formula eliminated pepsin as a major ingredient. By 1934 Pepsi-Cola had turned the corner and began purchasing bottling operations throughout the United States. Pepsi's net earnings had risen to more than $5.5 million by 1939.

Pepsi-Cola was disrupted yet again by World War II. In the United States, sugar rationing was imposed early in 1942, which drastically restricted the amount of soft drinks that Pepsi-Cola could produce. The Coca-Cola Company, on the other hand, received contracts from the U.S. government to supply America's military with soft drinks. After the war, Coca-Cola sales exploded as soldiers returned home and demanded "a Coke."

Even when the sugar restrictions were removed after the war, Pepsi had a hard time competing with Coke. By 1950 Pepsi-Cola was close to declaring bankruptcy for a third time, but a highly successful advertising campaign came to the rescue. Throughout the 1950s, Pepsi continued to expand aggressively abroad, particularly into Latin America and Europe.

Fruit-flavored Soft Drinks

An orange-based soft drink was invented by California chemist Neil C. Ward. He partnered with Clayton J. Howell of Cleveland, Ohio, to market the new beverage in 1916. During World War I, sugar was difficult to acquire and the new beverage languished until the war ended in 1918. Ward and Howell named their company Orange Crush Bottling Company and their drink "Ward's Orange Crush." It consisted mainly of sugar and carbonated water with enough orange concentrate to give the beverage a bright orange color. The product's name was subsequently shortened to Orange Crush. It became successful, in part because it was promoted as a health beverage. During the 1920s and '30s, Orange Crush dominated the market for orange soda. The company also added other citrus-flavored beverages, including lemon and lime.

Another soft drink was invented by Charles Leiper Grigg, proprietor of the Howdy Corporation in St. Louis. In 1927 Grigg began experimenting with lemon- and lime-flavored soft drinks. After two years of work, he came up with a beverage that blended seven different flavors; he called it "Bib-Label Lithiated Lemon-Lime Soda." Shortly thereafter, the name was shortened to just "7-Up." Prohibition ended a few years later, and 7-Up was marketed as a mixer for alcoholic drinks. Sales were so successful that in 1936 he changed the name of the Howdy Corporation to the Seven-Up Company. Within 10 years, 7-Up was the third largest-selling soft drink.

New Products

Diet soda was launched in 1952, when Kirsch Beverages began marketing No-Cal ginger ale and root beer. It was followed by many other diet sodas, including Royal Crown's Diet-Rite Cola (1958), Coca-Cola's Tab (1963), and Diet 7-Up (1979). Diet Coke and Diet Pepsi were released in 1982.

In 1980 Royal Crown released a decaffeinated cola, RC 100, and other soda manufacturers followed with caffeine-free colas of their own. About the same time, other soda companies began marketing decaffeinated sodas. As a backlash, in 1985 C. J. Rapp created Jolt Cola; it and other similar sodas, such as Surge and Josta, had 30–60 percent *more* caffeine than Coke and Pepsi.

During the 1960s Pepsi introduced several new soft drinks, including Mountain Dew. In 1965 Pepsi bought the Frito-Lay Corporation and renamed the new entity

PepsiCo. During the 1970s, PepsiCo acquired several **fast food chains**, including Pizza Hut, Taco Bell, and Kentucky Fried Chicken, which it saw as important outlets for its soft drink, as all its chains sold Pepsi products exclusively.

The Coca-Cola Company responded with many new brands of its own, including Sprite, Fanta, Fresca, Mr. Pibb, Mello Yello, Cherry Coke, and many more. Perhaps the most famous new Coca-Cola brand was "New Coke," created in the midst of the so-called cola wars.

Cola Wars

Coca-Cola and Pepsi have been at war for almost a century. For the first half of the 20th century, Coca-Cola dominated the soft drink world. Coca-Cola challenged other manufacturers in court, and when this failed, the company did its best to undercut competition. Coke's main rival, Pepsi-Cola, slowly gained market share beginning in the 1950s.

In the 1970s Pepsi-Cola's market share in Dallas was a dismal 4 percent—far behind Dr Pepper and Coca-Cola. To find out why, Pepsi ran a series of double-blind taste tests to see how people responded to the different soft drinks. Much to their surprise, the majority of testers—even die-hard Coke drinkers—preferred Pepsi. Pepsi launched a series of commercials, called "The Pepsi Challenge," showing Coke consumers stating in a blind taste test that they preferred Pepsi. This launched the "cola wars."

Coca-Cola responded with an ad that compared the Pepsi Challenge to two chimpanzees deciding which tennis ball was furrier. Other soft drink companies became involved: 7-Up, for instance, came up with a campaign that positioned it as the "uncola."

When Coke sales did not improve, the company launched another advertising campaign in 1981, with the slogan "Coke is it." Unfortunately, Coca-Cola sales continued to decline, and the company's own double-blind taste tests confirmed that most people preferred the sweeter taste of Pepsi to Coke. Company executives concluded that they needed to change the formula for Coca-Cola. In 1985, with great fanfare, the Coca-Cola Company introduced a sweeter "New Coke," which had been preferred in double-blind taste tests over both Pepsi and the old Coke. The company supported its introduction with a massive advertising campaign. However, many Coca-Cola drinkers were outraged at the change, and within months "Classic Coke" was back on the market. Sales of New Coke dwindled, and the company stopped marketing it nationally by the 1990s.

Consolidation in the Soft Drink Industry

Before World War II, hundreds of soft drink manufacturers dotted America. The war created difficulties due to the rationing of sugar and many the soft drink manufacturers went out of business. After the war, the survivors began to consolidate. In 1962 Crush International was acquired by Charles E. Hires Co., makers of Hires Root Beer. In 1986, 7-Up and Dr Pepper merged to form the Dr Pepper/Seven-Up Companies.

Schweppes expanded its global operation, merging with the **chocolate** manufacturer Cadbury to form Cadbury Schweppes in 1969. The combined company then began acquiring other soft drink companies, such as Hires Root Beer (1989), A&W

Beverages (1993), Dr Pepper/Seven-Up (1995), and RC Cola (2000). As of 2005, Cadbury Schweppes was the world's third largest manufacturer of soft drinks, behind Coca-Cola and PepsiCo.

Industry Problems

By the 1990s, soft drinks—which are full of sugar, salt, and caffeine—were being roundly condemned by many nutritionists. Advocates for limiting soda consumption have linked soda with tooth decay, delayed bone development, **obesity**, and diabetes. Diet sodas are not much better, because sugar substitutes also have potential risks. Aspartame, for instance, has been linked to a range of chronic disorders, including cramps, seizures, vertigo, and multiple sclerosis.

There is particular concern with the amount of soft drinks consumed by children and youth. In 1998 the Center for Science in the Public Interest (CSPI) study *Liquid Candy* reported that soft drinks "provided more than one-third of all refined sugars in the diet." Soft drinks, according to CSPI, are consumed by at least 75 percent of teenage children every day and are the single largest source of refined sugar, providing 9 percent of calories for boys and 8 percent for girls.

The CSPI study also reported that soft drink companies target schools for advertising and sales of their products. Soft drink manufacturers spend billions, as much as 25 percent of their entire revenue, on promotion and advertising, much of it targeting youth. Marketing efforts are aimed at children through cartoons, movies, videos, charities, and amusement parks. In addition, soft drink companies sponsor contests, sweepstakes, games, and clubs via television, radio, magazines, and the **Internet**.

With **vending machines** in schools, soft drinks are more accessible. Increased soda consumption has also been correlated with decreased milk consumption, which means that youth are not getting enough calcium and other **vitamins** and minerals. In 2006, the major soft drink companies agreed to remove soda with high amounts of sugar from school vending machines.

Soft Drinks Today

Despite the criticism, the soft drink industry has continued to expand throughout the world and to generate substantial profits. The basic costs of production for soft drinks are low, since water, carbon dioxide, sweeteners, colorings, and flavorings are inexpensive. The sales of soda are now more popular than **coffee**, tea, and juice combined. According to the American Beverage Association, soft drink companies gross almost $93 billion in annual sales in the United States alone, and the industry employees 211,000 people. Coca-Cola and PepsiCo sell more than 70 percent of the carbonated beverages in the world. Annually, Americans consume 52 gallons of soft drinks.

FURTHER READINGS: Allen, Frederick. *Secret Formula: How Brilliant Marketing and Relentless Salesmanship Made Coca-Cola the Best-known Product in the World.* New York: HarperBusiness, 1994; Ellis, Harry E. *Dr Pepper: King of Beverages Centennial Edition.* Dallas: Dr Pepper Company, 1986; Enrico, Roger, and Jesse Kornbluth. *The Other Guy Blinked: How Pepsi Won the Cola Wars.* New York: Bantam, 1986; Greising, David. *I'd Like the World to Buy a Coke: The Life and Leadership of Roberto Goizueta.* New York: Wiley, 1998; Hays, Constance L. *The Real Thing: Truth and Power at the Coca-Cola Company.* New York: Random House, 2005; Jacobson, Michael F. *Liquid Candy: How Soft Drinks Are Harming Americans' Health.*

2nd ed. Washington, D.C.: Center for Science in the Public Interest, 2005; Louis, J. C., and Harvey Yazijian. *The Cola Wars: The Story of the Global Corporate Battle between the Coca-Cola Company and PepsiCo*. New York: Everest House, 1980; Pendergrast, Mark. *For God, Country and Coca-Cola*. New York: Scribner's, 1993; Rodengen, Jeffrey L. *The Legend of Dr Pepper/Seven-Up*. Ft. Lauderdale, FL: Write Stuff Syndicate, 1995.

Andrew F. Smith

Spam Spam luncheon meat is a **canned**, precooked, spiced pork product created by the **Hormel** Foods Corporation in 1937. Through **advertising** and its distribution as food aid during World War II, Spam has become a worldwide food product, adapted to local cuisines, as well as a pop culture icon, inspiring a collection of haiku, a comedy routine, and a museum. The name is a contraction of "spiced ham." Today Spam is made in a variety of flavors, including low-sodium, hickory-smoked, garlic, "lite," honey, hot and spicy, and cheese.

Spam
The name of this canned pink product is a contraction of "spiced ham," but the ingredients tell a slightly different story: "Chopped pork and ham, salt, water, potato starch, sugar, sodium nitrite." That noncommittal "chopped pork" tells us little and has led to all sorts of grisly urban legends about exactly what parts of the pig might be included. "Ham" is certainly there—but one other thing is certain: there are no spices in those blue-and-yellow cans.

From its inception, Hormel has marketed Spam in the popular media, beginning with Spammy the Pig, a mascot who appeared on the *Burns and Allen* radio show. Spam entered a global stage in 1941, through America's Lend-Lease program, designed to support the Allied nations fighting World War II. Early Lend-Lease aid included food for civilian consumption in Britain and Russia, and Hormel began delivering four million cans per week to the U.S. government; the order quickly increased to 15 million cans a week. By 1944, 90 percent of Hormel's production was going to the government and, from there, around the world. After the United States entered the war, GIs also ate Spam, both as a staple in K-rations and in mess halls.

Spam is particularly popular in Hawaii, which leads the country in consumption with seven million cans per year. Its popularity can be traced to World War II, but also to the fact that Spam is an economical meat product easily shipped and stored, requiring no **refrigeration**. In Hawaii, it is often served with eggs and rice or as *musubi*. From the Japanese word *omusubi*, a rice snack, musubi is sushi that combines Spam with rice, wrapped in nori seaweed.

In Greece, Spam is still served to army conscripts, and in China, Spam is served as a Western food in sandwiches. In the United Kingdom, Spam was one of the few foods available during postwar rationing and even today is often featured at fish-and-chips shops, battered and fried.

A sketch by the British comedy troupe Monty Python inspired the term *spam* for electronic junk mail. The routine is set in a café where Spam appears in every dish and finishes with a Viking chorus chanting "Spam, Spam, Spam" drowning out any other communication, in the same way electronic junk mail obscures legitimate messages.

Hormel recognized the popularity of Spam and began marketing related gift products in 1992 at the Hormel Gift Center, selling more than 400 Spam-branded products, including golf tees, key rings, charm bracelets, and beach balls. In 2001, Hormel established the Spam Museum in the company's hometown of Austin, Minnesota. Exhibits include a memorial to Hormel employees who served in World War II; a replication of "Spamville," a South Pacific military camp; and a letter from President Dwight Eisenhower. Two cans of Spam are also part of the Smithsonian Institution's permanent collection, an original 1937 can and a contemporary one.

FURTHER READINGS: Cho, John. *Spam-Ku: Tranquil Reflections on Luncheon Loaf.* New York: Harper Perennial, 1998; Hormel Foods Corporation. http://www.spam.com; Wyman, Carolyn. *Spam: A Biography.* New York: Harcourt Brace, 1999.

Claudia Kousoulas

Starbucks. *See* Coffee and Tea.

Stuckey's In 1934, after an especially plentiful harvest, Williamson S. Stuckey opened a pecan stand in a shack on U.S. Route 23 in Eastman, Georgia. His wife, Ethel, provided her homemade pecan log candy for sale, based on a secret recipe of powdered **sugar**, white molasses, and roasted pecans. The business flourished, creating an excellent opportunity for expansion, as Route 23 was destined to become part of an interstate highway that would stretch south from Michigan to Florida by the 1950s. The success of the one roadside stand prompted Stuckey to expand and to offer other amenities needed by travelers. By the beginning of World War II, he had opened three stands, complete with gas pumps, a selection of whimsical souvenirs, and **cafeterias** that sold hot food. Stuckey's expanded to Florida in 1941, and by 1948 there were 49 establishments, mostly catering to highway travelers, long-haul truckers, and vacationers on their way to and from Florida.

The prototype "one-stop" family-owned facilities with the teal-colored roof became familiar to East Coast travelers by the 1950s, with the signature canopy over the gas area, outfitted with lunch counters and booths inside, accompanied by clean restrooms and **candy** and novelties sales area. The most important task of the business, and the key to its popularity, lay in the expected homogeneity and standardization of the food and décor of the restaurants, which lent a home-away-from-home sense of familiarity to travelers. The growth of the company saw more Stuckey's **franchises**, with locations expanding across the Midwest to Texas, and from the Great Plains to the Rockies. Eventually there were 350-plus Stuckey's throughout the continental United States.

The company was eventually sold in 1964 to Pet Milk, which also owned a variety of food producers, including Whitman and Son, and the H. Musselman Company. The corporate-run business became less personalized, and expansions slowed through the 1970s and '80s, and the chain was eventually repurchased by W. S. Stuckey Jr., son of the original owner and a former Georgia congressman. Stuckey assures customers in his welcome on the company's website of his plans to make the "Stuckey's name once again a prominent part of our country's landscape."

A family-run business again, Stuckey's corporate headquarters are located outside Washington, D.C., in Silver Spring, Maryland, while its shipping facilities are located in Atlanta. Stuckey's is an important icon in American highway history. An especially significant new part of the business is Stuckey's Express, a small outlet located inside other convenience stores and travel centers. Current sales are estimated at $3.09 million a year. The Stuckey's business ethic can be seen at work in the current popularity of the Cracker Barrel Old Country stores of Lebanon, Tennessee, first opened in 1969, and now spread through the nation.

FURTHER READINGS: Drinnon, Elizabeth McGants. *Stuckey: The Biography of Williamson Sylvester Stuckey, 1909–1977*. Macon, GA: Mercer University Press, 1997; Hollis, Tim. *Dixie before Disney: 100 Years of Roadside Fun*. Jackson: University Press of Mississippi, 1999; Jakle, John A., and Keith A. Sculle. *Fast Food: Roadside Restaurants in the Automobile Age*. Baltimore: Johns Hopkins University Press, 1999.

Margaret Coyle

Subway. *See* Fast Food Restaurants.

Sugar and Artificial Sweeteners The Western "sweet tooth" has fueled competition for vast profits for at least five centuries. Although other natural substances sweeten, sucrose has been the primary economic engine in the sweetener market. Sugarcane production harnessed millions of people into slave labor for three centuries. Pursuit of the sweetener market has also driven **research** efforts in search of substitutes for white sugar produced from cane. These experiments first bore fruit in the 19th century and continued to generate heat in the early 20th century. The current aim is to find a natural sweetener that tastes good (not just sweet) and adds no additional calories to foods and beverages while not threatening human health.

Sugar is perhaps the only food commodity to have given its name to a turning point in global economic history. Cane sugar came into wide usage in Europe after the 16th-century importation of sugarcane and production techniques into the Americas. At first, sugar was considered a **condiment** and was included in recipes in similar quantities as spices. As cane sugar from the Near East and the Americas became accessible to more people, it began to be used it in larger quantities as a sweetener.

Eating larger and larger quantities of sugar, which was the trend from the 16th through 20th centuries in the West, has become less appealing to some consumers. Even for those who give in readily to their sweet tooth, much sugar consumption has been replaced by high-fructose **corn** syrup, which is less costly than subsidized cane or beet sugar.

Current Sugar Production

Twenty-first-century consumers can choose from a variety of sweeteners, both natural and artificial—all subject to health claims. Natural sweeteners include maple syrup, honey, stevia, and corn syrup. Beet sugar was the first natural sucrose competitor, introduced industrially in the 19th century. Artificial sweeteners developed since then include saccharin, aspartame, and sucralose. The most well-known and heavily used sweeteners are produced from sugarcane and sugar beets: molasses (syrup from sugarcane), brown sugar (molasses syrup and sugar crystals), raw sugars (including turbinado, demerara, and muscovado, whose brown color has been removed to varying degrees), and white sugar (99.9 percent sucrose).

In 2005, the world produced about 148 million tons of sugar in a small number of countries. The top producer, Brazil, produced approximately 28 million tons of sugar, exporting about 60 percent of the total production. The **European Union** and India followed closely in production, but exported far less of their production. China, the United States, Mexico, South Africa, Australia, Thailand, and Russia complete the top 10 sugar producers in the world. Sugar is produced for the lowest cost in Brazil and costs more to produce in Cuba and Germany than in other sugar-producing countries. After Brazil, the top exporters were the EU, Australia, and Thailand.

However, most sugar is consumed in the country where it is produced. Per-capita consumption of sugar is currently highest in Brazil, Australia, the EU, Thailand, South Africa, and the United States. Brazilians consume almost 130 pounds each year, while U.S. citizens eat a little more than 65 pounds of sugar per year. Consumers pay more for sugar in Japan than in any other country in the world, with retail prices averaging just over 70 cents per pound in 2005. Domestic sugar prices are lowest in Brazil.

The Sugar Market

Countries compete to offer their sugar on the world market at the most attractive price, and most sugar-producing states offer subsidies or price supports to farmers. Trade is often affected by politics, such as the U.S. embargo on Cuban products. Countries subsidize the product to varying degrees and the elimination of subsidies is a regular topic of discussion in the World Trade Organization (WTO).

International trade agreements govern most sugar imports. Some of these are multinational, such as the **North American Free Trade Agreement** (NAFTA), Central American Free Trade Agreement (CAFTA), and WTO agreements, while others are bilateral **free-trade** agreements. In the United States, the **U.S. Department of Agriculture** (USDA) forecasts sugar demand for the year, then subtracts the commitments the United States has made in treaties to buy sugar from other countries. The rest of the demand is allocated to domestic producers. This program must operate at no cost to the federal government, so prices are controlled by regulating how much producers may sell or restricting imports of sugar from countries not covered by treaty obligations. Sugar producers who favor the current U.S. government sugar program take some heat from political opponents who claim the artificially high price hurts sugar users.

The European Union also supports domestic sugar production but embarked in 2006 on a program to reduce sugar subsidies and bring prices more in line with world prices. This move led to shifts in the industry and the announcement by a major sugar beet processor of the closure of five processing plants in Eastern Europe in 2006. (This producer, Tate & Lyle, intends to move away from sugar and toward the production of artificial sweeteners in a new factory in Singapore and an expanded facility in the United States.)

Sugar Production Process

Half of the sugar on the market in 2006 comes from sugarcane and half from sugar beets. Both cane and beets are produced using **labor**-intensive methods. While sugarcane must be processed as quickly as possible after harvesting to avoid losing sugar content, beets can be stored for several weeks. Processing beets is also easier than extracting the sugar from cane. Beets are transformed into white sugar in one step, while processing cane takes an additional step to whiten the crystals. White sugar from cane and beets is virtually identical.

Sugar beets thrive in northern climates and are harvested in the autumn and transported by truck to factories, where they are first washed and separated from leaves, dirt, and rocks. They are sliced to expose more surface to the hot water they will soak in to extract the sucrose. The slices are pressed to remove as much sugar as possible. The resulting liquid, called raw juice, contains about 14 percent sugar. The impurities are removed from the juice by *carbonatation* (using chalk to attract the nonsugar elements for removal). The sugar syrup is then boiled to stimulate crystallization. A centrifuge is used to separate the crystals from the remaining liquid and then the crystals are dried. This process is generally repeated three times to extract the most white sugar. Beet molasses, the sweet by-product of the process, is often used to make cattle feed.

Sugarcane is a tropical grass. Whereas the entire beet plant is harvested, sugarcane cutters leave the roots so the plant can regenerate for the next harvest. Cane fields must be close to processing factories, because the sugar content in the cane dissipates quickly. Within 24 hours of harvesting, the cane is crushed by large rollers. The fiber is boiled to extract additional sugar; the juice from this stage of extraction, while dirty, usually contains about 15 percent sugar. The impurities, such as dirt from the field, are removed from the syrup by evaporation using lime as in beet carbonatation. As in processing beet sugar, the syrup is then boiled to encourage crystallization. Unlike beet sugar, however, cane sugar must be refined to remove the brown color and distinctive taste from the crystals. Cane sugar also produces molasses, which can be used as a sweetener, added to cattle feed, or **distilled** to produce rum. Unlike the fiber by-product of sugar beet processing, the cane fibers can be burned to provide fuel to power the cane factory.

Pursuit of a Substitute for Sugar

More and more appearance-conscious Americans are turning to artificial sweeteners to avoid the calories (15 to the teaspoon) of white sugar. The stakes in the multibillion-dollar sweetener industry are high. Thousands of products—from cough drops to **soft drinks** to yogurt—incorporate artificial sweeteners and claim the designator "low-sugar" or "reduced sugar." Sales of reduced-sugar products in the United States were estimated at $5.9 billion for 2005.

Saccharin, the first artificial sugar substitute, was created by a German and American team of chemists in the late 19th century. Studies conducted in the 1960s suggested that this product causes cancer. Canada banned it, and the United States required a warning label until 2000.

The USDA approved aspartame for consumption in foods and beverages in 1981. A string of other sweet substances has followed, including acesufame potassium, isoglucose, isomaltulose, neotame, and sucralose. Each compound is created by a different process that usually results in a taste much sweeter than sucrose.

While aspartame (sold as NutraSweet and Equal in the United States) held a virtual monopoly on the market for artificial sweeteners in the 1980s and '90s, the current darling of the market is sucralose, a chemical alteration of cane sugar that produces a compound that is 600 times sweeter than sugar but has no calories. Splenda, a brand name for sucralose, accounted for about 60 percent of U.S. artificial sweetener sales domestically in 2006. In that year, Splenda sales reached $206 million annually.

Conflict over patents and marketing claims have come up periodically from the first creation of an artificial sweetener in the late 19th century. In the first case, Ira Remsen, the American partner in the creation of saccharin, sued his German partner over the patent for the substance. Recent conflicts concern infringement of the patent for aspartame and deceptive **advertising** claims related to Splenda.

In the early 21st century, prices for aspartame began to drop globally because of a glut of the substance on the world market after the patent on it expired. While the Chinese government established quotas on the production of aspartame, Tate & Lyle, the holder of the patent on sucralose, filed suit in the United States against a number of Chinese producers and U.S. importers alleging that the Chinese manufacturers have infringed the patent on the substance.

In an era when American consumers are beginning to abandon their fascination with artificial substitutes in favor of natural products, marketers of artificial sweeteners are searching for their products' links to nature, which is resulting in internal industry conflict and conflict with sugar producers. A series of suits and countersuits in the United States pitted the Sugar Association, an industry trade group, against the producers of Splenda in a dispute over the claim that Splenda "is made from sugar, so it tastes like sugar." The Sugar Association claimed that sucralose is a chloro-hydrocarbon created in a laboratory, not a natural product.

Health Concerns Associated with Sugar and Its Substitutes

American food and beverage manufacturers are currently under attack by some consumers and health professionals for contributing to what is now seen as an epidemic of **obesity** in the country. High-fructose corn syrup, made from cornstarch and now ubiquitous in processed foods sold in the United States, takes much of the heat.

Artificial sweeteners are advocated by some as a way to slake the craving for sweetness while also facilitating diets lower in calories, but this approach is criticized from at least two perspectives. First, the sugar industry points out that elimination of sugar from a food does not necessarily reduce its overall calorie count; other substances, which also contain calories, must be added to the food to achieve appropriate consistency or blunt the extra-sweet taste of the artificial sweeteners. Second, artificial sweeteners have been linked anecdotally with a variety of health problems, from headaches to cancer; although research studies do not support these claims, consumer movements continue to raise concerns.

FURTHER READINGS: Higman, B. W. "The Sugar Revolution." *Economic History Review*, n.s., 53, no. 2 (May 2000): 213–36; Mintz, Sidney. *Sweetness and Power: The Place of Sugar in Modern History.* New York: Viking, 1985; Sugar Knowledge International. "Welcome to the World of Sugar Technology." http://www.sucrose.com/home.html; Wilkinson, Alec. *Big Sugar: Seasons in the Canefields of Florida.* New York: Knopf, 1989.

Robin Bisha

Supermarkets Supermarkets emerged in the United States during the mid-20th century, but in many ways they are based on previous food systems. For almost 300 years, public markets were the primary retail and wholesale food source for urban Americans. Financed and regulated by municipalities, public markets were regularly scheduled events held in town one or two days a week. In rural areas, all-purpose general stores sold necessities and, occasionally, luxury items. As American cities grew larger in the late 18th and early 19th centuries, small grocery stores emerged. By the mid-1800s, privately owned grocery stores greatly outnumbered public markets.

The typical grocery store was small and family-owned. It sold mainly nonperishable **packaged** foods, which were stacked along the walls. Staple foods, such as flour, grains, and **sugar**, were sold from barrels or sacks. Counters separated clerks from customers. In the middle of the store was a wide aisle that permitted customers to view the food displays. Customers requested particular items, which the clerks then retrieved. The clerk wrote up the order and recorded it on the customer's account, which frequently was not paid until much later.

Chain Grocery Stores

In 1859 George F. Gilman, a prosperous New York businessman, and George H. Hartford started selling tea in New York City. Three years later, they named their business the Great American Tea Company. At the time, most grocers bought their stock from **middlemen**. Gilman and Hartford, however, decided to buy tea directly from the source in China and sell directly to the customer, thereby eliminating the middleman and dramatically lowering the price of tea. Buying in bulk, they were able to undersell their competition. Their system was so successful that by 1865 Hartford and Gilman had five small stores in New York City, thus creating America's first chain grocery store. When the transcontinental railroad was completed in 1869, Gilman and Hartford changed the name of their company to the Great Atlantic and Pacific Tea Company, subsequently shortened to A&P.

The early success of A&P brought condemnation from independent grocers. The *American Grocer*, a national trade publication, was launched in 1869, and it attacked A&P almost from its first issue for predatory pricing and destroying local businesses. Despite such continuous criticism, A&P expanded the number of stores and increased the number of products that it sold in its stores. **Coffee** was added in the 1870s; sugar, spices, and **canned** goods were carried during the following decade.

By turn of the 20th century, A&P had 198 stores. This number slowly increased until 1912, when A&P created the Economy Store—a small, self-contained module designed to fit into standard buildings. To reduce costs further, A&P stopped extending credit to customers and making home **deliveries**. The Economy Stores were similar in appearance to the independent grocery store and were about the same size—500 to 600 square feet—but because A&P bought in volume for all its stores, they were able to underprice their competition. A&P management rapidly expanded the Economy Stores; there were more than 14,000 such stores by 1925.

Other entrepreneurs saw the success of A&P and emulated its operation. In 1872 Grand Union was founded in New York, and by the early 20th century, it was the nation's second largest food retailer. Bernard H. Kroger began a Cincinnati-based chain store operation in 1883. Unlike A&P, Kroger began directly in the grocery trade. By 1900 the Kroger Company had almost 30 stores. In 1888, two Gristede brothers opened a small grocery store in New York. They were one of the first grocery stores to develop a meat department, enabling customers to buy meat from a butcher in a single store along with traditional groceries. After the repeal of Prohibition in 1933, Gristede's was the first grocery store to install liquor departments.

On the West Coast, in 1906 Charles Von der Ahe opened a store, which he called Von's Groceteria, in Los Angeles. The company's name was subsequently changed to Von's. Another Los Angeles grocery chain was launched by Sam Seelig in 1914. In 1926, Seelig merged with Marion Skaggs—who had launched the Skaggs Cash Stores in Boise, Idaho, in 1916—to create the Safeway chain.

Clarence Saunders launched the Piggly Wiggly grocery store in Memphis, Tennessee, in 1916,. It introduced the revolutionary concept of self-service: its shelves were open to customers, who collected their own groceries, placing them in small hand baskets, which were taken to cashiers in checkout stands. Self-service operations reduced **labor** costs, as fewer clerks were needed to serve customers. This revolutionized the business, and virtually all grocery stores since have followed this self-service model.

Chain stores had many advantages. They were better able to control overhead costs. Chains were also able to promote themselves through premiums, such as S&H Green Stamps, which were widely used after 1900. Chain stores usually had better insurance, so when struck by a catastrophe, such as a fire, they were more likely to survive. They were also more apt to survive economic hard times, as operators could close financially troubled stores while keeping more successful locations open. In addition, they also had the wherewithal to analyze and select the best sites for stores and to continually establish new outlets. Chain stores could hire buyers who specialized in certain product lines. Buyers maximized volume purchases and thereby reduced unit costs. In addition, some grocery chains launched their own product lines and brands, thus eliminating the middleman and reducing additional expenses. Finally, chains had the money to **advertise**. When radio and **television** advertising became possible, chain stores were able to advertise regionally and then nationally.

The small independent grocer hardly stood a chance against the chains. Eventually, independent grocers banded together to form associations that had many of the strengths of the chains. By the 1930s, the overwhelming majority of American grocery stores belonged to either corporate or affiliated independent chains.

The Supermarket

The chain-store system and the self-service concept were preconditions that shaped the supermarket. In many ways, the supermarket was an application of a concept previously developed in super-size department stores, such as those popularized by John Wanamaker in Philadelphia and Marshall Fields in Chicago during the early 20th century. Department stores had discovered that buying wholesale could reduce retail prices and that a greater volume of sales could increase profits. The term *supermarket* was first used in the grocery trade in Southern California during the 1920s. Los Angeles, a large sprawling metropolis, was highly dependent on the automobile. Land was relatively inexpensive, and two chains—Ralph's Grocery Company and Alpha Beta Food Markets—constructed large stores, which were organized by food departments. The major difference from other grocery stores was size: some of these stores covered 5,000 square feet—10 times more than an A&P Economy Store.

The success of the early supermarkets in Southern California was at first ignored by other corporate chains and affiliated independents, who believed they were just a passing phase. However, new supermarkets continued to open and grow larger. Michael Cullen, who had been an employee of the Kroger Grocery and Baking Company, in 1930 launched the King Kullen chain in Jamaica, New York. Cullen reduced his prices and increased profits by increasing the volume. To accomplish this, he built larger stores with 5,000–7,000 square feet of floor space. Because his supermarkets had parking lots, they were more convenient for suburban customers. Cullen also advertised in newspapers and radio, positioning his stores as "price wreckers" with prices so low that they could not be beaten. Two years later, Robert M. Otis and Roy A. Dawson opened their first Big Bear store on the first floor of a factory building in Elizabeth, New Jersey. With 15,000 square feet devoted to selling groceries, it proved an enormous economic success.

By the mid-1930s, A&P and other chains had closed their smaller stores and opened supermarkets. Independent grocers were unable to make the conversion, and tens of thousands went out of business during the late 1930s and early 1940s. The conversion from small stores to large supermarkets was helped by the Depression. Customers saw supermarkets as a practical means of saving money. They were willing to forgo the pleasant atmosphere of a small grocery store for the warehouse conditions of a supermarket that offered lower prices.

World War II slowed the growth of supermarkets, as wartime restrictions halted construction. Prior to the war, almost all clerks had been young men; as they went off to war, women filled their jobs. When the war ended, women continued to be employed by supermarkets.

During the war, many products, including meat, sugar, **chocolate**, canned goods, and imported foods, were rationed or otherwise unavailable. This necessitated changes in supermarkets. For instance, as the war effort required metal that would otherwise have gone to make food cans, **frozen foods** became more available for those stores with prewar freezers. Because so many of the traditional grocery store products were rationed, supermarkets expanded into nonfood products to fill in the empty spaces. After the war, management significantly expanded floor space for nonfood goods, frequently including kitchenware, medicines, cosmetics, books, magazines, records, kitchenware, hardware, toys, and clothes; where permitted, they also sold alcohol.

Postwar Expansion

The postwar growth of supermarkets was tremendous. Chain stores abandoned many inner-city locations and expanded into the suburbs with supermarkets. A number of new chains emerged in the postwar period. Albertsons, founded by Joe Albertson in Boise, Idaho, expanded rapidly after the war, for instance. Shop-Rite was launched in 1946 when several independent grocers began a cooperative to help lower costs by volume purchases. A Southern chain, Winn-Dixie, was created in 1955 when the Winn & Lovett chain acquired the Dixie Home Stores. C-Town was launched by independent grocery stores in 1975.

These challenges also caused a reorganization of existing supermarket chains. Some chains broke away from larger entities. Pathmark, for instance, broke away from Shop-Rite in 1968 and tried to make it on its own. In the same year, the German Tengelmann Group acquired control of A&P; shortly thereafter, Grand Union was acquired by an Englishman, Sir James Goldsmith. Both chains declined appreciably after their acquisitions, and their owners sold off many stores and chains. Other chains increased the size of their operations. Von's acquired a number of chains. Then in 1997, Safeway acquired Von's. Kroger acquired Ralph's, Food 4 Less, King Soopers, and many others. To compete with Wal-Mart and other large discount stores, in 2004 Kroger responded with superstores, called Kroger Marketplace. Today, Kroger is America's second largest grocery store.

In the past 50 years, the variety of inventory offered in supermarkets has grown substantially. In the 1940s, an average supermarket carried 3,000 different items; by the late 1950s, this had increased to 5,800, and by the 1970s, supermarkets stocked more than 10,000 items. Today, many large supermarkets sell twice that many products. Larger stores have had to be constructed to house these products. Some supermarkets have expanded to 30,000 square feet.

Technological Advances

Several advances in technology greatly enhanced supermarket shopping. The grocery shopping cart was invented by Sylvan Goldman in 1937 for his Standard Food Stores in Oklahoma City. The cart made it easy for customers to move their purchases from the cash register to their automobiles in the store's parking lot. A larger cart was an enticement to buy more. In 1947, "telescoping" shopping carts, which could be fitted into another empty cart thus creating a more compact way of storing them, were first used.

In 1940 Publix Supermarkets, launched by George Jenkins of Winter Haven, Florida, introduced the electric-eye door that opened automatically for customers as they entered and exited. Jenkins also equipped his stores with air conditioning, fluorescent lighting, and music. By 1956, 80 percent of all new supermarkets had piped-in music and air conditioning. In the 1950s, many supermarkets also included special areas and rides for small children.

Prices were stamped on items to reduce the time clerks spent writing down prices on each item, and price tags were installed on shelves so that consumers could easily see the cost of each product. Cash registers were redesigned to itemize purchases on the customer's receipt. To increase checkout speed, cashiers were trained to keep their eyes on the product price stamps, not the cash register keyboard. Bar code scanners were first installed into supermarkets in 1974. Although not commonly used until the 1980s, bar codes combined with computer analysis have revolutionized supermarket inventory tracking and have increased the ability to analyze customers' purchases. In 1996, self-checkout lines began to be installed in some supermarkets.

Technology has also been employed to prevent loss due to theft. Supermarkets have installed cameras in their stores and in parking lots. In addition, to prevent theft of shopping carts, a device has been developed to freeze the wheels of the cart when they are moved outside of a particular area.

Recent Developments

Today, supermarket chains are being challenged from four separate directions. The first is the return of the public market. Since the 1970s, green or **farmers' markets** have sprung up in many urban areas, selling produce and other food products. Many people prefer the fresh produce acquired from local farmers.

The second challenge is the rapid rise of small convenience stores. **Delicatessens**, bodegas, mom-and-pop shops, fruit stands, and chain convenience stores such as 7-Eleven and Stop & Shop have rapidly increased during the past three decades.

These stores typically stock only the most commonly purchased foods and their prices are substantially higher than those of supermarkets, but many customers patronize the smaller stores simply because they are closer or easier to get in and out.

At the opposite end of the spectrum from the convenience stores is the third challenge, large warehouse retail operations such as Costco and Wal-Mart that have begun to sell traditional grocery products. Costco was founded in Seattle in 1983 by James Sinegal and Jeffrey Brotman. Initially, the company sold mainly boxed products, but it has since expanded into selling other grocery products, including produce, meat, seafood, baked goods, and liquor, where permitted. Wal-Mart Stores was launched by Sam Walton in 1962, in Bentonville, Arkansas. It started as a retail store and at first it did not sell groceries. The company expanded rapidly in the United States and then abroad. By the 1990s, it was the largest retail store in the world. In the 1990s, Wal-Mart moved into selling bulk food at greatly reduced prices. It has been highly efficient in carrying out these practices, and today Wal-Mart is the largest seller of grocery foods in the world, with sales of more than $100 billion.

Finally, supermarkets have been challenged by new upscale chains such as **Trader Joe's**, **Whole Foods Market**, Fiesta Mart, and Central Market, which cut into the more profitable products traditionally sold in supermarkets.

Supermarkets have scrambled to meet these challenges, and they have not remained static. During the past few decades, many have added delis, and they are now selling more prepared foods. Supermarkets have also diversified their product lines and installed new departments, including **organic** and **vegetarian** foods, as well as **ethnic foods**, such as the Taquerias in Fiesta Marts, which sell Mexican food. Most stores issue membership or club cards that give shoppers additional discounts and ensure customer loyalty.

Supermarkets have also tried to reduce their costs. Wal-Mart and other supermarket competitors are nonunion. Because a major expense in grocery operations is staff, cutting costs inevitably created labor problems. Strikes have occurred at many traditional supermarkets, including Safeway, Kroger, Albertsons, Von's, and Fiesta Mart.

Many supermarket chains have found it difficult to meet these challenges, and several have filed for relief under Chapter 11 of the Bankruptcy Code. Grand Union did so in 1995 and again in 1998; Pathmark did so in 2000, as did Winn-Dixie in 2004.

Today, food has become a global business. Foods are shipped from thousands of miles away. U.S. supermarkets have set the world standards. American food corporations have been rapidly expanding abroad. Likewise, other countries have invested in American supermarket chains. With the implementation of agreements in NAFTA and the WTO, it is likely that globalization will influence supermarkets even more in the future.

FURTHER READINGS: Dumas, Lynne S. *Elephants in My Backyard: Alex Aidekman's Own Story of Founding the Pathmark Supermarket Powerhouse.* New York: Vantage Press, 1988; Humphrey, Kim. *Shelf Life: Supermarkets and the Changing Culture of Consumption.* Cambridge: Cambridge University Press, 1998; Kahn, Barbara E., and Leigh McAlister. *Grocery Revolution: The New Focus on the Consumer.* Reading, MA: Addison Wesley Longman, 1997; Marnell, William H. *Once upon a Store: A Biography of the World's First Supermarket.* New York: Herder & Herder, 1971; Mayo, James M. *The American Grocery Store: The Business Evolution of an Architectural Space.* Westport, CT: Greenwood Press, 1993; Seth, Andrew, and Geoffrey Randall. *The Grocers: The Rise and Rise of the Supermarket Chains.* 2nd ed. Dover, NH: Kogan Page, 2001; Seth, Andrew, and Geoffrey Randall. *Supermarket Wars: Global*

Strategies for Food Retailers. New York: Palgrave Macmillan, 2005; Walsh, William I. *The Rise and Decline of the Great Atlantic & Pacific Tea Company*. Secaucus, NJ: Lyle Stuart, 1986; Zimmerman, M. M. *The Super Market: A Revolution in Distribution*. New York: McGraw-Hill, 1955.

Andrew F. Smith

Swanson In 1896, 17-year-old Carl A. Swanson emigrated from Sweden to the United States. While working at a grocery store in Omaha, Nebraska, he met John O. Jerpe, who owned the Jerpe Commission Company. Jerpe's company acquired eggs and cream from local farmers, processed the eggs and manufactured butter from the cream, and sold these products to distributors, charging a commission to the farmers. In 1899 Swanson became a partner in the company. With Swanson on board, the company expanded its business to include the selling of chickens, turkeys, and other meats. Swanson bought the company in 1928, and during the 1940s he changed its name to C. A. Swanson and Sons.

Beginning in February 1936, Swanson guaranteed farmers that he would purchase chickens and turkeys from them at a particular price in the fall. As this was at the depth of the Depression when farmers were struggling to keep their farms, Swanson also advanced funds to farmers to help pay for feed and other expenses in the spring. This worked well during times of turkey scarcity, as Swanson would have a guaranteed supply while other processors would have to pay a higher price. In times of plenty, Swanson would freeze meat in the fall, when the price was low, and then sell them in the spring, when the supply was limited. These chickens and turkeys were also used to make **frozen** chicken and turkey pies.

In 1950, Swanson ended up with a huge quantity of birds—many more then he could expect to sell off in the following spring. His storage facilities filled up and he had to rent cold storage railroad cars for the overflow. By February 1951 Swanson had more than 20 **refrigerated** train carloads of frozen turkeys—with 52,000 pounds in each car—traversing the country because there was no market for them and no available cold storage facilities. The solution was using the turkeys in **TV dinners**, which was so successful that within three years, Swanson was selling 13 million turkey dinners annually. Based on this phenomenal success, the **Campbell's Soup** acquired C. A. Swanson and Sons in 1955.

Campbell's added new products to the Swanson brand, including desserts, a breakfast line, and Hungry-Man dinners. Campbell's later shifted the Swanson brand to Vlasic Foods International, which went bankrupt. In 2001 Pinnacle Foods Corporation bought the Vlasic and Swanson brands out of bankruptcy.

FURTHER READING: Smith, Andrew F. *The Turkey: An American Story*. Urbana: University of Illinois Press, 2006.

Andrew F. Smith

Swift Born in Sagamore, Massachusetts, Gustavus Swift (1839–1903) revolutionized the **meatpacking** industry in America. At the age of 16, he began buying heifers and selling meat. In 1859 he opened a store in Eastham, Massachusetts. He subsequently went into business with a partner, selling **beef** in Boston. At the time, live animals were shipped from railheads to meat-processing centers in major cities around the country. Swift purchased live animals and shipped them to his partner. Swift slowly expanded his operation from Massachusetts to Albany and Buffalo, New York.

Swift concluded that shipping live animals and slaughtering them in Eastern cities was inefficient. In 1875, Swift moved to Chicago, believing that the city was the right place to establish a large-scale meatpacking facility and national distribution center. He planned to slaughter and butcher animals in Chicago before shipping the carcasses to cities all over America. In the 1870s, Swift made improvements on existing **refrigerated** railroad cars, and he began employing his improved version in 1881.

Swift's cars were refrigerated with ice, which kept the meat cool. Since additional ice was needed along the way to replenish the melted ice, Swift went into the ice business, as well, setting up icehouses along the railroad lines that he used. In the process, he created the first nationwide distribution and marketing system.

His operation was such a success that he incorporated Swift & Company in 1885 and it quickly became one of most important meat packers and distributors in America. Swift's massive butchering operation generated considerable waste. Rather than throwing out the waste, he converted it into a diversity of other products, including glue, **fertilizer**, buttons, toothbrushes, and soap.

Swift & Company was one of the first vertically integrated businesses in America— it controlled all aspects of its products from the farm to the consumer. In 1902, Swift joined with its major competitors, including **Armour** and Morris, to create a trust called the National Packing Company. The combined company was challenged in court by the trust busters and was finally dissolved in 1912. Swift remained an independent company until the 1980s, when it was acquired by ConAgra in a leveraged buyout.

In 2002 Hicks, Muse, Tate, & Furst and Booth Creek Management Corporation acquired majority interest in ConAgra's fresh beef and pork processing business, and Swift & Company became independent once again. It is headquartered in Greeley, Colorado. In 2006, Swift was the world's second largest beef and pork processor, with an annual budget of $9 billion.

FURTHER READINGS: Carlson, Laurie Winn. *Cattle: An Informal Social History.* Chicago: Ivan R. Dee, 2001; Horowitz, Roger. *Putting Meat on the American Table: Taste, Technology, Transformation.* Baltimore: Johns Hopkins University Press, 2006.

Andrew F. Smith

T

Tabasco Tabasco-brand hot red pepper sauce has been spicing up food worldwide almost since the first batch was made on Avery Island, Louisiana. It remains America's best-selling hot sauce even as the category grows (some 1,000–2,000 hot sauces are now sold in the United States) and the use of Tabasco evolves. The family-owned McIlhenny Company has also had success with cobranding, food service placement, and foreign sales.

Edmund McIlhenny began by planting Mexican pepper seeds on the 2,200-acre island in 1868. The island remains the company's base and the site of its plant, toured by more than 100,000 people a year. Only 2 percent of the *Capsicum frutescens* Tabasco peppers used in the 700,000 **bottles** of sauce produced a year are still grown on Avery Island, but all the seeds for the next crop are. The peppers, some of the world's hottest, are harvested when bright red and then crushed. Growers in Mexico and Central America send the pepper mash to the island for processing. The mash is transferred to oak barrels, topped with salt mined on the island, and then covered with lids. After three years, the liquid is drained off, mixed with vinegar and salt, bottled, and labeled with the distinctive diamond-shaped labels and shipped to more than 160 countries.

Tabasco made only the fiery red sauce until 1994, when it introduced a green pepper sauce. In addition to six hot pepper sauces, the company now also offers steak sauces, a Bloody Mary drink mix, mustards, and more. The company began cobranding in 1999 by adding its logo to products made by the **Hormel** Foods Corporation, further increasing the range of foods featuring Tabasco. Nonfood Tabasco-themed items, including toys, are also offered.

The privately held company does not release sales figures, but estimates put its annual sales at $41 million and its share of the U.S. hot sauce market at about 30 percent. The brand's share of the food service market is about 50 percent. McIlhenny recognized more than a decade ago that home-cooked meals were declining and began promoting Tabasco to food service concerns as a table **condiment** as well as an ingredient. A wide variety of **restaurant chains** list their use of Tabasco on their menus in the United States and elsewhere.

The brand's popularity outside the United States began in the 1870s when it was exported to England. British fondness for the concoction resulted in its use throughout the empire. The sauce's ability to perk up military food and its popularity with U.S. troops also helped sales around the world. Tabasco continues to increase foreign market share by adapting its products and message to countries such as India, China, and Japan. In the United States, the company has increased outreach to Hispanic, African-American, and other **ethnic** markets, helping sales to grow an estimated 5 percent or more a year.

As carefully as McIlhenny cultivates its peppers, it also cultivates the hot sauce's image. The company has a staff historian and museum. It is known for promotions ranging from a traveling burlesque show in the 1890s to, more recently, its Super Bowl ads. All have helped to make the little bottle of red pepper sauce an icon (and a pantry staple) in America and around the world.

FURTHER READINGS: McIlhenny, Paul, with Barbara Hunter. *The Tabasco Brand Cookbook: 125 Years of America's Favorite Pepper Sauce.* New York: Gramercy Books, 1993; McIlhenny Company. http://www.tabasco.com; McNulty, Sheila. "How Tabasco Has Stayed a Hot Property." *Financial Times,* December 10, 2003.

Faith J. Kramer

Takeout Takeout or carry-out (as it is known in the United States and Canada), parcel (India), or take-away (Australia, Malaysia, and Great Britain) is any food that is sold as a meal (or meal replacement) and can be consumed on the go or at home. Takeout is an umbrella term that encompasses **fast food**, **delivery**, street food, convenience foods, and drive-thru **restaurants**. Restaurants specializing in takeout often do not provide table service, and if they do have seating, it tends to be uncomfortable and easy to clean, dissuading customers from loitering at their establishments. Takeout from a sit-down establishment may be purchased to go or may consist of leftovers from a meal eaten at the table; the container used for leftovers is commonly called a "doggy bag." Almost all restaurants have the means to produce food for takeout, but few nonchain high-end sit-down restaurants deliver. Customers may call in an order but will probably be expected to pick it up.

History

Takeout food has existed in its simplest form since **delicatessens** were popularized in America in the late 19th century. However, much of the food we associate with takeout service was dispensed through automats, **cafeterias**, **diners**, and lunchrooms. These enterprises sought to expedite the process of procuring a meal for busy workers with more disposable income. Vendors near factories sold food that was easy to wrap and eat on the go. They began with small lunch carts, but as business increased, they expanded operations to include indoor seats. A further development, the self-serve cafeteria, grew out of the need for workers to eat lunch quickly and then return to the factory.

The other major factor in the rise of takeout food service was the popularity of the automobile. As automobiles became more affordable, Americans of all social classes began to travel for pleasure in their cars, creating an instant market for roadside dining. The sheer novelty of the drive-thru window made eating in the car a popular activity for car-crazed Americans in the 1950s. Developments like drive-ins and carhops only increased the mania and spurred the growth of fast food **franchises**.

Takeout versus Fast Food

Takeout food is often fast food, but not always. Whereas fast food carries the connotation of a standardized product from a globalized **chain** or franchise, take-away operations encompass a wide variety of small businesses serving traditional, often **ethnic**, food without the **advertising** budget of a fast food franchise. Fast food options, however, are expanding as well. In addition to hamburgers, tacos, and fried chicken, fast food chains have added salads, soups, and wraps to their menu in an attempt to diminish their reputations as enablers of **obesity** and to appeal to an increasingly health-conscious consumer base.

Menus are expanding in other ways as well. Fast food franchises are consolidating with other operators to develop their menus to encompass all-day meal options. **Coffee** and doughnut chains have similarly begun to carry more lunch items as well.

To fill the gap between fast food and high-end takeout, many new chains are springing up with menus that specialize in more healthful **gourmet** convenience options. Designer sandwich chains a step above Subway or Quiznos are popular, as are gourmet Mexican food chains like Chipotle Mexican Grill and Baja Fresh, which pride themselves on higher meat quality and a dedication to freshness. The Starbucks coffee chain now offers a variety of sandwiches, baked goods, and even sushi.

Increasingly, American food chains that were traditionally sit-down family restaurants, such as Outback Steakhouse, the Cheesecake Factory, and Applebee's, are expanding takeout food service in their restaurants. These chains often have separate counters for takeout customers and a system to deliver food to a special "takeout" parking lot.

Delivery

Food that is delivered by a restaurant to a customer is also sometimes known as takeout, although it might be more properly labeled "bring-in." Customers generally order by phone (or increasingly online) and a driver brings the food to their home (or to whatever location is desired). Pizza and Chinese food are the most common examples of delivery-based takeout. In the United Kingdom, Indian food is a popular form of delivery take-away, as are Middle Eastern kebabs. Recently more eclectic cuisines are being added to the usual roundup of delivery foods, with the emergence of specialized businesses designed specifically to deliver food from a conglomerate of locally owned restaurants.

Packaging

Packaging for takeout foods is almost as diverse as the foods themselves. Industrial fast food chains like **McDonald's**, which once used Styrofoam as their primary packaging material, have shifted to more environmentally biodegradable materials such as wax-coated paper and recycled paper products. Styrofoam is still often used for takeout packaging, especially Styrofoam cups, which seal in heat better than paper. Plastic is another major material used in the take-out industry. Many high-end restaurants use sealed plastic containers of varying sizes for takeout orders. Aluminum dishes with specially fit lids are also customary for restaurant take-out orders. Desserts are usually carried out in plastic or Styrofoam containers with hinged lids. For certain takeout foods, the packaging is as iconic as the food itself. The folded paper containers of Chinese takeout are unmistakable in this regard.

Street Food

Street food is distinguished from takeout, junk food, **snack foods**, and fast food by its local flavor and by being purchased on the sidewalk without entering any building. Street food is food obtainable from a street-corner vendor, typically from a makeshift or movable stall. While most street foods are regional (New York City **hot dogs**, German curry-wurst), many are not, having spread beyond their region of origin. Most street food is both finger and fast food and is usually available for a low price.

Both takeout and fast food are typically sold from counters inside buildings. However, in some instances, there is no clear distinction between street food and takeout. Crêpe stands in France, for example, may be permanently situated as a kiosk or newsstand, but function primarily with takeout windows. When customers purchase coffee and **ice cream**, for instance, the expectation is that they will begin consuming the food immediately on the street.

Concerns over cleanliness and freshness often discourage people from eating street food. Lack of **refrigeration** for street food operations is often construed as a lack of hygiene; on the other hand, street food generally uses particularly fresh ingredients for this very reason. Cooking methods may reduce health risks as well. In Asian street food, for example, the high levels of heat required for wok cooking ensures that any **bacteria** are killed.

Supermarkets

Supermarket takeout, or prepared foods, is the fastest growing segment of the takeout market. Almost all large supermarkets are equipped with a steam bed where ready-to-eat foods like rotisserie chickens, mashed potatoes, ribs, and macaroni and cheese are prepacked and priced for easy carryout. The deli counters at supermarkets offer freshly prepared sandwiches (premade or constructed to the customer's specifications) and cold salad options. Supermarkets are also increasing their ready-to-heat options for consumers who want to buy, for example, a preassembled pizza or sealed plastic containers of soup that they can heat at home.

Convenience Food

Convenience foods are mainly packaged meals with a long shelf life and foods that can be prepared quickly and easily. These foods are often sold in convenience stores, such as the ubiquitous stores connected to gas stations that are open long hours and have a streamlined selection of foods (usually not fresh) for customers on the go. Most of these foods can be consumed on the spot, but some need to be heated. The frozen **TV dinner** created by **Swanson** in 1952 is the grandfather of today's convenience foods.

Another new market in convenience foods is known as "nutraceuticals," loosely defined as food products that have been infused with drugs, herbs, **vitamins**, and minerals purported to improve energy levels, reduce emotional tensions, or protect against disease. Examples include a vitamin-fortified drink called Power Frappucino currently being tested by Starbucks. Another rising trend are smoothie chains, like Jamba Juice, which offer smoothies enhanced with vitamins as a meal replacement. The most common form of nutraceutical is the energy bar. Marketed to people with active lifestyles or for dieters, energy bars are compact bars with the nutritional value of a meal, plus increased nutritional value in the form of protein or energy-enhancing ingredients.

Vending machines are the most important source of convenience foods because they are typically available 24 hours, can be placed virtually anywhere, and require no employees to make a transaction. These qualities make vending machines the ultimate in convenience for both sellers and consumers. Vending machines usually contain less substantial fare such as **candy** bars, Pop-Tarts, and chips. European vending machines tend to carry more variety of foods, while the Japanese versions contain such a diverse spectrum of products that it would be possible to eat from a vending machine every day without having to repeat a meal. The predecessor to the vending machine was the automat, where food was prepared in advance and then placed in glass compartments so that customers were able to see what they were buying directly before purchasing it. Automats sold sandwiches, pies, coffee, candy, ice cream, and soda. The heyday for American automats occurred in the 1950s.

See also Frozen Foods.

Sabrina Small

Tariffs Tariffs are taxes imposed on goods imported from foreign countries when they enter the domestic market. Tariffs are imposed when goods land on domestic soil, and the goods are not allowed to travel farther until collection is completed. Historically, these fees have been imposed primarily to protect domestic businesses. Although there is a growing movement toward globalization and **free trade**, tariffs are still widely present in agriculture in support of political and strategic objectives.

Types of Tariffs

There are two main types of tariffs: *ad valorem* tariffs and specific-value tariffs. *Ad valorem tariffs* are set as a percentage of the value of the imported item. Although flexible, this type of tariff creates uncertainty for taxation agencies that use them; if the price of goods being imported lowers too much, the tariffs will lower accordingly, limiting the protective and revenue nature of the tariff. Most tariffs worldwide are ad valorem, including 73 percent of those in Canada and 95 percent of Mexico's; by contrast, only 57 percent of U.S. tariffs are ad valorem.

Specific-value tariffs are not linked directly to the value of the goods. Instead, they are associated with other product characteristics such as weight, volume, or surface. These are harder to set in value and need to be constantly adjusted to reflect changes in the market and inflation. The United States is the heaviest user of this type of tariffs, followed by Canada and the Caribbean Community and Common Market (CARICOM).

Objectives of Tariffs

Tariffs exist for three main purposes: to create revenue for the country receiving the goods, for protective purposes, and for prohibitive purposes. *Revenue tariffs* are usually set to create a revenue stream for the taxing government, without inhibiting importation. *Protective tariffs* are used to artificially inflate the prices of products entering the domestic market, protecting local industries from international competition. By protecting local industries, tariffs are expected to reduce the loss of jobs and tax revenue that could result from the sudden influx of imported goods. Finally, *prohibitive tariffs* are usually set so high that the importation of the item is economically impossible or impractical except as a specialty item.

Tariffs in a Globalizing Market

Globalization has led to the emergence of free trade zones and customs unions. Free trade zones aim to lower tariffs to allow movement of goods freely within the area participating in the free trade, while customs unions usually have common external tariffs and agree to share revenues from tariffs on goods entering the customs union.

When reducing tariff rates, a variety of methods are employed by negotiating countries. These include single rate (tariffs are reduced to a single rate for all products), flat-rate percentage reduction (the same percentage reduction is applied to all products, no matter the starting point), harmonizing reductions (bringing different tariffs down to similar rates), or a combination of any of these methods.

To replace tariffs, some countries use alternative taxation tools known as *nontariff barriers*. The methods include quotas (physical limits to the number of goods that can be imported in a country during a set period of time), voluntary export restraints (a government restricts the number of items that can be exported, often at the behest of a trading partner), domestic subsidies (which are often used in agriculture), import deposits (a taxation agency requires the importer to give a deposit for importing goods), or safety and health standards specifications (which are often used to slow down or restrict importation).

Tariffs in Agricultural Markets

Agricultural products remain one of the most protected products worldwide; some reports estimate that global average agricultural tariffs hovered around 16 percent in 2006, ranging from no tariff at all up to as high as 530 percent for some products. The Uruguay Round Agreement on Agriculture (URAA) aimed to convert nontariff barriers (such as import levels and quotas) into bound tariffs established by the General Agreement on Tariffs and Trade (GATT). Also, developed countries agreed to reduce agriculture tariffs by a total of 36 percent. Still, major distortions exist, making this sector unlike others in international trade.

Debates over Tariffs

Tariffs can have negative impacts on the economies they are expected to protect. For example, as a result of artificially inflating price within a national economy, consumers are forced to purchase goods at a higher price than available in a free trade economy; this is especially penalizing if the goods are then used to produce secondary goods. Some believe that tariffs enable countries to artificially maintain inefficient local industries, when it would be better to let these industries collapse and be replaced by new more efficient structures. Studies have also shown that tariffs are not adapted to the rapidly changing landscape of commerce, and fixed tariffs render the movement of small food shipments economically unviable.

Those in favor of tariffs point to infant industries, maintaining that tariffs protect young domestic industries against established international products; tariffs allow these local industries to grow and become self-sufficient. Others point out that tariffs are important revenue streams for developing countries, as these countries do not always have the institutional ability to successfully collect income and sales taxes. Therefore, tariffs are a relatively simple way for a government to ensure revenues when compared to other forms of taxation.

FURTHER READINGS: Boyd, Shari, Jill Hobbs, and William Kerr. "The Impact of Customs Procedures on Business-to-Consumer e-Commerce in Food Products." *Supply Chain Management* 8, no. 3 (2003): 195–200; Gibson, Paul, Jon Wainio, Daniel Whitley, and Mary Bohman. "Profiles of Tariffs in Global Agricultural Markets." Agricultural Economic Report No. 796. Washington, D.C.: U.S. Department of Agriculture, Economic Research Service. Available at http://www.ers.usda.gov/publications/aer796; Ingco, Merlinda D., and L. Alan Winters, eds. *Agriculture and the New Trade Agenda: Creating a Global Trading Environment for Development.* Cambridge: Cambridge University Press, 2004.

Jean-François Denault

Taylorization Formally known as "scientific management," Taylorization is a controversial approach to human resource management named for its inventor Frederick Winslow Taylor (1856–1915). It was popular in the booming factory environment of his age and in the Depression years. In its day, it was one of numerous competing management strategies sharing a common paternalistic approach.

Taylor's method ultimately seeks to increase production, then consumption, then profit, by making each individual worker's body perform as much work as possible. As such, it is of most use in repetitive manual professions: indeed, it is in such high-turnover industries as **fast food** production that it retains strongest influence today. In its earliest form, the method aimed to increase profits for both employee and employer through structured work practices and rates of pay scaled to production. Later it was notoriously abused by employers seeking to increase worker productivity for little or no increased outlay, or simply to maintain profits during the Depression.

Born into a wealthy and well-educated Philadelphia family, Taylor trained as an engineer, but he preferred inventing to his work in the metals industry and was eventually to style himself as a freelance efficiency expert. His life's work, and subsequently the work of the Society to Promote the Science of Management (later the Taylor Society), was the attempt to find the single most efficient action for performing a given task and apply it in a "new factory system." His treatises on that project, *A Piece Rate System* (1895), *Shop Management* (1903), *The Principles of Scientific Management* (1911), and *Testimony before the Special House Committee* (1912) were widely disseminated in his lifetime, and all reformulated the same basic principles for different audiences.

These principles require a manager to observe and record how workers go about their tasks and how quickly they can work: one of his better-known inventions was a notebook with an inset timepiece that allowed him to time workers without their knowledge. Subsequently, the manager must experiment to discover the most efficient means of performing tasks, inventing and refining mechanical props where necessary before recording and disseminating the precise movements of this "best practice" work, so that new workers can replicate it quickly and easily. A piecework payment rate allowing a worker higher-than-average wages should be set as an incentive for reaching this new possible productivity high.

The system as a whole relies on ever greater consumption of the product in question. In *Principles of Scientific Management* (1911), Taylor presented his net theory of management and production in terms of an increased market for shoes resulting from cheaper, mechanized production:

> The cheapening of any article in common usage almost immediately results in a
> largely increased demand for that article. Take the case of shoes, for instance. The

introduction of machinery for doing every element of the work which was formerly done by hand has resulted in making shoes at a fraction of their former labor cost, and in selling them so cheap that now almost every man, woman, and child in the working-classes buys one or two pairs of shoes per year, and wears shoes all the time, whereas formerly each workman bought perhaps one pair of shoes every five years, and went barefoot most of the time, wearing shoes only as a luxury or as a matter of the sternest necessity. In spite of the enormously increased output of shoes per workman, which has come with shoe machinery, the demand for shoes has so increased that there are relatively more men working in the shoe industry now than ever before. (Taylor, *Scientific Management* [1972], 16–17)

Inasmuch as they did achieve increased production and consumption, Taylor's principles were instrumental in making possible the new Ford Motor Company type of American consumer economy with its cheap goods and in contributing to the enormous and rapid increase in national production capacity for the fast, cheap, pre-prepared food that now forms the greater part of a modern Western diet.

Apart from the rapidly increased capacity for low-cost production, Taylorization's strongest advantage in the turn-of-the-century factory world was that it encouraged invention, mechanization where possible for onerous tasks, and an open mind to change, in an industrial environment that had only recently discovered electricity and was still comparatively resistant to innovation. Its main disadvantages were its incompatibility with tasks requiring high-level skill or thought, its openness to managerial abuse, and its resistance to workers' needs falling outside the economic imperative— Taylorization treats workers' bodies as machines, for instance, calculating breaks according to how much time the worker's body needs to recover, rather than allowing for family or leisure time. This is because Taylor was convinced that the true interests of the two are one and the same—that worker happiness would directly follow a factory's successfully increased production. He relied on the employee's willingness to submit to routine work in order to benefit from team profit, writing, "In the past the man was first; in the future the system must be first."

The very financial success that Taylor sought for Americans has resulted in worker resistance to an occupation so determinedly profit-focused. Outsourcing of menial production, use of machines for routine tasks far outstripping that which Taylor could have imagined, and the increasing trend toward human relations schools of management, has seen Taylorization lose favor in the West, save in areas of production characterized by fast worker turnover and/or minimum wages.

FURTHER READINGS: Kanigel, Robert. *The One Best Way: Frederick Winslow Taylor and the Enigma of Efficiency.* New York: Viking, 1997; Nelson, Daniel. *Frederick W. Taylor and the Rise of Scientific Management.* Madison: University of Wisconsin Press, 1980; Nelson, Daniel, ed. *A Mental Revolution: Scientific Management since Taylor.* Columbus: Ohio State University Press, 1992; Taylor, Frederick Winslow. *Scientific Management: Comprising "Shop Management," "The Principles of Scientific Management," and "Testimony before the Special House Committee."* 2nd ed. Westport, CT: Greenwood Press, 1972.

Anne Brumley

Television "Food television" refers to the genre of food-related programming as well as to television channels dedicated entirely to food. Food TV has grown concurrently with television itself and, as one of the fastest growing sectors of the leisure industry, is directly related to the rise of the modern **celebrity chef** (including related commodities such as cookbooks, DVDs, branded food, and cookware).

As a genre, food TV broadly designates televised programs with content relating to food, cooking, and eating. It can be transmitted via cable, public broadcast television, or webcast (web-based broadcast). The food TV genre includes several subgenres: educational ("how-to"), lifestyle, game shows, reality shows, makeover shows, travelogues, and behind-the-scenes programs. Many of these showcase or are hosted by celebrity chefs.

History of the Genre

Food TV originated in the United Kingdom, where the first televised cooking demonstration was broadcast by the BBC in 1936 (also the year of the first TV broadcast ever). It featured Moira Meighn (née Phyllis Twigg, 1887–?), author of a recipe collection for cooking on a Primus Stove, *The Magic Ring for the Needy and Greedy*. Although Meighn's television appearance was short-lived and she is therefore rarely cited as the first television cook, the show's dual function of education and product promotion is an important precursor of many modern cooking shows.

The first program featuring a professional chef was the BBC's *Cook's Night Out* in 1937 with Xavier Marcel Boulestin (1878–1943), who is more commonly recognized as the first television chef. World War II prevented the genre from taking off, and the next significant British food show was *Cookery* (1946–1951) with Philip Harben (1906–1970), who focused on teaching people how to use their postwar rations. Harben was a regular on British television until the end of his third show, *What's Cooking?* (a.k.a. *Cooking Nook*) in 1956.

The BBC's first magazine show, *Designed for Women*, ran from 1947 until the early 1960s. Marguerite Patten (1915–), known as "the Doyenne of British Cookery" featured on the show's cooking segment. Patten worked for the British Ministry of Food during and after the war and is well known for designing nutritious recipes with rationed food such as **Spam**. Patten was awarded an OBE (Order of the British Empire) for "services to the art of cookery" in 1991 and has won numerous other lifetime achievement awards.

Other early and notable British food TV presenters include Fanny Cradock (née Phyllis Primrose-Pechey, 1909–1994), coauthor of "Bon Viveur," one of Britain's first newspaper restaurant columns (*Daily Telegraph*, 1950–1955). She hosted seven cookery shows, from *Kitchen Magic* (1955) to *Cradock Cooks for Christmas* (1975), often together with her husband Johnnie. The Cradocks, who entertained audiences with their extravagant food and marital banter, also presented one of the first food TV segments for children, "Happy Cooking" on *Tuesday Rendezvous* (1961–1963).

In the same year as Harben's TV debut, the first cooking spot on American TV went to James Beard (1903–1985). With a background in acting and cooking (including a food shop, Hors d'Oeuvres, Inc., which opened in 1937, and the first important appetizer cookbook, *Hors d'Oeuvres and Canapés*, 1940), Beard appeared on NBC's *For You and Yours* in a segment called "Elsie [the Cow] Presents James Beard in *I Love To Eat*" (1946). Production effects included using ink to highlight the mold on Roquefort cheese. In a 1980 interview with *Gastronome* magazine, Beard declared, "Food is very much theater." This statement is significant not only to his own success (a legacy that endures today in the James Beard Foundation) but also as an early indicator of the importance of performance in modern food TV.

Significant broadcasts following *I Love to Eat* include the cooking segment on WPTZ's *TV Matinee* (1947) with Florence Hanford, who went on to host *Television Kitchen* (sponsored by the Philadelphia Electric Company) until 1969. CBS followed in 1948 with *To the Queen's Taste*, featuring Dione Lucas (1909–1971). Lucas was renowned as the first woman to graduate from the Cordon Bleu School in Paris (she later founded the London and New York schools of the same name) and for having cooked for Hitler. Her TV show was recorded in her Bloomingdale's **restaurant**.

A pivotal moment in food TV came in 1963 with the premiere of WGBH's *The French Chef* featuring Julia Child (née McWilliams, 1912–2004). The show followed Child's appearance on PBS in 1962 as coauthor of the best-selling *Mastering the Art of French Cooking* (1961), where she had demonstrated how to cook an omelet. Running for an entire decade, *The French Chef* won a Peabody Award (1964) and was the first educational program to win an Emmy (1966). These accolades, combined with Child's engaging and unpretentious approach, inaugurated a prolific and award-winning career. By the time of her retirement in 2001, she had starred in 12 of her own food TV shows and authored 17 cookbooks. It is commonly held that, although Child was not the first television chef, she was the most widely watched and respected and therefore the first important one. In addition to inspiring a whole generation of cooking professionals and helping to make French cuisine accessible to the United States, Child and *The French Chef* launched a new television audience and a new era for food TV. Her studio kitchen is now housed at the Smithsonian's National Museum of American History.

The examples of Cradock, Beard, and Child show that personality played an important role in the early success of food TV as a genre. Yet its growth also follows that of the television industry in general, where more people were rapidly gaining access to this relatively new medium (which was inaugurated in Britain in 1936 and in the United States in 1939).

Australasia was no exception, where Graham Kerr (1934–), like Child, debuted on television with an omelet (1959). Kerr was the chief catering advisor for the Royal New Zealand Air Force, and his performance led to a food TV show, *Eggs with Flight Lieutenant Kerr*. The show ran for 12 episodes, despite, as Kerr has noted, there being only 50 TV sets in New Zealand by their first week on air in 1960. Kerr's greatest fame came a decade later with the Canadian hit series *The Galloping Gourmet* (1969–1971), syndicated by Fremantle International and produced by his wife Treena. Kerr is known for his flamboyant performances, including cooking in a suit of armor, and the success of the show (200 million viewers in 38 countries) was noteworthy for deconstructing the kitchen as a predominantly feminine space.

Keith Floyd (1943–) was another important pioneer of food TV. Floyd had run several restaurants by the time the BBC asked him to host his first cooking series, *Floyd on Fish* (1984). Sixteen different series ensued over the next two decades, typically beginning "Floyd on . . . ," followed by a destination (*Floyd on France*, *Floyd on Spain*, etc.). These programs were the first to take cooking out of the studio and in this way prefigured the combination of food and travel that have become standard templates of modern food TV.

Together, these early personalities laid the foundation for the genre. The next step was cable.

The Cable Network

Cable television, first known as Community Antenna Television, was launched in 1948. By 1958, there were 525 cable systems with 450 million subscribers operating across the United States. By 1987, 50 percent of U.S. households subscribed to cable; in 2005, it was nearly 85 percent.

The cable channel Foodnetwork (also known as TV Food Network, Food TV, The Food Network, TVFN, and Foodbytes) was launched in 1993 by the A. H. Belo Corporation as the first television channel dedicated entirely to food. In 1997, the channel was acquired by the E. W. Scripps Company, whose network division includes Home & Garden TV (HGTV), DIY Network, Fine Living, and Great American Country (GAC). In the year of Scripps's acquisition, the channel reached 15 million households. By 2002, Foodnetwork was the number-one midsize channel, catering to 35–68 million subscribers. A Scripps press release of May 2006 stated that Foodnetwork reached 89 million U.S. homes and that its overall revenue had seen an 18 percent rise since April 2005. Advertising revenue had increased by 16 percent. The growth of Scripps's interactive media (including acquisition of Shopzilla, uSwitch, and UpMyStreet) mirrors a prime feature of food TV: over and above entertaining and teaching people how to cook, Foodnetwork is a massive corporate enterprise.

Initially Foodnetwork ran four repeats of six hours of programming every 24 hours, and the shows—totalling 31—featured mainly how-to cooking. From 2000, the network started featuring more lifestyle, game, and reality food shows, with an increased focus on television values. This is reflected in the rise of nonprofessional-chef hosts and higher production values such as extreme close-ups of food. These developments have led critics to suggest that food TV is more about vicarious pleasure than about eating or cooking, giving new meaning to the term "**TV dinners**" and spawning the phrase "food porn." In line with higher-quality viewing, of the 62 different shows scheduled on the network in November 2006, approximately one-third were available in high-definition television (HDTV).

The Foodnetwork website (www.foodnetwork.com) gives a clear indication of the size and orientation of the food TV industry. In 2006 the website had six million unique visitors per month. In addition to schedules for standard and HDTV programming, including recipes for each show, the website also features:

- an online store for books, DVDs, and chef-branded products (allowing one to navigate by show, by host, or by brand)
- a Where-to-Find Guide to source featured products
- streaming videos with cooking demos and clips from shows
- video on demand (VOD)
- My Recipe Box (a customizable recipe collection)
- sections on chefs/hosts, health, travel, party cooking, and how to be on Foodnetwork (for example, on *The Next Food Network Star* or as a contestant on *Iron Chef*, a featured establishment on *Road Tasted*, or a participant in a makeover show)

Foodnetwork also offers Cable in the Classroom, "commercial-free, educational programming," available in more than 81,000 public and private schools as of the end of 2006.

One of food TV's leading products is the celebrity chef, such as Emeril Lagasse and Rachael Ray. Lagasse (1959–) joined Foodnetwork in its inaugural year as the host of *How to Boil Water*. Already an accomplished chef (his first restaurant, Emeril's, was *Esquire*'s 1990 restaurant of the year and Lagasse was named "Best Southeast Regional Chef" by the James Beard Foundation in 1991; "Outstanding Chef" was to follow in 1997), his TV show *Essence of Emeril* was launched in 1996. It was one of *Time*'s "Top 10 TV Shows" in 1996 and received Emmy nominations in 2001, 2002, and 2003. *Emeril Live* followed in 1997 and quickly became Foodnetwork's highest-rated show, winning a Cable Ace award for Best Informational Series. In 2005, Lagasse completed his 1,500th show for the network, and in 2006 he was inducted into the MenuMasters Hall of Fame. Lagasse's nonfood appearances include starring in an NBC sitcom (*Emeril*, 2001) and an ad for Crest toothpaste featuring his signature expression, "Bam!" (2006). With a dedicated Emeril Store on Foodnetwork.com, Lagasse typifies the symbiotic relationship between food TV and the modern celebrity chef. He is at once his own brand and a product of Foodnetwork.

Like Lagasse, Ray (1968–) is one of Foodnetwork's greatest assets. Her *30-Minute Meals* is one of the network's highest-rated shows, with 11 million weekly viewers and an Emmy for Outstanding Service Show (2006). Ray premiered on Foodnetwork in 2001 following appearances on WRGB (New York's CBS affiliate) and the *Today Show*. In addition to several other food shows, she hosts a daily talk show, *Rachael Ray*. One month after the show's debut in September 2006, Ray was voted America's "most liked TV host," outdoing Oprah Winfrey. Ray and Lagasse are two of the first celebrity chefs to prepare food to be consumed in outer space.

Foodnetwork can be viewed in 155 countries worldwide. Following its prototype, food TV channels are now broadcast from several other countries, including Canada (Food Network Canada), Australia (The Food Channel), New Zealand (Food TV), and the United Kingdom (BBC Food). Programming varies to include local content, but the global appeal of food TV as a genre and as a channel is clear from the number of shows that are shared across the networks, particularly those featuring celebrity chefs (Rachael Ray, Jamie Oliver, Nigella Lawson) and popular game shows (*Iron Chef*).

Nor is food TV is limited to food TV channels. Food-related programming (and product promotion) has become a regular feature in public broadcasting around the world. Other U.S. stations with regular food TV programming include Bravo, PBS, NBC, QVC, and TBS. Further examples of food TV include the frequent cooking segments on popular lifestyle and talk shows (*Oprah*, *The Tonight Show with Jay Leno*, *Late Show with David Letterman*) and amateur web-based channels (TasteTV, the Indie Food Channel).

FURTHER READINGS: Adema, Pauline. "Vicarious Consumption: Food, Television and the Ambiguity of Modernity." *Journal of American Culture* 23, no. 1 (2000): 113–23; Allfood.com. http://www.allfood.com; Buford, Bill. "TV Dinners." *New Yorker*, October 2, 2006, 42; Foodnetwork. http://www.foodnetwork.com; Humble, Nicola. *Culinary Pleasures: Cookbooks and the Transformation of British Food*. London: Faber & Faber, 2005; Jones, Evan. *Epicurean Delight: The Life and Times of James Beard*. New York: Alfred A. Knopf, 1990.

Signe Hansen

Terroir. *See* Wine Business.

Trader Joe's The Trader Joe's Company began as a local chain of convenience stores and has grown to more than 250 outlets by differentiating itself from traditional

supermarkets. The chain has a loyal customer base that eagerly shops its aisles of discounted, privately labeled **gourmet foods** and **wines**. Some industry analysts predict there could be more than 2,000 Trader Joe's stores across the United States by 2015. The privately held chain's sales in 2005 were estimated at $1,200 per square foot, about double the supermarket industry average.

In 1958, Joe Coulombe bought Pronto, a three-store Pasadena, California–based convenience chain. He added close-out and bargain gourmet and wine selections to appeal to well-educated and well-traveled consumers who were not necessarily well heeled. In 1963, when 7-Eleven, a national chain of convenience stores, entered the Southern California market, Coulombe decided his stores would meet the competitive challenge by concentrating on the discounted gourmet items and adopting a tropical theme. The chain's name was changed to Trader Joe's in 1967.

The concept that evolved of renting lower-cost buildings, offering a changing stock of unique, private-label items bought directly from suppliers, not relying on price-sensitive national brands, displaying a distinctive quirkiness (each store still features a tropical theme), keeping corporate overhead low, and not offering one-stop shopping differentiated it from its supermarket competitors and contributed to its success.

The company did very little **advertising**, relying on word-of-mouth and regular visits by customers wanting to discover the latest culinary bargain. By 1979 Trader Joe's had grown to 23 stores and was bought by the Albrecht family of Essen, Germany, which owns the Aldi chain of private-label, discount markets. Coulombe remained president until retiring in 1989, when there were 26 Trader Joe's locations with an estimated $145 million in sales a year.

Soon after, Trader Joe's began its privately financed expansion. By 2007, the chain, based in Monrovia, California, had stores in 22 states and Washington, D.C. The company does not disclose financial details, but analysts have put its 2005 sales at $3.6 billion or more. The first Trader Joe's, in Pasadena, is still in operation. Customers and community leaders in places not yet served by Trader Joe's often lobby the company to open a store in their area. A 2006 consumer survey ranked it as one of the top two supermarket chains in America (*Consumer Reports,* Oct. 2006).

The average Trader Joe's is about 12,000 square feet, about half the size of a typical supermarket, and stocks about 2,500–3,000 distinct items (supermarkets carry 25,000–55,000 items). About 80–85 percent of Trader Joe's nonalcoholic products are privately labeled, with names reflecting the cultivated whimsy of the corporate culture, such as Trader Ming's for Asian food products. The stores weed out less-popular items often and introduce about 20–25 new ones weekly, adding incentive for frequent customer visits. The chain is also known for responding to its customers' local preferences and their concerns about their foods. Many of its offerings are **organic**, and the chain refuses to stock genetically modified foods.

"Two Buck Chuck" is one example of the allure of Trader Joe's. The Charles Shaw label, bottled for Trader Joe's by the Bronco Wine Company of Ceres, California, was introduced in 2001. Charles Shaw was a way for Bronco to use surplus grapes by offering a wine that retails for $1.99 in California (higher in other locations). The demand for "Two Buck Chuck" was so great that at one point Trader Joe's was selling a million cases a month. Sales for the five Charles Shaw varietals now average five to six million cases a year.

FURTHER READINGS: Armstrong, Larry. "Trader Joe's: The Trendy American Cousin." *Business Week,* April 26, 2004. Available at http://www.businessweek.com/magazine/content/04_17/

b3880016.htm; Lewis, Len. *The Trader Joe's Adventure: Turning a Unique Approach to Business into a Retail and Cultural Phenomenon.* Chicago: Dearborn Trade, 2005; Rubow, Steven. "TJ'S Mystique: Cheap Thrills." *Private Label*, November/December 2005; Trader Joe's Company. http://www.traderjoes.com.

Faith J. Kramer

Transportation. *See* Airline Food; Delivery; Meat Packing; Middlemen; Refrigeration.

Tropicana Tropicana Products is one of the world's largest producers and marketers of fresh, ready-to-drink orange juice. Tropicana was founded in 1947 in Bradenton, Florida, by Anthony T. Rossi, an Italian immigrant. Rossi began by **packaging** and selling fresh fruit to department stores, hotels, and **restaurants** throughout the United States. In 1954 Tropicana engineers developed the process of flash pasteurization, which uses a lower temperature than regular pasteurization, but heats the liquid for a longer period of time. This process preserves color and **flavor**, while still making the juice safe to drink. This innovation meant a longer shelf life for fresh juice.

Tropicana has been praised for its system of transportation, using a system of "juice trains" to transport its fresh juice from production centers in Florida to distribution centers elsewhere. Before this, Tropicana used the S.S. *Tropicana*, a tanker ship, and the "Great White Juice Train." The S.S. *Tropicana* began service in 1957 and made its last voyage in 1961. The Great White Juice Train ran on an electric line from 1971 to 1976 and then was replaced by a more modern diesel railway.

In 1978 founder Rossi retired and sold Tropicana to Beatrice Foods. Tropicana was purchased by Seagram's the next year and then by PepsiCo in 1998. The acquisition of Tropicana provided PepsiCo with a brand to compete with Coca-Cola's Minute Maid product in the fresh juice market.

Tropicana Pure Premium, the company's flagship orange juice product, is one of the top-selling items in North American **supermarkets**. In addition to orange juice, Tropicana also produces and markets beverages targeted at different markets. One example is its Tropicana Essentials line, which features "healthy heart" and "low acid" juices.

In 1996 Tropicana became the corporate sponsor of Tropicana Field in St. Petersburg, Florida, the home to Major League Baseball's Tampa Bay Devil Rays. Tropicana's products are consumed throughout the world.

FURTHER READING: McPhee, John. *Oranges.* New York: Farrar, Straus and Giroux, 1967.

Eric Covey

Truth in Labeling. *See* Nutrition Labeling.

Tupperware Earl Silas Tupper, the founder of what is now the Tupperware Brands Corporation, was born on a New Hampshire farm in 1907. When his landscaping and tree-surgery business became a victim of the Depression in 1936, he worked for the DuPont chemical company for a year before leaving to start his own plastics company. At the end of the war, the challenge for the chemical industry was to adapt military production for domestic use, and Tupper achieved this in two stages. By

1942 he was able to produce clean, grease- and odor-free translucent plastic; by 1946, his home products were in the stores. The second, and defining, step was the invention of the famous "Tupperware seal"—an air- and watertight plastic lid based on the concept of the paint can—which he patented in 1947.

Sales initially proved disappointing in stores, but successful in the hands of representatives of Stanley Home Products, whose system of selling via "parties" in customers' homes enabled them to demonstrate the use of the seal. One of the most successful representatives was an ambitious woman named Brownie Wise, and in 1951 Tupper invited her to join the company to manage sales. With Wise as vice president, the company boomed. Her genius lay in her keen ability to judge the prevailing social mores of the 1950s. Tupperware products were taken off the shelves in 1951 and sold exclusively by the party-plan system—a method that enabled women to fulfill personal desires of earning income without compromising society's expectations of them as homemakers.

Wise left the company abruptly in 1958 amid rumors of a disagreement with Tupper, although the reason was never publicly disclosed. Within the year, Tupper sold the company to the Rexall Drug Company for $16 million. In 1986 Tupperware became part of Premark International, but it was split off in 1996 and the company was publicly listed on the New York Stock Exchange.

Tupperware entered the international market in 1960, and by 2005 an independent sales force of 1.9 million sold $1.2 billion of products (now expanded to include personal care products) worldwide. Almost all Tupperware is still sold in homes, with a party somewhere in the world every two seconds.

The Tupperware brand has been ranked by *HFN* magazine as the third most-recognized name in home furnishings (1997), listed as one of the greatest inventions of the 20th century by the Guinness Book of World Records, and described as one of the six most extraordinary designed products of the century by *Fortune*. Early Tupperware items also feature in the permanent collection of the New York Museum of Modern Art, but perhaps the most significant indicator of its iconic status is the appropriation of "tupperware" as a generic name for any plastic kitchen container.

FURTHER READING: Clarke, Alison J. *Tupperware: The Promise of Plastics in 1950s America.* Washington, D.C.: Smithsonian Institution Press, 1999.

Eric Covey

TV Dinners In 1935, the **Birds Eye** Company selected Carl A. **Swanson** to be its chief supplier of frozen turkeys. Swanson leased a large Colorado warehouse, which he converted into a cold storage facility, and built a sizable turkey-processing operation. By 1942, Swanson was the nation's largest turkey processor, with sales of $9 million. *Fortune* magazine dubbed him the "Turkey King."

During the late 1940s, Swanson decided to try to corner the turkey market and began a massive buying campaign from California to Minnesota. This drove up the price of turkeys, which encouraged more farmers to start raising turkeys. In 1950 the bubble burst with a glut of turkeys on the market: Swanson was stuck with a huge quantity of birds—many more then he could expect to sell off in the following spring. His storage facilities filled up and he had to rent cold-storage railroad cars for the overflow.

At an emergency meeting of the company, senior staff conferred on what to do with these unwanted turkeys. On the way to the meeting, Gerry Thomas, a company executive, met with one of Swanson's distributors—a company that prepared food for Pan Am Airways' overseas flights. These **airline** meals were packed in aluminum trays that could be heated in onboard convection ovens; they were not marketed to the general public. At the emergency meeting, Thomas proposed that Swanson make a similar meal for consumers, who, in postwar America, were interested in faster, more convenient meal preparation. He developed the concept of an aluminum tray with three compartments—one for a turkey entrée and two for side dishes. The original meal had giblet gravy and stuffing (in the compartment with the turkey), sweet potatoes, and green peas, and the whole was then covered by foil.

Swanson liked the idea and gave permission to test-market it. Thomas named his creation the "**television** dinner," thereby associating it with the new and exciting technology that was at the time just entering mainstream American life. Swanson created a six-color package for the meals. At the time, most **frozen food** packages were just two-color, and so the Swanson dinner stood out in the grocery store. A few thousand meals were test-marketed in cities from Omaha to Chicago in the spring of 1951. This was a risky venture: frozen foods were not yet a significant part of the American food supply.

During World War II, **canned** goods had been needed for the war effort and were in short supply, and frozen foods made with meat were rationed. However, frozen fruits and vegetables became more popular during wartime, and many Americans tried frozen foods for the first time. When the war ended, new frozen foods hit the market, and during the late 1940s, C. A. Swanson and Company had produced frozen chicken and turkey pies. Despite these successes, there were still obstacles in frozen food processing and marketing. Food processors did not fully understand the processes needed to manufacture the products. There were few **refrigerated** trucks to transport the frozen products to stores, freezers were not yet common in grocery stores, and not every home had a refrigerator or freezer to store frozen food. The packages often thawed and were then refrozen, which wreaked havoc with the quality of the food. There was little consumer enthusiasm for frozen foods in 1951.

Nevertheless, the idea of a prepared meal that could be eaten in front of the television set intrigued consumers. The test-marketing of the television dinner was successful, and Swanson capitalized on it by expanding the line to include chicken and **beef** entrées and by varying the side dishes. It also invested extensively in promotion and shortened the name of the product line to "TV dinner."

The new product was so successful that within three years, Swanson was selling 13 million turkey dinners. Based on this phenomenal success, **Campbell's Soup** acquired Swanson in 1955. The success of the frozen TV dinner encouraged others to jump into the market, and thousands of similar products have been marketed since. Swanson's TV dinners slowly lost market share to its varied competition. Pinnacle Foods Corporation acquired Swanson in 2001 and changed the name to "Swanson Dinners."

But the popularity of the TV dinner has continued to thrive. In 1986, an original TV dinner tray was placed in the Smithsonian museum. Thirteen years later, the TV dinner tray was placed on the "Walk of Fame" on the sidewalk in Hollywood. In 2003 Swanson celebrated the 50th anniversary of the TV dinner.

FURTHER READING: Smith, Andrew F. *The Turkey: An American Story.* Urbana: University of Illinois Press, 2006.

Andrew F. Smith

Uncle Ben's In 1937 a Texas rice broker named Gordon L. Harwell began selling "Uncle Ben's Plantation Rice." The image of a smiling, elderly African-American with a bow tie was employed by the company to promote its products. Harwell later claimed that Uncle Ben had been a real African-American rice farmer in the Houston area known for the quality of his rice, although no primary evidence has been offered in support of this claim, and the name "Uncle Ben" was commonly used prior to 1937. For instance, it was a cartoon character in the 1920s. Other African-American caricatures, such as Aunt Jemima and Rastus, were being employed to sell products. The image of Uncle Ben that appeared on the company's boxes, however, was that of Frank C. Brown, a Chicago **restaurant** maitre d' who posed for a portrait.

Harwell acquired a license from a British food chemist named Eric Huzenlaub to sell rice that had been converted or parboiled in such a way that the rice retained its nutritional value yet could be prepared quickly and easily. Harwell established a company, Converted Rice in Houston to market the new rice. By December 1942, he was selling converted rice to the American public, but most of his product went to the U.S. military during World War II. The military was particularly happy with converted rice as it proved impervious to weevils, in addition to its other qualities.

During the war, Forest E. Mars, the son of **candy** manufacturer Frank Mars, bought a controlling share of Converted Rice. In 1946, the company changed its name to Uncle Ben's Rice, and under Mars's direction, it began marketing Uncle Ben's Converted Rice in Canada and subsequently in Australia, the United Kingdom, and many other countries. At the time, rice was not a particularly important food for most Americans, so Mars's company, MasterFoods, pumped millions of dollars into **advertising** Uncle Ben's rice. By the 1950s it was the best-selling rice in the country, a position it held until the 1990s. Uncle Ben's rice became an American icon and today is one of the most famous brands in the world. Partly as a result of this and other rice advertising campaigns, Americans went from eating about 10 pounds of rice annually to consuming twice that amount by the 1980s.

In 1964, Forest Mars acquired control of Mars, Inc., the candy company launched by his father, and MasterFoods became a subsidiary. The Uncle Ben's product line has been expanded to include such products as nonstick and microwave rice. Today, the company markets a variety of flavored "ready rice," including Long Grain Rice,

Brown Rice, Long Grain & Wild Rice, Spanish Rice, and Roasted Chicken Flavored Rice. In 2007 Uncle Ben was featured in an advertising campaign to remake his image, now cast as CEO of his own company. It remains to be seen whether this makeover, like the subtle changes in the image of Aunt Jemima over the years, will be successful.

FURTHER READINGS: Kern-Foxworth, Marilyn. *Aunt Jemima, Uncle Ben, and Rastus: Blacks in Advertising, Yesterday, Today and Tomorrow.* Westport, CT: Praeger, 1994; Palmeri, Christopher. "Wake Up, Mars!" *Forbes,* December 13, 1999. Online at http://members.Forbes.com/1999/1213/6414178a.html

Andrew F. Smith

Unions. *See* Labor and Labor Unions.

U.S. Department of Agriculture (USDA) The Department of Agriculture oversees the nation's production, standards, and business of food. Headquartered in Washington, D.C., the department has offices in every state. Its general historical purpose has been to develop, promote, and implement policy on food, farming, and agricultural trade in the United States. Today, the USDA concerns itself with assisting farmers and ranchers with the production and sale of crops and food products in both domestic and world markets. It is additionally responsible for standards of **food safety**, assisting rural communities, protecting natural resources, and playing a national role in **nutrition education** and promotion.

History

Called "the people's department" by President Abraham Lincoln, the Department of Agriculture was established as an independent government agency in 1862 to support the agrarian economy, separating it from its previous homes within the Patent Office and the Department of the Interior. With many farmers from the North fighting in the Civil War, the expansion of public schools and agricultural colleges, and the absence of oppositional Southern congressmen, the government felt a pressing need to stimulate food production and relevant technologies. From its inception, the USDA was assigned two principal roles: to ensure a sufficient and reliable food supply; and to distribute useful information on subjects generally and comprehensively connected with agriculture to the U.S. population.

In the late 1800s, farmers and other agricultural interests successfully lobbied to have the Department of Agriculture directly represented within the presidential Cabinet. In the early 1890s, the USDA additionally began the task of translating new information, **research**, and scientific discoveries into dietary and nutrition advice for consumers. These first dietary recommendations established principles that govern USDA policies to this day: instead of recommending specific foods or combinations of foods, the recommendations grouped foods of similar nutrient content into five general categories—fruits and vegetables, meats, cereals, **sugar**, and fat.

By 1917, the agency had already produced at least 30 pamphlets that informed consumers about the role of specific foods in the diets of children and adults. Throughout the remainder of the 20th century and into the 21st, the USDA produced numerous sets of guidelines based on the "food group" approach. Its recommendations both emphasized the need to consume foods from certain groups in order to prevent nutritional deficiencies and encouraged the purchase of foods from the full range of available American agricultural products. These recommendations have been lobbied, supported, and protested by food and agricultural producers who understand that the market for their products is limited by the fact that the U.S. food supply is sufficient to provide adequate food to all of its citizens. As dietary recommendations have transformed over the years, the USDA's dual responsibilities for protecting agricultural producers and advising the public about diet have created increasing levels of conflict between the needs of the agriculture industry and consumers' dietary requirements.

The Department of Agriculture played an important role during the Great Depression of the 1930s by providing monetary and technical assistance for food production and distribution, especially in rural communities. By the end of World War II, farmers and food producers had come to view the USDA as their department, and its secretary as their spokesman, as they began to develop an increasingly industrialized system of agricultural production. Producers, together with USDA officials and members of the House and Senate agricultural committees, constituted the "agricultural establishment," ensuring that federal policies in such domains as land use, commodity distribution, and prices promoted their interests. The USDA also became increasingly involved after World War II in nutrition, poverty, and hunger through the National School Lunch Act in 1946, which provides low-cost or free school lunches to low-income children across the country to this day.

The USDA's conflict between agricultural interests and nutrition education continued through the second half of the 20th century, as the department became increasingly responsible for providing the public with dietary and nutrition advice. In the 1950s, national nutrition surveys indicated that the diets of many Americans were below normal for several important nutrients. To help the public choose foods more wisely, USDA nutritionists proposed a simplified guide, which would remain at the center of their nutrition policies for the next two decades, based on four groups— milk, meats, vegetables and fruits, and breads and cereals. This guide, for the first time, specified recommended numbers and sizes of servings.

There were other issues with Americans' diet during this time, however. The nutritional deficiencies of the past had declined in prevalence and been replaced by chronic diseases related to dietary excesses and imbalances, mainly related to fat and cholesterol levels. Early reports on the role of dietary fat in atherosclerosis were published in the mid-1950s, advice to reduce caloric intake from fat in 1961, and recommendations for dietary changes and public policies to reduce risk factors for coronary heart disease in 1970. By the 1980s, this message was well understood by nutrition scientists, dietitians, and consumer activists and was reflected in declining sales of whole milk and eggs. As these trends continued and as **beef** sales also began to decline, food producer lobbies became· much more actively involved in attempts to discredit, weaken, or eliminate dietary recommendations that suggested using less of their products.

Responsibility for providing food assistance to the poor was assigned to the USDA in the 1970s. The 1977 Farm Bill specified that the USDA was to be responsible for a wide range of nutrition research and education activities, including dietary advice to the public. After various disputes with food producers and their lobbies, new dietary guidelines were released in February 1980. These recommendations included the advice to eat a variety of foods; avoid too much fat, saturated fat, and cholesterol; eat foods with adequate starch and fiber; and avoid too much sugar and sodium. Because these guidelines had replaced the unacceptable "eat less" phrase with the vague advice of "avoid too much," agency officials did not expect objections from food producers. This lead role in dietary recommendations was reconfirmed in 1988, when the House Appropriations Committee declared that the federal government needed to speak with a single voice when it issues dietary advice.

Dietary Guidelines for Americans is currently published every five years as a joint project of the USDA and the Department of Health and Human Services. When the guidelines were revised in 1990, despite the apparent consensus among medical and scientific authorities, the 1990 committee—unlike previously appointed committees—consisted of nine nutrition scientists and physicians with few apparent ties to the food industry. However, during committee deliberations, 10 of the 13 groups that submitted written comments represented food producers, trade associations, or organizations allied with industry, again demonstrating the interconnectedness of U.S. nutrition policy with agricultural interests.

In 1991, the interference of food lobbies in policies around the dietary guidelines again came to public attention, this time over the guide best known as the Food Pyramid. The pyramid idea had originated a decade earlier in response to criticisms that consumers would have difficulty planning menus that met dietary recommendations. Its illustration displays grains and cereals at the wide base, vegetables and fruits in the band above, meats and **dairy** foods in the narrow upper band, and fats and sweets in the narrow peak. The band width represents the daily number of portions of each food group recommended by USDA, which also meant that the daily diet should include more servings of grains, fruits, and vegetables than of meats, dairy products, and fats and sweets. Through their connections in Congress and the USDA and use of their strong financial base, food lobbies successfully convinced government policy makers to alter the wording of their advice about meat and dairy products, the principal sources of dietary fat, from "eat less" to "choose lean meats" to "have 2–3 portions." This version of the Food Guide Pyramid was released in April 1992.

The dietary guidelines were revised most recently in 2005. This latest variant includes a dozen different Food Pyramids for different food intake patterns, for example, different levels of activity and age categories. Hundreds of comments received from the general public, nutrition professionals, and industry and trade associations informed the construction of these new recommendations.

The Multiple Hats of the USDA

In addition to serving the needs of the agriculture industry and public dietary guidelines, the USDA also works on social programs related to food and nutrition, including natural resource management and rural development. The USDA's numerous operational units include the following:

- The Agricultural Marketing Service (AMS) includes six commodity programs, which provide standardization, grading, and market news services: Cotton, Dairy, Fruit and Vegetable, Livestock and Seed, **Poultry**, and Tobacco. It also administers the Science and Technology Program, which provides laboratory, scientific, and statistical services, as well as managing agricultural transportation systems and policies. Additionally, the AMS manages the USDA's National **Organic** Program and supervises and promotes **farmers' market** initiatives around the country.

- The Animal and Plant Health Inspection Service (APHIS) chiefly handles issues of agricultural pests and disease management, especially the safety of importing and exporting of agricultural and food products. APHIS also contends with animal health, care, and welfare for animals as food and as pets, as well as administering the National Wildlife Research Center.

- The Food, Nutrition, and Consumer Services division administers governmental nutrition assistance programs, providing access to both food and information about nutrition. Established in 1969, the Food and Nutrition Services branch incorporates the **Food Stamp** program; school meal programs; Women, Infants, and Children (WIC) program for low-income women and their children; and Emergency Food Assistance programs, including disaster relief. The division also incorporates the Center for Nutrition Policy and Promotion, created in 1994, which is currently in charge of the *Dietary Guidelines for Americans*, including the Food Pyramid.

- The Farm Service Agency supervises farm commodity, credit, conservation, disaster, and loan programs across the United States through a network of federal, state and county offices. These programs, in addition to education and outreach work, are intended to provide economic stability for agricultural producers while maintaining conservation and environmental standards.

- The Food Safety Inspection Service (FSIS) is responsible for the safety and labeling of meat, poultry, and egg products, as well as all food products that contain more than 2 percent meat products.

- The National Agricultural Library (NAL) was created in 1862 as the departmental library for the USDA and became a national library on its centennial in 1962. It coordinates a national network of state land-grant and USDA field libraries of more than 3.3 million items. Internationally, it serves as the U.S. hub of an international agricultural information system, coordinating and sharing agricultural data and resources across the globe.

- The USDA's Rural Development programs have an $86 billion portfolio of loans and almost $16 billion in program loans, loan guarantees, and grants, which are used to provide financial and technical assistance to rural individuals, communities, and businesses. These programs support public services such as water and sewer systems, housing, health clinics, emergency service facilities, and electric and telephone service. They also provide technical assistance to help rural communities undertake community empowerment programs and start agricultural and other cooperatives.

See also Agribusiness.

FURTHER READINGS: Levenstein, Harvey. 1989. *Revolution at the Table: Transformation of the American Diet*. New York: Oxford University Press, 1989; Nestle, Marion. *Food Politics: How the Food Industry Influences Nutrition and Health*. 2nd ed. Berkeley: University of California Press, 2007.

Michaela DeSoucey

Vegetarian Food

History

Vegetarianism has a long history stretching from the Ancient Greeks to the modern day. Pythagoras, often called the "father of vegetarianism," believed that human souls transmigrate after death into animals, and thus killing them is tantamount to murder. Plutarch added the charges that killing animals degrades the human character and that flesh foods have deleterious effects on both the body and the intellect. Vegetarianism was, and continues to be, part of the ethical codes of several ancient religious traditions, including Hinduism and Buddhism. Even Christianity has its vegetarian sects, sometimes considered heresies in the Middle Ages.

In the Western world, the 19th century saw a renewed interest in vegetarianism as a religious-moral practice. In the United States in the 1830s and '40s, Presbyterian preacher Sylvester Graham and the early Seventh-Day Adventists spread the vegetarian message of physical and moral health. The Vegetarian Society was founded in 1850, three years after its sister organization in England. It was with this emergence of an organized movement that the term *vegetarianism* was coined.

A second wave of interest in the early 1900s was sparked by the work of Seventh-Day Adventist John Harvey Kellogg, whose **corn** flakes and granola represented a technological version of dietary purity. Around the same time in England, scientific arguments were invoked (by physicians such as Hereward Carrington) in an attempt to prove that the original and natural diet of humans was fruits and nuts. Although this idea persists, it is difficult to maintain that vegetarianism is "natural" in any meaningful sense of the word for, while meat may not have been part of the diet of early humans, adaptation to different environments and exploitation of the available food sources led inevitably to an omnivorous existence. Vegetarianism enjoyed resurgence in the counterculture of the 1960s and '70s, and since then has slowly entered mainstream culture, fueled by an increasing interest in claims of health benefits for vegetarian styles of eating.

Definition

Vegetarianism is not a unitary concept. There is a spectrum of practice among people who describe themselves as vegetarians, which entails partial or total exclusion of animal products from the diet.

The strictest form of vegetarianism is *veganism*. Vegans will consume neither animal flesh nor any product of animal origin, whether or not it involves the killing of the animal. This includes products with ingredients such as eggs or milk, or even animal enzymes such as rennet, which is used to curdle milk in order to make cheese. The strictest vegans will not consume honey, either. Vegans often eschew the use of animal-derived products in other aspects of their lives as well, for example, avoiding leather or fur clothing.

Lacto vegetarians exclude meat from the diet but do consume **dairy** products; *ovo vegetarians* include eggs; *lacto-ovo vegetarians* allow both dairy products and eggs; and *pesco vegetarians* also eat fish. Some people consider themselves to be vegetarian if they avoid red meat—even if they consume white meats such as chicken. *Fruitarians* eat only foods that do not kill the plant, mainly fruits, seeds, and some vegetables. *Macrobiotic* diets emphasize brown rice, sea vegetables, and legumes, but at lower levels of strictness may include fish.

Motivations for Vegetarianism

Practice of and attitudes toward vegetarianism are influenced by social, religious, philosophical, and political factors. A fundamental distinction should be made between vegetarianism as a normative sociocultural behavior and vegetarianism as a conscious individual choice. In the former case, vegetarianism is associated with specific religious beliefs or codes. Vegetarianism is a dietary tenet of Hinduism, Jainism, and Buddhism. Baha'is are encouraged, but not required, to follow a vegetarian diet; Seventh-Day Adventists also promote vegetarianism. Observance of religious dietary guidance varies depending on individual devoutness and social circumstances. Where vegetarianism is a personal choice, interconnected themes of health, economics, ecology, and spirituality arise. A useful distinction can be made between self-regarding and Other-regarding vegetarianism. The former is more to do with achievement of personal goals—whether corporeal or spiritual, while the latter evinces concern for others, including animals.

Health is the most commonly cited reason for vegetarian preferences in the United States, related to concerns over wellness, disease prevention, or weight management. Recent scares over meat safety, such as **bovine spongiform encephalopathy** (BSE) or "mad cow" disease have also played a part. Diets that emphasize fruit, vegetables, whole cereals, and pulses tend to be higher in bulk and lower in calories, **sugars**, and fats than a typical meat-centered regimen; thus, it is not surprising that some studies have shown vegetarians to weigh less on average than nonvegetarians and to have lower blood cholesterol levels and lower blood pressures. There is also evidence of lower cancer risks. The vegetarian health practices of Seventh-Day Adventists seem to have conferred nutritional benefits on them. As a group, they suffer less chronic diet-related disorders such as hypertension and cancer, and lower all-cause mortality, than does the general population. While poorly planned vegetarian diets may be low in some essential nutrients, well-balanced vegetarian diets that utilize a variety of foods are nutritionally sound. With more restrictive practices such as veganism or macrobiotics, there are greater concerns over the adequacy of some micronutrients, and care is needed to ensure that diets provide adequate zinc, **vitamin** B_{12}, calcium, and vitamin D.

People motivated by health are likely to be less committed to their vegetarian lifestyle than those motivated by ethical concerns. Whether religiously inspired or secular, ethical perspectives emphasize the need for compassion and respect for life.

Religious views emerge from the idea that humans are an interdependent part of creation and do not have any special claims over animals. This reasoning reaches its apotheosis in the Jain concept of *ahimsa*, or noninjury to living beings. Jain monks are fastidious in preserving life, for example, by sweeping the floor in front of them as they walk so as to avoid treading on insects and filtering water to avoid inadvertently swallowing any small creatures. Beliefs in *metempsychosis*, the transmigration of souls, similarly motivate orthodox Buddhists and Hindus. Vegetarianism thus becomes a means to spiritual freedom and an indicator of devotion to a moral life.

Secular ethical stances more frequently focus on the idea of **animal rights**, condemning both the eating of creatures that are said to have demonstrable interests and rights, and the rearing of animals under modern factory farm conditions that are seen to be inherently cruel. In this view, justice demands that animals be treated with the same ethical considerations as are accorded to human beings. Such arguments are rejected outright in philosophical stances that deny that animals can have natural rights.

The landmark publication in 1971 of Frances Moore Lappé's *Diet for a Small Planet* raised serious questions about the (in)efficiency of intensive livestock production and the sustainability of large-scale meat consumption as a normative human dietary pattern. A rising world demand for meat, epitomized by the meat-centered diet of North Americans, encourages the use of energy-intensive methods of food production, which, in turn, place tremendous pressure on ecosystems and on resource usage. The destruction of rain forest to provide land for animal grazing is a commonly cited example. By reducing the demand for meat, land and energy resources that are used for intensive animal-rearing could be freed to produce larger quantities of plant crops. In this way, it is argued, vegetarianism allows for a more equitable sharing of the world's resources and thus contributes to reducing world hunger and malnutrition.

While vegetarianism can be a deliberate choice, made for a variety of reasons, there are also cogent arguments that non–meat eating is primarily a consequence of want, not of choice, and that humans increase their dietary meat when it is economically feasible to do so. The term "meat-hunger" has been used to describe a supposed craving for meat, especially among people living at subsistence level. However, in many human societies, meat consumption is associated with wealth, prestige, and power so that it is possible to make a social argument for explaining the desirability of meat without invoking the slippery concept of "naturalness."

Vegetarians

British data since the 1980s indicate a gradual upward trend in the number of people considering themselves to be vegetarian and a marked upward trend in those who report avoiding red meat. Similar trends are evident in the United States, although the overall percentages are smaller. Estimates of the prevalence of vegetarianism in North America vary from 2 to 4 percent; it is more common on the West and East coasts and among young, middle-class whites, with females outnumbering males by two to one. The fact that vegetarianism is less common among lower socioeconomic groups may be at least partially explained by the role of meat as a high-status food. If "almost-vegetarians" are included, this number rises to 5–9 percent, while many more people claim to eat at least some meatless meals each week. Only a small percentage of self-identified vegetarians are vegan.

The Market for Vegetarian Food

With growing concerns over health, government advice to consume lower-fat and higher-fiber diets, health scares such as BSE, and concerns over cruelty to animals, vegetarianism has moved slowly into the mainstream market. While the number of true vegetarians appears to be relatively static, there is an increase in the number of "meat reducers" and red-meat avoiders that is creating a growing demand for alternatives to animal products. The U.S. market for meat and dairy substitutes and vegetarian entrees increased fivefold between 1996 and 2002 and is predicted to continue growing, albeit at a declining rate as the market matures. In response to increasing demand, vegetarian options are becoming increasingly available in the food market, at both retail and **restaurant** outlets. Prepared meals, including **snack** meals, account for the largest value share of the market, catering to convenience and busy lifestyles, with chilled products replacing **frozen** dishes as market leaders. The four largest segments of the chilled vegetarian foods market are pastry products, ready-to-eat meals, potato-based products, and snacks. While expanding market opportunities have spurred the development of a greater range of vegetarian products, including "**ethnic**" dishes, vegetarian alternatives to meat and dairy products such as flavored soy milks and nonmeat spicy "chicken wings" are often made to resemble their meat and dairy counterparts as possible. About half of the vegetarian food volume is sold through **supermarkets** and half through natural food stores.

Food Service

A high proportion of table-service restaurants in United States offer vegetarian entrees. **Fast food restaurants** now commonly offer veggie burgers or meatless sandwiches, while food services in shopping malls, **airlines**, workplaces, hospitals, sports venues, schools, and colleges increasingly offer vegetarian choices. On university and college campuses, up to 20 percent of students self-identify as vegetarian. As a result, food service companies have made efforts to provide vegetarian dining alternatives on many campuses. However, while there are growing opportunities for vegetarian options in all segments of the food and food service industry, it is apparent that products must meet traditional consumer expectations for taste, convenience, and cost.

See also Raw Food; Whole Food.

FURTHER READINGS: Fraser, Gary E. *Diet, Life Expectancy, and Chronic Disease: Studies of Seventh-Day Adventists and other Vegetarians.* Oxford: Oxford University Press, 2003; Iacobbo, Karen, and Michael Iacobbo. *Vegetarians and Vegans in America Today.* Westport, CT: Praeger, 2006; Lappé, Frances Moore. *Diet for a Small Planet.* Rev. ed. New York: Ballantine Books, 1975; Mangels, Reed, Virginia Kisch Messina, and Mark Messina. *The Dietitian's Guide to Vegetarian Diets.* 2nd ed. Sudbury, MA: Jones and Bartlett, 2004; Messina, V., R. Mangels, and M. Messina. *The Dieticians Guide to Vegetarian Diets.* Boston: Jones and Bartlett Publishers, Inc., 2004; Osborne, C. "Ancient Vegetarianism." In John Wilkins, David Harvey, and Mike Dobson, eds., *Food in Antiquity,* pp. 214–24. Exeter, U.K.: University of Exeter Press, 1995; *Restaurants USA,* January 1999; Sterba, James P., ed. *Earth Ethics: Introductory Readings on Animal Rights and Environmental Ethics.* Upper Saddle River, NJ: Prentice Hall, 2000; Vegetarianism UK 2000. Mintel Reports. http://reports.mintel.com/sinatra/reports/index/&letter=22/display/id=382&anchor=a382; Vegetarian Resource Group. http://www.vrg.org; Vegetarian Resource Group. "How Many Vegetarians Are There?" *Vegetarian Journal* 3, (2003): 8–9.

Paul Fieldhouse

Vending Machines The vending industry, dispensing a wide array of products, has a solid niche in the American marketplace. The top-selling categories—**soft drinks**, **candy**, and **coffee** (along with cigarettes, which began to decline in 1983)—have remained fairly stable for most of the $45 billion industry's 120-year history. While the variety of products sold has expanded and the machines that deliver them have modernized, vending sales today struggle to maintain their portion of the consumer's dollar.

The first vending machine patents were granted in 1886, followed, two years later, by the Thomas Addams Company's installation of a gum dispenser on an elevated platform in the New York City subway. During the 1890s, dozens of inventions appeared, most dispensing inexpensive goods such as penny candy, handfuls of peanuts, or gum. In its early years, the industry was composed of scores of small distributing companies that owned and serviced the machines. Most, paying a commission for their location, made at best a modest profit. Along with low margins on the inexpensive goods, vandalism and especially the use of slugs (coin-shaped pieces of metal) plagued the industry, a problem that continues to the present.

A period of innovation and growth followed World War I and lasted until the 1930s. Cigarettes were first sold by machine in the 1925, and the next year Sodamats, an early form of soft drink dispenser, were introduced. Two years later, there were 250 companies producing 400 different types of machines, most offering inexpensive everyday items. Hershey's introduced the first nickel candy bar in 1929; the Automatic Canteen Company (now part of the Compass Group) formed the same year and was, within a few years, operating a hundred machines, each offering five different selections of nickel candy bars.

During the 1930s, Americans spent $15 million buying candy and soft drinks from vending machines. The number of food items expanded to include fresh fruit, juice, milk, and baked goods. However, during the Depression, hiring a salesperson was less expensive than the cost of operating a vending machine, and with generally lower sales and increased pilferage, industry sales stagnated. Slugs continued to drain profits, and the American Merchandise Association was formed in 1931 in part to wage war on fraud. By 1939, Automatic Canteen was placing vending machines in factories, an ideal location with a captive audience, and by 1940, it had almost 230,000 machines in operation and annual sales of $10 million.

Once World War II began, sales and profits rose, as spending increased in the prosperous wartime economy. Because metal was allocated to the war effort, the production of new machines was curtailed, saving vending companies the investment costs involved in creating new models, which helped the industry regain its footing. During this period, the War Board estimated that 35 percent of all industrial plants had installed vending machines; one of the most lucrative locations was defense-industry factories, which, operating day and night, needed a quick and convenient way to feed their workers.

After the war, the use of electronically operated machines became more widespread, as sales continued to increase with a wider variety of products. The largest sellers remained candy, soft drinks, and cigarettes. Once machines were developed that could vend hot coffee in the mid-1940s, and office coffee breaks became a way of life in the 1950s, coffee joined the ranks of top-selling items. During this era, as factories moved out of cities into more remote locations, in-plant feeding became a necessity. Many firms either substituted or supplemented their **cafeterias** with large banks of vending machines. Various estimates in 1954 suggested that from 84 to 90 percent of large institutions has at least one vending machine, and a typical installation might include newly introduced **refrigerated** sandwiches, coffee, pastries, candy, and especially soda, which by the end of the decade accounted for 20 percent of sales.

Edible products made up almost 40 percent of industry totals in the 1960s. The introduction of the dollar bill-changing machine helped boost sales, as did soft drinks sold in cans. During this time, Automatic Canteen, now renamed the Canteen Corporation, had annual sales of $200 million. By the 1970s, schools became an important source of revenues for the vending industry, having first entered these locations in the 1950s. Water, one of the earliest products offered in vending machines in the 1880s, was reintroduced in the mid-1980s, and sales leapt 60 percent by 1990. Coffee made from freshly ground beans debuted in 1988 and the **gourmet** category expanded in 1991 with the machines serving cappuccino and espresso.

Today, the nation's largest food service corporations, such as Aramark Corporation, Compass Group Group, and Sodexho, all operate vending machines. Third-ranked Aramark began vending services in 1935, winning a contract to supply Douglas Aircraft four years later. A 1959 merger created the renamed Automatic Retailers of America (ARA), which became the largest U.S. vending corporation by 1961. Currently, the Canteen Corporation is the world's largest vending company, with machines in 18,500 sites and more than five million customers daily.

Large-scale industrial sites, traditionally a large percentage of vending sales, began to decline by 2006 as the number of manufacturing jobs diminished. Also expected to affect the state of the industry are concerns about **obesity**—many of the products sold through vending machines are high in calories—as well as a May 2006 agreement limiting the amount of **sugared** drinks in school vending machines.

Looking to new technologies to boost revenues, the vending industry is expected to expand the use of vandal-proof cashless machines, first introduced in 1985, which utilize debit or credit cards. These are expected to comprise one-quarter of the machines within the next few years. In addition to hindering fraud, payment by cards is expected to increase spending, since studies have shown that consumers spend larger sums on transactions while using cards. However, the expense of the new technology, plus soaring electricity costs for lighting and refrigeration, have created challenges for the vending industry.

FURTHER READINGS: Maras, Elliot. "Operators Slow to Invest; Sales Rise 3 Points in 2005." *Automatic Merchandiser* 48 (2006): 40–56; Segrave, Kerry. *Vending Machines: An American Social History.* Jefferson, NC: McFarland, 2002.

Joy Santlofer

Vitamin Deficiencies Vitamins are organic compounds needed in small amounts in the diet to maintain normal metabolic functions; along with minerals, they are known as *micronutrients*. The lack of regular adequate intake of a vitamin results in a specific deficiency disease.

Knowledge that certain foods protected health long predated the discovery and scientific understanding of vitamins. A classic example is the routine use of citrus fruit in the 18th-century British navy to prevent symptoms of scurvy arising in sailors on long voyages. Scurvy results from a deficiency of vitamin C in the diet, the richest dietary sources of which are fruit and vegetables. It is from this practice that the British became known as "limeys." Unpolished rice was known to protect against beriberi, before it was shown that the active compound, vitamin B_1 (thiamine), was lost in the polishing process used to produce refined rice. In the late 19th century, Frederick Rowland Hopkins, a British biochemist, proposed the existence of "accessory factors" in food that were as essential to health as the well-known components of protein, fat, and carbohydrates. Over the following decades, scientists identified a number of these accessory factors. The name *vitamin* came from a contraction of "vital amine"; even though it turned out that not all the active molecules were amines, they were certainly vital.

There are 13 known vitamins, which are divided into two broad groups: those that are water-soluble—vitamin C and the vitamin B complex, comprising B_1 (thiamine), B_2 (riboflavin), niacin, B_6 (pyridoxine), folic acid, B_{12} (cobalamin), and pantothenic acid—and the fat-soluble vitamins A, D, E, and K.

Vitamins are derived chiefly from dietary sources, where they may be either naturally occurring or added during fortification. They are also available as supplements in various dosages and forms. In addition, vitamin D can be synthesized in the body through the action of ultraviolet radiation or sunlight on the skin. Only vitamins A, E, and B_{12} can be stored in the body to any significant extent, so a regular daily intake of vitamins is essential to maintain health.

Vitamin deficiencies can arise for one or both of two reasons. Primary deficiencies occur when the healthy body does not obtain an adequate intake from the sources mentioned above. Secondary deficiencies may occur if something interferes with the absorption or metabolism of the vitamin or if disease conditions raise vitamin requirements above normal levels.

Primary deficiencies are the result of poor-quality diets that are missing sources of the vitamin in question. This situation is most common in developing countries where there is dietary dependence on a narrow range of nutritionally incomplete foods or where poverty prevents the acquisition of food. Vitamin A and folic acid deficiencies are endemic in many parts of the developing world; insufficient vitamin B is associated with widespread malnutrition in the form of beriberi and pellagra. In most developed countries, primary vitamin deficiencies are relatively rare; when they occur, they are associated with poverty, limited food intake due to poor appetite, or adherence to restrictive dietary regimens, such as macrobiotics or vegan **vegetarianism**.

Secondary vitamin deficiencies are more likely to be seen as a consequence of drug–nutrient interactions, drinking of alcohol, or smoking. Mild vitamin deficiencies may have effects at a subclinical level, compromising metabolic processes in the body associated with normal functioning and disease prevention. Prolonged or severe vitamin deficiencies result in classic deficiency symptoms such as rickets (from insufficient vitamin D), blindness (vitamin A), scurvy (vitamin C), beriberi (vitamin B_1), and pellagra (niacin).

In 2003, the National Institute of Medicine produced a series of reports that resulted in new dietary recommended intakes (DRIs), which form the basis for official government recommendations in both the United States and Canada. Meeting the recommended daily allowance provides assurance that the probability of inadequate dietary intake of the nutrient is less than 2–3 percent.

There are three basic components to preventing vitamin deficiencies. The first is to ensure access to an affordable food supply that permits a wide choice of foods to be made from among and within all food groups. Because foods have different nutrient profiles, no one food or food group can provide all the nutrients needed for human health. By consuming a wide variety of foods, a better overall nutritional intake is achieved.

Contemporary dietary advice in North America and around the world emphasizes the importance of variety and provides dietary guidance tools to assist consumers with healthy food selection. Examples include the U.S. Food Pyramid and Canada's Food Guide. Notwithstanding this, it is still the case that the dietary intake of several nutrients among the general population in North America is low enough to be of some concern; for adults, this includes vitamins A, C, and E, and for children, vitamin E. **Nutrition education** efforts are needed to increase consumption of these nutrients.

Other areas of potential concern are folic acid intake of women in their child-bearing years, vitamin B_{12} intake of older adults, and vitamin D intake of specific subgroups of infants and children whose exposure to sunlight is limited through geographic or sociocultural factors. Folic acid deficiency is associated with an increased risk of birth defects such as spina bifida and anencephaly. B_{12} deficiency, due to reduced ability of older adults to absorb dietary B_{12}, results in pernicious anemia. Vitamin D deficiency results in poor bone growth and ultimately rickets and may also play a role in protecting against other diseases. First described in 17th-century urban London, rickets is still seen today among children living in northern Canada.

The second preventive strategy is to add nutrients to the food supply through fortification schemes that focus on basic ingredients or on specific products. Fortification can also be used to restore levels of nutrients lost in processing and storage. For example, since 1998, all flour in the United States has been fortified with folic acid in a concentration of 1.4 parts per million (in Canada 1.5 parts per million). The result has been a decline of 20–50 percent in neural tube defects. In the United States, vitamin D is added to most fluid milk (and in Canada to evaporated milk, powdered milk, and goat's milk, as well as plant-based milks and certain margarines). Food manufacturers may also elect to fortify specific products within regulations set out by the U.S. Food and Drug Administration or Health Canada. Such nutrient additions are often used as a promotional tool in marketing.

The success of fortification schemes in industrialized countries has been only partly replicated in the developing world. There exists huge potential for the alleviation of suffering and prevention of disease through relatively inexpensive fortification interventions. However, while business has the knowledge and market mechanisms to do this, there is little profit to be made from a low-income market, and government action is required to directly sponsor programs or provide incentives to the private sector.

The third approach is to provide vitamins in the form of supplements, usually pills, which are consumed in addition to the normal diet. Many people take daily multivitamin supplements as a sort of nutritional insurance, and the market for these products is huge and highly competitive. There are advantages to obtaining vitamins from the diet, as food contains other nutrients and protective factors. However, while a balanced diet containing a wide variety of foods will generally provide adequate amounts of vitamins, there are physiological conditions, such as pregnancy and lactation, or age-related requirements of older adults, in which vitamin supplements are recommended. While taking vitamin supplements in moderation is nutritionally non-problematic, large amounts, or "megadoses," of vitamins A, C, D, and B_6 and niacin can have toxic effects.

See also Nutrition Labeling.

FURTHER READINGS: Subcommittee on Interpretation and Uses of Dietary Reference Intakes and the Standing Committee on the Scientific Evaluation of Dietary Reference Intakes, Institute of Medicine of the National Academies. *Dietary Reference Intakes: Applications in Dietary Planning.* Washington, D.C.: National Academic Press, 2003; UNICEF. *Vitamin and Mineral Deficiency: A Global Progress Report*, 2004. Online at http://www.micronutrient.org/reports/reports/Full_e.pdf; U.S. Department of Health and Human Services, and U.S. Department of Agriculture. *Dietary Guidelines for Americans.* Washington, D.C.: GPO, 2005.

Paul Fieldhouse

Wal-Mart. *See* Supermarkets.

Welch's Welch's Food is the manufacturing and marketing unit of the National Grape Cooperative Association. In this capacity, Welch's represents the interests of more than 1,300 growers whose products it is responsible for selling. Welch's is especially famous for its grape juice, though it offers other products as well.

Welch's existence was made possible by the 1849 development of the Concord grape by Ephraim Wales Bull in Concord, Massachusetts. In 1869, prohibitionist Dr. Thomas Bramwell Welch of Vineland, New Jersey, successfully pasteurized the juice of the Concord grape to create an "unfermented sacramental **wine**" that he marketed to churches.

In 1893 Welch's son, Dr. Charles E. Welch, offered samples of his family's grape juice to visitors at the Chicago World's Fair. Soon after, "Dr. Welch's Grape Juice" became simply Welch's Grape Juice. The younger Welch continued to market grape juice as a temperate alternative to alcohol by using the slogan "Get the Welch habit— it's one that won't get you."

Welch's received a free publicity boost in 1913 when Secretary of State William Jennings Bryan served Welch's Grape Juice instead of wine at a diplomatic gathering honoring retiring British ambassador James Bryce. A year later, Secretary of the Navy Josephus Daniels outlawed alcohol on Navy ships, replacing it with grape juice. Newspaper editors and cartoonists lampooned "Daniels' Grape Juice Navy."

Welch's began making Concord Grape Jelly in 1923 and introduced Welch's Homogenized Tomato Juice, its first nongrape product, in 1927. After Charles Welch died in 1926, Welch's languished until a competitor, Jacob M. Kaplan, purchased it in 1945. Kaplan was instrumental in expanding grape production in the United States, entering into a long-term contract with the growers of the National Grape Cooperative Association. Later, in 1952, these same growers would cooperatively purchase Welch's.

Over the years, Welch's has been a frequent sponsor of entertainment media. In the 1930s, Welch's sponsored *The Irene Rich Show*, a popular radio program. On **television** in the 1950s, Welch's sponsored *The Howdy Doody Show* and *The Mickey Mouse Club*, and in the 1960s, it sponsored *The Flintstones*.

During the 1980s, Welch's was one of the beverage companies **boycotted** by Jesse Jackson's Chicago-based People United to Save Humanity (PUSH). PUSH accused

Welch's of failing to hire enough African-American employees and not doing business with black-owned companies.

In recent years, Welch's has emphasized the possible health benefits of grapes as a way of marketing its product in an increasingly competitive market. It introduced the squeezable container in 1985, a juice concentrate that requires no freezing in 1996, and a plastic can for frozen juice concentrate in 1998. Welch's current product line includes **bottled**, **canned**, and **frozen** fruit juices; jams, jellies, and preserves; fruit juice bars; and dried fruit. The company has a branded fruit-flavored soda that is manufactured by Cadbury Schweppes's Dr Pepper/Seven Up unit.

Welch's corporate headquarters is in Concord, Massachusetts. In addition to the United States, Welch's products can be purchased in China, the United Kingdom, and Mexico.

FURTHER READING: "Almost Like Wine," *Time*, September 3, 1956.

Eric Covey

Wendy's. *See* Fast Food Restaurants.

Wheat A grass that belongs to the genus *Triticum*, wheat is grown on every continent and is the world's second most important cereal crop (in tons) after **corn**. Wheat is also one of the oldest cultivated cereals, having been farmed by Neolithic man as early as 7800 B.C. There are two varieties that are widely grown and consumed today— *T. aestivum*, or common bread wheat, and *T. durum*, pasta or durum wheat, which is ground for semolina flour. Other varieties such as *T. monococcum* and *T. dicoccum* were cultivated in ancient times but are rare today. *T. spelta* (spelt) is also cultivated in limited quantities but has recently enjoyed a resurgence in popularity due to its perceived health benefits.

This valuable cereal has been traded since antiquity and was one of the earliest commodities, along with oats, corn, barley, and so on, to be traded in large scale on the open market. Today, wheat is classified by three attributes on the commodities markets, and together these give rise to several classes of wheat that each have different uses and properties.

The *growth habit* refers to the time when wheat is usually planted in northern temperate regions. "Winter wheat" is planted in the fall and grows for a short period before becoming dormant for the winter months; growth then resumes in the spring and by midsummer, winter wheat is ready for harvest. "Spring wheat" is planted in the spring, grows over the summer, and ripens by late summer or early autumn. Winter wheat is generally preferred over spring because it gives larger yields (due in part to its earlier planting and longer growth period), but it can be grown only in regions with milder winters. In the United States, winter wheat makes up 70–80 percent of total production.

Wheat *color* is a genetically determined characteristic and is expressed through the presence of pigment in the seed coat or its absence: the former gives "red" wheat, and the latter gives "white."

Hardness is also an inherited characteristic, determined by the texture of the starchy endosperm. "Hard" wheat gives a coarser flour when ground and generally has a higher protein content that contributes to the formation of gluten. Hard wheat is therefore preferred for making leavened breads with a chewy, spongy texture.

"Soft" wheats are suitable for more delicate breads such as crackers, pastries, cakes, cookies, and noodles. In Europe, however, the terms are applied to distinguish between the two species of wheat: *T. aestivum* is soft, while *T. durum* is hard.

Wheat Classes

Most of the world has only two classes of wheat or does not bother to break them out at all. In contrast, there are six classes recognized in the United States.

- Hard Red Winter wheat varies in protein content and has good milling and baking characteristics. It is mostly used to produce bread, rolls, and, to a lesser extent, sweet goods and all-purpose flour. It is mainly produced in the Great Plains and is the largest class in terms of both production and export; about 40 percent is exported all over the world.
- Hard Red Spring wheat contains the highest percentage of protein. Its superior milling and baking characteristics make it an ideal bread wheat. The majority of the crop is grown in Montana, North Dakota, South Dakota, and Minnesota, and it is exported largely to Central America, Japan, the Philippines, and Russia, making up 20 percent of total U.S. wheat exports.
- Soft Red Winter wheat is low in protein, but achieves high yields and is milled for cake flour, pastry flour, and some self-rising flours. It is grown east of the Mississippi, is exported to China, Egypt, and Morocco, and makes up about 14 percent of total exports.
- Durum wheat, or pasta wheat as it is known in the United States, is hard, slightly translucent, and light in color. It is mostly used in the manufacture of pasta products and makes up about 5 percent of exports.
- Soft White Winter wheat is similar to Soft Red Winter. This wheat is grown mainly in the Pacific Northwest and to a lesser extent in California, Michigan, Wisconsin, and New York. It is low in protein but is a high-yielding variety and its flour is used for baking cakes, crackers, cookies, pastries, quick breads, muffins, and snack foods. It comprises 20 percent of total exports, mainly to the Middle East and Asia.
- Hard White Winter is the newest class of wheat, recently developed by researchers at Kansas State University to provide a high-yielding, light-colored wheat with the milling and baking properties of Hard Red Spring. Grown in Montana, Idaho, Kansas, and California, it has a milder, sweeter flavor and equal fiber content. In other words, this is a wheat that gives a product with the appearance and flavor of a white bread but the cooking and nutritional properties of whole wheat. Another advantage to this variety is its color, as soft and white wheats usually command higher prices than hard and red. In addition, hard wheats are generally harder to process and red wheats may need bleaching, steps that add to total processing costs. Hard White Winter wheat is used in a wider variety of products than Hard Red Spring, from yeast breads and hard rolls to tortillas and oriental noodles. Production quantities remain small and most is consumed by the domestic market, but there is much interest in this class and production is likely to increase.

Wheat Consumption and Trade

It should be remembered that wheat is important not only as a human food crop but also as a source of animal feed. Given that many different classes of wheat are grown for different purposes in very different agriclimatic conditions, it is logical that not every market is able to produce enough wheat to meet local demand. Thus, trade in wheat is extensive and their markets complex. Wheat is bought and sold in contracts on regulated **commodities exchanges** all over the world. In the United States, it is traded at the Minneapolis Grain Exchange, the Chicago Board of Trade, and the Kansas City Board of Trade.

FURTHER READINGS: Antle, John M., and Vincent H. Smith. *The Economics of World Wheat Markets.* Wallingford, Oxon, U.K.: CABI, 1999; Bajaj, Y. P. S., ed. *Wheat.* Berlin: Springer-Verlag, 1990; FAO Statistic Yearbook, Issue 1 – Cross-Section by Subject 2005–2006. *Production of Selected Agricultural Commodities, Group I (2004).* [Online, March 2007] United Nations Food and Agriculture Association web site. Online at http://www.fao.org/ES/ESS/yearbook/vol_1_1/pdf/b06.pdf

Karen Y. Lau

Whole Food "Whole food" is a broad term widely used to describe the body of foods also referred to as "natural foods" or "health foods." The hallmark of whole food is the primacy of wholesome food in a largely unprocessed and unrefined state, as in "whole grains." Processing and refining in this case result in reduced nutritional value.

Decline in the consumption of whole food coincided with the Industrial Revolution, specifically with the milling and chemical bleaching of wheat that resulted in refined flour. Whole grain bread was replaced by white refined bread. Later synthetic **vitamins** were added.

An early advocate of whole food was the reformer Sylvester Graham (1794–1851). Graham, a **vegetarian**, advocated whole wheat bread and a diet based in part on whole wheat as a solution to the nation's health problems.

The 20th-century attraction to whole foods was in part a reaction to the highly processed, refined foods available to the consumer after World War II. Modern food production methods that relied on the use of chemical **fertilizers**, pesticides, and herbicides and food technologies created during World War II led to an explosion of the consumer "convenience" food products. The results were foods that were highly processed, denatured, chemically laced, nutritionally deficient, high in sodium, and refined.

The late 1960s and early 1970s was a time of questioning of the Establishment by the counterculture. The concern for good nutrition and better health through whole food loosely coincided with the anti–Vietnam War protests and the Free Speech Movement. The back-to-the-earth movement manifested itself with the overarching demand for whole food. Many, though not all, whole food proponents were vegetarians who relied upon a plant-based diet. The results were questions about the ecological soundness and long-term implications of commercially raised foods, food production practices, and the consumption of junk food, with a corresponding resurgence in the study of nutrition. These concerns led to the cultivation of backyard kitchen and vegetable gardens with an emphasis on **organic** gardening and the consumption of organic, locally grown whole foods. Whole foods were the subject of magazines, cookbooks, and health and nutritional manuals.

Adelle Davis, née Jane Dunlap (1904–1974), was a nutritional authority who wrote several best-selling guides that emphasized the health benefits of consuming whole foods. She was an outspoken critic of processed foods and their manufacturers. Davis argued that improved health was based on the knowledge of nutrition, making better food choices, and proper cooking of foods.

Consumer demand for whole foods created a new market segmentation that spawned the rise of small, independent, whole food/natural food/health food stores, markets, and cooperatives. These stores often refused to carry processed foods and products made with white refined **sugar**. Instead, they specialized in whole grains, fresh vegetables, and organic foods in their natural state as an alternative to **supermarkets**. As the demand grew, mainstream supermarkets began to stock the whole food products that were once the exclusive domain of whole food stores. By the late 1980s, the small independent natural food stores were being brought up by the behemoths of the natural food segment, notably **Whole Foods Markets**.

Whole food **restaurants** and cooperatives began springing up across the country, particularly in college towns. Young people took the lead in starting such restaurants. Notable examples included the Whole Earth Restaurant at the University of California, Santa Cruz; Moosewood Restaurant in Ithaca, New York; and Modern Times in Cambridge, Massachusetts. These restaurants and cooperatives served whole foods with an emphasis on whole grains and fresh, organic vegetables. Some restaurants were vegetarian. Popular foods included brown rice, whole wheat bread, whole grains, organic steamed vegetables, and honey-sweetened desserts, often featuring carob.

Besides whole grains, the whole food movement emphasized naturally raised, cleaner, and safer foods. Naturally and humanely raised meats and **poultry** were preferred over feedlot-raised animals fed a steady **corn**-based diet laced with **antibiotics**.

Additionally, practitioners of the whole food diet and lifestyle rejected highly processed junk foods characterized by empty calories and products loaded with white refined sugar. Whole food advocates called for the use of uncooked, unfiltered honey in the placed of sugar. Carob (St. John's Bread) was used in place of **chocolate**; nonanimal proteins, including tofu (soy bean curd), tempeh, nuts, seeds, legumes, and brewers yeast, were widely used in place of meat; an abundance of whole grains, including whole wheat, bran, wheat germ, and old-fashioned rolled oats, were substituted for refined grains; and brown rice replaced white, converted rice. Sprouts such as alfalfa sprouts were grown at home and served on sandwiches. Soy milk replaced cow's milk. Yogurt was consumed for its healthful properties and promises of longevity. Whole wheat pasta replaced semolina pasta.

Whole foods are now one of the fastest-growing segments of the grocery industry.

See also Functional Foods and Nutraceuticals.

FURTHER READINGS: Davis, Adelle. *Let's Eat Right to Keep Fit.* New York: Harcourt, Brace, 1954; Gerras, Charles, ed. *Rodale's Basic Natural Foods Cookbook.* New York: Fireside, 1984; Katzen, Mollie. *Moosewood Cookbook.* Berkeley, CA: Ten Speed Press, 1977; Lappé, Frances Moore. *Diet for a Small Planet.* New York: Ballantine Books, 1975; Shapiro, Laura. *Something from the Oven: Reinventing dinner in the 1950s.* Waterville, ME: Thorndike Press, 2004.

Madonna L. Berry

Whole Foods Market From its humble beginnings as a single store employing 19 people in Austin, Texas, Whole Foods Market (WFM) has become the world's largest **whole food** retailer, with more than 40,000 employees in nearly 200 stores across the United States, Canada, and the United Kingdom. WFM is for some an example of how an innovative business that initially catered to a fringe population can, over the course of a few decades, redefine industry standards and become a business model that others emulate.

Many of the counterculture ideas that gained a foothold during the turbulent 1960s in America continued to feed a national subculture throughout the 1970s. Among them, a heightened concern for the environment and about agricultural practices fueled interest in regarding food choice as a social and political statement. This ideology, alongside burgeoning diet and fitness concerns, facilitated a growing demand for health and **organic** foods among consumers seeking alternatives to conventional, corporate food sources.

In 1978, John Mackey opened the Safer Way Natural Foods store in Austin. Two years later, Mackey merged his business with Austin's other alternative market, Clarksville Natural Grocery, creating Whole Foods Market, one of a handful of natural food **supermarkets** in the nation at the time.

"It's my belief that most of Americans are in denial about factory farms in America. They don't want to know what's happening. They don't want to look, because they're not willing to give up meat. And it's my belief that once we can really have animal-compassionate alternatives where people can buy this product and know that the animal was well-treated during its lifetime, that then they'll be willing to look at what the factory farm is all about. I think when that happens, across the United States, there's going to be outrage about factory farms."—John Mackey, founder and CEO of Whole Foods Market

Source: Amanda Griscom Little, "The Whole Foods Shebang: An Interview with John Mackey, Founder of Whole Foods." *Grist*, December 17, 2004, http://www.grist.org/news/maindish/2004/12/17/little-mackey

---

After opening two more stores in Austin (1982, 1985) and one in Houston (1984), and acquiring a store in Dallas (1986), Mackey reached into New Orleans, acquiring the local Whole Food Company stores in 1988. By the time WFM went public early in 1992, the company had 12 stores. With capital raised by an initial public offering, expansion continued, furthering WFM's transition from a regional purveyor of specialty goods to a specialty supermarket chain with a formidable national presence. Throughout the 1990s, the maturing company merged with or acquired former competitors across the nation, including the well-established Bread & Circus chain in New England (1992), Mrs. Gooch's seven stores in Los Angeles (1993), the 22-market Fresh Fields (1996), and Florida's Bread of Life markets (1997). Most WFM outlets offer customers a plethora of prepared foods, including hot entrees, sushi, and **gourmet** baked goods, alongside perishables (produce, seafood, meat, **dairy**), dry goods, **wine**, and health and skin care products.

With nearly 70 stores, WFM sales surpassed $1 billion for the first time in 1997. Expansion continues apace into the 21st century. In May 2002, the first Canadian Whole Foods opened in Toronto. By 2007, there will be four Whole Foods stores in Manhattan.

In addition to ongoing store openings, the company acquires product lines such as Allegro **Coffee**; cultivates specialty goods, including several private-label product lines; and develops comarketing and additional retail opportunities such as aligning with lifestyle company Gaiam. From the WFM World Headquarters and flagship store in downtown Austin, cofounder, chairman, and CEO Mackey leads the company with shrewd prudence and a social conscience. WFM's stock price has fluctuated with the vagaries of the stock market and as other retailers gain market share by luring customers with organic products and ready-made foods, the hallmarks of WFM. Nonetheless, through its ongoing demand for organic goods and ethical trade, WFM continues to inform dietary patterns, **agribusiness**, and food retailing.

As quickly as the company grew, so too did specific criticisms about its New Age capitalism. Among the most frequent complaints by advocacy groups have been that WFM is more committed to generating high returns for its shareholders than to providing good wages and benefits for employees or supporting fair working conditions for farm workers; that Mackey's anti-union stance is hostile to employee rights; and that WFM's rhetoric about the importance of local sourcing is misleading. Amid cries that WFM represents gluttonous gourmet consumerism, company leadership perpetuates WFM's carefully cultivated image by highlighting the foundational principles of supporting sustainable food systems and enhancing local communities.

FURTHER READINGS: Maloney, Field. "Is Whole Foods Wholesome? The Dark Secrets of the Organic-Food Movement." *Slate*, March 17, 2006. http://www.slate.com/id/2138176; Whole Foods Market. http://www.wholefoodsmarket.com.

Pauline Adema

Williams-Sonoma Williams-Sonoma was founded in 1956, when Chuck Williams opened a French kitchenware shop in the Northern California town of Sonoma. Over the next half-century, that small store would evolve into a multibillion-dollar retailer selling products to enhance every room in the home. Today, Williams-Sonoma operates more than 250 retail stores nationwide, a direct mail business that distributes some 50 million catalogs each year, and a flourishing e-commerce site. There are over 200 Williams-Sonoma cookbook titles, with the Williams-Sonoma Kitchen Library acclaimed as one of America's best-selling cookbook series.

The company has its roots in a 1953 vacation trip to Paris, where Williams became enamored of the local cuisine. Noticing that the high-quality French cookware greatly differed from the thin metal pots and pans typically used by Americans, Williams resolved to change this.

In 1958, Williams moved his store from Sonoma to nearby San Francisco, renting space in a Sutter Street building just off Union Square, the center of the city's shopping district. The Sutter Street store, specializing in French cooking equipment, quickly became a favorite among professional chefs and discerning home cooks alike.

During the next decades, Williams continued his annual buying trips to France and expanded the store's assortment to include products from England, Germany, and Italy. However, his selection criteria remained constant, always focusing on functional items with exceptional designs. Among the iconic products Williams introduced to American home cooks over the years are the Cuisinart food processor, the KitchenAid stand mixer, and the Waring blender. Williams also popularized such once-exotic specialty foods as balsamic vinegar and Dijon mustard.

With the creative assistance of Jackie Mallorca, a local copywriter, Williams published the first Williams-Sonoma catalog in 1972. Today, the award-winning catalog is still regarded as the brand's most successful marketing tool.

With the Sutter Street store thriving and the mail-order business growing, Williams sought the advice of customer and friend Edward Marcus of the Neiman-Marcus retailing group. Working with Marcus, Williams established Williams-Sonoma in 1972. Shortly thereafter, Williams-Sonoma stores opened in the upscale California communities of Beverly Hills, Palo Alto, and Costa Mesa. In 1978, Williams sold the company to entrepreneur W. Howard Lester, who assumed the role of president and CEO.

It was Lester's capital, business expertise, and vision that expanded the Williams-Sonoma brand into a retailing empire. Credited with launching the trend of retailers as lifestyle managers, Williams-Sonoma also includes the Williams-Sonoma Home, Pottery Barn, Pottery Barn Kids, Pottery Barn Teen, and West Elm brands. Lester currently serves as chairman of the board and CEO, while Williams merits the title of founder and director emeritus. Williams-Sonoma, which was taken public in 1983, is traded on the New York Stock Exchange under the acronym WSM.

FURTHER READINGS: Brenner, Leslie. *American Appetite.* New York: Avon, 1999; Williams, Chuck. *Celebrating the Pleasures of Cooking.* San Francisco: Weldon-Owen, 1997; Williams-Sonoma. http://www.williams-sonoma.com.

Laura Martin Bacon

Wine Business In the early 21st century, there are several imperatives that define the worldwide wine trade. These include the globalization of the wine business and the emergence of worldwide "brands" of affordable and highly drinkable wines; the growing worldwide acceptance, importance, and popularity of the varietal label (the name of the grape as the name of the wine); and the emergence of the New World—North America, South America, Oceania (Australia, New Zealand), and South Africa—as an important focus of wine production and consumption. With these trends, there has been a marked decrease in both the sales of French wine and per-capita wine consumption in the traditional wine nations of France, Italy, and Spain. Furthermore, wine has emerged as the most popular alcoholic beverage in the United States, which will soon be the foremost wine-consuming nation in the world. There has also been steady interest in "international" grape varietals, especially Chardonnay, Cabernet Sauvignon, Syrah/Shiraz, Merlot, and Pinot Noir, with wines made from these grapes in both traditional (e.g., Cabernet Sauvignon in Bordeaux) and nontraditional (e.g., Cabernet Sauvignon in Tuscany) settings. At the same time, experts have become particularly concerned about the immediate and long-range impact of global climate change and global warming on grape growing and winemaking.

Globalization

Until the last two decades of the 20th century, most wines were produced and consumed within their region or country of origin, and about 85 percent of the world's wine was produced in France, Italy, and Spain. If wine consumers in other countries wanted to drink fine wines, they looked to France first, and indeed until the early 1990s, sales of wines in white-tablecloth and exclusive **restaurants** in the United States were about 85 percent European wines, most of those French. Today, these statistics have been thrown on their head and reversed.

The U.S. market is considered to be perhaps the most important wine market in the world, and today wine drinkers in the United States drink between 75 and 80 percent wines produced in this country. The remaining 20–25 percent of U.S. wine consumption is spread out chiefly among Australia, Italy, France, Spain, and Chile. Australia is the number-one exporter to the United States (and the United Kingdom) in volume, while Italy is first in dollars spent. France is now third, behind both Italy and Australia in both categories.

The United States, Great Britain, and Australia have created global wine brands through the integration of **multinational** corporations, such as Constellation (the biggest wine company in the world, based in the United States), Diageo (the second largest, based in the United Kingdom), and Beringer Blass/Foster's (third, based in Australia). Other companies, such as Allied Domecq, Pernod Ricard, LVMH, Gallo, and Vincor—among many others—have created wine brands recognized around the globe and have focused on selling premium wines—most of them with varietal labels—at affordable prices. The Australians in particular have done an extraordinary job of marketing their brands, swearing almost-religious allegiance to the concept of "under-promise and over-deliver" and thereby creating a strong culture of perceived value in their wines, no matter the price level. A single Australian brand of inexpensive varietal wines, Yellow Tail, has become the most popular imported wine in the United States.

The trend toward globalization of the wine market is continuing and expanding. The reader need only visit any of the websites of these huge corporations to find out just how many popular brands they own and control (for example, Constellation now owns the Robert Mondavi wineries and nobody named Mondavi works there anymore; Beringer, a historic winery in the Napa Valley, is owned by Beringer Blass of Australia; Pernod Ricard of France owns Jacob's Creek, a well-known Australian brand). Wineries, both large and small, are being acquired by these corporations on a near-daily basis.

Varietal Labels

Most people are much more comfortable buying a **bottle** labeled "Chardonnay" than, for instance, a white Pernand-Vergelesses (which is 100 percent Chardonnay even though the name of the grape does not appear on the label). The popularity of varietal labels has created massive problems for the French wine industry, whose best *appellation contrôlée* wines are not allowed, by law, to place the name of the varietal or varietals on the label—just the name of the place, paying obeisance to the concept of *terroir*, which posits that *the place* the grape grows is far more important than the grape itself. Only the much cheaper and abundant *vin de pays* of France sport varietal labels, but there is a flood of these wines in the international market, and much of the wine-drinking public has rejected both the style of these wines (too dry, not enough alcohol) and their prices (not as cheap as Australian or Chilean wines made from the same varietals).

Problems in the French wine industry have reached crisis proportions (it is known as *la cris viticole* in France) and have led to violent demonstrations, sabotage, and worse. The *vignerons*—grape growers and owners of small wineries—have insisted that the government provide them with more price supports, but this is a Band-aid for a cancer that is spreading. France needs to figure out a way to compete with the New World and global marketing efforts if its wine industry is to regain health. Italy and Spain have focused on creating wines that people enjoy at all prices, some of them with varietal labels and some with increasingly well known and reliable place names (e.g., Chianti Classico, Rioja).

France's loss is Australia, the United States', and South America's gain. Wines from the New World all feature familiar varietal names, especially Chardonnay, Cabernet Sauvignon, Merlot, and Shiraz (or Syrah). It is easy to find drinkable versions of these wines for less than $10, and that seems to be the trend in purchasing wines. People are happy to splurge occasionally for an expensive wine, but most of the time they seek a wine that they can open at home and enjoy with their family and friends over an informal dinner.

The Emergence of the New World, Especially the United States

Nowhere has the paradigm shift in wine production and consumption made itself more visible than in the New World, and the United States in particular. Consider that by 2009, the United States is projected to be the world's number-one wine-consuming nation. This rise in consumption represents a true sea change for a country and culture that in the past has been far more identified with **beer** and **distilled spirits**. There are now more than 5,000 wineries in the United States, and every state, including Alaska and Hawaii, takes part in that total (although more than 90 percent of U.S. wine is produced in California). Twenty-five years ago, there were about 1,500 U.S. wineries; 30 years ago, only about 250. Forty of the 50 states have commercial vineyards (wineries in the 10 others buy grapes or juice from elsewhere). The wine industry contributes more than $100 billion to the U.S. economy and provides close to 600,000 jobs.

Americans seem to love their own wines, especially, but not limited to, the wines of California. Nationwide, Americans consume about 75–80 percent domestic wines. This patriotic percentage would probably be even higher if it were not for the price-attractive wines of Australia and Chile, which are also quite popular, accounting for about 15 percent of the total U.S. wine market.

Wine is perceived as—and has been scientifically proven by physicians and researchers around the world to be—a healthy beverage, when consumed with food and in moderation. So, in the minds of many Americans, wine has become a near guilt-free pleasure.

Americans also love to dine out in restaurants, and wine is an important part of that dining experience. Traditionally, "wine destination" restaurants are perceived as white-tablecloth venues where prices can be extravagant, but today dining and wine has become a lot more egalitarian and accessible. Starting in 2004, the Olive Garden, the well-known kind-of-Italian restaurant **chain**, put together a chain-wide wine list of just 38 wines, with 33 of the wines available by the glass, all of them available to taste for free. The result: Olive Garden sells a million cases of wine per year, making the chain the number-one restaurant venue for wine sales in the entire country. Clearly, wine has become a part of eating out, whether it is to grab a pizza or burger, a bowl of pasta and a salad, or an elaborate and formal multicourse dinner.

Since the mid-1990s there has been an increase of 35–40 percent in the total wine-drinking population of the United States, driven not only by people traditionally considered to be wine drinkers—male, white, middle and upper class, middle and upper aged—but also by women (who now account for close to 65 percent of the wine purchased in the United States) and younger wine drinkers—people in their 20s and early 30s—who love to try a wide variety of wines, especially what the industry calls "adventure brands": wines with curious and humorous names. "Smashed Grapes," "Smoking Loon," "Plungerhead," "3 Blind Moose," "Fat Bastard," "Mad Housewife,"

"Screw Kappa Napa," and, of course, "Cat's Pee on a Gooseberry Bush" (a New Zealand Sauvignon Blanc) are just eight examples among hundreds of such brands. These wines are tasty and fun and are also attractively priced for the "adventurous" wine consumer, usually less than $12 per bottle (although a bottle of California's "Used Automobile Parts" is $50).

Exports of American wines have grown exponentially and now stand at about $1 billion per year. About 60 percent of this wine is sold to the countries that make up the **European Union**, even though the European wine industry is heavily subsidized by government and very tough taxes and **tariffs** are placed on U.S. wines imported to EU member nations. In addition, Canada, Japan, and Mexico, the top three non-EU export markets, account for more than $225 million, or more than 20 percent of total wine exports. Ironically, U.S. per-capita wine consumption still is quite low, even when compared to the sliding European figures (an average of about 13 gallons per capita annually in Italy, France, and Spain, but only a little more than 2 gallons in the United States). However, the combined population of Italy, France, and Spain is about 160 million; the population of the United States is about 300 million. While the U.S. appears to have a growing and dedicated core of wine drinkers, less than 15 percent of American wine drinkers consume more than 45 percent of total wine consumed in our country. What this means is that the market has a lot of room to grow in both per-capita and total consumption, and since 1996 there has been steady annual growth in one or both of these metrics.

The Napa Valley is the hottest tourist destination in California (Disneyland is second). In addition, more than 750,000 people per year visit the vineyards and wineries of Virginia, and the spectacular Biltmore Estate vineyards and winery, located in Asheville, North Carolina, is the most visited winery in the United States. Wineries and vineyards have become tourist destinations, and wine has become a prominent symbol of a sophisticated, relaxed, and enjoyable American lifestyle, both at home and in restaurants.

Climate Change and Global Warming

In March 2006, the first conference of wine and global warming was held in Barcelona, Spain, and the information shared by climate scientists and winegrowers was sobering. Spain and Portugal are already suffering the impact of global warming to the point where winegrowers either cannot grow their classic grape varietals because they shrivel in the intense heat or have had to invest millions of euros to move their vineyards to higher ground where the vines can enjoy cool air currents. Winegrowers at the conference testified that they cannot control the sugars in their grapes and are making wines that do not come close to expressing true varietal character (the typical taste profiles of Syrah or Chardonnay, for example), much less a sense of place, the terroir of the vine.

The predictions by conference participants for the future of winegrowing, and by extension, agriculture, were uniformly dire. Large areas of central Spain that have now endured three straight years of drought are fast becoming a vast desert and will not be able to sustain life, much less grapes, possibly within 20 years; oceanic events will have greater impact on soils than greenhouse emissions as changes in climate will concentrate rainfall, creating flood conditions followed by drought conditions, necessitating sophisticated irrigation systems—now illegal in Europe's finest wine regions—in order to keep grape quality and flavor complexity high. An increase of just 1°C will deplete worldwide water resources by at least 15 percent by 2030; a rise of 2.5°C will mean a further 17 percent depletion by 2060 at current rates. In Europe, the average increase is more than 2°C by 2030; in Portugal, it's more than 4.5°C.

In 20 to 30 years, the Burgundy region of France will be too warm to plant its classic prized varietal, Pinot Noir, and might think about switching to Cabernet Sauvignon, because its climate will mirror today's warmer Bordeaux. Bordeaux, which will resemble the current Valencia, Spain, has to think about planting Syrah and Grenache, now grown in the much-warmer Rhône region. Southern England, usually considered too cool a region for anything but sparkling wines, may become a leading wine region, along with Canada, in the world of global warming. In California, the Napa Valley will become as warm as Stockton in the very warm Central Valley. Stockton will become warmer, as warm as Bakersfield. Barring genetic manipulation of grapes, much of California will become a wine wasteland.

See also Culinary Tourism; Gourmet Foods.

FURTHER READINGS: Kolpan, Steven, Brian Smith, and Michael Weiss. *Exploring Wine: The Culinary Institute of America's Complete Guide to Wines of the World.* 2nd ed. New York: Van Nostrand Reinhold, 2001.

Steven Kolpan

SELECTED BIBLIOGRAPHY

Books

Acs, Zoltan J., and Alan Lyles, eds. *Obesity, Business and Public Policy.* Northampton, MA: Edward Elgar, 2007.

Alberts, Robert C. *The Good Provider: H. J. Heinz and His 57 Varieties.* Boston: Houghton Mifflin, 1973.

Allen, Frederick. *Secret Formula: How Brilliant Marketing and Relentless Salesmanship Made Coca-Cola the Best-known Product in the World.* New York: HarperBusiness, 1994.

Allen, Gary. *Resource Guide for Food Writers.* New York: Routledge, 1999.

———. *The Herbalist in the Kitchen.* Urbana: University of Illinois Press, 2007.

Almond, Steve. *Candyfreak: A Journey through the Chocolate Underbelly of America.* Chapel Hill, NC: Algonquin Books, 2004.

American Poultry Historical Society. *American Poultry History, 1823–1973.* Madison, WI: American Poultry Historical Society, 1974.

Anderson, Oscar Edward. *Refrigeration in America: A History of a New Technology and Its Impact.* Princeton, NJ: University of Cincinnati by Princeton University Press, 1972.

Angelo, Rocco M., and Andrew N. Vladimir. *Hospitality Today: An Introduction.* 5th ed. Lansing, MI: American Hotel & Lodging Association Educational Institute, 2004.

Antle, John M., and Vincent H. Smith. *The Economics of World Wheat Markets.* Wallingford, Oxon, U.K.: CABI, 1999.

Avakian, Arlene Voski, and Barbara Haber, eds. *From Betty Crocker to Feminist Food Studies: Critical Perspectives on Women and Food.* Amherst: University of Massachusetts Press, 2005.

Avise, John. *The Hope, Hype and Reality of Genetic Engineering.* New York: Oxford University Press, 2004.

Bailey, Kenneth W. *Marketing and Pricing of Milk and Dairy Products in the United States.* Ames: Iowa State University Press, 1997.

Bajaj, Y. P. S., ed. *Wheat.* Berlin: Springer-Verlag, 1990.

Belasco, Warren. *Appetite for Change: How the Counterculture Took on the Food Industry, 1966–1988.* New York: Pantheon, 1989.

Beller, Anne Scott. *Fat and Thin: A Natural History of Obesity*. New York: Farrar, Straus, & Giroux, 1977.

Bijlefeld, Marjolijn, and Sharon K. Zoumbaris. *Food and You: A Guide to Healthy Habits for Teens*. Westport, CT: Greenwood Press, 2001.

Birkeland, Peter M. *Franchising Dreams: The Lure of Entrepreneurship in America*. Chicago: University of Chicago Press, 2002.

Boas, Max, and Steve Chain. *Big Mac: The Unauthorized Story of McDonald's*. New York: New American Library, 1977.

Borém, Aluizio, Fabrício R. Santos, and David E. Bowen. *Understanding Biotechnology*. Upper Saddle River, NJ: Prentice Hall, 2003.

Bottéro, Jean. *The Oldest Cuisine in the World: Cooking in Mesopotamia*. Trans. Teresa Lavender Fagan. Chicago: University of Chicago Press, 2004.

Bray, George A. *The Battle of the Bulge: A History of Obesity*. Pittsburgh, PA: Dorrance, 2006.

Brenner, Joël Glenn. *The Emperors of Chocolate: Inside the Secret World of Hershey and Mars*. New York: Broadway Books, 2000.

Brenner, Leslie. *American Appetite*. New York: Avon, 1999.

Brinson, Carroll. *A Tradition of Looking Ahead: The Story of Bryan Foods*. Jackson, MS: Oakdale Press, 1986.

Brown, Amy C. *Understanding Food: Principles and Preparation*. Belmont, CA: Wadsworth/Thompson Learning, 2004.

Brownstein, Bill. *Schwartz's Hebrew Delicatessen: The Story*. Montreal: Véhicule Press, 2006.

Bruce, Scott, and Bill Crawford. *Cerealizing America: The Unsweetened Story of American Breakfast Cereal*. Boston: Faber & Faber, 1995.

Burrough, Bryan, and John Helyar. *Barbarians at the Gate: The Fall of RJR Nabisco*. New York: Harper & Row, 1990.

Cahn, William. *Out of the Cracker Barrel: From Animal Crackers to ZuZu's*. New York: Simon & Schuster, 1969.

California's Finest: The History of Del Monte Corporation and the Del Monte Brand. San Francisco: Del Monte Corporation, 1982.

Campos, Paul. *The Obesity Myth: Why America's Obsession with Weight Is Hazardous to Your Health*. New York: Gotham Books, 2004.

Carlson, Laurie Winn. *Cattle: An Informal Social History*. Chicago: Ivan R. Dee, 2001.

Carney, George O., ed. *Fast Food, Stock Cars, and Rock 'n' Roll: Place and Space in American Pop Culture*. Lanham, MD: Rowman & Littlefield, 1995.

Casual and Fine Dining. Washington, DC: National Restaurant Association, 1990.

Chase, Chria. *The Great American Waistline: Putting It On and Taking It Off*. New York: Coward, McCann & Geoghegan, 1981.

Child, Julia, Louisette Bertholle, and Simone Beck. *Mastering the Art of French Cooking*. New York: Knopf, 1961.

Cho, John. *Spam-Ku: Tranquil Reflections on Luncheon Loaf*. New York: Harper Perennial, 1998.

Coe, Sophie D., and Michael D. Coe. *The True History of Chocolate*. London: Thames & Hudson, 1996.

Cohen, Lizabeth. *A Consumers' Republic: The Politics of Mass Consumption in Postwar America*. New York: Alfred A. Knopf, 2003.

Cohen, Rich. *Sweet and Low: A Family Story.* New York: Farrar, Straus, & Giroux, 2006.

Coles, R., D. McDowell, and M. Kirwan, eds. *Food Packaging Technology.* London: Blackwell, 2003.

Collins, Douglas. *America's Favorite Food: The Story of Campbell Soup Company.* New York: Harry N. Abrams, 1994.

Collins, James H. *The Story of Canned Foods.* New York: E. P. Dutton, 1924.

Counihan, Carole M. *Food in the U.S.A.: A Reader.* New York: Routledge, 2002.

Cowen, Ruth. *Relish: The Extraordinary Life of Alexis Soyer, Victorian Celebrity Chef.* London: Wiedenfeld & Nicolson, 2006.

Critser, Greg. *Fat Land: How Americans Became the Fattest People in the World.* New York: Houghton Mifflin, 2003.

Cronon, William. *Nature's Metropolis: Chicago and the Great West.* New York: W. W. Norton, 1991.

Cross, Gary. *An All-Consuming Century: Why Commercialism Won in Modern America.* New York: Columbia University Press, 2000.

Cummings, Richard O. *The American Ice Harvests: A Historical Study in Technology, 1800–1918.* Berkeley: University of California Press, 1949.

Datamonitor USA. *Fast Food in the United States: Industry Profile.* New York: Datamonitor USA, 2006.

David, Elizabeth. *Harvest of the Cold Months.* New York: Viking Penguin, 1995.

Davis, Adelle. *Let's Eat Right to Keep Fit.* New York: Harcourt, Brace, 1954.

Davis, John, and Ray Goldberg. *A Concept of Agribusiness.* Cambridge, MA: Harvard University, Division of Research, Graduate School of Business Administration, 1957.

Davis, Karen. *Prisoned Chickens, Poisoned Eggs: An Inside Look at the Modern Poultry Industry.* Summertown, TN: Book Publishing Company, 1996.

Davis, Karen. *More than a Meal: The Turkey in History, Myth, Ritual and Reality.* New York: Lantern Books, 2001.

Denker, Joel. *The World on a Plate: A Tour through the History of America's Ethnic Cuisine.* Boulder, CO: Westview Press, 2003.

Dicke, Thomas S. *Franchising in America: The Development of a Business Method, 1840–1980.* Chapel Hill: University of North Carolina Press, 1992.

Drinnon, Elizabeth McGants. *Stuckey: The Biography of Williamson Sylvester Stuckey, 1909–1977.* Macon, GA: Mercer University Press, 1997.

Drysdale, J. *Foodservice Equipment: Operation, Sanitation, and Maintenance.* Overland Park, KS: Hospitality Publishing, 2002.

DuBoff, Leonard D., and Christy O. King. *The Law (in Plain English) for Restaurants and Others in the Food Industry.* Naperville, IL: Sphinx, 2006.

Dumas, Lynne S. *Elephants in My Backyard: Alex Aidekman's Own Story of Founding the Pathmark Supermarket Powerhouse.* New York: Vantage Press, 1988.

DuPuis, E. Melanie. *Nature's Perfect Food: How Milk Became America's Drink.* New York: New York University Press, 2002.

Dyer, Betsey Dexter. *A Field Guide to Bacteria.* Ithaca, NY: Cornell University Press, 2003.

Edid, Marilyn. *Farm Labor Organizing: Trends and Prospects.* Ithaca, NY: ILR Press, 1994.

Ellis, Alice Thomas. *Fish, Flesh and Good Red Herring.* New York: Virago, 2006.

Ellis, Harry E. *Dr Pepper: King of Beverages Centennial Edition.* Dallas: Dr Pepper Company, 1986.

Enrico, Roger, and Jesse Kornbluth. *The Other Guy Blinked: How Pepsi Won the Cola Wars.* New York: Bantam, 1986.

Federal Trade Commission and Department of Health and Human Services. *Perspectives on Marketing Self-Regulation and Childhood Obesity.* Washington, DC: GPO, 2006.

Fildes, Valerie. *Breasts, Bottles and Babies: History of Infant Feeding.* Edinburgh: Edinburgh University Press, 1986.

Fischer, John W. *At Your Service: A Hands-on Guide to the Professional Dining Room.* Hoboken, NJ: Wiley, 2005.

Fishwick, Marshall, ed. *Ronald Revisited: The World of Ronald McDonald.* Bowling Green, IN: Bowling Green University Popular Press, 1983.

Fitzgerald, Deborah. *Every Farm a Factory: The Industrial Ideal in American Agriculture.* New Haven, CT: Yale University Press, 2003.

Fleming, Ciji A., and Richard K. Miller. *The 2005 Restaurant and Foodservice Market Research Handbook.* 6th ed. Loganville, GA: Richard K. Miller & Associates, 2005.

Frank, Dana. *Bananeras: Women Transforming the Banana Unions of Latin America.* Boston: South End Press, 2005.

Fraser, Gary E. *Diet, Life Expectancy, and Chronic Disease: Studies of Seventh-Day Adventists and other Vegetarians.* Oxford: Oxford University Press, 2003.

Fraser, Laura. *Losing It: America's Obsession with Weight and the Industry That Feeds on It.* New York: Dutton, 1997.

French, Michael, and Jim Phillips. *Cheated Not Poisoned? Food Regulation in the United Kingdom, 1875–1938.* New York: St. Martin's Press, 2000.

Friedman, M. *Consumer Boycotts.* New York: Routledge, 1999.

Fromartz, Samuel. *Organic, Inc.: Natural Foods and How They Grew.* New York: Harvest Books, 2007.

Fuller, Gordon. *New Food Product Development: From Concept to Marketplace.* Boca Raton, FL: CRC Press, 2005.

Funderburg, Anne Cooper. *Chocolate, Strawberry, and Vanilla.* Bowling Green, OH: Bowling Green State University Popular Press, 1995.

Fussell, Betty. *The Story of Corn: The Myths and History, the Culture and Agriculture, the Art and Science of America's Quintessential Crop.* New York: Alfred A. Knopf, 1992.

Gabaccia, Donna. *We Are What We Eat: Ethnic Food and the Making of Americans.* Cambridge, MA: Harvard University Press, 1998.

Gardner, Gary. *Underfed and Overfed: The Global Epidemic of Malnutrition.* Washington, DC: World Watch, 2000.

Gardner, Stephen. "Litigation as a Tool in Food Advertising: A Consumer Advocacy Viewpoint." *Loyola (Los Angeles) Law Review* 39 (2006): 101–20.

Gereffi, Gary, and Miguel Korzeniewicz, eds. *Commodity Chains and Global Capitalism.* Westport, CT: Greenwood Press, 1994.

Gerras, Charles, ed. *Rodale's Basic Natural Foods Cookbook.* New York: Fireside, 1984.

Global Strategy for Infant and Young Child Feeding. Geneva: World Health Organization, 2002.

Godlovitch, Stanley, Rosalind Godlovitch, and John Harris, eds. *Animals, Men, and Morals: An Enquiry into the Maltreatment of Non-humans.* New York: Tablinger, 1972.

Greising, David. *I'd Like the World to Buy a Coke: The Life and Leadership of Roberto Goizueta.* New York: Wiley, 1998.

Gutman, Richard J. S. *American Diner Then and Now.* Baltimore: Johns Hopkins University Press, 2000.

Harris, Jessica. *Iron Pots and Wooden Spoons.* 1st Fireside ed. New York: Simon & Schuster, 1999.

Hawkes, Corinna. *Nutrition Labels and Health Claims: The Global Regulatory Environment.* Geneva: World Health Organization, 2004.

Hays, Constance L. *The Real Thing: Truth and Power at the Coca-Cola Company.* New York: Random House, 2005.

Heasman, Michael, and Mellentin, Julian. *The Functional Foods Revolution: Healthy People, Healthy Profits?* London: Earthscan, 2001.

Heffer, Patrick, and Prud'homme, Michel. *World Agriculture and Fertilizer Demand, Global Fertilizer Supply and Trade, 2006–2007, Summary Report.* International Fertilizer Industry Association. Paris, 2007.

Heijbroek, Arend. *The Fighting Spirits: In a Competitive Mood.* n.p.: Netherlands: Rabobank, 2004.

Higgins, Cindy. *Kansas Breweries and Beer, 1854–1911.* Eudora, KS: Ad Astra Press, 1992.

Higgins, Vaughn, and Geoffrey Lawrence, eds. *Agricultural Governance: Globalization and the New Politics of Regulation.* London: Routledge, 2005.

Hightower, Jim. *Hard Tomatoes, Hard Times: A Report of the Agribusiness Accountability Project on the Failure of America's Land Grant College.* Cambridge, MA: Schenkman, 1973.

Hine, Thomas. *The Total Package: The Evolution and Secret Meanings of Boxes, Bottles, Cans and Tubes.* Boston: Little, Brown, 1995.

Hollis, Tim. *Dixie before Disney: 100 Years of Roadside Fun.* Jackson: University Press of Mississippi, 1999.

Horowitz, Roger. *Putting Meat on the American Table: Taste, Technology, Transformation.* Baltimore: Johns Hopkins University Press, 2006.

Hughes, Alex, and Suzanne Reimer, eds. *Geographies of Commodity Chains.* London: Routledge, 2004.

Humble, Nicola. *Culinary Pleasures: Cookbooks and the Transformation of British Food.* London: Faber & Faber, 2005.

Humphrey, Kim. *Shelf Life: Supermarkets and the Changing Culture of Consumption.* Cambridge: Cambridge University Press, 1998.

Hurst, Peter. *Agricultural Workers and Their Contribution to Sustainable Agriculture and Rural Development.* New York: FAO/ILO/IUF, 2005.

Iacobbo, Karen, and Michael Iacobbo. *Vegetarians and Vegans in America Today.* Westport, CT: Praeger, 2006.

Ingco, Merlinda D., and L. Alan Winters, eds. *Agriculture and the New Trade Agenda: Creating a Global Trading Environment for Development.* Cambridge: Cambridge University Press, 2004.

Inness, Sherrie A., ed. *Kitchen Culture in America.* Philadelphia: University of Pennsylvania Press, 2001.

Institute of Medicine. *Food Marketing to Children and Youth: Threat or Opportunity?* Washington, DC: National Academies Press, 2005.

Jacobson, Michael F. *Liquid Candy: How Soft Drinks Are Harming Americans' Health.* 2nd ed. Washington, DC: Center for Science in the Public Interest, 2005.

Jacobson, Michael F., and Bruce Maxwell. *What Are We Feeding Our Kids?* New York: Workman, 1994.

Jakle, John A., and Keith A. Sculle. *Fast Food: Roadside Restaurants in the Automobile Age.* Baltimore: Johns Hopkins University Press, 1999.

Jansen, Kees, and Sietze Vellama. *Agribusiness and Society: Corporate Responses to Environmentalism, Market Opportunities and Public Regulation.* New York: Zed Books, 2004.

Johnson, H. M., ed. *2005 Annual Report on the United States Seafood Industry.* Jacksonville, OR: Howard M. Johnson Publishing, 2005.

Jones, Evan. *Epicurean Delight: The Life and Times of James Beard.* New York: Alfred A. Knopf, 1990.

Kahn, Barbara E., and Leigh McAlister. *Grocery Revolution: The New Focus on the Consumer.* Reading, MA: Addison Wesley Longman, 1997.

Kamp, David. *The United States of Arugula: How We Became a Gourmet Nation.* New York: Broadway, 2006.

Kanigel, Robert. *The One Best Way: Frederick Winslow Taylor and the Enigma of Efficiency.* New York: Viking, 1997.

Katzen, Mollie. *Moosewood Cookbook.* Berkeley, CA: Ten Speed Press, 1977.

Kelly, Ian. *Cooking for Kings: The Life of Antonin Carême, the First Celebrity Chef.* New York: Walker, 2004.

Kern-Foxworth, Marilyn. *Aunt Jemima, Uncle Ben, and Rastus: Blacks in Advertising, Yesterday, Today and Tomorrow.* Westport, CT: Praeger, 1994.

Kirshenblatt-Gimblett, Barbara. *Destination Culture: Tourism, Museums, and Heritage.* Berkeley: University of California Press, 1998.

Kloppenburg, Jack Ralph, Jr. *First the Seed: The Political Economy of Plant Biotechnology, 1492–2000.* 2nd ed. Madison: University of Wisconsin Press, 2006.

Kroc, Ray, with Robert Anderson. *Grinding It Out: The Making of McDonald's.* Chicago: Regnery, 1977.

Kuh, Patric. *The Last Days of Haute Cuisine.* New York: Viking Press, 2001.

Kummer, Corby. *The Pleasures of Slow Food: Celebrating Authentic Traditions, Flavors, and Recipes.* San Francisco: Chronicle Books, 2002.

Kushner, Robert F., and Daniel H. Bessesen. *Treatment of the Obese Patient.* Totowa, NJ: Humana Press, 2007.

Labelle, Julie. "A Recipe for Connectedness: Bringing Production and Consumption with Slow Food." *Food, Culture & Society* 7, no. 2 (2004): 81–96.

Landy, Marc K., Marc J. Roberts, and Stephen R. Thomas. *The Environmental Protection Agency: Asking the Wrong Questions.* New York: Oxford University Press, 1990.

Lappé, Frances Moore. *Diet for a Small Planet.* New York: Ballantine Books, 1975.

Lea, Andrew G. H., and John R. Piggott, eds. *Fermented Beverage Production.* 2nd ed. New York: Kluwer Academic/Plenum, 2003.

Lebowitz, Daniel. *The Great Book of Chocolate: The Chocolate Lover's Guide, with Recipes.* Berkeley, CA: Ten Speed Press, 2004.

Leech, Harper. *Armour and His Times.* New York: D. Appleton-Century Co., 1938.

Leidner, Robin. *Fast Food, Fast Talk: Service Work and Routinization of Everyday Life.* Berkeley: University of California Press, 1993.

Levenson, Barry M. *Habeas Codfish: Reflections on Food and the Law.* Madison: University of Wisconsin Press, 2001.

Levenstein, Harvey. 1989. *Revolution at the Table: Transformation of the American Diet.* New York: Oxford University Press, 1989.

Levinson, Marc. *Guide to Financial Markets.* 3rd ed. Princeton, NJ: Bloomberg Press, 2003.

Lewis, Jerre, and Leslie Renn. *How to Start and Manage a Fertilizer and Pesticide Business.* Interlochen, MI: Lewis and Renn Associates, 2004.

Lewis, Len. *The Trader Joe's Adventure: Turning a Unique Approach to Business into a Retail and Cultural Phenomenon.* Chicago: Dearborn Trade, 2005.

Lien, Marianne Elisabeth, and Brigitte Nerlich, eds. *The Politics of Food.* New York: Berg, 2004.

Long, Lucy, ed. *Culinary Tourism: Eating and Otherness.* Lexington: University Press of Kentucky, 2004.

Louis, J. C., and Harvey Yazijian. *The Cola Wars: The Story of the Global Corporate Battle between the Coca-Cola Company and PepsiCo.* New York: Everest House, 1980.

Love, John F. *McDonald's: Behind the Arches.* Rev. ed. New York: Bantam Books, 1995.

Lovegren, Sylvia. *Fashionable Food: Seven Decades of Food Fads.* Chicago: University of Chicago Press, 2005.

Magdoff, Fred, John Bellamy Foster, and Frederick H. Buttel. *Hungry for Profit: The Agribusiness Threat to Farmers, Food, and the Environment.* New York: Monthly Review Press, 2000.

Mahoney, David J. *Growth and Social Responsibility: The Story of Norton Simon Inc.* New York: Newcomen Society in North America, 1973.

Mangels, Reed, Virginia Kisch Messina, and Mark Messina. *The Dietitian's Guide to Vegetarian Diets.* 2nd ed. Sudbury, MA: Jones and Bartlett, 2004.

Manley, Duncan J. R. *Technology of Biscuits, Crackers, and Cookies.* 3rd ed. Boca Raton, FL: CRC Press/Woodhead, 2000.

Manring, M. M. *Slave in a Box: The Strange Career of Aunt Jemima.* Charlottesville: University Press of Virginia, 1998.

Mariani, John F. *America Eats Out: An Illustrated History of Restaurants, Taverns, Coffee Shops, Speakeasies, and Other Establishments That Have Fed Us for 350 years.* New York: Morrow, 1991.

Marks, Susan. *Finding Betty Crocker: The Secret Life of America's First Lady of Food.* New York: Simon & Schuster, 2005.

Marnell, William H. *Once upon a Store: A Biography of the World's First Supermarket.* New York: Herder & Herder, 1971.

Martin, Roy E., and George Flick, ed. *The Seafood Industry.* New York: Van Nostrand Reinhold, 1990.

Mason, Laura. *Sugar-Plums and Sherbet: The Prehistory of Sweets.* Totnes, Devon, U.K.: Prospect Books, 2004.

Matz, Samuel A. *Snack Food Technology.* 3rd ed. New York: AVI Van Nostrand Reinhold, 1993.

May, Earl Chapin. *The Canning Clan: A Pageant of Pioneering Americans.* New York: Macmillan, 1937.

Mayo, James M. *The American Grocery Store: The Business Evolution of an Architectural Space.* Westport, CT: Greenwood Press, 1993.

McCool, Audrey C. *Inflight Catering Management.* New York: Wiley, 1995.

McDonald, Ronald L. *Ronald McDonald's Franchise Buyers Guide: How to Buy a Fast Food Franchise.* Philadelphia: Xlibris, 2003.

McGee, Harold. *On Food and Cooking.* 2nd ed. New York: Scribner, 2004.

McIlhenny, Paul, with Barbara Hunter. *The Tabasco Brand Cookbook: 125 Years of America's Favorite Pepper Sauce.* New York: Gramercy Books, 1993.

McLaren, Charles. *Scotch Whisky.* London: Octopus, 2002.

McPhee, John. *Oranges.* New York: Farrar, Strauss, & Giroux, 1966. Reprint, New York: Noonday Press, 1994.

Meyers, Herbert M., and Murray J. Lubliner. *The Marketer's Guide to Successful Package Design.* Chicago: NTC Business Books, 1998.

Mintz, Joel A. *Enforcement at the EPA: High Stakes and Hard Choices.* Austin: University of Texas Press, 1995.

Mintz, Sidney. *Sweetness and Power: The Place of Sugar in Modern History.* New York: Viking, 1985.

———. *Tasting Food, Tasting Freedom.* Boston: Beacon Press, 1996.

Mobius, Mark. *Equities: An Introduction to the Core Concepts.* Singapore: Wiley, 2007.

Moore, Elizabeth S. *It's Child's Play: Advergaming and the Online Marketing of Food to Children.* Menlo Park, CA: Kaiser Family Foundation, 2006.

Nasrallah, Nawal. *Delights from the Garden of Eden.* Bloomington, IN: 1stBooks, 2003.

National Research Council. *Nutrient Requirements of Dogs and Cats.* Washington, DC: National Academies Press, 2006.

National Restaurant Association Educational Foundation. *Servsafe Essentials.* 4th ed. Chicago: National Restaurant Association Educational Foundation, 2006.

Neaver, Louis E. V. *NAFTA's Second Decade: Assessing Opportunities in the Mexican and Canadian Markets.* Mason, OH: Thomson/South-Western, 2004.

Nelson, Daniel, ed. *A Mental Revolution: Scientific Management since Taylor.* Columbus: Ohio State University Press, 1992.

———. *Frederick W. Taylor and the Rise of Scientific Management.* Madison: University of Wisconsin Press, 1980.

Nestle, Marion. *Food Politics: How the Food Industry Influences Nutrition and Health.* 2nd ed. Berkeley: University of California Press, 2007.

———. *Safe Food: Bacteria, Biotechnology, and Bioterrorism.* Berkeley: University of California Press, 2003.

———. *What to Eat: An Aisle-by-Aisle Guide to Savvy Food Choices and Great Eating.* New York: North Point Press, 2006.

Ninemeier, Jack D., and Joe Perdue. *Hospitality Operations: Careers in the World's Greatest Industry.* Upper Saddle River, NJ: Pearson Prentice Hall, 2005.

Okun, Mitchell. *Fair Play in the Marketplace: The First Battle for Pure Food and Drugs.* De Kalb: Northern Illinois University Press, 1986.

Oliver, J. Eric. *Fat Politics: The Real Story behind America's Obesity Epidemic.* New York: Oxford University Press, 2005.

Packaged Facts. *The Condiments Market.* New York: Packaged Facts, 1991.

Paige, Howard. *Aspects of African American Foodways.* Southfield, MI: Aspects, 1999.

Panschar, William G. *Baking in America.* Evanston, IL: Northwestern University Press, 1956.

Papazian, Charlie. *The Complete Joy of Homebrewing.* 3rd ed. New York: Quill, 2003.

Parasecoli, Fabio. *Food Culture in Italy.* Westport, CT: Greenwood Press, 2004.

Parkin, Katherine. *Food Is Love: Advertising and Gender Roles in Modern America.* Philadelphia: University of Pennsylvania Press, 2006.

Parsa, H. G., and Francis A. Kwansa, eds. *Quick Service Restaurants, Franchising, and Multi-unit Chain Management.* New York: Haworth Hospitality Press, 2002.

Patton, Stuart. *Milk: Its Remarkable Contribution to Human Health and Well-being.* New Brunswick, NJ: Transaction, 2004.

Pearce, John Ed. *The Colonel: The Captivating Biography of the Dynamic Founder of a Fast-Food Empire.* Garden City, NY: Doubleday, 1982.

Pendergrast, Mark. *For God, Country and Coca-Cola.* New York: Scribner's, 1993.

Perren, Richard. *Taste, Trade and Technology: The Development of the International Meat Industry since 1840.* Aldershot, U.K.: Ashgate, 2006.

Peter, J. Paul, and James H. Donnelly Jr. *A Preface to Marketing Management.* 8th ed. Boston: Irwin/McGraw-Hill, 2000.

Petrini, Carlo, ed. *Slow Food: Collected Thoughts on Taste, Tradition, and the Honest Pleasures of Food.* White River Junction, VT: Chelsea Green, 2001.

———. *Slow Food: The Case for Taste.* New York: Columbia University Press, 2004.

Petrini, Carlo, and Gigi Padovani. *Slow Food Revolution.* New York: Rizzoli, 2006.

Pillsbury, Richard. *From Boarding House to Bistro: The American Restaurant Then and Now.* Boston: Unwin Hyman, 1990.

Planck, Nina. *Real Food: What to Eat and Why.* New York: Bloomsbury USA, 2006.

Playfair, John. *Living with Germs: In Sickness and in Health.* New York: Oxford University Press, 2004.

Pohl, Kathy, ed. *Pillsbury Annual Recipes, 2006.* Minneapolis, MN: Taste of Home Books, 2006.

Pollack, Penny, and Jeff Ruby. *Everybody Loves Pizza: The Deep Dish on America's Favorite Food.* Cincinnati, OH: Emmis Books, 2005.

Pollan, Michael. *The Omnivore's Dilemma: A Natural History of Four Meals.* New York: Penguin, 2006.

Powers, Tom, and Clayton W. Barrows. *Introduction to Management in the Hospitality Industry.* 8th ed. Hoboken, NJ: Wiley, 2006.

Quarles, John. *Cleaning Up America: An Insider's View of the Environmental Protection Agency.* Boston: Houghton Mifflin, 1976.

Raeburn, Paul. *The Last Harvest: The Genetic Gamble That Threatens to Destroy American Agriculture.* New York: Simon & Schuster, 1995.

Rama, Ruth. *Multinational Agribusinesses.* New York: Food Product Press, 2005.

Ray, Bibek. *Fundamental Food Microbiology.* 2nd ed. New York: CRC Press, 2001.

Richardson, Gordon L. *Food Packaging: Principles and Practice.* New York: Marcel Dekker, 1993.

Richardson, Tim. *Sweets: A History of Candy.* New York: Bloomsbury, 2002.

Rifkin, Jeremy. *Beyond Beef: The Rise and Fall of Cattle Culture.* New York: Dutton Books, 1992.

Rinzler, Carol Ann. *The New Complete Book of Herbs, Spices, and Condiments: A Nutritional, Medical and Culinary Guide.* New York: Checkmark Books, 2001.

Ritzer, George. *The McDonaldization of Society*. Rev. ed. Thousand Oaks, CA: Pine Forge Press, 2004.

Robert, Maryse. *Negotiating NAFTA: Explaining the Outcome in Culture, Textiles, Autos, and Pharmaceuticals*. Toronto: University of Toronto Press, 2000.

Rodengen, Jeffrey L. *The Legend of Dr Pepper/Seven-Up*. Ft. Lauderdale, FL: Write Stuff Syndicate, 1995.

Root, Waverly, and Richard de Rochemont. *Eating in America: A History*. New York: Ecco Press.

Rossant, Juliette. *Super Chef: The Making of the Great Modern Restaurant Empires*. New York: Simon & Schuster, 2004.

Royle, Tony. *Labour Relations in the Global Fast Food Industry*. London: Routledge, 2002.

———. *Working for McDonald's in Europe: The Unequal Struggle?* New York: Routledge, 2001.

Rozin, Elisabeth. *Ethnic Cuisine: The Flavor-Principle Cookbook*. Lexington, MA: Stephen Greene Press, 1983.

Russell, Cheryl. *Best Customers: Demographics of Consumer Demand*. 2nd ed. Ithaca, NY: New Strategist Publications, 2004.

Sacharow, Stanley, and Roger C. Griffin Jr. *Principles of Food Packaging*. 2nd ed. Westport, CT: AVI, 1980.

Saffron, Inge. *Caviar: The Strange History and Uncertain Future of the World's Most Coveted Delicacy*. New York: Broadway, 2003.

Said, Edward W. *Culture and Imperialism*. New York: Knopf, 1993. Reprint, New York: Vintage, 1994.

Salyers, Abigail A., and Dixie D. Whitt. *Revenge of the Microbes: How Bacterial Resistance Is Undermining the Antibiotic Miracle*. Washington, DC: ASM Press, 2005.

Sanders, Harland. *Life as I Have Known It Has Been Finger Lickin' Good*. Carol Stream, IL: Creation House, 1974.

Sargent, Ted. *The Dance of Molecules: How Nanotechnology Is Changing Our Lives*. New York: Penguin, 2005.

Sawyer, Gordon. *The Agribusiness Poultry Industry: A History of Its Development*. New York: Exposition Press, 1971.

Schenone, Laura. *A Thousand Years over a Hot Stove: A History of American Women Told through Food, Recipes and Remembrances*. New York: W. W. Norton, 2003.

Scheuring, Ann Foley. *Eighty Years of Excellence: A History of Diamond Walnut Growers, 1912–1992*. Stockton, CA: Diamond Walnut Growers, 1997.

Schilter, Benoit, and Anne Constable. "Regulatory Control of Genetically Modified (GM) Foods: Likely Developments. *Toxicology Letters* 127 (2002): 341–49.

Schlosser, Eric. *Fast Food Nation: The Dark Side of the All-American Meal*. New York: Perennial, 2002.

Schremp, Gerry. *Kitchen Culture: Fifty Years of Food Fads*. New York: Pharos Books, 1991.

Schwartz, Hillel. *Never Satisfied: A Cultural History of Diets, Fantasies and Fat*. New York: Free Press, 1986.

Schwartz, Marvin. *Tyson from Farm to Market: The Remarkable Story of Tyson Foods*. Fayetteville: University of Arkansas Press, 1991.

Segrave, Kerry. *Vending Machines: An American Social History*. Jefferson, NC: McFarland, 2002.

Seth, Andrew, and Geoffrey Randall. *The Grocers: The Rise and Rise of the Supermarket Chains.* 2nd ed. Dover, NH: Kogan Page, 2001.

———. *Supermarket Wars: Global Strategies for Food Retailers.* New York: Palgrave Macmillan, 2005.

Shapiro, Laura. *Perfection Salad: Women and Cooking at the Turn of the Century.* New York: Farrar, Straus, & Giroux, 1986.

Shapiro, Laura. *Something from the Oven: Reinventing Dinner in the 1950s.* Waterville, ME: Thorndike Press, 2004.

Sharples, Liz, Richard Mitchell, Nik Macionis, Brock Cambourne, and C. Michael Hall, eds. *Food Tourism around the World: Development, Management and Markets.* Oxford, U.K.: Butterworth-Heineman, 2003.

Shenton, James, ed. *American Cooking: The Melting Pot.* New York: Time-Life Books, 2003.

Shuler, Michael, and Fikret Kargi. *Bioprocess Engineering: Basic Concepts.* 2nd ed. Upper Saddle River, NJ: Prentice Hall, 2002.

Sim, Mary B. *Commercial Canning in New Jersey: History and Early Development.* Trenton: New Jersey Agricultural Society, 1951.

Simoons, Frederick J. *Eat Not This Flesh: Food Avoidances from Prehistory to the Present.* Madison: University of Wisconsin Press, 1994.

Sinclair, Upton. *The Jungle.* New York: Doubleday, Page, 1906.

Singer, Peter. *Animal Liberation.* New York: New York Review, 1975. Reprint, New York: Ecco, 2002.

Skaggs, Jimmy M. *Prime Cut: Livestock Raising and Meatpacking in the United States, 1607–1983.* College Station: Texas A&M University Press, 1986.

Smallzreid, Kathleen Ann. *The Everlasting Pleasure.* New York: Appleton-Century-Crofts, 1956.

Smith, Andrew F., ed. *The Oxford Companion to American Food and Drink.* New York: Oxford University Press, 2007.

———. *Peanuts: The Illustrious History of the Goober Pea.* Urbana: University of Illinois Press, 2002.

———. *Popped Culture: A Social History of Popcorn in America.* Washington, DC: Smithsonian Institution Press, 2001.

———. *Pure Ketchup: The History of America's National Condiment.* Columbia: University of South Carolina Press, 1996.

———. *Souper Tomatoes: The Story of America's Favorite Food.* New Brunswick, NJ: Rutgers University Press, 2000.

———. *The Turkey: An American Story.* Urbana: University of Illinois Press, 2006.

Smith, C. Wayne, Javier Betrán, and E. C. A. Runge. *Corn: Origin, History, Technology, and Production.* Hoboken, NJ: Wiley, 2004.

Smith, N. C. *Morality and the Market: Consumer Pressure for Corporate Accountability.* London: Routledge, 1990.

Smith, Page, and Charles Daniel. *The Chicken Book.* San Francisco: North Point Press, 1982.

Smith, W. H. *Biscuits, Crackers and Cookies.* London: Applied Science, 1972.

Snack Food Association. *Fifty Years: A Foundation for the Future.* Alexandria, VA: Snack Food Association, 1987.

Sokol, Ellen. *The Code Handbook: A Guide to Implementing the International Code of Marketing of Breastmilk Substitutes.* Penang, Malaysia: International Baby Food Action Network, 1997.

Spang, Rebecca L. *The Invention of the Restaurant.* Cambridge, MA: Harvard University Press, 2000.

———. *The Restaurant: Paris and Modern Gastronomic Culture.* Cambridge, MA: Harvard University Press, 2001.

Spedding, C. R. W., ed. *The Human Food Chain.* London: Elsevier Applied Science, 1989.

Spivey, Diane M. *The Peppers, Crackling, and Knots of Wool Cookbook: The Global Migration of African Cuisine.* Albany: State University of New York Press, 1999.

Sprague, G. F., and J. W. Dudley, eds. *Corn and Corn Improvement.* 3rd ed. Madison, WI: American Society of Agronomy, 1988.

Staller, John E., Robert H. Tykot, and Bruce F. Benz, eds. *Histories of Maize: Multidisciplinary Approaches to the Prehistory, Linguistics, Biogeography, Domestication, and Evolution of Maize.* Burlington, MA: Elsevier Academic Press, 2006.

Sterba, James P., ed. *Earth Ethics: Introductory Readings on Animal Rights and Environmental Ethics.* Upper Saddle River, NJ: Prentice Hall, 2000.

The Story of a Pantry Shelf, an Outline History of Grocery Specialties. New York: Butterick, 1925.

Stull, Donald, and Michael Broadway. *Slaughterhouse Blues: The Meat and Poultry Industry in North America.* Belmont, CA: Wadsworth, 2004.

Stull, Donald D., Michael J. Broadway, and David Griffith. *Any Way You Cut It: Meat Processing and Small-Town America.* Lawrence: University Press of Kansas, 1995.

Subcommittee on Interpretation and Uses of Dietary Reference Intakes and the Standing Committee on the Scientific Evaluation of Dietary Reference Intakes, Institute of Medicine of the National Academies. *Dietary Reference Intakes: Applications in Dietary Planning.* Washington, DC: National Academic Press, 2003.

Taylor, Frederick Winslow. *Scientific Management: Comprising "Shop Management," "The Principles of Scientific Management," and "Testimony before the Special House Committee."* 2nd ed. Westport, CT: Greenwood Press, 1972.

Thévenot, R. *A History of Refrigeration throughout the World.* Trans. J. C. Fidler. Paris: International Institute of Refrigeration, 1979.

Thomas, R. David, and Michael Seid. *Franchising for Dummies.* Foster City, CA: IDG Books Worldwide, 2000.

United Farm Workers of America. *The Wrath of Grapes.* Video. Wayne State University, 1986.

UNICEF. *Vitamin and Mineral Deficiency: A Global Progress Report*, 2004. Online at http://www.micronutrient.org/reports/reports/Full_e.pdf.

U.S. Department of Commerce, National Oceanic and Atmospheric Administration, National Marine Fisheries Service. *Fisheries of the United States, 1997.* Washington, DC: GPO, 1998.

U.S. Department of Health and Human Services, and U.S. Department of Agriculture. *Dietary Guidelines for Americans.* Washington, DC: GPO, 2005.

Van Wieren, Dale P. *American Breweries II.* West Point, PA: Eastern Coast Breweriana Association, 1995.

Veblen, Thorstein. *The Theory of the Leisure Class: An Economic Study of Institutions.* New York: Macmillan, 1899. Reprint, New York: Oxford University Press, 2007.

Wade, Louis Carroll. *Chicago's Pride: The Stockyards, Packingtown, and Environs in the Nineteenth Century*. Urbana: University of Illinois Press, 1987.

Walker, John R. *Introduction to Hospitality*. 4th ed. Upper Saddle River, NJ: Pearson Prentice Hall, 2006.

———. *The Restaurant: From Concept to Operation*. 5th ed. Hoboken, NJ: Wiley, 2007.

Walsh, William I. *The Rise and Decline of the Great Atlantic & Pacific Tea Company*. Secaucus, NJ: Lyle Stuart, 1986.

Watson, James L., ed. *Golden Arches East: McDonald's in East Asia*. Stanford, CA: Stanford University Press, 1997.

Who's Buying at Restaurants and Carry-Outs. Ithaca, NY: New Strategist Publications, 2004.

Wildman, Robert E. C., ed. *Handbook of Nutraceuticals and Functional Foods*. 2nd ed. Boca Raton, FL: CRC/Taylor & Francis, 2007.

Wilk, Rick, ed. *Fast Food/Slow Food: The Cultural Economy of the Global Food System*. Lanham, MD: Altamira Press, 2006.

Wilkinson, Alec. *Big Sugar: Seasons in the Canefields of Florida*. New York: Knopf, 1989.

Williams, Chuck. *Celebrating the Pleasures of Cooking*. San Francisco: Weldon-Owen, 1997.

Williams, E. W. *Frozen Food: Biography of an Industry*. Boston: Cahners, 1963.

Williams-Forson, Psyche. *Building Houses Out of Chicken Legs: Black Women, Food, and Power*. Chapel Hill: University of North Carolina Press, 2006.

Winter, Ruth. *A Consumer's Dictionary of Food Additives*. 6th ed. New York: Three Rivers Press, 2004.

Witt, Doris. *Black Hunger: Soul Food and America*. Minneapolis: University of Minnesota Press, 2004.

Wolf, Erik. *Culinary Tourism: The Hidden Harvest*. Dubuque, IA: Kendall/Hunt, 2006.

Woolrich, Willis Raymond. *The Men Who Created Cold: A History of Refrigeration*. New York: Exposition Press, 1967.

Wright, Clifford A. *A Mediterranean Feast: The Story of the Birth of the Celebrated Cuisines of the Mediterranean, from the Merchants of Venice to the Barbary Corsairs*. New York: Morrow, 1999.

Wyckoff, D. Daryl, and W. Earl Sasser. *The Chain-Restaurant Industry*. New York: D. C. Heath, 1978.

Wyman, Carolyn. *Spam: A Biography*. New York: Harcourt Brace, 1999.

Young, James Harvey. *Pure Food: Securing the Federal Food and Drugs Act of 1906*. Princeton, NJ: Princeton University Press, 1989.

Zimmerman, M. M. *The Super Market: A Revolution in Distribution*. New York: McGraw-Hill, 1955.

Zurborg, Carl E. *A History of Dairy Marketing in America*. Columbus, OH: National Dairy Shrine, 2005.

Websites

Agricultural Associations
   http://agrinet.tamu.edu/groups/default.htm

Directory of organizations, categorized as: general agriculture; fish and seafood; poultry; fruits and vegetables; grain; and livestock

Airlinemeals.net

http://www.airlinemeals.net.

Huge collection of photos and travelers' reviews of airline food, including meals from 1950s onward.

American Brewery History Page

http://www.beerhistory.com

Amazing collection of memories—both mild and bitter; frothy facts and foamy photos; links to other beer sites; a catalog of beer books, videos, and collectibles

The American Cheese Society

http://www.cheesesociety.org

"Educational resource for American cheesemakers and the public"; articles, industry news and research, contacts, calendar of events

American Frozen Food Institute (AFFI)

http://www.affi.com

Tradegroup site, with press releases, facts and statistics, and calendar of events

The American Meat Institute (AMI)

http://www.meatami.com

Meat industry news, research events—and some recipes

Bureau of Labor Statistics, U.S. Department of Labor. "Chefs, Cooks, and Food Preparation Workers." *Occupational Outlook Handbook, 2006–07*

http://www.bls.gov/oco/ocos161.htm

Job descriptions, working conditions, training, opportunities for advancement, earnings, etc. for kitchen workers

Business History Books—Food: Business History of Manufacturers

http://www.kipnotes.com/food.htm

Chronology, bibliography, and food history links

Center for Food Safety and Applied Nutrition, U.S. Food and Drug Administration

http://vm.cfsan.fda.gov/index.html

Links to government food science, nutrition, and food safety information

http://www.foodsafety.gov/list.html

Food safety news, articles and links from USDA's Food Safety and Inspection Service

Center for Science in the Public Interest. "Food Additives."

http://www.cspinet.org/reports/chemcuisine.htm

What these chemicals are, what to avoid, what's safe to eat, and what additives have been banned in the United States

Code of Federal Regulations, Title 21 (Food and Drink)

http://www.accessdata.fda.gov/scripts/cdrh/cfdocs/cfCFR/CFRSearch.cfm

Searchable database of U.S. government definitions of foodstuffs

Cookery Collection

http://www.lib.msu.edu//coll/main/spec_col/cookery/

Two thousand cookbooks in the Michigan State University Libraries: 18th-century British, 19th-century American, African-American, American regional and ethnic, church and charity, early works, international, Jewish/kosher, unusual

Emergence of Advertising in America, 1850–1920

http://scriptorium.lib.duke.edu/eaa/

Duke University's Hartman Center for Sales, Advertising and Marketing History, including the Nicole Di Bona Peterson Collection of Advertising Cookbooks, 1878–1929

Fish Information and Services

http://fis.com

"Global seafood industry information"; members get access to daily market information and more, but there are plenty of free data and links

Food History News

http://foodhistorynews.com

Food historian Sandy Oliver's mecca for food historians: booksellers, calendar of events, culinary history groups, food products for food history, hearth cooking classes, heirloom seeds and plants, historic recipes, learning opportunities, libraries, museums, reproduction cooking equipment, speakers and consultants, miscellaneous, FAQ, newsletter subscription info

Food Institute Daily Update

http://www.foodinstitute.com/dailyupdate.cfm

Subscription-based food industry news, with a free version and a more comprehensive version for a fee

Food Museum

http://www.foodmuseum.com

Articles on current exhibits, info on other food museums, great links

Foodnavigator

http://www.foodnavigator.com

"Breaking news and analysis on food ingredients"; provides news, market reports, and science on food safety, fibers, proteins, and enzymes for the bakery, beverage, and dairy industries

Food Production Daily

http://FoodProductionDaily.com/nl/archives.asp

"Breaking news on food processing and packaging"; archive of back issues

Food Reference Website

http://www.foodreference.com

Culinary history, facts, trivia, quotes, humor, poetry, crossword puzzle, recipes, newsletter

Fruit Online

http://www.fruitonline.com

Fruit industry news, trends, statistics, import/export data, links

Gateway to Government Food Safety Information

http://www.foodsafety.gov

Links to all government programs on food safety, consumer advice, educational programs, assistance to the food industry, and issues of foodborne illnesses

History of Kitchen Innovations

http://inventors.about.com/library/inventors/blkitchen.htm

From apple peelers to waffle irons and more—including links to lots of food history

Home Economics Archive: Research, Tradition, History (HEARTH)

http://hearth.library.cornell.edu

Free core electronic collection of books and journals in home economics and related disciplines that were published between 1850 and 1950

How Products Are Made
> http://www.madehow.com
> History and technology behind things of interest to food writers, from aspartame to candy corn, chopsticks to condensed milk, fruit leather to imitation crab meat, ketchup to popsicles, rice cakes to Teflon, TV dinners to yogurt—and a host of nonfood products as well

International Association of Ice Cream Vendors
> http://www.iaicv.org
> Trade group site for manufacturers and purveyors of frozen treats

International Dairy Foods Association
> http://www.idfa.org
> Trade group site with news, industry facts and statistics, news about legislation and economic analyses, access to publications

"Irradiation." Foodsafety.gov: Gateway to Government Safety Information.
> http://www.foodsafety.gov/~fsg/irradiat.html
> Links to federal and state sites dealing with irradiation of foods

"It's a McWorld After All"
> http://www.salon.com/books/review/2005/12/10/hungry_planet/print.html

Language of the Food Industry
> http://www.fmi.org/facts_figs/glossary_search.cfm
> Glossary of arcane supermarket terminology

Manufacturing of Foods in the Tenements
> http://www2.arts.gla.ac.uk/www/ctich/eastside/foods12.html
> 1906 account of commercial food production in New York's Lower East Side—focusing on unsanitary conditions, but revealing much more

National Council of Chain Restaurants
> http://www.nccr.net
> Trade group site with news, press releases, industry facts and discussion of government regulation of the industry

National Marine Fisheries Service
> http://www.nmfs.noaa.gov
> The science, technology, conservation and protection—by the government—of saltwater seafood species

National Restaurant Association
> http://www.restaurant.org
> Trade group site with news, press releases, discussions of careers, education, food safety, nutrition, and recent research

Nationwide Food Consumption Survey
> http://www.barc.usda.gov/bhnrc/foodsurvey/home.htm
> USDA's Food Service Research Group looks at "What We Eat in America"

New York Food Museum
> http://www.nyfoodmuseum.org
> Exhibits on New York City foodways as they used to be: production, distribution, history, economics; links to wonderful period photos and other historical resources

Organic Agriculture Information Access
> http://www.hti.umich.edu/n/nal/

Searchable collection at the Alternative Farming Systems Information Center, a part of the National Agricultural Library

Prepared Foods

http://www.preparedfoods.com

Online trade magazine's site includes a Wellness and Organic Ingredients Directory with listings of suppliers with addresses, phone numbers, key contacts, and other critical information; the Food Master Ingredient Directory, the "phone book" of the food industry; calendar of events; list of food associations; index of back issues; and links to media kits, product literature, and Cahner's other trade magazines: *Dairy Foods, FoodExplorer, Food Manufacturing, Foodservice Equipment & Supplies, Packaging Digest,* and *R&I Marketplace*

Sodamuseum.com

http://www.sodamuseum.bigstep.com

History of, and myths about, some favorite brands of soft drinks

Sugar Knowledge International. "Welcome to the World of Sugar Technology"

http://www.sucrose.com/home.html

How sugar is made, the technologists who work with sugar, industry news, jobs available in the industry, a library of industry facts, and a sugar forum

UC Davis Viticulture Department

http://wineserver.ucdavis.edu

University of California at Davis is *the* place for American winemakers to get their education; its site features a news journal, home winemaking information, wine books, links to wine websites, wine and health, the aroma wheel, Trellis Alliance; facilities, weatherpests, a library, wine yeast, brandy science, wine research, thesis search, viticultural areas, and wine regulations

U.S. Department of Agriculture, Food and Nutrition Service. "Food Stamp Program"

http://www.fns.usda.gov/fsp

How the program works, informational materials available, nutritional education, research

U.S. Patent and Trademark Office

http://www.uspto.gov/patft/index.html

Search through all the U.S. patents to get the details about ingredients and processes, back to 1790

U.S. Poultry and Egg Association

http://www.poultryegg.org

Industry news and press releases

INDEX

Note: **Boldface** page numbers refer to main entries.

ABOUT THE EDITORS AND CONTRIBUTORS

Pauline Adema is a culinary anthropologist who studies contemporary food culture and place.

Ken Albala is a professor of history at the University of the Pacific in Stockton, California. He is the author of several food books, including *Eating Right in the Renaissance* (2002), *Food in Early Modern Europe* (Greenwood, 2003), *Cooking in Europe* (Greenwood, 2006), *The Banquet* (2007), and *Beans: A History* (2007). He is also series editor for *Food Culture around the World* and *Cooking Up History*, published by Greenwood.

Gary Allen is an adjunct professor at Empire State College, Highland, New York; Webmaster for the ASFS; and food history editor at LeitesCulinaria.com. His books include *The Resource Guide for Food Writers* (1999) and *The Herbalist in the Kitchen* (2007).

Laura Martin Bacon has been a writer and culinary historian for Williams-Sonoma since 1996.

Madonna L. Berry is a chef instructor in the Roger A. Saunders School of Hotel and Restaurant Management at Newbury College, Brookline, Massachusetts.

Robin Bisha is an assistant professor of communication studies at Texas Lutheran University, Seguin, Texas.

Gwendolyn Blue is an assistant professor of Communication and Culture at the University of Calgary, Alberta.

Barrett P. Brenton teaches in the Sociology and Anthropology Department of St. John's University, Queens, New York.

Anne Brumley is a master's candidate in literary studies at the University of Melbourne, Australia.

Joseph M. Carlin is a nutritionist and American food historian, proprietor of the Food Heritage Press, and one of the founding members of the Culinary Historians of Boston.

Jeffrey Charles is an associate professor in the History Department of California State University, San Marcos.

Janet Clarkson is a medical practitioner in private practice, a senior lecturer at the school of medicine, University of Queensland, Brisbane, Australia, and a culinary historian.

Alfredo Manuel Coelho is associated researcher at Unité Mixte de Recherche; Marchés, Organisations, Institutions et Stratégies D'Acteurs; Centre International D'Etudes Supérieures en Sciences Agronomiques, Montpellier, France. He is the author of W^2D—World Wine Data, a database covering mergers, acquisitions, and partnerships in the world wine and spirits industries.

Eric Covey is a graduate student in American studies at the University of Texas at Austin.

Margaret Coyle is a visiting assistant professor in theatre at Allegheny College, Meadville, Pennsylvania.

Jean-François Denault works as a consultant in the life sciences segment, while completing his graduate studies in communications at the University of Montreal.

Joel S. Denker is an independent scholar and writer. His publications include *Capital Flavors: Exploring Washington's Ethnic Restaurants* (1989) and *The World on a Plate: A Tour through the History of America's Ethnic Cuisine* (2003).

Michaela DeSoucey is a Ph.D. candidate in sociology at Northwestern University, Evanston, Illinois.

Jonathan M. Deutsch is an assistant professor and director of the Culinary Management Center in the Department of Tourism and Hospitality at Kingsborough Community College, City University of New York. He serves as secretary of the Association for the Study of Food and Society and is education editor of the journal *Food, Culture and Society*.

Nate Eastman is a doctoral candidate at Lehigh University, Bethlehem, Pennsylvania.

Paul Fieldhouse is an adjunct professor of nursing at the University of Manitoba and nutrition research and policy analyst for Manitoba Health. He has written *Food and Nutrition: Customs and Culture* (2nd ed., 1995) and coauthored *The World Religions Cookbook* (Greenwood, 2007), among other works.

Ellen J. Fried is an adjunct clinical assistant professor in the Department of Nutrition, Food Studies, and Public Health at New York University.

Cayo Gamber is an assistant professor of writing at the George Washington University, Washington, D.C.

Signe Hansen is a doctoral candidate in film and media at the University of Cape Town, South Africa.

Lisa Heldke is a professor of philosophy at Gustavus Adolphus College in St. Peter, Minnesota. She is the author of *Exotic Appetites: Ruminations of a Food Adventure* (2003) and coeditor of *Cooking, Eating, Thinking: Transformative Philosophies of Food* (1992).

Jerri A. Husch is a sociologist at the University of Massachusetts, specializing in human and policy aspects of drug abuse, primary health care, and health management.

Cathy K. Kaufman has taught culinary history at New York City's Institute of Culinary Education for more than a decade and is the author of *Cooking in Ancient Civilizations* (Greenwood, 2006).

Carly Kocurek is a graduate student in the Department of American Studies at the University of Texas at Austin.

Steven Kolpan is a Certified Wine Educator and professor and Endowed Chair of Wine Studies at the Culinary Institute of America. He is the author of *A Sense of Place: An Intimate Portrait of the Niebaum-Coppola Winery and the Napa Valley* (1999) and coauthor of *Exploring Wine* (1997, 2001).

Sarah Kornik is completing the joint graduate program in communication and culture at Ryerson and York Universities, Toronto.

Claudia Kousoulas is a food writer and a member and past president of Culinary Historians of Washington, D.C.

Bruce Kraig is professor emeritus of history at Chicago's Roosevelt University and an adjunct at Kendall College Culinary School.

Faith J. Kramer is a writer and researcher from Oakland, California.

Michael Krondl is on the faculty of the New School's Culinary Center. He is the author of several books, including *Around the American Table: Treasured Recipes and Food Traditions from the American Cookery Collections of the New York Public Library* (1995) and *The Taste of Conquest: The Rise and Fall of the Three Great Cities of Spice* (2007).

Samantha Kwan is a Ph.D. candidate in sociology at the University of Arizona.

Karen Y. Lau is a freelance writer based in Washington, D.C.

Marianne LeGreco is a doctoral candidate in organizational and health communication in the Hugh Downs School of Human Communication at Arizona State

University. She also holds a faculty associate position with the College of Nursing and Health Innovation at Arizona State.

Lucy M. Long focuses her work on popular culture in the International Studies and American Culture Studies Program at Bowling Green State University, Ohio.

Marty Martindale is a food writer living in Largo, Florida.

Renee Marton is an adjunct professor at Lehman College, City University of New York on the Concourse, New York.

Nora Maynard is a freelance writer based in New York City.

Alice McLean is the Honors Teaching Fellow at Sweet Briar College in Virginia and the author of *Cooking in America, 1840–1945* (Greenwood, 2006).

Bonni J. Miller is the proprietor of Chez Marché Cafe in Waupaca, Wisconsin.

Jeffrey Miller is an assistant professor in the Department of Food Science and Human Nutrition and program coordinator in the Restaurant and Resort Management Program at Colorado State University. He is also a Certified Executive Chef and Certified Culinary Educator.

Malden C. Nesheim is a professor of nutrition emeritus and provost emeritus of Cornell University, Ithaca, New York.

Marion Nestle is the Paulette Goddard Professor of Nutrition, Food Studies, and Public Health and Professor of Sociology at New York University, and is the author of *Food Politics* (rev. ed., 2007), *Safe Food* (2003), and *What to Eat* (2006).

Molly O'Neill has been a chef, cookbook author, and food journalist for *The New York Times*, and is a culinary anthologist. Her most recent book is *American Food Writing: An Anthology: With Classic Recipes* (2007).

Fabio Parasecoli is the U.S. correspondent for *Gambero Rosso*, Italy's authoritative food and wine magazine. He teaches courses in food history and food and culture in the program for Communication and Journalism in Food and Wine at the Città del Gusto School in Rome and in the Department of Nutrition, Food Studies, and Public Health at New York University.

Gabriella M. Petrick is an assistant professor of food studies at New York University.

Wendy W. Pickett is an instructor in the Boston University English Department specializing in American poetry.

Jeffrey M. Pilcher, a professor of history at the University of Minnesota, is author of *¡Que Vivan los Tamales! Food and the Making of Mexican Identity* (1998), *The Sausage Rebellion: Public Health, Private Enterprise, and Meat in Mexico City* (2006), and *Food in World History* (2006).

Jeri Quinzio is the author of *Ice Cream: The Ultimate Cold Comfort* (2007).

Jorge Abril Sánchez is a Ph.D. candidate and a lector of Spanish at the Department of Romance Languages and Literatures of the University of Chicago.

Joy Santlofer is an adjunct instructor in the Food Studies Program at New York University.

Molly G. Schuchat is a cultural anthropologist who has long studied the social and symbolic setting of food habits.

Jeff Shantz teaches at Kwantlen University College in Vancouver, British Columbia.

Bonnie J. Slotnick is an editor and writer and has worked in cookbook publishing for more than 20 years.

Sabrina Small is completing her master's degree in gastronomy from Boston University and currently works as a sous chef in Los Angeles.

Andrew F. Smith teaches culinary history and professional food writing at the New School in Manhattan and serves as the general editor of the Food series at the University of Illinois Press. He is the author or editor of 16 books, including the *Oxford Companion to American Food and Drink*.

Rebecca Tolley-Stokes is an assistant professor at East Tennessee State University, Johnson City.

Leena Trivedi-Grenier is a freelance food writer in Chicago.

Penny Van Esterik is a professor of anthropology at York University, Toronto, where she teaches nutritional anthropology, advocacy anthropology, and feminist theory. Her publications include *Beyond the Breast-Bottle Controversy* (1989), *Materializing Thailand* (2000), *Taking Refuge: Lao Buddhists in North America* (1992), and the edited reader *Food and Culture* (1997).

Andrea S. Wiley is a professor of anthropology at James Madison University, Harrisonburg, Virginia.

Psyche Williams-Forson is an Assistant Professor of American Studies at the University of Maryland, College Park. She has written extensively on African-American foodways and is the author of *Building Houses out of Chicken Legs: African American Women, Food, and Power*. In 2006, she won the Elli Köngäs-Maranda Prize, of the Women's Section of the American Folklore Society.

Darius Willoughby is a freelance food writer in Bozeman, Montana.

Mark Zanger is a restaurant critic and food historian in Boston.